D0023065

# The Social Psychology
## of Clothing

# The Social Psychology of Clothing

■ ■ ■

## Symbolic Appearances in Context

### SECOND EDITION

**Susan B. Kaiser**

UNIVERSITY OF CALIFORNIA, DAVIS

*Macmillan Publishing Company*

NEW YORK

Editor: Helen McInnis
Production Supervision: Till & Till, Inc.
Text Design: Russell H. Till
Cover Design: Blake Logan

This book was set in Galliard by C.L. Hutson Co., Inc., printed and bound by R.R. Donnelly & Sons. The cover was printed by Phoenix Color Corp.

Copyright © 1990 by Macmillan Publishing Company,
a division of Macmillan, Inc.

Printed in the United States of America

All rights reserved. No part of this book may be reproduced or transmitted in any form or by any means, electronic or mechanical, including photocopying, recording, or any information storage and retrieval system, without permission in writing from the Publisher.

Earlier edition, entitled The Social Psychology of Clothing and Personal Adornment, copyright © 1985 by Macmillan Publishing Company.

Macmillan Publishing Company
866 Third Avenue, New York, New York 10022

Collier Macmillan Canada, Inc.

**Library of Congress Cataloging-in-Publication Data**

Kaiser, Susan B.
    The social psychology of clothing: Symbolic appearances
in context / Susan B. Kaiser.—2nd ed.
        p.   cm.
    Rev. ed. of: The social psychology of clothing and personal
adornment. c1985.
    Includes bibliographical references.
    ISBN 0-02-361882-5
    1. Clothing and dress—Psychological aspects.   2. Clothing and
dress—Social aspects.   I. Kaiser, Susan B. Social psychology of
clothing and personal adornment.   II. Title.
GT524.K36   1990
391'.001'9—dc20                                                89-37219
                                                                CIP

Printing:     2  3  4  5  6  7       Year:     1  2  3  4  5  6

*To the Memory of*
*My Parents*

# *Preface*

On a daily basis, we are confronted with a variety of clothing styles—in our wardrobes, on other people, and in mass media. On an almost unconscious level, we continually assess what we should wear, what meanings clothing carries about people and situations, and what is currently happening in our culture. Clothes are tangible objects, and yet they provide a frame of reference for interpreting more abstract social processes, including how people relate to one another. Clothes are generally not seen by themselves (except in a closet or a store), but are inextricably linked to other, related cues that comprise our personal appearances. These cues include hairstyles, accessories, and facial and bodily characteristics.

The social psychology of clothing, then, encompasses the study of clothes within the larger context of appearance in general. This study includes: (a) how we use clothing and personal appearance cues as stimuli that help us to understand ourselves and the world around us, and (b) the influences of social relations on our daily decisions and thought processes involving clothing and personal appearance. Moreover, because some of the meanings we associate with clothing and appearance are provided by the particular culture and the times in which we live, it is important to place the study of clothing and appearance within their larger cultural and historical contexts.

As visible, material objects that are relevant to everyday life, clothes help us to organize, and make sense of, our social experiences. In the process, clothes are linked to different levels of everyday experience: (a) how we see ourselves as individuals, (b) how we interact with other people, and (c) how we are influenced by, and contribute to, the cultural milieu in which we live.

A theme that runs throughout this book is the importance of the social meaning of appearance, how it is established, how it is interpreted, and the importance of the social and cultural contexts in which these processes occur. Readers who are familiar with the first edition of *The Social Psychology of Clothing* (1985) will discover that this second edition has been extensively revised and rewritten. These changes reflect growth and development in the social psychology of clothing, as well as in related areas of study. This edition incorporates a stronger emphasis on the broader issue of appearance as a whole; on linkages between social-psychological processes and culture; on the connection between clothing, gender, and the body; and on the importance of context in the study of clothes. The new subtitle, "Symbolic appearances in context," reflects these emphases. Just as clothing and appearance are embedded in social and cultural contexts, the *study* of clothing and appearance is embedded within the intellectual movements that cut across disciplines in the social and human sciences. This study is similar to a web or a network of discovery—about everyday life, social meaning, and culture. As we explore the dynamic processes through which styles of clothes, as well as their meanings, emerge and change, we catch an illuminating glimpse of the essence of social-psychological processes.

The book is organized into five parts, beginning with a framework to view the social meaning of appearance, and then proceeding to discussions on individuals, their social interactions with others, and the importance of cultural context, change, and continuity. Part One introduces the social psychology of clothing as an area of study, by presenting its basic concepts and its development as influenced by related areas of study. Additionally, the theoretical perspectives that enable us to explain clothing as a component of social and cultural contexts are introduced and illustrated through an analysis of gender. Part One will set the stage for understanding the study of clothing and related cues in conjunction with the self (Part Two), interpersonal relations and communication (Part Three), appearance in cultural context (Part Four), and culture change and continuity (Part Five). Throughout, the emphasis is on viewing people as individuals who implicitly relate to clothing as a means for ordering, understanding, and shaping everyday life.

Readers of this book will find it helpful if they have had some preliminary background in the social or human sciences. However, many students have commented that it is helpful to study the social psychology of clothing and introductory sociology or psychology concurrently. Because clothing is so grounded in our everyday experience, it is sometimes easier to grasp abstract concepts (for example, the self, status) when we can relate them to clothing or other artifacts of culture. As readers of this or any other book, we bring to the *process* of reading a wealth of experiences, meanings, and ideas. It is this amalgamation of reader characteristics that shapes our understandings of the subject matter. One of the most exciting aspects of studying clothing pertains to the fact that we all have unique, individual perspectives on clothes that we rarely articulate but can bring to the surface in the course of reading and discussing. When we relate subject matter to everyday experience, our study becomes accessible and personal. That is, it becomes contextualized, or embedded in the contexts of our everyday lives.

With this theme of context in mind, several suggestions are offered for the reader who is new to this area of study and to the social and human sciences in general. These suggestions have been shared by students themselves, who note that it is helpful to: (1) read the abstract at the beginning of the chapter to obtain a "nutshell" view of its content, and (2) flip through the chapter to peruse the headings and subheadings; while doing so, look at the pictures and drawings and read the captions; also read the "Social Foci," designed to provide an elaboration on a theme or concept for purposes of illustration. At this point, do not be too concerned if all the ideas are not clear. As you begin your more careful reading of the chapter, you will have some "images" in mind that will help to contextualize your understanding. As you read, think of other examples of the concepts that relate to your own experiences. Imagine ways the pictures or drawings could be altered or imagine different ones altogether. In this way, you will be engaged in the process of understanding more abstract concepts by relating them to everyday life.

*S.B.K*

# Acknowledgments

Many people have contributed directly or indirectly to the completion of this edition. I am indebted to Joan Chandler and Carla Freeman for their continual, enthusiastic support, as well as their coordination of the complex process of acquiring illustrations, along with the necessary permissions. They both read earlier drafts and provided valuable suggestions throughout the project. Joan Chandler also provided tremendous assistance during the process of indexing. Wendy Dildey and Molly Greek also assisted greatly by taking photographs, doing their best to keep the files organized as I rummaged through them, tracking down references in the library, and (most of all) providing insights into students' points of view. Graduate students who have served as teaching assistants at the University of California at Davis have also provided a wealth of suggestions and helpful materials such as media clippings: Linda Boynton, Anthony Freitas, Yong-Ju Kim, and Marcia Wynes. Undergraduate students continue to provide fresh perspectives on clothing and appearance, and to share their ideas and suggestions freely.

The faculty in the Division of Textiles and Clothing at the University of California, Davis and numerous colleagues in the Association of College Professors of Textiles and Clothing have provided an abundance of encouragement and support throughout the project. Professors who have used the first edition in their classes have made numerous suggestions that have been incorporated into this edition. The reviewers provided inspiring ideas for revision in a most constructive way, and I appreciate their contributions very much. Mary Lynn Damhorst has continued to shape my thinking in our numerous, offbeat and informal discussions. I have also been influenced as well as supported in numerous ways by the following colleagues: Carolyn Balkwell, Joann Boles, Anna Creekmore, Fred Davis, Leslie Davis, JoAnn Eicher, Betty Feather, Judith Forney, Jean Hamilton, Robert Hillestad, Marilyn Horn, Sandra Hutton, Jane Lamb, Sharron Lennon, Richard Nagasawa, Rachel Pannabecker, Nancy Rabolt, Mary Ellen Roach-Higgins, Margaret Rucker, Nancy Rudd, and Soyeon Shim. And many,

many other colleagues have shared their insights, as well as reference materials, in the context of professional meetings, workshops in theoretical development, and informal dialogue.

I am also very grateful to the staff at Macmillan Publishing Company for their patience and guidance. Julie Alexander was a tremendous supporter, sensitive to the goals of the project, as editor in the early stages, and Helen McInnis has been extremely understanding and effective as Executive Editor in the final stages. I am also indebted to Russell Till, who has been especially adept and competent, as well as encouraging in handling the production of the book.

Finally, I am especially grateful for the consistent and abiding commitment to the project on the part of my family. My husband Mark has taken many of the photographs and has served as a constructive critic throughout. Most notably, he has persevered as a sincere advocate of shared responsibility in the home; without his continual support and genuine contributions, this edition would not have been possible. Additionally, I appreciate the understanding and enthusiasm on the part of my son Nathan and daughter Carolyn. They have provided encouragement for the project and fuel for the imagination, reminding me on an ongoing basis about the concept of everyday life.

*S.B.K*

# Contents

*Part Three*                                                    **211**
● ● ●
*Appearance Communication in Context*

# Part One
# ...
# Symbolic Appearances in Context

WHAT exactly is the social psychology of clothing? How and why did this area of study emerge? How do we go about studying clothes and related cues as pertinent to social behavior? Part One explores the intellectual context of this area of study, to illustrate how and why it emerged. Part One also examines the basic topics and ideas that contribute to an understanding of clothing and human behavior. We will see that the social psychology of clothing draws from different disciplines or areas of study (for example, anthropology, consumer behavior, cultural studies, psychology, and sociology).

Chapter One addresses the basic concepts or terms used to define clothing and related cues and examines the social psychology of clothing as an area of knowledge. Some of the history of this young discipline is presented, along with an explanation of how different, older disciplines have contributed to our understanding of clothing and human behavior.

Chapter Two presents three perspectives from different disciplines and then introduces the contextual approach to the social psychology of clothing. The contextual approach integrates elements of three different perspectives and emphasizes the importance of situational factors in the interpretation of clothing, within larger cultural and historical contexts. Chapter Two also explores how theoretical perspectives structure and increase our knowledge of clothing and human behavior, to lay the foundation for understanding basic concepts and research findings presented throughout the remainder of the book.

Chapter Three explores how clothing and appearance are related to social thinking about gender. The contextual approach is illustrated by focusing on how males and females use clothes to frame their social experiences. Gender is a pervasive aspect of how humans are socialized to use clothing in everyday life; understanding this topic enables us to examine other social-psychological concepts more critically.

# Chapter One
...
# The Social Psychology of Clothing: Defining the Discipline

*Clothing is part of a larger context of appearance. In this chapter, some of the basic definitions related to the social psychology of clothing and appearance are provided. We will see that appearance is managed and perceived in everyday life, and that the social psychology of clothing encompasses many other areas of study in order to address the question of not only* what, *but also* how, *appearance means. How did the social psychology of clothing emerge as an area of study? We will trace its historical development to address the contributions of diverse areas of knowledge, and to examine how the questions that it has addressed have shifted from why people first wore clothes to how people use clothing in their daily lives, within larger cultural and historical contexts.*

It is hard to imagine how clothing could be more relevant to everyday life, more concrete as an illustration of basic social processes, or more visual in terms of its impact. Yet we are accustomed to thinking about clothes in a fairly routine and matter-of-fact, almost unconscious, way. Only when our attention is drawn to them do we actively realize that we analyze clothes. As everyday objects and topics of study, clothes are both public and personal. People of all cultures wear clothes or otherwise decorate their bodies in some manner. Both males and females deal on a daily basis with decisions related to their own clothing and interpretations of other people's appearances. Factors such as culture and gender may lead people to *think* differently about clothes because of varying social backgrounds and experiences. Still, the social psychology of clothing crosses the socially created boundaries of gender and culture, and these factors must be considered when selecting and defining our terminology.

Distinctions need to be clarified between everyday usage of clothing-related terms and conceptual usage of the same words, as we attempt to study clothing and human behavior. At times, confusion may be created by the connotations words have for us in everyday life as contrasted with their conceptual definitions.

*TABLE 1-1*
*Everyday and Conceptual Clothing Terminology*

| | |
|---|---|
| **Adornment** | Any decoration or alteration of the body's appearance. [Roach and Musa, 1980, have pointed out some disadvantages to the use of this term; namely, it may have subjective connotations: "Perhaps problems have stemmed from the difficulties inherent in determining the aesthetic perspectives of people from a time far removed. Ultimately our task is to separate contemporary predispositions in aesthetic judgments from those of people actually wearing the dress of a particular time, and regarding it as beautiful" (p. 9).] |
| **Apparel** | A body covering, specifically referring to actual garment constructed from fabric (Sproles, 1979). (This is a term often used by industry.) |
| **Appearance** | The total, composite image created by the human body and any modifications, embellishments, or coverings of the body that are visually perceived; a visual context that includes clothing as well as the body. |
| **Clothing** | Any tangible or material object connected to the human body. |
| **Costume** | A style of clothes belonging to a particular cultural or historical context (often used to refer to ethnic or historical clothing, as well as clothing designed for performances or rituals—drama, Halloween, etc.). |
| **Dress** | Verb: the act of altering appearance; noun: the total arrangement of all outwardly detectible modifications of the body itself and all material objects added to it (Roach and Musa, 1980). |
| **Fashion** | A dynamic social *process* by which new styles are created, introduced to a consuming public, and popularly accepted by that public (Sproles, 1979, p. 5); *as object*: a style accepted by a large group of people at a particular time (Kefgen and Touchie-Specht, 1986). |
| **Style** | A distinctive characteristic or way of expression; style in clothing describes the lines that distinguish one form or shape from another (Kefgen and Touchie-Specht, 1986). |
| **Wearable Art** | Use of clothing as a medium for artistic communication, to reflect the uniqueness and personal creativity of the artist and designer; a strong movement in the United States growing out of the attitude of the 1960s that rejected anonymous mass production (Stabb, 1985, p. 208). |

For example, the word *dress* may conjure an image of a female's article of clothing, whereas clothing scholars use the term to refer to a more generic idea. Ideally, ways of speaking about clothes as human behavior would be similar for laypersons and clothing scholars alike, but since this is not always the case, some definitions of clothing-related terms, as used throughout the book, are provided in Table 1-1.

## Basic Terms

*The social psychology of clothing is concerned with the various means people use to modify the appearance of the body, as well as the social and psychological forces that lead to, and result from, processes of managing personal appearance.* Some of the terms used to describe the various forms of appearance modification should be clarified, along with the processes involved in creating these different forms.

The term *clothing* refers to any tangible or material object connected to the human body. This definition encompasses such items as pants, skirts, tops, and other related body coverings. For purposes of our discussion, it will also include material items often thought of as accessories—shoes, gloves, hats, bows, ties, jewelry, and the like. *Clothing*, then, applies to those objects that we obtain (by buying, receiving, or constructing) and attach to or wear on our bodies.

**Clothing and Appearance**

A broader and more inclusive term than clothing is *appearance*, which refers to the total, composite image created not only by clothing, but also by the human body and any modifications to the body that are visually perceived. This concept enhances our understanding of clothing by also considering related processes of body modification—including dieting, hairstyling, using cosmetics, tattooing, and piercing. Appearance is similar to the "big picture" that we see when we observe ourselves and other people in everyday life; it is a context in and of itself. Therefore, it is important to study clothing within the context of appearance, appreciating that clothes are generally viewed in conjunction with bodies, which are themselves modified (see Figure 1-1).

Some social scientists emphasize that appearance is not only a visual image, but also a process when thought of in terms of social relations (Stone, 1965). This approach would lead us to consider two processes contributing to and emerging from the way we appear to ourselves and others: appearance management and appearance perception.

**Appearance management** encompasses all attention, decisions, and acts related to one's personal appearance (that is, the process of thinking about and actually carrying out activities pertaining to the way one looks). This concept includes all activities and thought processes leading to the purchase and wear of clothing items, as well as processes of body modification (for example, dieting and exercising). Appearance management encompasses what we do to and for our bodies visually, as well as how we plan and organize these actions (for example, making decisions about attire to buy and wear and assessing the personal and social implications of such decisions). Individuals may vary in their level of involvement with clothing and appearance concerns. However, appearance management is a universal concept. All individuals engage in some form of appearance management on a daily basis.

A frequently used term that encompasses acts and forms of appearance management is *dress*. As a verb or a process, *dress* refers to the *act* of altering or adding to appearance. (Appearance management, as a more general concept, also includes processes of planning, thinking about, or assessing the social consequences of one's appearance.) *Dress* may also be a noun, referring to the "total arrangement of all outwardly detectable modifications of the body and all material objects added to it" (Roach and Musa, 1980). Three different forms of dress are defined and illustrated in Table 1-2 and in Figures 1-2 through 1-10: (1)

**FIGURE 1-1**

*Appearance and its elements: If we focus on the male in this picture, we may notice (**a**) the body, including its form and size; (**b**) the clothing, including the styles worn, how they are worn, and the presence or lack of brand labels; (**c**) hairstyle; and (**d**) additional accessories that are carried (the backpack, and how it is worn). Additionally, this male's appearance is observed in a social context, so, for example, a perceiver may imagine what his relationship is with his female friend. Photo by Michelle Small.*

**TABLE 1-2**
*Three Types of Dressing*[a]

---

1. **Body Modifications**—includes any temporary or permanent changing or redesigning of the body itself (the color, texture, or shape of the body might be modified).
   a. Modification of body color: dyeing or lightening the hair; tattooing, powdering, painting, tanning, or lightening the skin; using makeup or nail polish (see Figures 1-2 through 1-5).
   b. Modification of body texture: curling or straightening the hair; smoothing the skin through plastic surgery; using creams or lotions to soften the skin (see Figure 1-6).
   c. Modification of body shape: styling hair, trimming beard or mustache; reshaping the body through the use of undergarments; reshaping the body through dieting, exercising, weight lifting, or plastic surgery (see Figures 1-6 and 1-7).
2. **Body Enclosures**—includes the envelopment and covering of the body or some part of the body; the item may be wrapped around the body, suspended from a part of the body, preshaped to fit a part of the body (for example, gold ring, rubber boot, parts of garments designed to be formed around the contours of parts of the body), or combinations thereof (see Figures 1-8 through 1-10).
3. **Attachments to the Body or to Body Enclosures**—the covering of small areas of the body or the body enclosures to which they are fixed.
   a. Insertions: earrings for pierced ears; barrettes or ribbons interlaced in the hair (attached to body); cufflinks or pins (attached to body enclosures) (see Figure 1-9).
   b. Clips: earrings (attached to body) or clip-on bow ties (attached to a body enclosure—a shirt).
   c. Adherends: false eyelashes; artificial fingernails.
   d. Items hung from the shoulder or hand-held: shoulder bag, purse, umbrella, walking stick (see Figure 1-10).

---

[a] Adapted from Roach and Musa, 1980.

body modifications (see Figures 1-2 through 1-7), (2) **body enclosures** (see Figures 1-8 through 1-10), and (3) **attachments to the body or to body enclosures** (see Figures 1-9 and 1-10) (Roach and Musa, 1980).

Appearance perception is the opposite of appearance management—the process of observing and making evaluations or drawing inferences based on how people look. Appearance perception is a daily occurrence. In fact, we rely on it, almost unconsciously in many cases, to make sense of everyday life. We engage in appearance perception when we are confronted with appearances in face-to-face encounters with other people, in media presentations where imagery may be used to cast a character, and in stores—where we are likely to observe the clothes worn by sales personnel or other shoppers, or shown in displays, where they exist as objects for purchase, apart from being worn yet suggestive of potential uses. Because the way we perceive clothing in real life is rarely disconnected from appearance perception in general, this term will be used to encompass clothing perceptions.

Even in situations where we perceive clothing apart from a more general appearance, we are still likely to deal in an implicit way with a kind of "imaginative" appearance perception (how the clothes would look and what they would represent in the broader context of appearance on one's own or other persons' bodies,

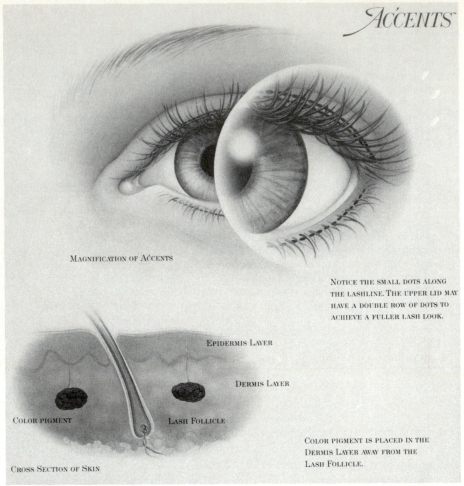

MAGNIFICATION OF AĆCENTS

NOTICE THE SMALL DOTS ALONG THE LASHLINE. THE UPPER LID MAY HAVE A DOUBLE ROW OF DOTS TO ACHIEVE A FULLER LASH LOOK.

EPIDERMIS LAYER

DERMIS LAYER

COLOR PIGMENT

LASH FOLLICLE

CROSS SECTION OF SKIN

COLOR PIGMENT IS PLACED IN THE DERMIS LAYER AWAY FROM THE LASH FOLLICLE.

**FIGURE 1-2**
*The process for obtaining a permanent form of eyeliner by adding permanent color (normally shades of black, brown, or gray): This form of body modification represents a collaboration between medical science and cosmetology. (Trained physicians insert color pigment in small dots along the lashline.) Courtesy of Dioptics.*

including what could be worn with them). For example, imagine going into a women's clothing store that carries separates and accessories. As you observe a large scarf that you find attractive, you imagine how it will be worn, over what clothing, and the like.

Although clothes are tangible and concrete, they are taken for granted in terms of communication. Even so, they may lead to rich interpretations as people engage in appearance perception. In complex societies, in particular, there is a wide array of competing appearances. Responses to and interpretations of clothing and appearance can range from almost automatic and unconscious perceptions to uniquely developed scenarios, as a perceiver contemplates all of the possible meanings of a style and the implications of these potential meanings for social interactions. It becomes virtually impossible to attend to all of the images we

**FIGURE 1-3**
*Tattooing involves a permanent change in body color based on the insertion of an indelible dye in punctured skin. Here, a Malaysian man displays tattoos that are traditional to his culture. Photo by Katharine Hoag.*

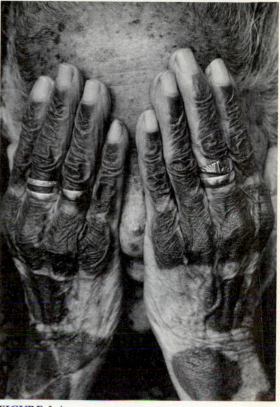

**FIGURE 1-4**
*Okinawan woman with tattooed hands. This practice was adopted, in part, to prevent women from being taken as prisoners by foreign invaders at a critical point in Okinawa's history. Photo courtesy of Richard O. Ward.*

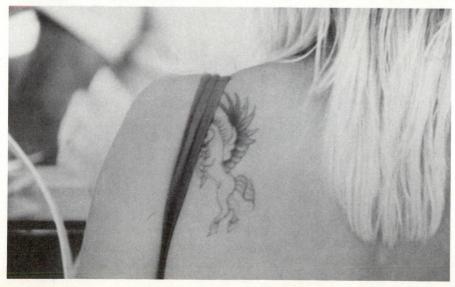

**FIGURE 1-5**
*A popular form of tattoo among beach crowds in southern California. Photo by Mark Kaiser.*

**FIGURE 1-6**
*Modification of body texture through the creation of a raised or relief pattern from scar tissue. The lip disk worn by this Mursi woman from southern Ethiopia is an example of body shape modification. From childhood on, a series of clay plates have been fitted into a hole in the lip, until the skin has been stretched to the desired size. Photo by Robert Caputo.*

**FIGURE 1-7**
*Modification of body shape: During infancy, the head of this Kwakiuti Indian of Vancouver Island was molded. Photo courtesty of the Library Services Department, American Museum of Natural History.*

**FIGURE 1-8**
*Body enclosure: Turban wrapped around the head of this Middle Eastern man. Other body enclosures include all of the clothes worn by the individuals in this picture. Photo by Susan B. Kaiser.*

*FIGURE 1-10*
*Note the attachment to the body in the form of a shoulder bag. The clothes worn by these men, of course, represent body enclosures. Photo by Susan B. Kaiser.*

*FIGURE 1-9*
*Body enclosure: Turban wrapped around the head of this American woman. The pierced ears and nose are examples of body attachments by insertion. Photo by Carla M. Freeman.*

see, so we tend to "screen" the appearances we see to interpret those that are most interesting, attractive, or important to us. Other appearances may be processed automatically, ignored altogether, or viewed as inexplicable.

The processes of appearance management and appearance perception may be considered a means for framing (composing guidelines or boundaries for understanding) our social experiences (see Figure 1-11). Engaging in these processes helps us to make sense of the world around us and, therefore, serves to shape social life. In a fluid and dynamic way, appearance management and perception allow for creative expression and interpretation, as well as aesthetic stimulation.

At this point it should be clear that although clothing items are concrete (visible and material), it is necessary in the social psychology of clothing to become more abstract in one's thinking—and to be able to apply abstract concepts or perspectives to clothing.

**FIGURE 1-11**
*Appearance management and appearance perception both occur as individuals dress themselves for a social occasion and then observe one anothers' choices of clothing in that social situation. In the process, individuals frame their social experiences by determining and comparing how they and other persons "fit" into a social situation. In this cartoon, how do the individuals shown use clothes to identify social differences and to "frame" social boundaries? Drawing by Koren; © 1987, the New Yorker Magazine, Inc.*

*"I'm afraid California just isn't me."*

## History of Knowledge on Clothing and Human Behavior

At various times in the history of different areas of study contributing to our knowledge about clothing, questions have arisen about the nature of its relation to human behavior. The pursuit of answers to these questions has led to new questions and ideas about clothing and human behavior. As we look at these questions, several overriding themes will become apparent:

*1.* The study of clothing as human behavior has been influenced and shaped by social movements or trends, as well as intellectual currents. However, by using theories that incorporate change to study clothing phenomena, underlying social and psychological processes can be uncovered that explain, and in some cases surpass, this change.

*2.* A number of academic disciplines, predominantly in the social sciences and humanities, have contributed to our understanding of clothing and human behavior. Therefore, we may regard the social psychology of clothing as a **transdiscipline**—an area of knowledge that has emerged because of theories and research findings that cross traditional disciplinary boundaries. To the extent that such knowledge has been integrated by clothing scholars, the social psychology of clothing is also **interdisciplinary**.

*3.* Ideas derived from a variety of disciplines need to be examined *critically* as they are used to explain clothing as human behavior. This critical examination involves (*a*) evaluating how adequately ideas describe and explain the social-psychological aspects of clothing, (*b*) exploring the sources of these ideas, including the historical context in which scholars developed their points of view or interests, (*c*) delving into the basic assumptions about humans that have influenced the kinds of questions asked in the history of the social psychology of clothing, and (*d*) tracing the influence of ideas across time.

The nineteenth century marked the transition in Europe and the United States from rural or preindustrial societies to industrial societies. Some of the earliest questions on the relation of clothing to human behavior emerged as a result of social and intellectual movements in the nineteenth century (Roach and Eicher, 1973). One movement that caused controversy and active discussion of social and ethical issues related to clothing was the feminist movement of the nineteenth century. Feminists strived to reform women's clothing by promoting styles that were more functional, less restrictive, and more comfortable than the styles in that century. It became apparent that clothes have not only physical but also social implications: They can serve as means of socially organizing our understanding of the differences between males and females, including the extent to which these differences are socially and artificially imposed. Questions such as the following emerged: What does clothing convey about the way gender is socially structured? How and why have males and females managed their appearances to illustrate their roles at different times in history? These questions are still applicable today and are considered in more detail in Chapter Three. Gender is important in the social psychology of clothing, because its definition constitutes one of the most fundamental social meanings expressed and shaped by clothes. Historically, gender has also influenced who has pursued clothing for purpose of study and why or how they have done so.

*Early Interest in the Social Aspects of Dress*

Another event that sparked scholarly interest in the social significance of apparel, from a socioeconomic perspective, was the Industrial Revolution and, consequently, the transition from agrarian to city life. Fashion became even more important than it previously had been, as the variety of social roles increased and a marked distinction emerged between private and public life. Emerging from industrialization was the idea of factory-made clothes, instead of custom or made-at-home styles. Between 1890 and 1910 the clothing industry expanded rapidly in England and the United States (Wilson, 1985, p. 76). (See Figure 1-12.) As the effects of this change were realized, fashion became more democratic and available to the general public. Sociologists and economists became interested in the implications of this tendency for social class structure in society. They considered such questions as: What impact does industrialization of a society have on the clothing its members wear and on the nature of fashion change? How has the spread of new styles changed, and, specifically, what are the implications of industrialization for social class structure in society?

**FIGURE 1-12**
*Shown is a typical garment workroom during the early days of apparel manufacturing in New York City. Mass production of apparel influenced social thinking about fashion, including who could afford it and how it spreads throughout society. Photo courtesy of the International Ladies Garment Workers' Union Archives.*

Sociologists and economists addressed these issues as part of their attention to industrialization and social class as related to society as a whole. Economist Thorstein Veblen (1899) focused on individuals' desires to appear prosperous. He noted that in an industrialized society, women's roles were linked to the display of their husbands' wealth. (His ideas will be explained in further detail in Chapter Thirteen, which deals with social differences.) Sociologist Georg Simmel (1904) also focused on social class as a factor in the purchase and use of clothing. He theorized that fashions "trickle down" from the upper classes to the lower classes, with the tendency for social classes to imitate those immediately above them in order to move up the social ladder. (His theory, and later theories on fashion change, will be considered in Chapter Fifteen.) Another economist, Paul Nystrom (1928), indicated that fashion changes on the basis of such social-psychological factors as overcoming boredom, craving for diversity, striving for personal uniqueness, expressing rebellion, imitating others, or obtaining companionship.

## Early Theories on Why People Wear Clothing

When social and behavioral sciences were becoming established at the turn of the century, one of the first questions to interest anthropologists and psychologists was, *Why do people wear clothes?* Many theoretical explanations were developed to address this basic question. Due to a trend in psychology at the time to attribute basic human motives to instinct, some of the earliest theories were developed around the question: *Why did people first wear clothing?* Some anthropologists who attempted to answer this question were influenced by the cultural biases of their time. Clothing scholars Cynthia Jasper and Mary Ellen Roach-Higgins (1987) point out that some of this early theorizing and field work also reflected the influence and bias of evolutionary thought, building on the assumptions that (*a*) clothing, like other artifacts, evolved from the most simple (primitive) to the most complex (civilized) forms, and (*b*) the motives of contemporary, non-Western "primitive" people are identical to those of the first humans. Therefore, it is important to examine critically the four theories emerging from these earliest writings and to consider them in the context of the times in which they were developed. In spite of the obvious shortcomings of these earliest theories, they set the stage for understanding early academic writings on the social nature of clothing. They provide some "food for thought" and the opportunity to think critically about clothing.

The **modesty theory** suggests that people first wore clothing to cover or conceal the "private" parts of the human body. This theory was derived from a Christian, biblical explanation of clothing—namely, that clothes were initially worn by humans (Adam and Eve) to cover nakedness because of instinctive shame. The modesty theory was based on the idea that morality is dependent upon modesty, as expressed through the concealment of the human body. Psychologist Dunlap (1928) noted that because moralist writers were frequently males, there was an inordinate emphasis in their writing on female sexuality and the maintenance of morality through the covering of the female body. Moreover, he noted, the theory was accepted largely because it fit the assumption that the wearing of clothes was based on a cause, rather than the result of experimentation with the body. Arguments against this theory are that young children are not instinctively modest and that, instead, modesty is socially learned. Also, standards of modesty vary from one culture to the next and one historical era to the next. Yet modesty is frequently acknowledged as a factor in why people continue to wear clothes, although numerous other factors exist that are equally, if not more, compelling. (See Figure 1-13 as an example illustrating the limitations of focusing exclusively on modesty as an explanation of dress.)

Recognizing that humans not only cover their bodies but also display them to attract others, psychologist Westermarck (1921) focused on **immodesty**, or sexual attraction. Proponents of this explanation point out that individuals may have first worn clothing in order to attract attention to, rather than to conceal, the sexual organs. This theory was based on the doctrine that familiarity breeds indifference, whereas concealment breeds interest. Though many have since agreed that clothes do serve a function of sexual appeal, few accept the idea that immodesty was the reason for wearing clothing. How would early humans have known of this alluring effect, and how can cross-cultural differences be explained? For example, Tuareg males in the Middle East wear a veil to cover the mouth, which is perceived to be as erotic as the sexual organs. In Japan, the back of a woman's neck has traditionally been considered sexually erotic. The clothes that have been worn in these cultures have most likely promoted perceptions of eroticism. Psychologist Dunlap (1928) argued that both the modesty and immodesty theories may be refuted. He pointed out that historical evidence supports neither of these explanations. Furthermore, individuals may appear either clothed or nude before others with accompanying feelings of either modesty or immodesty.

**FIGURE 1-13**
*Clothing usage is more complex than a modesty explanation alone can handle. The attire of this woman in the latter part of the nineteenth century might be interpreted as depicting Victorian standards of modesty. Yet a closer analysis of women's attire in this period reveals some cultural ambivalence about such values. For example, feminists regarded the appearance of tight-fitting dresses with bustles (introduced in the 1870s) as increasing the tendency for a woman's body to be viewed as an object (Banner, 1983, p. 61). Rather than merely concealing the body, the bustle actually emphasized it. Photo courtesy of the Juanita Franklini Collection, City of Sacramento, Museum and History Division.*

A third explanation of why people first wore clothes was provided by the **adornment theory**. This theory refers to the decorative nature of clothes and other forms of appearance modification for purposes of display, attraction, or aesthetic expression. Anthropologists around the turn of the century frequently identified adornment, or ornamentation, as the initial reason for wearing clothes, citing evidence that "savages" may be naked but still adorned, as compared to the modestly covered "civilized" Western people. The assumption underlying this emphasis on adornment was that people "evolved" from merely decorating their bodies to the wearing of clothing, and once they wore clothing they became modest without it and also realized the functional advantages of clothing. The following passage is an example of early writing attributable to this reasoning, which reflects the influence and potential bias of evolutionary thinking (as noted by Jasper and Roach-Higgins, 1987):

> Ornament is never lacking—clothing often is. . . . There are tribes who, when first discovered, lived naked. . . . All these people, dwelling in a state of nudity, seemed to have no idea of shame on that account. . . . It seems to us, from these facts, that the idea of clothing as a modest covering is relatively recent, and that it is subsequent to dress development. . . . Dress has generally developed out of ornament. . . . As soon as man hung an ornament. . . , dress evolution had begun (Starr, 1891).

The fallacy in this thinking lies in the implication that "advanced" standards of modesty and status displays evolved from simple decoration of the body. There has always been room for a great deal of variation in appearance management among unclothed persons of the world. The various forms of appearance management they have used are likely to have had rich cultural meanings in and of themselves; thus unclothed but decorated bodies should be regarded as more than "previews" to modern clothing. (See Figure 1-14 for an illustration of the potential for bias when studying unclothed people from an evolutionary perspective today.)

In 1930, psychologist Flügel noted that anthropological evidence for this theory consists primarily of the fact that there exist unclothed but not undecorated people. He indicated that psychologists were not likely to contradict anthropologists' explanations but rather were likely to focus their attention on other matters, such as unconscious emotions reflected in clothing (Flügel, 1950, p. 17). (See Social Focus 1-1.)

A fourth and final explanation of why people first wore clothing was provided by the ***protection theory***, which suggests that clothes protect humans from the elements, animals, or even supernatural forces (see Figure 1-15). Although protection is an important function of clothing, this explanation as an initial motive for wearing clothing has been largely discredited because clothing is thought to have originated in tropical regions of the world where there was the least need for protection against the climate. However, psychologist Dunlap (1928) proposed that clothes were originally adopted to protect humans not from the weather but from insects, as people wore hanging strips of leaves or animal hides that flapped along with the movements of the body (serving as types of fly swatters). Later, he argued, people began to focus on how clothes could enhance social status, particularly when costly materials and expensive dyes were developed. He went on to say that modesty probably arose as the upper classes began to conceal themselves, using costly materials. A critical examination of Dunlap's ideas points once again to some biases prevalent in the social thinking of his time—namely, the assumption that people evolved from savages in clothing-like insect swatters to higher orders of cultured classes. The danger of applying such a line of thinking to the study of clothing today is that one might judge some cultures as more advanced than others on the basis of clothing cues, therefore leading to cross-cultural bias.

**FIGURE 1-14**
*Ecuadoran Indians, as shown here in the 1980s, dress their bodies by altering the shape of the ear (woman in the back) and wearing necklaces. Social-evolutionary theory might explain the use of the loin cloth by males in terms of protection and would predict that modesty "would come later." However, the tropical climate is well-suited to a relative lack of clothing; what would be the advantage of gradually adding more? Some have hypothesized that the Indians who have covered selected body parts have done so at the urging of missionaries, or for the benefit of visitors to their region, rather than for natural, evolutionary purposes. Photo by Stephen Cunha.*

Some anthropologists and psychologists focused on the psychic or magical protection provided by ornaments or clothing that did not physically protect, but instead served religious functions or unconscious protection. For example, psychoanalysts pointed out that clothing envelops and protects the body, not unlike a mother's womb.

***Toward an Understanding of Basic Human Needs***

As more writers dealt with the topic of early motivations for wearing clothes, it became clear that there were a number of possibilities. Instinct theories of motivation largely fell into disfavor by psychologists as they realized that too many instincts would be required to explain behavior, and therefore the theories would become too cumbersome to be useful (Ryan, 1966).

Theories of human needs, such as individual requirements for health and social adjustment, took the place of instinct theories. Identifying clothing as a basic human need, along with food and shelter, psychologists began to focus on the needs clothes fulfill. For example, Dearborn (1918) developed a list of ways in which clothing, in some time or place, protects individuals from various kinds of fears, including fear of ridicule; fear of being judged as inefficient, stupid, immodest, poor, lacking good taste or self-respect; fear of being unattractive; and fear of skin irritation or discomfort. This list was based on personal observations and some speculation.

Later, psychologist Elizabeth Hurlock (1929) studied motivation in fashion among over 1,400 people, aged 16 to 51. Through a questionnaire, she examined whether individuals dress to please their own sex or the opposite sex, dress to appear prosperous, choose clothes to enhance their best physical assets, or use modesty as a factor in clothing choice. These questions were derived from need theories of motivation, but also reflect some of the thinking of instinct theories. Although the methods used by Hurlock, in terms of how questions were phrased, are open to dispute (Ryan, 1966), this research does represent an early, systematic attempt to address the question of why people "need" clothes (now in the

**FIGURE 1-15**
*Interpreting the use of the black leather pants worn by these motorcyclists in Germany (in the summer of 1986) requires a more complex explanation than protection alone. Of course, leather pants protect a motorcyclist's legs from chafing, but they are also likely to be hot. And, consider the social and cultural context of the situation. German influence on black leather fashion has been fairly consistent since the First World War (Farren, 1985). Therefore, black leather garments might be interpreted differently in Germany than they are in some other countries. Other factors, including group affiliation and leisure preference, may also be critical to a complete understanding. Photo by Mark Kaiser.*

# Psychoanalytic Thinking and Interpretations of Clothing

Although the immodesty theory as an explanation of why people first wore clothes may not have received widespread attention or acceptance among psychologists, many did choose to focus on the sexual significance of clothing. An intellectual movement initiated by psychologist Sigmund Freud, the founder of psychoanalysis, focused on sexual instincts (in part, based on preservation of the species) and shaped some of the thinking on this topic. Psychologist Flügel (1950) used psychoanalytic ideas to explain clothing and human behavior, focusing on the concept of **ambivalence** created by contradictory tendencies—the use of clothing to display, as well as to hide, the body.

> Clothes, in fact, as articles devised for the satisfaction of human needs, are essentially in the nature of a compromise; they are an ingenious device for the establishment of some degree of harmony between conflicting interests. In this respect the discovery, or at any rate the use, of clothes, seems, in its psychological aspects, to resemble the process whereby a neurotic symptom is developed. Neurotic symptoms, as it is the great merit of psychoanalysis to have shown, are also something of a compromise, due to the interplay of conflicting and largely unconscious impulses (Flügel, 1950, pp. 20–21).

Flügel went on to theorize that when clothes do conceal the body, they serve to symbolize the sexual organs they hide (for example, the man's tie as a symbol of the penis). It was common among psychoanalysts to interpret the meanings of clothes on the basis of unconscious feelings about sexuality. The problem with this kind of analysis lies in detecting, in Freud's words, when "a cigar is just a cigar" (and not a symbol of a sexual organ). Also, case studies of psychologically disturbed individuals may not be indicative of the general public's conscious or unconscious thinking about clothing.

Although few scholars continue to focus on psychoanalytic ideas about fetishistic symbolism in clothing, the psychoanalytic concepts of ambivalence and the unconscious have had a more lasting, although not necessarily consistent, impact on our thinking about clothes. Clothing scholar Mary Lou Rosencranz (1962, 1965) noted the need to use measures that tap unconscious interpretations when studying the meaning of clothing. Later, American sociologist Fred David (1982) called for a return to the use of indirect measures to tap symbolic meanings or hidden messages in clothing. Moreover, what Flügel applied in the 1930s to psychological motivation in clothing, a British sociologist named Elizabeth Wilson (1985) applied in the 1980s to fashion and culture. In her book, *Adorned in Dreams: Fashion and Modernity*, Wilson treats clothing as a cultural phenomenon—as an "aesthetic medium for the expression of ideas, desires and beliefs circulating in society" (p. 9). And, some of these ideas, desires, and beliefs, she notes, may be beyond the realm of conscious emotions:

> Fashion clearly does . . . tap the unconscious source of deep emotion, and at any rate is about more than surface. Fashion, in fact, is not unlike Freud's vision of the unconscious mind—we may view the fashionable dress of the Western world as one means whereby an always fragmentary self is glued together into the semblance of a unified identity (Wilson, 1985, p. 11).

Also, like Flügel, Wilson regards fashion as a medium for responding to ambivalence:

> Fashion acts as a vehicle for fantasy. . . . There will never be a world without fantasy, which expresses the unconscious unfulfillable. All art draws on unconscious fantasy; the performance that is fashion is one road from the inner to the outer world. Hence its compulsiveness, hence our ambivalence, hence the immense psychological work that goes into the production of the social self, of which clothes are an indispensable part. . . . This ambivalence is that of contradictory and irreconcilable desires, inscribed in the human psyche by that very "social construction" that decrees such a long period of cultural development for the human ego. Fashion—a performance art—acts as the vehicle for this ambivalence; the daring of fashion speaks dread as well as desire; the shell of chic, the aura of glamour, always hide a wound. . . . Fashion reflects also the ambivalence of the fissured culture of modernity, is only like all modern art in expressing a flawed culture. . . . Like all art, it has a troubled relationship with morality, is almost always in danger of being denounced as immoral. Yet also, like all art, it is likely to become most "immoral" when it comes closest to the truth (Wilson, 1985, p. 246).

Therefore, although it is unlikely that clothes *only* serve to communicate unconscious feelings about sexuality, the

## Social Focus 1-1 (continued)

psychoanalytic idea of focusing on the unconscious has left its mark on the possibilities for exploring meanings of clothing. In particular, the idea that clothes (and other cultural objects) provide a means for communicating unconscious thoughts or cultural values still promotes theoretical analysis of clothing today. Given the visual and dynamic nature of clothes, they may convey not only personal feelings that are difficult to express verbally, but also contradictory cultural values that are closely intertwined in social life.

present tense). Hurlock's research suggested that people dress more for their own sex than the opposite sex. She also found that looking prosperous was not a motive for following fashion, although modesty and the desire to enhance one's best features were. However, as Ryan (1966) pointed out, the wording of the questions may have induced a negative response in relation to looking prosperous, and people are not likely to admit that they seek status. (To do so may sound snobbish or pretentious.)

A few years later, when research techniques were improved in terms of questionnaire construction, Barr (1934) conducted a study among 350 women to examine personal desires related to conformity, economy, comfort, modesty, self-expression, sex, and femininity. Her research indicated that the desire to conform with the clothing of others was the most frequent or pervasive motive indicated and even overlapped with some other motives such as modesty. Like Hurlock, she found that most individuals do not indicate a desire to look prosperous, but they do want to bring out the best in their personal appearance and express themselves.

A more comprehensive study relating clothing behavior to human needs was undertaken by clothing scholar Anna Creekmore (1963), who studied 300 college women and found some correlations between the following:

1. The needs for belonging and self-esteem, and behavior related to the use of clothing as a status symbol.
2. The need for self-esteem, and the use of clothing as a tool to enhance personal appearance.

Although few studies today focus on motives in everyday dressing, the studies mentioned earlier provide some foundation for understanding the complexities involved in examining the purposes of clothes. Some of the problems in trying to determine *why* people wear clothes are illustrated in the early work pursuing this question—basically, that clothes serve multiple purposes for individuals, and some motives or needs may be easier to admit or acknowledge than others. Furthermore, motives or needs are likely to be of varying importance depending on the social situations for which a person is dressing.

British sociologist Elizabeth Wilson (1985) raised another point about the study of clothing and fashion in relation to human needs. She argues that scholars have often failed to remember that fashion is a form of art, and, in terms of artistic expression, we need not necessarily expect all clothes to be justifiable strictly in terms of human needs. Instead, a range of clothing styles, when viewed from a cultural-aesthetic point of view, reflects variations in aesthetic tastes and sensibilities.

Hence, clothes not only serve individual, social-psychological, and physical needs but also are cultural representations and art forms. The realization of the subtle complexities involved in understanding clothing has generally led scholars to focus on *how people use clothing in their daily lives, within a larger cultural and historical context.* This approach produces a more fruitful and observable way of approaching clothing and human behavior, allowing for the study of social-psychological processes as well as aesthetic and cultural influences on these processes. The implications of this approach may be realized in the realm of everyday life and social interaction, as well as in consumer behavior (that is, decision-making, purchase, and actual use of clothes).

## 1940s to the Present

Clothing scholars in the 1940s and 1950s, housed in home economics programs in colleges and universities, began to focus on the social and psychological implications of clothing. Prior to this time—back as early as the turn of the century—the more physical aspects of clothing (for example, construction or design and textiles) were emphasized, and the history of clothing was studied, with particular interest in history as a source of ideas for designing clothing (Jasper and Roach-Higgins, 1987).

In 1947 a group of clothing scholars joined some social scientists at Columbia University to explore mutual interests and concerns, which resulted in some new insights and questions. The following year a psychologist named George Hartmann, who had attended a previous meeting, spoke at a conference of textiles and clothing college professors, and further stimulated thinking on connections between clothing and human behavior (Horn, 1965; Ryan, 1966). Hartmann (1949) wrote an article in the *Journal of Home Economics* stressing the "double" aspect of clothes, namely, how they deal with personal concerns and social issues. In his challenge to clothing scholars, he noted that clothing is a "persistent 'interest center' in everyone's life," varying greatly in intensity and expression but nevertheless a fundamental part of life (Hartmann, 1949, p. 295).

In 1949 and 1951 seminars were held at Michigan State College (now Michigan State University), where different sociological, anthropological, and psychological theories were considered, along with appropriate research methods, for use in the explanation and study of clothing as human behavior (Rosencranz, 1950; Ryan, 1966, p. 3). In 1956 a group of leaders in the clothing field organized a work conference in Maryland to outline basic concepts and propositions related to social-psychological and other factors associated with the use of clothing, followed by a second work conference at the University of Illinois in 1961. As a result of these conferences and the efforts of clothing scholars, the emphasis in this emerging area of study was placed on the study of clothing in the context of its cultural, social, psychological, physical, economic, and aesthetic relations (Horn, 1965). The social psychology of clothing has further developed in its own right. Still, it is important to consider social-psychological factors as part of a broader nexus of factors, including cultural factors such as mass media, physical factors such as body type, economic factors such as social class, and aesthetic factors such as clothing perceived as art.

Interest in the social-psychological aspects of clothing increased as scholars wrote about the relation of clothing to the social order, compiling and integrating works from a variety of disciplines (Roach and Eicher, 1965; Horn, 1965; Ryan, 1966). Research studies on this topic also began to emerge. In 1965, Mary Lou Rosencranz wrote that 50 to 60 years of psychological interest in clothing had elapsed. She noted that motives related to clothing are often disguised, complex, and numerous—even for a single situation. Therefore, Rosencranz (1965) suggested the need for a focus on meanings in social situations and for a consideration of *how* as well as *why* clothing has meaning.

> Clothing adaptations, covers, and extensions to the body appear over and over again in different places; however, their meaning and functions may differ. Always there is a need to ask "why?" and to ask how particular clothing is an expression of a particular culture or people (p. 29).

Around the same time, some sociologists were considering fashion change and clothing from a theoretical perspective. One perspective that was seen to be quite applicable to clothing usage is known as **symbolic interaction**. This perspective focuses on social processes related to how meanings are constructed and reconstructed in everyday life. So, it was only natural that symbolic inter-actionists and clothing scholars would begin to recognize a common focus on *how* personal appearances have meaning. (This perspective is explained in much more detail in Chapter Two.) This school of thought was based largely on the works of George Herbert Mead (1934), a social psychologist at the University of Chicago in the early part of the twentieth century. He emphasized that social interaction should be studied as a dynamic process rather than as a static entity.

One of Mead's students, Herbert Blumer (1969a), later coined the phrase symbolic interaction and elaborated on many of Mead's concepts. Through his writings and teaching at both the University of Chicago and the University of California at Berkeley, Blumer (1969a) expanded on the idea of interaction as a process of people sharing meanings and fitting their lines of action together. He also applied the perspective to his study of fashion processes (Blumer, 1969b). Another symbolic interactionist, Gregory Stone (1965), wrote a theoretical article on "Appearance and the Self," in which he linked appearance, and more specifically clothing, to how individuals are socialized in a society and how appearance is a factor in the development of their self-concepts.

Erving Goffman, a student of Blumer's at the University of Chicago, was also a sociologist who dealt with the topic of clothing in the late 1950s and 1960s. His work, along with Stone's, lays the foundation for much of our understanding of appearance management and the self. He focused on strategies people use when they present themselves to others in social interaction (Goffman, 1959). His perspective has been called *dramaturgy*, because it uses the analogy of the stage to explain much of human behavior. This perspective emphasizes the use of clothing as a "costume" that enables individuals to assume social roles with some degree of credibility, as discussed in Chapter Six.

Although much of the thinking in sociological literature about clothing was based on the perspective of symbolic interaction, social psychologists in psychology departments in universities and colleges in the late 1960s and early 1970s began to consider the potential of clothing as a variable to be manipulated in experiments. This interest was stimulated by a convergence of a social trend for clothing to reflect social-political attitudes and theories focusing on how people perceive one another. "Inconspicuous consumption" became a prevalent norm among youth in the 1960s, as characterized by worn-out jeans, T-shirts, and sandals. A distinction between "hip(pie)" versus "straight" attire prompted an interest among psychologists in the study of how attire reflected social-political attitudes, as perceived by other people. Theories dealing with how people form impressions about other people were developed under the rubric of a **cognitive perspective**, focusing on how people simplify their perceptions and develop judgments about other people on the basis of certain cues.

The cognitive perspective may be traced back to some of the research in the 1920s and 1930s, focusing on the accuracy of first impressions about people's intelligence and personalities when the appearance of the person being judged was the only information available to them. Although the accuracy of such judgments was frequently quite low, it became clear that appearance perception did occur (Ryan, 1966, p. 29). Also, some of the work by psychologist Kurt Lewin in the 1930s and 1940s on the mental worlds of individuals contributed to the cognitive perspective (Gergen, 1985). Fritz Heider (1958) also began to formulate ideas about balance in thought processes and, later, to deal with how people explain the world around them. Around the same time, Lewin's student Leon Festinger (1957) developed *dissonance theory* under the rubric of the cognitive perspective to explain the mental conflict people experience when they have conflicting thoughts about a stimulus.

By the 1950s and 1960s, much of the research in social psychology dealt with attitudes and attitude change. Affluence in the 1960s, as well as the growth of a youth culture, brought about a shift in societal emphasis from material success to meaningful social relationships. Psychologists followed suit by exploring how people are attracted to one another (McGuire, 1985), and appearance was one variable they began to manipulate. When hip versus straight attire became indicative of social-political attitudes in the late 1960s, social psychologists began to explore how people use these cues and what effects they have on their responses, as well as the degree to which such cues reflected actual attitudes.

Much of the focus of social psychologists in the 1970s and thereafter has been on how people perceive one another and social situations. In the 1970s and 1980s, research has continued and burgeoned on appearance perception (to a greater extent than that on appearance management), focusing not only on different clothing styles (for example, career versus casual attire) but also physical attractiveness. This work has been conducted by both psychologists and clothing scholars, as well as by scholars of communications and consumer behavior (in business or marketing programs) in some cases. Addressed in this work has been the question of how people use appearance as a cue in perceiving others, encompassing not only *what appearance means* but also *how appearance conveys meaning*, that is, how thought processes and social interactions influence the assignment of meaning to personal appearances.

In addition to the research described earlier, clothing scholars have continued to pay attention to special or unique, everyday needs related to clothing. The special clothing needs of certain age groups (predominantly adolescents and the elderly) and people with special needs (for example, people with physical disabilities) have been studied by clothing researchers, frequently with the intent of addressing physical and social needs that can be met through more effective clothing design and marketing.

During the 1960s and 1970s, marketing researchers studied the characteristics of individuals who follow fashion at various stages in the cycle of a new style, with the purpose of understanding how early adopters of styles can be influenced. The assumption underlying much of this work is that if "innovators" and "fashion leaders" can be appealed to through more effective marketing and advertising procedures, they will, in turn, influence other consumers to adopt a new style. In the 1980s, marketing scholars have been influenced by the intellectual perspective known as **semiotics**, or the study of how cultural meanings are produced and conveyed. Consumer and marketing researchers have paid more attention to how clothes as consumer products (*a*) communicate about the culture in which we live, and (*b*) may be advertised so as to convey socially desirable meanings.

Semiotics has influenced marketing researchers, but on a much broader scale, there has been a revitalization of the **"culture" concept** in the social sciences and humanities. This newer, interdisciplinary approach to culture addresses the symbolic realm of social life, encompassing the study of the cultural forms and social relations as related to (*a*) the arts, (*b*) the media, and (*c*) historical and contemporary value systems or ideologies characterizing a culture or groups within a culture. This approach incorporates a strong focus on **expressive culture**, or the artifacts or products of culture, including clothing fashions. As anthropologist Clifford Geertz (1973, p. 14) notes, culture is a context that can be "thickly described." Clothes lend themselves to rich and "thick" description, as clothing researchers have appreciated and acknowledged (Roach and Eicher, 1973; Hamilton, 1987).

Contributing to a renewed interest in culture is the **cultural studies** movement that emerged in the 1970s, beginning in England and spreading to North America. Cultural studies may be described as an interdisciplinary area of study, incorporating concepts and methods from cultural anthropology, literature, semiotics, social history, and sociology (Allor, 1987; Coughlin, 1989). Cultural studies calls for the use of the human sciences to examine social practices and relations from a cultural point of view (Johnson, 1986–1987). There is an interest in how (and why) certain cultural artifacts (such as clothes) are produced and used. Cultural studies emerged in part as a critical, theoretical outgrowth of social movements of the 1960s (for example, the civil rights, peace, and women's movements). Social critique of ideas, as well as cultural products, is fundamental to cultural studies. Feminists have contributed to cultural studies, for example, by illustrating social inequities related to gender, citing such cultural products as cosmetics and uncomfortable garments as representations of these inequities.

Part of the impetus for a renewed focus on expressive culture in the 1980s was the breakdown of aesthetic and social criteria for art forms, associated with a cultural condition referred to as *postmodernism* (Berg, 1987; Gitlin, 1989). Styles emerging from the punk subculture of the 1970s and 1980s illustrated some of the ambivalence associated with the postmodern period. (Postmodernism will be discussed in further detail in Chapter Twelve.) Using a semiotics' and cultural studies' approach, Dick Hebdige (1979) focused on the subcultures' development of their own products to convey meanings that diverge from a larger culture—again, with an emphasis on social practice and social relations.

Meanwhile, during the 1970s and 1980s, in clothing and textiles programs around the country, fashion merchandising became an increasingly popular area of study. Clothing scholars began to explore the potential linkages between the social psychology of clothing and apparel marketing, in terms of fashion change, media communications (for example, music videos as an additional fashion influence of the 1980s), and international trade (in a time of growing apparel imports and a need to assess consumers' preferences and perceptions of apparel from different parts of the world). The implications of studying social-psychological processes with sensitivity to clothing customs and fashion as forms of expressive culture have become evident. It is critical in merchandising-oriented research to uncover social meanings that both *direct* and *explain* consumer behavior toward appearance-related products (clothes, makeup, and hair products) (Hamilton, 1988). Hence, there is a convergence between the social psychology of clothing and market-related concerns, all within a cultural context (see Figure 1-16).

It becomes clear when examining the history of the social psychology of clothing that influences have been numerous, rapid change has been inevitable, and various theoretical perspectives must be critically evaluated in terms of their ability to explain clothing as a form of human behavior. It also becomes evident that the complexity of studying clothing and appearance is further increased by the fact that prevalent apparel modes change so rapidly, and individuals have a variety of options they may pursue at different times. Knowledge in this area, as well as in any other area, must be evaluated in relation to larger societal issues and trends. As necessary, theoretical perspectives will continue to be modified.

Questions are still emerging on appearance management and appearance perception as basic social processes, linked not only to social interactions but also to culture itself (for example, the mass media, larger social issues, and patterns of power). The underlying goal in the social psychology of clothing is

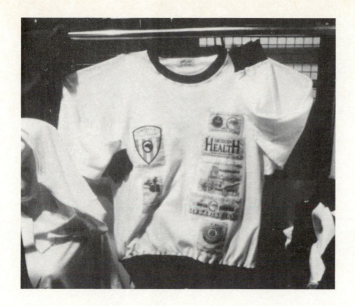

**FIGURE 1-16**
*Fashion merchandising uses concepts of semiotics and "expressive culture" to promote sales. This window display of a store in a Paris mall is part of a promotion on American activewear. Although the merchandise is not manufactured in the United States, the use of the English language and American sports themes on the apparel communicates the intended message. A thorough study of cultural communications in fashion merchandising would explore how consumers interpret such messages and apply them in their usage of clothing in everyday life. Photo by Susan B. Kaiser.*

to understand the relation of clothing to the everyday lives, aspirations, and fantasies of individuals and groups of individuals. The focus in this quest is on the meanings that clothing and related appearance cues hold for individuals, how these meanings change (as do the cues themselves), and how people rely on meaning to orient their actions toward one another. The ways in which people organize their thinking about clothes vary tremendously. Still, some common themes, concerns, and hopes underlie this thinking. In Chapter Two, we will explore a conceptual framework to attempt to organize our study of social thinking about appearance.

## Suggested Readings

Hutton, S. S. 1984. State of the art: Clothing as a form of human behavior. *Home Economics Research Journal* 12(3):340–353.
    Hutton reviews the state of concepts and methods used to study clothing as a form of human behavior and provides insights on what is needed to advance inquiry in this area.

Kaiser, S. B., and Damhorst, M. L. eds. 1990. *Critical linkages in textiles and clothing: Theory, method, and practice.* Monument, CO: Association of College Professors of Textiles and Clothing.
    In this book of readings, conceptual linkages across the various components of textiles and clothing are explored in a series of papers dealing with theoretical issues.

Nagasawa, R. H., Kaiser, S. B., and Hutton, S. S. 1989. Theoretical development in clothing and textiles: Are we stuck in the concrete? *Clothing and Textiles Research Journal* 7(2):23–31.

A model for inquiry into the study of textiles and clothing is presented, and the need to be able to move freely between concrete and abstract themes in the study of textiles and clothing is addressed.

Ryan, M. S. 1966. *Clothing: A study in human behavior*. New York: Holt, Rinehart & Winston.

Ryan provides an extensive summary of research available to date in the 1960s, as well as a critical look at the basic questions and methods underlying this research.

# Chapter Two
...
# *Toward a Contextual Perspective*

*The contextual perspective, introduced in this chapter, leads us to explore the various contexts or circumstances in which we can understand the social meanings of clothes. These meanings are embedded in, and altered by, the appearances in which they are found, in social situations, and in larger cultural/historical contexts framing space and time. To understand meaning and its potential for change, we can draw from three different theoretical perspectives which, in turn, inform a contextual perspective: (a) cognitive, (b) symbolic-interactionist, and (c) cultural. These three perspectives address how people structure their thought processes about clothing, how people negotiate meanings of clothes in social encounters with others, and how culture promotes continuity as well as change in social meanings. Together, they set the stage for a sensitivity to context as we study clothing.*

In the social psychology of clothing, we are not only concerned with what clothes mean but also with (*a*) the *processes* by which people come to associate clothing and appearance with certain meanings, and (*b*) the social *consequences* of these meanings. These processes and consequences may at first elicit a "so what?" kind of response. However, with closer reflection, some of the most taken-for-granted aspects of everyday life become fascinating yet puzzling, obvious yet elusive. It is particularly difficult to explain human behavior that on the surface seems mundane but that exerts a profound influence on our social interactions. Appearance and clothing are so familiar and visible that we do not often consider the significance of them in everyday life. Only when our attention is directed toward them do we realize how they provide exciting and relevant prospects for a better understanding of personal expression and social relations.

## Symbolic Appearances in Context

Part of the complexity in the social significance of clothing may be attributed to the dynamics of **context**—the social circumstances or more complete framework of daily life in which clothing is worn, within the visual context of personal appearance. Appearance messages do not exist in limbo; instead, they are embedded in context. A context may consist of a setting or a relationship, or may even lie within ourselves, as when we are attempting to understand ourselves or others. Context includes the attributes of a wearer and a perceiver of clothing, as well as the entire history of their relationship and the nature of the setting in which the interaction occurs. Even more generally, the culture in which individuals live and the historical meanings associated with their clothes represent a more general context influencing how people relate to one another (see Figure 2-1).

**FIGURE 2-1**

*How are clothes interpreted on the basis of context in this picture? To illustrate the importance of context, first look at the clothes in relation to the individuals' entire appearances. Then, consider the social circumstances involved—including the setting as well as the identities of, and relationship between, the wearers. Also, look at the larger, more abstract cultural and historical context in which we interpret the social context of these clothes. How and why has the concept of service station changed in the last 40 years? Our perceptions of the roles of service station attendants influence our actions as well as our expectations. Photo courtesy of the California State Library Collection, City of Sacramento, Museum and History Division.*

Scholars studying clothing and appearance as aspects of human behavior have asked a variety of questions and pursued many lines of inquiry. It does not require an academic degree, however, to tell us that clothes are used on a daily basis in terms of planning, dressing, grooming, cleaning, as well as perceiving or "reading" certain aspects of others' thoughts and behavior. Therefore, it might be helpful to focus first on the everyday aspects of appearance management and perception and then consider how these compare with the social psychology of clothing as a discipline of study.

*Everyday Life*

Clothing and appearance may be explored in relation to everyday life—by considering how people themselves use clothing to frame and explain their social experiences. In these terms, people engaging in appearance management may be regarded as "lay designers" or "lay stylists." The processes of planning what one is going to wear and combining different elements of appearance parallel some of the processes apparel designers and stylists use as they select, combine, coordinate, and reconfigure elements of clothing to create new styles.

At the same time individuals manage their appearances and function as lay stylists or designers, they try to interpret other individuals' appearances. Psychologist Gordon Allport (1968) once described a social psychologist as someone who attempts to understand, explain, and predict how individuals influence one another's thoughts, feelings, and actions. Many authors have pointed out that it is not only scholars who make such attempts on a regular basis. Psychologist Fritz Heider (1958) noted that we are all "naive" (natural or everyday) social psychologists. In our daily observations, we form ideas about others and about the social situations in which we are involved. We have a basic desire to understand the meanings behind others' appearances and actions, so we try to interpret and explain them in hopes of better predicting future behaviors.

In comparing the interpretations of lay social psychologists with those of social scientists, Heider (1958, p. 5) said: "Though these ideas are usually not well formulated, they often function adequately. They achieve in some measure what a science is supposed to achieve: an adequate description of the subject matter which makes prediction possible." Social scientists attempt to structure their knowledge to make it more cumulative, so that one set of research findings leads to new questions that build upon existing knowledge. Essentially, a basic difference between common-sense, or practical, lay thought and scientific thought is the emphasis in scientific thought on becoming more useful than common sense by contributing to *shared* knowledge (Douglas, 1970, p. 28). To further shared knowledge in scientific inquiry, it is necessary to articulate the basic assumptions about humans that lead to further inquiry. Yet a sensitivity to the basic tenets of everyday life is essential if our knowledge about clothing and human behavior is to be grounded in social contexts as people experience them. Therefore, a careful study of common-sense meanings and actions in everyday life, in people's own terms, must be pursued systematically. Then, observations based on such an understanding can be accumulated and systematized to further knowledge and increase understanding.

There are a number of **perspectives** from which we can approach the social psychology of clothing. To have a perspective is to reflect on a subject using critical thinking, to analyze patterns of relationships within an articulated viewpoint, and to develop a framework that spells out the basic questions one is trying to answer. In this way, meaningful coherence and direction are provided for pursuing further knowledge (Williams, 1986). A perspective includes the values, beliefs, and meaning that provide a framework and a point of view for study (Theodorson and Theodorson, 1969). By clarifying one's perspective, the ideas and compatible **methodologies,** or ways of discovering new knowledge, become clearer. So the following question may be addressed as we consider a perspective: How does this perspective provide a focus or framework for understanding clothing as human behavior?

In this chapter, three perspectives that come from different disciplines of study will be addressed: (1) the cognitive perspective from psychology, (2) the symbolic-interactionist perspective from sociology, and (3) the cultural perspective that emerges from a variety of disciplines in the humanities and social sciences (as discussed in Chapter One). In this discussion, various points of view will be identified in relation to clothing, appearance, and everyday life. From these perspectives, more specific *theories* may be identified, which will be referred to throughout the book. A theory serves to describe, explain, and predict how people relate to clothing and use it in appearance management and perception. The basic component of a theory is a **concept,** or a term that expresses an abstract idea by describing or explaining basic social processes or relationships among social objects. For example, clothing is an observable or concrete object, but a concept enables us to go beyond the obvious or visible to a more abstract level of thinking—one that would point to the relation between different kinds of clothing that may on the surface seem to be quite different but reflect the same kinds of social-psychological processes. (See Figure 2-2 for a diagram of perspective, theory, and concept and how they guide our pursuit of knowledge.)

Concepts are used to develop **generalizations,** or general statements that indicate what we know about human behavior based upon observations or research findings. The kinds of generalizations we make about clothing and human behavior are largely related to the level of **social organization** to which we are referring. The concept of social organization refers to the study of different levels or contexts of human behavior, ranging from "micro" (individual) to "macro" (collective) levels. It is important to clarify whether we are explaining and describing appearance processes as they relate to the self, to the way people interact, to group or organizational behavior, or to subcultures or society as a whole. The following perspectives vary somewhat in this regard.

The cognitive perspective focuses primarily on the micro level, by considering how individuals' thought processes lead to social perceptions. However, this perspective also provides a point of view that helps to predict the consequences of such perceptions for social interaction. The symbolic-interactionist perspective deals with the self as well as social interaction; it also helps to clarify some aspects of appearance symbolism in subcultures, as well as fashion change (at

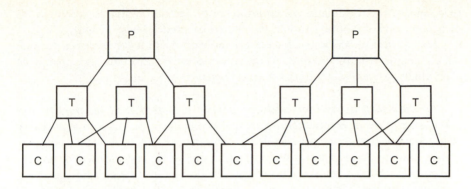

**P** = **Perspective**—larger framework for organizing knowledge and guiding inquiry; guided by a system of values, beliefs, and meanings that provide a point of view for study
**T** = **Theory**—set of ideas that describe, explain, and predict outcomes and relationships; guides the development of research hypotheses
**C** = **Concept**—basic component of a theory; a word that expresses an idea to describe or explain basic social processes

*FIGURE 2-2*
*Perspectives, theories, and concepts guide the way we approach inquiry, or the pursuit of new knowledge, in the social psychology of clothing; they also enable us to make predictions that can be tested in the form of research hypotheses. Once we have some research evidence or observations about clothing and human behavior, we can make some generalizations and organize the new knowledge using a perspective. Also, research findings may yield new concepts and thories to explain social life.*

the macro level). Finally, a cultural perspective leads us to consider symbolic appearances in a larger context of shared beliefs and values. All of these perspectives, as we will see, deal in some way with meaning and context, yet they approach these concepts with different points of view. The **contextual** perspective incorporates those concepts and methodologies, derived from the other three perspectives, that best describe and explain social meanings of clothes, with sensitivity to the contexts in which they are found.

## *Cognitive Perspective*

The cognitive perspective focuses primarily on appearance perception— specifically in terms of how people form impressions about one another and, to some extent, about themselves. This perspective, then, focuses on individual thought processes. Clothing and appearance are viewed as providing clues about what a person is like. These cues make up what we might think of as "the tip of the iceberg" (Zerubavel, 1982, p. 98). We can never see the entire iceberg, especially the part that is nonvisible or beneath the surface. However, we do have some information to go on, and using that information, it is clear that people form impressions about one another. In this respect, clothing is regarded as a stimulus that leads to the formulation of an impression. Factors leading to certain kinds of perceptions of clothing should also be considered (Davis, 1984a).

So, a cognitive perspective focuses primarily on the thought processes through which people use and retrieve information about individuals and groups of individuals, particularly in relation to personal traits or qualities.

## Basic Assumptions

*1. Cues such as clothing and appearance are often used to simplify and make sense of social interactions.* This premise is based on the idea that reality is too complex to be comprehended in its entirety. To deal with a complex reality, humans develop means such as mental shortcuts to enable them to process information. Such mental shortcuts might include cognitive systems for classifying or categorizing people on the basis of appearance cues. Within a given category (for example, "yuppie" or punk) there may be a cluster of traits or attributes to explain what a person classified in that category would be like. This cluster of traits might be called a **cognitive structure.** In a cognitive structure, some traits or qualities may be regarded as more central or dominant than others. Observers tend to assume, in the absence of conflicting information, that a person appearing a certain way has not only one quality that is inferred, but also a related set of traits that are linked to that one quality. Therefore, there is an assumption that traits or qualities are linked together and that if one of these traits is true, then the rest of the traits will also hold true (Schneider, 1973). For example, if an observer infers that an artistically dressed male is creative, that observer might also be likely to expect him to have a sense of humor. Perceivers may have their own distinctive cognitive structures, consisting of traits that they expect to be related.

Cognitive theorists would indicate that we are not overtly aware of how we use cognitive structures; instead, they are often used at an implicit or subtle level of consciousness. So, appearance may be used to provide information about an observed person, as a perceiver calls on private "theories" about what that person is like. In the process, appearance is likely to be linked to a category and a set of expected traits or qualities. Therefore, appearance perception may serve as a kind of strategy for responding to the complexities of social life. However, a cognitive perspective would suggest that although people's thought processes tend to be structured, these processes are used with a remarkable degree of flexibility as people move from one context to the next (Taylor, 1981). This flexibility is necessary because people often do not fit into existing "categories," and inevitably some of the traits in a cognitive structure will prove to be inaccurate.

*2. People strive for some consistency and continuity in their appearance perceptions.* This premise stems from the cognitive assumption that people strive for a psychological state of internal adjustment and that people actively work to maintain consistency and continuity in their thought processes. Fritz Heider (1958) assumed that humans have a goal to maintain cognitive equilibrium or balance. Similarly, Leon Festinger (1957) focused on the importance of **cognitive consistency** as a goal, referring to the "fit" among different pieces of information.

FIGURE 2-3
*We may tend to have mental pictures or images of a "southern California surfer." When we see people who do not fit that mental image, there may be a sense of cognitive inconsistency. Once this occurs, we may need to evaluate and perhaps reshape our mental images and the social categories to which they refer. These surfers are Indian Sikhs who are wearing what is comparable to the undergarment of their traditional turbans. Photo by Mark Kaiser.*

For example, perceivers might find it perplexing or troubling if a person's appearance seemed to contradict his or her role in a situation (see Figure 2-3).

This desire for consistency does not mean that perceivers do not alter their thought processes. In fact, fashion change and social situations are often likely to lead perceivers to question and revise their cognitive structures. To do so requires a more active level of consciousness than might ordinarily be used in perceiving a person who fits cognitive categories and structures. Moreover, the degree to which a person strives for consistency or balance is likely to be affected by social context. At times some contradiction, particularly in the realm of clothing and fashion, might be stimulating.

*3. Humans seek and use aesthetic stimulation in their environments.* Just as they strive to simplify reality, they also desire stimulation and fulfillment (McGuire, 1985). (See Figure 2-4). In the visual realm, clothing and appearance can provide such stimulation and, with fashion change, it is inevitable that novel stimuli will continue to be produced and perceived. The degree to which people seek aesthetic stimulation may vary, and context is also likely to influence the degree of desire or tolerance for diversity and novelty. For example, aesthetic stimulation is likely to be sought or expected in the appearances of rock stars or fashion models.

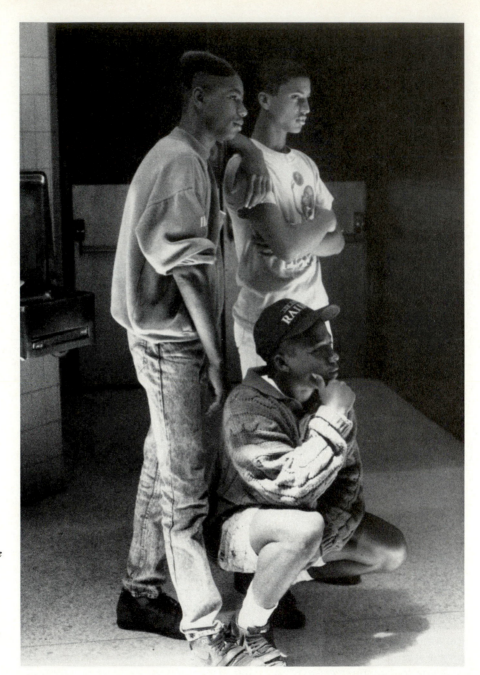

**FIGURE 2-4**
*These young men display enough consistency across their individual looks to provide a sense of cognitive balance to a perceiver. At the same time, the cognitive need for novelty and visual stimulation is provided by the degree of individual expression they display (for example, as in the unique hairstyle of the male on the left). Photo by Joan L. Chandler.*

**4. *Humans are motivated to explain social occurrences or outcomes in terms of people or situations.*** Heider (1958) used the term **attribution** to refer to individual desires to determine causality. He indicated humans have a basic mental need to indicate why events occur as they do and why people act as they do. This process of making attributions is not merely internal in nature, but involves external information that perceivers evaluate and weigh (Jones and Davis, 1965; Kelley, 1973). Clothing and appearance are likely to be cues that enable perceivers to evaluate the source or cause of a social outcome. According to attribution theory, people may explain a social outcome in terms of the people involved, and the appearances of these people may provide clues to their role and to personal traits or qualities. Or, perceivers might explain a social outcome based on the situation or context, including factors that are outside the control of the people involved. Even so, clothing might be used to explain or define the context. In Chapter Eight, research focusing on these two kinds of possibilities will be discussed. In the meantime, however, it is important to focus on how context enters into people's thought processes as a potential "cause" of a social outcome. The idea that perceivers are trying to make sense of everyday life by developing explanations guides the methods cognitive theorists use to study appearance perception.

## Methodology

Cognitive social psychologists tend to study the effect of clothing and appearance cues on people's perceptions by manipulating them in experiments. Of course, clothing lends itself to considerable manipulation; once a "look" has been created by a researcher that is to be compared with another kind of appearance, all appearances are pretested to see if the desired effect is being created. Clothes serve as stimuli in these studies and are either viewed on real people, photographed, or illustrated. Then the different appearances are incorporated into an experimental design. These experiments are conducted either in a laboratory or in a field setting.

Cognitive social psychologists generally use research methods that are conducive to **quantitative analysis,** consisting of a coding of responses in a format that lends itself to statistical analysis on a computer. (See Social Focus 2-1.) The goal in many cases is to test whether or not certain variables influence or cause outcomes, for example, whether a change in clothing changes a perceiver's judgments. This type of approach ordinarily involves the formulation and acceptance or rejection of hypotheses. Appearance manipulations, then, can be assessed statistically to see if they produced the expected outcome, at a level that would be expected beyond chance.

Quantitative analysis is also conducive to assessing the degree of consensus on a certain judgment. For example, how many perceivers really attribute intelligence to people who wear glasses? Statistical analysis enables researchers to see if a significant number of perceivers do so and also to determine differences among perceivers on the basis of certain attributes (gender, age, and attitudes). Quantitative analysis allows researchers to process large amounts of data with efficiency, using tools such as computers and statistical software packages. The

# Examples of Methodology in Cognitive Social Psychology of Appearance

The cognitive perspective calls for an understanding of how people attempt to understand others' appearances to make sense of their everyday worlds. To this end, methods for studying appearance often attempt to tap perceivers' thought processes. Here we will focus on a form of measurement known as the **semantic differential scale**, which is frequently used to explore perceptions based on appearance. Sarah Sweat and Mary Ann Zentner (1985) examined perceptions of four types of female appearance styles: dramatic, natural, classic, and romantic. One goal of the study was to examine the *differences* in perceptions among these four styles; by using quantitative, statistical analyses, such differences were discerned. For purposes of illustrating the semantic differential technique, however, let's focus on just one of the styles: romantic. Each of 360 students (170 males and 190 females) rated a line drawing of a woman wearing a dress that had a soft, flowing skirt and a blouse with a relatively low V-neckline decorated with a ruffle.

Thirty-six semantic differential scales were used. Each of these consisted of a set of bipolar adjectives, or descriptive terms, at two extreme (opposite) ends. Let's look at several examples used in the study:

*friendly* \_\_\_\_:\_\_\_\_:\_\_\_\_:\_\_\_\_:\_\_\_\_:\_\_\_\_:\_\_\_\_ *unfriendly*
*soft* \_\_\_\_:\_\_\_\_:\_\_\_\_:\_\_\_\_:\_\_\_\_:\_\_\_\_:\_\_\_\_ *hard*
*warm* \_\_\_\_:\_\_\_\_:\_\_\_\_:\_\_\_\_:\_\_\_\_:\_\_\_\_:\_\_\_\_ *cold*

Individuals could put an *X* in the blank according to the degree to which the woman in the drawing was perceived as friendly as compared with unfriendly, and so on. (Note that there are seven blanks in these scales; the number may actually vary from one study to the next, depending on such factors as the preferences of the researchers and the specific requirements for the study.) Once the students had completed all of the scales, a statistical technique known as **factor analysis** was used to identify *groupings* of the adjective scales. For purposes of analysis, it becomes necessary to simplify and organize the data in a manageable form. Factor analysis allows researchers to determine relations *among* adjective scales in order to reduce the number of variables and to derive variables that are broader in nature, conceptually speaking. So, for example, the 36 scales were reduced to four groupings or "subscales." One of these was labelled by the researchers as *social–unsociable*, because it included the scales listed earlier, as well as other scales related to sociability. The other three groupings or subscales were *nontraditional–traditional*, *formal–informal*, and *weak–strong*. The average ratings for the romantic style, for each of these groupings of scales, were as follows: nontraditional–traditional (3.13), sociable–unsociable (2.46), formal–informal (2.91), weak–strong (3.65). Given that the averages could have been as high as 7, it becomes clear that the style was perceived as sociable. Through further analysis comparing the ratings across the four appearance styles, the researchers determined that this style was the only one that was near the "weak" side of the weak–strong grouping (although an average of 3.65 is not far from the neutral point of 4.00). Additionally, statistical techniques allowed the researchers to compare males' and females' responses toward the styles. Females perceived the romantic style to be significantly more nontraditional than did the males.

Clearly, as this study shows, quantitative methods are extremely valuable in allowing researchers to conduct studies that have enough people to obtain a good cross-section of views, that consider many variables and then reduce them to a manageable size, and that provide meaningful comparisons (across styles as well as perceivers). Although methods such as these are commonly used in conjunction with the cognitive perspective, other methods may also be used. For example, when a researcher has little basis for knowing which adjectives should be selected for the perceivers and styles involved, it is valuable to use methods that allow perceivers to make free responses, or to use their own words. With any method of a researcher's choice, there are advantages and disadvantages; the goal is to select a method that provides the best opportunity for meeting the major objectives of the study.

drawback of quantitative analysis, however, is that researchers may find significant results and not be able to explain them in very great detail. The "why" behind the findings may seem to be lacking in some cases, especially when unexpected or novel findings emerge. To discover these deeper insights, the symbolic-interactionist perspective offers some useful concepts and methods.

## Symbolic-Interactionist Perspective

Whereas the cognitive perspective focuses primarily on appearance perception, the symbolic-interactionist perspective deals with both appearance management *and* appearance perception. Thus two-way interaction is a major focus. Accordingly, the term *meaning* tends to be used more in this perspective, as compared with "information," used more prevalently within the cognitive perspective. Yet it is important to understand that the two are not necessarily distinct from one another. Information may or may not be meaningful to a person. It could be considered more meaningful, in symbolic-interactionist terms, if two people process the same bits of information similarly, or if they jointly construct an interpretation using the same information. On an individual level, information could become meaningful if a person regards that information as salient or personally relevant. Another difference between these two perspectives may be found in approaches to the study of appearance perception. Whereas cognitive researchers tend to look for causality as attributed either to people *or* situations, symbolic interactionists would maintain that people and their appearances cannot be isolated from social context, so they should be looked at jointly (as people fit their lines of action together in a context). Again, however, it is important to note that this difference is more closely aligned with a frame of reference and mode of inquiry than it is with a basic conceptual difference. Both cognitive and symbolic-interactionist researchers would probably acknowledge that individuals should be studied in relation to social context, but *how* they would approach this study would vary.

Symbolic interaction is a perspective that pursues the study of social actions and social objects (McCall and Simmons, 1966). The point of view guiding this perspective is that humans fit their "lines of action" (streams of behavior or social actions) together to make sense of the situations in which they find themselves (Blumer, 1969a). Let's explore some basic concepts and assumptions of symbolic interaction by discussing Figure 2-5. Imagine that you are an attorney in San Francisco wearing business attire who needs a document to be delivered several blocks away. As you meet the bicycle messenger in the photograph, how will symbolic-interactionist concepts be illustrated?

First you must interpret his appearance to understand who he is. The concept of **self-indication** refers to people's attempts to understand the social world by defining or identifying the objects and people that comprise that world (Morrione and Farberman, 1981). If you make a self-indication identifying the person in Figure 2-5 as a messenger (as he is also making a self-indication about

**FIGURE 2-5**
*Imagine that you are an attorney with a small law firm in San Francisco and that you have a document that needs to be delivered to an office several blocks away. You walk outside to make the delivery and remember that an important client may be trying to phone you. The messenger in this picture rides by; how will you respond toward him? (See the discussion of symbolic-interactionist concepts and premises or assumptions of this perspective to see the point of view from which this picture might be interpreted.) Photo by Carla M. Freeman.*

you), this will help you fit your lines of action together. In other words, you may request his services and he will respond accordingly.

Through people's joint actions, the meanings assigned to clothing and appearances in certain social situations are *socially constructed* or mutually defined. It may be necessary for people interacting to "work out" their interpretations of clothing, so their interactions and communication will proceed smoothly. In our hypothetical interaction, as you begin to communicate with one another, you may both continue to confirm and evaluate your self-indications (to make sure you want to do business with each other). You may then continue to assess some of the symbols you find in one another's appearance, even as you talk. Your self-indications about one another may be altered or refined as necessary so your interaction can occur.

A symbolic-interactionist perspective focuses on this process of *negotiation*, and individuals are said to have communicated meaningfully when the same response is evoked in an observer as in the self. (You understand each other.) This response may take such forms as an emotion, an interpretation, a judgment, a sensation, or an expression of taste. For example, you may be relieved to see one another, because you both need the delivery to take place.

Many jointly constructed meanings are not exactly the same, but may be more accurately described as "approximately the same" associations (Davis, 1982). In other words, individuals come to associate the appearance or clothing item with the same kind of related objects, relationships, or social categories of people. Although you may have successfully planned the delivery by interpreting each other's appearance and acting accordingly toward one another, you still may have only "approximate" understandings of what different aspects of your appearances mean to you. You may also assume that you have different attitudes about some social or political issues. Your interpretations about these finer points of appearance perception may or may not be totally accurate, but you have had a sufficient understanding of one another's identities to communicate smoothly and to be mutually satisfied.

Now that we have considered how a symbolic-interactionist perspective leads us to view people constructing meanings in everyday life, we can turn to some of the basic assumptions this perspective uses to guide an understanding of appearance management and perception:

*1. Humans create their own realities, in part, by managing their appearances.* A symbolic-interactionist perspective assumes that humans are capable of developing their own ideas and actions (Denzin, 1970, pp. 260–261). Appearance management includes both ideas and actions. Clothing selections, in particular, may be altered and modified to fit a given situation or to create a special type of impression. We present personal information to others through our appearances and convey such messages as age, taste, occupation, philosophy of life, ideas about social conformity, and the like. Furthermore, we are aware that others do so at the same time. Let's return to our messenger example and imagine how he might manage his appearance to create his own reality. He has a job that allows a great deal of freedom in terms of appearance, so he can express his preference for a nonconformist lifestyle. As an attorney, you need to wear businesslike attire to fit into your social world.

As consumers of fashion, in general, fit into their social worlds, they do not merely buy, in a passive manner, what manufacturers and retailers offer to them. Instead, consumers actively and selectively use what is available to them to shape their own realities, to express themselves visually, and to join their actions with those of others in everyday life. Consumers may also combine

**Basic Assumptions**

clothes, modify the way they are worn, or wear them in new contexts, in ways that may be different from what manufacturers and retailers could have ever visualized (see Figure 2-6).

*2. To fit their lines of action together, people use symbols.* People live in a world that is understood in terms of how they indicate it to themselves, and it is necessary to examine the symbols that they use to do so if joint actions are to be understood (Morrione and Farberman, 1981). *Symbols* have shared meanings for people; they may or may not be physical or concrete, but in either case they do include an abstract component. Clothing and appearance symbols may be concrete or material objects, or they may be stored in memory as an image that evokes meaningful responses. We use symbols to define or represent our realities. In an interview with Morrione and Farberman (1981), Herbert Blumer noted that symbols allow for some expression of feelings and for a kind of merging or blending of social experiences. Symbols help to initiate responses, provide cues to behavior, organize behavior, focus attention on critical elements in a social situation, and permit us to organize our actions as appropriate (Stryker, 1980, p. 56). Symbols derive their meanings from social contexts and are sustained in them; they enrich the way we view everyday life. They serve to provide some degree of continuity and structure from one context to the next, as well as to present some variety and change, because of the way people are able to manipulate them (Franks and Seeburger, 1980).

By using symbols in this way as they fit their lines of action together, humans are able to develop a sense of living in a social world that is shared with others. This sense of commonality is fundamental to social interaction (Wilson, 1970).

*3. We act toward other people, in part, on the basis of the meanings their appearances hold for us.* This premise is derived from Blumer's (1969a) assertion that people act toward objects and other people on the basis of meanings. In other words, we use the cues provided by their appearances, interpret them, and attempt to organize our actions toward them accordingly. Once some semblance of meaning of symbols can be agreed on, social interaction can flow along more routine or customary lines (Denzin, 1970, pp. 260–261). We tend to live in a world of objects or commodities for which we have no responsibility in creating. Clothes and related accessories may be designed and produced by the apparel industry, and some meaning may have already been given to them by fashion designers, writers, and retailers who have suggested potential contexts for wear. However, when people have occasion to question these objects or to imagine different uses, new meanings may be constructed. Humans have the capacity to break out of these old routines and develop new frameworks for interacting. Creative appearance management and perception afford opportunities to do so.

*4. Meanings associated with appearance symbols emerge from social interactions with others.* Blumer (1969a) noted that people come to social contexts with a storehouse of meanings, and this storehouse is developed and refined over time based on social interactions. Meanings are not just passively received; each person must learn, discover, or develop a meaning on his or her own. This

**FIGURE 2-6**
*One can imagine all the ways a second-grade boy might wear this outfit to create his own reality. He can roll the sleeves and pants legs up or down. He may also remove the suspenders, which may have appealed more to his mother than to him. Alternatively, he may enjoy wearing the suspenders and the idea of making a statement among his peers, if this outfit is perceived as such in his social circles. Photo by Susan B. Kaiser.*

process of discovery is generally linked to social experiences or quasisocial exposure to appearances (such as the media). For example, a second-grade boy wearing the outfit shown in Figure 2-6 may discover how peers will respond to suspenders; he may learn to differentiate (implicitly) people who would wear them versus those who would not. In contrast, his mother's preference for this outfit may have been formulated while viewing children's fashion catalogs or magazines.

If we are to understand social interactions and meanings, we must take into account the viewpoints of different people in a situation. One context gives rise to a new context and, in this way, meaning changes. A symbolic-interactionist perspective accepts change and fluctuation of meanings as normal, because humans are creative and dynamic as they attempt to construct meaningful lives for themselves and others with whom they are connected (Straus, 1981). Within this fluctuation, however, there are strands of continuity that seem to influence ongoing actions and social order.

5. *Meanings assigned to clothing and appearance are manipulated and modified through interpretive processes* (Blumer, 1969a). Symbolic interactionists contend that there is often a tentative nature to meaning. Even after we have arrived at a given meaning of a clothing symbol, we are likely to exert some effort in either maintaining or altering this meaning as required by subsequent interactions (Davis, 1982). Therefore, perceived purpose or meaning of clothes in certain contexts is always provisional and subject to revision or reinterpretation (see Figure 2-7). Referring back to Figure 2-5, you might arrive at some tentative interpretations of various components of the messenger's appearance (the spiked wrist bands, the pierced nose, the scarf, the strips of fabric tied around the hands), but you realize that these interpretations are subject to revision.

Revision is accomplished through interpretive processes, or the means by which people define and redefine clothing and appearance as necessary. The process orientation in the symbolic-interactionist perspective leads us to consider that when people come together with different interpretations some newer or modified joint interpretations are likely to emerge. An analogy to interpretive processes might be the game "telephone," when people sit in a circle and, in turn, whisper the same message to the person adjacent to them. By the time the last person has received the message, it has inevitably changed. The same is true of appearance perception, except in this case we are dealing with the visual realm. As we are influenced by the images of others with whom we come into contact, we construct interpretations and even possibly consider ways we could wear similar garments in the same or different contexts. In this way, meaning evolves because of the very nature of social life and human creativity.

There are many shades of differences between what we might consider interpretive and noninterpretive (automatic) processes. At times our assessments or identifications of other people are so automatic that we are barely conscious we are making them; at other times, we are required to concentrate and more actively construct an interpretation. It would be tiring to have to construct interpretations actively all of the time, but it would be boring and tedious to never do so. Those interpretations that require more active interpretation and social construction are most likely to lead to new alterations in meaning, because under these circumstances either automatic meanings do not exist for people or people have chosen to question existing meanings.

*Methodology*    The premises mentioned earlier point to the overriding idea that humans use appearance management and perception to fit their lines of action together. By

**FIGURE 2-7**
*Imagine you are in San Francisco's Chinatown and need directions to return to your hotel. You see this man on the street and wonder if he speaks English so that you can ask for help. When you ask him, he cheerfully responds that he is an English professor who taught in China before coming to the United States. The more you come to know about him as your interaction progresses, the more fascinated you become with his background and experiences he shares (in addition to the directions). You may need to reformulate your interpretation of his appearance in light of your interaction with him, and especially after coming to a general understanding you are likely to realize the complexities involved in assigning meaning. Photo by Carla M. Freeman.*

doing so, they are generally able to anticipate and interpret the social contexts in which they find themselves. The key to this process is meaning, which is used in conjunction with symbols to make sense of social interaction. Symbolic interactionists maintain that to understand people's social worlds, a researcher must try to discover their understandings or frames of reference. How individuals frame and interpret social context must be understood to accomplish this task. This philosophy on method has been described as "antielitist," because the actor's view cannot be denied. Who is to say which way of knowing or interpreting is correct? Symbolic interactionists would say that expertise should be viewed as located in ordinary people's lives (Wellman, 1988); researchers should not presume to know the "real" reason for how and why people dress as they do.

How does the symbolic-interactionist perspective promote the study of clothing and appearance in everyday life? First, it places the topic of study in the world of everyday experience—people using, defining, and interpreting clothes in contexts as part of a larger picture of reality. Second, a person researching clothing content as well as fashion change does not presume to understand the social worlds of others in advance of study. With these basic guidelines in mind, different methods of study may be used. Typically, symbolic interactionists have used methods of inquiry that involve close contact with the individuals under study—through such means as *participant observation*, where the researcher becomes immersed in the subjects' social worlds, and in-depth interviews, where the subjects are free to provide meanings of their own. These types of methods employ **qualitative analysis.**

Qualitative researchers, then, tend to work in the field, more closely with people in their everyday contexts (rather than in a laboratory, for example). These researchers must locate a specific group and gain access to observe it closely. The idea is to get the insider's view. The advantages of such analysis are that the data are extremely rich, fascinating, and grounded in everyday contexts. (See Social Focus 2-2). The disadvantages are that volumes of data are collected, frequently through field notes, and it is often laborious and time-consuming to sift through all of these data to identify underlying threads of continuity and develop conclusions. It may be difficult at times to assess consensus in meanings among subjects, because they may construct their interpretations or phrase their responses quite differently. Moreover, researchers must be extremely cautious to avoid injecting their own perceptions as to what is important. If this problem can be avoided, however, qualitative methods do provide a picture of reality that is close to everyday life and that yields fresh insights and interpretation that cannot be provided through other means. Qualitative researchers often try to use a variety of methods (for example, observations plus interviews) to check and recheck their interpretations.

In recent years, symbolic interactionists have been more open to other modes of analysis, but the basic principle of considering the viewpoints of participants in social interaction when constructing explanations of those interactions must still be met (Stryker, 1987). This philosophy on how to study social life is not very different from that employed in a cultural perspective.

# Qualitative Approach to the Study of What It Means to Be Beautiful

Qualitative methods are especially well-suited to the study of meanings that people assign to phenomena in their everyday lives. Numerous studies in social psychology have explored how beautiful people are *perceived* by others. Typically, these studies are based on the cognitive perspective and employ such techniques as semantic differential scales (discussed in Social Focus 2-1). Instead, drawing heavily from the symbolic-interactionist perspective for guidance, Jacque Lynn Foltyn (1989) used a different approach in her doctoral dissertation at the University of California at San Diego. She wanted to determine how being beautiful affects the lives of women, in their own words.

Accordingly, she conducted in-depth, open-ended interviews with 110 respondents. (This is a relatively large number of respondents for a study of this type.) The interviewees included 50 beautiful women (25 of whom were professional models or actresses), 20 women of average appearance, 30 men, and 10 arbiters of beauty (for example, modeling agents). Some of the interviews lasted several hours and took longer than one session. Although a list of questions and topics were used as a base for the interview format, these were tailored according to the individual's situation, and the respondents were allowed to pursue topics they wanted to discuss in great depth.

Let's look at some examples of the type of information that pertained to the process of becoming a beautiful self, derived from Foltyn's interviews. She found that perceiving the self as beautiful was contextual. Only 7 of the 50 beautiful women could not remember a time when they were not considered (by others or themselves) as beautiful. Some were not born beautiful; others were very attractive as children but were less so during adolescence; some became beautiful only in their adult years; and some actively constructed their beauty through makeup or even plastic surgery. The following accounts are representative of the women's processes of "discovering" their beauty. (The names of the subjects are fictitious.)

Allysa, 30, "blossomed" during adolescence and recalled that she was mystified in high school when people first began telling her how beautiful she was.

> I was treated really special. It seemed like I was an object of curiosity. People acted flattered if I spoke with them (Foltyn, 1989, p. 257).

Debbie, 26, was a model and former international beauty queen who described herself as a "cute" (but not beautiful) child who developed an interest in makeup and fashion.

> I started modeling when I was 15 and I remember I just wanted to do it. So it wasn't like somebody came up and said, "You are beautiful; you have to model." . . . And at these sessions . . . photo sessions or commercials . . . people would say, "Gee, you really are beautiful, you know." And I'd say, "Well, thank you." I was almost surprised they would stop and take the time to tell me that.

> I was about 16 the first time I really looked in the mirror and analyzed my face and realized that it was put together all right. And I could see the difference between myself and other people. It was OK. I suddenly began to realize that pretty could apply to me (Foltyn, 1989, p. 271).

In contrast, some respondents had been extremely attractive children who "lost their looks" during adolescence, then "recovered" them in their late teens or twenties. For example, Lisa, 23, remembered looking at herself in the mirror during her mid-teens and deciding that her confident assessment of her attractiveness was no longer valid. By 19, however, she was beautiful again, but would protest when people told her so: "Oh no—I'm not now. I was really a beautiful child, but not any longer."

For the respondents, being beautiful had its ups and downs. For example, men had pursued some of the beautiful women because of their looks, and some less-than-meaningful relationships had been formulated on that basis. Some women had experienced sexual abuse. Many suffered from identity confusion because being beautiful was not necessarily a constant throughout the life cycle.

Based on her research, Foltyn (1989, p. vii) concluded that being beautiful is "an exaggerated and paradoxical female experience, fraught with distinct privileges and problems, revealing of such larger social issues as the formation of identity, gender role socialization, and trends in mass society." In addition to the richness and significance of the data that led her to this conclusion, a major advantage of the methodological approach lies in its ability to pinpoint ambivalences and complexities in being beautiful. Studies based on quantitative data alone may lead one to miss some of these insights that can only come from individuals' own accounts and interpretations.

## *Cultural Perspective*

To place our study of clothing and appearance into a larger, cultural framework, it is helpful to consider the contributions of different disciplines focusing on cultural objects and their relation to belief systems. The cultural perspective discussed throughout this book is interdisciplinary and therefore draws from theories and concepts from a variety of human sciences, as described in Chapter One. These areas of study include anthropology, consumer behavior, cultural studies, ethnic studies, semiotics, sociology, and women's studies. Clearly, the concept of culture crosses disciplinary boundaries, and there has been a renewed academic focus on culture in recent years. For example, the interdisciplinary field of cultural studies has been profoundly influenced by feminists who have pointed to gender inequities as perpetuated by culture (Allor, 1987).

It has become evident that almost anything can develop cultural significance as it comes to be regarded as meaningful, whether by design or by serendipity. Clothing is certainly no exception. People of all cultures modify their appearances in some way, yet the symbolic systems and codes used to decipher and interpret clothing are likely to vary. In cultural studies, culture is regarded as a kind of "structure of feeling" (Allor, 1987) or a context within which people experience and evaluate their lives. Therefore, the social psychology of clothing must consider meaning not only within social contexts, but also within a larger cultural context.

The essence of culture, from a semiotic viewpoint focusing on how meaning is produced, lies in the interplay between a kind of "historical" memory (the history of meaning) and social resistance to this memory (MacCannell and MacCannell, 1982, p. 27). For example, how males and females relate to one another is symbolized by clothing differences, and the meanings we associate with some of these clothes may be traced back to earlier, historical memories that are hard to "shake." Therefore, a cultural perspective enables us to view the meanings of clothing as they have developed over time, as one historical context leads to another one (see Figure 2-8).

The Swiss linguist Saussure (1959, p. 66) called for a semiotics that would some day encompass not only the study of language but also that of other cultural forms (such as clothing). He called for a link between semiotics and social psychology, because he recognized the need to understand social relations within a larger context of cultural meanings. Whenever people share a common culture, they are likely to be exposed to a network of tangible products. The buying, selling, and wearing of clothes all contribute to **signification** or the development of meaning associated with cultural objects. So it is not just the product that results in the process of signification, but it is also the *way people relate to these products and what they do to or with them.* In fact, a fundamental idea behind a cultural perspective, derived from semiotics, is that *the perceiver of a cultural message is a vital part of the process of signification* (MacCannell and MacCannell, 1982).

*FIGURE 2-8*
*Some appearance styles seem to carry with them a kind of "historical memory," as is the case with this classic skirted suit. It was designed by Coco Chanel in Paris in the mid-1960s, but is reminiscent of the 1940s and similar to styles of the late 1980s. Photo courtesy of the Trustees of the Victoria and Albert Museum.*

*1. Collective values are produced and reproduced through cultural forms.* In other words, certain appearances or material artifacts come to represent *shared* values within a culture. These shared values often are linked to cultural belief systems (Johnson, 1986–1987). **Cultural forms** then are tangible aspects of culture that somehow represent more abstract ideas that are ingrained within the culture. These forms often refer to *social relations*: how people relate to one

**Basic Assumptions**

**FIGURE 2-9**
*The appearances of these two males in India may be contrasted with that of the female American tourist (left). The specific appearances of the individuals in this picture visually represent more abstract American and Indian **cultural forms**. Specific appearances, as well as the more general cultural forms to which they refer, should be interpreted within their contexts. Photo by Stephen Cunha.*

another on the basis of such qualities as gender, social class, age, and ethnicity. Some meanings of clothing and appearance symbols are provided and transmitted by culture, and we interact with one another within this context of cultural meaning. A cultural form may specifically refer to a kind of abstract, composite appearance or clothing style that is used to socially "categorize" people (see Figure 2-9).

How do cultural forms arise? From a cultural perspective (drawing from semiotics), *meanings are regarded as arising from oppositions and contrasts in social life*. These oppositions and contrasts might include the following: "youth versus age, masculinity versus femininity, androgyny versus singularity, inclusiveness versus exclusiveness, work versus play, domesticity versus worldliness, revelation versus concealment, license versus restraint, and conformity versus rebellion" (F. Davis, 1985, pp. 24–25). Cultural forms tend to represent or bring to the surface such contrasts. For example, the manner in which gender is socially organized may be represented by the tendency for women's attire to be "softer" (less severe) in appearance than men's.

The nature of social relations are subject to change, or at least to some cultural expression of tensions based on these relations (Johnson, 1986–1987). Instabilities may also exist in social identities, and fashion provides a forum for expressing these instabilities or tensions—in fact, for bringing them to the surface.

By whatever operation, when successful fashion manages through symbolic means to resonate exquisitely with the shifting, highly self-referential collective tensions and moods abroad in the land. Indeed, in so doing it more than lends expression to them; it helps shape and define them as well (F. Davis, 1985, p. 25).

Consumers may also respond to collective tensions as they manage their appearances. They contribute to the development of cultural forms by juxtaposing different symbols or by transferring symbols from one social identity to another or from one context to another. For example, in the 1980s, rock singer Boy George (and David Bowie before him in the 1970s) used androgyny or "gender bending" as a theme for defying traditional perceptions of the male appearance. Later, he displayed through a more traditional (but still fashionable) appearance style that he could switch from one mode to another. Even within a given appearance, symbols of masculinity and femininity can be juxtaposed. For example, rock singer Annie Lennox of the Eurythmics wore a very short ("masculine") hairstyle and, at times, a man's suit; these symbols would be juxtaposed with ("feminine") makeup, however, to create an overall impression that was unique. Rock stars such as these can become cultural "figures" that come to represent more generic and abstract "forms" (androgyny).

*2. Cultural beliefs and values tend to be perpetuated when they are represented on a relatively unconscious level.* **Ideology** consists of the principal beliefs and values that characterize a culture, group, or movement. Ideology may be reflected in everyday objects that people do not question and that they interpret with relative ease because of shared meaning. Cultural messages of this sort form the basis of the construction and transformation of cultural knowledge, according to French semiologist Roland Barthes (1972). These messages are like ideas, yet they are expressed through such tangible cultural objects as clothing. Ideological messages deal with more than meaning; they deal with *values* by defining who or what is more worthwhile (as in the case of status symbols). These cultural messages are created through the process of **representation.** This process may involve selecting, presenting, structuring, and shaping elements of reality, by either reinforcing the status quo or creating new meanings (Hall, 1982, p. 64). Apparel designers and fashion advertisers, for example, may step out of existing ideological frameworks and develop new ones. Humans are also able to "break out" of these frameworks if they use clothing and appearance objects imaginatively (see Figure 2-10).

*3. People have the potential to transform their own realities by manipulating the objects in their cultural worlds.* Culture provides clothes and other tools or objects used for appearance management. It also provides images and ideas. However, individuals may use these objects, images, and ideas in imaginative ways. Even when one's repertoire of these objects is limited—and some of these limitations are based on culture—he or she may reorganize them, find new ways of combining them, juxtapose elements or images that are not often seen together, or try out looks in new contexts. In this way, cultural conventions may be applied in new ways or may be broken or bent. Through individual

**FIGURE 2-10**
*In what way do stores such as this one "break out" of some of the existing ways of thinking about retailing and fashion goods? The process of **representation** is illustrated here in the selection and display of "post-punk" and new wave clothes and paraphernalia, in a store that blatantly indicates that the customer gives "cash for chaos." Photo by Susan B. Kaiser.*

actions, people make what we commonly think of as "fashion statements" (Barthes, 1972; Simon-Miller, 1985).

In terms of appearance perception, people also are able to transform their realities through the means they develop to see the world. Two kinds of perception of cultural images (messages) may be identified: naive and participant. Perceivers are *naive* in contexts where they are convinced the image observed is a passive picture of reality. In contrast, perceivers are active *participants* when they are involved in the process of signification (or making things mean) (von Uexkull, 1984). This distinction is important when considering cultural forms that are ideological, because these forms are not likely to be hidden. They are out in the open and visible, but they may not seem to be terribly important. For example, cartoons on television may represent stereotypical images of social groups, but we are not likely to consider cartoons as ideological. Or, some fashion ads may perpetuate social thinking about gender (for example, women as sex objects); yet when we are focused on clothing styles or fashion messages we may not think about ideological messages. However, these media are not necessarily passively accepted as indicative of reality. In fact, observers may develop new interpretations of images viewed, and these interpretations may differ from old ideological views as well as from the intent of the "media makers." An active participant in signification is more likely to become aware of the importance of cultural objects than one who passively endorses reality as it is represented, from a semiotic perspective. So it is important to consider contexts in which individuals may be more or less likely to be naive or participant in their perceptions of cultural appearances.

4. *Culture provides abstract pictures or representations of social life.* Media images, for example, tend to depict abstract or hypothetical representations of life, which may not be identical to everyday life (Johnson, 1986–1987). Media clothing imagery may be caricaturized or exaggerated for purposes of easy identification (for example, an old woman on a television cartoon). Or, media clothing imagery may be outrageous, fantastic, or stimulating to the imagination. People experience their lives, within a larger culture, at many levels of experience, from the practical to the imaginary. A cultural approach, drawing from semiotics, provides a framework for interpreting cultural stories, images, dreams, and fantasies that allow people a means for escape or for making sense of who they are and what they are doing.

Abstract, cultural forms may be compared and contrasted with the more specific and concrete clothing styles in everyday life. Although cultural representations of social life may be shared by the public, they are often experienced in private contexts (for example, watching television at home), and the experience of being exposed to cultural representations actually becomes part of everyday life as people interpret cultural appearances. Cultural representations also may provide some ideas for personal appearance management. For example, in Brazil in the late 1980s a female model and singer became an extremely popular cultural figure in children's television. Xuxa (pronounced "shoo-sha") became a common figure on lunch boxes, posters, billboards, and the like. She even endorsed her own clothing line, along with toiletry and other items. Young girls throughout Brazil wanted to achieve the Xuxa "look," typified by pigtails and brightly colored bows (all over the head), high boots, and very short, colorful skirts and separates.

5. *People use codes to decipher the meanings of cultural representations of social life.* A semiotic approach to cultural representations entails delving into the cultural meanings that lie beneath the surface of messages. This approach also assumes that the world is coded (Lavers, 1982, p. 50) and that meaning abounds in everyday cultural objects as well as in abstract cultural representations. According to semiologist Umberto Eco (1979), a **code** is the "habitual patterning of an expression and meaning." Certain forms of expression or meaning become routine to the extent that the same object or set of objects almost always conjures up the same or similar meanings. A code is not a concrete object itself, but rather it is an abstract pattern, a type of cultural knowledge, that forms the taken-for-granted reality of a culture. Clothing and appearance imagery involves a kind of "silent language" through which meanings are coded and from which shared understandings emerge (F. Davis, 1985). Codes may involve logical relations, associations, or networks among clothing and appearance items, for example, between a business suit and a briefcase. When we talk about appearance we consider the way elements are combined or juxtaposed.

**FIGURE 2-11**
*Codes for business wear on Wall Street in New York include the patterning of the various components of an ensemble (for example, jacket, skirt, blouse, hairstyle). In the context of walking on the street, the code has been modified to allow for comfortable footwear. (Her shoes for the office are likely to be in her bag.) Perceivers are likely to take context into account as they implicitly interpret appearances using cultural codes. Photo by Margery Freeman.*

Codes also include the guidelines or culturally provided ways of thinking that enable us to interpret appearance messages similarly to other people. Codes guide the way symbolic materials are patterned so as to shape the creation and re-creation of culture. Appearance codes are linked to aesthetic, visual, and tactile experiences (F. Davis, 1985, p. 16). So they are likely to allow for creativity in terms of interpretation. Cultural guidelines underlying the interpretation of messages may be difficult to put into words, when they tap the realm of emotions or feelings rather than tangible rules. Codes can also serve as "rules" that imply what articles of clothing and accessories should be worn together (see Figure 2-11).

*Methodology*    What methods do a cultural approach to the study of clothing and fashion change lead us to use? To study the impact of cultural forms on social life, it is necessary to study both public forms, such as those found in the media, and private forms, or people's appearances. Cultural forms may be produced and represented publicly and, therefore, shared among many individuals, but they are used and interpreted privately, alone or with people with whom one interacts (Johnson, 1986–1987).

Therefore, the study of cultural appearance forms may take two directions, and ideally this study would encompass both elements: First, cultural forms may be *content analyzed*. The way they are represented and their content can be assessed. For example, images of women in Saturday morning television can be analyzed in relation to their role portrayals. Second, individual interpretations of cultural forms may be assessed as people are asked to respond to appearances derived from the media or indicative of social relations. To carry through the example from Saturday morning television, young boys and girls may be interviewed on the nature of female cartoon characters' roles. Typically, scholars in the humanities have used techniques similar to those of literary criticism to assess cultural forms. This has involved social critique of books and other cultural media to analyze changing meanings. Although such critiques may be rich and insightful, difficulties may arise if scholars' own interpretations are assumed to be the same as those of people in everyday life who are also exposed to cultural forms (Johnson, 1986–1987). There is no assurance that people in everyday life see cultural forms the way a scholar does. However, a cultural focus does provide a sensitivity to forms that depict social relations, and this sensitivity can be combined with the study of everyday meanings-in-use for a more complete understanding of the connections between culture representations and individual interpretations (Davis, 1982).

Therefore, by integrating social-psychological methodologies with cultural critique, people's actual interpretations may be studied and assessed from a cultural perspective. In this way, the more concrete and private moments of interpreting culture may be explored. Examples of such studies may include a study of how adolescents respond to the appearances portrayed in music videos, or how young children interpret images of males and females in cartoons.

To study specific cultures or subcultures, a methodology commonly used in anthropology is **ethnography.** This typically involves immersion in the culture or subculture, frequently different from that of the person undertaking the study. Ethnography involves rich and detailed description of cultural forms, as well as interpretation and analysis based on an unravelling of the interlinked networks of cultural forms and social actions. Culture, in this type of analysis, is regarded as a context that can be richly described (Geertz, 1973). The researcher thinks not only *about* the phenomena observed, but also *with* these phenomena through creative and participative analysis (Geertz, 1973). It becomes important for a researcher immersed in a field setting (in a cultural context) to strive to empathize. For example, imagine an American female researcher studying the use of the veil among fundamentalist Iranian women. Rather than impose her own cultural frame of reference in her interpretation of the veil, it becomes important for her to think *with* (while wearing) the veil and to see what the experience is like from the inside. The interconnected aspects of culture are more likely to become apparent when the material artifacts through which culture is readily experienced are used.

## Summary

All three of the perspectives deal in some way with interpretations and implications of clothing and appearance. Yet they approach these topics in diverse ways. Table 2-1 summarizes the differences and underlying similarities among these perspectives by considering how they approach the concept of meaning in clothing and appearance.

**TABLE 2-1**
*Comparison of Three Perspectives*

| | *Symbolic Interactionist* | *Cognitive* | *Cultural* |
|---|---|---|---|
| **Meaning** | | | |
| For whom? | Interacting individuals | Perceivers | Individuals sharing a common culture |
| How is it produced? | Socially constructed through individuals' joint actions | Perceivers use their cognitive structures to interpret | Cultural representation of social relations and ideology |
| How does it change? | Through processes of interpretation and reinterpretation by different individuals | When perceivers' cognitive structures do not adequately explain social realities | Cultural and fashion change, influenced in part by unresolved ambivalence about the social order (for example, young/old; male/female) |
| **Relative Strengths** | Give and take of social interaction; human potential for creative appearance management and perception | Implicit perceptions and basic mechanisms for processing appearance cues | Cultural context for understanding linkage between social relations and appearance codes |
| **Methodologies** | Qualitative; focus on everyday life | Quantitative; experimental | Ethnographic; critique of cultural forms |
| **Common Assumption** | | | |
| Humans use appearance to make sense of everyday life | Explained in terms of humans fitting their lines of action together to communicate | Explained in terms of perceivers trying to simplify reality using somewhat structured thought processes | Explained in terms of cultural codes that we take for granted |

**FIGURE 2-12**

*A woman in Tibet observes a skirt worn by an American tourist. The skirt was made by a Tibetan refugee living in Nepal, and this tourist purchased the skirt in Nepal before traveling to Tibet. The style and materials and especially the brightness and newness of the skirt are most meaningful to this Tibetan observer, who has been under Chinese rule since the 1950s. The Chinese have precluded the making of new skirts in this type of pattern, and the necessary materials are no longer available to this woman. Thus, this Tibetan woman (and many others) has been wearing either her old, faded skirt or Mao suits. For her, seeing the new skirt in a familiar pattern with bright, vibrant colors is an emotional experience. This interaction may be interpreted within a contextual framework (see discussion under the assumptions of this framework). Photo by Stephen Cunha.*

All the perspectives share the basic assumption that humans use such cultural objects as clothing to make sense of everyday life. In doing so, each brings a different "focus" or point of view to this understanding. In this way, each perspective can deal with a different issue. Let's consider the picture in Figure 2-12 and imagine that we are looking at the appearances of the females through a camera lens. The way the images become focused or clear depends on which of the three perspectives one is using to assess this picture. In other words, one's point of view or angle may lead to a different emphasis, interpretation, or question.

In Figure 2-12, the Tibetan woman is observing a skirt worn by an American tourist. This skirt was purchased earlier by the tourist in Nepal (from a Tibetan refugee), and she was not aware of its significance for older Tibetan women until she arrived in Tibet and noticed a great deal of interest on their part. A symbolic-interactionist perspective would lead us to consider the communications between the Tibetan woman and the American tourist (most of which would be nonverbal since they do not share a common language). The feedback on the skirt and the way the American tourist internalizes and interprets this feedback would be a major focus. Also, the way her interpretations might be altered or reinforced as she meets other Tibetan women would be considered. (For example, she notes that younger women do not notice or respond to the skirt.) She discovers that the materials in the skirt, as well as the style itself, have not been seen by older Tibetan women since the Chinese invaded Tibet in the 1950s. A symbolic-interactionist perspective would focus on the meaning this skirt holds for the Tibetan woman, as well as the emerging understanding of this skirt on the part of the tourist. Also, the tourist's perceptions of the Tibetan woman's attire would be considered.

A cognitive perspective would lead us to focus on the appearance perception depicted in Figure 2-12. The Tibetan woman's observation and interpretation of the skirt might be considered in relation to (*a*) the social category of people she associates with the skirt, (*b*) the personal qualities she might assume the American tourist to have, and (*c*) the possible cognitive inconsistency induced by seeing the skirt on an American female, worn with items the Tibetan woman would not expect to see. According to a cognitive point of view, the Tibetan woman will need to modify her cognitive structure relevant to this skirt. Moreover, the social category of people who would wear the skirt will need to be broadened.

A cultural perspective would lead us to consider the skirt as a cultural form. The cultural context in which the skirt was originally produced, its history and symbolism for Tibetan women, as well as the current cultural context would be considered. Any reference to social relations (for example, gender) would be explored, as well as any ideological significance. A cultural perspective would also lead us to study the manner in which the skirt historically and/or presently represents social reality for Tibetan women.

## *Contributions*

The three perspectives have their differences, but if we approach the study of meaning in clothing by considering them jointly, the big picture is considered and different aspects of meaning may surface. These perspectives may be subsumed and used as appropriate under the rubric of a **contextual perspective.** This framework leads us to study how people manage and perceive appearances in everyday life, *considering the actual social situations, as well as the larger cultural or historical context, in which people find themselves.* The situation depicted in Figure 2-12 illustrates a social interaction within a cultural context, and the historical significance of the skirt also is critical to an understanding of what is taking place. (Table 2-2 reveals how components of the symbolic-interactionist, cognitive, and cultural perspectives contribute to a new framework emphasizing context.)

A contextual approach enhances our understanding not only of appearance from people's viewpoints but also how common such viewpoints are within a culture or larger group. It enables us to focus upon situational dynamics and to explore the meaning of clothes within their larger contexts.

**TABLE 2-2**
*Contextual Framework*

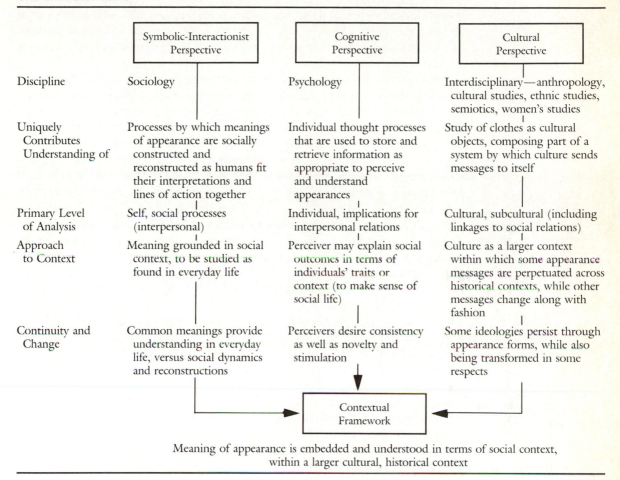

| | Symbolic-Interactionist Perspective | Cognitive Perspective | Cultural Perspective |
|---|---|---|---|
| Discipline | Sociology | Psychology | Interdisciplinary—anthropology, cultural studies, ethnic studies, semiotics, women's studies |
| Uniquely Contributes Understanding of | Processes by which meanings of appearance are socially constructed and reconstructed as humans fit their interpretations and lines of action together | Individual thought processes that are used to store and retrieve information as appropriate to perceive and understand appearances | Study of clothes as cultural objects, composing part of a system by which culture sends messages to itself |
| Primary Level of Analysis | Self, social processes (interpersonal) | Individual, implications for interpersonal relations | Cultural, subcultural (including linkages to social relations) |
| Approach to Context | Meaning grounded in social context, to be studied as found in everyday life | Perceiver may explain social outcomes in terms of individuals' traits or context (to make sense of social life) | Culture as a larger context within which some appearance messages are perpetuated across historical contexts, while other messages change along with fashion |
| Continuity and Change | Common meanings provide understanding in everyday life, versus social dynamics and reconstructions | Perceivers desire consistency as well as novelty and stimulation | Some ideologies persist through appearance forms, while also being transformed in some respects |

Contextual Framework

Meaning of appearance is embedded and understood in terms of social context, within a larger cultural, historical context

Given the nature of fashion change and the manner in which people's own interpretations lead to new meanings of clothes, it is important to discover how meanings may be resolved in one situation and then lead to a new set of questions or new contexts of discovery. This process of **contextualizing** allows us to see changes in the meaning of clothes as contexts dissolve into one another (Kaiser, 1983–1984). Clearly, one historical context leads to a new one, one cultural context influences another one as there is intercultural contact, and one social context influences people's interpretations of another one. Moreover, context serves as a pervasive backdrop that interacts with people's own actions and interactions. Contexts are also created by people themselves, so there is a dynamic relation between individuals and the contexts in which they find themselves. An understanding of these connections and transitions related to contexts leads to a fuller understanding of how clothes have meaning for people, including the conditions under which these meanings are altered, where these meanings arise and how they are modified by social interactions, and how individual manipulations of clothing and appearance contribute in their own right to a larger cultural context.

A contextual social psychology of clothing, then, studies the richness of meanings not only within, but also across, contexts (Kaiser, 1983–1984). Culture is one larger context within which appearance styles arise and influence social processes. Culture does not exist strictly to dictate meanings to individuals; instead social-psychological processes lead to new meanings, which are interpreted within a cultural framework. A social-psychological focus that integrates culture in this regard can enable us to explore how individuals influence and are influenced by cultural processes.

**Assumptions**

1. *Meanings of clothing and appearance are altered and enriched by the contexts in which they are found.* Clothes and appearances do not exist in limbo, but rather they are connected to individual experiences and social relations. As the symbolic-interactionist perspective indicates, meanings are grounded in everyday life perceptions, including how people define situations. A cognitive perspective also suggests that people interpret causality in terms of situations. Therefore, context influences how perceivers explain why people dress and act as they do, and why interactions lead to certain outcomes. A cultural perspective indicates that cultural forms provide clues to social relations, and these forms are intertwined with other forms to provide a dynamic foundation for individual interpretations. This perspective also sensitizes us to cross-cultural variations in meaning and usage of clothing.

2. *Meanings of clothing and appearance arise as part of a dynamic process of historical and fashion change.* One historical context leads to another one, just as one fashion context leads to a new framework for interpreting novelty. Everyday life acts present themselves in contexts that illuminate their distinctive features and meanings, and there is likely to be an element of continuity and familiarity, as well as one of emergence and transition, across such acts. If we look at historical contexts dissolving into one another, we may focus on three components related to time: (1) the past, where meanings of clothes were initiated, (2) the present, where situational conditions or social relations sustain or modify their present meanings, and (3) the future, where new meanings and consequences are yet to be discovered.

3. *Social life is a complex mixture of confusion and continuity.* This complex mixture comes to light when we view people's appearances and reflect on their meanings. Some dimensions of social life point to a sense of order, completeness, and continuity, whereas others point to novelty, ambiguity, and change (Georgoudi and Rosnow, 1985). The clothes worn in large organizations versus those worn by individuals immersed in the fashion industry point to this diversity. Often diversity of this sort is more abstract in nature and found in a given article of

clothing or a given appearance style. Moreover, the social psychology of clothing deals with continuity as well as changes in meanings. Therefore, a multifaceted approach to the study of clothing is most likely to capture the diversity of human experience and expression. Such an approach integrates individual thought processes and interpretations with social interactions and cultural processes and forms.

There are likely to be some underlying continuities, as well as dynamic processes of change, in meanings that emerge across historical, cultural, and social contexts. A symbolic-interactionist perspective points to the dynamics by which meanings are socially constructed as people fit their interpretations and lines of action together. It, however, also acknowledges that some meanings are provided for people before they interact. From a cognitive point of view, there is an emphasis on perceivers' desires not only for consistency and continuity, but also for novelty and stimulation. And a cultural perspective would illuminate the processes by which cultural forms emerge and change, as well as endure. So all three of the perspectives allow in some way for continuity and change, but they focus on different levels of social organization: the individual level, the social or interpersonal level, and the cultural level.

*4. Discovery about the meanings of clothes and appearance is an exploratory process of change and continuity.* Although there are underlying regularities or processes that are likely to endure across contexts, what we know about people's use and interpretation of clothing is not necessarily absolute. Therefore, the study of clothing must include a sensitivity to historical and fashion context, while also examining underlying commonalities across these contexts. So confinement of attention to the meaning of clothes to one historical context, without considering contexts that precede and follow that context, is likely to miss or overlook continuities that may exist. In the same vein, no one perspective is likely to answer all of the questions that emerge on the relation of clothing to human behavior; consequently, there are benefits to examining alternative perspectives.

A contextual approach promotes the idea of studying phenomena through active participation, in order to have the insight to decipher transitions and continuities. Thus discovery is a continuous process of confirming, modifying, and reconstructing theories (Georgoudi and Rosnow, 1985). Knowledge in the social psychology of clothing may be regarded not only as a product but also as a process of discovery. The ultimate goal is to discover contexts in which a given theory leads to relevant insights, as well as contexts in which it is misleading (McGuire, 1985). In this way, the meanings and implications of theories may be clarified. A contextual approach submits that each of several different theories may be right in some context; therefore, theories need not necessarily contradict one another but rather bring different explanations to the surface, as appropriate.

## Methodology

A contextual framework of inquiry suggests a creative and critical use of methods (McGuire, 1985). This approach leads us to question whether any single method can demonstrate the truth conclusively. Therefore, the use of multiple methods

CONTEXTUAL MODEL OF CLOTHING SIGN SYSTEM

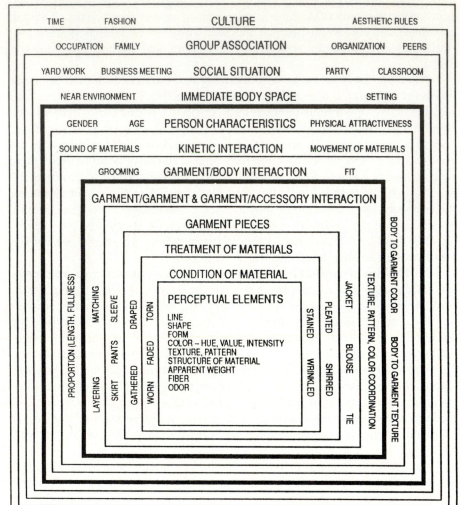

**FIGURE 2-13**
*This model illustrates how contexts are embedded within one another and how these can be studied using a contextual approach to the study of clothing. Clothing and all of its perceptual elements are embedded in the larger context of appearance, which includes garment/garment and garment/accessory combinations as viewed in conjunction with a person's body. The social situation in which a person is observed provides a context for viewing his or her appearance, which may be framed in terms of group associations. Culture provides a larger framework for interpreting that appearance according to aesthetic rules, historical context, and fashion. Model by Mary Lynn Damhorst (1989).*

is encouraged. Social-psychological processes lead to new cultural meanings, and culture provides a larger context for the interpretation and use of clothing and appearance. Individual thoughts, social interactions, social relations, cultural forms, and historical and fashion processes all influence the way clothes are viewed and used. The study of clothing and appearance in everyday life entails individual plans and cognitions along with dynamic patterns of relations and cultural and historical conditions. Important connections among these aspects of human behavior can only be discovered through the use of multiple methods. Therefore, the combined use of qualitative and quantitative methodologies is promoted, with a regard for the contexts in which they are most appropriate and in which they may be combined.

Another methodological principle in a contextual approach to the study of clothing and appearance is the importance of studying them within contexts (Damhorst, 1989). Two principles underlie this type of study: (1) In real life, we seldom see clothes divorced from social context, and (2) it has been demonstrated that interpretations of clothing vary along contextual lines (Damhorst, 1985). Therefore, it is important that the meanings of appearances are examined in light of context. Clothing falls within a context of appearance, which is part of a larger social context, which takes place within a cultural-historical context. Thus, the linkages within and across contexts need to be brought to light in order to understand similarities and differences in the assignment of meaning. See Figure 2-13 for a contextual model that shows how contexts are embedded within one another. This model by Mary Lynn Damhorst (1989) incorporates an analysis of the structure of appearance, considering the perceptual elements of dress (line, shape, form, and color, for example), condition and treatment of material, garment pieces, garment/garment or accessory interactions (wearing a top with a skirt and belt), and garment/body interactions (how clothes fit or hang on the body, for example). This context of appearance is embedded within social situations as well as within the larger cultural context.

Another advantage of a contextual approach is that it illustrates the connections between "micro" (individual) levels of analysis and larger, "macro" levels (for example, society). Social-psychological processes may be seen as contributing to culture change, while also being influenced by cultural context.

## Suggested Readings

Damhorst, M. L. 1985. Meanings of clothing cues in social context. *Clothing and Textiles Research Journal* 3(2): 39–48.
> This research explores the importance of context in perceivers' assignments of meaning and uses both quantitative and qualitative methodologies.

Davis, L. L., and Lennon, S. J. 1988. Social cognition and the study of clothing and human behavior. *Social Behavior and Personality* 16(2): 175–186.
> Davis and Lennon provide a helpful discussion of methodological issues relative to the manipulation of appearance in dress perception studies. They also evaluate the various ways perceivers are allowed to respond in these studies.

Kaiser, S. B. 1983–1984. Toward a contextual social psychology of clothing: A synthesis of symbolic interactionist and cognitive theoretical perspectives. *Clothing and Textiles Research Journal* 2: 1–9.
> Potential linkages between symbolic-interactionist and cognitive perspectives are addressed, and the benefits of a contextual approach to the study of clothing are noted.

# Chapter Three
...
# Clothing, Appearance, and the Social Construction of Gender

*Gender is a social construction. Accordingly, in everyday life, appearance becomes a medium with which we can shape our impressions of what it means to be male or female. We will explore an understanding of gender and appearance at this point in the book for two overriding reasons. First, these topics illustrate the contextual perspective and, hopefully, bring it to life as we consider how appearance leads us to* think *about gender, how meanings of gender can be shaped and altered by social processes linked to appearance, and how culture provides a framework for persistent beliefs about gender, while also allowing for some change. Thus, we can examine meanings of gender across social as well as historical and cultural contexts. Second, gender is a pervasive, but often hidden, theme in the social psychology of clothing. A contextual perspective leads us to consider not only differences, but also similarities in males' and females' experiences in and across contexts.*

Two young children look at a picture of Adam and Eve in an illustrated Bible. One child asks, "Which is which?" The other child replies, "I don't know, but I could tell if they had their clothes on" (story by Samuel Butler, as described in Roberts, 1977). The moral behind this anecdote is actually not as facetious as it may seem. In fact, this anecdote illustrates the social nature of gender. By definition, **gender** is socially created and reconstructed. In contrast, **sex** refers to the biological differences between males and females. At birth, infants' genitalia are examined, and they are labelled accordingly. In everyday social life, genitalia are covered by clothes, and hairstyle and other forms of appearance management are used to construct a masculine or feminine image (see Figure 3-1). Research indicates that children as young as two years of age use clothing to classify people according to cultural codes or rules of gender, before they are likely to understand biological differences (Thompson, 1975; Weinraub et al., 1984). Clothes, like verbal labels (*boy* and *girl*), comprise the early basis for mental

**FIGURE 3-1**
*Whether or not one can read French, the differentiation between male and female restrooms can be easily interpreted because of appearance coding. Photo by Susan B. Kaiser.*

"filing" systems, used to classify and understand others and the self. What symbolic and cognitive purposes do these filing systems serve? To understand the expansive linkages between clothing, appearance, and gender, we must turn to cultural ideology and the structure of gender relations. Cross-cultural studies have indicated that in virtually every cultural context, male activities are recognized as being more important than female activities (Rosaldo, 1974).

Culture provides a way of socially organizing our thoughts about gender categories. And, because only two gender categories exist, social expectations about what it means to be male or female tend to be differentiated in an oversimplified manner. Most commonly, females are expected to be immersed in the fashion and beauty culture, whereas males are not. That is, there is a strong link between femininity and beauty (Freedman, 1986). Girls are traditionally encouraged to be concerned with appearance; beauty, then, becomes a kind of duty (Paoletti and Kregloh, 1989). In contrast, males are often regarded with suspicion if they seem to pay too much attention to their looks or to fashion. Yet we know that males, like females, wear clothing, although unfortunately few studies have considered how males use clothing to frame or understand their experiences. All too often, the social psychology of clothing has addressed females' orientations toward clothing or has compared males' and females' perceptions of women's clothing. If we are to understand how appearance management and perception contribute to the social construction of gender, we must consider *social relations* between females and males. That is, it is necessary to identify how clothing and appearance cues are used to designate gender boundaries as well as to explain the nature of relationships.

**FIGURE 3-2**
*Males and females alike wear skirts in Bali, yet gender differentiation is indicated by their methods of draping the fabric around the body. Males' skirts are draped to allow for more freedom of movement (as shown here). Photo by Margery Freeman.*

All societies differentiate in some way between the appearances of males and females (Rosaldo, 1974). (See Figure 3-2.) It is important to consider cultural context when deciphering gender symbolism, along with historical developments that have led to present meanings. In this chapter, we will focus on the cultural and historical bases for gender coding through appearance. The implications of meanings linked to gender-typed appearances for everyday life will also be examined, using a contextual approach.

## Appearance Coding and the Social Construction of Gender: A Contextual Approach

A contextual framework provides a basis for exploring when individual behavior is attributable to gender as opposed to other social variables (for example, roles and situations). This framework also allows us to understand symbolic and cognitive factors leading to the social construction of gender, within a larger cultural and historical context. To set the stage for understanding the social construction of gender, let's look at three perspectives (cultural, cognitive, and symbolic-interactionist) in terms of gender.

**Cultural Perspective**

A cultural perspective on gender draws from semiotics, cultural studies, and feminist theory, and provides a general basis for understanding **gender ideology**, or beliefs about how male and female roles should be socially structured. This perspective encourages us to explore consumers' interpretations of cultural images of men and women. (See Figures 3-3 and 3-4.) Some cultural beliefs about male and female roles and relationships seem to endure despite dramatic alterations in the realities of everyday life (for example, the growing population of women in the workforce). It may take a while for ways of *thinking* about gender to catch up with the actual implications of gender in social contexts.

In the midst of contradictions between old ideas and new realities, fashion often captures the essence of the resulting tensions by bringing them to the surface. Fundamental to the history of dress, however, is the symbolic separation of men and women (Schreier, 1989). The *forms* (fabrics, colors, shapes in clothing) of this symbolic separation have varied with time, but the idea of gender *difference* has endured. Nevertheless, cultural conceptions of gender can change, as can the appearances associated with being a man or a woman. For example, note the shift in cultural images of women in West Germany following the Second World War:

> Women were constrained to search beyond national boundaries for female cultural forms untainted by aftertastes of Nazism. To don the accoutrements of an American female ideal—nylon stockings, scarlet lipstick, narrow skirts and high-heeled shoes—was in part to register a public disavowal of fascist images of femininity: scrubbed faces shining with health, sturdy child-bearing hips sporting seamed stockings and sensible shoes (Carter, 1984, p. 213).

**Cognitive Perspective**

A basic premise underlying a cognitive perspective on gender is that people try to simplify their understanding of others around them in order to make sense of everyday life. Part of this simplifying process involves the placement of individuals into binary categories according to gender. As indicated earlier in the chapter, children learn from an early age to distinguish males and females on the basis of clothing and hairstyles. They also begin to assign expected behaviors and personality traits to individuals on the basis of appearance cues.

Although people's cognitive filing systems for organizing their perceptions of others may become relatively complex in terms of their applications, a cognitive

*FIGURE 3-3*
*In recent years, the media have sometimes portrayed men as sex objects. A look at this high school girl's bedroom wall suggests that men's appearances are not unimportant. Still, as historian Valerie Steele (1989b) points out, "cheesecake is more common than beefcake, and male objectification remains very different from the representation of women as sex objects" (p. 49). Photo by Susan B. Kaiser.*

**FIGURE 3-4**
*In this French billboard, traditional cultural ideology (declaring woman as sex object) is reinforced along with an advertising appeal to "do it yourself" (supposedly in the context of home improvement). The ad copy may be loosely translated as, "Would you like to 'do it yourself' (or be a handyperson) with me?" The model's appearance and pose add to the prospect that additional, none-too-subtle interpretations will be assigned to the advertisement. Photo by Susan B. Kaiser.*

perspective suggests that perceiving people prefer to take "the easy way out" and respond almost automatically to appearance symbols that seem straightforward, especially if these symbols are consistent with culturally communicated messages about gender. Although perceivers use cognitive structures to perceive images of gender, they are capable of using these structures with remarkable flexibility when called on to do so in everyday situations (Kaiser, 1989).

## Symbolic-Interactionist Perspective

A symbolic-interactionist perspective on gender leads us to consider the dynamic aspects of gender in social contexts. Also, this perspective focuses on the *meanings* of gender-coded appearances in everyday life. (See Social Focus 3-1.)

Symbolic interactionists would argue that the richest interpretations of gender-related symbolism arise when a perceiver is challenged to interpret in greater detail than an automatic tendency to categorize a person would allow (see Figure 3-5). In other words, when people do not neatly fit into categories we have in our heads, we are forced to engage in a more interpretive kind of thinking, taking into account situational variables and possibilities and deriving additional information from social interactions. What arises from this kind of interpretation? Newly constructed meanings, restructured mental categories (designed to incorporate more novel interpretations), and meaningful communication are possible outcomes.

# Gender Symbols and Meaning in Everyday Life: Interpretations of "Bossiness"

A symbolic-interactionist perspective on gender promotes attention to the dynamics of meaning, derived from social contexts in everyday life. In a study of young girls' (aged 7 through 13) interpretive processes relative to personality traits (Kaiser, 1989), the girls were asked to select one of four clothing styles for a girl who is "bossy." These styles ranged from jeans and a T-shirt (the most androgynous) to a frilly dress (the most feminine). (The two styles in between included a somewhat feminine pants set and a plain dress.) The two most extreme styles were matched most often with the trait of bossiness, with the frilly dress being selected by 51 percent of the girls and the jeans by 26 percent.

More informative, perhaps, than the selections were the explanations provided by the girls. It became clear from their comments that there are two kinds of bossiness, interpreted on the basis of gender symbols. There was a tendency for the girls to clarify and qualify their selections through narrative or contextual explanations suggestive of diverse gender "scripts" (that is, a prissy, spoiled girl versus a tough tomboy script). What themes can you identify in the following quotes that reflect the interpretive processes distinguishing the two styles?

*Assignment of "Bossy" Attribute (Kaiser, 1989)*
*Explanations for Selection of Frilly Dress*

"Nelly, in a story, has nice clothes and is bossy." (7-year-old girl)

"She likes things done her way." (7-year-old girl)

"Some girls who have cute dresses boss people around—like Margo on 'Punky Brewster'." (7-year-old girl)

"She'd be spoiled, so she'd be bossy because everything had always been done for her." (8-year-old girl)

"She always wears nice clothes and tells on others." (9-year-old girl)

"She thinks she's pretty, and she thinks she's so good. She says, 'I'm not going to play with you.'" (9-year-old girl)

"When I was a kid, girls with nice dresses thought they were better." (11-year-old girl)

*Explanations for Selection of Jeans*

"She tells everyone what to do." (6-year-old girl)

"If you are somewhere playing and being bossy, you are probably sitting on the ground getting dirty." (7-year-old girl)

"She probably likes to kick a lot." (7-year-old girl)

"She looks like a tough person." (9-year-old girl)

"She would get in a fight, and she's mean to others, and her pants rip." (9-year-old girl)

"A bossy person might wear it." (10-year-old girl)

"Bullies wear jeans." (12-year-old girl)

**FIGURE 3-5**
*Some appearances may be intriguing and require us to reexamine traditional gender categories. A perceiver viewing this male may need to reevaluate the traditional notion that only females spend a great deal of time and effort on their appearances. Photo by Mark Kaiser.*

*Gender-Coded Appearances in Context*

Let's look at some possibilities for more mindful interpretations of gender-related appearances and see how social interaction can lead to the recasting of gender perceptions. Imagine yourself as an American tourist in France, traveling around the country in a rental car. In the city of Orléans, you pull into a gas station and see the woman in Figure 3-6 putting gas in the car in front of you. What would be your first (most automatic) interpretation of her role in this situation? Would you think that she is putting gas in her car, and that this is a self-service station? (If these are your assumptions, note how they relate to what would be expected in the context of most American gas stations.) As this woman finishes putting gas in the car as shown, she does something that disrupts your flow of implicit interpretation. Instead of getting in this car and driving off, she walks back to your car and motions to you as though she wants to speak to you. You roll your window down, but do not understand what she is saying in French. She pleasantly points to your car keys as though she wants to take them, and then she points to the gas cap on your rental car. Finally, you realize that she works at the gas station, and that you have been mistaken in placing her in the identity of a self-service customer. Now, let's look at how a contextual perspective would analyze this scenario.

First, conceptual linkages exist between (*a*) cultural ideology that we do not question, and (*b*) the implicit tendency to categorize or stereotype others according to gender. Connections between cultural and cognitive perspectives lead to this kind of understanding. In the scenario described earlier, an American tourist may first interpret Figure 3-6 in terms of American cultural expectations. Also, the woman's appearance may not automatically indicate that her role is that of a service station attendant.

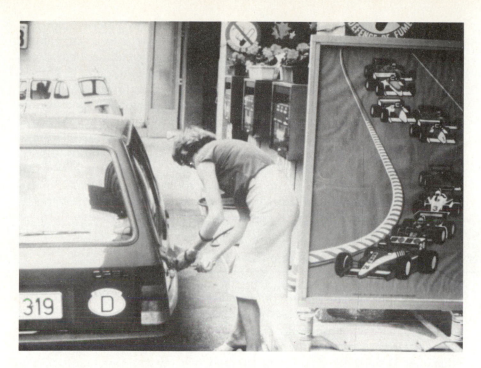

*FIGURE 3-6*
*What are your automatic assumptions about this woman's identity and the context in which it is being interpreted? (See discussion under "Gender-Coded Appearances in Context.") Photo by Mark Kaiser.*

Second, linkages exist between (*a*) the tensions resulting from social *thinking* about gender roles versus the *realities* of gender roles in everyday contexts, and (*b*) the ambiguity (or intriguing confusion) that results when gender-coded appearances seem out of context. Cultural and symbolic-interactionist perspectives contribute to an understanding of the need for interpretive analysis when gender ideology does not mesh with everyday life. In the earlier scenario, there are some culturally derived expectations that may not apply in the context of a different culture. And, the social interaction described is critical to more interpretive analysis and the emergence of new meanings.

Third, ambiguity created by differences between cultural gender ideology and everyday contexts can lead perceivers to restructure their gender categories or definitions. This restructuring becomes necessary when existing mental filing systems are found to be inadequate for interpreting an appearance in context. Symbolic-interactionist and cognitive perspectives jointly contribute to an understanding of how ambiguity in everyday contexts can lead perceivers to restructure their gender categories and related cognitive structures.

The way we are socialized to think about the cultural meanings linked to gender is critically linked to the manner in which gender is socially organized. Gender ideology pertains not only to gender categories themselves, but also to the relation between these categories and the tensions resulting from an ideology that overemphasizes the importance of personal appearance for females and underemphasizes it for males.

An in-depth analysis of gender ideology is necessary to understand present meanings. Such an analysis includes how we are socialized to accept cultural definitions of gender, how it is culturally communicated to us, how it changes, and how it applies to the everyday lives of both males and females. In popular culture, gender is socially organized to portray males more frequently in active or adventurous roles of *doing*, whereas females are more often found in roles of *being*, depicted as less active, romantic, and decorative (Rosen, 1985; Kaiser et al., 1986). This dichotomy of doing versus being, while obviously artificial and oversimplified, is one cultural mechanism for socially organizing gender. How has this cultural ideology been perpetuated, and in what ways has it changed? A historical look at American ideas about males and females sheds some understanding on the larger context within which everyday perceptions of gender have been constructed and reconstructed.

## *Historical Context of Gender Coding in American Culture*

Costume historians have pointed out that gender distinctions within fashionable circles (the wealthier classes) were not as strongly marked before the nineteenth century as they have become since (Laver, 1937). During the eighteenth century, both men and women of the aristocracy wore what we currently regard as effeminate symbols of appearance: lace and rich velvets; elaborate footwear, wigs, and hats; and cosmetics, including powders and rouges (see Figures 3-7 and 3-8).

As European and American societies were transformed from predominantly rural to urban, industrial entities, values emerged to coincide with these changes, including the Protestant work ethic, the strong desire for economic advancement, the move to industrialization and modernization, and the growth of democratic institutions (Weber, 1947; Davis, 1988). All of these values were applied to the domain of males, rather than to females (see Figures 3-9 and 3-10). Indeed, the adult middle-class male eventually became the visible symbol of these societal transformations (Davis, 1988).

The serious and hard-working ethic for males was translated into a somber uniform of sorts. Black became a prominent color for men's wear, as compared with the more colorful attire prior to the 1850s. Historian Valerie Steele points out that the gradual shift toward darker and less elaborate men's attire had actually begun earlier, around the 1750s, and that this more somber, tailored attire was associated with the active leisure wear of the English aristocracy, as well as with middle-class capitalists and democrats (Steele, 1989a, p. 17). Nevertheless, men's clothing came to epitomize the commercial or business spirit. Thus, the beginning of what we now think of as the business suit was born. Part of the rationale and ideology behind this uniform was an ethic of conservative utilitarianism and a belief that "time has commercial value"; therefore, what was needed was a simple ensemble that could easily and quickly be coordinated (Banner, 1983, p. 234). By the 1880s, the business suit was considered acceptable

**FIGURE 3-7**
*Male apparel in eighteenth-century Europe (an English suit of cut and uncut silk, circa the 1760s). Courtesy of the Trustees of the Victoria and Albert Museum.*

**FIGURE 3-8**
*Female apparel in
eighteenth-century Europe
(an English dress of figured
silk, circa the 1760s).
Courtesy of the Trustees of
the Victoria and Albert
Museum.*

*FIGURE 3-9*
*Male apparel in nineteenth-century Europe (an Irish double-breasted frock coat with woolen twill trousers, circa 1871). Courtesy of the Trustees of the Victoria and Albert Museum.*

**FIGURE 3-10**
*Female apparel in
nineteenth-century Europe
(an English dress and
mantle, circa mid-1840s).
Courtesy of the Trustees of
the Victoria and Albert
Museum.*

office wear. At the same time, cartoons ridiculing men's dress were common, as were those depicting men as unattractive, unmanly, or effeminate. Costume historian Jo Paoletti (1985) suggests that a fear of ridicule compelled men to assert an image of masculinity; hence, the shift from traditional context-specific dress to the all-purpose business suit—deemed appropriate for both formal and office wear. Social-psychological research suggests that contemporary men are still motivated by the fear of ridicule to avoid wearing clothing styles they view as connoting any feminine qualities (Kaiser, 1987).

The phrase "clothes make the man" was profoundly accurate in the nineteenth century. Men's clothes showed no sign of frivolity, femininity, or humor. Historian Helene Roberts (1977) has described the difference between their clothes and women's in the following way:

> More than identifying each sex, clothing defined the role of each sex. Men were serious (they wore dark colors and little ornamentation), women were frivolous (they wore light pastel colors, ribbons, lace, and bows); men were active (their clothes allowed them movement), women inactive (their clothes inhibited movement); men were strong (their clothes emphasized broad shoulders and chests), women delicate (their clothing accentuated tiny waists, sloping shoulders, and a softly rounded silhouette); men were aggressive (their clothing had sharp definite lines and a clearly defined silhouette), women were submissive (their silhouette was indefinite, their clothing constricting (p. 555).

Despite all of this conservatism and seriousness, there were subtle indications that style was still important to men. New York City tailors displayed fashion plates of the latest styles from London in their shop windows. In 1865, Harriet Beecher Stowe compared men's and women's clothing and wrote that men's clothes "have as many fine, invisible points of fashion, and their fashions change quite as often; and they have as many knick-knacks with their studs and their sleeve-buttons and waistcoat buttons, their scarves and scarf-pins, their watch-chains and seals and sealrings" (Banner, 1983, p. 234).

Despite the subtle indications of males' continuing concern about appearance management, if not fashion per se, cultural codes of gender were becoming clarified for what we think of as modern social life. Men had come to be assigned a highly *restricted* dress code, whereas women continued to be immersed in an *elaborate* code that had been evolving for them for centuries (Davis, 1988). Why did male attire become more narrowly defined in terms of appropriateness, while female clothing continued to become more aesthetically complex? A look at the structural relationship between males and females during the nineteenth century sheds some light on this question.

The general ideology in terms of gender relation in the nineteenth century revolved around the concept of separate but equal spheres. Females were assigned to the social world of the home: the *private* sphere. They were permitted to take part in activities outside this sphere in terms of church work or related activities, but the *public* sphere, including the world of business and industry, was the domain of males. Appearance management became aligned with the world of aesthetic sensitivity and moral responsibility, versus that of commercial and worldly enterprise. While females were socialized to value beauty as a means of power for obtaining (and keeping) a husband, males were immersed in a world of building character for purposes of achievement in the outside (public) world. Therefore, a contrast between being and doing was accentuated. Yet the complexities of these gender roles defy easy interpretation. Females had considerable influence within their domestic or private spheres; in fact, they were responsible for the continuity of moral virtue (as contrasted with the sometimes "corrupt" business world). At the same time, women were, in a sense, placed on a pedestal, with the idea that they were virtuous and would remain so if they were confined to the domestic sphere. And, it was the responsibility of males to see that women maintained their virtuous qualities. Thus a seemingly passive, but responsible, role was assigned to women. This role was further complicated by the creative aspect of being immersed in the fashion and beauty culture and maintaining an aesthetically pleasing home interior. In this way, the home became a welcome refuge for males who were immersed in an increasingly complex, industrial world.

Perhaps the most constricting aspect of the nineteenth-century fashion and beauty culture for women was the corset, which was designed to change the shape of the body to mesh with the feminine ideal of a small waist and enlarged hips and bust. This undergarment also constricted the diaphragm, when laced tightly, making breathing difficult and further diminishing the prospects of activity. Roberts (1977) suggests a link between the wearing of corsets and women's moral responsibilities in the home. The uncorseted woman of the nineteenth century was perceived as "loose" morally, whereas tight lacing was consistent with the notions of personal discipline and self-restraint.

By the last third of the nineteenth century, public commentary on the pros and cons of the corset had swelled to illustrate the social nature of clothing. Medical dissertations and journals, lectures, books on clothing and physical education, and popular press and cartoons all commented on the issue. Yet in this commentary, as historian David Kunzle (1977) has pointed out, it is often difficult to discern if the writer approaches the subject from a profemale or antifemale perspective. The *Times* in England editorialized that "tight lacing creates more domestic unhappiness than any other domestic circumstance in life" (as cited in Kunzle, 1977). To some writers, tight lacing was proof that women were beyond reason. It has been debated by historians how extensively tight lacing with the corset was practiced (Roberts, 1977; Kunzle, 1977; Steele, 1989b).

Despite the widespread criticism of fashion in popular literature, by the 1850s women's fashionable attire was particularly unreasonable. In addition to the corset, long skirts dragged in the mud, covering the heavy crinoline and layers of petticoats. The alternative to this style, introduced by nineteenth-century feminists, was not socially accepted, however (see Figure 3-11).

In 1851 in Seneca Falls, New York, feminists Elizabeth Cady Stanton and Amelia Bloomer began a campaign for "rational" clothing—costumes consisting

**FIGURE 3-11**
*The Bloomer costume of the nineteenth century became associated with the women's dress reform movement, but women who wore the outfit were ridiculed. American society of the 1850s was not ready for the sight of women in a two-piece garment—one piece of which was pants or trousers (Foote, 1989).*

of dresses shortened to mid-calf and worn over baggy Turkish trousers (Banner, 1983; Foote, 1989). Public commentary had led to this crusade. A local newspaper had written a satirical article on women's clothing and had jokingly suggested a similar costume. Amelia Bloomer wrote a rebuttal to the publication's antifeminist stance in a journal she edited. By coincidence, feminist Elizabeth Smith Miller had designed a reform outfit, similar to that described by the newspaper columnist, for gardening and housework. She inspired Cady Stanton and, eventually, Bloomer to adopt this costume, which came to be known as the "bloomer" by journalists. Within a few months, it had become a reform uniform—a symbol of a movement. What began as favorable publicity quickly degenerated into a kind of hysteria. Journalists were not impressed with women's new alternative (as they often had not been with fashionable attire), and stories emerged about males' jeering reactions to the bloomer. In reality, there was fairly widespread consensus among doctors, educators, women authors, feminists, and reformers to the effect that there was a need to modify fashionable clothing for women. Yet the bloomer alternative did not seem to do the trick.

Two related movements fostered the public's consciousness about dress reform: the popular health movement and the physical exercise movement. Even *Godey's Lady's Book* advocated moderate exercise for women, "however unfashionable the sentiment will appear to some of our more than usually romantic and fastidious readers" (Banner, 1983, pp. 86–91). *Godey's* still identified housework as the best exercise for women, and when it did feature exercise alternatives, it was "to counteract nervousness and invalidism, not to make athletes" (Banner, 1983, pp. 86–91).

Although the impact of the physical exercise movement had some impact on thinking about women's health and attire, it had a profound impact on males in the nineteenth century. Dubbert (1979) writes that males during this era realized that their old frames of reference, the frontier and rugged individualism, were no longer a reality in the era of industrization and materialism. Unlike the legendary heroes (for example, Daniel Boone and Davy Crockett) who blazed the trails around 1800, males were now confined to a particular space within a community. Males were "involved in the worldly pursuit of things—manipulating objects and making deals" (Dubbert, 1979, pp. 16–17). By the latter half of the nineteenth century, however, masculinity and physical strength had become interwoven as males realized that their space was more confined in the commercial world, and they would have to make an effort to achieve masculinity. There were still separate spheres for men and women (public versus private), but women began to ride bicycles, unfasten their corsets, and find jobs that had been held by men (for example, librarians and teachers).

One way of excluding women from some jobs was to emphasize sex differences in terms of physical strength. Males rallied by creating organized male athletics and the Boy Scouts of America. Ernest Seton, who founded this organization, blamed females for boys' flabby muscles. Prior to this time, women, who had been largely confined to the domestic sphere of influence, had been charged with rearing moral male children, molding their characters so that they would be good and successful citizens. By the 1870s, the imagery of the moral male child had been carried to an extreme by some mothers, in the minds of many men. The perfect boychild had hair in soft ringlets and effeminate clothing, as epitomized in the Little Lord Fauntleroy look (Dubbert, 1979, p. 18). Young boys' clothes retained some of this feminine influence into the twentieth century, as shown in Figure 3-12 (Paoletti and Kregloh, 1989).

Thus men became concerned that women had too much control over developing images of masculinity and sought organizational means for instilling an ethic of physical competition and individualism in young males. The ideology of this era has been noted by Franklin (1984, p. 8): "One thing appears certain, and that is that the meaning of being masculine shifted . . . to being the opposite

**FIGURE 3-12**
*Imagery of the "perfectly moral" male child remained popular in portraits into the early part of the twentieth century. Somewhere between the ages of 5 and 7 years old, boys received their first short haircut. This ritual was portrayed in the popular literature as a step toward independence—a painful step for mothers and sons alike (Paoletti, 1987). How would this appearance of a little boy be regarded today? Courtesy of the Joseph W. Clary Collection, City of Sacramento, Museum and History Division.*

of feminine." Maleness came to be defined in terms of avoiding effeminate pursuits, including the realm of involvement with fashion and concern with personal appearance.

By the turn of the century, the culturally preferred male images were of sports figures such as boxer John L. Sullivan, as well as businessmen and industrialists. Western cowboys were also admired (see Figure 3-13).

With respect to the emerging masculine models around the turn of the century, historian Lois Banner (1983) writes:

> The male aggressiveness exhibited on the football field and the battlefield in these years, the violence that the tales of Tarzan and the cowboy implicitly condoned, was a part of male behavior. But we are unfaithful to the historical record not to realize that other models were also current, models both humorous and serious and appropriate to an age of reform that at its best moments was infused with the millennial vision that the nation might lead the world in righteousness, that all women might be beautiful and all men gentlemen, motivated by the highest standards of ethical conduct and of concern for others (p. 248).

As Banner points out, gender ideology was extreme yet conducive to humanistic reform. The doing versus being ideology, so prominent in the nineteenth

**FIGURE 3-13**
*During the 1950s in the United States, cowboy figures were admired and emulated by young boys. Courtesy of the Department of Parks and Recreation Collection, City of Sacramento, Museum and History Division.*

century, was still with us at the turn of the century, but society was becoming increasingly complex and the realities of everyday life did not coincide neatly with cultural ideology.

In the twentieth century, female clothing has changed with remarkable rapidity, whereas males have continued to be influenced by the restricted code of the commercial work ethic (as symbolized by the ubiquitous business suit). As in the nineteenth century, it has been complicated to discern which changes in female attire have been profemale and which have not. Part of this complexity stems from the multitude of factors influencing changing styles of dress. For example, the flapper style of the 1920s revealed the influence of industrialization in the apparel industry, with its simple lines that could be mass produced. Yet it also was consistent with the new freedoms experienced by women who had become economically independent during World War I, when women were needed in the labor force while men fought in the service. Feminist Susan Brownmiller (1984) reflects on the flapper style in the following way:

> The evolution from long skirts to short in the 1920s was an important advance in the history of women's rights. By a cut of the scissors in a dressmaker's salon, women were able to walk and move with greater freedom than they had been allowed for centuries. Gone was the dragging weight of several layers of petticoats, and yards of heavy fabric that swirled around the ankles were thrown aside in

a single stroke of fashion. From breast to thigh, the torso was liberated from the restraining corset. But the transformation of women's legs from a bodily part that was hidden in modesty to a glamorous appendage that was whistled at and admired may not have been a remarkable gain. Both extremes of fashion derived from a belief in the seductive nature of female, sexuality, and both sought to minimize the true function of legs (p. 84).

Even though the flapper style offered freedom of movement, some residue of the old ideology—shaping and revealing the female form as though it were an object—lingered. Breasts were bound with undergarments designed to create a flat appearance to go with the new boyish hairstyles. The borrowed symbolism from masculine appearance reflected the power differential to some degree. This power differential was further indicated by the emergence of beauty contests for women, to which feminists have continued to object (see Figure 3-14). By 1921, fashion and beauty had clearly become big business. As women abandoned corsets, they began wearing heavy makeup and would continue to do so throughout

**FIGURE 3-14**
*Feminists voice their objections to beauty contests with humor as well as protest. Here, former fashion model Ann Simonton wears a "beef bathing suit" to point out that to judge a woman strictly on the basis of beauty is to reduce her to a sex object or a "piece of meat." Photo courtesy of Media Watch.*

the 1950s. (During the late 1960s, the ideal became a more natural one.) Banner (1983, p. 272) notes that neither the Great Depression nor World War II had an adverse effect on the growing cosmetics industry.

Three historical themes may be identified for changing gender ideology in the twentieth century (Banner, 1983, pp. 274–278). First, there is what Betty Friedan called the feminine mystique, the twentieth-century version of nineteenth-century Victorianism, with domesticity, motherhood, and sexual attractiveness as central to women's lives. The feminine mystique flourished in the 1950s (see Figure 3-15), when the ideal woman was devoted to her home as well as to her own beauty (Friedan, 1984, p. 59). The feminine mystique, according to Friedan, "says that the highest value and the only commitment for women is the fulfillment of their own femininity. It says that the great mistake of Western culture, through most of its history, has been the undervaluation of this femininity," which is "so mysterious and intuitive and close to the creation and origin of life that man-made science may never be able to understand it" (Friedan, 1984, p. 43).

Females were not the only ones to have an air of mystique surrounding their roles, according to Joe Dubbert (1979), author of *A Man's Place: Masculinity in Transition*

> Just as women have been trapped by a historical identity and role definition known to some as the feminine mystique, men too have been trapped by a masculine mystique. There is an assumed framework of doctrines emphasizing male power, superiority, and domination in the sexual, social, political, and intellectual life of the United States (p. 2).

Dubbert identifies many contemporary males as suffering from distorted views about themselves as compared with what they think society has always expected of them, to achieve success and superiority and to be athletic or, at least, able to identify vicariously with athletes through intelligent observation and analysis of strategies.

A second theme in gender roles, evident throughout the twentieth century, has been the increasing role of women in the workforce. Banner (1983) notes that despite women's impact in this regard, they have historically had lower pay and power. She contends that a mere surface analysis of the women's movement into the workforce is not sufficient for understanding, continuity, and change in gender ideology.

In the late 1970s and early 1980s, career women seemed to shift their emphasis from aesthetics in appearance management to one of strategy (that is, to be taken seriously in the business world (Solomon and Douglas, 1985). Another way of looking at the rise of the skirted business suit for women in professional fields might be to look at the shift from elaborate to restricted codes to accommodate the business world, dominated so long by the commercial spirit and work ethic. Yet by the mid-1980s, the "dress for success" look had become a kind of cliché, and work attire for women evolved away from the tailored, conservative look. Perhaps this shift could be attributed to the rising number

**FIGURE 3-15**
*The shirtwaist dress became a virtual uniform for many women who worked (stayed) at home in the 1950s. Hose and high heels were also part of the uniform, although this image did not mesh with everyday life experience. Such television mothers as June Cleaver in "Leave it to Beaver" and Lucy Ricardo in "I Love Lucy" promoted the idea that a woman's place was in the home. Illustration by Molly Greek.*

of women assuming previously male-dominated positions (Steele, 1989c). Also, research suggests that with longevity in one's career and the corresponding sense of self-assurance come a willingness on the part of working women to experiment more with appearance by obtaining ideas from fashion media and by becoming less reliant on one's co-workers for fashion guidance (Rabolt and Drake, 1985). Of course, it is also important to note that years of socialization to value fashion and beauty probably deterred women from sticking to somber business suits.

From a social-psychological viewpoint of clothing, the general issue that arises from women's entrance into the business world is, How can women simultaneously fulfill cultural demands of the female role (beauty) while also being taken seriously in a traditionally man's world? This question has generated a great deal of research on male and female perceptions of women's business suits (to be dealt with in more detail in Social Focus 11-1).

Although research has largely documented that women are perceived as more competent in businesslike attire than in traditionally feminine or sexually attractive attire, it also has pointed to the either/or nature of women's options, basically, emphasizing personal attractiveness versus competence. (Social Focus 3-2 delves into these options in light of shoe symbolism.) Generally, business uniforms adopted by women are perceived as reflecting their ability and willingness to do what is required of them in the workplace, whereas traditional female appearances have tended to place women in positions that require them to be passive but moral creatures placed on pedestals or to be objects of sexual delight. Thus, basic tenets of an oversimplified and outdated gender ideology remain in the midst of roles in an active and constant flux; they remain in the form of everyday choices that both men and women make about their appearances and their actions.

A third historical theme that may be identified in twentieth-century gender ideology revolves around the changing nature of males' roles. In terms of business attire in white-collar professions, men's wear increasingly conformed to organizational demands. William Whyte's (1957) book, *The Organization Man*, focused on the consciousness of the American public in the 1950s on the type of conformity and lack of individualism perpetuated by bureaucracy. Social commentators wrote that while the masculine mystique may perpetuate the myth of individualism among males, the reality was much more mundane and routine, as symbolized by the conservative business suit, following the restricted code of masculinity. Several forms of symbolic escape were available to males at this time, however. Among these were the "beat" and "playboy" movements of the 1950s, identified by some writers as means of evading the mundane commitments of everyday life (Ehrenreich, 1983). These movements preceded the women's movement of the 1960s, so both males and females had expressed frustration with the limitations of gender ideology and the resulting masculine and feminine mystiques.

By now it should be apparent that as one historical context has merged into a new one, some realities have changed in gender roles, while some ideologies have persisted.

# Cultural Ideology and Gender Symbolism in Shoes

Writing from a cultural perspective, Dick Hebdige (1979) noted that ideology may be coded in mundane, everyday objects, which he described as "perceived—accepted—suffered." A study of 261 consumers' perceptions of males' and females' shoes pinpointed the either/or nature of symbolism pertinent to gender ideology (Kaiser, Schutz, and Chandler, 1987). The most positively evaluated shoe for females was a high-heeled, strappy sandal. It was viewed as the most feminine, the most formal, the least comfortable, the sexiest, the most fashionable, and the most prestigious of the 10 women's shoes photographed for the study. In contrast, a basic career loafer was perceived as unsexy, conservative, comfortable, appropriate for work, and moderately low in status. Attractiveness and discomfort tended to be perceived as compatible qualities in a desirable woman's shoe, and status seemed to be linked more to attractiveness than to a career.

In contrast, men's shoes were not distinguished from one another on the basis of qualities such as sexiness. One positively received shoe was the man's loafer, which was extremely similar in appearance to the woman's loafer noted earlier. The man's loafer was perceived as expensive, comfortable, masculine, relatively high in status, and moderately sexy. It appears from these data that males need not make the same kinds of choices that women do in terms of shoe selections—that is, attractiveness versus comfort, attractiveness versus status, and the like.

The perceptions identified in this study are consistent with the findings in a 1986 Gallup survey of 1,033 American women, commissioned by Scholl, Inc., and the American Podiatric Medical Association. More than half (59 percent) of the women reported wearing high heels on a daily or regular basis as a badge of feminine beauty, an emblem of fashion savvy, or as a symbol of their professional status. Women with higher occupational, educational, and economic status were more likely to consider wearing high heels as a sign of "making it." Thus, success and status appear to be intricately linked to attractiveness, as suggested in the preceding study. White-collar workers and business and professional women not only wore high heels more frequently when working than did blue-collar women or housewives, they also were more likely to wear high heels when dressing up for social events. However, 60 percent of those surveyed never wore high heels while in transit to their jobs. Instead, sneakers or jogging shoes were worn en route to work—with good reason: More than one-half of those who wore high heels regularly indicated they have experienced discomfort in the balls of their feet.

In this nationwide Gallup survey, positive self-image proved a significant factor. More of the women who wore high heels daily (73 percent) rated themselves as physically attractive as compared with the nondaily wearers (54 percent). Additionally, those with a positive physical self-image were more likely to wear high heels more often and for longer periods of time than did those who did not view themselves as attractive.

What then accounts for women's attraction to physically uncomfortable yet (seemingly) socially comfortable shoe styles? Is social status coded in women's shoes along with the feminine mystique? Mimi Pond (1985) provides a tongue-in-cheek response to this question in her book, *Shoes Never Lie*:

> Shoes are totems of Disembodied Lust. They are candy for the eyes, poetry for the feet, icing on your soul. They stand for everything you've ever wanted: glamour, success, a rapierlike wit, a date with the Sex God of your choice, Barbie's wedding dress. Shoes hint that attaining these things is just as easy as slipping them on your feet. . . . Women who love shoes know this. . . . They know that shoes, and not men, are God's gift to women (p. 13).

## Doing versus Being: An Artificial Dichotomy

Historical perceptions of males as active agents in the public sphere, increasingly confined to restricted appearance codes, may be contrasted with notions of females' concern with *appearing rather than acting*. Clearly, numerous social contexts exist where these perceptions do not apply (for example, when females are in career or sports contexts or when males are concerned with appearance). Nevertheless, it is important to understand and critically analyze the basis for gender dichotomies because they influence our social perceptions.

Table 3-1 contrasts physical effectiveness, the goal promoted by the masculine mystique, with physical attractiveness, as valued by the feminine mystique. Popular culture has tended to classify media or fiction intended to appeal to males or females according to *adventure scripts* emphasizing action, aggression, or strategical conquest, or *romance scripts* emphasizing the value of a woman's beauty in attracting a male (Rosen, 1985). The fairy tale of Cinderella, for example, is based on a romance script, where a poor girl uses her ingenuity (and the help of a fairy godmother) to be appropriately dressed for the ball. Of course, this effort "pays off" in the end.

As Table 3-1 reveals, social relations with respect to power may also fall under the headings of doing and being. Inasmuch as Western culture tends to dictate that females acquire their power through more covert and indirect sources than do males (Lips, 1981, p. 55), females are likely to be socialized to expect more rewards for their appearance than for their overt actions or accomplishments. A dual system of power contrasts the *agonic* mode of power, which involves the direct use of aggression or active force (a form of doing), with the *hedonic* mode, which is based upon the ability to command the attention of others through display (Morgan, 1972, pp. 186–188; Freedman, 1986, pp. 73–75).

Figures 3-16 and 3-17 illustrate the power dichotomy by comparing football players on the field—where the "action" is—with cheerleaders off the field. The artificiality of this power dichotomy becomes clear with closer analysis of roles and consideration of social context. For example, some collegiate and professional football players have begun to display creativity in appearance through unusual hairstyles and accessories. And clearly cheerleaders are far from inactive; their

**TABLE 3-1**
*Coding of Gender Ideology: "Doing" versus "Being" (An Artificial Dichotomy)*

| Doing | Being |
|---|---|
| Emphasis on achievement and action | Emphasis on appearance and attraction |
| Physical effectiveness | Physical attractiveness |
| Adventure script in popular media | Romance script in popular media |
| Agonic (aggressive and active) power | Hedonic (indirect and attracting) power |
| Ideology of building character | Ideology of maintaining character ("placed on a pedestal") |

**FIGURE 3-16**
*Football players typify the kind of aggressive, direct, and active means of obtaining power—known as* **agonic**. *Photo by Susan B. Kaiser.*

**FIGURE 3-17**
*Cheerleaders are often associated with hedonic power, based on attractiveness and indirect means of obtaining power. This association, however, oversimplifies the cheerleader role, which generally requires a high level of athletic ability. How does it compare to the activity associated with agonic power? Photo by Susan B. Kaiser.*

**FIGURE 3-18**
*Male athletes are often depicted in fashion publications, in part to assure the male audience that one can be fashionable and still be masculine. How do these portrayals influence social thinking about traditional "doing" and "being" roles? Photo by Wendy Dildey.*

performance requires athletic ability and coordination. So the reality of gender roles, in this context as well as in many others, is more complex than we are socialized to believe. Clearly, it is the way we think about gender rather than the more complex implications of gender in everyday contexts that is reflected in ideological systems that propose dichotomies. However, only by understanding such social categories can ideology be understood and interpreted.

How does the fashion industry combat gender ideology when the goal is to promote male fashion? Suggesting through ads that interest in fashion and physical ability are compatible qualities may be one strategy, as illustrated in Figure 3-18. Similarly, apparel advertisers striving to appeal to professional women may use symbols to suggest that women look both businesslike and attractive.

In addition to focusing on cultural and historical representations of gender, a contextual perspective leads us to consider changing emphases in appearance for males and females in terms of gender relations in everyday life, the manner in which we restructure our thinking about gender as necessary to make sense of social contexts, and the implications of gender ideology for appearance management and perception. Gendered appearance symbols, and the meanings to which they refer, are dynamic components of everyday life. What it means to be (and look) masculine or feminine may vary in different social, historical, and cultural contexts. What seems to remain relatively stable is the principle of some degree of visual separation and binary classification, and the implications of this principle must be negotiated in everyday relations between men and women through social-psychological processes.

## Suggested Readings

Freedman, R. 1986. *Beauty bound*. Lexington: Heath/Lexington Books.
    In this book, Freedman explores the issue of the beauty myth and describes how and why there are differences in the kinds of power that men and women have traditionally exercised.

Kaiser, S. B. 1989. Clothing and the social organization of gender perception: A developmental approach. *Clothing and Textiles Research Journal* 7(2):46–56.
    This article summarizes the findings from a two-part study on the meanings young girls assign to girls' clothing styles. The artificial distinctions between "doing" and "being" are revealed in the girls' associations between clothing and behaviors and personality traits.

Kidwell, C. B., and Steele, V., eds. 1989. *Men and women: Dressing the part*. Washington: Smithsonian Institution Press.
    In this book of readings, the historical relation between outward appearances and definitions of masculinity and femininity are explored. A common theme throughout is the tendency for clothing to be used as a device to separate men and women into different spheres. Some interesting historical variations in gender symbols are provided, and it becomes evident after reading this book that there is nothing intrinsically masculine or feminine about certain colors or styles in clothing.

McRobbie, A., and Nava, M., eds. 1984. *Gender and generation*. London: Macmillan Education.

This series of articles explores the relational aspects of gender in adolescents' lives, focusing primarily on British culture. It is shown how everyday activities and appearances are linked to cultural discourses on the meaning of adolescence and femininity.

Paoletti, J. B. 1987. Clothing and gender in America: Children's fashions, 1890–1920. *Signs 13*(1):136–143.

Paoletti provides a historical overview of children's clothes. Of particular interest are the observations that little boys were dressed in skirts and had long hair until the First World War and that the gender color coding system (pink versus blue) we know so well today was not common until the 1920s. Paoletti notes that as children's clothes have become more gender-typed, adult women's clothes have become more androgynous.

# Part Two

### ...

# Appearance and the Self

THEORIST William James once wrote, "The old saying—that the human person is composed of three parts—soul, body, and clothes—is more than a joke" (James, 1890, p. 292). The **self** consists of an individual's consciousness of being and that being comprises a tangible dimension (body and appearance symbols), as well as a conceptual or perceptual dimension (how one defines and appraises the self). James used the concept **material self** to refer to the physical and possessive dimensions of the self. Through the body, as well as other objects with which we surround ourselves (clothes, cars, and even bumper stickers), we communicate to others and to ourselves who we are and what we view as important in life. Terms such as the *visible self* (Roach and Eicher, 1973) and the *second skin* (Horn and Gurel, 1981) refer to the closeness of clothing to the self.

It is important to place the self in context of social interactions and social life. No person exists in a vacuum or forms impressions about his or her own appearance apart from others. These contexts of everyday life influence how we see and evaluate our bodies and appearances, how we formulate ideas about who we are and what we are striving to accomplish, and how we present ourselves to others.

In Part Two, we will explore how our physical appearances and clothes come to have meaning for us as we strive to make sense of our social realities. As we approach the subject of our personal appearances and how we modify and manipulate them for social purposes, it is important to remember that we do so as a function of inner thoughts and feelings and understandings of the cultural milieu in which we live.

In this part, we will consider three dimensions of the self in relation to appearance: (1) body, (2) perceptions and evaluations of self

95

in a social sense, and (3) appearance management and the self in social contexts. It seems logical when approaching a study of the individual in relation to clothing to begin with some understanding of the body—the **physical self**. The questions we are concerned with here include: How do cultural ideals about bodies influence the way we evaluate our own bodies? Are these cultural ideals differentiated on the basis of gender? What are the consequences of these feelings about the body, or how and why do we strive to shape our bodies to achieve certain appearances? Chapter Four will address these and other questions about the physical self.

In Chapter Five, the focus will be on what we know about ourselves as individuals, and how we use clothing to clarify this type of understanding. This understanding refers to the *self-concept*, or how we think about and identify ourselves. Self-concept is developed, maintained, and modified as necessary to place and understand the self within the context of social life. This chapter will address such questions as: How are my conceptions of self and appearance formulated? What role do clothes play in the process of becoming socialized into one's culture? To what extent do people's identities mirror or reflect the feedback they receive from others?

**Self-presentation** involves the relation of self to actual behavior in social situations. Appearance management facilitates self-presentation, by enabling us to appear before others as we see, or would like to see, ourselves. **Identity** is a kind of self-in-context—a self that is embedded in social relations and situations. These considerations are influenced by social expectations and cultural symbolism. At times, the following issue may plague individuals: Am I me or am I merely following a social script? As most of our presentations of self are dependent on social contexts, it becomes difficult to draw a line between the self and social contraints. For example, we tend to dress and behave differently when interacting with various individuals and/or when we find ourselves in diverse contexts. Are our "true" selves reflected when certain roles or situations are emphasized in our appearances? Chapter Six deals with these issues and others connected to processes of appearance management.

By viewing the self within larger social, cultural, and historical contexts, we are reminded that meaning arises from everyday life experiences and changing imagery of desirable appearances.

# Chapter Four
**• • •**
# The Body in Context

*In this chapter we focus upon the body as a component of appearance. The ways we perceive our bodies are linked to social as well as cultural and historical contexts, and are influenced by gender as well as other factors. There are fashionable bodies just as there are fashionable clothes. In fact, we can alter the appearances of our bodies through diet, exercise, and clothing choices. The extent to which we are satisfied with our bodies influences our feelings about ourselves in general. Thus, cultural images of attractiveness affect self-development because we see our own bodies through the filter of culture, and others respond toward our appearances based upon idealized (as compared to stigmatized) appearances.*

One obvious fact about human beings is that "they have bodies and they are bodies" (Turner, 1984, p. 1). The body is similar to a vehicle for carrying around an individual's thoughts, feelings, and perceptions. It is at once a part of nature (an environment) and a part of culture (medium of the self) (Turner, 1984, pp. 38–39). The body may be regarded as a link between an inner person and some of society's most important values. In every culture, there are powerful forces that "aim to bring the individual's body under control" (Fisher, 1986, p. 137). The desirability of certain body forms and prescriptions on how the body should be displayed are evidence of cultural influence. Cultural imagery of bodies abound in fashion magazines, beauty contests, sports events, and calendars. Even toys depict social values, as in the "hard bodies" of svelte and elongated Barbie dolls as opposed to the male and female muscular action figures.

The way people feel about their bodies is indicative of cultural ideology, social relations, and personal activities. In this way, bodies become signifiers; they refer to individuals as social beings within a larger cultural and historical context. On a personal level, people use their bodies as markers for self-assessment. Bodies lie at the center of many social and political struggles, especially in relation to gender, aging, and cultural ideals. Therefore, it is important to explore the social importance of the body in relation to the changing meanings of clothes.

Our bodies are likely to become particularly meaningful to us in certain contexts, when they are called to our attention (for example, working out in a health club, observing others at the pool or beach, trying on clothes while shopping, or engaging in physical activity). There is a cognitive tendency to classify one's own and other bodies in accordance with physical cues and cultural norms. All of our thought processes, physical and social experiences, and perceptions of cultural values surrounding bodies are intertwined and linked to context (see Figure 4-1).

We will now consider psychological concepts that deal with an individual's perception of the body, as linked to social, cultural, and historical forces. First, we will explore people's ways of visualizing and assessing their bodies, and then we will look at the dynamics of cultural and historical contexts within which personal evaluations of the body are formulated.

## Body Image

The concept of **body image** refers to the mental picture one has of his or her body at any given moment in time. This picture may or may not be accurate or consistent with others' perceptions of that body. Nevertheless, self-image affects our feelings about ourselves and represents a vital component of the physical self. Fisher (1968) described body image as a body concept or scheme. The organization of body experience is clearly multidimensional and complex, incorporating a collection of feelings and perceptions about the body. For example, these may include overall awareness of the body, perception of body boundaries, attention to parts of the body as well as the whole, perception of size of parts and the whole, position in space, and gender-related perceptions (Fisher, 1986b, p. 633). (See Figure 4-2.)

During infancy body image is initiated through visual and tactile exploration of the body. Around six months of age infants can distinguish themselves from the rest of the environment and become aware that they are separate individuals (Fisher and Cleveland, 1968). Some of our earliest meaningful contacts with the world are likely to be body-oriented (Fisher, 1986, p. xiv).

Clothing may be perceived differently by individuals in relation to body image. For example, a female may shop for a large jacket to wear over dresses or tops worn with either skirts or pants, with the intention of hiding certain parts of the body she perceives as flawed. As a kind of "second skin" or extension of the body, clothes represent the nearest aspect of one's environment (Horn and Gurel, 1981). At the same time clothes extend the body, they are not quite part of it. Sociologist Elizabeth Wilson (1985, p. 3) notes that clothes not only link the body to the social world, but also more clearly separate the two. Clothing also may confound the process of developing a personal body image to some extent, especially when the clothes do not closely fit the shape of the body.

**FIGURE 4-1**
*The physical ideal preferred by males tends to be a muscular physique, as epitomized by this student from France who does not take steroids, follows a basically vegetarian diet, and works out (lifting weights) at least two hours daily. For males, muscles become a sign of strength, endurance, and physical effectiveness. Photo by Carla M. Freeman.*

**FIGURE 4-2**
*During pregnancy, especially in the final stages, the multidimensional aspects of body image become apparent. The distinction between physical and social-emotional issues is likely to become increasingly blurred as body perceptions are embedded more and more in anticipated changes in social relations and personal plans. Additionally, the body becomes a salient symbol for perceivers, who are likely to respond accordingly. Body image may include all of the following, as well as other dimensions: (1) awareness of body size; (2) the personal-social meanings of physical changes; (3) one's position in space (possibly involving the tendency to bump into objects or to overestimate one's ability to fit through tight spaces); (4) evaluation of one's feelings about motherhood; and (5) anticipating the return of the body to its normal size (and possibly looking forward to wearing styles that include such features as belts). Photo by Carla M. Freeman.*

"It seems fairly obvious, from a commonsense point of view, that body attitudes influence the character of the clothes people choose to wear . . . Theoretically, it should be possible to determine the kinds of assumptions people make about their appearance by analyzing their clothing styles" (Fisher, 1986a, p. 135). Aside from the need for more research on the linkages between body image and clothing, the difficulty of making the kinds of predictions that Fisher hypothesizes should be possible stems from the multidimensional nature of both body and clothing perceptions. Both of these constructs are complex and multifaceted, but they may also pursue different directions of social experience in different contexts.

### Perception of Body Size

Although all individuals have some concept of body image, research has indicated that there is considerable variation in the way they process information relevant to such specific aspects of body image as weight. For example, some persons evaluate a wide range of stimuli in relation to body weight (Does he weigh more than I do? Will I look thinner in this black dress? Will the exercise equipment advertised on television really help me reduce the size of my waist?) Such persons have been called **schematics,** because they develop schemas or knowledge structures that are interrelated with one another and are activated when they perceive body weight. In contrast, **aschematics** are unlikely to evaluate stimuli in relation to body weight. Although they may vary in size, aschematics do not consider body weight important and do not focus on this characteristic of the self. Consequently, they process information differently than schematics because they lack an integrated knowledge structure, or way of thinking, with respect to body weight (Markus, Hamill, and Sentis, 1987).

Body image may become distorted when bodies change in size or when people focus or dwell unusually on the size or shape of the body. The expression, "being fat is *thinking* fat," used by many organized weight-reduction groups, seems to have some basis in fact with respect to body image (Markus, Hamill, and Sentis, 1987). As one woman who had lost a great deal of weight remarked, "When I was 130 pounds, I still looked in the mirror and saw a fat person" (Chapkis, 1986, p. 159). Researchers have studied subjects' estimates of their body sizes and evaluations of their bodies through a variety of quantitative and qualitative techniques. Table 4-1 provides a summary of common quantitative measures of body image.

Although quantitative techniques are most common for assessing differences between estimations of body size and actual body size, there are times when open-ended interviews—in which people can talk freely about how they feel about their bodies—are especially revealing. In a study involving in-depth interviews with overweight women, sociologist Marcia Millman (1980) found, for example, that one social-psychological mechanism for coping with a negative body image was "disembodiment of the self," or mentally splitting the body from the mind. She found that some overweight people think of themselves in terms of "the neck up," with the body being an "alienated, unwanted appendage of the headself," as illustrated in the following comment:

> I feel so terrible about the way I look that I cut off connection with my body. I operate from the neck up. I do not look in mirrors. . . . I have receded from the physical world. . . . I block out the feeling of my body being used, looked at, put to work, employed, any of these things—adorned, dressed (Millman, 1980, pp. 194–195).

Many obese women commented that they disliked shopping, because it is a context that forces them to confront the reality that they are overweight. One woman noted that it forces her to view her backside in three-way mirrors: "I would have to see what my body looked like from the back, without my face there to distract it." Almost all of the overweight women Millman interviewed had had the expression "such a pretty face" directed at them; the face may be the last part of the body to be pushed out of shape by obesity (Millman, 1980, pp. 196–198).

*TABLE 4-1*
*Measuring Individuals' Estimations and Evaluations of the Body[a]*

| | |
|---|---|
| Body Distortion Questionnaire | 82-Item questionnaire using a three-response format (yes, no, undecided) to identify abnormal attitudes. |
| Body Parts Satisfaction Questionnaire | 25-Item revision of an earlier version; uses a 7-point scale to assess a person's satisfaction with body parts. |
| Distorting Picture Technique | Subject is photographed in a bathing suit; a slide is then shown to the subject through a slide projector with an anamorphic adjustable lens. The subject sees his or her image at size 20 percent larger or smaller than it really is and adjusts the projected image until it matches his or her perception of actual body size. |
| Open Door Test | Subject opens a door to the width that he or she believes will permit sliding through the door sideways. Then the actual width needed to do this is measured and compared with the estimated width. |
| Image Marking Procedure | Subject marks the perceived width of her or his face, shoulders, waist, and hips on a large sheet of paper affixed to a wall. This perceived width is compared to the body parts' actual widths. |
| Moving Caliper Technique | Two lights are mounted on a horizontal metal bar, on a pulley system. The experimenter moves the lights, as instructed by the subject, to meet her or his estimated size of a specific body part. |
| Kinesthetic Size Estimating Apparatus | Two calipers glide along a tape measure fastened to a metal frame. The subjects stand with their eyes closed and move the calipers inward with their hands until they match their perceptions of the size of a specific body site. |

[a] Adapted from Gleghorn et al. (1987).

Research has indicated that people with a variety of shapes and sizes of bodies may have distorted images of their bodies (see Figure 4-3). Most commonly, there is a tendency to overestimate the size of one's body—a tendency found among obese persons (Slade and Russell, 1973b), pregnant women at four months (Slade, 1977), and individuals with eating disorders such as anorexia nervosa (Slade and Russell, 1973a; Crisp and Kalucy, 1974; Wingate and Christie, 1978; Garner et al., 1976) or bulimia (Gleghorn et al., 1987). Those with anorexia starve themselves to achieve thinness, whereas bulimics engage in binge-eating, followed by self-induced vomiting or use of laxatives to maintain a desirable body weight. The ultimate goal of the person with anorexia is to lose

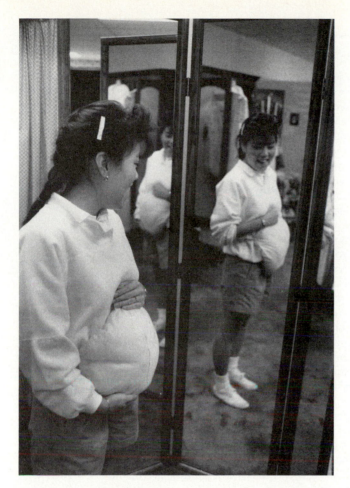

**FIGURE 4-3**
*In the early stages of pregnancy, one experiences the sensation of physical changes and becomes acutely aware of these changes. This awareness may promote the cognitive tendency to distort the size of the body—to feel larger than one really is—and to anticipate what it will be like to feel and look even larger in the later stages of pregnancy. Maternity shops provide padded pillows that can be used to enable a woman to envision how she will look in clothes that will be worn later in pregnancy. Photo by Carla M. Freeman.*

weight, whereas the aim of the bulimic is to eat without gaining weight. Some patients move from one disorder to the other, most often beginning with anorexia and then progressing to bulimia (Muuss, 1986). (See Social Focus 4-1 for information on the cultural nature of anorexia nervosa.)

In most studies evaluating body image among certain groups of individuals (usually females), there has been a tendency to compare a group of anorexics or bulimics, for example, with a "normal" control group without any easily recognized eating-disorder symptoms. One researcher reexamined the data from many of these studies and discovered that the normal women also often overestimated their body size (Thompson, 1986). To evaluate this trend further, he conducted a study of more than 100 women with no eating-disorder symptoms and found that more than 95 percent of the women overestimated the size of four body parts—on average, 25 percent larger than they really were. Most often the size of their facial cheeks was overestimated, followed by the waist,

# Anorexia Nervosa

Anorexia nervosa may be best described as voluntary self-starvation. The term actually means "loss of appetite," but in reality individuals afflicted with this eating disorder are obsessively preoccupied with food, yet deny themselves the privilege of eating. The most typical victim of anorexia nervosa is a bright, young, achievement-oriented female from a middle- or upper-socioeconomic class. Those with anorexia appear to feel personally ineffective as compared with individuals with normal eating patterns (Woods and Heretick, 1983–1984). One way of exerting some control over one's life is to manipulate the size of the body.

Although the disease has also been identified among males (for example, long-distance runners), 90 to 95 percent of those with anorexia are female. An estimated 2 percent of the population suffers from anorexia nervosa, but it is important to note that anorectic eating patterns may range from "subclinical anorexia" to emaciated hospital cases. The following characteristics are associated with anorexia nervosa: a fear of becoming obese, disturbance of body image, significant weight loss, refusal to maintain a normal body weight, and amenorrhea, or cessation of menstrual periods among females with anorexia. Also, individuals with the disease say they "feel fat" even when they are emaciated and display a preoccupation with the body. Even individuals who are down to a skeletal condition may tell doctors that they feel a little heavy. Clothes can confound the abilities of others to diagnose the disease, because many of those suffering from anorexia either look good in their clothing (similar to fashion models) or they use clothes to hide their shrinking bodies from others.

Particularly vulnerable to the disease are ballet dancers, gymnasts, and models, who are apt to maintain an artificially low weight for professional reasons (Anorexia, 1982). That these individuals' appearances may be emulated by adolescent girls points to the social implications of the disease. In fact, anorexia nervosa does seem to have strong connections with cultural ideology about desirable appearances, especially for females. Anorexia nervosa has been labelled (*a*) an "illness of abundance" because it is most common in wealthier, industrialized nations (Turner, 1984), and (*b*) a postmodern disorder, even though cases of female anorexia were documented as early as the thirteenth century (Morris, 1985). Feminists have pointed out that gender and cultural ideology about social relations should not be ignored when analyzing the illness. The association of a woman's status and character with her thinness is a cultural issue that may produce continual body dissatisfaction on the part of females.

Dissatisfaction with the bodily self is encouraged by countless television and magazine ads, which virtually accuse women of irresponsibility to loved ones and to society (but to self?) unless they purchase such improving agents as wrinkle removers, feminine hygiene sprays, and diet aids. Products are offered to hide every stage of the normal woman's development. Almost without exception, models used for these commercials are atypically tall, thin, small-breasted professionals, many of whom are anorexic themselves. The question is not why so many women become anorexic in this society, but why more are not (Morris, 1985, p. 95).

Similarly, in the book *The Obsession*, Kim Chernin (1983) describes the "tyranny of slenderness" as "more than even a struggle between mind and body" and characterizes anorexia nervosa as "tempestuous warfare against our bodies (which) involves no less than a woman's identity as a woman" (p. 65). Other social theorists have noted the need to locate anorexia within the historical context of the general position of women in society. Along with hysteria in the nineteenth century and depression in the twentieth century, anorexia nervosa may be viewed as an illness that "gives expression to the structural limitations placed on women" (Turner, 1984). Through a complex, oppositional reality, those with anorexia nervosa reproduce the norm of female beauty, but in a disobedient way (Turner, 1984, p. 196). Other authors have linked the social problem of anorexia nervosa to the need for a more ethical consciousness on the part of the fashion industry, which seems to persist in using thin models to display styles that have been designed to look good only on the thin (Giddon, 1985).

Using a cultural perspective drawing on semiotics, Probyn (1987) notes the need to keep in mind the complex and ambiguous nature of cultural discourses (for example, media messages) and interpretations on gender and bodies. Modern culture's obsession with narcissism (that is, self-love, quest for praise from others, and concern about

## *Social Focus 4-1 (continued)*

aging) and consumption or materialism may contribute to anorexia, according to Turner (1984):

> Anorexic self-obsession with appearance may be simply an extreme version of modern narcissism. Anorexia is thus a neurotic version of a widespread "mode of living" which is centered on jogging, keep-fit, healthy diets, weight-watching, and calculating hedonism (p. 203).

Probyn (1987) notes that anorexia may symbolize contradictions with respect to social ideals and gender identities. For example, a female's starvation may simultaneously indicate a desire to return to a childlike, undeveloped figure, as well as a desire to conform with cultural ideals that prescribe dutiful subservience and self-control. Attempts to combat the disease are similarly complex and ambiguous. One of the primary problems of treating anorexia is the socially desirable, achievement-oriented nature of anorexic behavior. Those suffering from anorexia are, at least initially, likely to hear the following kinds of comments from their peers: "I wish I were as thin as you are." "You sure have will power." Indeed, the American female ideal of beauty appears to be consistent with the achievement-oriented ethic that "thin equals win" (Morris, 1985). A person with anorexia nervosa may experience a feeling of accomplishment not unlike one associated with athletic prowess or achievement. The aim of reaching a certain weight—a goal that continues to shift downward—is distorted into the sheer pleasure of losing weight (Freedman, 1986, p. 159). In the process, we are reminded that bodies and feelings toward them are linked to cultural beliefs about gender, personal accomplishment, and social rewards.

---

thighs, and hips. Some women seemed to have undue concern about the size of a particular body part. [Two perceived one body part to be at least 50 percent larger than it really was (Thompson, 1986).]

In a follow-up study, women overestimated their body size more (25 percent) on the average than did men (13 percent) on overall measurements, as well as on facial cheeks, waist, and hips. Both sexes were equally inaccurate (approximately 22 percent) when it came to the size of their thighs (Thompson, 1986). However, in another study females consistently considered themselves heavier than they really were, whereas males underestimated their body size (Gray, 1977).

Why do people have distorted images of their bodies? The difficulty in approaching this question stems from the need to link cultural influences with personal, cognitive perceptions. And, such a linkage is not easy to capture in the quantitative measures used by most researchers. It seems likely that people implicitly compare themselves with fashion models or other media figures; when they feel that they do not look the same way as those models, they may begin to dwell on certain parts of the body (or the body as a whole) that they view as being problematic. More qualitative studies are needed to delve into this issue and to connect body-image (micro-level) perceptions with cultural (macro-level) imagery.

Some researchers attribute the problem of distorted body image to perceptual difficulties, while others emphasize emotional or cognitive factors (for example, wishing to be thinner). Although the question of why people have distorted body image cannot yet clearly be answered, it is clear that the disadvantages of a distorted body image are more apparent among females, who appear to feel worse about themselves the more inaccurate they are about their body sizes (Taylor and Cooper, 1986). Also, women who tend to feel negative about themselves and perceive themselves as unattractive to some degree are more prone to exhibit behaviors consistent with such eating disorders as anorexia nervosa (Grant and Fodor, 1986). A study of 751 high school cheerleaders indicated that those who expressed a strong desire for thinness were most likely to report disordered eating patterns and weight-control behaviors associated with bulimia (Lundholm and Littrell, 1986). The social importance of striving for thinness, especially among females, becomes apparent when considering the prevalence of this goal. In a study of 385 adolescent females, of whom 81 percent were assessed to be within the range for ideal weight or underweight, 78 percent preferred to weigh less. This tendency was most prominent among older girls (14-year-olds as compared with 12-year-olds) (Eisele, Hertsgaard, and Light, 1986).

In addition to body-size estimation, a dimension of body image with social-psychological ramifications is one's perceptions of the boundaries of the body.

## Body Boundary

Seymour Fisher and Sidney Cleveland (1968) described the concept of **body boundary** as a person's tendency to distinguish the space of the body from surrounding space. This concept is linked to the sense of firmness or definiteness of body boundaries. A clearly bounded person differentiates highly between the self and the nonself (Fisher, 1986b, p. 329). Therefore, perceived body boundaries may be linked to social relations.

> The whole concept of body-image boundaries has implicit in it the idea of the structuring of one's relations with others. It would seem to follow that if the body-image concept has something to do with the kind of defensive barriers an individual establishes . . . an understanding of these barriers should tell us something about the nature of that person's interactions with others (Fisher and Cleveland, 1968, p. 206).

Body boundary is a theoretical, not a tangible, construct that is largely unconscious. Therefore it cannot be easily measured directly in research; instead, how an individual structures boundary regions is measured through indirect methods. Through the projective task of describing a series of ink blots, people have been shown to vary in terms of the characteristics they assign to the peripheries and the definiteness of the imaginative structure's boundaries. These imaginative accounts appear to mirror the way people feel about their own body boundaries. The more they view their own boundaries as well-articulated, the more likely they are to view ink blots as having distinct boundaries. For example, the following imaginative constructs are indicative of a "barrier" response: cave with rocky walls, man in armor, mummy wrapped up, and turtle within shell. Barrier responses depict themes of enclosing, concealing, and protecting (Fisher, 1986b, pp. 329–331).

In contrast, some individuals use descriptors that emphasize the weakness, lack of substance, or penetrability of persons and objects: mashed bug, broken body, torn coat or ghost or shadow (Fisher, 1986b, p. 331). People with poorly defined boundaries may be more defensive and/or more likely to seek ways to convert the body, either by reconstructing it to create muscular boundaries or by wearing clothes with strongly contrasting patterns that advertise the body surface. Fisher (1986b, p. 411) suggests that some males may initially participate in sports as an attempt to compensate for feelings of body inadequacy. However, it seems that the longer one participates in sports, the more definite body boundaries become. Fisher interprets the available research in this area by asserting that an indefinite body boundary may contribute unconsciously to one's seeking athletic activities to bolster it, which may, in turn, contribute to a more defined body boundary, especially if it involves the build-up of muscles (Fisher, 1986b, p. 411).

It appears that clothing is also linked to body boundary, in terms of both fabric preferences and change in styles worn. A series of studies explored fabric preferences as a variable in body image, using the Compton Fabric Preference Test (Compton, 1962), beginning with a study by Compton (1964). In this study, schizophrenic women with poorly defined boundaries preferred bright clothes with saturated colors and strong figure-ground contrasts. Subsequent studies among other populations of women were reviewed by Fisher (1986b, pp. 411–418) and interpreted to suggest that individuals with weak body boundaries may try to strengthen them by wearing bright or contrasting clothes. In contrast, those with definite boundaries seem less often to feel the need to use clothing as a way of compensating for feelings of body weakness or penetrability. They have less motivation to wrap themselves in materials that loudly advertise: "This is the outside of my body that clearly represents a line of separation between me and you" (Fisher, 1986b, p. 417).

Paradoxically, a person with weak body boundaries may feel compelled to experiment with clothing, to put outfits together in novel ways to provide the self with a sense of reassurance (for example, female style leaders, who are likely to experiment with clothing, have lower barrier scores than nonleaders) (Kernaleguen and Compton, 1968). Fisher (1986b, p. 417) notes that this use of clothing for boundary reinforcement may be quite sensible, given that there is some evidence that a major change in clothing style may have a boundary-strengthening effect. Nuns who switched to a new style of clothing (away from the traditional habit) strengthened their body boundaries, as evident through a significant increase in barrier scores (Brocken, 1969).

Although there has been little research on men with respect to clothing and body boundary, there is some evidence that males who have tattoos on the body surface have high barrier scores, as noted with male prisoners (Mosher, Oliver, and Dolgan, 1967) and male narcotic addicts (Hassan, 1976). The feeling of being covered with potent symbols and signs may generate a sense of boundary (Fisher, 1986b, p. 413).

Research that identifies relationships without focusing on cause and effect is difficult to interpret with respect to the need for strengthened boundaries versus the impact of clothing and exercise practices. Among the studies on body boundary and clothing, the Brocken (1969) study has most directly pointed to the influence of clothing on body boundary. More research on the causal nature of the relation of body boundary to clothing could illuminate the link between body image and clothing.

## Body Cathexis

**Body cathexis** is a concept closely related to body image. It represents the degree of *satisfaction* with the body, however, rather than the image per se. There is more of an evaluative dimension to body cathexis. In general, people are more likely to say that they like rather than dislike their bodies. However, some caution should be exercised when interpreting body cathexis research based almost exclusively on self-ratings of satisfaction with specific body parts and overall appearance. Respondents may provide answers (being satisfied) that are deemed to be socially desirable (Fisher, 1986a, p. 133). Still, some consistent findings associated with body cathexis, beginning in the 1950s, have indicated that body cathexis is positively related to satisfaction with the self (Secord and Jourard, 1953). Body satisfaction appears to be closely linked to one's feelings toward the self in general, which is consistent with the idea that the body is a self-container.

Many researchers have studied people's degree of satisfaction with their bodies as a whole, as well as with specific body parts. There is some evidence of "perceptual groupings" of interrelated body parts that are relevant in predicting overall body cathexis and/or feelings about the self. Clearly, body cathexis is a complex, multidimensional construct. For example, differential cultural ideals for males and females influence the degree of satisfaction one has with the body. (This will be discussed in the section on gender and the body, to follow in this chapter.)

In a comprehensive study of body cathexis among 751 high school cheerleaders, who would be expected to be concerned with personal appearance as a crucial element of their public performances, neutral to somewhat positive feelings were expressed about several groupings of body parts (Damhorst, Littrell, and Littrell, 1987). Their degree of satisfaction was lowest for the midsection of the body, specifically including the waist, hip, and thigh areas. [Dissatisfaction with this portion of the body has also been found among female college students (L. Davis, 1985b).] Satisfaction with the bust was only slightly higher. Dissatisfaction with the midsection of the body was also related to dieting and purging behaviors (Damhorst, Littrell, and Littrell, 1987).

Some researchers have explored therapeutic means of improving body cathexis. Cognitive therapy techniques appear to be most effective for improving satisfaction with the body. These techniques focus on changing negative self-statements into more positive ones by identifying, analyzing, and evaluating automatic thoughts about body image and then reframing them into more positive, rational beliefs. This therapy, coupled with cognitive behavior therapy techniques (involving additional behavioral techniques of self-reinforcement and a fantasy exercise), can lead to more positive feelings about the self (Dworkin and Kerr, 1987).

Several researchers have studied the possible implications of body cathexis for grooming practices and orientation toward clothing and fashion. Rook (1985a) studied body cathexis in relation to consumers' usage of certain grooming products. Among the consumers expressing a high degree of satisfaction with certain body parts, there was a tendency to report high usage of certain grooming products. Men were significantly more positive than women on 14 body features.

Although there is some evidence of a relation between body cathexis and use of certain grooming products, degree of interest in clothing is not necessarily related to body cathexis (Littrell, Damhorst, and Littrell, in press). Leslie Davis (1985b) reported that the way female undergraduates perceived their bodies in terms of size was unrelated to their interest in clothing and fashion. Therefore, body perceptions and interest in clothing may be somewhat distinct dimensions. Further research is needed to clarify the nature of the relation, if any, between body perceptions and perceptions and usage of clothing. Females, in particular, are likely to be socialized to place emphasis on clothes and fashion on an everyday basis; therefore, it may be difficult to distinguish among females on the basis of interest in clothing. In other words, they may tend to be interested in clothing and fashion regardless of body perceptions (L. Davis, 1985b).

One issue that should be explored further is the extent to which body cathexis is culturally influenced. How do Americans compare with individuals in other cultures? A comparison of body cathexis scores between Japanese and American adolescents revealed that Japanese adolescents had less favorable views of their bodies' attractiveness and effectiveness. However, the Japanese data challenged the idea that a link between self-appraisals and body evaluations applies cross-culturally (Lerner et al., 1981).

Therefore, the issue of cultural influence on body cathexis merits further research attention, as do the implications of body cathexis for personal approaches to appearance management. Since ideas about ideal bodies are socially constructed and managed, the following section will consider the cultural and historical contexts in which these ideals are formulated.

## Body in Cultural and Historical Context

Our bodies and our perceptions of them represent an important part of our sociocultural heritage. As we learn to have a body, we also begin to learn about our "social body"—our society (Polhemus, 1978, p. 21). If changing body ideals are explored within their cultural and historical contexts, how these ideals are perpetuated and/or transformed becomes more apparent. Physical ideals vary from culture to culture and from one historical era to the next, but in most cultures and periods of time it is clear that humans strive to improve nature. So what is natural?

It is apparently a difficult concept for most people to accept that there is no "natural" way for men and women to look. . . . In different historical contexts bodies have been stylized in part by the clothes that they would have worn, which in turn reflected cultural conceptions of the ideal body type. The "natural" human body does not exist; but most people accept as natural the clothed figures that they are accustomed to seeing, or, to some extent, what they would like to see (Steele, 1985, p. 244).

Like clothing styles, cultural ideals about the body are subject to changes in fashion. In fact, there is a close relation between physical ideals and apparel styles at a given point in time. Because we are accustomed to seeing the body in a clothed state, there is a tendency to view nude bodies with clothed bodies in mind (Hollander, 1976).

Thus there are historical variations in "ideal" bodies. For instance, the fifteenth-century woman in Europe strived for a pregnant-like appearance because of the social importance of fertility following the plague that depopulated Europe (see Figure 4-4). This look was achieved through the use of a very full gown worn with whatever stuffing underneath (for example, a pillow) was required to provide the appearance of a rounded stomach.

Some social theorists contend that themes of female reproduction and sexuality may be discerned in later fashions as well. The corset became a simultaneous "affirmation of female beauty and a denial of female sexuality" (Turner, 1984, p. 197). Like anorexia, Turner notes, the corset had the important medical side effect of suppressing menstruation. Thus while slimness may be a norm of sexual attractiveness, the means of achieving it may ironically represent a denial of sexuality and fertility (Turner, 1984, p. 199).

Historian Valerie Steele (1985) argues, however, that if nineteenth-century fashion is placed in historical context, it becomes clear that the female body did not necessarily cease to be perceived as an "instrument of production." She cautions against stereotyping historical eras in terms of body attitudes, noting that corsets in some form had been worn since the sixteenth century.

Between 1820 and 1850, women were depicted in art and fashion with tapered arms and drawn-in waists. In the nineteenth century, the unrestricted body form, especially that of the female, has been interpreted by some historians as a symbol of "moral license," with the "loose body" reflecting "loose morals." At the same time, the wearing of the corset to constrict the waistline, especially in American and British culture, was a sign of the family being wealthy enough so that the corseted woman did not need to perform manual labor.

The ideal male of the early nineteenth century was also slender and elegant and wore close-fitting trousers and coat. In the 1860s, men abandoned form-fitting attire in favor of fuller pants and jackets, and males with less-than-sleek figures were publicly less conspicuous than women with fuller figures. Valerie Steele (1985) notes that some historians seem to have assumed, naively, that women's bodies, in particular, really changed along with fashion, whereas in reality, women were likely to have had approximately the same range of body

**FIGURE 4-4**
*In this painting by Jan van Eyck (1434), known as the* Arnolfini Wedding Portrait, *the desirability of a "fertile" look is exemplified. Although this bride is not pregnant, she strives for a bodily shape that fits the physical ideal of the times. This ideal was shaped by the need in Europe to replenish the population following war and the plague. Courtesy of the National Gallery in London.*

types that they currently have. As particular images became popular, however, women were likely to use foundation garments (see Figures 4-5 through 4-7), diets, optical illusions with clothes, and specific ways of standing or posing to approximate the current ideal (Steele, 1985, p. 224).

From the end of the Civil War to the turn of the century, the female ideal hovered between a slender, innocent figure to a "femme fatale" or ambitiously

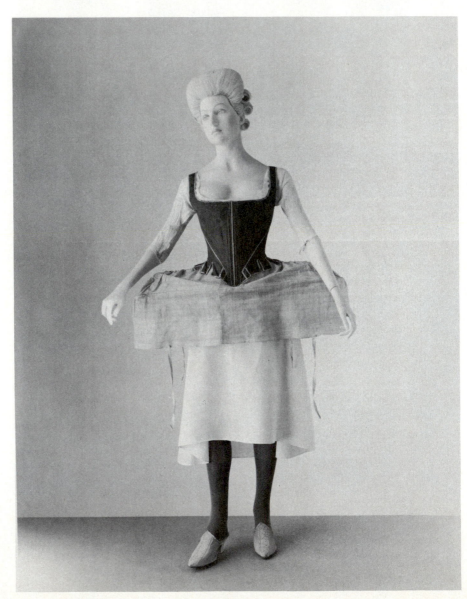

**FIGURE 4-5**
*Undergarments have traditionally been used to shape and reshape women's bodies in accordance with physical ideals across historic contexts. Shown here is an English corset, circa the 1770s and 1780s. Courtesy of the Trustees of the Victoria and Albert Museum.*

seductive and shapely figure (Schwartz, 1986, p. 93). Edwardian dress around the turn of the century gave the impression of buxom stateliness. After the turn of the century, the corset did not immediately disappear. Rather, new forms of corsets emerged on the market that were less rigid, and corset ads began to boast that they provided for "the corsetless figure so much admired" (Steele, 1985, p. 228). Designer Paul Poiret created corsetless fashions at a time when

*FIGURE 4-6*
*A crinoline frame was designed to shape the female body, circa the 1860s in England. Courtesy of the Trustees of the Victoria and Albert Museum.*

**FIGURE 4-7**
*A bustle was designed to enlarge and mold the appearance of the derrière, circa 1884 in England. Courtesy of the Trustees of the Victoria and Albert Museum.*

women were realizing that such physical movements as dancing were facilitated by removing the corset.

World War I accelerated the changes in body imagery that had been evolving. By 1919, for the first time in more than 100 years, women's summer clothes actually weighed less than those of men. However, for women whose figures were less than consistent with the current ideal, the new freedom was not altogether cause for celebration. The art of illusion replaced the art of managing layers of clothing (Schwartz, 1986, p. 161). During the 1920s, a boyish figure was the ideal, and a "teddy" was worn under short, sheathlike dresses to flatten the breasts. However, undergarments that molded the body into a tubular line were only a partial solution to achieving the ideal look, because part of the charm of the 1920s look was deemed to be the suppleness of the sleek physique—a kind of "boa constrictor," streamlined and flexible chic. Middle-aged females were at a particular disadvantage. Achieving the look of a slim, active body required dieting, at a time when the cosmetics industry was also creating and promoting the need to look young (Steele, 1985, p. 241).

Whereas the styles of the 1920s minimized the maternal bosom, by the 1950s (see Figure 4-8), women desired voluptuous curves and achieved them through the use of the padded bra. By the latter part of the 1960s, however, the physical ideal for females was a very thin body (see Figure 4-9).

The "thin is in" notion seems to have prevailed since the 1960s; yet, it is no longer sufficient *just* to be thin. In the 1980s a new ideal of female beauty emerged, emphasizing muscle tone and fitness along with a slim physique (see Figure 4-10).

> It is a body made for motion: for long, purposeful strides across the backcourt, through the mall, into the boardroom. It is a body that speaks assurance, in itself and in the woman who, with will power and muscle power, has created it. It is not yet, and may never be, for everybody, but for many men this feminine physical assurance can be galvanizing; there can be an allure to equal-

**FIGURE 4-8**
*Shapelier and heavier figures were considered beautiful in the 1940s and 1950s, as compared with today's standards for beauty contestants. Courtesy of the Department of Parks and Recreation Collection, City of Sacramento, Museum and History Division.*

**FIGURE 4-9**
*During the 1960s, an extremely thin figure was viewed as the physical ideal for women, as illustrated by these fashion models' bodies. Photo by Wendy Dildey.*

**FIGURE 4-10**
*Bodybuilding became a popular sport for women in the 1980s. This bodybuilder describes her body not as a taken-for-granted object, but rather as a "presence," in which "each muscle can be felt, seems to be vibrant." Along with visible muscles, a very slim physique is a major goal. Courtesy of Trish Mayer; photography by David Mayer.*

ity. . . . As a symbol of status, health, or sex appeal, the strong body is a sensible goal—and not only for those women whose livelihoods depend on the rigorous care and feeding of their bodies (Corliss, 1982, pp. 72–73).

How pervasive is concern with muscle tone and fitness among females? In a survey among *Psychology Today* readers, women tended to evaluate their fitness more harshly than men (Cash, Winstead, and Janda, 1986). However, females still placed less importance on fitness than males and were not as likely to strive on a regular basis to improve it. Many women noted the importance of being fit and exercising regularly, but they often did so in relation to some aspect of appearance, particularly their weight, in contrast to feeling good about their bodies, which was the theme transmitted by men (Cash, Winstead, and Janda, 1986).

Whether the emphasis on physical fitness and muscle tone for females is a blessing or another cultural manipulation is an issue debated by scholars of physical education and gender. On the one hand, physical strength may increase a woman's sense of personal power, just as a build-up of muscles may provide definition to her body boundaries. However, there is another feminist perspective:

Fitness may not represent a revolution in female beauty standards as much as it does the latest in beauty fashion. . . . And it echoes the very old promise that beauty is the answer to both. . . . While female muscles may be in, pretty clearly only certain kinds of muscles on certain kinds of recognizably feminine bodies are really acceptable. The model of the youthful and physically fit woman ultimately is not a symbol of power so much as it is a symbol of the beauty of feminine control over appetites and age (Chapkis, 1986, pp. 12–13).

In her book *Beauty Bound*, Rita Freedman (1986) attributes the link between body-building and beauty to the convergence of the feminist movement of the 1970s with a worldwide fitness craze. "Athleticism has been superimposed onto a superthin beauty ideal," requiring not only diet but also exercise. She argues that "if the drive to stay in shape derives mainly from insecurity about attractiveness, then the goal of looking good can undermine the goal of feeling good" (Freedman, 1986, pp. 163–166).

One study examined the influence of participation in an aerobics class versus a class on "professional image and dress" on females' body cathexis. There was a significant difference in the students' change in body cathexis as a function of participation in the two courses. Body cathexis did not change appreciably among the aerobics students. However, among the students in the professional image class, who were exposed to such topics as figure analysis, there was a significant *reduction* in body cathexis. This research suggests that a focus on appearance in a way that may induce self-analysis and self-critique also may be a deterrent to positive evaluation of the body, although it is still not clear whether physical exercise has any effect on body cathexis (Lawson, Pedersen, and Markee, 1987).

Whether or not women have been well-served by the "thin and strong" body ideal, apparently the active sportswear market has profited from cultural imagery of this body type. As some activewear companies become increasingly segmented to appeal to specific markets (such as runners and bikers), others cater to spectators who want to *look* like active sports participants or persons appreciating the comfort and practicality of sportswear during leisure time. The industry's terminology has changed accordingly:

> Activewear is no longer as accurate a term as it once was. Athletic wear and performance wear covers one end of the spectrum while phrases like spectator wear, weekend wear, leisure wear and street wear are some of the terms used to define the other end (Lettich, 1986, pp. 35–38).

Styles such as leotards, running shoes, jogging shorts, running tights, headbands and wristbands, leg warmers, and sweatsuits (not to mention specialized sports gear) emerged as fashionable items not necessarily restricted to the gym, track, or dance studio (see Figure 4-11), and some of these styles are unisexual. However, important differences between male and female physical ideals still exist.

**FIGURE 4-11**
*What would once have been considered active sportswear became fashionable as "weekend" or leisure wear in the late 1980s. As physical fitness assumed a prominent place within cultural value systems, the "fitness ideology" was transformed into a fashion message that had little to do with sweat or exertion. This college student wears cycling shorts with a long shirt and other accessories —not for biking, but for studying. Photo by Wendy Dildey.*

## Gender and the Social Construction of the Body: A Contextual Perspective

A contextual perspective is appropriate to the study of how males and females differentially construct definitions and assessments of ideal body types. The importance of context becomes critical in the interpretation of gender and appearance management (as discussed in Chapter Three), and it becomes increasingly so in relation to the social, as well as the physical, construction of the body. While the influence of cultural and historical context on individual body perceptions was considered in the previous section, here the focus is on social processes leading to different perceptions on the basis of gender.

The integrative nature of a contextual approach leads us to consider the social worlds of individuals and how these worlds influence the meanings they construct and reconstruct to interpret male and female bodies (derived from a symbolic-interactionist perspective). The contextual approach also allows us to consider the means for classifying individuals on the basis of body type and the resulting gender stereotypes about personality traits or behaviors and cultural sources of body imagery and the processes by which changing cultural images transform as well as perpetuate gender ideology. (Table 4-2 summarizes the differences in gender ideology relative to the phenomenal self.)

Basically, males have traditionally focused on their bodies in relation to physical achievement, whereas females have derived self-confidence from physical attractiveness (or at least this distinction has dominated social thinking). There are contexts in which this distinction becomes blurred and yet even in such contexts, gender ideology as we know it remains a factor in people's *interpretations* of changing physical images. Due to cultural ideology, interpretations of a woman's muscular body, for example, are likely to be linked to standards of female beauty and sexuality. These standards may supercede a concern with muscle definition and mass symmetry.

Similarly, in television cartoons, superheroines tend to have muscular bodies, but because they wear skimpy and/or form-fitting leotards, viewers perceive them as predominantly sexy, with physical strength as a secondary attribute (Kaiser et al., 1986). (See Figure 4-12.)

Both males and females feel better about themselves when they view their own bodies favorably. However, they appear to vary in how they *think* about their bodies, in the criteria they use to evaluate their bodies, and in the meanings

TABLE 4-2
*Gender and Body Ideology*

| How One Looks | What One Does |
|---|---|
| Emphasis on physical attractiveness | Emphasis on physical effectiveness |
| Achievement of slimness and fitness through diet and exercise | Achievement through athletic performance and strength |
| Goal: svelte, well-toned figure | Goal: muscular physique with little body fat |

**FIGURE 4-12**
*Superheroines in television cartoons may reflect the "best of both worlds"* with respect to physical attractiveness and effectiveness. *However, the issue of sexual attractiveness prevails amidst issues of bravery and strength or ability. In a study of 126 different character appearances, Ariel, from the cartoon "Thundarr," was evaluated by college students as the second most sexy (the first was a receptionist). Ariel was perceived as having the following attributes, in rank order (on a 5-point scale): (1) sexy (average rating = 4.73); (2) brave (average = 4.69); (3) feminine in appearance (average = 4.36); (4) attractive (average = 4.29); and (5) problem-solving (average = 4.27). Photo by Susan B. Kaiser.*

their bodies hold for them. These differences stem from distinct social worlds, to some extent, fostered by active sports for boys and pretty dresses (along with compliments) for girls. In part, the emphasis on *physical effectiveness* in males' self-evaluations, as contrasted with *physical attractiveness* as a criterion in females' views of themselves, may be linked to traditional gender ideology focusing on such personality traits as assertiveness and achievement for men and nurturance and warmth for women (Lerner, Orlos, and Knapp, 1976).

A gender focus leads us to consider the *relational*, rather than merely dichotomous, variations in body imagery, as well as the distinction between popular beliefs and social-psychological realities. Physical effectiveness and physical attractiveness are relative, not absolute, concepts, and they are not mutually exclusive. Research shows that relative to adolescent females, for example, adolescent males evaluate their bodies as more physically effective. As compared with adolescent males who focus on the effective use of their bodies, adolescent females tend to perceive their bodies as effective by means of attractiveness (Grant and Fodor, 1986).

In recent years, females have become increasingly concerned with physical effectiveness as have males with physical attractiveness (as discussed previously), but gender ideology seems to be slow and complex in the extent to which it changes. Some women contend that through the discipline of exercise, they are "forging a new unity between mind and body" and improving self-image in the process (Freedman, 1986, p. 165). However, Freedman points out that it is still mainly upper-middle-class women who have the time required to pursue the "jock chic" look. Moreover, the message of physical fitness is not so different from that found in traditional fashion and beauty magazines for women, except this time the message is cloaked in a more masculine image (Freedman, 1986, p. 166). Female fitness, it seems, has not *replaced* concern with appearance, but rather has become an *additional* concern. The *Psychology Today* survey indicates that women are more critical of their bodies than males on dimensions of appearance, physical fitness, health, and sexuality (Cash, Winstead, and Janda, 1986). However, the majority of both males and females tend to be relatively satisfied on these dimensions. The *relative* satisfaction as a function of gender is the issue at hand.

## The Male Body in Context

A muscular physique is a culturally valued body in a male (Staffieri, 1967; Tucker, 1982). Such a body becomes a sign of physical effectiveness. Chest circumference, in addition to voice and facial features, predicts overall satisfaction with the self among young adult males (Mahoney and Finch, 1976).

As males' bodies deviate from this muscular ideal, their satisfaction with their bodies also declines (Tucker, 1982). Viewing one's body as underweight has an adverse effect on males, especially as compared with females. A contextual perspective would lead us to look at the social and cultural meanings associated with being underweight, in relation to gender. As one male said in the study by Cash, Winstead, and Janda (1986), "Women are slender, men are skinny."

Adams (1977b) found that males who saw themselves as being too angular and thin also felt they were unattractive. These body characteristics were also related to the following personal traits in the males: emotionality, feelings of not being liked, anxiety, and external control (a belief that fate has control over a person's life).

One male commented in an interview on appearance management that if males want to draw attention to themselves, it should be through something "genuine" such as muscles (Kaiser, 1987). The process of being involved in a weight-training program does appear to be conducive to more positive feelings about the self on the part of males (Tucker, 1982). A look at the social worlds in which males are socialized to value a body that performs is helpful in understanding their emphasis on strength and effectiveness. The world of organized sports, for example, involves activities that are framed in the context of achieving and winning. Males report more competence in using their bodies effectively than do females (Lerner, Orlos, and Knapp, 1976). More research is needed on body imagery among females in relation to physical effectiveness, in order to discern the relation between gender and context.

How do males and females compare in terms of preferences for male physiques? Females appear to consider the male chest to be the most sexually stimulating part of the male body (Wildman et al., 1976). However, a somewhat large chest in males is preferred by females over an "Atlas"-type physique or a small chest (Beck, Ward-Hull, and McLear, 1976). In other words, a moderately muscular physique in males is preferred by females over a tremendously muscular one. One study found that women who are traditionally feminine show a preference for traditionally masculine physiques, such as tapering "V" physiques, whereas less traditional women have less stereotypical preferences (Lavrakas, 1975). Another study indicated that for men, there was congruence among the following perceptions: (*a*) their perceptions of their current figures (as identified in a range of drawings), (*b*) their ideal figures, and (*c*) the figure they feel is most attractive to the opposite sex. However, the last judgment was actually heavier than females' ratings, so it seems that men distort women's preferences to bring them in line with their own current figures (Fallon and Rozin, 1985). (See Figure 4-13.)

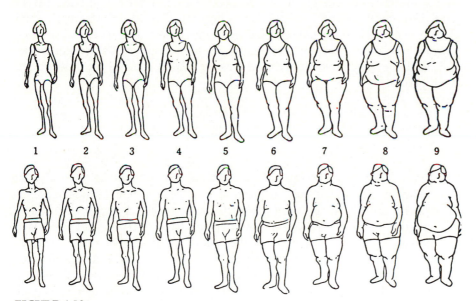

**FIGURE 4-13**
*In a study at the University of Pennsylvania, psychologists April Fallon and Paul Rozin (1985) asked students the following questions: (1) Which body is the closest to what you look like? (2) Which body is closest to how you want to look? (3) Which body represents the body type that is most attractive to the opposite sex? The average man selected body number 4 as what he would like to look like, and also thought he actually did look like that drawing. He also thought women were most attracted to that type, although women actually said they prefer leaner men. The average female was likely to think she was somewhat slimmer than body number 4 and thought men would be most attracted to body number 3 (men actually preferred women a little plumper). She also wanted to be even thinner than the body number 3 standard—significantly thinner than she thought would be most attractive to men. Courtesy of April Fallon and Paul Rozin.*

The socially learned emphases on global perceptions of the male body include height as well as body build. Numerous studies indicate that tall men are judged to be more attractive than shorter men. Additionally, a person's height tends to affect perceivers' evaluations of that person's traits or abilities, such as level of authority and status (Dannenmaier and Thumin, 1964; Wilson, 1968; Koulack and Tuthill, 1972). In several studies, subjects have been requested to estimate the physical heights of men when they had some previous information on the men's level of status. Lechelt (1975) found male and female students rated or estimated the physical heights of men in different occupations as a function of the esteem or prestige they accorded to these occupations. For instance, lawyers were estimated to be taller than plumbers or clerks. Additionally, male politicians have been more successful in attracting voters when they have been taller than their opponents (Kassarjian, 1963).

Apparently height can interact with other appearance cues such as glasses to influence people's perceptions. In a study by Elman (1977), students were asked to judge photographs of male upper bodies. The photographs were identical except the experimenter wore glasses in one photo and did not in the other. The students were also given two heights: 5'4" and 6'4". The taller height tended to produce significantly higher ratings on the traits of extraversion and attractiveness. When the glasses were worn, the person was perceived as more sensitive and gentle. The most "feminine" traits (for example, sensitivity, fearfulness, and passiveness) were attributed to the target person who was both short and wore glasses.

## The Female Body in Context

The sense of fullness and swelling, of curves and softness, of the awareness of plenitude and abundance which filled me with disgust and alarm, were actually the qualities of a woman's body.

—CHERNIN, 1981, p. 18

From an early age, young girls in American culture tend to favor a gaunt female figure (Staffieri, 1972). It seems that adolescent females would like to have bodies similar to fashion models and Barbie dolls. Approximately three-quarters of American women feel they are prone to be overweight. Leslie Davis (1985b) reported that 78 percent of the college females in her study displayed such a discrepancy between their perceived body size and the ideal. As compared with underweight men, underweight women are more likely to consider themselves normal. Similarly, normal-weight women, as opposed to normal-weight men, tend to view themselves as overweight (Cash, Winstead, and Janda, 1986). In the Cash, Winstead, and Janda study, one underweight woman commented: "I get two reactions about my weight. Some people tell me I would look even better if I put on a little weight, but many of my friends are envious. I don't know how many times I have heard someone say, 'I hate you, you're so thin.'"

Weight obsession is now one of the most common clinical disorders among females. The problem stems from a conflict between the cultural ideal and the reality of being female. Estrogen provides the female body with more fat than the male body, so women are prone to deviate from a lean and muscular physique (Freedman, 1986, p. 147). Heavy males may still be successful athletes (especially in football), whereas culture equates heaviness in females with lack of attractiveness and, therefore, with failure. Because a woman's form tends to be viewed as symbolic of character, an obese woman is perceived not only as fat but also as out of control (Turner, 1984, pp. 196–197).

A unique method for measuring and evaluating female figure attractiveness, using real people for stimuli, was developed and used by Douty and Brannon (1984). The technique of *somatometry* is based on photographs of actual silhouettes. Using this measure, Douty and Brannon (1984) found that females consistently rated female figures lower than males did. Males seemed to be more general and global in their assessments of the female figures or less critical of specific body details. Of the 29 female figures evaluated, the three perceived as most attractive were slim and had relatively smooth contours on the surface of the body. In contrast, all five of the figures in the lowest ranks were heavy or fat and uneven or lumpy in contour. The perceivers talked about the images in the pictures as objects that could be molded; females were especially critical of excess weight and protruding abdomens (Douty and Brannon, 1984).

Is the thin-is-in standard for women initiated and perpetuated by men, by women, or by cultural media? Most likely, some combination of the three accounts for this standard. There has been a significant decrease in weight over 20 years (1959–1978) in *Playboy* centerfolds and Miss America Pageant contestants, and it is primarily males who observe and evaluate women's bodies in both contexts. It should be noted that judgments of women's bodies became quantifiable in the form of beauty contests, from which the concept of a perfect "10" was derived (Riverol, 1983).

Both males and females are likely to be influenced by cultural codes in the media, which tend to promote a thin standard of body attractiveness for women. In a comprehensive study of media imagery, Silverstein et al. (1986) reported that 69 percent of observed female television characters were thin, whereas only 17.5 percent of observed male television characters could be classified as thin. Only 5 percent of females were heavy, as compared to 25.5 percent of males. In an analysis of magazine articles or ads about body shape or size, women's magazines contained 96 articles as compared with 8 in men's magazines. At the same time, women's magazines contained more messages (228) about eating and food than did men's (10). Women's magazines carried 63 ads for diet foods, whereas men's carried only 1. Thus conflicting messages are conveyed to women about food and bodies: Stay in shape and be slim but also think about food and cooking. Between 1901 and 1980, the size of women's bodies displayed in bathing suits and underwear in the *Ladies Home Journal* and *Vogue* dropped fairly steadily, as shown in Figure 4-14. The same pattern was identified in the bodies of popular movie actresses during this period, at least since the 1930s and especially since the 1960s.

Can the pressure on women to be thin be attributed to males? The evidence suggests that factors other than appealing to men influence the pursuit of thinness.

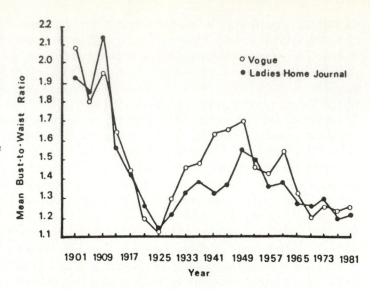

**FIGURE 4-14**
*This graph depicts the average bust-to-waist ratios of models appearing in* Vogue *and* Ladies Home Journal *at four-year intervals during this century (Silverstein et al., 1986). Note the decline since the 1960s, as well as the valley around 1925, when busts were deemphasized—the only other time in the century when fashion models have been as noncurvaceous as they are now. It is interesting to note that an epidemic of eating disorders was reported around that time in history, just as such disorders have been prevalent since the 1960s. Reprinted by permission from* Sex Roles 14 (9–10, 1986), *"The role of the mass media in promoting a thin standard of bodily attractiveness for women," by B. Silverstein, L. Perdue, B. Peterson, and E. Kelly, p. 530.*

As we have seen, cultural imagery is likely to be an influencing factor. Moreover, females' ideal figures are slightly thinner than what they perceive to be most attractive to males, so females are aware that there is some discrepancy (Fallon and Rozin, 1985). Establishing control over their lives and the social desirability of thinness, apart but not distinct from sexual attraction, may also explain the pressures on women (Fallon and Rozin, 1985).

With respect to specific body parts, college males prefer larger breasts than women typically possess, and males identify the breast as the most sexually stimulating part of the female body (Wildman et al., 1976). (See Figure 4-15.) Breast augmentation surgery is the most common form of cosmetic surgery among women, although breast reduction surgery is also on the rise. Among 64 females seeking breast augmentation surgery, 10 percent were normal-sized but viewed themselves as too small (Beale, Lisper, and Palm, 1980). Yet in the study by Douty and Brannon (1984), small breasts were not necessarily evaluated negatively in terms of attractiveness. It seems that large breasts are not necessarily an advantage except in the context of sexuality. Otherwise, large-breasted female stimulus figures have been evaluated as associated with lack of intelligence, incompetence, immorality, and immodesty. In contrast, small-breasted women are evaluated as more intelligent, competent, modest, and moral (Kleinke and Staneski, 1980). The apparent contradiction between perceived attractiveness and other positive traits of character points to the complexities involved in body perception and gender ideology.

## Physical Attractiveness

Culture provides ideals not only of desirable bodies but also of attractive faces to be connected with them. A number of studies have pointed to the social

**FIGURE 4-15**
*In recent years, a more curvaceous figure has become fashionable once again. Yet along with the popularity of this more curvaceous look, an ideal of thinness still prevails, and women are likely to exercise with that ideal as a goal. Photo by Molly Greek.*

importance of physical attractiveness, or lack thereof, in people's lives. A "beauty is good" stereotype exists and applies when people observe other people who are judged to be attractive. This stereotype is inconsistent with the belief that it is not fair to judge a "book by its cover." Nevertheless, research clearly indicates a bias in people's perceptions in favor of attractiveness. Facial attractiveness may differ from figure attractiveness by being relatively more stable throughout an individual's life. In some research studies, the focus is more on facial attractiveness, whereas in others, the entire body serves as the stimulus. Both bodies and faces contribute to impressions of attractiveness (Alicke, Smith, and Klotz, 1986).

Smith (1985) found that college students' evaluations of facial and full-length photographs of young children were highly correlated, but Smith and Krantz (1986) reported there may be gender differences. They compared perceptions of facial shots of third-graders with those of full figure shots of the same children engaged in outdoor play. The ratings of female attractiveness were fairly consistent across the different types of imagery, but the ratings of male attractiveness were less consistent. Freeman (1985) had subjects rate photographs of bodies (in bathing suits, without the heads) and found that people with moderately attractive bodies were associated with more socially desirable characteristics and were said to experience more life happiness than people with unattractive or highly attractive bodies. We will now consider the impact of the "beauty is good" bias on socialization to different life stages and, as a consequence, perceptions of self. (Later, in Chapter Thirteen, the consequences of physical attractiveness for social relations will be discussed.)

## Childhood

From an early age, the advantages of being attractive become apparent. Infants receive different treatment consistent with the notion that what is beautiful is good (Power, Hildebrandt, and Fitzgerald, 1982; Hildebrandt and Fitzgerald, 1978). A cuter infant is likely to be perceived as smart, likable, and a "better" baby (attached to mother, healthier, and more cheerful), whereas unattractive infants are expected to cause more problems (Stephan and Langlois, 1984).

Children's personalities and actions are judged and interpreted by being "filtered" through perceptions on the part of parents (Adams and LaVoie, 1975) and preschool teachers (Adams, 1978). When fifth-grade teachers were asked to evaluate an average student's report card attached to an attractive facial photograph, the child was rated as having a higher IQ, higher educational potential, and better relationships with peers than when an unattractive facial photograph accompanied the report card. The teachers also expected the parents of the physically attractive child to be more interested in the school (Clifford and Walster, 1973). If this set of expectations is applied to a teacher's interactions with a child and his or her parents, the child's success in school could be influenced. In fact, there is some evidence that teachers react more positively toward attractive children in classroom contexts (Adams and Cohen, 1974). Although there is no evidence that attractive children are actually brighter than unattractive children, attractive children receive significantly higher grades (Salvia, Algozzine, and Sheare, 1977; Lerner and Lerner, 1977). The same findings have resulted from a study of Lebanese schoolchildren (grades 5 through 12) (Zahr, 1985). Wheeler, Adams, and Nielsen (1987) explored the possibility of scoring bias in intelligence tests when degree of attractiveness is known. They found no evidence of a physical attractiveness bias in scoring, as long as careful controls are used for objectivity, including specific technical training. However, more positive personality and social characteristics were attributed to attractive than to unattractive children. This finding suggests that unattractive children are likely to be at a disadvantage when it comes to more subjective assessments.

Adult perceivers are also more likely to attribute antisocial behaviors to unattractive children, as compared with attractive children (who are viewed as less dishonest; Dion, 1972). Accordingly, unattractive children are more likely to be expected to repeat a negative behavior (Dion, 1972) and therefore to be punished more severely (Berkowitz and Frodi, 1979). Unattractive children may also be the more likely recipients of child abuse as compared with attractive children (Roscoe, Callahan, and Peterson, 1985). Even pediatric nurses expect attractive young patients to be less responsible for a hypothetical disturbance in a hospital and to attribute the problem to situational causes, as compared with their perception of an unattractive patient, who is more likely to be regarded as having emotional problems (Bordieri, Solodky, and Mikos, 1985).

Children themselves learn the what-is-beautiful-is-good stereotype at an early age and apply it in their own perceptions of one another. Even 3-month and 6-month-old infants gaze longer at adult faces judged to be attractive by adults (Samuels and Ewy, 1985). Children's evaluations of one another based on attractiveness appear to be similar to their teachers' and parents' evaluations (Adams and Crane, 1980). In addition to cultural factors pointing to children's evaluations of appearance, there are cognitive and developmental factors promoting their usage of appearance to judge others. It is easier for children to perceive *peripheral* (outer, concrete) cues such as appearance than it is for them to perceive more inner, abstract qualities such as personality traits (Livesley and Bromley, 1973). Children are even more likely than adults to pay close attention to appearance cues, because such cues are obvious and straightforward. Children appear to learn the subtle aspects of facial attractiveness, for example, as a result of minor oral surgery, as early as 7 years of age (Rumsey, Bull, and Gahagan, 1986).

What are the implications of children's perceptions of physical attractiveness in others? In terms of peer relations, preschool children are perceived as "nicer" and more popular when they are attractive than when they are unattractive (Adams and Crane, 1980). Attractive children are also thought by their peers to have more control over their destinies and to be more capable of achieving their goals. Conversely, unattractive children are expected to have less control over their lives, and are regarded as looking "frightened" and/or "scary" (Dion and Berscheid, 1974). Attractive children are more likely to be chosen as potential friends (Dion, 1973) and to be more successful than unattractive children in influencing attempts directed toward opposite-sex peers (Dion and Stein, 1978). Smith (1985) found that while attractive girls were treated more favorably by their peers than unattractive girls, in boys there was no relation between their level of attractiveness and peers' actions toward them. Thus the what is beautiful is good stereotype seems to be applied more stringently toward girls than boys, perhaps because femininity tends to be equated with attractiveness.

## Adolescence

During adolescence, physical attractiveness assumes a new kind of importance in the lives of both males and females, in a broadened span of social contexts as peers become increasingly influential in feelings of self. Physical appearance and clothing alike become magnified in importance because the adolescent has not yet fully outgrown the orientation to concentration on peripheral, concrete qualities in a person. The teen still retains some of the egocentrism of childhood but becomes increasingly aware of the self in relation to others, experiences concern about "appropriate" appearance and behavior in the self, and feels that everyone else notices his or her appearance and behavior to the same degree. During puberty, physical changes occur that are related to sexuality. Perceived changes in others' bodies affect feelings about one's own body.

Research indicates that positive feelings abut the body are related to a positive self-concept in adolescents (Lerner, Orlos, and Knapp, 1976). Among females, body attractiveness is more important than effectiveness, and *interpersonal* attractiveness is more important than *individual* physical effectiveness. Conversely, among males individual physical effectiveness is more important than interpersonal attractiveness in determining self-feelings.

Unattractive adolescent girls perceive themselves as less popular with both boys and girls than do attractive girls. They are less satisfied with their bodies and weight. Also, girls who experience pubertal changes are less satisfied with their weight than are undeveloped girls (Zakin, Blyth, and Simmons, 1984). Changes in the body must be taken into account when assessing the self. Despite the social advantages of attractiveness, puberty has been shown to interact with attractiveness and influence self-evaluations in general. Attractive girls who undergo early pubertal changes appear to feel less positive about themselves in general than their unattractive counterparts. How can this difference be explained? It is important to look at the *relative* perspective of the attractive and unattractive girls. An attractive girl is likely to be accustomed to receiving favorable treatment because of her looks. Therefore, when she begins to experience pubertal changes, they may seem riskier and more traumatic to her than to a physically unattractive girl, who may welcome the onset of puberty and hope for favorable body changes (consistent with the popular myth of the ugly duckling). In other words, the attractive girl has more to lose, whereas the unattractive girl has more to gain by pubertal change. Another factor that might make an attractive, developing girl more uncomfortable is the increased impact of her appearance on others (especially males), along with corresponding increased emotional demands and stress (Zakin, Blyth, and Simmons, 1984).

Personal attractiveness in high school students has been found to be related to the clothes they wear. Creekmore (1980) compared the personal attractiveness of 228 high school students to the attractiveness of their clothing. She found that attractive students generally wore attractive clothing and conformed to clothing styles worn by the peer group. Attractive students were also more likely than unattractive students to be accepted by their peers and to participate in school activities.

## Adulthood and Aging

As an individual ages, changes are expected in terms of physical appearance. Aging is often associated with body changes, including shifts in distribution of weight and increased weight. Female age appears to be more important than male age in determining perceptions of physical attractiveness. As males age, their judgments of their attractiveness decrease, especially among young adult males. However, this pattern does not appear to apply to female judges' ratings of male adults. Females of certain ages (10 to 14, 20 to 29, and 40 to 49 years) do seem to be more critical of older women's attractiveness, although males do not necessarily evaluate males more negatively on the basis of age (Mathes et al., 1985).

Cash, Winstead, and Janda (1986) reported a tendency of the older adult subjects in their study to be less interested in appearance than the younger adults, with one exception: women over 60 years of age. However, older people did not necessarily report a poorer body image; in fact, young adult women were the most dissatisfied with their bodies. Perhaps people's standards shift as they age, or perhaps the older generation's socialization to the importance of body imagery differs from that of younger adults. Older adults tend to be less satisfied with their fitness and to place less emphasis on it, and more satisfied with their health, and to place greater emphasis on it. Younger people may be more likely to take health for granted (Cash, Winstead, and Janda, 1986). In a study of 242 women, aged 20 to 89, satisfaction with the body and with clothing did not necessarily tend to decline with age. In fact, women between 20 and 39 years were less satisfied with their bodies than older women between 70 and 89 (McLean, 1978). The youngest women may have been unable to attain the desired "ideal" figures, whereas the oldest women may have focused more on maintaining their physical capabilities, in lieu of appearance, to allow continued involvement in activities. Although advanced age may bring with it body infirmity and a decline in attractiveness as culturally defined, there is little consistent evidence that self-assessments decline correspondingly (Fisher, 1986a, p. 250).

What culture defines as physical attractiveness, even in faces, may be fleeting with age, particularly in American society where a youthful look is perceived to be more desirable and where the physical attractiveness stereotype can work against even the physically attractive as they age. As the appearance of a physically attractive individual, and especially a woman, changes over a period of years, that person is placed in the position of being at a relative disadvantage. This situation is somewhat similar to that described earlier for physically attractive female adolescents experiencing puberty, except it is likely to be worse. A physically attractive adult would not be accustomed to negative self-evaluations, and a loss of positive feelings about the self might be expected.

Berscheid and Walster (1974) reported a relation between the physical attractiveness of a woman at college age and her happiness in life 20 years later. The attractive women in their study appeared to be at a relative disadvantage when it came to the aging process because they tended to compare their current looks to their previous appearances. The more attractive a woman was judged to be at the age of 20 (as evaluated by college students evaluating her yearbook picture), the less happy and the less well-adjusted she was in her current life (20 years later). This relation did not apply to men. In fact, the attractive men who had aged appeared to be socially and professionally well-adjusted. Attractive men indicated they were as happy as they had been 20 years before. There also was some evidence that the attractive men were wealthier 20 years later than were the unattractive men. Therefore, a double standard exists when it comes to aging and gender, with women being at a distinct disadvantage. Although culture seems to define the appearance codes associated with old age among men with a distinguished appearance, older women's appearances are defined as unattractive.

These findings may be understood by looking at the history of attitudes about women's appearances. Throughout the nineteenth century, women in the United States were considered to be old at ages much younger than men. Men were described as youthful even when they were in their middle to late thirties. In contrast, once a woman married, she was eliminated from the category of "youth," and most people simply disregarded the importance of her physical appearance. With the emergence and dominance of the commercial beauty culture (cosmetics and fashion) in the twentieth century, some of these ideas about

**FIGURE 4-16**
*Women in their sixties are likely to maintain an interest in appearance (Cash, Winstead, and Janda, 1986). Such an interest may entail working to keep a slim figure and following fashion trends. At the same time, research has indicated that by their seventies or eighties, women tend to have distinct clothing preferences that are likely to be linked to physical changes (for example, dresses with jackets to increase comfort when body temperature fluctuates, and V-necklines, which are more comfortable than those that fit close to the neck). Photo by Carla M. Freeman.*

aging changed, and older women were faced with a new paradox: They were now free to be concerned with appearance after marriage, yet they had to contend with new, almost unattainable standards of attractiveness (Banner, 1983, pp. 219–220).

One of the more recent images of attractive women is the over-40, physically fit, midlife beauty (for example, Jane Fonda and Raquel Welch).

> To be beautiful, they seem to say, is to look a constant twenty whether biologically twelve or forty-five. Now that foundation garments and heavy make-up (which provided the illusion of youth) have fallen out of fashion, older women must literally remake their bodies in the pursuit of beauty. . . . Even with the growing visibility of older women, their most striking quality is their apparent youth (Chapkis, 1986, pp. 8–10).

The physical changes that occur with aging tend to affect clothing preferences. Almost all of the available research in this regard has involved only older women. The physical changes older women tend to experience include sagging bustlines, thickened waists, and loss of muscle tone in the upper arms. These changes may limit the range of clothing options because of fitting problems. Older females have been found to prefer waistless designs, A-line skirts, front closures, set-in sleeves, dresses with jackets, three-quarter-length sleeves (to conceal the upper arms), and the color blue (Bartley and Warden, 1962; Ebeling and Rosencranz, 1961; Smathers and Horridge, 1978–1979; Richards, 1981). (See Figure 4-16.) The apparel industry is faced with a dilemma when trying to cater to this market, in part due to the negative connotations of aging in American culture. It is difficult for apparel marketers to cater to the older adult market without labeling it as old in the process, thereby stigmatizing it to some extent (Kaiser and Khan, 1980). At the same time, there is a tendency for new styles to be produced with youthful figures in mind.

## Stigma and the Physical Self

In a society where physical attractiveness is highly valued, individuals who deviate in some way from appearance norms and ideals are likely to be at a social disadvantage. The term *stigma* is often used to refer to socially disqualifying attributes. The term *stigma* originated with the ancient Greeks, who used it to refer to bodily marks or brands that were designed to expose disgrace (for example, that a person was a slave or a criminal). Today, the word is used more widely to refer to attributes that are socially discrediting or that reduce an individual to a marginal status.

Sociologist Erving Goffman (1963) defined stigma as a "special kind of relationship between attribute and stereotype," indicating that when an attribute is undesirable or difficult to understand and makes a person different from others, that attribute becomes a stigma. Obesity, physical disability, and mastectomy are some of the physical attributes that may socially disqualify an individual (see Social Focus 4-2).

# Appearance and Women Postmastectomy

One in 10 women develops breast cancer at some point in her life. In addition to life-threatening issues surrounding breast cancer (there is a 5-year survival rate of 68 percent versus 88 percent with early detection), women who have one or both breasts removed surgically have important social and psychological needs. Culturally, the female breast is glorified and equated with femininity, sexual attractiveness, and nurturing behavior. Along with the loss of a breast, women with mastectomies may have to contend with postsurgical treatments resulting in an altered appearance, including hair loss, weight change, and arm-swelling.

Additionally, a woman postmastectomy is faced with the possibility of social stigma. By wearing a prosthesis and concealment through clothing, a woman postmastectomy "covers" her apparent difference and may "pass" as normal, in the words of sociologist Erving Goffman (1963). (Since the 1960s, when Goffman wrote about the stigma of mastectomy, there has been increased social awareness and acceptance of the disease, due in large part to women in the public eye who have spoken out about mastectomy in the media.) By "covering up," the stigma is concealed from unknowing persons and eased for those who do know. Therefore, clothing and prosthesis represent means for appearance management on a daily basis, and using such means to present oneself to others is essentially no different from the strategies used by all individuals as a part of everyday life.

However, women postmastectomy have some practical problems when using clothing and prostheses. Research indicates that as many as one-half of the women who wear a prosthesis are dissatisfied in some way, with problems ranging from poor fit, skin irritation, heaviness, and feeling hot, to actual pain (Tish-Knobf, 1985). One-half of the women in one study noted that they could not wear all styles of clothing because of their surgery; particular problems occur during warm weather in contexts calling for more revealing garments (Feather and Lanigan, 1987).

In a survey of 979 women postmastectomy, clothing and prosthesis concerns were perceived as more important than social and sexuality issues, but less of a concern than health-related issues (Feather, Kaiser, and Rucker, 1989). Having a professional fitter made a big difference in the degree of satisfaction with the prosthesis. The women who were dissatisfied with their prostheses tended to reserve wear for certain contexts, whereas those who were more satisfied wore them a greater portion of the time. Attitude toward appearance was the most important factor in determining how satisfied the women were with the prosthesis. Younger women, who were more likely to be working outside the home, were more likely than older women to wear the prosthesis during the day (Feather, Kaiser, and Rucker, 1989). In general, garments that emphasized the bust or revealed a large amount of shoulder bareness were most problematic. For example, swimwear, nightwear, and formals presented more difficulties than casual, office or work, or dressy garments (Feather, Rucker, and Kaiser, 1989).

Large-breasted women were especially likely to have appearance concerns as the following comment indicates: "I plan to have a second mastectomy because I am large breasted and would rather be flat. I feel too lopsided."

In follow-up personal interviews, it was evident that for some women appearance was an important concern:

> *The most stressful time was before I could wear a bra and things would just hang, all those bandages. The appearance I think bothered me the worst . . . I wear my prosthesis all the time; I look horrible without it.*

Many women expressed concerns that related directly to their bodies, including the extent of the scarring, not liking to look at themselves in the mirror, and the feeling that the loss of a body part was a constant reminder of the disease. When clothing was mentioned, it was often in reference to covering bodily signs of the disease.

> *When I take a shower I sure do feel that I've lost something, so I try to take it real fast and after I get my clothes on, I don't think about it very much. I'm more careful about going to the bathroom; I just don't care to look in the mirror that much. I think that's why a lot of people get reconstruction.*

> *I am more careful in what clothes I buy. I won't wear anything that is sleeveless or shows my arms because of the edema (arm swelling). So I've gotten rid of those kinds of clothes.*

For women who have had mastectomies, appearance management with clothing and prosthesis represents a

## Social Focus 4-2 (continued)

strategy for asserting control over the potentially stigmatizing aspects of breast cancer. The psychological importance of this control becomes evident when considering that the women who were more satisfied with their appearance felt better about themselves in general (Feather, Kaiser, and Rucker, 1988). For some women, reconstructive surgery appears to contribute to a "complete" and symmetrical female image (Feather, Kaiser, and Rucker, 1989). The use of prosthesis and clothing, on the other hand, is likely to be more context-dependent in relation to body image, with some situations calling more attention to bodily difference than others.

---

After World War II in the United States, consumerism was characterized by an intensified emphasis upon materialism and personal appearance. Obesity became increasingly stigmatizing, stereotyped as indicative of a lack of personal control, slovenliness, and poor performance (Turner, 1984, p. 202). As slimness was increasingly equated with being modern and fashionable, obese people came to be regarded as "stuck in the past," with the "modern world passing them by" (Schwartz, 1986, p. 322).

### Obesity

Ironically, there appears to be a conflict between cultural ideology about the size and fitness of the body and the realities of Americans' bodies. The United States population ranks among the world's heaviest. Since the Civil War when the first statistics on body height and weight were collected, American adults have been growing both taller and fatter, as have their offspring. These statistics have been attributed to American diet and eating habits.

Being overweight has become synonymous more with "deviation" than "variation," as height-weight charts came to be associated with physical ideals rather than physical averages (Schwartz, 1986, p. 153). Technically, the term *obesity* applies to those at least 20 to 30 percent over their "best" weight, whereas those who are 14 to 19 percent over this "ideal" are considered overweight.

The stigmatizing effects of being overweight have been increasingly applied to children. What had been considered to be innocent "baby fat" during the 1920s and 1930s became a source of social concern to parents (Schwartz, 1986, p. 285). Having an overweight child was a source of embarrassment to parents, a poor reflection on the parents themselves (Millman, 1980, p. 75). By the 1960s, research indicated that overweight children were regarded by their peers as having the following traits: nervous, likely to cheat, argumentative, likely to be teased, forgetful, lazy, sloppy, naughty, mean, ugly, dirty, and stupid (Staffieri, 1967). In contrast, children with more socially desirable physiques were attributed favorable personal traits. There is cross-cultural evidence that heavier children experience more social distance from their peers (Lerner, Karabenick, and Meisels, 1975).

What are the personal consequences of being stigmatized due to large size? Lack of social acceptance among peers may be manifest in such social-psychological problems as disturbance or preoccupation with body image, antagonism toward more obese persons, and envy of thin persons. However, there is some evidence that whatever stigma some groups attach to being overweight, it does not necessarily make heavy people miserable about themselves. In other words, overweight people do not necessarily view their size as negatively as do others (Hayes and Ross, 1987). Nevertheless, some of the stigmatizing aspects appear to be internalized by people who are extremely overweight (obese) or who are very concerned about their weight.

Millman (1980) reported three common themes indicating the complexities of overweight women's self-judgments. First, there was concern that in others' eyes as well as their own, obesity represents a violation of what it means to be a female. That is, an overweight woman is regarded in American society as being unfeminine, unattractive, and "out of the running," sexually speaking. Yet in an almost unconscious way, some regarded excess weight as an expression of "excessive or forbidden sexuality" (Millman, 1980, p. 98). Second, for many women obesity was symbolic of disorder, of being unable or unwilling to exhibit personal control. Paradoxically, overeating was also regarded as a means of controlling one's experiences in the world, for example, as a way of fighting with one's parents and exercising autonomy. Finally, many overweight women had "before and after" fantasies, similar to media depictions and advertisements of how people's lives have changed once they have lost weight. These fantasies are indicative of a fascination with the "mutability of the self" (that is, transforming the self while also identifying that which is stable and constant (Millman, 1980, pp. 98–99).

The socially stigmatizing aspects of obesity, which are likely to be taken for granted or are relatively unconscious on the part of those who are not directly affected, become apparent when conceptualizing how different society would be if being fat were socially accepted. Schwartz (1986) depicts the utopia of a "fat society" in the following way:

> In a fat society, fat people would dress expressively. Their fashions would no longer be called "oversize" or "half-size", and they would have the same choice of fabrics and designs as everyone else. Not just panty-hose but all clothes would be "Just My Size." Full-size models would be featured in the salons of *haute couture*; full-size fiberglass mannequins would pose with others in the most elite shop windows. Fat people would no longer need to buy their clothes at specialty shops like The Forgotten Woman and Catherine Stout, or discreetly through the mails from Lane Bryant, Roaman's and King-Size. A fat woman could wear dramatic colors and horizontal stripes when the fancy struck; a fat man could indulge a secret desire to wear a large-checked light gray suit (p. 325).

The fashion situation has improved somewhat for large women in recent years, as it has become apparent to the apparel industry that the market can reap big profits (see Social Focus 4-3 and Figure 4-17).

### Physical Disability

People with visible physical disabilities tend to encounter uncomfortable social situations, especially in initial-contact contexts. A physical disability can become a novel stimulus for perceivers, and the desire to observe this stimulus conflicts with social restraints against staring. This conflict can lead to stifled or controlled

# The Large-Size Women's Apparel Market

Even though obesity may be a social stigma, the large-size apparel market has burgeoned in recent years. Prior to the 1980s, however, clothes available to large women were drab and lacking in fashion appeal, as a female carpenter (weighing over 200 pounds) noted in Millman's (1980) study:

> I remember shopping in Los Angeles shopping malls and going into and out of one boutique after another, and there was nothing I could fit into. Nobody ever thought of manufacturing for me. If you're fat you're just left out—cold. So I'm very thankful for the overalls at Penney's because they've gotten me through some very rough times and times when I didn't have to think about what I was going to wear and could think about other things. . . . A fantasy I have is dressing up and looking elegant and going shopping in San Francisco in nice shops and being socially acceptable—being thin and beautiful. But you can't live off that every day (p. 118).

Because being overweight is more problematic for women than it is for men, due to cultural ideology, being fat has become a feminist issue. In the popular press, feminist publications have addressed the stigma of being fat, and how this stigma is applied to "rules" about dressing. For example, an article in *Ms.* magazine reported that one large woman who had accepted her size and had created a personal style (with a range from African clothes to pink pedal pushers) received the following feedback from a neighbor: "You have a lot of nerve to wear a pair of pants that color. A person like you should wear dark, subtle colors to hide the fat." The woman replied, "Listen, I like the color. I'm entitled to wear something pretty. I'm overweight, not in mourning" (Fat, flashy—and fashionable, 1984).

Magazines such as *Big Beautiful Woman* and *Radiance* have catered to large women's needs not only with information about clothing and fashion trends, but also with editorials that encourage women to be self-accepting first and to diet later (Burgard, 1986).

In the 1980s, manufacturers and retailers have placed increasing emphasis on the large-size women's market. This move has not been altogether altruistic; there clearly is money to be made. Estimates indicate that over one-third of American women wear a size 16 or larger. Retailers are realizing the importance of using large-sized man-

nequins for display, as well as large-size models in fashion shows. Sales personnel need to be trained, as do buyers, to understand physical as well as social needs of the large-size woman (Novotny and Walsleben, 1986).

In fashion magazines advertising large styles, models wearing sizes 12 to 14 are most commonly shown. In contrast, runway and showroom models are more likely to be larger (up to size 18). The dilemma is one of *relative* size. In mainstream fashion magazines, the models are so thin (the industry "standard") that a model of average size looks large. In other words, we are culturally conditioned to expect models to look thinner than we do. Nevertheless, many large women would prefer to have the opportunity to see the styles they buy on larger models (Lebow, 1986).

Despite the lucrative nature of the business, there is still hesitancy on the part of some manufacturers or retailers to acknowledge the market. As one designer and president of a large-size apparel firm noted: "There's still a lot of prejudice out there against large-sized women. Many major stores don't even want her in them." Many companies that manufacture misses and juniors sizes do not want their name affiliated with large sizes, so if they do manufacture in this market, they have a different label for it. Retailers who are more successful in catering to the market include those who are "up front" with their departments and displays. Customer service is deemed to be the most important element in the specialty store business (McReady, 1987).

The large-size women's market has been described as the "pot of gold at the end of the rainbow," and one industry analyst noted that "the real treasure is that the category pays off for manufacturer, seller *and* consumer." Because their needs have been overlooked for so long, large women are perceived by the industry as willing to pay virtually any price for fashion-forward, quality apparel (Richmond, 1985).

The styles manufactured and marketed for large women may be similar to those produced for smaller women, with some adaptations, such as tank straps in lieu of spaghetti straps (to accommodate bra straps); designers are realizing the fashion tastes of the large-size woman are no different from those of any other woman (Schloderer, 1986). Many retailers, as well, are quite aware that large-size fashion is becoming a prosperous business. As

## Social Focus 4-3 *(continued)*

the divisional manager for special sizes at Bullock's department store noted, the large-size customer's "closet is not full. She doesn't already have 50 tops. Her ability to choose is new. There were no designers in this before. So she comes in and buys what she likes. If she sees it, she has to buy it, because it won't be there next time" (Adams, 1988).

Body type is not a lifestyle, just as style is not equated with size. Yet large women probably have to pay more than thinner women for the privilege of being in style.

---

interactions between physically disabled persons and able-bodied persons in face-to-face situations (Kleck, Ono, and Hastorf, 1966; Kleck, 1968; Comer and Piliavin, 1972). Moreover, a person who deviates from the physical norm may have difficulties with social relations or feelings of rejection and essential difference from others.

The impressions formed about people with physical disabilities are affected by clothing cues as well as physical disabilities (Miller, 1982). On the part of the physically disabled students themselves, there is evidence of them holding less favorable attitudes toward clothing, as compared with able-bodied students (Feather, Martin, and Miller, 1979), even though students with physical disabilities tend to value the importance of clothes in appearance management and social interactions (Kaiser, Freeman, and Wingate, 1985).

Part of the clothing problems associated with physical disability stems from the lack of available clothing in the apparel marketplace to suit individual differences (Hallenbeck, 1966; Kernaleguen, 1978; Shannon and Reich, 1979). Yet specially designed, functional clothing, designed to incorporate self-help and/or special-fit features, as available from some mail-order firms, may not be desirable either, due to distinct differences from social norms. Ambivalence may result from the conflict between a person's unique needs and those based on cultural norms (Cuber, 1963). Special features of garments designed for people with disabilities (for example, Velcro, large zippers, and other such features in unconventional places) may be sources of stigma that further differentiate physically disabled from able-bodied persons. This clothing may be both positively and negatively received by persons with physical disabilities, in that it may be both functional and different from the norm. "Since the handicapped may have different and special needs, clothing designed to meet these needs can easily become 'special clothing' which emphasizes, rather than minimizes, a handicap" (Kernaleguen, 1978, p. 3). (See Figures 4-18 and 4-19.) The following responses of physically disabled students when shown slides of functional clothing in interviews illustrate this dilemma:

*When I saw it, I looked at it and said, "Made especially for a handicapped person? That has a label on it."*

*I don't want to look any different. You don't want to look sick. I feel like that when I see a zipper like that—kind of sick, different, because other people don't wear them.*

*FIGURE 4-17*
*Fashion magazines catering to larger women have reinforced the idea that big can be beautiful, as well as fashionable.* Courtesy of Big Beautiful Woman, *photography by Jak McDonnell.*

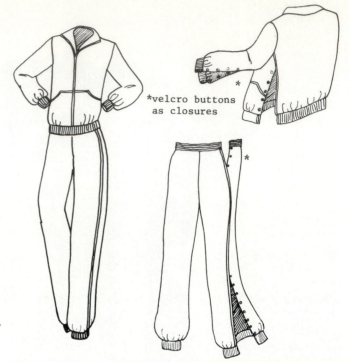

*velcro buttons
as closures

**FIGURE 4-18**

*Perceptions of this jogging suit by male and female college students with physical disabilities varied in accordance with the gender-typed issue of attractiveness and fashionability versus physical effectiveness. In a national survey conducted by Wingate, Kaiser, and Freeman (1986), males regarded this style as less attractive than did females. Females focused on the fashionability of jogging suits, whereas males framed their interpretation of this style in terms of physical effectiveness. Accordingly, males in wheelchairs, in particular, were concerned that a man in a wheelchair who wears a jogging suit may be viewed as "inconsistent."*

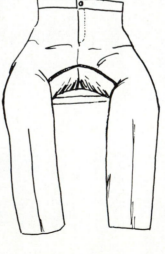

*zipper in inseam of pants
from mid-thigh to mid-
thigh

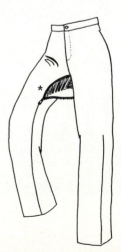

**FIGURE 4-19**

*When college students with physical disabilities were shown this drawing with information about the zipper feature in the crotch (as opposed to the drawing without additional information or another view of the pants unzipped), they evaluated the pants as significantly less common, less likely to be worn, less fashionable, less applicable to their disabilities, less comfortable, less modest, and more conspicuous (Wingate, Kaiser, and Freeman, 1986). In interview discussions, concern was expressed about the stigmatizing aspects as well as the dysfunctional nature of this style (which can cause pressure sores or zipper marks in areas of the body that are paralyzed and therefore that are not sensitive to this pressure) (Freeman, Kasier, and Wingate, 1985).*

*It was ugly. I wonder with all that Velcro because you bend, and when you're sitting in all that Velcro it would pucker and look funny. Then you not only are disabled, but you look like you dressed in a dark closet (Freeman, Kaiser, and Wingate, 1985–1986).*

At times the functionality of the garment seemed to be an advantage, but the social consequences were not perceived as being worth the cost, as one student noted: "It might be kinda nice to own, but I wouldn't want to be seen in public in it" (Freeman, Kaiser, and Wingate, 1985–1986).

Basically, just knowing that an article of clothing is "functional" or "specially designed" was enough as a general rule to stigmatize the garment in the eyes of students with disabilities (Wingate, Kaiser, and Freeman, 1985–1986). How do the perceptions of physically disabled persons compare with those of able-bodied students? In general, able-bodied students appear to be more positive than disabled students in their perceptions of the same functional clothing styles. Also, able-bodied students appear to be less likely to distinguish function as a separate cognitive dimension; instead, they tend to make more global perceptions of the styles (Freeman, Kaiser, and Chandler, 1987). Moreover, themes of the differential emphasis of males and females on physical effectiveness and physical attractiveness, respectively, were evident in the students' perceptions of a jogging suit (see Figure 4-18). Females tended to rate this style more favorably than males, in terms of attractiveness. Males who were born with their disabilities were especially unlikely to find the style attractive. These males may have been socialized to associate the jogging suit with physical effectiveness and, therefore, inconsistent with physical disability. One male in a wheelchair described the jogging suit as looking "severely able-bodied"; another male in a wheelchair indicated that the sight of a disabled person wearing a jogging suit in a wheelchair is something of a paradox. In contrast, females may have been more conscious of the appropriateness of the jogging suit for a range of social contexts or as fashionable and comfortable beyond the realm of physical activity or sports (Wingate, Kaiser, and Freeman, 1985–1986). Thus cultural gender associations are likely to have influenced the students' personal, symbolic, and cognitive assessments of the style. In this case, it becomes clear that *meaning* must be considered alongside function if the apparel needs of individuals are to be met.

For some students the overall concept of functional or special clothing was a source of ambivalence:

*I don't like to be categorized, but I think if there's clothing available that could make it easier for someone and make them more independent. . .*

*At the moment I might say "damn it all, who cares if I really need it, what if the world looks at me." I'm certain I would have ambivalence on those articles of clothing, depending on who saw me and what context it was in.*

Several points were made by the students about how their clothing needs could be better met (Freeman, Kaiser, and Wingate, 1985–1986). First, a number of students indicated that they prefer the idea of altering ready-to-wear apparel over the concept of special clothing, although they recognized the technical difficulties involved. They noted that people with special training could be available in department stores to help in the selection of clothes that could be altered for personal needs of any kind. A second suggestion was to develop means for sharing tips or strategies among physically disabled persons themselves. One of the most fascinating aspects of the interviews was the sharing of ingenious strategies for adapting and using clothing, for example, removing back pockets from jeans in order to avoid pressure sores or sewing sheepskin into the seat of jeans to avoid sitting on welt seams. Social mechanisms such as networking might facilitate the sharing of such strategies generated by physically disabled persons themselves. A third suggestion or theme that emerged from the interviews was the need for increased functionality in *all* clothing. The idea here was that "whatever's comfortable is comfortable to everybody" (Freeman, Kaiser, and Wingate, 1985–1986).

The marketability of clothing for persons with physical disabilities differs from special-size markets (for example, large sizes and petites). The market is not likely to be as large and profitable as many special-size markets, because individual disabilities involve unique fitting problems and dressing abilities. Therefore, mass production does not tend to be economically feasible. However, the markets for large sizes and functional clothing (for physically disabled persons) do tend to share some degree of social stigma. Historically, the apparel industry has catered to "average" bodies that do not necessarily exist even among able-bodied, slim persons. Although the needs of people with special sizes are being increasingly met by the apparel industry, persons with physical disabilities are largely left to their own devices. Both heavy and physically disabled persons could benefit from more cultural awareness of their needs, as well as from informal groups urging self-acceptance and social-political consciousness. Self-acceptance is closely related to how individuals view their bodies, and it is hard to separate these perceptions from cultural images and social-psychological processes, whether or not people's bodies match what is socially perceived as ideal.

## Suggested Readings

Chowdhary, U., and Beale, N. V. 1988. Plus-size women's clothing interest, satisfactions and dissatisfactions with ready-to-wear apparel. *Perceptual and Motor Skills* 66: 783–788.

A study of the interests, satisfactions, and problems of 71 large women (size 16 and over) is reported. The women were relatively satisfied with most types of apparel, but opinions differed according to size and age. Heavier and older women tended to be less satisfied with their clothing, especially in relation to fit and size.

Fisher, S. 1986a. *Development and structure of the body image* vol. 1. Hillsdale: Lawrence Erlbaum.

Fisher, S. 1986b. *Development and structure of the body image* vol. 2. Hillsdale: Lawrence Erlbaum.

In this two-part series, Fisher reviews and summarizes the numerous studies related to body image. The concept of body-image boundaries is explored in depth, and the relation between this concept and clothing is addressed.

Lennon, S. J. 1988. Physical attractiveness, age, and body type. *Home Economics Research Journal 16*(3): 195–203.

Age and weight in women are explored as variables in judgments of physical attractiveness. The findings document that thinness and youth tend to be equated with attractiveness.

Millman, M. 1980. *Such a pretty face: Being fat in America.* New York: W. W. Norton & Co.

Millman draws on qualitative data to explore the meaning of obesity in women's lives. The concept of body image becomes much clearer after reading how heavy women describe their bodies in relation to everyday-life activities and interactions.

Seid, R. Pollack. 1989. *Never too thin: Why women are at war with their bodies.* New York: Prentice Hall Press.

Seid uses a social-historical approach to explain why women have become so obsessed with thinness. The book includes several chapters tracing the historical development of this obsession and establishes connections among thinness, fashion, and beauty.

# Chapter Five
# ...
# *Appearance and Self-Concept*

*How do we go about the business of evaluating our appearances and incorporating these evaluations into our perceptions of who we are as individuals? This question addresses the crux of the issue in the study of appearance and the self. Dressing and experimenting with appearance afford opportunities for exploring who we are. Information about the self may be gleaned from the responses of others, visual comparisons with others' appearances, and internal thought processes that lead us to attribute explanations to our own clothing choices and preferences. In turn, how positively or negatively we feel about our selves in general can influence our clothing choices, as we manage how we look either to express a positive view of self or to bolster a less-than-positive view. As we attempt to define who we are, we have a wide array of appearance symbols at our disposal to experiment with, as well as to complete, the picture of self.*

*I have some very bright, colored sweaters and sweatshirts. . . . The first time I wore them, I couldn't figure out why everybody was looking at me. . . . First it made me uncomfortable, like maybe I shouldn't have worn this because it is too startling, but . . . I decided that I like it and think it's part of me, so I continued to wear it.*

—FEMALE COLLEGE STUDENT

*There are some times (not every day) you can wear your favorite clothes, and when you do, it takes a burden off. . . . When you're wearing clothes that you just don't like or you have to because everything else is dirty or something, you just kind of feel self-conscious.*

—MALE COLLEGE STUDENT

Clothes are linked to the way we view and evaluate ourselves. These thought processes do not emerge in a vacuum. Rather, everyday social contexts and clothes that are special (or not special) to us bring these thoughts to our attention. The self, after all, is an individual's consciousness of being, and personal appearance is part of that consciousness. In this chapter, the relation between self and clothing and appearance will be considered, beginning with a discussion of concepts linking the two. Then we will explore the social factors that influence our perceptions of self and appearance, by looking at how a person is located within society, as well as how values and ideals in society come to be incorporated into the person. Then the sources of information we use to know and define the self will be discussed, followed by a focus on the consequences of this knowledge: (1) feelings about the self and (2) seeking self-completion in areas that need to be bolstered.

Through clothing and other forms of appearance management, the body becomes a malleable form of self-expression. On a daily basis, individuals use clothes to communicate desired aspects about the self to others, and those others, in turn, respond to this self-symbolizing and provide new insights to others about themselves.

A contextual approach to the study of self leads us to focus on the **social self.** This means that self-reflection is a social construction. As a person reflects on the self, the perspectives of others (real or imagined) are taken into account (see Figure 5-1). Drawing primarily from a symbolic-interactionist perspective in sociology, the self is studied in terms of social arrangements and transactions, as well as the influence of these social factors on a developing sense of self. Self-conceptions are not static; rather, as people move into new contexts and life

**FIGURE 5-1**
*A young girl who has her hair crimped for the first time critically studies her reflection in the mirror and contemplates not only how she* thinks *it looks but also how she* imagines *others will respond to her new hairstyle. Photo by Susan B. Kaiser.*

situations (*a*) requiring new clothes and/or (*b*) inducing reconsiderations about the meaning of their appearance, ideas about the self are reconstructed and refined. The socialization process, which begins with early childhood and continues throughout the life cycle, promotes continual assessment of self. Viewing a person within a larger cultural and historical context, it is also important to consider social change and fashion change as they influence perceptions of socially appropriate clothes and identity.

The sources of information that an individual uses to develop and modify the self-concept are largely social in nature, including such processes as social feedback and social comparison. There are some basic psychological processes, however, that also influence the self-concept and strategies for appearance management.

## *Self and Appearance*

How do the clothes we wear affect the way we see ourselves? To answer this question, it is necessary to delve into several concepts related to the self. The concept of self is derived from the works of theorists such as William James (1890), Charles Horton Cooley (1902), and George Herbert Mead (1934). **Self-concept** is a global perception of who one is. People internalize and integrate personal qualities and other characteristics to define the self. Although we may have self-perceptions for every role we play in life, most theorists feel that we also have more global concepts of who we are. Drawing on social experiences in different contexts, one's concept of self is developed, maintained, and modified. Through self-related processes, individuals experience and interpret social interactions and thus shape their course.

### *Proximity of Clothing to Self*

Clothes are not only contiguous to the body in a physical sense, but they also may be close to the self in a psychological sense, according to Suzanne Sontag and Jean Schlater (1982). They asked husbands and wives, "How do you feel about your clothing?" and "How do you feel about your self?" The subjects responded to these questions on a scale from "delighted" to "terrible." Then they were asked to write an essay on the following question: "What are some of the most important reasons *why* you feel as you do about your clothing?" Almost half (44 percent) of the people indicated some degree of proximity of clothing to self in their essays, with women more likely to do so than men. More men than women, however, indicated a relation between clothing and how they evaluated and felt about themselves. More women than men indicated close proximity between their clothing and body satisfaction. This research suggested that people differ with respect to clothing perceptions as linked to the body and the self. Moreover, proximity of clothing to the self is likely to be a multifaceted construct, incorporating (*a*) structured ways of thinking about clothing and the self, (*b*) internalization of others' judgments and awareness of self when self-symbolizing with clothing, (*c*) body satisfaction (cathexis), and (*d*) evaluations of self resulting in positive or negative feelings (Sontag and Schlater, 1982). Let us consider the first two dimensions: self as structure and self as process. (Body cathexis was discussed in Chapter Four, and evaluations of the self will be discussed later in this chapter.)

## Self as Structure

The term *structure* implies that the self is a psychological construct, involving systematic mental perceptions that are integrated into some kind of order. A structural model of self is derived from the cognitive perspective and suggests that self-image involves structured thought processes that are likely to be relatively stable until they no longer function adequately or apply to one's life. When these structured thought processes change, then, the change occurs at a cognitive or mental level. Some change in clothing style may also result. Comments such as the following may typify responses about the self that fit a structural model: "My dress is me." "It [clothing] fits my character" (Sontag and Schlater, 1982, p. 4).

A tangible example of a structural model of self may be seen in the case of a person who feels compelled to view his or her clothes as one with the self or with a dominant identity within the self. Taken to an extreme, one might tend to dress the same in different social contexts, or to a lesser extreme, modify his or her appearance slightly, but still maintain a central theme that is synonymous with the self. For example, Alex P. Keaton on the television show *Family Ties* was known for his politically and economically conservative views and his own career aspirations; his fairly consistent tendency to wear a tie (whether with a sportscoat, a three-piece suit, or a sweater, depending on the context) could be characterized as symbolic of a highly structured view of the self—integrating qualities of ambition, goal-directedness, conservatism, and sensitivity (when least expected). At the same time, some accommodations are made for social situations calling for different levels of formality.

### Self-Schema

The term *self-schema* may be used to refer to structured thought processes that organize, modify, and integrate qualities assigned to the self. Self-schema may include visual images as well as verbal descriptions, as people determine what looks "like the real me" versus "not like the real me" (Yarmey and Johnson, 1982). (See Figure 5-2.)

Harvey Pines (1983) conducted a series of studies to see how self-image might be structured around clothes that illustrate "me" versus "not me." He found that although female college students could decide quickly which pictures of clothes were most me and least me, it took more time to classify styles that fall somewhere in between. The students could also later recall the styles that were most me more easily than the other styles. This identification of what is me is likely to parallel people's self-schemata as they shop and identify "just what they are looking for," although of course these schemata may be restructured or redefined, at least in part, as fashion changes (Pines, 1983).

What is the difference, if any, between "clothes that are me" versus "clothes that I like"? Pines and Roll (1984) found that there was a relation between me

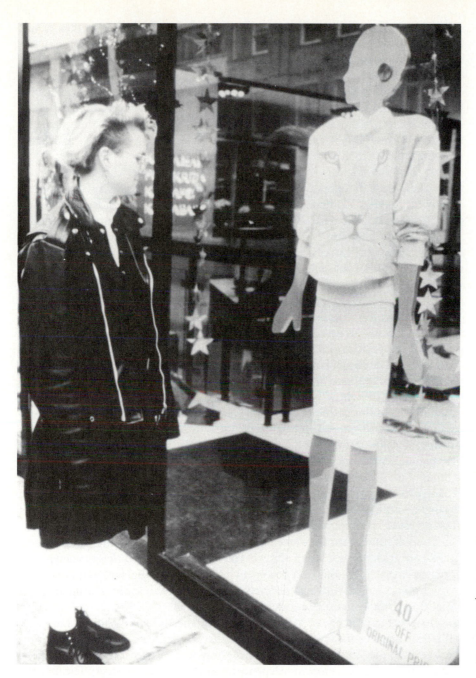

**FIGURE 5-2**
*When shopping, one can identify styles that are clearly "me" or "not me" fairly readily. This young woman shopping in London knows after seeing this style in a store window that it is "not me." Photo by Susan B. Kaiser.*

and "liking"; however, ratings of liking tended to be higher than ratings of me. In other words, people may like a clothing style, but indicate "it's not me." In contrast, few would say, "It's me, but I don't like it." Some people seem to distinguish between me and "liking" more than others.

How do self-schemata relate to social context? Pines and Kuczkowski (1987) found that the more like me clothes are, the more situations females could identify where they would wear those clothes. Also, it took less time to begin thinking of situations when the clothes were included in a person's self-schema (like me), rather than when the clothes were not like me.

So while people may have structured thoughts about what clothes typify themselves, those thoughts are likely to be filtered, in part, through social contexts and perceptions of others. This tendency leads us to consider the self as process—with a sense of fluidity as a person moves from one context to another.

Persons emphasizing "self as process" are likely to emphasize the importance of social responses from others about one's clothes and to equate these responses with feelings about the self, as the following quote suggests: "I've always been very conscious of how I look to others. If people tell me I dress nice, I feel good" (Sontag and Schlater, 1982).

Symbolic interactionists tend to view the self as a process, emphasizing that social experiences are dynamic enough to cause us to continually examine and refine our perceptions of self. Moreover, appearance per se is likely to be regarded as a social process by symbolic interactionists. That is, as we present our appearances to others, they are used by those others to understand our identities and subsequently influence how we interact with one another. Gregory Stone (1965) noted that clothing and appearance play a vital part in the development, maintenance, and modification of one's sense of self (see Social Focus 5-1).

Experiencing and interpreting social interactions are components of a process that symbolic interactionists call **self-indication** (Blumer, 1969a). Self-indication is similar to a conversation within the self, through which one defines and explains to one's self. The self-indication, or inner dialogue, leading a person to label a garment as me or not me (as in Figure 5-2) illustrates this process of defining and explaining to the self.

The self, then, may be viewed as a context of inner dialogue, almost like a "miniature society" (Fisher, 1978, p. 167) comprised of different viewpoints or perspectives. Self-indication becomes the essence of social interaction because of the human potential to act creatively and uniquely while also considering the social desirability of one's actions.

George Herbert Mead (1934), following the ideas of William James on self-understanding, believed that the self may be separated into dual entities: the **I** and the **me.** These components may only be distinguished hypothetically, because in reality they are interdependent in their consequences. The I is the active component of self that is prepared to behave or initiate an action in a relatively impulsive or unorganized manner. The me helps to control the I by providing a social conscience that incorporates the concept of "other"—social norms, community attitudes, group values, and the like. The me provides a

# Appearance as Process: Programs and Reviews

Symbolic interactionist Gregory Stone (1965) defined **appearance** as a phase of a social transaction, during which the identities of people interacting are initially established and the stage is set for further communication.

> Appearance *substitutes* for past and present action and, at the same time, conveys an *incipience* permitting others to anticipate what is about to occur. Specifically, it represents our action, past, present, and future, as it is established by the proposals and anticipations that occur in every social transaction (p. 229).

This view of appearance as a process laying the foundation for interaction is illustrated in the context of a customer entering a store, being greeted by a sales associate. Of course, the social transaction that may follow this initial greeting could lead to a sale.

Stone further identified two concepts that are relevant in the appearance process: programs and reviews. **Programs** involve responses made about the wearer by the wearer. They represent the intended meaning about the self or the relevant identity that the wearer is trying to convey. **Reviews,** on the other hand, are the responses or interpretations made about the wearer by *others*.

Imagine the program of a customer who is entering a store, and assume that she is attempting to convey a casual shopping image. She does not want to buy the most formal and expensive clothes in the store, but she needs to acquire an outfit that she can wear to a campus interview with a career counselor, to discuss her potential future in an advertising firm. Therefore, she needs something that is moderately conservative and/or career-oriented, but informal enough to be suitable for other contexts as well. She would like some help in selecting an appropriate outfit.

The sales associate engages in a review of the customer's appearance, as is common when trying to assess style preferences and economic abilities of customers. Let us assume that she acknowledges the casual shopper look and takes into account that she needs to talk with the customer to assess her apparel needs, before assuming the customers' present clothes are similar to those she wishes to buy. At the same time, she does not necessarily expect the customer to go straight to the most formal or expensive clothes in the store and is sensitive to the customer's needs and preferences. The stage is set for meaningful communication.

When programs and reviews coincide, that appearance may be described as meaningful, according to Stone (1965).

> In appearances, then, selves are established and mobilized. As the self is dressed, it is simultaneously addressed, for, whenever we clothe ourselves, we dress "toward" or address some audience whose validating responses are essential to the establishment of our self. Such responses may, of course, also be challenges, in which case a new program is aroused (p. 230).

Through the course of social interactions, then, individuals may reevaluate their own appearances and retain that information for future appearance management, that is, for the development of new programs. If the customer in our example had received poor treatment from a snobbish sales associate, she might have reconsidered how she should dress for shopping in the future. Since that was not the case, the program, at least for this store and this sales associate, has been evaluated as appropriate.

As individuals interact with one another, they define to themselves the identities of themselves as well as the others with whom they are interacting. Thus, appearances of individuals cannot be separated from social contexts, and even with fashion change and changes in personal situations, the programs people initiate are likely to take into account past reviews of their own and others' clothes.

sense of direction to the I and tends to make human behavior less random or more predictable. Both entities interact within the self through a kind of internal discussion. A storehouse of past experiences and interpretations are embodied in the me, which comprises what is known about the self. It contains the consciousness and past experiences of the acting self (I), as well as observations of others' experiences. In this way, the I and the me jointly provide the self with the ability to appear or act a certain way and to interpret the appropriateness of this action or appearance for a given context. The I discovers, feels, and interprets experience as it occurs, subjectively, while this experience is evaluated and judged in relation to the self by the me, which is capable of taking satisfaction (or identifying concerns) in what is observed or experienced.

It is almost as though there are multiple me's in addition to a more global one, because individuals have a sense of appropriate behaviors and appearances for a variety of others and contexts. This sense allows individuals to adapt their appearances and behaviors so they can identify with others as appropriate to given situations. The I may (but not necessarily) be impulsive, creative, and spontaneous; it contains the potential for action, whereas the me restrains the self and reminds it of the social consequences of appearance and/or behavior. The me provides a form of self-control and retains information about others' responses to one's appearance for future reference.

Therefore, the I and the me jointly have the potential to provide a sense of balance between creativity and social constraint. This balance is critical to the self when interacting with others, because responses and appearances almost always need to bear some relation to a given social context (Aboulafia, 1986).

A dialogue between the I and the me is likely to take place each time we shop for clothes. When a style is first observed, it is the I that initiates a response toward it ("That's me," or "That's intriguing."). The style may be further contemplated or even tried on, and the me is likely to begin to evaluate the implications for the self ("Where will I wear this?" or "What will people think?" or "Is this what people have come to expect of me, and if not, how will others respond to a new image?").

Pines and Kuczkowski (1987) found that it takes longer for female college students to think of places where a clothing item may be worn if it is for the self, as opposed to the "average" woman. This additional time in generating social contexts could possibly be explained by the inner dialogue between the I and the me, which is applied to the self, but not necessarily to the "average" woman. If the style is for the self, there is more at stake than when it is for someone else. There is also likely to be a more elaborate and complex storehouse of knowledge upon which the me can draw.

How does a person come to develop a knowledge base about the self and how it fits into social life? In the following sections, we will consider how a person is located within a society, and then examine how the values of that society, as well as socially desirable appearances, become incorporated into the self.

Part of growing up is learning what society expects in terms of actions and appearances. Humans are born into a social configuration of beliefs and values, at a certain time in history, in a specific geographic area. In addition to cultural and historical context, an individual has little control over attributes *ascribed* or assigned at birth: sex, age (as initiated in a historical context), family structure and socioeconomic class, and ethnicity. These attributes have predetermined social meanings. One's location on a hypothetical social map may be pinpointed at the intersection of all of these attributes, within a cultural and historical context. This abstract point of intersection may be referred to as **social location** (see Figure 5-3).

**FIGURE 5-3**
*Social location is illustrated in this young Chinese boy's Mao suit and hat. This concept incorporates where and when a person is born, as well as the specific social-political ideologies that are prominent in one's culture and family. Just as sex, ethnicity, and age are predetermined for an individual, one is likely to have little control over the historic, cultural, and family context into which he or she is born. All of these factors place an individual socially, and appearance affords a means for displaying this placement. Photo by Stephen Cunha.*

Sociologist Peter Berger (1963) described social location as follows:

> We are located in society not only in space but in time. Our society is a historical entity that extends temporally beyond any individual biography. Society antedates us and it will survive us. It was there before we were born and it will be there after we are dead. Our lives are but episodes in its majestic march through time (p. 92).

Some of the meanings associated with what males and females can wear and when, or what people of different ages, social classes, and ethnic groups wear, then, are not only defined by our contemporaries through social interaction but also predefined by predecessors. There are areas where society allows individuals free choice, but some ideas—even about clothes, which are influenced by fashion change—last beyond our lifetimes. So, certain dimensions of a person's perception of self are culturally supplied, based on social location. The self stands "at the center (that is, at the point of maximum pressure) of a set of concentric circles, each representing a system of social control" (Berger, 1963, p. 73). The me within the self is likely to integrate what it means to be a black female in an upper-middle-class family in the United States in the 1990s, for example. By changing any one of six factors—sex, age, family background, ethnicity, and cultural and historical context—the picture of self is likely to change.

The concept of social location does not necessarily imply that people are mere pawns in a chess game, moved and constrained against their will. The way people dress and act can never be totally predicted, partly because of the impulsiveness and responsiveness of which the I component of the self is capable. Depending on the nature of one's social location and social experiences, creativity and ingenuity may be displayed through appearance. Another factor suggesting that people are not necessarily moved and constrained against their will is the orientation of the person. Most of the time, people *want* to obey the rules or to "dress the part." It is the preference to play by the rules on the part of most persons that makes society possible (Berger, 1963, p. 94). Socialization of the self contributes greatly to a person's preference to "dress the part."

## Socialization and Appearance

Socialization is the process through which individuals become socially adjusted to the standards and values of the community and society. Two kinds of socialization may be identified: primary and secondary. **Primary socialization** involves those processes through which we initially form our conceptions of self, for example, during childhood and adolescence. Through primary socialization, we come to know ourselves as objects or entities distinct from the environment. Mead (1934) believed that one has a self when he or she (*a*) is aware of the self as the object of others' evaluations and as an acting entity and (*b*) is able to empathize with the viewpoints or perspectives of other persons— to mentally place one's self in another person's place.

**Secondary internalizations,** on the other hand, involve the socialization processes that allow us to maintain and/or refine our self-concepts (Berger and Luckmann, 1966). The socialization process, then, is not finite; instead, the self is emergent, or is continually in the process of becoming. Clothing and appearance changes symbolize this fluidity in self-concept. They allow us to experiment with new identities [or in Stone's (1965) words, to develop new appearance "programs"] and to adapt to social changes. (See Figure 5-4.)

A person's developing conception of who he or she is cannot be separated from social interactions. Just as identities are formulated in contexts, more global perceptions of self are intricately linked to social life. Mead (1934) indicated that one has a self when he or she can interact in a meaningful way with others. Symbolic interaction requires that the individual shares the meanings that other persons associate with social and physical objects. These meanings are learned

*FIGURE 5-4*

*The socialization process continues into young adulthood, when a person refines, revises, and/or maintains a sense of self-concept through continuing internalizations of self in relation to social expectations. This student enjoys integrating cues such as multiple earrings into an overall, collegiate appearance. Mixing and combining appearance elements in a variety of ways allows an individual to juxtapose different aspects of the self, and to create and mediate a unique, general perception of self. Photo by Carla M. Freeman.*

as the individual develops a self-concept through a *play* and a *game* stage (Mead, 1934). During the play stage, the child acts out roles through the manipulation of objects and assesses the responses of others. In the game stage, a child's sphere of influence expands to include the collective attitudes of many individuals. Gregory Stone (1965) elaborated on Mead's conceptions and related them to appearance socialization; he also added another stage that precedes the play and game stages: the pre-play stage. As we consider these stages, it is important to keep in mind that the self-concept is not fixed or constant, even when the final stage is reached. Even as we complete these stages, we may repeat some of them throughout the various phases of our lives, particularly as we face new contexts requiring new forms of appearance management and identities. Initially, however, the primary socialization process linked to appearance begins with the pre-play stage.

## Pre-Play Stage

The **pre-play** stage is initially associated with infancy and early childhood, and is characterized by **investiture**—meaning that one does not select his or her own clothing. At this stage, an individual does not yet know how society expects him or her to dress. The most obvious identity at this stage is gender. Adults (parents or guardians) are likely to have control over an infant's appearance and are likely to develop gender "programs" that may or may not be traditional. Yet in a larger sense, it should be remembered that forces pinpointing social location are also at play, including the cultural and historical context into which an infant is born, as well as his or her sex, ethnicity, and family background (see Figure 5-5). Moreover, the social location of the parents or guardians is an important factor in investiture, as are available clothes in the marketplace and the general expectations of society. Social Focus 5-2 deals with the role of the mother in the pre-play stage.

Although an infant has little say as to appearance, he or she is still likely to be influenced by others' responses or "reviews." From the moment of birth, adults respond differently toward boys versus girls and have differential expectations. When parents were asked within 24 hours after delivery to evaluate their first-born infants in relation to a range of characteristics, daughters were described as soft, beautiful, cute, pretty, delicate, and little. Sons, on the other hand, were viewed as firm, strong, large-featured, well-coordinated, and hardy. The infants in question had been carefully matched so that they were equivalent in length, weight, and level of responsiveness. Nevertheless, their parents viewed them differently on the basis of gender labels ("boy" versus "girl") (Rubin, Provenzano, and Luria, 1974). As little boys and girls are dressed and groomed differently to communicate gender to the outside world, perceivers identify sex on the basis of appearance symbols and respond accordingly.

Given that the most vivid example of investiture is gender symbolism, it is not surprising that adult observers are accurately able to discern an infant's sex on the basis of clothing cues (Shakin, Shakin, and Sternglanz, 1985), and children themselves are able as early as 2 to 3 years of age to classify clothes and hairstyles in this way (Thompson, 1975; Weinraub et al., 1984).

**FIGURE 5-5**
*Through investiture, parents can communicate how an infant is located socially in terms of gender and status. Appearance "programs" are used to convey messages to perceivers in the pre-play stage of socialization. How might this appearance be interpreted or "reviewed" by perceivers? They are likely to try to interpret sex on the basis of hair and color of the sleeper (it is blue). Status may be inferred from a designer label. In reality, this is a girl with only a little bit of hair, and the sleeper was inexpensive, having been purchased at a fashion discount store that stocked the style in large quantities. Photo by Susan B. Kaiser.*

When can children's clothes be attributed to their choices rather than to investiture? This question is difficult to answer; some selections are exclusively adults, whereas some represent compromises between child and adult purchaser. By the preschool years, children themselves are likely to experiment with appearance management.

The second stage of the primary socialization of the self is the **play** stage. During this phase, the individual experiments with various identities and takes note of the reactions of others. Children discover who they are while learning what society is; in the process, a variety of appearances and manners may be assumed and the significance assigned to them by others is assessed. Stone (1965) indicated that clothing helps us in testing definitions of self and rendering credibility to them. Certain individuals' opinions and attitudes are likely to be especially

*Play Stage*

# Investiture and the Ubiquitous Mother

During infancy, or Stone's (1965) pre-play stage, the appearance of the infant is imposed. Dressing the child in blue invests that child with masculinity, whereas dressing the child in pink invests femininity. Costume historians Jo Paoletti and Carol Kregloh (1989) note that this "color coding" is the reverse of the gender symbolism in the beginning of the century in the United States. Then, pink was for boys and blue was for girls. Between 1900 and 1940 the colors were used interchangeably; it took about 40 or 50 years for the present system to evolve.

In the 1960s, Stone noted that the process of investiture is primarily accomplished by the mother. In the 1980s, evidence still suggested that mothers assume primary responsibility for selecting young children's clothes, although fathers may make some special occasion or gift purchases (Rucker, Boynton, and Park, 1986).

Stone described the mother as "ubiquitous" (everywhere at the same time or "doing it all" with respect to investiture). He indicated that some of the male adults of the 1950s, who had been children in the 1930s or earlier, reported in interviews that their mothers had dressed them in "fussy" clothing or knee pants which resulted in the label *sissy* by their peers. Stone (1965) noted the relative disadvantage of investiture for young males (as compared with young females).

> Dressed as someone he is not, by a ubiquitous mother, in clothing that is employed arbitrarily by his peers (and himself) to establish who he is, the American male may, indeed, have been disadvantaged very early with respect to the formulation of a sense of sexual identity. Advantages, rather, accrued to the female, who from the earliest age was dressed as she was by a mother from whose perspective she was provided with an adequate conception of herself in sexual terms (p. 236).

Scholarly attention to issues of gendered appearances have been influenced in the intervening years by the women's movement and feminist concerns about "blaming" mothers for all problems associated with childhood socialization. With increasing attention to overcoming gender stereotypes, rather than reinforcing existing ideas about gender identity (as noted in Stone's preceding comment), the role of mothers (and fathers) in the pre-play stage of childhood socialization is becoming increasingly complex.

Should the mother be identified as ubiquitous, as Stone suggested? The picture that is emerging from ongoing research on mother–daughter relations suggests that a variety of factors impinge on the clothes young girls wear, and the processes leading to these selections should be placed in their social, cultural, and historical context (Kaiser, 1990). In other words, it seems that even in addition to mothers' preferences, their daughters' wardrobes are influenced by other factors such as gifts (especially from grandparents), hand-me-downs from friends and relatives, the apparel marketplace, the media, and last but certainly not least—the preferences of young girls themselves and their peers, who by 2 to 3 years of age are aware of gender differences and generally prefer very feminine styles until they approach middle childhood (beginning around 7 or 8 years) (Kaiser, 1989).

In a study involving in-depth interviews with 60 mothers of preschool daughters (Kaiser, 1990), the mothers were asked how they had expected to dress their daughters versus what had actually occurred. A common theme was a tendency for them to have underestimated how feminine they would want or allow their daughters to dress. These mothers had been influenced by the women's movement and in some cases had strong feelings about gender equality. Accordingly, they frequently displayed feelings of ambivalence about their daughters' clothes and issues of gender:

> I told myself before she was born that it wouldn't matter, and I'd probably dress her in greens and yellows. She was born bald; she stayed bald for two years, and yes, she wore lots of pinks and purples and scotch-taped bows on her head so that we knew she was a girl. It hurt my feelings when they said, "Oh, what a nice son you have."

> I thought I would never sex differentiate or sex discriminate—let them mold themselves. Yet after having five boys, I was so delighted that I had a girl that I really wanted her to look very feminine, but she's not turning out that way, and it's okay.

> When I was pregnant and before I had my daughters I was very convinced that my kids would go around in jeans and tennis shoes and shirts, whether they were boys or girls. I was very committed to the idea that children develop their sense of identity and their sense of . . . their place in the world, not

## Social Focus 5-2 (continued)

*by what they are wearing, but by how you treat them. . . . But I've found myself succumbing to—whatever it is—the marketing, I don't know what—my past, when I was a little girl. I don't know what it is, but yes, I do find myself dressing her much more femininely than I would have thought (Kaiser, 1990).*

Another theme in the mothers' responses pertained to the difference between the enjoyment of selecting clothes and dressing a "doll" versus the recognition that a daughter is a young person with an individual personality and specific appearance preferences. These preferences are clearly indicated by the preschool years and can and should be developed as a means of self-exploration. This distinction between "investing" the child's appearance in conjunction with a mental picture a mother has in her head versus allowing a child to experiment becomes evident in the following mothers' comments:

*I . . . wanted a girl so I could pick the little clothes and stuff.*

*When she was an infant I did get into the frills and dressed her like a little doll, but now that she's her own*

*person, she doesn't allow that type of thing. We did get her ears pierced at a young age because she was mistaken for a boy. Not solely because of that, but that's just one feminine thing.*

*I'd rather have her experience more than I have. I want her to go out and buy some of these wild clothes and wear them and enjoy them because I think it's really an expression of how they feel.*

*I guess I want her to be her own person, so whatever she wants to dress . . . I mean if she wants to dress like a punk, what can I do? . . . . It's more important to me for her to feel good about herself, than for me to feel good about what she's wearing (Kaiser, 1990).*

As research continues on family relations and gender socialization through appearance, with males as well as females, the issue of the ubiquitous mother will most likely be a recurring theme. Yet it is important to qualify our understanding of the mother's role in gender socialization by considering the social and cultural context, including the complex dynamics in family life, peer influences, and gender imagery in the media.

---

important at this stage in gauging the suitability or desirability of appearances. These individuals are referred to as **significant others.** During primary socialization, children's significant others may include parents, teachers, siblings, and playmates. Gradually, children acquire the ability to differentiate and integrate their opinions and attitudes (Denzin, 1977). There are two types of appearance experimentation that reflects two forms of socialization: anticipatory and fantastic (Stone, 1965).

As children engage in play that involves assuming an identity that they could realistically assume in later life, this play may be characterized as anticipatory socialization. Gender as well as more specific, often gender-related occupational or parental roles are common ground for experimentation (see Figure 5-6). Preschool girls tend to prefer feminine styles of clothing over more androgynous styles as they experiment with cultural meanings of being female (Kaiser, 1989). They also tend to recognize that dress and personal appearance wield some degree of interpersonal power. In an observational study of young girls in a preschool setting, Joffe (1971) noted that young girls were more likely to receive compliments on personal appearance on the days they wore dresses, as opposed to pants. Receiving this type of feedback from significant others most likely contributes to an emphasis on appearance by young females.

*Anticipatory Socialization*

**FIGURE 5-6**
*Tangible symbols of the objective self allow this young boy to interpret how he and others evaluate the self and/or the more specific role he is assuming. These symbols concretely identify the role he is playing and represent his possessions. Photo by Mark Kaiser.*

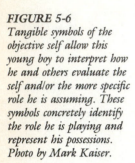

By approximately 5 years of age, children develop a sense of **objective self,** with an emphasis on tangible and physical qualities linked to the self, including the body, clothes, and objects such as toys. (See Figure 5-6.) This objective self is presented and evaluated by intimate circles of people. By approximately 10 years of age, the **subjective self** has developed, emphasizing internal, more abstract attributes and abilities, and acknowledging the difference between self and others (Leahy and Shirk, 1985). (See Figure 5-7.)

Stone's (1965) research indicated that girls more frequently engage in play that involves dressing up in parental-role costumes than do boys. However, boys are also likely to learn what it means to be male by observing and selecting clothes accordingly. For example, a little boy may refuse to wear pull-on elasticized pants or lightweight socks because these are perceived as feminine. Children tend to become aware of even subtle cues of gender identity by the preschool years.

Anticipatory socialization is achieved in part through play that provides children with social contexts for developing joint actions with others. Play is closely associated with the construction of social order, which aids children in becoming prepared to interact with more than one person at a time and to take on the collective attitudes of the community (Denzin, 1977). Are appearance symbols of gender linked to gender-typed play? Although children are attentive to gender symbols at an early age and use them in the development of stereotypes about play behavior, they do not necessarily apply the same gender stereotypes to themselves (in their own behaviors) that they apply to others (Kaiser and Phinney, 1983; Kaiser, Rudy and Byfield, 1985). Still, we would expect children's *conceptions* of clothes to be more lasting in importance than their *overt behaviors,* because overt behavior (especially play) is more spontaneous than developing perceptions of gender identity.

**FIGURE 5-7**
*By middle childhood or preteen years, a sense of subjective self has emerged. The subjective self, as compared with the objective self, emphasizes more abstract attributes and abilities, as shown in the case of this boy who excels at gymnastics and displays his interest in the sport through his T-shirt. Photo by Susan B. Kaiser.*

After primary socialization, it is still likely that we encounter situations in life that require experimentation through appearance. Take for example a male law student who begins to dress in a three-piece suit in anticipation of job interviews and a subsequent career. The situation would be similar to anticipatory socialization experienced by young children. Significant others in this case, however, might include law professors, peers, and professional attorneys.

*Fantastic Socialization*

Clothing and appearance can also provide opportunities for engaging in fantasy behavior—by appearing in an identity that does not mesh with probable present or future reality. Fantastic socialization allows a child to engage in creative appearance management and to assume an identity that is conducive to imaginative play. For example, children might dress and assume the roles of cowboys and Indians, or even elephants and cats, while engaging in fantastic socialization. Costumes that are fantastic in nature might include the clothes worn by superheroes or superheroines, princesses, witches, Dracula, or other characters depicted in cultural fantasies. As in anticipatory socialization, there is a tendency for young children to dichotomize fantasy appearances with respect to gender. For example, a young boy is more likely to pretend to be Superman than is a young girl (she might be Wonder Woman). (See Figure 5-8.)

The tendency to fantasize may facilitate the normal evolution of self-concept, which is just beginning to develop prior to adolescence. By trying out new identities, it is possible to expand the range of possible extensions of self (Elliott, 1986).

Fantasizing through appearance management may be seen after primary socialization, usually in specific contexts that afford adults with the opportunity to dress up (for example, Halloween, Mardi Gras, and costume balls). (See Figure 5-9.) Are such opportunities healthy, in terms of providing some means for "escaping" from mundane daily routines, as well as for expression of creativity? Unfortunately, little is known about fantasy dressing; this is an area with a great

**FIGURE 5-8**
*The distinction between anticipatory and fantastic socialization is illustrated in these four-year-old girls' Halloween costumes. The girl on the right dresses as a cheerleader—a role that she could realistically assume later in life and evaluate in terms of others' responses to her costume. The girl on the left is dressed as a fairy princess—a fantasy role that she is not actually likely to pursue in the future. Nevertheless, she still evaluates feedback others provide based on her appearance, and her internalization of this feedback is likely to influence her socialization to more general interpretations of gender. Photo by Susan B. Kaiser.*

**FIGURE 5-9**
*Adults have opportunities in specific social contexts to experience fantastic socialization, as is the case when they dress up and act differently than they do in their ordinary, day-to-day routines. Here, adults dress in a manner that would be expected at a Renaissance fair, which may constitute a form of escapism from the routine aspects of everyday life. Photos by Mark Kaiser.*

deal of potential for contributing to an understanding of creativity and self-expression. Some contend that fashion per se acts as a vehicle for fantasy and, that through fantasy, the "unconscious unfulfillable" is expressed (Wilson, 1985, p. 246).

Significant others continue to be important throughout life, and individuals are likely to continue to experience forms of anticipatory and fantastic socialization. Significant others may be context-dependent; for example, we may value some people's opinions about our appearances more than others, whereas other significant others' perspectives may be more valuable with respect to other areas of life (for example, parenting and career paths).

*Game Stage*

The third stage in the socialization of the self is the **game stage.** Certain abstract self-thought processes are developed by means of this stage. Individuals eventually learn that they can take on the attitudes of the community as a whole, or generally understand collective norms and values. Whereas during the play stage children evaluate the "reviews" of their appearance by significant others in sequence, higher levels of abstraction are required to coordinate and integrate the perspectives of diverse others into a collective sense of what is socially acceptable. This understanding is reflected in the me side of the self; those others in one's social world whose norms and values are internalized compose the **generalized other.** During primary socialization, the game stage may be associated with late childhood or preadolescence, when conformity with one's peers as a whole assumes great importance. Clothing becomes a very important symbol of belonging to certain peer groups. Gradually, adolescents become more abstract, flexible, and general in their self-assessments.

Although clothes are more often a source of positive feelings toward the self than negative feelings for most adolescents, for some they may be a source of embarrassment and social discomfort. It seems that those adolescents who dress for themselves tend to be more self-accepting, whereas those who dress to please others are less self-accepting. Less self-accepting adolescents are also more likely to feel their clothing is inadequate. Involvement in organized activities seems to be associated with reduced feelings of clothing deprivation (Drake and Ford, 1979). Such involvement is likely to require the ability to generate a sense of generalized other, by taking the attitudes and perspectives of a variety of individuals into account. Thus there may be a distinction between dressing for others because of a lack of self-assurance and dressing with a more abstract sense of "generalized other" in mind.

Both males and females are likely to learn that there are multiple means of assessing the self through others and, perhaps, multiple me's. Correspondingly, there are a variety of clothing and appearance styles from which to pick and choose. The potential for compromising between extreme conformity and extreme individuality is realized as relevant identities (of self and others) and contexts are taken into account.

By middle to late adolescence, a person has developed a **subjective-process level** sense of self (see Figure 5-10). Such a self-concept allows one to integrate personal traits and appearances that seemingly conflict with one another—in line with *contextual* considerations (Leahy and Shirk, 1985). By young adulthood, then, values appear to be determined more by self-chosen principles, although sets of generalized others still remain important, especially in certain contexts (Leahy and Shirk, 1985). Once the self is set in motion, a person is increasingly capable of self-determination and is prepared to exert a *mediating* influence in social relations (Aboulafia, 1986, p. 101). In other words, the self influences social arrangements just as these arrangements influence the self. Yet there is a continuing tendency to assess the self, drawing on diverse types of information.

## Assessing Appearance and Self

The socialization process is never totally complete; self and culture reciprocate in their influence on one another. Once a self-concept is acquired, we continue to assess it for accuracy and relevance in light of culture change and social context. This reasoning follows the symbolic-interactionist conception of self as process rather than thing. As individuals acquire new information about themselves and as fashion and cultural changes provide impetus to self-discovery, perceived self-image is also likely to change. Where do we acquire information about ourselves to enable self-assessment? Let's consider three sources: feedback from others, personal comparison with others, and self-perception.

*Social Feedback*    "Evidence suggests that we first acquire a self—and then lose it—in a mirror" (Brandt, 1980). How we see our appearances as part of our selves is more

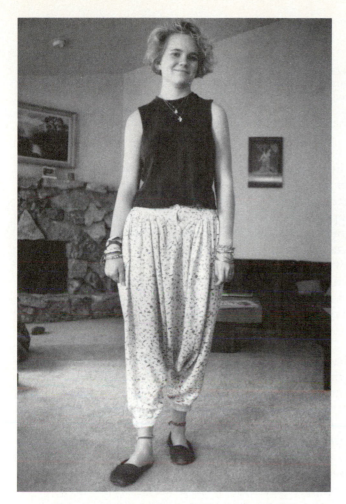

**FIGURE 5-10**
*During the adolescent years, the subjective-process level view of self is likely to develop. Diverse personal traits and appearances are internalized and integrated. The importance of the generalized other is interpreted in light of social context, as one moves toward the ability to evaluate the self in terms of self-chosen principles. This young woman is able to explore feelings about the self by expressing her creativity through appearance management and developing an individual sense of style. Photo by Susan B. Kaiser.*

complex than a mirror image. Although a fair amount of information about appearance can be obtained from a mirror, we never see our own appearances exactly as others do. In fact, we are likely to be surprised about our appearance when we hurriedly catch a glimpse in a mirror. Similarly, photographs are often startling. ("No, that doesn't *really* look like me, does it?") Therefore, we rely on others to supply us with feedback about what we look like, as well as how attractive and appropriate our clothes are perceived to be.

Social worlds often revolve around the kinds of feedback we receive from others. We tend to be concerned with how we appear to others, at least implicitly. In the process of constructing images of self, we may ask ourselves questions such as "Who am I?" and "How do I appear before others?"

Charles Cooley (1902) termed this process of perceiving ourselves through our imaginations of others' impressions as the **looking-glass self.** A looking glass, or a mirror, then, becomes a metaphor for social feedback as interpreted by the self:

> As we see our face, figure, and dress in the glass, and are interested in them because they are ours, and pleased or otherwise with them accordingly as they do or do not answer to what we should like them to be; so in imagination we perceive in another's mind some thought of our appearance, manners, aims, deeds, character, friends, and so on, and are variously affected by it (Cooley, 1902, p. 152).

In other words, our impressions of our own appearances are largely based on **reflected appraisals,** or we see ourselves, in part, through the eyes and impressions of others. Three stages are involved in the process of social feedback: (1) our imagination of our appearances (and other behaviors) to others; (2) our imagination of others' judgments or appraisals of that appearance; and (3) the emergence of self-feeling (for example, pride versus humiliation).

How do we know what others think about how we look? Also, when do we think about it? Self-attention is not a constant phenomenon. Awareness of one's own appearance is likely to be induced when our attention is focused on it because of personal or social factors (for example, new clothes, a photograph, or a mirror image, as well as social feedback).

*Verbal Feedback*    At times, social feedback comes in the form of direct comments. As perceivers become socialized with regard to standards of tact, they are not as likely to be blunt or frank with comments about appearance, so verbal feedback on appearance is seldom blatantly negative. Therefore, we are likely to "read between the lines" to make sense of social feedback in relation to appearance management. The following comments from interviews with college students reveal this tendency.

> *I've had people come up and go, "Do you do modeling?" . . . A lot of stuff I wear is more dressed up or whatever than people mostly around. . . . I feel more comfortable in jeans and a sweatshirt walking around on campus than I do in most of the things I wear. . . . It just makes me feel weird (dressing up here) because . . . I don't know, I just feel out of place sometimes. (Female)*

> *Sometimes I just dress because I feel like I just want to be loud and obnoxious. . . . Once I wore this shiny green shirt to work and I walked through Ghirardelli Square where I work and a street performer had a microphone and speakers, and he made a comment about my shirt . . . "Oh, that green!". . . I was kind of embarrassed that he would draw attention to my shirt. I knew it was pretty loud, and I've never really worn it again, but this was a one-time thing and I knew what I was doing. (Male)*

*Nonverbal Feedback*    Often, we are likely to rely on nonverbal feedback, including raised eyebrows, stares, whistles, wistful looks, smiles, or even spatial distance. We become attuned to many sources of information or cues, particularly from significant others and from individuals who we do not know very well and whose impressions matter (for example, a campus recruiter or a first date). The following remarks are from students indicating how they respond to nonverbal feedback from others. Their imaginations of what others are thinking about them and their attempts to understand attention from others are apparent.

> *If people look at me I tend to think that there's something wrong or something like that. (Female)*

> *Sometimes when I walk the street a lot of people turn their heads and different things like that. . . . I know they're doing it just because it's different or something (wearing suspenders). . . . I know it's not because I'm so outstanding and so it doesn't do that to me. . . . I do like to be noticed and to be different. And from that sense it makes me feel good. (Male)*

At times, it may be a relief to have people comment verbally, especially after they have been staring. Verbal comments can clarify what others are thinking, as the following comment suggests:

> *I was wearing a shirt that had a woven outside and printed inside—so when you rolled up the sleeves, it had two different prints and the collar had a different print. And, someone came up to me and said "I like your shirt.". . . I had noticed that the person had been watching me for quite a while and I was kind of uncomfortable because I didn't know why they were watching me and so I was relieved when they came up and just were watching me because of my shirt, and I didn't have something on my back or something like that. (Male)*

Social feedback tends to be evaluated in relation to the particular others supplying it. We are likely to factor in others' tastes (as we perceive them), how generous they tend to be with compliments, how attentive they are to detail, and other qualities. We may also be especially attentive to feedback from others whom we are trying to impress or whom we know will notice some effort in appearance management.

*Considering the Source (Audience)*

> *I'll wear something . . . depending on like how many . . . or what kind of guys are going to be there. . . . Like if there's a lot of good looking guys that are real fashionable. . . . I'll wear something real nice or something expensive because I'll know that they can notice the difference between like Ralph Lauren sweaters and just a regular sweater. . . . Or if I'm going to go somewhere where everybody is just kind of like the football guys that don't know what they're wearing . . . their mom bought their clothes for them and stuff, I'll wear something a little more just casual. (Female)*

*I would never dress to stand out like a sore thumb. I would dress so that if there were any differences at all, they'd be very subtle and only someone that can maybe appreciate the things that I can get would notice those subtleties and so if I . . . was aware that somebody noticed the way I was dressing, I know it would . . . feel good. (Male)*

*Sometimes like if a girl turns her head . . . Someone's looking at you and you know they are and you kinda feel uncomfortable 'cause you do not know what to do. Especially, I don't know, if they are cute, then it feels good I guess. And if they are not cute, then you feel kinda weird 'cause you don't know how to react, and you don't know what to say. (Male)*

*Accuracy of Reflected Appraisals*

How accurate are reflected appraisals? An early study sought to test the basic hypothesis that self-evaluation is dependent on the opinions of others (Miyamoto and Dornbusch, 1956). College students were asked to rate themselves repeatedly on a set of four traits: intelligence; self-confidence; physical attractiveness; and likeableness. The first of the self-ratings was based on the subjects' actual self-perceptions. The second was that individual's perceptions of the ratings that each other member of the group would give him or her (reflected appraisals), and the third was the perception of the way "most persons" (the generalized other) would view him or her. Each subject rated all of the other members of the group as well. Three general findings emerged, which were in support of symbolic-interactionist thought. First, the self-rating was quite close to the actual rating of the individual by other members of the group. Second, the self-rating was close to the perceived rating by others. Third, the individuals' self-ratings were closely related to the perceived rating by the generalized other; this association was even closer than the association between self-rating and perceived rating by other members of the specific membership group.

Clothing researcher Ryan (1965) investigated individuals' concepts of their appearance versus the concepts of members of a group. In order to operationalize the looking-glass self-concept, college females rated themselves as well as the others of their group on five rating scales: extent of being well-dressed; physical appearance of face; appearance of figure; individuality in dress; and self-confidence. In order to incorporate the concept of the looking-glass self into the study, the females were also asked to estimate how they thought the group had rated them. The most common pattern that resulted was that the self-rating was equal to the estimate of the group-rating, rendering support to the looking-glass self-concept. The next two most common patterns were those where the self-rating was equal to the estimate of the group-rating, which was either higher or lower than the median group-rating.

One factor that Ryan (1965) found to be related to the ratings was the degree to which the group was acquainted with the individual. The more closely they were acquainted, the higher the ratings tended to be with respect to the degree of being well-dressed. Other related factors were the size of the town and the economic level. The larger the town and the higher the economic level, the higher the rating on being well-dressed. Furthermore, there was a highly significant relation, as one might expect, between an individual's interest in clothes and her self-ratings and those of the group.

Felson (1985) studied the effect of reflected appraisals on self-appraisals, noting that there may be a problem of accuracy when people project their own opinions onto others. He found that reflected appraisals are a factor in the development of self-appraisals of physical attractiveness. Appearance is likely to be defined through the responses of others; some other aspects of self-concept may not be as likely to be defined in such a way.

Overall attractiveness seems to be more important in predicting self-concepts in females than in males (Lerner and Karabenick, 1974). In general, however, physically attractive people tend to have more favorable self-concepts than unattractive people, and this advantage is likely to be based, at least in part, on social feedback (Adams, 1977b; Lerner and Karabenick, 1974; Lerner, Karabenick, and Stuart, 1973; Lerner, Orlos, and Knapp, 1976). Physically attractive people are also less anxious socially (Adams, 1977b) and are more individualistic (Krebs and Adinolfi, 1975).

How do perceptions of self in relation to physical attractiveness differ from those related to clothing worn? Physical attractiveness is more consistent across time or has greater longevity when compared to clothing, which is more likely to be linked to perceptions of self in particular contexts.

By late adolescence, people may be less dependent on how they believe others view the self. Also, there appear to be some gender differences in terms of self-appraisals. See Social Focus 5-3 for a discussion of gender differences with respect to clothing preferences and the self.

Adolescent females tend to have a higher orientation toward relationships with others, for example, than do males, so females might be expected to receive, and to be more attentive to, social feedback (Leahy and Shirk, 1985, pp. 131–132). There is evidence that physically attractive males tend to possess a higher sense of responsibility for their own behavior, such as effectiveness in social activities. In contrast, attractive females tend to emphasize self-confidence and positive self-evaluation—but more in terms of attraction than effectiveness (Adams, 1977b).

In addition to developmental and gender differences when interpreting and internalizing social feedback, another potential problem with reflected appraisals is that people may already have impressions about how attractive they appear. In other words, there may be a self-serving bias in perceptions of social feedback. If someone thinks he or she looks good and feels good about what he or she is wearing, then validation of that feeling may be sought, and other information may be ignored, as the following comments suggest.

> *I think if I dress nicely, I think I feel good about what I'm wearing. If I wear something I like, people tend to notice me more. (Female)*

# Gender Differences in Self-Concept: Framing Social Experiences through Clothes

> Men act and women appear. . . . Women
> watch themselves being looked at. . . .
> Thus she turns herself into an object—
> and most particularly an object of vision:
> a sight
>
> —JOHN BERGER, 1972

Is this the whole story on how women view themselves, as opposed to how men view themselves? As we have seen in our discussions of gender (Chapter Three) and the body (Chapter Four), males and females seem to evaluate themselves in terms of attractiveness and effectiveness, respectively. But do women view themselves primarily as "objects of vision," and do men necessarily see themselves in perpetual motion, without regard for appearance? Also, how does the concept of "looking-glass" self apply to both males and females? In short, how do they differ in the extent to which they rely on others for evaluation of personal appearance? There is some evidence that males are more autonomous than females with respect to such evaluations. Among adolescents, females appear to be influenced more by friends in terms of their clothing choices than are boys (May and Koester, 1985). In one study, 45 percent of the adolescent boys indicated that they trust their own opinions about what looks good on them (Warden and Colquett, 1982). Other males reported being influenced by their mothers (15 percent), friends (14 percent), girlfriends (12 percent), and sisters (5 percent). Drake and Ford (1979) reported that adolescent females were more likely than males to report dressing for others and feeling deprived about their clothes.

Clothes still appear to be important to males, but perhaps in different ways than they are to females. Adolescent boys may admit that they are interested in wearing clothes that show off their muscles (Warden and Colquett, 1982). Self-concept in males seems to be enhanced by an increase in muscular strength and girth, such as that achieved in regular weight training (Tucker, 1982).

Research by Leslie Davis (1985c) points to the complexity of understanding gender and self-concept in relation to clothing. She found that males and females do wear clothes appropriate to their own sex, but their clothes do not necessarily symbolize a tendency to internalize masculine and/or feminine personality traits into the self-concept. In other words, there does not seem to be a relation between actual clothes worn and internalization of personality traits traditionally associated with being female (for example, affectionate) or male (for example, assertive).

However, males and females may frame their social experiences differently in terms of clothing and self-evaluation. A qualitative study among 30 male and 30 female undergraduates was undertaken to look for differences in this regard (Kaiser and Freeman, 1989). The students were asked to bring a favorite article of clothing to the interview. They discussed what they liked about the clothing, what they felt it represented about them, what associations they made with the clothing, and what kind of feedback they had received. The major gender difference emerging from the study related to the manner in which clothing was viewed in connection with the self and others. Males were more likely than females to ground their associations with a favorite article of clothing to a particular context in the past. The males' discussions of their experiences emphasized the **mnemonic value** of favorite clothing. That is, the clothes reminded them of personal accomplishments (for example, athletics or becoming a fraternity member) or sentimental associations with special dates or parties.

Females were less likely than males to link their favorite articles of clothing to a tangible referent. Instead, females related accounts of personal feelings (for example, happy, cheery, or friendly) they experience when they wear these clothes. The concept of self as process, or "becoming" through a sense of connection with other people, was reflected in the females' discussions. A typical comment among females was, "When I feel more comfortable, I'm more relaxed, at ease with people" (Kaiser and Freeman, 1989).

Why would females emphasize feelings, self as process, and connectedness with other people, as compared to the more autonomous discussions about favorite clothing from males? One explanation may relate to the greater likelihood that females receive more social feedback on appearance than do males. Females also tend to frame their social experiences by empathizing with, and expressing sensitivity toward, particular others who are different from the self—on a case by case or context-dependent basis (Gilligan, 1982, p. 11). In other words, females are socialized to emphasize cooperation with others, as well as interpersonal

## *Social Focus 5-3 (continued)*

attraction (Gilligan, 1982, p. 11). Males, on the other hand, are likely to be left to their own devices to explain why their clothes are important to them, because they are less likely than females to receive social feedback. Also, males are socialized to focus on competition and independence while relating to others on a more abstract level. Thus they appear to interpret the importance of their own clothes in relation to personal considerations. They also are likely to wear their clothes longer than females, because male fashion changes less rapidly than does female fashion. Therefore, males have more time than females to develop sentimental (albeit autonomous) associations with their clothes, which they view as personal possessions signifying *what they have done or accomplished*. In contrast, females are more likely to emphasize *how they appear, how others respond, and how they feel* in favorite clothing (Kaiser and Freeman, 1989).

---

*I was wearing something that I thought was good. I thought I looked good . . . a few people smiled at me and talked to me or something. . . . That was cool. I could handle that. (Male)*

*Usually I have never gotten any negative comments. If I do, I try not to listen to them, so I don't really remember them. But I've had a lot of people just walk up to you and just say, "Oh, I really like that" . . . It makes me feel good. (Female)*

*I was wearing an outfit I just bought (suspender pants and a bright red shirt) . . . and all these people would look at me. . . . I liked the outfit so I was pretty sure it was positive stares. (Male)*

*Like if you're at a party or something and you're wearing 501s and a shirt or something, you figure, some girl is probably looking at you someplace. (Male)*

### Social Comparison

Selves exist not only in relation to other selves, but also in relation to an awareness that the self and other selves *differ* in some respects. Social psychologist Leon Festinger (1954) noted that humans have a basic need to compare themselves with others, for purposes of self-evaluation. Social comparison becomes a source of **comparative appraisals.** Appearance is so peripheral or so visible that it becomes an easy target for social comparison. Social comparison can be combined with perceptions of others' responses. Together, social feedback and comparison of self with others can become valuable in terms of assessing the self.

The following quotes by college students suggest a tendency to compare the self with others and to be aware that others do the same.

*You might think your friends are comparing with you, with how you dress. They might want to look better than you. (Female talking about clothes worn at dances.)*

*My senior ball in high school—everyone had these huge dresses and really alive pastels, and that was just the thing to buy and that's what all the magazines and advertisements were promoting that year, and instead I bought this like gold lamé dress, and it was really tight-fitting. And, it was really different and it just really stood out. . . . It made me feel really good, just that I, you know, took a little more effort because I really had to go and look for something different. (Female)*

One study revealed that comparison processes are used in making comprehensive self-evaluations ("I'm a good person" versus "I'm a bad person") (Morse and Gergen, 1970). In this study, male undergraduates were asked to fill out a questionnaire measuring general self-evaluation. They were divided into two groups. While they were filling out the forms, an experimenter entered each of the two rooms and also began to fill out some of the questionnaires. One of the experimenters was nicknamed "Mr. Clean," because he was attractive, well-dressed, and appeared highly competent. In the other room, the experimenter was "Mr. Dirty," a poorly groomed student who wore ragged clothing. He carried a tattered copy of a paperback of questionable taste. The results of the study supported the social comparison theory: (1) The students exposed to Mr. Clean showed a decrease in self-evaluation from the first portion of the test to the second portion of the test, and (2) the students exposed to Mr. Dirty showed an increase in self-evaluation from the first part to the second part of the test. Thus, the clothing and general appearance of the experimenter provided a source of information that was apparently used by the subjects in evaluating themselves.

Musa and Roach (1973) compared high school juniors' self-evaluations of appearance with their evaluations of their peers' appearances. Most commonly, the adolescents' self-ratings of their own appearances equalled those they assigned to their peers. However, an important gender difference emerged in the data. Boys were more likely than girls to rate their own appearances as more desirable than that of their peers', and a larger proportion of girls rated their own appearances lower than they rated their peers' appearances. In other words, boys tended to be more self-confident than girls about their own appearances when using social comparison as a means for assessing the self. The girls whose own appearance ratings were equal to those they assigned to their peers were also personally adjusted in terms of self-concept, whereas the girls whose appearance ratings were lower than those they assigned to their peers were low in terms of personal adjustment. No relation existed for males in terms of self-evaluation of appearance and personal adjustment. These findings reinforce the assertion, presented in Chapters Three and Four, that females define themselves in terms of appearance more than do males (who use criteria of effectiveness).

A later study indicated that most adolescent boys compare their own wardrobes as typical or average in relation to those of their peers (Warden and Colquett, 1982). In contrast, female adolescents are more likely than males to feel deprived in relation to clothes (Drake and Ford, 1979).

In general, then, we rely on feedback from others to aid us in formulating a self-image and in determining how we want to appear to others. This self-image helps us in deciding what kinds of clothes and accessories are consistent with our images of who we are. Of course, we vary our modes of dress depending on the persons with whom we are interacting and on the roles that we are playing.

We have special relationships with ourselves, and just as we engage in appearance perception (of others) we also engage in self-perception. However, because we realize that our feelings and attitudes are complex, we are more careful in making assumptions or categorical statements about ourselves than we are about doing the same for others. However, Wegner and Vallacher (1977) contend that we select, generate, and organize information in order to develop perceptions about ourselves, just as we do to form impressions about others.

Psychologist Daryl Bem (1967, 1972) indicated that self-attributions are a very special form of perception. Based on our observations of our own behaviors and our actions toward others, we make attributions regarding our motives and attitudes. Fortunately, we also have access to "inside" information. Clothes are likely to enhance this process, as we make self-attributions based on them, often in the form of questions we pose to ourselves ("Why did I buy this bizarre outfit?").

Bem (1967) contends that self-descriptive statements can provide a cue to self-perception processes. However, it is likely that one may not wish to express some perceptions of self verbally, but may instead prefer to express them non-verbally, such as through dress. An individual's attitudinal statements are viewed as inferences made by the individual about his or her behavior, using cues in the process: "I must like popsicles. I'm always eating them." It is also probable that one makes inferences from cues such as clothing: "I must like red. I'm always wearing it." Furthermore, Bem suggests that we use some of the same cues to perceive ourselves as others do to perceive us. Therefore, it is likely that common meanings may be established.

There appear to be both *internal* and *external* cues that may be used for self-perception. The internal cues would include those to which only we have access (for example, about our motives for wearing a certain garment). Information that is not readily available to others, or internal cues, often play a role in self-perceptions. However, if obvious and explicit patterns of dress (as well as patterns of behavior) are used to convey a message, others may make attributions similar to one's own self-perceptions. They may, therefore, be using cues similar to those that the wearer is using (the clothes themselves). In other words, clothes are generally external cues that are accessible to both ourselves and others for observation. One may tend to dress in a certain style of clothing in an almost automatic fashion, out of habit. Once in a while, it is common to step back and wonder: Why am I dressing this way? Am I trying to impress someone? Why do I prefer this style?

This inference process may sound a bit backward. However, at times we cannot explain our own behavior on the basis of social feedback or social com-

## Self-Perception

parison; in such cases, our "inside" information about ourselves comes in handy.

Individuals may use any combination of social feedback, social comparison, and self-perception, as appropriate, to derive self-concept and to guide appearance management and behavior.

## Self-Esteem

Once we have developed at least a semipermanent idea of who we are, we tend to formulate some opinions about how we feel about ourselves. **Self-esteem** involves individual feelings of self-worth. It is based on the part of the self (the me) that is capable of not only judging and responding to the self as object, but also taking satisfaction in what is observed and explained. A person with high self-esteem is self-accepting and self-tolerant, likes the self, and has proper respect for the self's worth. In contrast, low self-esteem is associated with depression, unhappiness, and anxiety (Rosenberg, 1985).

Some degree of self-esteem is needed for healthy psychological functioning. People need to feel that they are valuable within the context of everyday life and culture, that is, that they have some belief that (*a*) human life, within the larger drama of culture, is meaningful and (*b*) they as individuals play a significant part in that drama. Cultural symbols, including fashion, can enable individuals to maintain a certain degree of faith in the reality and significance of cultural drama and one's personal role within it (Greenberg, Pyszczynski, and Solomon, 1986). Appearance management is likely to serve a similar function. An important part of self-esteem is feeling that one matters. One way to matter is to be the object of other people's attention. Otherwise, one might feel invisible. Appearance management may be conducive to feeling that one matters and therefore to bolstering self-esteem. Anna Creekmore (1974) noted that clothing may serve an *adaptive function* when self-esteem is low, by helping to bolster assessments of self. In contrast, clothes may provide an *expressive function* when self-esteem is high. In other words, some individuals who feel positive about themselves may express those feelings visually.

Much of the research linking self-esteem to clothing and appearance is correlational. This means that a relation exists, but it may be difficult to assess if self-esteem is a cause or an effect of appearance or interest in appearance management. For example, research has indicated that self-esteem is related to satisfaction with the body (body cathexis), as discussed in Chapter Four. Yet we cannot easily determine whether high body cathexis is conducive to high self-esteem or vice versa, or if a causal relation exists.

Also, it is not clear whether lack of attractiveness is necessarily a problem, or whether unattractive people may be able to adapt and function adequately by emphasizing non-appearance-related assets (for example, intelligence or talent). Some research suggests that lack of attractiveness is not necessarily related to negative evaluation of self; rather, unattractive individuals tend to be less positive about themselves *as compared with attractive individuals*. So, there is a relative but not necessarily an absolute difference between attractive and unattractive people's assessments of self. For example, unattractive adolescent males indicate they "sometimes" to "often" view themselves positively and feel happy, whereas attractive adolescent males are more certain, in a positive direction, about self-feelings and happiness (Agnew, 1984).

In terms of the relation between clothing and self-esteem, the research does suggest support for Creekmore's (1974) concept of adaptive functioning. It seems that people who evaluate themselves less positively tend to use clothing for means of social approval. As the need for social approval by means of clothing increased in a study of adult women, the level of satisfaction with the self decreased (Tyrchniewicz and Gonzales, 1978). Or, as the level of self-satisfaction increased, the desire for social approval decreased.

Male and female college students who are more clothes-conscious appear to be more likely to be anxious and compliant to authority, while those lacking clothes consciousness are more independent and aggressive (Rosenfeld and Plax, 1977). Darlene Kness (1983) reported that adolescents who are more satisfied with clothing tend to feel more secure socially, whereas those who feel deprived in terms of their clothing are socially insecure. Self-esteem was positively related to satisfaction with clothing, as well. In a study of self-esteem among Japanese people, high conservativeness in clothing was found to be related to lower ego strength and greater sensitivity to the evaluations of others (Fujiwara, 1986).

Low self-esteem has been linked to depression and insecurity. Depression per se, however, may fluctuate with mood. What is the relation between depression and perceptions of personal appearance? Depressed persons tend to be less satisfied with their bodies and view themselves as less attractive than nondepressed persons, even when outside raters can see no appreciable differences between the individuals' appearances in the two groups. Depressed people seem to distort their self-image in a negative manner, while nondepressed people appear to distort self-image positively (Noles, Cash, and Winstead, 1985).

Dubler and Gurel (1984) conducted a study to assess daily fluctuations in mood and feelings about clothing and appearance. Twenty-five women completed daily questionnaires for four weeks. Of these, six were depressed to some degree. As level of depression rose, so did positive feelings about clothing and appearance. It seems that appearance management may take on greater importance for depressed people and may be used to boost morale.

Research findings on depression, together with those on self-esteem, suggest that appearance management is viewed differently by people with varying feelings about themselves at a given point in time. In general, it seems that for persons who are depressed or have low self-esteem, appearance management serves an adaptive function—to bolster oneself in social life. For persons who feel positively about themselves, clothes may be used as a form of self-expression, in the eyes of self more than others.

Self-esteem tends to have a motivational component. People with high self-esteem are likely to work to maintain it, whereas those with low self-esteem labor to improve it (Elliot, 1986). In addition to general, global feelings about the self, people have particular self-definitions or identities (for example, student, young upwardly mobile professional, and religious person) and may be motivated to "complete" these self-definitions as necessary to feel good about the self.

## Self-Symbolizing

Although self-esteem refers to a global evaluation of self, more specific evaluations are also possible. The self is comprised of numerous **self-definitions.** Self-definitions are particular statements of self that may vary greatly by the context and the person, for example, football player, intellectual, creative, and able to speak French. Self-definitions are also *goals* that humans pursue (Wicklund and Gollwitzer, 1982). These goals have implications for future behavioral and thinking patterns; they may be broad and general, or they may be very narrow. Self-definitions may involve occupational roles, but they are not merely social roles. Self-definitions may include human qualities as well, for example, creative or thrifty (Wicklund and Gollwitzer, 1982, p. 31).

The building blocks of these self-definitions are symbols used to strive for a sense of completion. A person engages in **self-symbolizing,** or the use of symbols to build and retain a complete self-definition, when he or she senses a lack of completion (Wicklund and Gollwitzer, 1982, p. 9).

Four conditions may be identified in what Wicklund and Gollwitzer (1982, p. 38) refer to as **symbolic self-completion**:

*1.* A person must be committed to a self-defining goal. Let us assume that a self-defining goal is one of being "creative" with respect to appearance. A person with this goal wants to follow a course of action in appearance management that will reinforce this goal (by selecting and coordinating clothes accordingly).

*2.* Symbols are available within one's culture that pertain to self-definition. For example, one person pursuing a "creative" self-definition may find cultural symbols in the form of unusual hairstyles, innovative color combinations of clothing items, self-made or self-modified apparel, and the like.

*3.* The person experiences a sense of incompleteness. That is, one's progress toward achieving the self-defining goal is interrupted in some way, and an evaluation follows (in the me), resulting in a sense of incompleteness. For example, the person in our example may find it difficult to find the "right" symbols of creativity, may feel unsure about what constitutes appearing creative, or may not know how to coordinate outfits without making "mistakes."

*4.* A person has access to at least one route of self-symbolizing. Routes of self-symbolizing for a person striving to appear creative may be to consult magazines and shop to get ideas, to experiment with different color combinations, or to observe clothes worn by others perceived to be creative.

Symbolic self-completion theory draws from the cognitive and symbolic-interactionist perspectives. Early cognitive theorist Kurt Lewin (1935) and his students focused an individual's needs to reduce states of tension through whatever means necessary, including pursuing goals. The goal-directed dimension of self-symbolizing parallels this need for reducing the tension created by feelings of incompleteness. The symbolic-interactionist perspective provides insight with respect to the me, in the process of evaluating and knowing the self so as to sense the need for completion. When do we sense incompleteness? Wicklund and Gollwitzer (1982) explain this tension state in relation to the concept of "generalized other":

> If a self-definition is composed of multiple symbols, and this system of symbols is defined within the community, then disrupted individuals will evaluate the self in line with the way society would view their standing on the self-definitional dimension (p. 36).

If a negative self-evaluation is made with respect to a particular self-definition, an individual will pursue a substitute source of symbolic completeness. Yet symbolic self-completion involves more than just attaining a wardrobe of suitable symbols; it also involves constructing, and exerting control over, one's social reality. This sense of social reality is necessary before one can feel he or she actually possesses self-definition. Others can acknowledge self-definition and provide that sense of self, as well. However, self-symbolizing can be somewhat self-destructive when a person relies too heavily on symbols and fails to take the perspective of others into account. The danger lies in not understanding the needs of others and not communicating responsively (Wicklund and Gollwitzer, 1982, p. 36).

Several studies have tested symbolic self-completion theory and have found support for the idea that individuals lacking a sense of completeness with respect to a self-definition are most likely to make use of available cultural symbols to pursue a sense of completeness. These studies have dealt with self-definitions relative to careers and religion; there is even some evidence of symbolic use of clothing for purposes of acquiring an acceptable self-definition with respect to gender.

## Career Self-Definitions

A study of male business graduate students focused upon factors that might contribute to a sense of incompleteness (height, grade point average in the master's in business administration program, number of months in the program, and job offers and interviews) (Wicklund and Gollwitzer, 1982, pp. 153–156). Students who showed little success in their graduate programs and little promise in terms of future careers were most likely to surround themselves with symbols culturally associated with success in business, including an expensive watch and expensive shoes and accessories. The most committed and relatively incomplete students used these symbols the most.

Solomon and Douglas (1985) note that women in the early stages of their careers are most likely—due to commitment as well as a possible sense of incompleteness—to use clothing as a kind of strategy for acquiring a sense of success—hence, the dress-for-success look. Sticking to the "letter of the law" in terms of business attire may reflect means for compensation for a lack of self-assurance early in one's career. Later on when the career self-definition has become a social reality in the eyes of self and others, one might feel freer to experiment with appearance and/or pursue other self-definitions. Some support for this idea was suggested in research by Nancy Rabolt and Mary Francis Drake (1985), who found that women accepted more information about clothing from others when clothing was viewed as important, when they were anxious in careers, when they felt there was an expected dress code, when they had worked a short time in their careers, when they were less confident about dressing professionally, and when they were aware of their own and others' clothes. Older women were less likely to seek information from work associates, perhaps due to a greater sense of completeness in the career role.

## Religious Self-Definition

In a study of religious self-definition, students from families of heterogeneous religious backgrounds (for example, Catholic mother and Lutheran father) were compared with students from families of homogeneous religious backgrounds (for example, both parents as Methodists). Students from heterogeneous families were more inclined to wear or display such religious symbols as bracelets, crosses, stars of David, pins, bumper stickers, Bible, T-shirts, and rings. These symbols were worn or displayed in more places and more frequently by the students from the heterogeneous families. This finding was explained by the fact that "the social reality afforded by a religiously-heterogeneous family leads the child to a mixed, uncertain sense of self-definitions regarding religious identity" (Wicklund and Gollwitzer, 1982, pp. 160–163).

## Gender

Gender may be a type of self-definition, especially in the early phases of gender acquisition when a child is just learning about cultural rules equating objects (clothes, hairstyles, and toys) with being male or female (Constantinople, 1979; Kaiser, 1989). During the preschool years, in particular, young children are likely to prefer traditional gendered appearances. One factor contributing to this is the exaggeration of gender for the purpose of establishing a solid gender self-statement ("I am a boy" or "I am a girl"). Some cognitive developmental psychologists contend that children do not fully realize the *constancy* of gender until the approximate age of 5 years. That is, gender constancy is associated with the cognitive realization that one's sex does not readily change with a change in clothing or grooming (outer, surface characteristics). A lack of gender constancy parallels the idea of a tension state. Before they establish this concept, young children may think that even an anatomically correct male doll would change to a female doll if a dress and wig were put on it (Thompson and Bentler, 1971; Thompson, 1975). However, there is some controversy as to when children develop a sense of gender constancy and when they distinguish "real" from "pretend" changes in gender. The age of gender constancy may be as young as 4 years if a real response mode is sought instead of demonstrating gender change on a doll (Martin and Halverson, 1983). Still, there is clearly a strong preference during the preschool years for like-sex clothes, with a corresponding exaggeration of masculinity and femininity.

Numerous possibilities exist for revealing additional relations between the symbolic use of clothes and self-definitions. The advantages and disadvantages of self-symbolizing is of particular interest in terms of clothing and human behavior. Gollwitzer and Wicklund (1985) note that self-symbolizing is not the same as self-presentation (to be discussed in the next chapter); it is similar to self-construction. The danger in self-construction lies in the potential for becoming too absorbed in pursuing the self-definition and failing to be attentive to others' judgments of self (Gollwitzer and Wicklund, 1985).

In the next chapter, we will consider appearance management as a factor in self-presentation. Although individuals will vary to the extent that they are concerned with appearance management, it is an everyday process that can shed some light on how and why we present ourselves to others.

## *Suggested Readings*

Feather, B. L., Kaiser, S. B., and Rucker, M. 1989. Breast reconstruction and prosthesis use as forms of symbolic completion of the physical self. *Home Economics Research Journal 17*: 216–227.
   The concept of symbolic self-completion is explored in relation to women's perceptions of their bodies after they have had mastectomies, as well as their related practices and preferences linked to prosthesis use and intentions with respect to breast reconstruction.

Sontag, M. S., and Schlater, J. D. 1982. Proximity of clothing to self: Evolution of a concept. *Clothing and Textiles Research Journal 1*(1): 1–8.
   Sontag and Schlater provide data documenting different orientations to clothing as connected to the self. Among these orientations are tendencies to see the self as process versus the self as structure.

Wicklund, R. A., and Gollwitzer, P. M. 1982. *Symbolic self-completion*. Hillsdale: Lawrence Erlbaum Associates.
   In this book, the concept of symbolic self-completion is explored in great depth. Several studies related to clothing and appearance are reviewed, and the findings suggest that clothing can be used as a prop to bolster a sense of self when some component of self seems incomplete.

# Chapter Six
∎ ∎ ∎
# Appearance Management and Self-Presentation

*In everyday life we are caught up in the act of appearing before others. As we do so, we present existing and idealized images of self. Of course, there are variations in how self-conscious we are likely to be, based upon individual and situational differences. In different contexts, the self can assume varying identities, and by managing our appearances we can try to shape others' understandings of our identities. In this chapter, the metaphor of drama and the stage is used, in part, to explore clothes and other appearance manipulations as props that enable us to move from one role to the next. At the same time, it is important to remember that we are not just actors/actresses appearing before an audience, but that we are also individuals striving to mesh our lines of action together—to interact with one another.*

> *Last week one time, I just sat and put together different combinations of clothes that I'd never worn before—holey jeans and this oxford shirt that I really like, and then just a sweatshirt over that. And I thought it looked good. . . . I can remember times now when I'm trying to impress somebody . . . I just put on different shirts and they look stupid, and I take them off and put on . . .*
>
> —MALE COLLEGE STUDENT

> *I think if I were to wear skirts and high heels, people would look at me different, even if my personality was exactly the same.*
>
> —FEMALE COLLEGE STUDENT

As these comments suggest, appearance management is not only a process that is enacted with others in mind, but also one that involves experimentation and self-expression. In this way, appearance management becomes a means for **self-presentation**—a process of displaying an identity to others in social context.

Our lives are interwoven with those of others around us; accordingly, our actions and appearances are not totally random. Most of us strive for some sense of order in our daily interactions and perceptions. Our clothing selections and styles of grooming are influenced by how we would like others to see us. Appearance management becomes a means not only for creating a visual picture of self but also for understanding the self by defining the meaning of appearance symbols across situations.

Consideration of cultural, as well as social, context is critical to an understanding of self-presentation. The elements of self-definitions (discussed in Chapter Five) are provided by culture. Within the cultural repertoire, there are numerous *identity kits* (Goffman, 1961a) available for personal use and self-symbolizing. Clothing and appearance symbols provide an outlet for bringing to the surface—or to life—some of our personal feelings about cultural prescriptions, social factors over which we may have little control, and expressions of creativity and who we strive to be. With these symbols, we can play and experiment as well as conform to cultural expectations.

In this chapter, self-presentation will be discussed in terms of appearance-managing strategies, identity as a self-in-context, and issues of acting versus interacting. A contextual perspective will be used, along with a consideration of the perspective of **dramaturgy**, which uses a life-as-theater analogy to understand selves in contexts.

## Self-Presentation

Our self-concepts, as discussed in Chapter Five, provide some guidelines for dressing ("that's me" versus "that's not me"). At times, however, our *perceived* selves, or self-concepts, do not necessarily coincide with our *ideal* selves, or the selves we are striving to be. Appearance management affords an outlet for approximating visually, as closely as possible, one's ideal self.

### Private versus Public Self

Social psychologists often distinguish the self in terms of private versus public contexts. The *private* context of self deals with introspection and self-understanding. Are we likely to dress differently when we are alone, rather than when we are interacting with others? The private context of self is likely to involve inner dialogue and thought processes, but it can also include some experimentation with appearance, as well as fantasy. Joanne Eicher (1981) uses the term *secret self* to refer to the self that may not be shared with any other person and notes that the secret self can dress to fulfill fantasies. Fantasy clothes may be sexual or may represent bold colors that would not be worn in public. Secret self-image may also be a basis of psychiatric analysis. For example, conflicts of gender and age may be apparent in the secret appearances of some troubled adolescents, as noted by Michelman and Michelman (1986). Dressing in a private context may eventually become a type of "dress rehearsal" for future interactions. Because the private context of self is more difficult to measure and is not as commonly discussed as the more public contexts of self, little research has been conducted in this area and there is tremendous potential here for a fuller understanding of appearance management from the perspective of the self.

The *public* context of self is especially likely to include concern about others' perceptions of us. In this context, cultural expectations of appropriate appearances according to factors like age, gender, and occupation are factored into self-presentations. This is the context of self that is most often observed and discussed in everyday life, as well as in popular media.

What motivates us to think about our self-presentations? In part, we may be motivated by the desire to seek and maintain some sense of personal control or power to exert influence over present and future events. We may wish to engage in self-presentation for purposes of individually or socially induced concerns. Public expression of self also becomes an arena for constructing a kind of compromise between actual and ideal self-image (Baumeister, 1986). Through **self-construction**, a concept of self may be tested out publicly through assessment of others' responses to one's appearance. In this case, one's conception of the ideal self may be the criterion used to evaluate favorable self-presentation. **Self-promotion**, on the other hand, has a social basis for self-presentation and involves appearance display for the perusal of others, to further the self in some way—as is common in a job interview or politics. In other words, self-promotion is not motivated strictly for the purpose of satisfying one's own picture of self, but rather for the purpose of pursuing social opportunities (see Figure 6-1).

## Self-Consciousness

Through dialogue within the self (self-indication), individuals can experience the self in action and also be aware of how others are viewing and evaluating the self. When do we become self-conscious about our appearances? Obviously, we cannot spend all of our time focusing on how we look. In some public contexts, we become acutely aware of ourselves as social objects. Some examples include job interviews, public speeches, participation in fashion shows, and other contexts in which we are focused on how we appear. (See Figures 6-2 and 6-3.) Research has suggested linkages between feelings about various aspects of clothing and fashion and feelings of public self-consciousness. In other words, males and females who are concerned about their appearance and the general impression they make on other people tend also to feel that clothes have an influence upon their moods at a given time; they make an effort to be dressed in newer styles and think that what others wear influences their perceptions of those others (Solomon and Schopler, 1982).

People who are high in public self-consciousness, then, view themselves as social objects. A study with 60 females indicated that those high in public self-consciousness were more interested and involved in clothing with regard to others' perceptions. Publicly self-conscious persons may actually be more fashionable and more concerned with conformity to social norms than people who are not as self-conscious in public contexts. Public self-consciousness is also associated with self-presentations and possibly anxiety when appearance and/or knowledge about fashion is criticized or questioned. It seems that persons who

**FIGURE 6-1**
*This young girl may engage in either self-construction or self-promotion, as she contemplates which accessories she prefers to wear in her hair. If she is engaging in self-construction, she may be using cultural criteria linked to femininity, and she can test this self-concept by gauging others' responses to the accessories she chooses. If, however, she is engaged in self-promotion, she may have some specific social opportunities in mind. For example, she may be motivated by the popularity a feminine look seems to provide girls in her preschool. Photo by Joan L. Chandler.*

**FIGURE 6-2**
*These pregnant women in the early 1970s were likely to have felt some degree of public self-consciousness when they first exposed their abdomens. Yet once they did so and it became the natural thing to do, they were able to make a visual statement about the role of pregnant women. Photo by Larry White.*

**FIGURE 6-3**
*This woman from India is likely to experience some degree of public self-consciousness as she dances in a performance before others. Photo by Katharine Hoag.*

are high in public self-consciousness may use clothing as a means for reducing social anxiety by "creating a public image that corresponds to a socially desirable image" (Miller, Davis, and Rowold, 1982).

Leslie Davis (1984b) studied females' responses to ambiguous information about fashion (what kinds of clothes would be fashionable in the future). She found that females high in public self-consciousness tended to conform more with others' judgments of what will be fashionable in the future than with judgments as to what is currently fashionable. This finding was even stronger among the individuals high in private self-consciousness, that is, who were attune to their inner thoughts and feelings, or self-reflective. It seems that individuals who focus attention on themselves are sensitive to the subtle nuances of their own responses to social pressure (Davis, 1984b).

How do males and females compare in terms of relationships to clothing and self-consciousness? Solomon and Schopler (1982) found that males with a higher sense of public self-consciousness (as compared with males who are not as self-conscious) appear to be more interested in clothing and more influenced in their daily clothing decisions by the situations they expect to find themselves in (for example, class, work, and making a presentation). In addition, these males experience more of a psychological "lift" when they buy new clothes, express a greater sense of self-consciousness when dressed inappropriately for an occasion, and are more likely to expect their clothes to influence others' impressions of them. These relationships did not tend to apply as much to females. Clearly, females as a whole express a greater involvement with clothes than do males, and this might be expected because of the cultural and historical emphasis in female socialization on the importance of personal appearance. Thus females may not be differentiated as readily on the basis of such attributes as public self-consciousness, because appearance concerns may become a general way of life for females as a whole. Solomon and Schopler (1982) noted that males may be freer than females to elect their own level of clothing interest and that males who are high in public self-consciousness may "capitalize to a greater degree . . . on the strategic utility of clothing for . . increasing the value of the self as a social commodity on the interpersonal marketplace" (Solomon and Schopler, 1982, p. 514).

In part, concern with personal appearance is a matter of how one is located socially (as discussed in Chapter Five). Yet individuals are free to some extent to "break out" of social scripts, within certain boundaries. The concept of identity can be considered in greater depth if we look at how people come to view themselves in social contexts, as influenced both by cultural demands and personal interpretations and responses with respect to these demands.

## Identity and Appearance: The Visual Self in Context

A concept that enables us to understand perceptions of self across contexts is **identity**. An identity is the organized set of characteristics an individual perceives as representing or defining the self in a given social situation. Although people have only one self-concept, they have many contextually relevant identities (Troiden, 1984). For example, people are likely to dress and behave differently in class than they would at a party, or when interacting with their mothers as opposed to their dates. Identity can also pertain to qualities that people perceive the self to have in a context. For example, one might feel creative or original at a Halloween party or fashion-conscious when interacting (and comparing oneself) with friends who do not emphasize fashion.

Through a process of **self-identification**, individuals place (locate or identify) and express their own identities. Appearance management allows them to anticipate what identities they would like to have in a social situation, so they can present themselves accordingly to others. Self-presentation enacted with others in mind—in a public context—is often referred to as **self-disclosure**. Thus self-identification, as well as the more specific act of appearance management, is like a transaction involving a *person* (and his or her self-image, goals, or mood), an *audience* (others with whom one interacts), and a *situation* (with all of its attendant opportunities and constraints) (Schlenker, 1986).

Just as an audience may be comprised of other people, it may also be comprised of the self. Self-identification that occurs in a private context represents **self-reflection**. In this way, appearance management can enable people to understand themselves and to reflect on identity. The self can become a kind of audience (as when looking in a mirror) that evaluates one's own image and places it in context.

Yet people cannot hold on to particular identities by themselves. Identities tend to be constructed, revised, and reconstructed in social transactions. The basis for these identities, however, may be linked to one of two processes. Identities may be *ascribed*, as when they are assigned and attributed to individuals by society, or they may be *achieved*, as when people earn or create their own. In either case, the meanings and appearances associated with an identity are socially constructed. (Gendered appearances, as discussed in Chapter Three, are a prime example of an ascribed identity that is socially constructed.)

Some authors do not include variables associated with social location (as discussed in Chapter Five), including gender, socioeconomic status, age, and ethnicity, in their definitions of identity, because they contend that these aspects of self are never enacted independently in social contexts (Hoelter, 1985). However, the way we are located socially becomes intricately linked to identity because people respond to us, in part, on the basis of clothes or other appearance cues that place us as males versus females, young versus old, or wealthy versus poor. Social location, like other aspects of identity, assumes varying importance in different contexts. For example, gender is likely to become a salient identity when one is the only female in a group. If this female dresses in a particularly feminine or provocative manner, her gender may become an even more prominent identity.

*Ascribed Identities*

An achieved identity may relate self-identifications linked to one's abilities or accomplishments in one's career, leisure activities, social life, politics and other contexts over which a person has some control. To assist us in defining ourselves and establishing identities, we select and display appearance symbols our culture provides and defines for us. However, individual spontaneity and group dynamics provide means for new forms of self-expression and identity achievement.

To what extent are people free to manipulate and personalize their appearances? Culture provides some prescriptions or expectations in relation to conventional systems of dress meaning (for example, pink for baby girls and blue for baby boys), but there is also room for individual selection and combination of appearance elements. We might think of these individual acts of expression as "fashion statements" (Simon-Miller, 1985). *Individual* acts can provide a means for personal

*Achieved Identities*

expression, flexibility in conveying a message or combination of messages, and creativity. So, culture may provide "identity kits" (Goffman, 1961a) that assist us in assuming conventional identities, but we may break out of traditional identity kits provided for us by rearranging, juxtaposing, and combining elements of different kits. Through experimentation, a person can play or experiment with identity kits, as well as use them to conform. In this way, one can bring to the surface how he or she feels about, or responds to, cultural conventions. At the same time, identity is constructed and used to negotiate desired impressions for one's self and/or for others (see Figure 6-4).

Some identities (especially achieved ones that are not linked to institutionalized dress codes) provide opportunities for individual choice and interpretation. But even when institutionalized dress codes exist, people may adopt means for personalizing these codes, or at least their self-reflections. To some extent, people want to feel that they are unique or special, and if they cannot present this visually in a context, they may still perceive themselves as comprising a unique set of qualities (that may not be visible to others). As a person brings a set of identities to a social context, one way of personalizing the situation is to identify which identity is most salient.

## Identity Salience

As a form of choice behavior (Serpe, 1987), **identity salience** is a process of determining when a particular identity becomes important for defining the self, as opposed to other identities. An identity becomes a kind of self-in-context. The word *identity* is not a substitute word for self; rather, when one has identity, he or she is *situated* within the realm of social relations. By dressing in a police uniform, for example, a female police officer announces a career identity. When peceivers validate that announcement by placing her in that career, then that identity becomes a meaningful component of the (more complex) self (Stone, 1965, p. 223).

## Identity Negotiation

At times, the identity that we wish to convey to others is overshadowed by another identity (less salient to us at the moment) that is highly visible or obvious to those others. In these cases, it is necessary to *negotiate* with others, or to vie for the identity that one wants to be recognized in a given context. If a female police officer comes home from work and greets her preschool daughter and friend, the identity that is likely to be most salient in this context is "mother," yet the daughter's friend may focus on the uniform and find it difficult to get past that identity. In this case, negotiation could occur if the mother continues to talk to her daughter's friend and reveals some of the qualities this friend identifies in her own mother.

The process of **identity negotiation** occurs when a wearer and a perceiver are able to come to a shared understanding of the wearer's identity through a process of give and take, interpretation and reinterpretation, using not only appearance but also verbal communication as a guide. Appearance management is important as a contributing factor to identity salience in the eyes of the self. The amount of effort people expend to create a desired appearance, consistent

**FIGURE 6-4**
*Opportunities for unique presentations of self are provided in thrift stores, as shown here. One can mix and match second-hand garments and accessories with other items in the wardrobe, thereby creating an individualistic appearance. Photo by Susan B. Kaiser.*

with an identity, is likely to focus their attention on the importance of that identity to the self.

When we realize others are responding to an identity, even when it is not the most salient to us at the moment, it is a form of social feedback that we may interpret and use in understanding ourselves through the eyes of others. But we do not necessarily have to "settle" for the social labels or identities they assign to us, if we prefer for another aspect of the self to be emphasized. Social Focus 6-1 provides an illustration of a type of identity that may be salient in the eyes of observers because of high visibility, even when it is not the most salient identity in the eyes of an observed person. Appearance management among persons with physical disabilities is discussed in terms of how individuals can negotiate or bargain for preferred social labels (identities).

In everyday life, negotiation is a necessary part of identity construction. One factor that contributes to negotiation is the cultural restlessness about identity that may be characteristic of modern life. Fashion invites, and even pressures, individuals to revise themselves—to seek new forms of self-expression and self-definition (Klapp, 1969, p. 73). This tendency of fashion is part of a larger cultural drama that refers to unresolved issues in people's lives, for example, how they want to be viewed as males or females vis à vis other identities. This cultural approach to the study of identity will be discussed later in Chapter Fourteen, as it pertains to culture theory. For now, however, the drama of everyday life may be looked at in terms of social interactions and self-presentation.

## Dramaturgy and Appearance

> *All the world's a stage*
> *And all the men and women merely players:*
> *They have their exits and their entrances;*
> *And one man in his time plays many parts.*
> *As You Like It*—Act 2, Scene 7

Let's look at this excerpt from a Shakespearean play. *Is* all the world a stage, with all people as performers of roles? In looking at self-concept and appearance, we have seen that clothes most likely represent more in our daily personal and social lives than costumes for performances before others. Yet appearance management as a form of human behavior may be characterized in part by performance of the self in context. The social-psychological perspective in sociology known as dramaturgy draws analogies between human behavior and the theater. A major premise of this perspective is that people are dependent on one another for their identities; building up identities is a continuous, lifelong process—as is the more basic self-concept that subsumes these identities. Identities are formulated in social context and—as individuals move from one context to another—reformulated. This fragile, somewhat staged nature of the self was captured in the work of sociologist Erving Goffman (1959). In *The Presentation of Self*

# Appearance Management among Persons with Physical Disabilities

People with physical disabilities, like any other individuals, do not necessarily accept the labels society assigns to them in a passive manner. Appearance management affords a possible outlet for ameliorating the consequences of visible differences. A symbolic-interactionist perspective on appearance-managing strategies on the part of physically disabled persons focuses on their ability to *negotiate social outcomes*—that is, to vie for preferred social labels by presenting appearance symbols that communicate about other aspects of the self—pointing out that the disability is not the only or the most important aspect of the self (Hanks and Poplin, 1981; Kaiser, Freeman, and Wingate, 1985). Through the manipulation of clothing and accessories, persons with disabilities may emphasize other aspects of the self, even if total concealment of the disability is not possible. Appearance management is regarded by some persons with physical disabilities as a potential means for improving on the social impact of a physical disability, but it is realistically expected to serve a secondary role in appearance perception on the part of others. Those persons who regard appearance management as a means of compensating for a disability tend to be more likely to view that disability as central to personal identity. University students who use wheelchairs tend to be less optimistic with respect to the ameliorating consequences of appearance management than are physically disabled students who do not use wheelchairs. Also, wheelchair users are more likely to agree with the statement, "People I don't know tend to notice my disability first, and my clothing second" (Kaiser et al., 1987).

*A lot of times, I think people look at the chair before they look at who's in it.*

*I must tell you that the overriding way to characterize them [others' responses] is in relation to my handicap. I suspect that they're noticing my dress . . . second or third (Kaiser, Freeman, and Wingate, 1985).*

Overall, 64 percent of the students with physical disabilities (both wheelchair users and nonusers) agreed with the statement, "If I'm attractively dressed, people are more likely to notice me rather than my disability" (Kaiser, Freeman, and Wingate, 1985). In order to draw attention to the person, rather than to the disability, a variety of appearance-managing strategies were reported by the students in interviews and on questionnaires:

## Concealment

Some students reported that they could reduce the impact of a disability by concealing it. For example, a woman with one arm would conceal the missing arm by avoiding short sleeves.

## Deflection

Another strategy was to deflect attention away from the disability and toward another attribute that is not totally positive but is still considered by the wearer to be less discrediting than disability. Several students reported that they wore T-shirts with slogans alluding to drinking habits, for example, as a means of emphasizing an aspect of identity other than physical disability.

## Compensation

One way of gaining legitimacy in social encounters is to compensate for a disability by expressing mastery in an area usually closed to physically disabled persons and/or important to a particular context for which the stigma is irrelevant. By doing so, a person communicates that the disability "isn't all of me." Some students reported a strong interest in fashion or clothing, indicating that others respond accordingly toward the clothing rather than the disability. Other students emphasized occupation aspirations, social-political views, or other aspects of the self through T-shirts with slogans: "Social workers do it in the field," "No nukes," "Joe Cool," "I'm a wild and crazy guy," and "Short and sexy."

## Emphasizing Social Uniqueness

A few students indicated that they enjoy the extra attention they receive from others, and they take advantage of this attention by making noticeable clothing choices. This was

## Social Focus 6-1 *(continued)*

not a common response among the students as a whole, but it does point to one potential avenue for self-expression that deemphasizes physical disability. One student commented as follows:

*I like bright colors. I used to think that I didn't like that extra attention, but in the last year I've noticed that I like it. I used to resent all the extra attention I got being in a chair, but I kind-of am finding that I like the extra attention, so I take advantage of it (Kaiser, Freeman, and Wingate, 1985).*

A few students emphasized their physical uniqueness with humor. During an interview, one male student in a wheelchair relayed an experience in which his unexpected response to staring disrupted that staring and provided a personal sense of satisfaction. He was in a pizza parlor with his mother when every person in a group at a nearby table began to stare at him. Finally, he started waving and smiling at them; they were so disconcerted that they got up and moved to a new table where they could not see him. Other examples of humor were noted in the T-shirt slogans some students reported displaying: "I'm no quad; I'm just tired of walking," "Guess which part of me is not bionic," and "High-level quads do it with a joy stick." Again, students who called attention to themselves in this way were in the distinct minority; however, it is clear that for these students, at least, emphasizing social uniqueness may be as effective a strategy as "normalizing" appearance through concealment, deflection, or compensation is for other students with physical disabilities.

---

*in Everyday Life*, Goffman focused on the self as a staged production or a series of masks that people present to the diverse audiences they encounter. From this perspective, then, the self becomes the result of interaction between actor and audience (Allen, Guy, and Edgley, 1980, p. 177).

How does appearance enter into this interaction? As clothes are changed, hairstyles recoiffed, and makeup reapplied for different social contexts, different identities may be assumed. Drawing from the works of Goffman and literary critic Kenneth Burke (1975), we can consider four elements of the dramaturgical perspective that may be merged with a discussion of appearance management and self-presentation: (1) the performance (the "act"), (2) the setting (the "stage"), (3) the audience, and (4) self as actor or actress. These elements jointly make up the social context: what one does, where one does it, and for (and with) whom.

### Performance: The Concept of Role

Humans are immersed in actions and appearances; in short, they *behave* and they *appear* before others. Together, actions and appearances make up performances, in dramaturgical terms. To explore the connection between actions and appearances in self-presentation, let us consider the concept of role (as compared with identity), as well as the impact of appearances on individual actions and audience perceptions of performance credibility.

### The Concept of Role

Part of individual performances tend to be prescribed by social convention. Although there is some controversy over the concept of role in the social science literature, one common way of defining **role** is a "typified response to a typified expectation" (Berger, 1963, p. 95). A role is similar to a position a person occupies in a social situation; for this position, society has already provided a "script" for one to follow. Being cast in a role is facilitated by "looking the part" and dressing in a costume that others have come to expect of a person in that role.

Role theory is rooted in the symbolic-interactionist perspective, although role theorists have tended to pursue a different direction for explaining human behavior, focusing on the role an individual plays in the larger play or drama of society. According to these theorists, we acquire masks to adopt certain roles for performances, and our perceptions of self are shaped by these masks. The words *person* and *personality* are derived from the Latin word *persona*, which means "mask." Our personae become our public self-presentations, which should not necessarily be regarded as deceitful or even totally purposive. In contrast, they are likely to be so well-ingrained in everyday life actions that we take them for granted and rarely focus on them. Rituals associated with appearance management are also relatively unconsciously enacted.

In a sense, the range of an individual person is measured by the number of roles he or she is capable of performing. A person is likely to internalize a large number of roles (and their scripts), yet is likely to use only a subset of these roles for defining the self (Hoelter, 1985). How does the concept of role differ from that of identity? Whereas a role tends to be associated with structural requirements for a fairly routine or automatic performance (with a script provided), an identity is more of self-definition, being more abstract and personal. A role is closer to "what a person does," whereas an identity refers more to "who one is." One may or may not incorporate a role or performance into an identity. As shown in Figure 6-5, role performances are not always included in self-

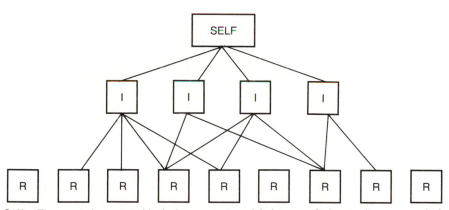

**Self:**  The most abstract and inclusive concept; a global sense of who one is, composed of a subset of identities

**Identity (I):**  Self-in-context; constructed and negotiated through social processes (person interacting in context); composed of a subset of roles

**Role (R):**  Typified response to a typified expectation; most tangible of the three concepts— refers to performance or enactment (person acting, following a script that is prescribed); may or may not be included in an identity

*FIGURE 6-5*
*Schematic illustration of self, identities, and roles.*

definitions; some roles may be enacted because they are obligatory and do not necessarily reflect one's view of self. Yet dramaturgists would say that many of our roles or performances do become incorporated into identities. As Figure 6-5 reveals, we tend to have many roles, which are subsumed by a smaller number of identities, which, in turn, make up the global view people have of themselves. It is important to remember that identity is not a "given"; rather, it is constructed and bestowed through a process of social negotiation, in context. One brings multiple identities to a context; these identities intersect one another, and some are likely to become more salient than others, as we have seen. In contrast, a role is more of a "given" in a social situation, and it may or may not be incorporated into one's view of self.

We tend to express whether or not a role or performance is part of an identity through our appearance, by providing clues about how fully we relate to a given role. Goffman's (1961b) concepts of role embracement and role distance help to explain how we communicate these clues. **Role embracement** refers to a close link between a particular role or performance and an identity, meaning that the role is likely to be integrated into one's self-concept. (Through enactment of the role, or following the script provided by society, we come to know ourselves.) **Role distance**, on the other hand, refers to a lack of inner identification with a role. A person may want to communicate "this role is not all of me" or "this role is not part of my identity." By distancing ourselves from roles, we demonstrate that we are not merely roles whose parts are neatly cast (we are more complex). A young male military recruit has little say over the type of haircut he receives. However, during leisure hours he may be able to express through his choice of clothes (for example, T-shirts with slogans) that there is more to him than his military role. His haircut is still visible, yet he is able in the leisure context to distance himself from the role it represents.

Role embracement and role distance are concepts that rely on human agency to display the degree of relation between role (what one does) and self (who one is, as composed of identities). Another issue related to individual performances, in a dramaturgical sense, is the extent to which roles or performances influence human behavior. As a component of these roles or performances, appearance (including clothes and grooming) may influence our actions.

## The Influence of Appearance on Behavior

Do our appearances influence the way we act? To answer this question, it is important to distinguish our more stable physical attributes from our clothes and personal grooming, which may be altered for individual "performances." With respect to the impact of physical attributes on behavior, there is some suggestion in the literature that physically attractive people are more assertive than unattractive persons when it comes to correcting an impolite person (Jackson and Huston, 1975) or speaking up quickly and succinctly (Campbell et al., 1986). In terms of the impact of clothing per se on behavior, there is mixed support for a direct relation. Wass and Eicher (1964) surveyed ninth-grade girls on their attitudes about appropriate clothing for different situations. Over one-half of the girls believed that they behaved differently on school days that were designated as "dress-up" days. The majority of them (over two-thirds) felt that student behavior was different on these days—specifically, more mature or better behaved. Over 80 percent of the girls believed that certain styles of clothes induced them to act in certain ways.

The Wass and Eicher (1964) study relied on self-report data; however, an observational study by Tharin (1981) produced similar findings. Tharin studied the relation between clothing and behavior in roller rinks. She found differences in behavior between the regular nights and those when dress codes were enforced. The enforcement of dress codes appeared to result in fewer accidents, fewer confrontations, and less noise. Furthermore, skaters who wore more modest attire (as measured by the amount of skin revealed) had fewer accidents.

It may be that clothes are more of a factor in behavior displayed in specially defined contexts, as compared with routine or everyday contexts. In both studies, clothes helped to define special contexts, incurring a higher degree of formality than is normally encountered. It is also possible in the roller rink study that people who are attracted to the evening when dress codes are enforced may be better behaved anyway.

Do clothing changes affect individual behavior in more routine contexts? Observations of girls' free-play behavior in preschool settings did not reveal any differences on the days the girls wore pants, as compared with dresses. Girls were just as likely to be active when they wore dresses. They were also just as likely to engage in traditionally feminine play activities (for example, playing with dolls) when they wore pants, despite the fact that perceptual measures indicated they *believed* girls typically dress differently for various play activities, along gender-stereotyped lines (Kaiser, Rudy, and Byfield, 1985). Dramaturgists might explain the lack of a direct clothing-behavior relationship in routine contexts on the fact that people are likely to be immersed in the actions of everyday life and not necessarily prone to analyze their clothes before initiating behavior, especially when the options for behavior are fairly well-defined. However, as self-perception theory (discussed in Chapter Five) would also suggest, people often step back and examine the meanings of their behaviors after the fact. In the preschool study, some girls were observed wearing dressier clothes than usual and engaging in activities where clothes may become soiled or stained (for example, painting). When spills occurred, the girls became upset (after the fact). Children, especially, may not always stop and question the appropriateness of their clothes for a particular activity before acting; awareness of appearance is not constant, and people are immersed in actions. However, in contexts that are novel or unique to a person or when new and different clothes are worn, self-awareness may be increased and the impact of clothes on one's behavior may be more evident. Further research is needed to explore this possible distinction between routine and "special" contexts.

"Appearance is a dimension of all reality, and it is, of course, real itself" (Stone, 1977, p. 10). Part of the relation between appearance and reality pertains to others' perceptions of one's credibility in a "performance." To what extent do

*Appearance and Reality: Performance Credibility*

our appearances convince others about who we are? (Refer to Figures 6-6 and 6-7 as examples of this; also see Figures 6-11 and 6-12.) A related question is whether or not appearances render credibility to behavior. A dramaturgical approach leads us to pursue the study of clothing as a "prop" or costume enabling a credible performance. Meaning, according to dramaturgists, emerges from the behavior of selves acting and interacting in context (Brisset and Edgley, 1975). Clothes are likely to contribute to credibility of performances and therefore to the meaning that arises from social interaction.

Individuals dress in part on the basis of their interpretations of audiences' expectations in order to anticipate approval from others, especially when these individuals want their actions or words to be taken seriously. The issue of credibility in performances touches on many aspects of everyday and media life. Politicians want potential voters to believe in their promises and agendas if elected, actors and actresses want the audience to believe they are the characters played, career women want to be taken seriously at board meetings, and newscasters want to look and sound credible and effective. Researchers have found that conservative apparel—a navy blue suit jacket, blouse, or shirt and tie suitable for professional wear—promotes an audience's perceptions of male and female newscasters' credibility and effectiveness (Harp, Stretch, and Harp, 1985). Similarly, Kaiser (1982) found that some city managers referred to their navy blue suits as those appropriate for appearing sincere.

## Setting

Goffman's approach to the study of everyday life has been characterized as follows: "Even if the world is a stage, . . . it is a stage made out of real boards and real curtains; to recognize the way multiple realities are constructed does not mean that they are any less real or necessary" (Collins, 1986). The settings of everyday life include the more permanent backdrops for performances (for example, a home, a library, a church, or a bar) (Schlenker, 1986). Using the stage metaphor to analyze social settings, it becomes clear that settings come to have certain associations because their meanings are socially derived. Yet the social context may vary in a given setting, just as there may be a variety of theatrical renditions on a stage. For example, a park may become the physical backdrop for a number of social activities: a softball game, a picnic, or a wedding. As compared with a physical setting, clothes and other movable props are less permanent and more conducive to change according to personal preference or an audience. Together, clothes (and other changeable props) and setting help to define a context for social interaction, as do the people themselves. (See Figure 6-8.)

Dramaturgists describe interactions as being either *on* or *off* stage. Changes of clothing are often used to symbolize this movement back and forth, between acting and relaxing between roles or performances.

Specifically, clothing represents our action, past, present, and future, as it is established by the proposals and anticipations that occur in every social transaction. Without further elaboration, I think that this can be clearly seen in the doffing

**FIGURE 6-6**
*This woman's neat yet casual appearance (complete with stethoscope) renders credibility to her role as a nurse in a community clinic. If she were dressed too formally, her rapport with low-income patients might be diminished. On the other hand, if she were dressed sloppily, her appearance could be taken as a sign of disregard or incompetence. Photo by Carla M. Freeman.*

**FIGURE 6-7**
*An everyday-life example of appearance enabling a perceiver to identify another person's role is depicted in this beach scene. Does the male in the "high seat" appear credible as a lifeguard? The situational cues and props, as well as his hat, whistle, special red trunks, and tan, well-conditioned body are all likely to contribute to such an interpretation. Photo by Mark Kaiser.*

**FIGURE 6-8**
*The dramaturgical perspective would lead us to examine how a London toy store can be transformed into a stage for a Christmas performance. The singers' costumes help to create this impromptu transformation, as do their performances of such songs as "Jingle Bells." Photo by Susan B. Kaiser.*

of dress, signaling that an act is done (and another act is about to begin), the donning of dress, signaling the initiation of a new act, and the wearing of dress, signaling that action is going on (Stone, 1965, p. 229).

Goffman (1959) distinguished between two regions that pertain to roles and performances: front and back regions. The **front region** is the actual stage or setting where the self interacts with others. An important component of the front region is the **personal front**, which consists of **appearance** (clothing, makeup, and hairstyle) and **manner** (behavior, gestures, and style of speech). In the front regions of everyday life, it is easier to exert control over manner than it is appearance. We mainly deal with appearance management when we are backstage, in dramaturgical terms.

**Back regions** are backstage settings or situations, in which it is not as necessary to be concerned with appearance management (see Figure 6-9). We may identify three functions of back regions in everyday life: (1) preparation for interactions with others in front regions, or grooming, (2) relaxation between social interactions that must be on stage (changing into something more comfortable upon returning home from work), and (3) performing backstage tasks that can be better accomplished alone, without the distraction of props and concern with appearance (for example, working at the office on the weekend, wearing jeans and a sweatshirt).

Does this dramaturgical perspective on front and back regions seem to characterize everyday life as artificial? Are we as likely to worry about how we look when we are alone, as opposed to interacting with others? Dramaturgists would argue that, far from being unnatural, appearance management characterizes some of the rituals and feelings that make us social creatures, and that, in general, dressing for the eyes of others is not necessarily distinct from dressing for the

**FIGURE 6-9**
*A small specialty store may be distinguished into two contexts: the front region where the image presented to customers is carefully managed, and the back region that the public does not see and where the retail staff complete office work. Photos by Carla M. Freeman.*

self. The dramaturgical perspective's focus on front and back regions becomes a heuristic device, or a tool, to help us observe, explain, and understand the importance of appearance management—by distinguishing and clarifying contexts that require being on versus those without such a requirement. Of course, front regions are likely to vary in terms of the importance of appearance. In some contexts, appearance may not be an important factor, or individuals may be more engrossed in their actions than in their appearances. What becomes a front region to one person may be a back region to another; people also vary in their interpretations of the settings of everyday life. The nature of one's audience is an additional factor influencing what is construed as a front stage.

## *Audience*

When we dress, we also *address* some audience whose responses are essential to the establishment of our ideas about ourselves (Stone, 1965). In Stone's terms, we receive *reviews* from our audiences, which come in the form of social feedback as well as challenges to develop new *programs* (appearances). Thus the audiences of everyday life implicitly inspire as well as criticize appearance programs.

Often, it seems that audiences coincide with roles and performances. What happens when they do not coincide, when we are dressed for the wrong part? Goffman (1959) contends that we attempt to keep our audiences separate when the roles that we perform for them are incongruent, and he calls this process **audience segregation**. A theme of "shattering" the personal front pervades Goffman's writings on self-presentation; he notes that we often try to keep our role performances intact for the appropriate audiences. (See Figure 6-10.)

The term *role strain* is often used to describe contexts in which an individual finds that the multiple roles a person performs conflict with one another or add up to a feeling of overload on the part of an actor. Moving from one role to the next on a regular basis, especially if different clothes are required for the different roles, can be exhausting. What are the consequences if it is not possible for an actor to change between roles? Most likely, many observers are able to deal with the confusion because they understand that modern life is characterized by multiple roles and that it is impossible to alter one's appearance for every role. In fact, the perceivers comprising the audiences of everyday life are likely to construct interpretations for out-of-context attire (Kelley and Sweat, 1983–1984). For example, if a young couple wearing very formal attire (a male in a tuxedo and a female in an evening dress) are observed at a convenience store on a Saturday evening in spring in the United States, observers are likely to construct the following interpretation: They are on their way to their prom. It may be difficult for a foreign visitor to construct this interpretation, if he or she is not familiar with the custom of prom night. Thus cultural factors contribute to audience interpretations of actors' and actresses' appearances.

Even when personal fronts are shattered, symbolic interactionists maintain that the consequences are not necessarily negative. Interactions may be risky, but they are also rewarding. Once others come to know us as more than the roles we play, we derive more benefit or gain from our relationships with those others. For example, imagine the case of a female who carefully manages her

*FIGURE 6-10*
*Whether the audience finds this role performance convincing is dependent on the costume. If this Santa's beard drops off his face, his personal front may be shattered. Moreover, Santa's other personal fronts (accountant during the tax season, member of the church choir) that are presented to different audiences are kept distinct from the present role performance. Photo by Mark Kaiser.*

appearance with makeup, attractive clothes, and styled hair before all of her dates with a significant other. Although her personal front may have been crucial to the impression she made upon this significant other when they were initially getting to know one another, it is a distinct possibility that once this person is allowed to see her without extensive appearance management, a more genuine level of appreciation will be attained. That is, there may be less concern with appearance and more emphasis on understanding one another's feelings and needs.

Individuals are likely to vary in the extent to which they cater to an audience and monitor their appearances accordingly. In the next section, research aimed at deciphering individual (actor) differences in this regard will be addressed.

## Self-Monitoring

All people are not equally concerned with appearance management and its consequences in everyday social contexts. Some people are more attune to, and conscious of, their own appearances along with other situational cues. Social psychologist Mark Snyder (1987) provided an extension to Goffman's ideas about self-presentation and dramaturgy by developing a means for measuring individual differences in monitoring the self, in an attempt to answer the following questions:

Why do some people appear to be living lives of public illusion, while others are content just to "be themselves," without constantly assessing the social climate around them? Why do the public and private person seem to mesh so well for some, when others project a kaleidoscope of changing appearances? (p. 4).

The premise behind **self-monitoring** is that people differ in the extent to which they observe, regulate, and control the public appearance of self (Snyder, 1987, p. 4). Goffman (1959) had noted that appearance management can occupy a great deal of time, and he had pointed out an irony by showing that the people who make the best impressions may do so because of their appearance and ability to monitor the self. High self-monitors tend to be sensitive to interpersonal cues, and they manage appearance and behavior accordingly.

The implications of a high degree of self-monitoring become clear in such contexts as political campaigns, where it may be critical to survival in an age of constant visual media portrayals. If a politician is not sensitive to interpersonal cues, then he or she is likely to hire a consultant to assist in the creation and maintenance of an appropriate image, which may be modified as necessary for different social contexts.

As compared with high self-monitors, low self-monitors do not tend to be as concerned about situational appropriateness and personal management of appearance and behavior. Low self-monitors are not as likely to have developed an elaborate repertoire of self-presentational skills; their self-presentations are more likely to be controlled by inner values and dispositions than to be molded by the situation. There may be more congruence for low self-monitors between who they are and what they do. They are likely to take the following maxim seriously: "To thine own self be true" (Snyder, 1987, p. 4). Therefore, the expressiveness of a low self-monitor may be taken at face value, whereas the expressiveness of a high self-monitor is more purposely controlled. This is not to say the high self-monitors lack feeling, but rather that they control the way these feelings are expressed to others.

## Self-Monitoring Scale

To measure individual differences in self-monitoring, Snyder developed a scale to distinguish high from low self-monitors. This scale consists of 25 self-descriptive statements, to which people respond with true or false answers. High self-monitors are likely to respond to the statements in a way that suggests what they say and do does not always reflect their beliefs. They tend to endorse, or agree with, the following statements:

*I would probably make a good actor.*

*In different situations and with different people, I often act like very different persons.*

*I'm not always the person I appear to be (Snyder, 1987, p. 16).*

On the other hand, low self-monitors do not tend to believe they have the self-presentational skills to be other than "themselves." They tend to respond positively to the following statements.

*I have trouble changing my behavior to suit different people in different situations.*

*I can only argue for ideas which I already believe.*

*I would not change my opinion (or the way I do things) in order to please people or win their favor (Snyder, 1987, p. 17).*

Snyder notes that the statement that best seems to discriminate high from low self-monitors is, "I would probably make a good actor." He describes high self-monitors as "social chameleons who can fashion public images tailored to the dictates of a wide variety of situations" (Snyder, 1987, p. 22). High self-monitors tend to emphasize others more than the self, so they are conscious of the audience's perspective (p. 24). This consciousness may induce high self-monitors to strive for audience segregation, whereas low self-monitors may initiate and encourage contact between people from different areas of their lives (p. 62).

*Relation of Self-Monitoring to Appearance Management*

The self-monitoring scale has been used to seek relations with measures tapping various aspects of appearance management. To appear and act appropriately for a range of social encounters is likely to require a wide range of clothes, as well as other artifacts such as books, records, and magazines. The wardrobes of high self-monitoring males have more different items of clothes in more styles than do those of low self-monitoring males (Snyder, 1987). The same finding does not appear to apply as much to females, probably because female socialization stresses the need for a diverse wardrobe, and individual differences are not as likely to occur among females as they are among males. [This explanation is supported by the finding of Solomon and Schopler (1982), reported earlier, in terms of the relation of public self-consciousness to clothing variables. This relation was found to apply more to males than to females, and the authors interpreted this difference by noting that males can elect to emphasize appearance, whereas for females such an emphasis is an integral part of socialization.]

However, Leslie Davis and Sharron Lennon (1985) did find that females may be distinguished in terms of fashion behavior. They extended an understanding of self-monitoring by addressing its relation to individuality and conformity and fashion leadership among 55 female undergraduates. Both individuality and conformity in clothing were emphasized more by high self-monitors than by those with low self-monitors. Additionally, high self-monitors were more likely to exhibit characteristics of fashion leadership. There was also a trend for them to place more importance on usage of clothing for purposes of security.

In a later study of 88 female undergraduates, Lennon, Davis, and Fairhurst (1988) reported that high self-monitors were more favorable toward image-oriented fashion advertisements, whereas low self-monitors preferred ads emphasizing product quality. High self-monitors were also more willing to pay more for some products (Guess jeans and a Jordache denim jacket) than were low self-monitors.

Thus it seems that self-monitoring is a fruitful concept for understanding individual differences in appearance management and consumer decision-making. Future research addressing gender differences in this regard is likely to be especially revealing. The concept of self-monitoring, along with the dramaturgical perspective, also raises the issue of whether people use appearance management for purposes of deception.

## *Restrictions from Misrepresentation of Self*

Self-monitoring is likely to contribute to the use of appearance in people's constructions of a sense of reality. Hypothetically, if a person (a high self-monitor) misrepresents the self by adopting a fraudulent appearance (for example, a civilian dressing in a police uniform), then a perceiver is likely to develop an inaccurate impression of that person. However, there are two points that bear on this possibility. First, perceivers may develop a less-than-accurate impression regardless of an observed person's intent. For this reason, negotiation becomes a critical component of mutual identity construction in social interaction; other forms of communication (verbal comments, gestures, and behavior) normally contribute to this negotiation, along with appearance. Therefore, it is important to remember that appearance is only one part of communication. However, at times appearances can be extremely convincing, overriding other forms of communication. If other cues are less prominent or if limited information about a person is available, then a perceiver may develop an inaccurate impression on the basis of appearance.

The second point is linked to the fact that people do not purposefully deceive others by dressing and acting deceptively. Symbolic interactionists emphasize that people are not "con artists." Generally, people do not strive to deceive others by presenting false fronts. Marilyn Horn and Lois Gurel (1981) agree with this assertion and identify several factors that restrict people from misrepresenting the self through appearance:

*1. Intrinsic restrictions* pertain to a lack of resources to effect a misrepresentation of self. For example, one may not have the money to buy a fur coat and present the self as affluent.

*2. Moral restrictions* refer to ethical considerations related to the presentation of self. People are likely to feel that it is morally wrong to pretend to be a police officer, a nun, or a physician, for example. To do so may be harmful to others.

*3. Organic restrictions* are linked to the physical self. One's body may restrict a person from pretending to be an athlete. Simply donning a football uniform may not be sufficient to convince perceivers that one is a football player, if one's body does not "fit" this role.

**FIGURE 6-11**
*When interpreting this transvestite's appearance, more is involved than evaluating the clothes and makeup. If one is to present a credible cross-gendered appearance, several obstacles must be overcome: ability to attain the right symbols, ethical considerations (in some contexts), physical attributes, and conditioning that influences the way one sits and gestures. Photo by Larry White.*

   **4. *Cultivation and socialization*** may also prevent people from presenting themselves in roles they are not prepared to perform. For example, one may be able to assume the props necessary to impersonate the opposite sex, but subtle nuances (walking, sitting, and gesturing) may be as likely as organic restrictions to betray one's sex (see Figure 6-11). Self-monitoring and especially acting ability may assist a person in overcoming the restrictions of cultivation and socialization, in some cases.

   Self-monitoring helps to explain individual variations in appearance management. Like the dramaturgical perspective, it also raises the issue of the extent to which people act (appear and perform for others) versus interact (communicate with others).

## Acting versus Interacting

In everyday life, the distinction between acting and interacting tends to become blurred, because people do not act in a vacuum but within the context of social interaction. The concept of role tends be linked to performance or acting *for others*, in dramaturgical terms, whereas the concept of identity is more compatible with the use of clothing and appearance as means for communication and interaction *with others*, in symbolic-interactionist terms. Regardless of whether one feels as if he or she is acting or interacting, one is likely to be aware of continuity and differentiation in self-expression across contexts.

**Continuity and Differentiation**

Two characteristics of self-expression—continuity and differentiation—shed light on appearance management in relation to acting and interacting. **Continuity** represents a sense of unity across time or social contexts, or a feeling that one is the same person today as yesterday or last year or as he or she was in another situation. Certain clothing preferences may transcend time and context and allow one to develop a dimension of self-concept that is continuous. At the same time, appearance symbols may be used to create a sense of **differentiation** from others and from past self-definitions that no longer apply (Baumeister, 1986, p. 18). This simultaneous need for continuity and differentiation is essential to a fluid and healthy self-concept, and appearance management affords a tangible way of expressing this need.

Although it is probably more evident how clothes are adopted to play roles, because of the prescribed nature of roles (especially those requiring uniforms or standardized forms of apparel), envisioning how clothes are linked to identity is perhaps more difficult because of a higher level of abstraction—as linked to the self in context. However, in everyday life certain identities become habitual, so one's friends come to expect certain attributes in a person. The concept of **personality** refers to the relatively organized set of typical behavioral patterns and attitudes and values that are characteristic of a person and are recognized as such by the public self and others. People may come to expect some consistency, even across contexts, in a person's appearance as well—at least in terms of general themes or standards such as degree of modesty, creativity, conservatism, and the like.

Dramaturgists and role theorists tend to differ from some other social psychologists in their emphasis on actions and behaviors, rather than personality traits. There is a common adage that clothes reflect one's personality, which probably points out that one's clothes tend to be relatively consistent with how we have come to expect that person to appear. Dramaturgists and role theorists stress a focus on the processes of appearance management and self-presentation *in action* as guides to understanding human behavior, however, preferring this emphasis over one focusing on stability in individuals' personality traits. Symbolic interactionists take this emphasis on action a step further, focusing on the social contexts in which interaction occurs and people present their appearances to one another and construct identities.

**TABLE 6-1**
*Dramaturgy versus Symbolic Interactionism:*
*Acting as a Component of Interacting*

| Dramaturgy | Symbolic Interactionism |
|---|---|
| Acting | Interacting |
| Awareness of self in enactment of role | Awareness of self and most salient identity in a context |
| Awareness of audience perceptions of self | Process of identity negotiation involving mutual constructions of identity |
| Taken to an extreme, tendency to be illustrated by prescriptive requirements (for example, uniforms and dress codes) | Taken to an extreme, tendency to be explained by absence of prescriptions and presence of complex social constructions (for example, creative or ambiguous outfits requiring interpretation) |
| Role-playing | Role-taking |

Table 6-1 summarizes the differences between the dramaturgical and symbolic-interactionist perspectives and points out that acting and interacting are not necessarily mutually exclusive processes. Acting can be subsumed under the more general framework of interacting; in this way, appearance management and concern with image can be understood in terms of everyday actions that are carried out not only to promote the self but also to allow one to join his or her actions with those of others. Therefore, clothes may be viewed not only as props in the performance of a role but also as means for negotiating an identity in social contexts (see Figure 6-12).

Individuals strive to understand both their own roles and those of others with whom they interact. Symbolic interactionists emphasize that we not only *perform* our own roles but also *interpret* others' roles by attempting to place ourselves mentally into the roles those others are performing. The concept of **role-taking** refers to this cognitive ability people have to imagine themselves in another person's role and see a situation from that person's point of view as well as their own (Mead, 1934). Symbolic interactionists indicate that role-taking is critical to meaningful communication. By understanding another person's appearance in a way that fosters role-taking ability, one is able to interpret who that person is and what is occurring more accurately. Symbolic interactionists remind us that roles do not interact, people do, and their identities are the linkages between their self-concepts and the roles they play. Thus individual interpretations of a role may vary from one person to the next, despite institutional or prescribed role requirements. For example, female police officers may conform to institutional requirements in terms of dress codes and still express a personalized form of gender identity.

Some sociologists contend that playing it "safe" in prescribed social roles may hinder human development (Foote, 1975; Becker, 1975). There are creative,

*Symbolic-*
*Interactionist and*
*Dramaturgical*
*Perspectives*

**FIGURE 6-12**
*This woman in Rothenburg, Germany, dresses in traditional costume to render credibility to the handcrafted product she sells. Yet she is not only acting for, but is also interacting with, tourists and other passers-by. Her attire allows them to construct an interpretation of her identity, just as she probably attempts to interpret theirs (to determine if they are tourists or locals). Photo by Susan B. Kaiser.*

as well as threatening, aspects to social interaction, which may produce pleasures we cannot totally anticipate. If one is caught appearing or performing in a role by the "wrong" audience, symbolic interactionists argue that human potential for expression and interpretation of identity may be expanded.

## Suggested Readings

Davis, L. L., and Lennon, S. J. 1985. Self-monitoring, fashion opinion leadership, and attitudes toward clothing. In M. R. Solomon, ed. *The psychology of fashion*, pp. 177–182. Lexington: Heath/Lexington Books.
A relation between self-monitoring and use of clothing is established in this study. Fashion opinion leadership is also linked to self-monitoring behavior.

Goffman, E. 1959. *The presentation of self in everyday life*. Garden City: Doubleday.
Goffman's dramaturgical framework is presented in this classic book on self-presentation. Clothing is considered as a costume allowing us to move effectively from one "stage" to another and from "front stage" to backstage.

Lennon, S. J., Davis, L. L., and Fairhurst, A. 1988. Evaluations of apparel advertising as a function of self-monitoring. *Perceptual and Motor Skills* 66:987–996.
This study reports on the relation between self-monitoring behavior and perceptions of apparel ads.

Snyder, M. 1987. *Public appearances, private realities: The psychology of self-monitoring*. New York: W. H. Freeman.
    Drawing on Goffman's dramaturgical perspective, Snyder presents the concept of self-monitoring, describes how it can be measured, and reviews the available evidence on this concept to date.

Vaughan, J. L., and Riemer, J. W. 1985. Fabricating the self: The socialization of fashion models. *Sociological Spectrum* 5:213–229.
    Using Goffman's metaphor of front stage and backstage, this study examines the lives of fashion models. Qualitative data on their self-presentations are provided.

# *Part Three*
# ...
# *Appearance*
# *Communication*
# *in Context*

**D**AILY life consists of numerous interchanges between self and others. These interchanges require that we continually shift or alternate (move freely) between a focus on self-presentations and on others' appearances: in other words, between appearance management and appearance perception.

In Part Three, our concern is with the intricate process of **appearance communication**, which is the meaningful exchange of information through visual personal cues. Mutual processes of appearance management and appearance perception contribute to appearance communication. Both senders (observed persons) and receivers (perceivers) bring unique qualities, past experiences, and frames of reference to social interaction. Moreover, appearance messages are unique and complex in their own right, and they are perceived in a way that involves a filtering of personal experiences and expectations.

What is required for appearance communication to be meaningful? It may be described as meaningful when the way we look "calls out essentially, if not precisely . . . the same images and associations in ourselves as it does in others" (F. Davis, 1985, p. 21). As we will see in Chapter Seven, appearance messages have certain characteristics that make it somewhat unusual for these messages to elicit *exactly* the same definitions, associations, or emotions in senders as they do in receivers. Nevertheless, meaningful communication can proceed when a sender and receiver can sufficiently mesh their interpretations to develop a sense of shared understanding.

We will proceed in Part Three from a discussion of appearance as a visual context per se, drawing from semiotics (in Chapter Seven), to a focus on processes of social cognition influencing appearance perception (Chapter Eight). Then, because appearance perception is only one component of the two-way process of appearance communication, Chapter Nine will consider the qualities perceivers bring with them to social contexts that influence, and set the stage for, appearance communication. (As perceivers, we vary in how we see and understand the world around us.) Finally, in Chapter Ten the various pieces and processes of appearance communication will be pulled together to explore mutual negotiations of meaning in everyday life.

# Chapter Seven

### ···

# The Underlying Context of Appearance

*As we have seen in our contextual study of clothing, appearance is a context in and of itself. In this chapter, we will explore how the "parts" of appearance fit together to convey an overall, visual impression. Culture provides guidelines about what items of dress we should wear together, or which appearance elements are associated with one another (for example, a man's shirt with a tie). At the same time, appearance elements are manipulated on a daily basis by individuals who actually participate in the process of making meaning through everyday choices and combinations of these elements. Specific appearance elements acquire meaning, then, in the context of a visual system that allows for the emergence of meaning. The overall impression of a person's appearance is a medium for conveying messages about the self, and appearance as a mode of communication holds some unique properties that will be examined in this chapter.*

In everyday life, personal appearance becomes a context in and of itself. This visual context of personal appearance may be distinguished from what we might refer to as the larger social context, which consists of the appearances of whomever is interacting (as shown earlier in Figure 2-14 in Chapter Two). What is the difference between appearance per se and social context? Appearance is a component, of course, of social context. Whereas appearance as a context addresses the way all the elements (that is, body, different clothes and accessories, and grooming) "fit" together as a whole, the larger social context is concerned more generally with how separate appearances compare with one another to define the situation.

Appearance is a whole—a framework or configuration—that is often ordered by rules or principles of interpretation and placement. These rules are often supplied by culture and enable perceivers to make sense of the appearances they behold. Culture provides guidelines as to how we can interpret the meaning of clothes and/or what articles of clothing should be worn together. For example, take note of the German man's appearance in Figure 7-1. German culture provides the "rules" that compel him to wear knee socks with shorts (*lederhosen*) and to wear a green hat. We can look at this appearance and the way all of these parts "fit together" based on these rules of association. Then, looking at the appearance as a whole, we can interpret that this man is German based on rules of interpretation. Of course, the setting—a small town in Bavaria—also helps. Nevertheless, his appearance may be contrasted with that of persons surrounding him, such as the man observing him to the right. This man also wears traditional German attire, but his appearance is governed by different rules. Still other passers-by might be American tourists whose appearances are set apart from these men's. These differences among appearances help to make up the social context that set the stage for rules of interpretation. Therefore, we seldom see a person's appearance in a vacuum; rather, we use surrounding cues to make sense of that appearance.

In this chapter we will focus on the qualities and characteristics of appearance as a visual context, considering:

**FIGURE 7-1**
*Bavarian culture in Germany provides the "rules" that guide what items this man wears together—lederhosen (leather shorts), knee socks, a hat, and so on. Appearance becomes a context in and of itself, with each of the component parts fitting together to compose the whole. Photo by Susan B. Kaiser.*

*1.* How clothes and styles of appearance management derive their meanings.

*2.* How elements of appearance (body, hair, hat, shorts, and socks), taken together, make up a visual context. Here we are interested in the underlying guidelines on what articles of clothing can or should be worn together. For example, a man's business suit is often associated in people's minds with a tie. We also tend to "connect" socks with shoes, pajamas with robes, and tank tops with shorts. See Figure 7-2 for an illustration of the associations that tend to guide perceivers' impressions of males' and females' business suits.

In this chapter, we will also explore the basic elements of appearance and characteristics of appearance messages as compared with other forms of communication. In this way, we can address the unique qualities of appearance messages and understand how these qualities influence our perceptions.

**FIGURE 7-2**
*Research by Scherbaum and Shepherd (1987) indicates that perceivers evaluate a man's appearance more favorably when he wears a vest with a suit jacket as opposed to a vest without a suit jacket. This distinction between wearing and not wearing a jacket is not as critical in perceptions of a woman's appearance. Additionally, perceivers are more receptive to a woman wearing a red suit than they are to a man in a suit of that color. These findings suggest that the cultural rules linked to a businesslike appearance are still more stringent for men than they are for women. That is, in the professional context, women are afforded more latitude than men in terms of aesthetic codes governing how clothes should be layered and what colors they may be. Drawing by Wendy Dildey, adapted from Scherbaum and Shepherd (1987).*

## Appearance Signs

**Material versus Symbolic Properties**

Clothing has a dual role: It functions as a tangible thing and also as a **sign** (Bogatyrev, 1976; Delaporte, 1980). The concept of sign has been defined various ways by different authors. Some of these differences may be attributed to the types of signs they have written about (for example, words versus objects); still other variations are due to usage of the term in different disciplines. For our purposes, a sign is anything that has *social meaning* or that refers to something else. The close connection between thing and sign in one object is not unique to clothing. A car is also likely to be a sign, as are any other consumer products that are valued by the owners. Yet clothing is one of the most eloquent and powerful products we use; it is an *expressive* medium, or a concrete way of revealing particular ideas in the mind that cannot be otherwise articulated (McCracken, 1988). The object and sign are linked in a way that is highly visual, connected intimately with the person (owner), and conducive to every social dimension of daily life.

What is the difference between a thing and a sign? Essentially, the world around us displays two kinds of material objects: those with and those without any ideological significance (reference to other cultural beliefs). Yet even the most ordinary object may become a sign. For example, a person may take a sea shell from the beach into the home and turn it into a decorative object for the bathroom. It now is not only linked to the beach, as in nature, but is also likely to be associated with the homeowner's aesthetic taste and feelings about the beach. The sea shell has become a *sign* as people interpret what it implies about the homeowner and to what it refers. Virtually all clothes and accessories are likely to become signs, or to *signify* information. Yet it is essential to remember that clothes and accessories do not have intrinsic meanings of their own. In other words, their meanings are not merely established when the objects are created and then ingrained as *the* meaning. A designer may have a meaning in mind while creating, but regardless of his or her intent, consumers themselves assign meaning to clothes and accessories as they interact and influence one another. The meanings we associate with clothes emerge and change as a function of social interaction. We obtain our ideas about what clothes *mean* from our observations and interpretations in everyday life. We learn, for example, that a bathing suit would be considered inappropriate for a formal restaurant, that men seldom wear skirts in most Western societies (with the exception of the Scottish kilt), and that certain items of women's attire (for example, spiked high-heeled sandals and teddies) have erotic connotations.

At the same time, clothes tend to have a practical function; they can serve more than one purpose. Let's look at an example of how we can view clothing in more than one way, depending on our knowledge of how it can signify (mean) certain information. This example comes from Bogatyrev's (1976) study of Russian folk costume:

> Let us imagine that we obtain the dresses of a rich peasant woman and of a
> poor peasant woman from some village, for instance from Vajnor in the Bratislava

area where formerly rich peasant women embroidered their sleeves with gold and the poor only with silk, and that we send these dresses to a secondhand dealer in town. Even if the dealer should not know that both costumes were symbols of class distinction between peasants, he still would appraise the sleeves differently, judging them as material objects (p. 15).

In this example, the appraiser is likely to rely on the material properties of the sleeves to assess the worth of the costumes, whether or not he or she knows about the more abstract, social-class meanings.

Bogatyrev goes on to note that in certain special cases, however, the social distinctiveness of clothing may appear as a sign only. For example, a military uniform has certain details that indicate the rank and rights of the wearer in the army. When a private sees a uniformed officer, he or she knows the implications of the uniform; the quality or aesthetics of the uniform is irrelevant. A secondhand dealer who is unaware of military symbolism would be unlikely to "appreciate" the differences between a private's and a colonel's uniform, and therefore would evaluate the "worth" of these two uniforms equally, based on their material properties.

Bogatyrev (1976) also notes that some of the functions of folk costume are also derived solely from its property as a sign. For example, an unwed mother may be obligated to wear certain items of costume, and neighbors note that she wears this type of attire rather than those appropriate for a "maiden." The quality of material and the aesthetics of the garment are irrelevant; what is relevant is the social meaning attached to the costume, known only to those who understand the culture.

## The Parts and the Whole

Here, our focus is not so much on *what* appearance means as it is on *how* appearance means, and part of the "how" involves culturally patterned ways of thinking about appearance. For example, we can consider the various components of a police officer's appearance: a hat, shirt, badge, belt, pants, shoes, and tools and weapons. Each component part is distinctive, but the effect it has on our perception is derived from the whole ensemble. When one part of the ensemble—one sign unit—is altered, the entire appearance context is altered (Manning, 1987). For example, a baseball cap may be substituted for a traditional police hat; this baseball cap may then be contrasted with the message supplied to an observer by the gun. (A baseball cap may seem to contribute to a friendly impression, whereas a gun is viewed as serious.) Also, the entire uniform serves to differentiate the police officer from the average citizen.

It becomes clear at this point that if we want to understand how appearance *means*, we need to pursue three tasks: (1) dissect the appearance into component parts and interpret the meanings of these parts, (2) identify the rules of association among the component parts (Holman, 1980), and (3) compare the meaning of one appearance (as a whole) with another "whole" appearance. The way the parts and the whole of appearance communicate in everyday life works in part on the *principle of contrast* (Manning, 1987): (*a*) by what *is* versus *is not* carried or worn, (*b*) by how different elements of appearance may seem to contradict one another, or (*c*) by how one person's appearance may be distinguished from another person's. Let's explore these points by considering the appearance in Figure 7-3. First, we can look at the specific elements that make up this appearance (hat, sunglasses, "public enemy" T-shirt, baggy shorts, and high tops). Each of these items may be interpreted separately and contrasted with what *is not* worn. One might imagine the difference in the ensemble if the hat were missing, or if a tuxedo jacket was worn instead of the T-shirt. Second, we can examine how the different articles of dress "work together" to make up a visual image. Does the hat seem to "contradict" the shirt? Do certain articles seem to go together, like the sunglasses and hat, to create a certain mood or impression? Would you find it unusual, in conjunction with the rest of this appearance, if this male were wearing knee socks like the German man in Figure 7-1? Third, we can consider this appearance as a whole and contrast it to other images (male police officer or college professor).

**FIGURE 7-3**
*How does the "principle of contrast" apply to this male's appearance? Note the combination of the "public enemy" T-shirt, the long shorts, the high-top tennis shoes, and the sunglasses with a traditional man's hat. Photo by Wendy Dildey.*

## *Semiotic Analysis of Appearance*

You will recall from Chapters One and Two that semiotics involves the study of signs and that semiotics may be explored within the cultural perspective. Semiotics provides concepts and methods for analyzing the visual context of appearance and its potential in communication:

> Clothing usage forms a semiotic system. Because clothing can be easily manipulatable by the individual, it falls into the realm of voluntary activity. It is, in fact, the most easily controllable aspect of the external environment of the individual (Holman, 1980).

Semiotic analysis encourages us to note the significance of the sender and receiver of signs, as well as the message, the channel used and the style of its communication. Again, it is important to stress that the meaning of signs is not *intrinsically* linked to the signs themselves, but rather that the signs acquire their meanings through processes of interpretation. The meanings associated with signs in general, and appearance in particular, tend to be tentative, or subject to change. In everyday social contexts, signs begin to hold some associations for us or make sense to us. Signs serve to represent social values, illustrate or express personal feelings and ambitions, and depict what we wish to convey about ourselves.

Semiotic analysis provides methods for pursuing the understanding of appearance, focusing on the component parts of appearance and how these parts influence one another. For example, consider the South American women's hats in Figure 7-4. In North American culture, these hats may be evaluated as masculine, but in the context of the cultural context depicted in the picture, North American observers are able to surmise that these hats hold different associations in South America. Even when we lack a cultural framework for interpretation, then, we are influenced by the other cues (clothes and gender) in a given appearance.

Semiotics also deals with how messages can develop in one context and possibly move across contextual boundaries (Manning, 1987, p. 44). For example, in the 1980s the rock singer Madonna "borrowed" appearance cues normally associated with religious contexts (for example, a cross or crucifix necklace), juxtaposed these cues with those holding erotic cultural connotations (black bra, corset, and black leather), and created a new kind of appearance context. Thus, her appearance as a whole context required a new framework or set of rules of association, for purposes of interpretation. Individual cues (cross and black bra) moved across contextual boundaries (religious and erotic, respectively) into a new appearance context calling for a new mode of perception.

Semiotic analysis is largely based on two principles in relation to appearance. First, there is the idea that a system or structural context exists and precedes the emergence of a particular sign or symbol. For example, a black bra was part of an erotic appearance context even before Madonna used it. The bra itself,

*FIGURE 7-4*

*Traditional bowler or derby hats are worn by Aymará Indian women in Peru and Bolivia. This style might be construed as masculine by North American and European standards; clearly, it is important to view the hats within their cultural context and to avoid imposing the rules or codes of one's own culture on them. Photo by Stephen Cunha.*

then, served to represent a more general erotic context, and Madonna used it for those purposes, as a component part in her own appearance. After she devised her own visual context, some new associations emerged for the black bra. Now it could be seen as being associated with a new set of appearance elements, including religious ones. Second, this system or structural context designates the nature of the associations among signs (Manning, 1987, p. 26). Madonna's appearance developed a new set of associations among such cues as crosses, black leather, lace, and black bras. Despite the presence of a system or structural context, however, signs are human constructions, and they make communication possible. Wearing certain clothes and engaging in various appearance-managing processes are part of this vital process of *making things mean*. Therefore, although culture tends to provide guidelines or systems for managing and perceiving appearance, there is often a great deal of room for individual freedom and expression.

Once we have discovered the underlying rules of association that compose a "system," it becomes easier to bend these rules, distort or exaggerate them, or break them. Fashion change promotes such an interplay with appearance-related rules. Designers are especially likely to manipulate these rules, but consumers are also prone to do so as they coordinate ensembles, mix and match, and reconcile a total look by "softening" its impact or integrating component parts.

See Figure 7-5 for an extreme example of this kind of manipulation of rules. A clown purposely juxtaposes signs that were derived from distinct systems (for example, a tie from a business context and a Mickey Mouse sweatshirt from leisure context). A more subtle form of manipulating and "breaking" rules is depicted in Figure 7-6.

We can distinguish two concepts that help to clarify the contrast between culturally provided rules of association and individual manipulation of these rules. **Code** refers to the rules of association or underlying patterns provided by culture. It is like a kind of protocol or "etiquette" for dressing. This concept is derived from that of *language* in semiotics (Barthes, 1988; Simon-Miller, 1985). Culture provides the tools we have with which to groom and dress ourselves and affords certain principles to guide how we can, should, or must use these tools. For example, by convention, a male wearing a business suit also wears (a shirt and) tie.

    In contrast, the concept of **message** refers to individuals' own manipulations of appearance rules and is derived from the semiotic concept of *speech* (Barthes,

## Code and Message

**FIGURE 7-5**
*Clowns help to create a context of "play" by manipulating and breaking traditional "rules" about what elements of appearance "fit" together. Photo by Mark Jordan.*

**FIGURE 7-6**
*Unique appearances can be constructed in everyday life by combining garments and accessories as shown here. The resulting look evolves from a manipulation of rules and represents a new concept that has little to do with the component parts' (petticoat, high tops) previous associations. Photo by Jock Sturgus.*

1988; Simon-Miller, 1985). Through expression, individuals fashion (make or create) their own appearances. Symbolic interactionist Gregory Stone (1965) would have called these created appearances "programs." By developing such programs, individuals can derive a sense of personal style or derive "fashion statements." Table 7-1 summarizes the differences between code and message. Note that code is *culturally* prescribed, whereas message is *individually* created. This distinction is illustrated in Figure 7-7.

It becomes evident that codes provide a cultural frame of reference for interpreting appearance. In other words, we come to expect certain combinations of appearance parts. Imagine a male wearing a tie, but no shirt, to a job interview. Granted, he has taken his roommate's advice and has worn a tie, but his appearance (and lack of a shirt) violates the convention of appropriate interview attire. Now

**TABLE 7-1**
*Appearance Codes and Messages*

| Appearance Code | Appearance Message |
| --- | --- |
| Convention | Expression |
| Cultural schema | Individual act |
| Fashion as institution | Personal fashion statement |
| Facilitates expression (individual acts) | Produces new conventions (cultural codes) |
| System of meaning | Meaning as process |

let us look at this same appearance in a different social context—a nightclub for women only. Now the appearance context in question shifts from a possible meaning of inappropriateness to one of sexual suggestiveness. Different rules of association are applied in these two social contexts, and it becomes evident that appearance context structures meaning, being mediated by social circumstance.

Thus a structuralist point of view suggests that we should consider how much our thinking (the mental images we hold or rules of association we apply) produces social meanings or interpretations. At the same time, changing social realities create new ways of thinking (Manning, 1987, p. 31). Once a perceiver has seen a male wearing a tie without a shirt, that appearance context no longer seems implausible, but is still likely to be associated only with particular social contexts, because the principles guiding the association of a shirt with a tie are still linked to strong cultural convention.

On the other hand, there are infinite possibilities for the act of expression, especially outside the realm of uniforms or career apparel. Expression allows for "active consumer participation in the sign production process (by encouragement of flexibility and creativity rather than conformity to a socioeconomic code or to a fashion consensus)" (Simon-Miller, 1985, pp. 80–81). Acts of expression keep individual contributions to fashion change alive and help avoid the translation of personal style into an institutional mode.

Now we have considered signs within the context of appearance, as well as the manipulation of the rules of association governing these signs through the coordination of, and interplay between, convention and expression. At this point we need to turn to a closer inspection of signs and consider how they come to assume meaning in the minds of beholders.

## Analyzing Signs

Since by definition a sign represents or stands for something else, two component parts of signs may be delineated for purposes of closer scrutiny: signifier and signified. The **signifier** is the vehicle through which a sign conveys its message. Clothes and other accessories, as well as hairstyles and other grooming styles, can be conceptualized as vehicles that have the potential for carrying a message. Once the message becomes time-worn, irrelevant, or unexciting, then the vehicle may cease to convey the message in question. This point raises some critical questions, if we desire to compare appearance messages to words. Why do some ordinary words such as *cat* and *dog* continue to hold their meanings after hundreds of years of usage, whereas other words (*groovy* and *radical*) seem to be more

**FIGURE 7-7**
*African culture is an important part of the lives of these black newlyweds from Philadelphia (spending their honeymoon in San Francisco). They have just had a traditional Yoruban wedding, and they are authors of short stories based on folktales of African origin. Their appearances draw on codes in African as well as North American cultures. Yet these codes are combined as different ethnic elements are mixed together and interpreted in a way that makes the resulting appearance messages personally satisfying and meaningful. Codes are culturally based, whereas messages are individually constructed. Photo by Carla M. Freeman.*

time-bound? A parallel may be seen when we contrast "classic" styles such as business suits with trendy styles such as bicycle shorts. Still, appearance messages, as *signifiers*, are extremely complex because of the potential for mixing and matching, fashion change, and other characteristics related to the visual realm. Whereas the signifier is the medium that *carries* the message, the *signified* is the actual content of the message, as shown below.

$$\textit{\textbf{sign}}$$
$$\swarrow \qquad \searrow$$

| *signifier* | *signified* |
|---|---|
| *artifact* | *message* |
| *vehicle* | *concept* |
| *tangible* | *abstract idea* |
| *image* | *ideology* |

A signifier may be a complete appearance (a whole) as well as a particular unit or element of that appearance (a part—a shoe, a hairstyle, or a garment). In fact, we normally see people's appearances in their entirety, so it is important to recognize that signifiers may be complete appearances or images. Consider the ensemble in Figure 7-8. This style was introduced to the public after World War II and was labelled the "New Look." What was *signified* by this ensemble

**FIGURE 7-8**
*Designer Christian Dior's 1947 "New Look" (like any other look or even a single element of a look) illustrates the concept of signifier. The signifier (image, look, or silhouette) is the medium or vehicle that carries a message (what is signified —in this case, newness and change from the styles of the Second World War). Photo courtesy of the Trustees of the Victoria and Albert Museum.*

was newness and a rather drastic change from the shorter, narrower skirts during the war period.

The signifier, then, is the tangible, concrete, visual, and physical artifact (clothes) or image (appearance) through which meaning is conveyed. The signified, on the other hand, is more abstract and intangible; it is the concept or idea to which a signifier refers. How do these two concepts connect and relate to the concept of appearance sign? The appearance sign is the union of the signifier and the signified; it is similar to a composite of a tangible artifact (part) or image (whole) and an intangible idea or message. Therefore, an appearance sign is at once concrete (tangible) and abstract (intangible).

The union or linkage of the signifier and signified is made possible through codes of interpretation or understanding. The concept of **code**, introduced in Chapter Two, becomes the principle of association that enables us to link the signifier with the signified, all within our minds (and influenced by social context). We have already considered the rules of association that link one sign with another in an appearance context; such rules of association also may be referred to as codes. Therefore, there are two types of codes that are relevant to a discussion of appearance: (1) those that link signifier with signified within a specific sign, and (2) those that link the signs themselves within the context of an appearance. See Figure 7-9 for an illustration of these two types of codes.

Therefore, a code, in the more general sense, is an underlying set of rules governing signs (connecting signifier with signified) and linking signs into a larger system of signs. A code makes it possible for appearance to convey meaning (F. Davis, 1985; Simon-Miller, 1985).

The fit between signifier and signified, or the code that links them, may range from tight and precise to diffuse and ambiguous. The next section shows how signs may be distinguished on the basis of this fit.

## Variations in Appearance Signs

Sociologist Nathan Joseph (1986) distinguishes between two kinds of appearance signs, on the basis of the degree of complexity of the codes used to interpret them: signal and symbol. A **signal** is a relatively straightforward, easy-to-interpret appearance sign, based on a simple cognitive link between the signifier and the signified. The cognitive process involved in making straightforward connections between signifier and signified may be referred to as **signaling**. Some examples of appearance signals might include a police uniform or a business suit, when they are worn in contexts where a perceiver would normally expect to see them and does not need to concentrate on (or even consciously note) their meaning(s). The cognitive link between police uniform and police officer, or business suit and professional, is relatively straightforward. However, if these clothing styles are worn in unexpected contexts or by persons one would not expect to see wearing them, then they do not necessarily function as signals. For example, if a uniformed police officer walks into a college classroom, more interpretation is required than if she is seen in a police car. Therefore, the social context becomes a critical factor in whether or not a specific appearance functions as a signal.

**FIGURE 7-9**
*Let's consider two types of appearance codes. First, there is the type of code that links the signifier with the signified. This student's tie-dyed T-shirt, accessories, and apron compose an appearance that signifies (refers to) her identity as the "bagel lady" at a natural-food coffee house. That is, the code helps us to link the signifier (appearance) with what is signified (her identity). Her fellow workers as well as her customers (especially the "regulars") are well aware of this code and have come to develop a mental association between the signifier and the signified, especially in this situational context. Second, we can consider the type of code that links the different elements of her appearance together. The tie-dyed T-shirt, accessories, and natural look (lack of heavy makeup) all "fit" together, because there is a late-1960s-influenced association (or late 1980s version thereof) that provides a historical and cultural context for her appearance. Photo by Wendy Dildey.*

A **symbol**, on the other hand, is more complex and intricate, in terms of the link between signifier and signified. This link is not as likely as that found in a signal to be simple or straightforward. The cognitive activity of **symboling** is required when more interpretation is needed. It may be that the appearance in question conveys meanings about values, beliefs, and emotions. These meanings are harder to put into words, the codes are more complex and variable, and more concentration or conscious attention is required on the part of a perceiver. Accordingly, social interactions become critical as participants negotiate and renegotiate or socially construct and reconstruct meaning.

A sign, then, can be either a symbol or a signal depending on the kind of mental activity or type of cognitive processing in which the perceiver (and wearer, too) is involved. Social context may trigger one activity or the other (signaling or symboling). Whether appearance signs function as signals or symbols is not dependent on the items of clothes themselves, or hairstyles, facial hair, or makeup. The difference between a signal and a symbol is not absolute and distinct then, but is dependent on the context in which appearance signs are viewed and the mental processes participants use to interpret them. *Signification* is a process of making things mean, and a perceiver is a vital part of this process (MacCannell and MacCannell, 1982). Thus, social-cognitive processes are critically linked to the interpretation of appearance signs. At the same time, it is important to recognize that convention provides the means for interpreting some appearance signs more readily than others.

At times, culture provides an explicit code or close or tight fit between signifier and signified. The concept of **semanticity** refers to the degree of associative "fit," or the correlation or close connection between an appearance sign and its referent (Harrison, 1985). A code that is high in semanticity is likely to be linked to conventional attire and to clothes that function as signals. On the other hand, a "fuzzy" connection between signifier and signified, or a lack of specific rules for interpretation, is likely to promote the functioning of clothing as a symbol—arousing emotion and referring to values but not neatly pigeonholed.

The concept of meaning is central not only to a cultural and semiotic point of view but also to the symbolic-interactionist perspective, which promotes the idea that everyday interactions must be studied in process, in naturalistic contexts as they occur, if we are to understand how meaning is conveyed through the give and take of social life (Blumer, 1969a). In the symbolic realm of appearance, meanings enable us to (1) interpret what is occurring and (2) organize our actions toward one another.

In everyday life, appearance signs are used as a cue for understanding others with whom we come into contact. Because appearance is a seemingly silent and visible form of communication, as contrasted with conversation, it is classified in the realm of nonverbal communication.

## Appearance as Nonverbal Communication

All too often, the importance of appearance is disregarded or overlooked in the study of communication, which tends to suffer from a "discursive bias" (Stone, 1965). This means that when we think of communication, we ordinarily think of having the ability to *discuss* during the course of interaction. If we want to change the subject when we are speaking, we can easily do so. If we want to clarify a point that seems uncertain, there are means for accomplishing this when engaging in conversation. And, if we want to elaborate on a theme or argue an alternative viewpoint, language and the act of conversation provide adequate mechanisms. In contrast, when we *appear* before others, we cannot discuss through this medium of communication. We have decided before interaction occurs (in the "backstage" of grooming and dressing rituals) what messages we would like to convey and to whom we especially want to convey them. Yet once interaction begins (in the "front stage"), we cannot easily shift the subject of our appearances (change what is signified) or repair unwanted messages through appearance alone. If we desire to negotiate the meaning of our appearances with others, it becomes necessary to resort to conversation, to explain who we are and what we represent and what we anticipate for interaction.

At the same time, it is important to recognize that appearance is a form of communication in its own right, and it is not the only type of communication that is frequently overlooked or taken for granted. Other nonverbal forms of communication, many of which are to varying degrees discursive (for example, gestures, facial expressions, and bodily positions) are also studied less than conversation, a linguistic form of communication (based on language).

Communication is based not only on language, but also on the senses, including vision, tactile sensations (feel), smell, and taste (Wilden, 1987, p. 137). Vision is the most fundamental sense involved in appearance communication, but the other senses function as well, for example, when clothing is touched or worn or the aromas of others are smelled. (In cases where perceivers are visually impaired, tactile sensation of clothes and a sender's physical features, as well as the sense of smell, become increasingly significant.)

The realm of nonverbal communication, then, includes personal appearance as well as gestures, facial expression, and bodily positions. Where do clothes and appearance fit into larger schemes of communication? It is helpful to look at different types of nonverbal communication, based on varying codes and functioning through diverse channels. Four types of nonverbal codes may be distinguished: artifactual, body, media, and spatiotemporal (Harrison, 1985). Each of these codes is broader in scope than is their relation to appearance. The first two codes most directly bear on personal appearance, but the other two may be intricately linked to it as well.

*Artifactual Codes*

Culture provides objects and artifacts that are imbued with meaning in the domain of consumer behavior. Products that consumers select and use are associated, in a cultural sense, with qualities or attributes they would like others to assign to them. Obviously, clothes are consumer products, and therefore cultural artifacts, as are shoes, jewelry, or any other commodities that serve to express identity or intent. Artifacts that carry meaning are both things and signs.

Variables such as color, texture, pattern, form, and design influence how garments, parts of garments, or combinations of garments are perceived. These variables appear to be subject to aesthetic rules (principles of design such as balance and proportion) as they blend with social and cultural rules (see Figure 7-10). Social Focus 7-1 considers this blend of rules that influence perceptions of clothing.

Although clothing is clearly classified as an artifactual code in communication, it interacts with the other three codes in the sphere of nonverbal communication. Personal appearance per se is connected with, and made up of, the interplay between artifactual and body codes. Similarly, clothing-related elements and body-related elements are what jointly compose an appearance context (Hillestad, 1980).

*Body Codes*

Body codes arise from personal appearance and the movement of the body and face. These codes govern and link variables such as physical attractiveness, size

**FIGURE 7-10**
*Let's consider the variables subject to aesthetic rules and cultural codes in this gown and jacket designed by Mariano Fortuny around 1920. Note how a visual sense of balance and proportion is created through the use of lines, textures, and shapes. Cultural codes connecting the resulting design to qualities such as formality and elegance may also be deciphered in this style. Photo courtesy of the Trustees of the Victoria and Albert Museum.*

of the body, facial expressions, gestures (for example, waving, pointing, or saluting), and bodily positions (how one sits, stands, or moves). Therefore, the appearance of the body when it is still or moving comprises the domain of body codes. Clearly, communication through the body can be more discursive when movement is involved, but even when still its visibility conveys messages.

Robert Hillestad (1980) regards the body as a vehicle for dress and distinguishes three kinds of bodily expression: body form, body surface, and body motion. Body form refers to the shape of the body or its constituent parts. The

# Aesthetic Rules in Context

The aesthetic experience of perceiving clothing is based in part on its structure. However, in recent years there has been a breakdown of many conventional aesthetic rules. Punk and postpunk aesthetics relied on experimentation with, and exploitation of, such rules. Fashion change, then, is intricately linked to changing ideas about aesthetic rules. What is considered beautiful in one period of time may be viewed as unpleasing to the eye in another.

Aesthetic rules are culturally derived and tend to change with fashion, but in part they are based on fundamental principles of design (that is, proportion, balance, emphasis, and rhythm). The complexity of understanding apparel structure stems from the blending of aesthetic codes and social and cultural trends. It seems that apparel designers command considerable latitude in their interpretations of aesthetic rules, according to a study conducted by Elizabeth Lowe (1984). She examined magazine pictures of women's evening apparel from 1926 to 1980, to see if the theories about aesthetic rules were consistent with the empirical reality. The dimensions of skirt length, waist length, décolletage (neckline) length, skirt width, waist width, and décolletage width were measured and then converted to relational ratios.

Lowe found that there was a lack of uniformity in these ratios. Skirt width seemed to have greater freedom to vary than did waist length or width. The aesthetic rule of avoiding too much sameness (for example, too much width in all dimensions) was broken in some cases; in fact, some designers seemed to have actively sought to achieve sameness. Still, they did not combine wide waists with wide décolletage. Perhaps this may be explained in part by the Western ideal of beauty, in which there is a marked preference for vertical emphasis.

It seems that designers were careful not to cut the body in half with the position of the waistline relative to the hemline, nor did they create skirts that were as wide as they were long. Overall, however, Lowe (1984) concluded that several of the rules associated with design principles were simply not supported empirically and proposed three alternative conclusions: (1) The rules are wrong, (2) the designers are creating an abundance of poor designs, or (3) they are breaking rules but still somehow are creating pleasing designs by compensating in some way. Lowe indicated that she is inclined to believe that a "hierarchical structure exists in the ordering of these rules such that some rules may be broken with greater impunity than others and still a pleasing effect may be achieved," especially if compensating elements are operating (Lowe, 1984, p. 181).

To enhance our understanding of the importance of aesthetic rules, it is important to consider consumers, as well as designers. Although research is needed to see if consumers rely on aesthetic rules in their evaluations of apparel, it is clear that aesthetics in general are important to them. Research indicates that aesthetics are likely to win out over utility in terms of how female consumers value apparel (Morganosky, 1984). Showing good taste and enhancing one's own beauty seem to be among the most important factors influencing the apparel selection of female consumers (Woods, Padgett, and Montoya, 1987). In a study of male and female consumers, aesthetic appeal appeared to be more closely related to clothing preferences than were economic and performance characteristics (Lubner-Rupert and Winakor, 1985). Clearly, consumer aesthetics "matter" and deserve further attention. Part of the complexity in studying consumer aesthetics is that evaluative or appreciative responses interact with other variables (for example, fashion change and social context). Moreover, consumers vary in their interpretations of what is beautiful. There is "meaningful heterogeneity" in their preference structures (Holbrook, 1986).

As we attempt to understand the role of aesthetic rules in perception, it is important, then, to recognize that aesthetic judgments are participatory. That is, consumers take part in a process that evokes feelings and emotions. In other words, we do not live by rules alone; neither do designers—they may actually manipulate and bend rules as they create. To focus strictly on aesthetic rules about what "works" is to promote the idea that aesthetic judgments are always analytical and detached. There is a paradox in aesthetic judgments of clothing in that some degree of this type of detachment is probably necessary to enjoy the visual qualities of a garment, but conformance to aesthetic rules alone are not enough to "make" a successful garment.

Active enjoyment of beauty involves a certain paradox. Detachment is required, and yet the attitude of the detached observer, sensing the surface and discerning the form of an aesthetic object, is not enough. Pure detachment is aesthetically barren (Wheelwright, 1960, p. 357).

appearance of body form can be altered through the use of articles of clothing and accessories. Factors such as fit, clinginess of a fabric, and actual configurations of garment parts (for example, sleeves and skirts) can visually create or re-create body form. Body surfaces include such factors as the color and texture of skin and hair (see Social Focus 7-2 for a discussion of the color of clothing as it relates to that of physical features). The appearance of body surfaces may be visually altered through the use of cosmetics or apparel. For example, hose tend to change the surface characteristics of legs. Body motions include individual posture, gait, gestures, and facial expressions. Again, clothes can influence the manner in which body motions are visually perceived. A dancer wearing and using scarves in her routine can accentuate her bodily movements, for example.

Awareness of bodily shapes in one's self or others may complement an awareness of clothing elements, but it may also supersede awareness of clothing in importance. For instance, a man may notice a woman's curves or legs as accentuated by clothes and shoes (for example, a tight skirt and high heels), but he may not later be able to describe the clothes and shoes, or even consciously notice them during the actual observation. The concern here is with the way the body looks, rather than with the clothes themselves.

Of course, we rarely see bodies without clothes in social situations. So it is important to consider how clothes function with body codes to alter, clarify, exaggerate, or contradict those codes (see Figure 7-11).

Research suggests that perceivers have the ability to distinguish between impressions made on the basis of bodies and clothes (Conner, Peters, and Nagasawa, 1975). Subjects were shown a series of photographs of three different females. One female appeared rather athletic in appearance, with a stocky build and short hair. Another female appeared intellectual, with a slightly more serious expression and her hair in a bun. The third female was intended to look friendly and sociable. She had long hair and a smile on her face. Three forms of dress were manipulated as variables in conjunction with the bodily types used. One costume was meant to be sociable, one intellectual, and one athletic. The costume (clothing style) was more important than the body type in the perceivers' development of impressions of sociability, whereas the body was more important in determining the impression of being athletic, as measured by the use of such adjectives as *robust* versus *frail*. Even when the athletic person was pictured in the sociable or intellectual clothing, the impression remained athletic. The individuals without the athletic body type did not appear to be more athletic as a result of wearing the athletic costume. Neither the body nor the costume communicated an intellectual impression to a significant extent. The social impression was highest when the models were consistent with the clothes on them. In other words, the models were seen as more social when the athletic costume was on the athletic body, the social costume on the social body, and the intellectual costume on the intellectual body. Apparently the consistency between the two was an important factor in the subjects' impressions. Basically, this study tells us that although there is a tendency for perceivers to view appearances holistically, they do have the perceptual ability to distinguish the

## Personal Color Analysis

Most women grew up with an elaborate set of rules, which were usually passed on by their mothers, concerning the relationship between color in dress and the natural color of their hair and skin. Some black women were told not to wear red. Others were told not to wear black. . . . Redheads were constantly warned against wearing red or pink. As a blond, I was told I shouldn't wear yellow because it made my hair look so yellow. A childhood friend of mine whose distinguishing features were emerald-green eyes was cautioned against red on the ground that it "makes you look like a Christmas tree." With these endless injunctions in mind, it's hardly surprising that many women regard color as a minefield and fall back on neutral choices that are unlikely to give offense.

— JACOBY, 1986

What was left at one time to a kind of personal color folklore, passed on from one generation to the next, was transformed in the 1970s into big business. Rules related to personal color were organized into "systems" based on the premise that each individual looks best in a specific set of colors that are determined by skin, hair, eye color, bone structure, and sometimes even personality (Rasband, 1983). Towns and cities throughout the United States today have personal color analysts or wardrobe consultants who categorize their clients based on their "reading" of the clients' personal features. Ironically, this process emphasizes that each consumer has individual uniqueness, even though each one is "squeezed . . . into one of three or four molds" (Abramov, 1985).

The most prevalent system has been the "seasons" system, in which consumers are typed as fall, winter, spring, or summer. Systems such as this one are used to develop "personal palettes" for consumers; these palettes composed of the consumer's "ideal colors" govern his or her choice in clothes, jewelry, shoes, and sometimes even interior decorating and automobile color. Academics who study color are concerned that individual choice and creative expression are diminished by color typing. In the process, what is probably the complex and stimulating element of design is oversimplifed, and consumers may feel locked into a system in which they are eventually likely to experience: (1) boredom with wearing only the "right colors" (and, indeed, often great difficulty even finding them in the marketplace) or (2) feelings of guilt if they take their color palettes seriously but instead wear their old "wrong" favorites (Rasband, 1983).

Other concerns stem from the fact that color systems are supposedly based on more than rules of etiquette (merely opinions of arbiters of good taste and behavior). In fact, they are said to be based on rules with a factual basis. Yet color science does not support the concept of color palettes or categories such as those promoted by these systems. Moreover, there is no good evidence (1) that facial colorings can be categorized or that facial coloring determines color preference, (2) that color preferences and personality are related to each each other, or (3) that individuals' lives will improve if they wear colors in their palettes (Abramov, 1985).

Moreover, even if we assume the systems are valid in the first place, anecdotal evidence abounds that they are not applied consistently by analysts. Some clients have received diametrically opposed advice from different analysts (Abramov, 1985).

I have, on separate occasions, been typed a Winter (most common), an Autumn, and also a Summer. Typed as a Winter by a Beauty For All Seasons analyst, I was told I "should never wear" my favorite olive-green Austrian cape because it was attractive on Autumns only. . . . Over the years, I have been told, I'm never supposed to wear black, always supposed to wear black, and sometimes supposed to wear black—as long as it's accompanied by tan or beige. I've been told to wear white but not ivory, or ivory but not white. I've been instructed to wear only silver jewelry but not gold, and gold but not silver. In Phoenix, Arizona, I wore a mixture of silver and gold chain necklaces. A woman from the audience asked me to remove the silver because "the ladies in our group have learned that gold and silver can't be mixed harmoniously." At an autograph party some months ago, a woman who identified herself as a color analyst complimented me for choosing a dress harmonious with my Winter warm tones. Within an hour at the same party, another analyst expressed regret that I was wearing a color so obviously inappropriate for my Season—Autumn (Rasband, 1983).

What is needed to sort out some of this color confusion is research on how people actually perceive themselves and others in certain colors, how and why people vary

**233**

## Social Focus 7-2 *(continued)*

in their perceptions of personal and clothing color combinations, and how these perceptions are influenced by contextual factors such as culture, fashion, and social meanings for certain situations.

Cross-cultural research has suggested that there are physiological, environmental, and cultural explanations for how we perceive color and its affective (feeling- and preference-oriented) meanings (Adams and Osgood,

1973). Perceptions of clothing color in the context of its visual impact against a background of skin, hair, and eye color are even more complex than perceptions of color alone. Hence, as we attempt to understand the meanings people assign to color in the context of personal appearance, it becomes imperative to factor in a range of variables and to acknowledge the intricacies in color choices and perceptions.

---

most relevant cues for the type of impression formed. In other words, appearance perceptions factor in the *context* of the type of impression in question. Therefore, the body is a more relevant cue than clothes in the formation of athletic impressions, but clothes are more relevant than the body in formulating impressions of sociability. The combined effect of the two is also important.

Clothing also serves to communicate jointly with discursive body codes. For example, a military salute (a discursive body code) is easier to interpret if an observed person is also wearing a military uniform, especially if individuals facing one another are not on a military base—a context in which military personnel in civilian attire often salute. Thus either the uniform or the setting can provide a context conducive to interpretation and definition. Similarly, a hitchhiker's chances of getting picked up are probably enhanced by a neat appearance. While a neat appearance may convey positive attributes about a hitchhiker, the "thumbing" gesture is imperative to conveying his or her intent. Thus perceivers driving by (or stopping) are likely to factor both appearance (including artifactual as well as body codes) and gestures (relying upon body codes) into their evaluation and decision as to whether to offer a ride.

*Media Codes*    In concert, the body and clothes make up appearance contexts that are visible and tangible, yet also refer to more abstract *social forms* having cultural and interpersonal significance in context. Culture provides appearance imagery through mass media, and the images we behold are likely to shape our perceptions of desirable appearances, of what is current or fashionable, of what it means to be male or female, and of how social reality is ordered. Movies, cartoons, television, music videos, advertisements, and magazines may all influence our interpretations of appearance in everyday communications.

In media life, appearance can become a kind of **format**. We come to expect certain styles of appearance in particular media, and these styles serve to facilitate shared understanding (Altheide and Snow, 1979). At the same time, the media may perpetuate stereotypes about different groups of people (see Figure 7-12).

*Spatiotemporal Codes*    Some codes refer to individuals' use of time and space in terms of social interaction. For example, studies indicate that males occupy more space in terms of bodily

**FIGURE 7-11**
Bodily movements give form to the body as well as to one's clothing. Note how this model's attire accentuates the impression conveyed through body codes. Photo by Mark Colman.

**FIGURE 7-12**
*Media codes or formats are used in animated cartoons to create a kind of "communication to the quick" (Harrison, 1981). Part of these codes or formats is based on a principle of exaggeration by means of caricatures or stereotypes. What are the various stereotyped characters in this cartoon? Photo by Susan B. Kaiser.*

position as compared to females. Males are more likely to spread their legs apart or fold their arms behind their heads (Henley, 1977).

Clothes are likely to be a factor in the amount of space one takes up because of bodily position. Goffman (1963) observed the public behavior of women in mental hospitals, to assess the degree of what he called "situational harness," and noted a link between body codes (manner of sitting) and artifactual codes (a dress) that is often taken for granted:

> The universality in our society of . . . limb discipline can be deeply appreciated on a chronic female ward where, for whatever reason, women indulge in zestful scratching of their private parts and in sitting with legs quite spread, causing the student to become conscious of the vast amount of limb discipline that is ordinarily taken for granted (p. 27).

Use of time is also governed by nonverbal codes. Studies indicate that males guard their time more carefully, and there seems to be a cultural idea that males' time is more valuable—that every second counts (Henley, 1977). Sommer, Gemulla, and Sommer (working paper) studied men's and women's watches and found that artifactual codes ordering perceptions of watches are linked to these cultural, gender-based distinctions. Males' watches tended to be more precise, being more likely to contain second hands and other mechanisms for scheduling time, evaluating how much time an event takes, and setting alarms. Females' watches, on the other hand, were more likely to be decorative and less precise in terms of "making every second count."

## *Characteristics of Appearance Messages*

Appearance signs serve to communicate at various levels of complexity in social interaction. In the simplest case, they denote or validate claims to membership in a particular group, cultural category (gender, age, social class, and ethnicity), or occupation, and verbal labels come to mind almost unconsciously: "female executive," "police officer," "football player," "ballet dancer," "fraternity member." Media codes may exaggerate these kinds of claims to membership by using "communication to the quick" (Harrison, 1981), based on codes that are high in semanticity through signs that function as signals, as Figure 7-12 revealed.

On the other hand, some appearance messages are rife with ambiguity, emotion, and expression. The meanings or associations connected with these messages are difficult to put into words or to describe, but sensibilities are aroused and experienced (see Figure 7-13). No ready labels come to mind.

Most everyday appearance messages fall somewhere in between total precision and total ambiguity. In real life, some interpretation and negotiation are required because of the interplay between person and context. The degree of fit between a clothed appearance and a context influences the degree of complexity of a visual impression. In fact, even when an appearance message seems relatively straightforward in its own right, the social context in which it is found can transform its meaning or raise new questions as to the appropriate interpretation.

**FIGURE 7-13**
*The messages associated with "wearable art" tend to be hard to pinpoint because no ready labels come to mind to characterize them (as compared to the stereotyped appearances in Figure 7-12). Wearable art deals with aesthetic qualities and evokes evaluative responses in perceivers. The designer of this ethnic-styled garment, Gayle M. Bon Durant, desires to convey a feeling of "richness and ceremony" in her work. Thus the message she intends by the piece is in the emotional realm of experience. Courtesy of Gayle M. Bon Durant; photo by Kathi Silva.*

To complicate matters further, seldom is only one meaning associated with an appearance message. More commonly, a range of possible meanings exist or meanings are layered on one another, almost creating a rainbow effect of meaning. Some meanings are derived from cultural experience, some are negotiated during social transactions, and some are conjured independently in the minds of participants. For two-way, meaningful communication to occur, the meaning intended by a programmed appearance should roughly coincide with that reviewed and interpreted by a perceiver. Note that the meaning does not need to be exactly the same; in fact, often a rough approximation of jointly constructed interpretation is sufficient to allow participants to understand one another and to proceed with communication. Alternatively, they give and take, clarify, and rearrange potential interpretations to mesh with some semblance of understanding. Even after meaning is assigned, there may be some "effort-after-meaning" (Davis, 1982) as potential interpretations are checked, refined, and modified.

By looking at specific characteristics of appearance messages, we can better understand how these messages are shaped and interpreted. In everyday life, the following characteristics tend to be interrelated and interconnected; together they shape the course of appearance as a unique form of communication.

## Nonlinguistic Characteristics

Appearance as a form of communication is transmitted primarily in the visual mode. A receiver's gaze is required (Enninger, 1985), and information is processed visually. As a general rule, appearance messages are *not* interpreted on the basis of a linguistic code (relying on words). Rather, they tend to be interpreted using *aesthetic codes*. There is a distinction between verbal cognition and visual cognition that parallels the contrast between the use of linguistic and aesthetic codes.

The nonlinguistic, aesthetic quality of appearance messages assumes significance in two ways. First, words seem to fail us when we attempt to *describe* appearance; it is difficult to express appearance through words to others in a way that evokes an image (picture) in their minds. This characteristic becomes evident when a friend describes what he or she plans to wear to a party. The receiver of the verbal message may conjure an image of an outfit and then be surprised to see the actual outfit at the party. Often, the verbal and the visual do not match. It is virtually impossible to describe all visible attributes (Peacock, 1986, p. 21). Therefore, when we perceive an appearance-related object, as well as a total appearance, we tend to rely on those attributes that are most salient to us.

Second, it is difficult to verbalize the *meaning* of an appearance message. Words may not exist to describe the emotions aroused or the feelings of appreciation or disgust. Receivers may find it challenging to express what they like or dislike about an appearance.

Clothes can convey messages that are inaccessible or inappropriate to language. So, given that appearance messages tend to be nonlinguistic, what does this mean in relation to the nature of their communicative value? Frequently, their meanings or significance cannot be verbalized, because aesthetic impressions are involved, just as we see paintings or sculptures with nonlinguistic eyes. It is difficult to "put into words" the emotions, sentiments, and intangible associations that clothes often convey. Appearance messages actually rely on codes that lie somewhere between aesthetics and language. At the aesthetic end of the continuum are signs such as wearable art, laden with emotional content. Often preferences and moods fall near this aesthetic side as well, when they are invoked on the basis of observing certain appearances. It may be possible to *feel* when observing appearances, but be unable to put these feelings to words, to like or dislike without really being able to explain why. Because appearance is visual and taken for granted in everyday life, there is probably a tendency not to verbalize messages conveyed, but rather to implicitly note them in passing (unless they require more diligent attention and interpretation). Therefore, it may become somewhat annoying if clothes become a prominent topic of conversation, in a context where the sender would prefer for them to speak silently, yet effectively.

In the everyday world of communication, then, appearance signs are often used to construct social realities, without verbalizing these realities. Who wants to be told "Oh, I see you are trying to impress me," or "You must be depressed; you've been wearing dark colors all week"? In essence, most individuals probably welcome compliments but not trilogies on the essence of meaning of appearance signs. Sociologist Harold Garfinkel (1967) contends that everyday worlds involve taken-for-granted meanings that interactants want neither to be disrupted nor to emerge as the focal point of attention, in a manner that may disrupt the smooth and nonstressful flow of interaction. Of course, the extent to which this preference applies is likely to relate to the context and the participants in interaction.

Language possesses a different kind of potential to convey messages, and expresses those messages through a different medium, with a different effect. Therefore, it is inappropriate or misleading to speak of "clothing as language" (Enninger, 1985; McCracken, 1988). Before understanding what appearance messages can and cannot convey, it is important to explore *how* they convey. Whereas language "materializes in sounds or graphics, . . . clothing materializes in fabrics of certain shapes and colors" (Enninger, 1985, p. 81). The aesthetic code is like an underlying pattern or system that links fabric, texture, color, pattern, volume, silhouette, and occasion (F. Davis, 1985). The body also materializes visually and is perceived aesthetically. Therefore, we should be careful not to impose the structure of language on that of clothing, or more generally, on appearance. To do so may limit our thinking about the nature and potential of appearance messages. Language is only one of many sign systems; appearance is another. Each system has its own range of possibilities for signifying, stimulating, and shaping meaning.

> We might consider whether the nonlinguistic codes of material culture communicate things that language proper cannot or, characteristically, does not. Do cultures charge material culture with the responsibility of carrying certain messages that they cannot or do not entrust to language? (McCracken, 1988, p. 68).

However, at times it is useful to *compare* clothing and appearance to language. At times, appearance signs seem to resemble linguistic signs. They are both relatively complex in terms of their organization, and both rely heavily on social context in order for a message to be comprehended (Delaporte, 1980). In some cases, linguistic messages actually appear on clothes, as in the case of T-shirts with written slogans, labels, or proverbs. Through linguistic messages, T-shirts can display political and social attitudes, loyalty to a school, the location of one's vacation(s), taste in music or food, sense of humor, and so on, as shown in Figure 7-14.

Other uses of linguistic codes in relation to clothing apply when verbal labels may be used to identify a wearer on the basis of his or her clothes: "police officer," "businessperson," "baseball player," or "punk." Receivers may be able to establish the "look" of an appearance before them and place that look into a category with a ready-made, verbal tag. But often, such linguistic labels do not exist and the meanings are not easily put into words. Interpreting appearance then becomes more similar to solving a puzzle than to labeling.

In an analysis of Russian folk costume, Bogatyrev (1976) noted that perceivers can more easily determine the social position, cultural level, and taste of a wearer through his or her appearance than through speech. The appearance can convey messages that languages cannot, and these messages cannot necessarily be conveyed in words.

At times, clothing is clearly more aesthetic or artistic in terms of communication than it is linguistic. This is especially true when "emotions, allusions, and moods

**FIGURE 7-14**
*Linguistic messages are illustrated on this T-shirt in a shop window in Paris. Photo by Susan B. Kaiser.*

. . . are aroused" (F. Davis, 1985, p. 15), and meanings assigned defy simple cognitive interpretation. Davis goes on to note that clothing can sometimes make a statement as does language and arouse feelings as does art, or possibly accomplish both at the same time. That is, our appearances can explicitly state who we are while "alternatively or simultaneously evoking an aura that 'merely suggests' more than it can (or intends to) state precisely" (F. Davis, 1985, p. 15).

Appearance in general, and clothing in particular, has the capacity for "interference-free transmission of unlimited numbers of messages" (Enninger, 1985). Multi-messages are the number of distinct meanings that may be associated with or linked to a single signifier such as an item of clothing (Sebeok, 1985, p. 465). The choice of interpretation depends on the time, place, and social circumstances surrounding the signifier.

*Multimessages and Ambiguity*

Clothes rarely convey single meanings; more often, their messages may be described as consisting of *layers of meaning*, with some layers more applicable than others in a specific context. For example, if one asks "what do jeans mean," it is difficult to answer with a single meaning. As Joseph (1986) notes, jeans have variously "meant" membership in groups such as agricultural laborers, civil rights, youth subcultures, and foreign communist elites with access to Western consumer goods. They have also signified "designer" goods, unisexuality, comfort, earthiness, and sexiness. Because clothes are social artifacts, they have the potential to derive meaning in and from a variety of social and cultural contexts.

Given that an article of clothing has many possible meanings, there is likely to be a certain degree of ambiguity as to which is "correct" (Delaporte, 1980). Moreover, the articles of clothing that are worn together may have numerous possible meanings, and they also interact with one another to produce additional ambiguities. To interpret, perceivers are likely to refer to the appearance context, as well as the social context, for additional guidance. These contexts are important factors in any interpretations of appearance messages, but become especially critical when a range of possible meanings may be identified.

Ambiguity, in fact, becomes an overriding characteristic in clothing and appearance messages (Delaporte, 1980; F. Davis, 1985). Ambiguity is present when a receiver (*a*) cannot simply or easily interpret because of a variety of possible meanings and, therefore, does not know which one to select (see Figure 7-15), or (*b*) lacks a frame of reference to understand an appearance, while also possibly being able to loosely relate the appearance to a similar one from his or her past experiences, as shown in Figure 7-16. Ambiguity can be created by the presence or absence of certain items of clothing, that is, in how the parts of the appearance context work together, just as it can evolve from the social context when one attempts interpretation (Delaporte, 1980).

When people perceive a sender's appearance, they are not likely to "read" it from top to bottom, or in a linear progression from one part to another (McCracken, 1988). Rather, it seems that appearance tends to be perceived in

*Nonlinear, Gestalt-like Characteristics*

**FIGURE 7-15**
*One form of ambiguity is illustrated in the way this woman is dressed in her city office for what has been declared "1950s day" (although few people are actually dressing up for the occasion). Namely, there are multiple messages that we can "read into" her appearance, and it is difficult to know which one (if any) is "correct." Is she dressed this way to achieve a 1950s look? (Her appearance is neither distinctively 1950s enough nor sufficiently different from a 1980s look to be certain.) Or, is she simply dressing a little more casually than usual? Photo by Mark Kaiser.*

its entirety, all at once, as an integrated system. Even if perceivers were to move systematically from one part of the body to another, interpretation would not involve a simple "adding up" of the meanings of all of the parts to arrive at a sum (total) meaning of appearance, because the interaction among the parts of the appearance influences the assessment (Lennon and Miller, 1984–1985).

Anthropologists frequently use the concept of *holism* to refer to the interconnectedness of parts in human experience. To perceive holistically is to see the parts in relation to the whole, to avoid stripping the part from its larger context. When we fail to see holistically, we are more likely to be blinded by our own perspectives (Peacock, 1986, p. 11).

The psychological concept of **Gestalt** (Asch, 1946) is useful in understanding holistic perceptions. *Gestalt* is the German word for "shape" or "form," but it is often used to describe holistic perceptual processes enabling us to organize our impressions with respect to the parts in relation to the whole—in this case,

**FIGURE 7-16**
*A second form of ambiguity (see Figure 7-15 for the first form) is depicted in this picture. Unless one is familiar with the University of Texas Cowboys (the service organization that promotes spirit at football games), these males' appearances may seem ambiguous or difficult to interpret. That is, a perceiver must have some frame of reference to interpret an appearance in a given context. Otherwise, the meanings or possible meanings are vague or unclear. Photo by Mark Kaiser.*

the visual context presented by a person's appearance. The concept of Gestalt emphasizes that the whole is often greater, or more powerful in its impact, than the sum of the parts. (For an example of this, refer back to Figure 7-13 and note how each element of appearance contributes to a unique whole that must be perceived in its entirety; also see Figure 7-17.)

Appearance, as presented and received, is a kind of "formed expression," created through the use of fabrics, shapes, and colors combined in and across articles of clothing, and through the way an entire ensemble of clothing looks on one's body (based on its size, coloring, and other features). As we have already seen, the parts of appearance work together to convey an impression on the base of an underlying aesthetic code. The concept of Gestalt, as applied to appearance, refers to the aggregate impression made possible through aesthetic codes that present "rules of well-formedness" (Enninger, 1985). Each time a creative individual develops a new ensemble by combining garments and accessories that have not previously been seen together, a new Gestalt is formed (Enninger, 1985). Figures 7-5 and 7-6 are good examples of "created" Gestalts.

The concept of Gestalt can apply either to a given article of clothing or to an integrated system of clothing articles, accessories, and the body. Let's look first at a given article of clothing. Here we can focus on the parts of the garment, including the colors, textures, and forms that compose it. When single garments are disassembled, they can no longer be interpreted in the same manner as when the parts are a composite unit of dress (Wass and Eicher, 1980). Garments can be subdivided into component parts, as can composite, clothed appearances. Yet the manner in which the parts of a garment or a total appearance connect is vital to interpretation. Whether we are concerned with a single item of clothing or a total appearance as an integrated system of parts, underlying aesthetic codes influence appearance management and perception. These codes provide the glue

**FIGURE 7-17**
*The concept of **Gestalt** is illustrated in this male's appearance. That is, the whole is greater than the sum of the parts that compose it. Each time articles of clothing, accessories, and modes of grooming are combined or recombined into a new look, a new Gestalt is created. Photo by Larry White.*

that connect component parts and distinguish meaning on the basis of "what is worn with what." An awareness of how component parts of appearance are interconnected and interdependent refers to the Gestalt nature of appearance messages.

How are interpretations influenced by the "breaking" of aesthetic codes? Some evidence suggests that cognitive forces lead perceivers to try to simplify their understandings of others. When the pieces of the appearance puzzle do not fit together and perceivers cannot explain the appearance on the basis of a Gestalt, they may experience *cognitive dissonance* (Festinger, 1957). That is, there is a lack of mental "balance" in one's perception and some cognitive tension may result. When the parts of appearance do not "gel," a less-than-positive impression may be produced in the mind of a perceiver. At the same time, many perceivers have the cognitive flexibility to provide some rationale or explanation for an unusual combination of appearance parts. In a study by Gibbins and Schneider (1980), subjects were shown a woman clothed in a 1900-style coat paired with an incongruent style of pants—harem pants. The subjects interpreted that the woman must be "basically dressed in the harem outfit" but needed to throw "the coat on over it for warmth or from embarrassment." The subjects could not believe that anyone would *choose* to wear the two at the same time, together.

Because appearance codes change with time and fashion, appearances inducing a sense of cognitive dissonance also change. For example, a woman wearing a business suit with jogging shoes on a city street was, at first, an image that seemed inconsistent. The parts did not go together. Over time, however, this Gestalt became accepted.

The context in which any message is transmitted influences its interpretation. All kinds of messages are more or less context-sensitive (Sebeok, 1985, p. 454). Clearly, appearance messages are complex, prone to be ambiguous, and holistically emitted and received. Therefore, they rely heavily on context for meaning, and they also serve to alter the meaning of context. There are three kinds of contexts we can consider in relation to appearance messages: (1) the appearance context per se, (2) the social context, including the people involved and the nature of the interaction, and (3) the cultural and historical context.

*Context- Dependence*

Changes in clothes facilitate and accommodate changes in contexts (Joseph, 1986). Even the slightest alteration in a person's appearance can alter the meaning of the appearance context. At the same time, the total appearance context (Gestalt) is used to interpret individual clothing or appearance cues. An identical material such as the black gauze of a funeral veil "means" something very different when it is sewn into the bodice of a nightgown (F. Davis, 1985). In this case, the black gauze is part of a larger appearance context and therefore becomes part of a Gestalt-like image.

Similarly, clothes not only help to define the social and cultural and historical contexts but also rely on those contexts for meaningful interpretation. A jogging suit has a very different meaning when one is lying on the couch watching television, as compared with when he or she is running around a track or shopping in a grocery store. Wearing blue jeans "meant" something very different in the late 1960s and early 1970s (unisexuality, deemphasis of materialism, comfort, and earthiness—back to nature) than it did in the 1980s (designer goods and sexiness).

Although all types of verbal and nonverbal messages are more or less dependent on context for meaningful interpretation, it seems that this context-dependency especially applies to appearance messages. Why is this? Sociologist Fred Davis (1985) notes that there is a high degree of social variability in the link between signifier and signified when it comes to appearance. Different groups of people attach different meanings to the same signifier (style, appearance). As compared to many other expressive products of modern culture:

> meanings are more ambiguous in that it is hard to get *people in general* to interpret the same clothing symbols in the same way; in semiotic terminology, the signifier-signified relationship is quite unstable (F. Davis, 1985, p. 18).

In other words, different groups of people (for example, age groups or occupations) can use different codes to interpret the same signifiers. For example, what is considered to be "fashionable" differs between persons immersed in the world of fashion (designers, retailers, and journalists) and the consuming public. Retailers have different concepts of what shoes are fashionable, high in status, and expensive than do consumers (Kaiser et al., 1985). Within the general public, as well, there are a variety of perceptions about applicable meanings for given clothing and appearance styles, as people interact in different spheres of social interaction, have different social identities, have differential access to fashion (where they live, what they can afford, and how interested they are), and pursue different leisure activities regardless of social class. Due to the visible nature of appearance, styles may be imitated and adopted without involving social interaction to ascertain their meanings to senders. Therefore, they may be "stripped" from their original contexts and take on totally different meanings that need to be constructed by the people who have adopted them and others with whom they come into contact. For example, head scarves used by the Palestinian Liberation Organization became fashionable in the late 1980s in the streets of New York. Consumers adopted them after seeing these scarves on television for a number of years. Most of these consumers were probably not as concerned with ideological connotations as they were with aesthetics.

## Unfocused Characteristics

Appearance messages are often unfocused in nature, meaning that senders cannot readily control who receives the messages conveyed through appearance. Given that different groups of perceivers may interpret the same cues in various ways, this characteristic can lead to unintentional sending of messages, to individuals with whom one may not be attempting to communicate. Whereas with speech a sender can separate people in conversation and direct messages to particular receivers, it is not possible to "focus" appearance. It is available as a form of communication to all potential receivers within sight. Once clothes are placed on the body, one's hair is fixed in a certain style, makeup is applied, and a person enters a social context, the resulting appearance functions much like a "broadcast signal" (Enninger, 1985; McCracken, 1988). That appearance is "turned on" and emits signals until the person leaves the context.

A male trying to impress a female may dress accordingly but may impress others instead. Similarly, unsolicited or unwanted whistles from admiring males on the street are likely to annoy women who are on the way to important business meetings, wearing skirted suits. Depending on the awareness of the individuals with whom we come into contact, any or all of them may receive messages intended for a select few.

Relative to the nature of appearance as a "broadcast signal," it is also important to note that people cannot *discuss* with appearance once they are interacting in a social context. The adjective "discursive" refers to the movement from one topic to another. Any planning of a particular appearance message on the part of a sender must be done in advance of interaction, for the most part (in the backstage). Appearance does not "fade" as a message, unlike discursive forms of communication. A sender cannot free the channel for new signals, because the signal is constant throughout interaction—the whole time actors are on stage (Enninger, 1985, p. 88).

*Nondiscursive Characteristics*

In contrast, in verbal communication a variety of subjects can be discussed in the same encounter, and if communication is not going well, it is possible to change the subject or to apologize for a previous statement.

The nondiscursive quality of appearance makes it difficult (if not impossible) to "repair" messages that were not intended or that have been received poorly. In everyday appearance communication, senders lack the ability to exert total control over how a message is conveyed in the *front stage*. Once clothes have been donned and appearance has been groomed (behind the scenes of interaction) and a sender is now engaging in social discourse, it is difficult to alter the message. It is not easy to shift from one message to another or to change the topic or tone of conversation, because appearance is visual and omnipresent. (It is hard to change clothes or restyle one's hair in the middle of a social transaction; senders of appearance messages tend to be "stuck" with what they are wearing.) However, appearance communication can be a little more discursive in some contexts than in others. Imagine a male college professor removing his jacket, rolling up his shirt sleeves, and loosening his tie. A male stripper also engages in a discursive act.

Clothes, in particular, are not only forms of communication used at the discretion of senders. They are also *commodities*, or consumer products that are purchased at a cost. These signs are sold, in contrast to words or discursive nonverbal messages. They involve expense and are therefore not equally accessible to all potential users.

*Characteristics as Commodity*

As commodities and signs, clothes (and other accessories and forms of grooming that are purchased) are part of the extended self. Consumer objects have no inherent meanings; rather, their meanings are formed in their production, marketing, and use. Despite fashion advertisements, store displays, and fashion shows, however, the meanings of clothes as commodities are rarely entirely shared (Belk, 1987).

A Gestalt approach may be taken to understand how groupings of products tend to be clustered together in consumers' minds and to carry some of the same meanings: "All goods carry meaning, but none by itself. . . . The meaning is in the relations between all the goods, just as music is in the relations marked out by the sounds and not in any one note (Douglas and Isherwood, 1979, pp. 72–73).

Research suggests that products are grouped along symbolic rather than functional lines. In one study, 80 business graduate students were asked to form a mental picture of a person described in terms of his or her occupation. Then they were asked to picture any products this person would be likely to own. What resulted were products grouped in constellations for each occupational social role. For example, for the occupational label *professional*, the products generated included a Seiko watch, Burberry raincoat, Lacoste shirt, *Atlantic* magazine, Brooks Brothers' suit, Bass loafers, silk tie, French wine, and a BMW. In contrast, the label *blue collar* elicited the following products: Schaefer beer, AMF bowling ball, Ford pick-up truck, Levi's jeans, Marlboro cigarettes, RCA TV, *Field and Stream*, Black and Decker tools, and McDonald's. Almost half the products came from three categories: clothing, electronic equipment, and cars. Clothing was the most frequently mentioned product, which is not surprising given its communicative value, not only as a commodity but also as a part of personal appearance linked to one's occupation (Solomon and Assael, 1987).

Fashion marketing and merchandising can effectively make use of the principle of product clusters and/or a Gestalt effect of groupings of products based on symbolism rather than functionality. For example, innovative consumers may be encouraged (in advertisements) to wear layers of shirts and tops to create their own "Gestalts." By wearing layers of outerwear shirts, the traditional distinctions among underwear, indoor-wear, and outerwear are blurred; the idea of wearing the shirts together is symbolic rather than merely functional (Kehret-Ward, 1987).

Similarly, retailers may promote the idea of combining products in use. However, traditionally products have been grouped, shelved, and displayed in departments according to similar attributes rather than on the basis of social meaning or the same consumption goal. For example, shoes are generally found with other footwear in shoe departments, jewelry with other accessories, and so on. More and more manufacturers are urging or even forcing retailers to display their products (including clothes, accessories, and shoes) together, grouped symbolically as they might be worn and with a particular consumption occasion and goal in mind (rather than separated into different departments). Manufacturers who produce complete costumes had been complaining that retailers failed to accessorize clothing displays, refused to stock their entire line, and lacked the space to make a full presentation of the manufacturer's complete collection. Accordingly, manufacturers began to get more involved in how their merchandise is sold and presented, and the result has been boutiques within major department stores (for example, an Esprit boutique within Macy's and Bullock's stores (Kehret-Ward, 1987).

The commodity characteristic of clothing and accessories interconnects with the multimessage characteristic, as well as the Gestalt quality. Given that different consumer groups may assign various meanings to a particular clothing style or brand, fashion advertisers may strive to use this potential to convey multiple meanings to their advantage. The world of advertising is essentially a system of symbols, pulled together from the range of culturally determined ways of knowing and establishing a sense of consumer need and desire. Advertisers would like for consumers to regard the products as relevant to their social experiences. Therefore, advertising is more than a system of creating messages; it is a system of discerning or discovering meaning (Sherry, 1987). The idea is to appeal to a variety of consumers in different ways, by playing with the multimessages, the Gestalts, as well as the other characteristics of appearance messages. Without multiple potential meanings, an extensive and diverse audience could not be attracted to a product (Zakia, 1986).

In summary, appearance becomes a visual context in its own right. The visual nature of appearance, coupled with its direct and personal association with a sender, provides it with some relatively unique characteristics that distinguish it from other forms of communication and contribute to its complexity. In the course of interpretation, like the proverbial customer, the interpreter is always right (or thinks he or she is and proceeds accordingly, in the absence of any disqualifying information). Thus researchers need to focus on consumers' interpretations, in their own words (Mick and Politi, 1989). Therefore, in the next two chapters, we will look more closely at (*a*) the process of social cognition (Chapter Eight) and (*b*) the qualities perceivers bring to social contexts (Chapter Nine).

## *Suggested Readings*

Davis, F. 1985. Clothing and fashion as communication. In M. R. Solomon, ed. *The psychology of fashion*, pp. 15–27. Lexington: Heath/Lexington Books.
Davis explores the characteristics of clothing and fashion that distinguish them from language. He draws from semiotics and the symbolic-interactionist perspective to consider the changing nature of aesthetic codes and suggests that underlying ambivalences about identity provide fuel for fashion change.

DeLong, M. R. 1987. *The way we look: A framework for visual analysis of dress*. Ames: Iowa State University Press.
DeLong presents a framework for analyzing appearance, with a sensitivity to the visual and aesthetic dimensions of perception. The apparel-body construct is explored as a means of visually interpreting appearance as a whole entity.

Enninger, W. 1985. The design features of clothing codes: The functions of clothing displays in interaction. *Kodikas/Code 8*(1/2):81–110.
Using a semiotic approach, Enninger examines a number of characteristics making clothing a unique form of nonlinguistic communication.

Hillestad, R. 1980. The underlying structure of appearance. *Dress 5*:117–125.
Appearance is conceptualized in relation to interactions between the body and clothing. The visual impact of these interactions is explored using a structural approach.

McCracken, G. 1988. *Culture and consumption*. Bloomington: Indiana University Press.
In this book on a cultural understanding of consumption, McCracken includes a chapter on clothing as a form of communication and argues persuasively that the metaphor of language is inappropriate and inadequate to comprehend clothing—a nonverbal and nonlinguistic medium.

# Chapter Eight
# • • •
# Appearance and Social Cognition

One hundred tellings are not as good as one seeing.
—TRADITIONAL CHINESE PROVERB

*In this chapter, our focus is on how we interpret the appearances of people we see. Essentially, we are dealing here with cognitive processes, or ways of thinking and knowing about people and their appearances. What personal traits or characteristics do we attribute to particular clothing cues? How do we organize our thoughts to keep track of all of the information conveyed through a person's appearance? How and why do we classify individuals into categories or groups based upon like appearances? While there is a tendency for perceivers to simplify the process of understanding others through the use of "shortcut" avenues such as classification, at the same time perceivers tend to be stimulated by new, fascinating appearances that cannot be easily placed into categories. Underlying perceivers' attempts to understand other people is a cognitive need to explain the causes of social outcomes.*

How do we come to formulate impressions about one another on the basis of appearance? In this chapter, we will address the social and cognitive processes that lead to interpretations of a sender's personal characteristics, expectations for his or her actions, and explanations of behavior. Cognitive social psychology contributes to our knowledge of **social cognition**. Social cognition involves "the use of cognitive psychological processes with social objects, that is, people" (Lennon and Davis, 1989, p. 41). Social cognition, then, is an "umbrella" concept that incorporates a variety of thought processes relative to appearance perception. Thus, we rely heavily on the cognitive perspective in this chapter, but we also consider symbolic-interactionist assumptions and concepts that contribute to an understanding of social cognition. We are concerned with perception as a *one-way* process. That is, the social-cognitive processes through which perceivers or receivers make assessments and judgments about senders on the basis of their appearances is the primary focus.

When are receivers especially likely to rely on senders' appearances to understand those senders? First-impression contexts are among those in which appearance is an especially critical factor in judgments of others. A favorable first impression can stimulate perceivers to learn more about an observed person, can influence the nature of the search for new information, and can affect the way this information is interpreted. It also may serve as an invitation to associate or identify with that person (Huston and Levinger, 1978). Since many professional and social contacts in modern life are fleeting and impersonal in nature, first impressions assume added significance in social cognitions.

Yet, appearance is also important in everyday encounters with others whom we may know, as we attempt to interpret or explain the basis for, and outcome of, social contexts. However, we have more information available to us in these more familiar types of social encounters, so we are less dependent on appearance alone. Much of the research drawing from a cognitive perspective has dealt more with first-impression types of contexts, that is, requiring evaluation of drawings or photographs of unknown persons, where receivers have little else to go on besides appearance. In real life, perceivers may rely less on appearance as a source of evaluation when they actually interact with senders rather than simply observe them (Damhorst, in press). Nevertheless, the available research provides a wealth of information about personality traits receivers assign to unknown senders (Damhorst, in press). Although we know that many other types of information are likely to be provided by a sender's appearance (as we will discuss in Chapter Ten), our focus will be on perceptions of personal traits and processes of *attribution* (explanations of the causes for social occurrences).

You will recall from Chapter Two that a major assumption of the cognitive perspective is that receivers strive to simplify their perceptions so as to make sense of social reality. Also, receivers may be regarded as "naive scientists," because they have a basic need to interpret the everyday motives of senders. In the process, they develop private, implicit theories of explanation.

## Cognitive Structures

As naive social psychologists, receivers try to make sense of the world around them, including the people with whom they interact. To do so, perceivers develop **cognitive structures**. These structures are part of a network of thought that enables perceivers to respond to stimuli such as appearance (Wegner and Vallacher, 1977). Cognitive structures also allow receivers to organize their thoughts and to simplify their perceptions, so they do not have to consciously struggle for interpretation each time a person is observed. Cognitive structures provide an easy sense of order and predictability for the purpose of clarifying expectations and explaining behaviors related to senders.

Perceivers tend to assume that the attributes or qualities assigned to others on the basis of appearance are interrelated. In other words, there is a tendency to "cluster" or group person-attributes or person-qualities. Accordingly, receivers implicitly assume that if one attribute in the cluster is assigned to a sender, it is likely that other attributes in that cluster will also be assigned. For example, elementary-school-aged girls tend to associate a girl who wears frilly dresses not only as being concerned with her appearance, but also as popular (Kaiser, 1989). Perceivers may also view such traits as intelligence, competence, and industriousness as interrelated, and these traits may compose a cognitive structure assigned to an observed person on the basis of appearance cues such as a business suit and briefcase. (See Figures 8-1 and 8-2 for other examples of the use of cognitive structures.)

How fixed or stable are receivers' cognitive structures? Everyday life is complicated and enriched by social contexts that alter the applicability of receivers' cognitive structures. Thus the use of a cognitive structure frequently needs to be tailored to a particular context in order to be useful. Moreover, fashion and social change, as well as a sender's creativity in appearance management, lead to a variety of appearances for which perceivers may not have already formulated a cognitive structure. Therefore, cognitive structures need to be used flexibly to meet the demands of everyday appearances and occurrences. Although implicit systems for organizing information may be highly structured then, perceivers' abilities to use them are "remarkably fluid and dependent on the features of the context in which persons are observed" (Taylor, 1981). This context may include the total appearance context presented by a sender, the social circumstances in

**FIGURE 8-1**
*A perceiver interpreting this man's appearance at a Renaissance fair might use a variety of adjectives to describe it, and, through processes of inference, find ways of describing his personal qualities as well. For example, some perceivers might describe him as creative, talented, romantic, and sensitive. The context is taken into account as perceivers develop their* **cognitive structures** *and, hence, construct a profile of traits perceived as interconnected to associate with his appearance. Photo by Mark Kaiser.*

**FIGURE 8-2**
*In a study by Hongo and Kaiser (1989), this male was perceived in a manner consistent with a "macho" cognitive structure when he wore the clothes pictured. He was viewed as masculine and likely to endorse the following products in an ad: domestic beer, season football tickets, liquor, and cigarettes. Photo by Susan B. Kaiser.*

which a sender is observed, and the cultural and historical context influencing social judgments. Thus, when perceivers find that their cognitive structures no longer adequately apply, they are motivated to change them accordingly.

Receivers are especially prone to call upon their cognitive structures to explain the appearance of a sender when that sender seems to fit neatly into a category. Categorization seems to be an inescapable part of all perception, because it is virtually impossible to look at an object (or person) without identifying or classifying in some way (Lennon and Davis, 1989).

## Cognitive Categories

Part of a receiver's streamlining of reality involves the tendency to categorize senders into clusters of social groupings. Note the illustrations in Figures 8-3

**FIGURE 8-3**
*Cues such as steel-toed boots may be used to place individuals into social groupings or categories, with labels such as "punk" or "post-punk." These boots may be worn by persons in different subcultures, of course, depending on the other garments or forms of grooming that go with the boots. Nevertheless, cues such as these boots are frequently used to categorize or "place" individuals, in a social and cognitive sense. Photo by Mark Kaiser.*

and 8-4; what kinds of classifications or categories do you call on to understand what is pictured? And, once you call on these categories, what cognitive structures do you call on for interpretation?

Thus there is a tendency to place observed persons in mental categories; we tend to see an individual as a member of a group based on available cues such as clothing (Taylor, 1981). Although it is a natural cognitive tendency to categorize others and most persons engage in categorization almost unconsciously, categorization is the first cognitive process that may lead to **stereotyping**. Stereotypes are "pictures in the head," or mental images that receivers use to place others into categories and then to apply certain cognitive structures. The danger of stereotyping is evident in contexts where a sender does not actually fit the category in question and/or the cognitive structures applied result in an over-simplified, exaggerated, or inaccurate assessment. Stereotyping processes become overgeneralized when some or all of the traits in a perceiver's cognitive structure do not apply to the observed person but are still assigned because they are part of the cluster.

Stereotypes are not necessarily negative in their consequences. They may be viewed as strategies for simplifying and sorting the complex array of information supplied by appearance and for reducing uncertainty and apprehension in initial interactions with others. The concept of **prejudice**, however, does have negative implications for interactions. Prejudice results when (1) the stereotypes that are held are rigid and (2) any information about a person that conflicts with the assigned stereotype is disregarded or incorrectly perceived. Stereotypical expectations may bias perceivers implicitly from receiving information openly and

**FIGURE 8-4**
*This woman's knitted (red) cap is symbolic of the Rastafarian religious subculture that originated in Jamaica and spread to North America and the United Kingdom. Perceivers who are aware of this symbolism are likely to use the cap as a means of placing her into a social category. Photo by Susan B. Kaiser.*

objectively, even when they strive to avoid feelings of prejudice. In symbolic-interactionist terms, stereotyping consists of making an identification *of* another person (placing that person in a category or labeling that person) without identifying *with* that person (Stone, 1965). As we will see in Chapter Ten, a receiver's ability to identify *with* a sender facilitates meaningful communication. If a receiver cannot relate to a sender's appearance or finds it distasteful in some way, then that appearance poses a barrier to a meaningful exchange of information.

The use of cognitive structures and categories is linked to receivers' attempts to organize their perceptions. To organize perceptions efficiently, perceivers select and simplify (Eiser, 1980). The process of perceiving and understanding others involves the selection of personal cues that may be used to develop *inferences* about those others' characteristics or probable behaviors. Inferences based on appearance derive from receivers' tendencies to deduce, to assume, to hypothesize, and to conclude, rightly or wrongly.

## Appearance Perception and Inference

When perceiving others, four stages of thought processes may be identified (Livesley and Bromley, 1973). As a social-cognitive *process*, appearance perception leads to inferences and states of expectation as a result of these processes.

*1. Selection of cues.* Although perceivers frequently perceive holistically, seeing the parts in relation to the larger appearance as a whole, they may also select and focus upon particular appearance cues. Therefore, the process of selecting cues may either entail a holistic perception or a focus on a particular cue. For example, a hairstylist is probably more likely than the average person to use hairstyle as a cue to understanding others. Or a shoe sales associate is likely to focus on shoes when perceiving customers, for a variety of reasons. What appearance cues do you tend to select to understand the appearance of the person depicted in Figure 8-5 on the next page?

*2. Interpretative inference.* The process of inferring meaning begins as a perceiver interprets the appearance cues selected and, using cognitive structures, associates them with a few primary or central personal characteristics. Let's look at the illustration in Figure 8-5 and consider possible central characteristics of the person pictured.

*3. Extended inference.* Once perceivers have developed an interpretation of an appearance cue or larger appearance structure, they may make additional "cognitive leaps." Often this process is referred to as relying on *halo effects*. That is, perceivers refer to one personal trait or cluster of traits to which they feel the appearance is linked. Then, in turn, another personal trait or grouping of traits seem to be logically connected to the appearance, because perceivers logically connect the traits in question in their minds with other traits in a cognitive structure. Judgments are prone to be somewhat tenuous in the case of extended inferences. For example, just because a person is perceived as competent does not mean he or she is intelligent, and actual warmth and sensitivity are not necessarily equated with a tendency to make a favorable first impression.

*4. Anticipatory set.* The final stage of appearance perception involves the observer's readiness to respond toward the other person on the basis of inferred traits. The resulting expectations may be either explicit (readily verbalized) or implicit (subtle or almost unconscious). Children are particularly fascinating to study in terms of anticipatory sets because they will often talk about their inferences in a manner adults have been socialized to regard as inappropriate. ("It is not nice to judge a book by its cover.") Although adults certainly judge others by appearance, as volumes of research studies indicate, they often do so

**FIGURE 8-5**

*This young boy wears an army-green camouflage T-shirt with a peace sign superimposed (painted) on it. His father, who has fairly long hair and wears a tie-dyed T-shirt reminiscent of the late 1960s, watches his son play from a nearby park bench. Let's consider the four stages of person perception to interpret this boy's appearance. First, let's assume that the stage of **cue selection** leads us to focus on his T-shirt. Second, we make the **interpretative inference** (based in part on his father's appearance) that the son wanted the camouflage shirt and the father (who is concerned with world peace, according to our inference) talked him into adding a peace sign as a way of softening the militaristic impression of the shirt. Thus, as we formulate an impression about the boy shown here, we make the inference that he is learning to balance issues of war and peace. Next, we enter a deeper stage of inference known as **extended inference**. Here we make some mental leaps and attribute other traits to this boy. Let's suppose we think of him as friendly and sociable, yet prone to get into fights at times. We can see here that our inferences are becoming increasingly tenuous as we make assumptions that may or may not be true. Finally, we enter the final stage of **anticipatory set**, in which we formulate an approach (implicitly or explicitly) for interacting with him and/or his father. We could ask him, for example, if he likes movies or video games related to war, or we could just talk to him as though we expect him to be friendly. We might also engage his father in a conversation. Topics related to war and peace could be raised in the conversation, if we expect him to have some concern about these types of social-political issues. Photo by Susan B. Kaiser.*

on a more implicit, complex level, as compared with children. In contrast, children are apt to verbalize their inferences in a more frank and forthcoming manner. For example, in a study of appearance perceptions of young girls (Kaiser and Phinney, 1983), one preschool boy associated the behavior of kicking with a feminine, frilly dress. He explained this association by recounting an incident when a girl in a frilly dress had kicked him (the "chicken's way of fighting").

He described her as highly emotional, and noted he had to "calm her down" after he had responded to her kick by using "karate" on her. Because of this incident, he associated kicking with girls who wore frilly dresses.

"The hunches, intuitions and revelations of human experience take place" in the context of appearance perception (Mick, 1986, p. 205). Thus, while the process of developing inferences about a person on the basis of appearance seems to be straightforward and precise when we break it down into stages, in reality a lot of subtle nuances, contextual considerations, and contradictions often enrich as well as complicate everyday perceptions. See Social Focus 8-1 for a discussion of physical attractiveness as a cue with implications for anticipatory set in the context of being evaluated for a job.

## The Case of Novel Stimuli

Social life would certainly be simpler and require less conscious interpretation if we observed the same appearances every day and/or were able to use the same thought processes to interpret appearances, but it would also be less interesting or energizing. Along with the cognitive need to simplify perceptions, receivers desire some stimulation. Thus when appearances that are novel (unusual, unfamiliar, innovative, fresh, and/or fascinating) are presented to receivers, they ordinarily want to attend to them or to pay extra attention to senders and their actions. We tend to emphasize and remember novel appearances and to use them to understand social outcomes, although we may lack the cognitive structures and categories (as well as the social experience) to apply to them. On the other hand, it appears to require a more novel appearance, or one that somehow confounds our typical perceptions, to change our minds about a person, style, or issue. An unexpected appearance such as one that seems inconsistent with a person's role may "arouse" receivers to change their minds about a social-political issue (Cooper, Darley, and Henderson, 1974) or view senders as more sincere (McPeek and Edwards, 1975). Out-of-role behavior may be seen as more sincere, in some contexts, than role-consistent behavior. Perceivers may infer that if a sender is daring enough to ignore role requirements for the sake of an important issue, he or she must have strong inner convictions. Furthermore, an unexpected appearance is likely to be stimulating and to cause perceivers to contemplate an issue at hand and, therefore, possibly to change their attitude about that issue. For example, a conservative businessman who supports women's rights may change another person's views on women's issues more than a woman whose appearance fits a feminist stereotype in a perceiver's mind. Or, a businesswoman who begins to dress in more colorful and fashionable styles may induce perceivers to question the necessity of a fixed business stereotype. Of course, perceivers' own views and tendencies will influence the extent to which attitude-change effects occur.

Novel appearance stimuli are basic to fashion change. Fresh or innovative styles may appear inappropriate when first introduced, but their novelty is essential to the arousal of interest on the part of perceivers. An old expression in the

# Judgments of Being Qualified for the Job: The Effects of Physical Attractiveness

In the world of job-seeking and interviewing, judgments are made on a regular basis about a candidate's qualifications. How well-qualified an applicant is judged to be is likely to be linked (implicitly or unconsciously, at least) to perceptions of competence. Often, as in an interview context, a perceiver is influenced greatly, especially in the first few minutes, by an applicant's personal appearance. Favorable judgments of this appearance are likely to contribute to other positive inferences that may not necessarily be logically related. That is, a halo effect operates, in that when a person is judged to be attractive, then he or she is also evaluated as having other positive traits (for example, competence), and therefore, as being the best person for the job. At a time when women are increasingly striving to move up the corporate ladder and to be taken seriously in the business world, there understandably has been a great deal of research on the role of women's appearances in hiring decisions. This research has followed two lines of inquiry, focusing upon physical attractiveness and clothing, respectively. In this discussion, we will focus primarily on the dimension of physical attractiveness. In Social Focus 11-1, the effects of women's clothing choices on first impressions of competence will be addressed.

Regardless of an interviewer's sex and own level of attractiveness, highly qualified applicants tend to be preferred over poorly qualified applicants. Moreover, males tend to be preferred over females, and attractive candidates are preferred over unattractive ones. Thus, discrimination appears to operate along the lines of gender and physical attractiveness stereotypes. However, bias against female applicants appears to be diminished when they are moderately attractive (which appears to be better than being either highly attractive or unattractive). Also, women with low qualifications who are also unattractive are especially likely to elicit a negative evaluation. Female interviewers appear to be as biased as male interviewers, and unattractive interviewers as biased as attractive interviewers (Dipboye, Arvey, and Terpstra, 1977). This gender effect was reinforced in a later study in which male perceivers tended to ignore appearance altogether, whereas female raters were favorably influenced by candidates with average to above-average appearance (Quereshi and Kay, 1986).

Contextual considerations come into play in hiring decisions. Physical attractiveness has been found to be an advantage for males pursuing either managerial or clerical jobs, whereas it is an advantage for women only in clerical jobs (Heilman and Saruwatari, 1979). It seems that a high degree of attractiveness may "backfire" for a female applicant when the job in question emphasizes the need for instrumental or masculine skills (such as making decisions quickly and accurately under pressure), because highly attractive women are stereotyped as being too feminine for the job. However, in a managerial context requiring a high degree of interpersonal skill, such as managing a furniture department in a large department store, attractiveness appears to be an asset (Cash and Kilcullen, 1985). Similarly, in "appearance-relevant" jobs such as personnel interviewing or counseling, physical attractiveness is more of an advantage in hiring decisions than it is in "appearance-irrelevant" positions such as safety administration or working with personnel records (Beehr and Gilmore, 1982).

One study manipulated the level of female attractiveness and appropriateness of dress for a hypothetical entry-level management position within a large corporation (Bardack and McAndrew, 1985). It found that both attractiveness and being well-dressed are assets, with physical attractiveness being weighted more heavily. An unattractive person could increase her chances of being hired from 68 to 76 percent by dressing well, whereas an attractive woman could enchance her chances from 82 to 100 percent. Female perceivers were especially hard on an unattractive applicant; only 58 percent indicated that they would hire her. In contrast, 80 percent of the men said they would (Bardack and McAndrew, 1985).

Attempts to draw general conclusions from these and other similar studies should be tempered by a few qualifications. Often, students have been the perceivers used in these studies rather than individuals who are especially likely to make the hiring decisions. Some research has suggested that there may be differences between students' and professional interviewers' judgments of candidates (Gilmore, Beehr, and Love, 1986). Also, differences in the ways researchers manipulate physical attractiveness (and the unique physical qualities of the individuals they use) may account for some discrepancies from one study to the next. Additionally, it is difficult to know whether perceptions of photographs (the most common stimulus

## Social Focus 8-1 (continued)

in these studies) actually simulate what occurs in the everyday business world, where people are influenced by other nonverbal and verbal cues in conjunction with appearance. Nevertheless, some common threads run through these studies and point to the relevance of both physical attractiveness and clothing in the context of hiring decisions. It seems that when physical attractiveness is used as a cue for understanding a person, a variety of inferences can lead to an anticipatory set in the mind of an evaluator. The result may be getting or not getting a job.

retailing business is "Show royal blue; sell navy blue." Whereas brighter or more flamboyant stimuli may attract the attention of consumers (for example, in the display window), many of these consumers are probably more likely to purchase and wear a more "toned-down" version of an avant-garde style. Nevertheless, the avant-garde style is the stimulus that leads to interest or arousal. This principle was illustrated in a study of female students' responses to a series of photographs of a female college student who was either very, fairly, slightly, or not similar to themselves. The students were less likely to accept new fashion suggestions when they thought they came from the pictured female who was very similar to themselves. New fashion suggestions were received more favorably from a dissimilar source (Leavitt and Kaigler-Evans, 1975). It seems that receivers may prefer to interact with people whom they perceive to be similar to themselves; they may be influenced more in some contexts by dissimilar and/or novel appearances because of the arousal or stimulation these appearances may provide in order to be noticed (see Figure 8-6).

As we will see in the following section, a sender's novel or noticeable appearance may also lead to the tendency to explain social outcomes by attributing them to him or her. Focusing on people because of their appearances may make us extra attentive to their degree of control over a situation.

### Attribution

Attribution theory falls under the general umbrella of a cognitive perspective and focuses on the inferences used by a perceiver to explain the causes of outcomes in interaction (Heider, 1958). Attributions may be either dispositional or situational. In the case of a **dispositional attribution**, it is assumed that the stimulus person is responsible for the outcome in social interaction. For example, a female wearing a seductive dress to a party may be perceived as "responsible" for attracting advances from males at the party. When a **situational attribution** is made, it is assumed that external forces, outside the control of the observed person, are responsible. A female who is attracting attention and is wearing a modest outfit is an example of situational attribution.

**FIGURE 8-6**
*In the context of a culture different from one's own, a perceiver is likely to be in a state of cognitive arousal. For example, a female fashion designer who travels to India may be visually stimulated by the style of clothes she sees (as shown here) to the extent that she creates some new styles of pants or "pegged" skirts, and uses scarves and other separates to create new looks. Photo by Stephen Cunha.*

When do perceivers make dispositional attributions, as opposed to situational ones, and how does appearance enter into this process? An actor's appearance may attract an observer's attention and thus result in a dispositional attribution. In contrast, if an actor's appearance is not sufficiently novel to attract a perceiver's attention, then that perceiver is likely to attribute a social outcome to the situation, rather than to the actor. For example, consider the male's appearance in Figure 8-7, and note how a perceiver might make a dispositional attribution by focusing primarily on his appearance, a situational attribution by considering factors linked to his role in this context, or some combination of the two.

Research has shown that perceivers are more likely to make a dispositional attribution when an actor's clothes are eye-catching. In contrast, a stimulus person whose "differentness" is more subtle (for example, more similar in style with other group members' attire) appears to call more attention to the social context (the group with which he conformed), producing situational attributions (McArthur and Post, 1977).

Dispositional attributions are likely to proceed from the observation of a person's *overt act* (for example, a woman wearing a skirted suit) to decisions about that person's *knowledge or ability* (for example, success or competence) to inferences about her *intentions* ("dressing for success," or trying to succeed in her job). It is on the basis of these inferred intentions that stable personal attributes, or *dispositions* (for example, intelligence and ambition) may be inferred (Jones and Davis, 1965). Perceivers must sort out whether these inferences can be tied to the person or merely to the situation (for example, high conformity required in office attire). If the person's attire is unique to the setting (for example, wearing only skirted suits when everyone else wears sundresses), perceivers are most likely to decide that the cause is not the situation, but rather the person. Thus, trait inferences are more likely to be assigned. Perceivers are more likely to decide that the situation is the "culprit" (in the context of a negative outcome) if the person being judged is well-known and liked (Solano, 1979).

Whether observers attribute the meanings of others' clothing to the observed person's dispositions or to the situation is a topic deserving further research

*FIGURE 8-7*
*Are you likely to interpret this male's appearance using a dispositional attribution, a situational attribution, or a combination of the two? A dispositional attribution may stem from some impressions about his ability or strength or from his pride in his body (because he wears running tights to work along with a muscle-revealing tank top). A situational attribution, on the other hand, might revolve around an explanation of his appearance based on contextual factors beyond his immediate control. For example, we might assume that he just came from a workout at the gym and did not have time to change his clothes (or else he would have been late to work). In many cases, perceivers are likely to use a combination of dispositional and situational attributions to interpret a person's appearance, to make sense of it, and to place it into a context. Photo by Carla M. Freeman.*

attention. Moreover, as a symbolic-interactionist perspective would suggest, the link between people and contexts in which they are observed is critical to the emergence of social identities. Therefore, dispositional and situational attributions are not necessarily mutually exclusive. It is especially difficult to tease apart the types of attributions defined by appearance cues, because clothes help to define situations as well as identify others. When we view problematic situations, we tend to rehearse (imaginatively) the various alternative reactions to these situations. We consider the identities of the observed persons in relation to the possible consequences of those persons' actions. Therefore, we do not necessarily make either dispositional *or* situational attributions, but in fact may link the two in our interpretations.

Some support for this linkage between observed persons and the contexts in which they are found was provided in a 1970s' study of deviant behavior (Deseran and Chung, 1979). The researchers had college students view videotaped scenes depicting rule-breaking (shoplifting) and non-rule-breaking (nonshoplifting) behavior of a "deviant" (hippie) versus a "straight" actress. In the hippie condition, the actress wore a long denim skirt, sandals, and a black sweater with no bra. Her hair was frizzy, and she wore no makeup. In the straight condition, she wore a moderate amount of makeup, a stylish skirt, blouse, and shoes; and her hair was pulled neatly into a bun. A pair of modern sunglasses also were worn over the head. The college students tended to make negative dispositional attributions in relation to moral attributes—not being trustworthy, moral, responsible, reliable, or honest—with (a) the shoplifting behavior in either style of dress or (b) the hippie appearance in the non-rule-breaking behavior. Appearance was used to make dispositional attributions related to morality in the straight condition, but appearance was not as important as the act itself when a deviant act (shoplifting) was observed.

Interestingly, though, the effect of appearance was more extreme than the effect of the behavior when it came to the "imagined" severity of the impact of shoplifting. The students thought that the consequences of shoplifting would be more severe in the straight condition than in the hippie condition. Why would they make such an attribution about the consequences of the deviant act? The hippie attire may have been seen as more consistent with shoplifting, as compared with the straight attire, based on some of the (not necessarily accurate) stereotypes of the 1970s. In addition, the students may have identified more *with* the actress in the straight condition and thus may have been more concerned about the possible outcome of the behavior.

Most studies have focused on clothing and other appearance cues as factors in trait inferences, although other kinds of dispositional information are also conveyed by a sender's appearance. Mary Lynn Damhorst (in press) analyzed 97 studies of dress perception and found that almost all of these produced significant effects as a function of dress. Among the traits assigned by receivers based on clothing, Damhorst identified four major categories: evaluation, potency, dynamism, and quality of thought.

## *Trait Perceptions Based on Clothing*

The basic positive or negative component of a person or relationship makes up his or her *evaluation*. Evaluation may deal with moral qualities, how a sender is expected to relate to others, interpersonal attractiveness, and affect (whether or not the receiver likes him or her).

*Evaluation*

A person may be evaluated as basically good or bad on the basis of appearance. Adjective scales such as sloppy–neat or trustworthy–untrustworthy are included in this subcategory under evaluation. Females dressed in conservative or casual styles are judged as more sincere, trustful, and reliable than those wearing dressy or "daring" (more sexually provocative) styles (Paek, 1986). In terms of the body itself, women with large breasts are viewed as less moral than women with small breasts (Kleinke and Staneski, 1980).

*Character*

Whether or not an observed person is seen as friendly and sociable is linked to his or her clothing (see Figure 8-8). Sociability encompasses judgments of how a person relates to others, as well as of that person's likableness and attractiveness as a potential friend. Trait scales such as cool–warm, pleasant–unpleasant, sociable–unsociable may be included in this subcategory. In-fashion or popular styles of clothing appear to communicate a stronger impression of sociability than out-of-fashion styles (Johnson, Nagasawa, and Peters, 1977). Very dressy or sophisticated styles of clothes worn by females appear to elicit judgments of their being less popular, cheerful, and sociable than those women wearing conservative, casual, or provocative styles. A dressy appearance may connote excessive concern about appearance and a lack of self-confidence on the part of a wearer (Paek, 1986). In a study that compared perceivers' judgments of males and females based on whether they wore either revealing or nonrevealing attire, those who wore nonrevealing attire were judged as more likable, kind, and warm (Abbey et al., 1987). It seems that women wearing revealing attire are perceived as sexually attractive and desirable, but not necessarily nice.

*Sociability*

Part of evaluating a sender may involve inferences about whether he or she feels good or bad about the self or situation. In one study, school counselors and law enforcement officers were asked to evaluate a male adolescent in the context of an office visit (Littrell and Berger, 1986). Attributions about his attitude were more negative when he was poorly groomed than when he was nicely groomed. The poorly groomed male was described in the following way:

*Mood*

- Thinking about what he's going to say.
- His attitude appears to be, "let's get this over with."
- Worried about the outcome of this conference as he may be sent for rehabilitation (Littrell and Berger, 1986).

**FIGURE 8-8**
*Research indicates that people wearing popular styles tend to be perceived as sociable or friendly (Johnson, Nagasawa, and Peters, 1977). Thus, if tie-dyed T-shirts, short skirts, and long hair are fashionable (as in the late 1980s due to a revival of many styles from the 1960s) or are commonly worn and accepted among one's peers, then impressions of sociability will be enhanced. This student's facial expression probably also contributes greatly to impressions of sociability. She also happens to be in a sorority, and this social involvement may add to a perceiver's impression of sociability. Photo by Wendy Dildey.*

This study illustrates the value of allowing receivers to use free-response assessments, rather than predesigned trait scales, when assessing an observed person's mood.

*Potency*

Potency judgments are linked to the strong and weak dimension of perception and are among the most commonly studied types of trait inferences. In Damhorst's (in press) analysis of 97 studies of dress perception, potency information was conveyed through clothing in 80 percent of the studies. Part of the concern with potency in research studies may stem from concerns about image and power in business, law enforcement, and other contexts in which potency is relevant (Damhorst, in press).

*Power*

Assessments of a sender's power pertain to perceptions of physical strength, interpersonal power, and perceived control over others and the environment.

Qualities of boldness, aggressiveness, and powerfulness are associated with the dimension of power (Bassett, 1979).

Power may also be conceptualized as the "ability to move others, spatially or otherwise" (Dabbs and Stokes, 1975). Uniforms tend to convey power in this way. In a military setting, a uniform symbolic of high rank has been found to increase the physical distance between interactants (Dean, Willis, and Hewitt, 1975). (The receivers allow more personal space for a higher ranking officer.) Similarly, more personal space is allowed for persons wearing formal or high-status business apparel (Fortenberry et al., 1978) or for physically attractive persons (Powell and Dabbs, 1976; Dabbs and Stokes, 1975).

Power may also revolve around judgments of legitimacy or authority. In one study, a guard in a uniform commanded more compliance to a request than did a milkman in uniform or a civilian in a sports jacket and tie. The guard's uniform may have rendered legitimacy to his request for passers-by to pick up a paper bag, to give a dime to a stranger, or to move away from a bus stop (Bickman, 1974).

Similarly, the addition of a hat to a police officer's uniform can enhance perceptions of his or her authority (Volpp and Lennon, 1988). In one study, clothing cues were carefully controlled for experimental purposes. The *style* of hat commanded different levels of authority for male and female officers. For males, the helmet was viewed as most authoritative, whereas for females the derby was evaluated as most authoritative. Accordingly, Volpp and Lennon (1988) concluded that "wearing a hat is more important for female officers than male officers if authority is to be conveyed" (p. 821).

However, clothing cues in other studies of power-related perceptions have not been controlled so systematically. For example, Bassett (1979) manipulated men's clothing along the dimension of occupational status (business suit versus blue-collar attire) and women's clothing along the dimension of status accrued by means of attractive attire. Hence, there was a tendency on the part of the researcher to conceptualize power along the traditional lines of agonic (direct) versus hedonic (indirect) power, as discussed earlier in Chapter Three. It is important for researchers to strive toward a more objective and systematic use of appearance cues (as per the Volpp and Lennon study) if we are to move toward a better understanding of gender, power, and dress.

*Competence*

Appearance influences judgments of a sender's competence (ability or expertise), even when the task at hand is unrelated to appearance. The extent to which a person is judged as qualified–unqualified, frivolous–serious, youthful–mature, successful–unsuccessful, or even able to write well may be influenced by clothing. Lapitsky and Smith (1981) studied 160 female students, who gave significantly higher ratings to an author (whose photograph they saw) when she wore attractive clothing. The attractively dressed writer was judged as having written a more creative essay, with more ideas and better general quality (but not necessarily organization) than was the less attractively dressed writer.

Males in white-collar attire are judged as more qualified and expert than males in blue-collar attire (Bassett, 1979). Of course, the question that comes to mind is, in what context? This question points to the need for research assessing competence to provide some sense of context for the receiver, such as he or she would find in everyday life.

*Intelligence*  Assessments of basic intelligence, level of education, and shallowness—deepness may also be based on clothing. The most prevalent cue of intelligence produced in studies has been glasses (Manz and Lueck, 1968; Hamid, 1968; Lennon and Miller, 1984). Other cues producing a dispositional attribution of intelligence for female models include conservative clothing consisting of skirted suits (Paek, 1986) or a blazer (Lennon and Miller, 1984). In contrast, very dressy styles are not as likely to convey an image of intelligence (Paek, 1986). Males, but not females, judged a male model in one study as less intelligent when he wore trendy attire, as compared with more classic casual attire (Hongo and Kaiser, 1989).

Appropriately enough, context has been found to influence judgments of intelligence. In one study, intelligence was based on the appropriateness of style of dress for the social context (Rees, Williams, and Giles, 1974). A male student was viewed as more intelligent when wearing a tie to an interview but less intelligent when wearing it to a lecture/tutorial. In the latter context, a tie may have been perceived as an attempt to compensate for a lack of intelligence. Or, the male may have been perceived as not knowing how to dress appropriately for the lecture/tutorial context.

## Dynamism

The category of traits linked to dynamism includes those referring to the degree of inertia in physical and mental activity (Damhorst, in press). This category may be further divided into subcategories of *activity* (for example, fast—slow), *control* (for example, relaxed—tense), and *stimulation* (for example, interesting—dull).

One of the earlier studies in appearance perception involved the effect of lipstick on evaluations of a female. Male students judged a female in an interview as more frivolous, more talkative, and more anxious when she wore lipstick than when she did not (McKeachie, 1952).

## Quality of Thought

Quality of thought inferences pertain to attributions about belief structures and modes of thinking, or the manner in which an observed person approaches problems and events. Quality of thought may include judgments associated with *flexibility* (imaginative, adventurous, open-minded, individualistic, and creative), *objectivity* (empirical—theoretical and idealistic—realistic), and *tangibility* (clarity and complexity of thinking).

More "daring" or provocative clothing styles worn by women are associated with self-oriented and individualistic traits (Paek, 1986). Research conducted in the 1970s, when beards and long hair were associated with a liberal world view, indicated that bearded males were perceived as not only more open-minded, but also more educated, intelligent, outgoing, and reckless than a clean-shaven male. Similarly, a male with long hair was viewed as more open-minded and reckless than a short-haired male (Pancer and Meindl, 1978).

*Summary*

Research has clearly indicated that appearance influences trait perceptions, but as Damhorst (in press) has noted, researchers may tend to "stack the deck" by providing trait scales for receivers that they may not ordinarily use. There may be adjectives that would be more meaningful to perceivers than those provided by a researcher (Davis and Lennon, 1988). Additionally, much more information is provided by appearance than traits alone. As we will see in Chapter Ten, appearance simultaneously conveys a multitude of information about a person's identity, attitude, values and mood, as well as about the social context itself. In everyday life, as compared to the experimental tasks required of perceivers in research studies, social cognition is uncontrolled by external forces and open to numerous context effects. Moreover, receivers are concerned not only with understanding other persons but also with *communicating* with them. Thus social cognition may be subsumed by the larger, two-way process of communication.

Accordingly, the symbolic-interactionist approach to communication, which is more inclusive and less specific in terms of receiver thought processes than the cognitive perspective, is useful for exploring mutual processes of appearance management *and* perception. The broader symbolic-interactionist approach does not preclude an emphasis on cognitive processes (Quin, Robinson, and Balkwell, 1980). Even more broadly, a contextual approach, which includes a sensitivity to cultural context, allows us to view appearance communication from a perspective in terms of social constraints and expectations, that is, individual processes in larger social structures (Pettigrew, 1981; Kaiser, 1983–1984). A contextual approach reminds us that perceivers have unique social experiences that they bring with them to social interactions, and these past experiences (along with the expectations and emotions) become part of any social context.

*Suggested Readings*

Bandura, A. 1986. Social foundations of thought and action: A social cognitive theory. Englewood Cliffs: Prentice-Hall, Inc.
> Bandura reviews various models of human nature and causality, using a (social) cognitive perspective. He notes that "theoretical conceptions on human nature can influence what people actually become" (p. 1).

Buckley, H. M. 1985. Toward an operational definition of dress. *Clothing and Textiles Research Journal* 3(2):1–10.
> Buckley draws on a cognitive perspective in an elaborate study of perceivers' categorizations of women's clothing styles. The data suggest that perceivers use both structural and contextual criteria to classify clothes.

Damhorst, M. L. In press. In search of a common thread: Classification of information communicated through dress. *Clothing and Textiles Research Journal*.
> Damhorst provides an analysis of dress perception studies, classifies the type of information

communicated through dress, and calls for new methodologies to expand the scope of inquiry in this area.

Lennon, S. J., and Davis, L. L. 1989. Clothing and human behavior from a social cognitive framework. Part I: Theoretical perspectives. *Clothing and Textiles Research Journal* 7(4):41–48.
Lennon and Davis summarize the various theoretical insights a (social) cognitive perspective provides and classify existing research to suggest the need for new directions of study.

Miller, F. G. 1982. Clothing and physical impairment: Joint effects on person perception. *Home Economics Research Journal* 10:265–270.
Miller presents a study on the interaction between clothing and physical disability cues. The concepts of dispositional and situational attributions are employed in the study.

# Chapter Nine
# · · ·
# Perceiver Variables

*Appearance perceptions are influenced not only by the images that are observed and evaluated, but also by the characteristics of the perceivers themselves. Perceivers bring with them to any social context a variety of personal backgrounds that shape what and how they see. Similarly, as consumers, perceivers respond toward specific items of apparel or accessories based upon similar background characteristics. In this chapter, we will explore variations among perceivers based upon self-related characteristics (self-esteem, sensitivity to appearance, awareness, values, attitudes, and interests) as well as demographic variations based upon such variables as gender, age, social class, occupation, and ethnicity. In this way we can consider how males and females differ in their interpretations of clothes and appearance, for example, or how individuals who are interested in sports differ in their perceptions of active sportswear from persons who do not hold such an interest. Our focus is on perceivers as selves with unique attributes and understandings.*

In everyday life, individuals construct and interpret images through processes of appearance management and perception. Just as appearance management is an active albeit implicit activity, so is the process of understanding others through their appearances. At times, appearance perception is on a more conscious plane than other times, but the important thing to remember is that perceivers are not merely passive receivers of information. Perceivers bring unique characteristics to social interactions, and these characteristics influence their frames of reference, world views (how they see the world), and levels of awareness. In this chapter we will explore personal, demographic characteristics that influence how receivers see and interpret appearances differently. We will also look at how basic values and related attributes shape the extent to which individuals use clothing and appearance in everyday interpretations.

## Self as Perceiver

A fundamental proposition may be stated in relation to appearance perception: What is perceived in a social situation is determined by characteristics of the perceiver as well as characteristics of a clothed appearance. Each perceiver brings something unique to a social situation, and an understanding of self-as-perceiver qualities is a critical prerequisite to understanding appearance communication as a two-way process—involving both appearance management and perception.

The self is not only observed but is also an observer. Therefore, in appearance communication it is important to look at characteristics of individuals as both senders (observed) and receivers (observers). Granted, everyone is not equally tuned in to appearance, and socialization influences *how* interpretations of appearance are formulated.

We need to delineate the difference between the characteristics of perceivers and the appearance contexts they perceive (Lapitsky and Smith, 1981; Littrell and Berger, 1986), because meanings associated with appearance are *assigned* by people. These meanings are not intrinsically tied to appearances. Identity-linked characteristics such as gender, age, social class, occupation, and ethnicity are among the perceiver variables studied by researchers. Self-esteem, personal values, and interest in and awareness of clothing also help to set the stage for appearance management *and* perception.

## Identity-linked Variables

### Gender

Studies exploring gender differences in perceptions of appearance have produced some important similarities and differences. The similarities often seem to pertain to general preferences that may relate to aesthetic codes (Lubner-Rupert and Winakor, 1985). Additionally, males and females seem to have the same kinds of expectations in certain social contexts (for example, in counseling sessions, as found by Paradise, Zweig and Conway, 1986). Yet some critical distinctions in male–female appearance perceptions have been identified across studies related to physical attractiveness, perceptions of sexuality, aesthetic judgments of own-versus opposite-sex attire, and assessments of business-social attire. Most of the existing research focuses on gender differences in perceivers' evaluations of *females'* appearances. Less is known about the meanings of males' appearances in general, much less about *differences* in perceivers' evaluations of males as a function of gender.

### Physical Attractiveness

Studies comparing male and female perceivers of sender's physical attractiveness have produced some mixed results that may be attributable to context effects. In some cases, females have been found to be more lenient than males in their judgments of physical attractiveness. Men may be particularly likely to rate other men, pictured in photographs, lower in terms of attractiveness because of a homophobic reaction (Maret and Harling, 1985). On the other hand, other research has indicated that opposite-sex persons are rated more positively when viewed in real life. In a laboratory study, male subjects rated attractive female experimenters more positively than unattractive female experimenters, whereas female subjects rated attractive male experimenters more positively than unattractive male experimenters (Barnes and Rosenthal, 1985).

In a study on personnel decisions, women were especially critical of an unattractive female stimulus person who dressed poorly. Only 58 percent of the female (student) subjects indicated that they would hire her; in contrast, 80 percent of the men said they would. Otherwise, males and females were similar on their evaluations (Bardack and McAndrew, 1985). It seems that females may not be as tolerant of other females who do not dress well, especially when those females are not as physically attractive. This relative lack of tolerance may be attributable at least in part to the salience of the context, as in the case of one involving an employment decision.

Another study reinforced the idea that females are favorably influenced by a physically attractive appearance of job candidates, at least for two of three jobs—tax manager and postmaster, but not vice principal. Although males tended to ignore appearance altogether in their ratings of the candidates' resumés, females were favorably influenced by resumés of candidates with average to above-average appearances (Quereshi and Kay, 1986).

Males and females also differ in perceptions of females' sexuality. This difference is in the direction of male perceivers focusing more on sexuality and/or finding female appearances more sexually attractive than female perceivers. This variation in perceptions, while fairly consistent across studies, is a *relative* difference or evident in terms of a matter of degree. Also, despite this consistent trend, there are some findings on gender differences that reveal the complex and sometimes paradoxical nature of these differences. *Sexuality*

For example, one study explored the question: How do males and females compare in the amount of time they spend looking at male and female appearances (Rosenwasser, Adams, and Tansh, 1983)? Not surprisingly, men looked longer at slides of women than they did at slides of men. However, women looked longer at slides of clothed women than they did at slides of men. Overall viewing times were ranked as follows: (1) men looking at women clothed, (2) women looking at women clothed, (3) women looking at men in bathing suits, and (4) men looking at women in bathing suits. In a laboratory setting, males may have known that it is not socially desirable to stare a long time at a scantily clad female, so the amount of time males spend looking at women in bathing suits may differ in private contexts (when they do not suspect their perceptions are being observed). Still, there was a pattern for men to look longer at (clothed) women than they did at (clothed) men, and this pattern may be explained in terms of attraction. The fact that women looked longer at clothed women than any other stimuli may be accounted for by the aesthetic complexity of a clothed female appearance, or by intrasex competitiveness (Rosenwasser, Adams, and

Tansh, 1983). This study points to the intricate nature of gender differences in appearance perception.

Given the choice, it seems that males generally prefer to see females in less-than-modest attire, although not necessarily obviously provocative attire. In a study of female models' attractiveness, which was based on different clothing styles ranging from blatantly provocative to modest, males tended to prefer more revealing clothes on the female models than did female receivers (Williamson and Hewitt, 1986). Males preferred short shorts over boxer-length shorts and miniskirts over regular-length skirts. However, males did not necessarily prefer blatantly provocative styles such as an unbuttoned shirt or a no-bra look emphasized by a wet T-shirt. And, such obviously provocative styles actually *reduced* perceived attractiveness on the part of female receivers. Females rated women as less attractive in the no-bra, unbuttoned shirt, and miniskirt conditions; however, they did find the short shorts to be more attractive than the boxer shorts. (It should be noted that this study was most likely completed before boxer shorts became fashionable for women later in the 1980s.) Therefore, it seems that subtle forms of sexually alluring attire do make a woman more attractive in the eyes of men, whereas more blatant forms of sexually alluring attire do not increase a woman's attractiveness in the eyes of men and actually reduce it in the eyes of women (Williamson and Hewitt, 1986).

Additional research also suggests that differences in male–female perceptions of females are a matter of degree. In a study of perceptions of women in magazine advertising, males did find some of the ads to be quite sexist, but they judged them as significantly less sexist than did females. Moreover, males still gave more favorable ratings to sexist ads than did females (Rossi and Rossi, 1985).

Gender differences in perceptions of females' appearances must consider the "visual-stimulant" dimension of clothed female appearances. For males, sensuality is emphasized in this dimension, as evident by their responses on scales evaluating attractiveness, sexiness, temptation, and femininity. In contrast, females appear to emphasize, or be visually stimulated by, fashion and social status indicators in clothed female appearances (Kaigler-Evans and Damhorst, 1978). (See Figure 9-1.)

Male adolescents, more than female adolescents, seem to attend to female clothes as a sign of sexual interest or availability (Zellman and Goodchilds, 1983). In general, research indicates that heterosexual males regard female appearances as more sexy and seductive than do heterosexual females. In contrast, males do not consistently perceive males more sexually than do female perceivers (Abbey et al., 1987).

The implications of gender differences in sexually-related appearance perceptions of females will be explored more thoroughly later in Social Focus 10-1.

*Aesthetic Preferences*      One of the few studies using both male and female clothing as stimuli compared the responses of 30 married couples to clothing styles (Lubner-Rupert and Winakor, 1985). Generally, the males and females ranked men's suits and women's

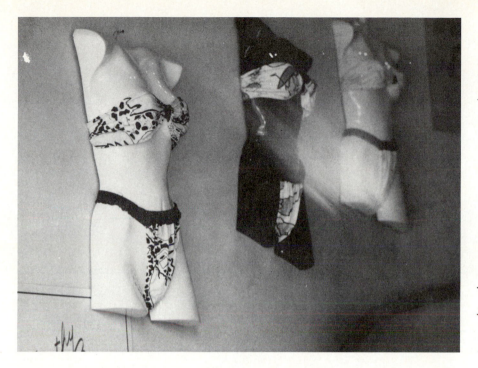

**FIGURE 9-1**
*Research suggests that males are more likely than females to focus on characteristics of sensuality and sexiness in women's clothing. Thus, one can imagine the potential differences in focus that lead to interpretations that might arise if a female wears a swimsuit of this style on the beach. For example, a woman might be aware that this swimsuit is likely to be perceived as sexy, but her focus is on fashionability. To a man, however, the question of fashionability is likely to be less of an issue than sexiness. Photo by Susan B. Kaiser.*

dresses similarly. However, males and females tended to judge their own-sex clothes more harshly than those of the opposite sex. Other-sex clothing was judged more favorably in terms of such bipolar scales as ugly–beautiful, handsome–homely, and appealing–unappealing. Overall, however, there were many more similarities than differences between males and females (Lubner-Rupert and Winakor, 1985).

In a study exploring gender differences in perceptions of male clothing styles, the idea that own-sex perceptions are more critical than opposite-sex judgments was reinforced (Hongo and Kaiser, 1989). Basically, females tended to be more lenient than males in terms of some forms of evaluation. The females evaluated a male model pictured in five different clothing styles as slightly more intriguing (less boring) than males did. The males and females did not differ in their judgments of updated–outdated. However, females were less likely than males to evaluate the pictured male as effeminate, regardless of his attire or the altered grooming, including gelled hair and an earring in some conditions. Also, there was a trend for females to judge the more fashionable male appearances as creative (Hongo and Kaiser, 1989).

Other research suggests that males and females use somewhat different aesthetic criteria in the evaluation of male appearances. One study explored the aesthetic "rules" about what types of patterns (solids, stripes, or plaids) should be worn together in men's outfits (jacket, slacks, tie, and shirt) (Holbrook, 1986). (See Figure 9-2 for the stimuli used in this study.)

**FIGURE 9-2**
*This graph depicts preference vectors for men and women with high-versus low-verbalizing/visualizing tendencies. [M = male; F = female; HVV = high visualizing (highly sensitive to Gestalt-like patterns and cue configurations); LVV = low visualizing (less sensitive to Gestalt-like perceptions).] Note that males tend to "play it safe" in their preferences, regardless of verbalizing/visualizing tendencies, whereas females may be differentiated more in terms of these tendencies (compare the upper right and lower right vectors). Reprinted by permission of the* Journal of Consumer Research 13 *(December 1986), "Aims, concepts, and methods for the representation of individual differences in esthetic responses to design features," by Morris B. Holbrook, p. 340.*

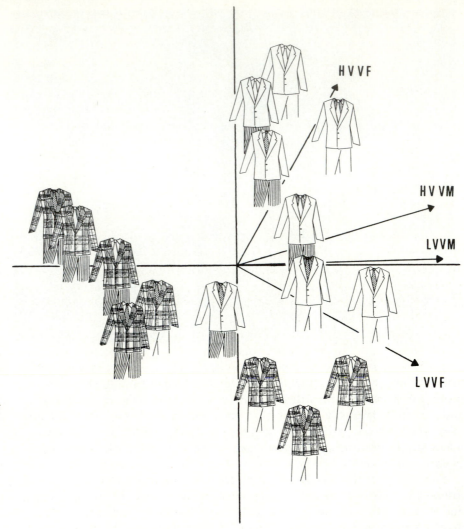

Also explored in this study was the distinction between visualizing and verbalizing tendency. Visualizing tendency refers to a Gestalt-like perception, including the degree of holistic sensitivity to patterns and cue configurations. Verbalizing tendency, on the other hand, relates to the degree of analytic attention to particular stimuli and/or isolated cues. As compared to females, men did not tend to vary much in terms of their preferences for men's ensembles on the basis of verbalizing and visualizing tendency. Men tended to be basically neutral or indifferent about nonclashing outfits (with no more than two striped or plaid features); however, they strongly disliked clashing combinations. Men seemed to "play it safe" in terms of their preferences. (Note that they hover around the right-hand side along the horizontal axis in Figure 9-2). Females, on the other hand, varied more on the basis of verbalizing and visualizing inclinations. Highly visual women tended to prefer simple combinations with plain jackets and no more than one or two sets of stripes (in a tie, pants, or shirt.) (See the upper-right-hand quadrant in Figure 9-2.) They did not like any of the suit ensembles including plaid jackets, so they did not really distinguish among them. In contrast, more verbal (less visual) women actually tended to prefer plaid jackets, but only when they were combined with no more than one striped article of clothing (for example, a striped tie or shirt), as shown in the lower-right-hand quadrant in Figure 9-2. The highly verbal women tended to be relatively neutral in their evaluations of any outfit including a solid jacket, but they had a strong disregard for any clashing combinations with three or more striped and plaid features (Holbrook, 1986).

Several studies have explored gender differences in perceptions of female attire that may or may not be suitable for business or professional contexts. In general, these studies have suggested that females are more receptive to women's business attire than are males. Or, at least, males respond to different criteria in women's business attire. One study indicated that males' and females' perceptions of female business attire were generally similar overall, although formality was emphasized more by males in perceptions of appropriate business attire (Dillon, 1980). Another study expanded the range of clothing styles shown to include social as well as business attire (DeLong, Salusso-Deonier, and Larntz, 1983). Overall, the males' responses showed less variation than female responses, or, male response patterns were more consistent. [Note that this difference supports the finding of the Holbrook (1986) study.] Males responded to female attire as relatively more sexy, conspicuous, formal, and elegant than did female receivers. As in Dillon's (1980) study, formality was more important in the male response. Males tended to like business dress somewhat less, view it as less fashionable, less attractive, and less exciting than social dress. Females differentiated business from social dress more than did males; females were also more sympathetic to the idea of business dress (DeLong, Salusso-Deonier, and Larntz, 1983).

*Women's Attire: Social-Business Evaluations*

This receptivity toward female career appearance on the part of females was reinforced in another study (Kelley et al., 1982), where females had more favorable views of line drawings of career appearances than did males. Also, females were more favorable about the concept of appropriate work-role attire. One explanation for this gender difference is that females may place more faith in the ability of a female career appearance to present a favorable professional impression.

A similar gender difference was noted in a study comparing different styles of female appearances (Sweat and Zentner, 1985). Although both males and females rated a classic appearance (skirted suit) as conventional and dominant, the females regarded it as more conventional and more dominant than did the males. Females also considered a more feminine, romantic style to be more submissive than did the males. (See Figure 9-3.) These differences in males' and

**FIGURE 9-3**
*Research by Sweat and Zentner (1985) indicated that this appearance style was perceived by both males and females as approachable and submissive, as compared with other less feminine appearance styles. Females, however, viewed this style as much more submissive than males did, consistent with a trend for females to rate the appearance styles closer to stereotypic images than did males.*

females' assignments of meaning to women's dress may, in part, result from women's greater knowledge of women's dress (including knowledge about gender stereotypes). Additionally, there is some evidence that women are more sensitive to nonverbal messages than are men (Henley, 1977). Because gender differences of this sort are likely to be influenced greatly by socialization, we will look next at differences in children's perceptions of dress as a function of gender.

*Children*    The idea that females, to a greater extent than males, are socialized to connect diverse female appearances with specific attributes is further supported by a study comparing young boys' and girls' (aged 3 through 6 years) associations of play behaviors with girls' clothing styles (pants versus skirts) (Kaiser and Phinney, 1983). Only 31 percent of the males under 5 years old associated doll play with a girl in a skirt, whereas 79 percent of the females under 5 years made that association. Similarly, the girls in the study were more likely to associate the girl in the dress than the one in pants with the activity of cooking, regardless of age. One-third of the boys under 5 years of age made this association, in contrast to 80 percent of the males over 5 years.

Thus, like-sex associations appear to develop very early, whereas opposite-sex symbolic associations emerge a little later in childhood. Deeply ingrained gender-symbolic connections appear to be especially salient when applied to one's own sex. (At least, this appears to be true with females; there is a need for more research with males in this area.)

Research with elementary-school-aged children revealed that boys were less likely than girls to attribute popularity, wealth, happiness, and good looks to product usage (Mayer and Belk, 1985). Girls admired persons wearing designer jeans and popular shoes; they associated these styles with popularity, happiness, intelligence, good looks, and wealth, to a greater extent than males. The girls were more sensitive to clothing cues than boys. In general, females held stronger stereotypes than did males for different products. Also, the children most clearly inferred user characteristics for products likely to be owned by members of their own sex. The greater cue sensitivity among females was most pronounced for products likely to be owned by girls. Moreover, girls were more likely than boys to envision designer-jeans owners as female (Belk, Mayer, and Driscoll, 1984).

*Summary*

Some general themes emerge from the various studies noting gender differences in perceptions of appearance. Like-sex evaluations appear to be more critical than opposite-sex evaluations. Opposite-sex perceptions appear to be more lenient. Perhaps like-sex judgments are made on the basis of additional knowledge, sensitivity, or attentiveness to detail. Or, opposite-sex judgments may be mediated by attraction. In some cases, like-sex perceptions are actually more stereotypical than those of the opposite-sex. An important exception to this rule is noted in the case of males perceiving sensuality in female appearances. Whereas females appear to use a frame of reference based on the criteria of fashion and aesthetic details for evaluating female appearances, males are more likely to employ a frame of reference using criteria of sensuality.

The limited data that are available on male appearances suggest that some important differences may be attributed to the gender of the stimulus person as well as to the perceiver's gender. Since most of the existing research deals with female appearances, clearly there is a need for more studies on male appearances to see if the same gender differences apply there as well.

It is also important to note that some studies have revealed contexts in which gender is not a significant perceiver variable. For example, in a study exploring perceptions of a counselor's professional and personal attributes and influence, there were no differences in males' and females' perceptions. Also, the sex of the counselor did not matter (Paradise, Zweig, and Conway, 1986). This points to the importance of understanding gender in context. Although most studies look at stimuli stripped from social context, in real life a variety of contextual factors influence how males and females perceive clothing and, more generally, appearance.

*Age*

Young children make extensive use of appearance when forming impressions of others. Physical appearance and clothing are peripheral cues that can be observed in a concrete manner. In contrast, personality traits are abstract and less easily observed and understood by young children (Barenboim, 1981; Livesley and Bromley, 1973).

As early as 2 years of age, children use clothing and hairstyle as cues to differentiate between males and females according to cultural "rules" of gender typing (Thompson, 1975; Weinraub et al., 1984). Children develop mental male and female filing systems, and appearance cues are most likely the earliest symbols to be included in such systems. Children at the age of 26 months are aware, for example, that adult men and women wear and use different artifacts, as indicated by their ability to differentiate between (*a*) men's suits, shirts, and hats and (*b*) women's dresses, blouses, purses, and makeup (Weinraub et al., 1984).

Young girls' clothes are further differentiated according to the kinds of behaviors with which they are associated, for example, wearers of dresses are associated with doll play (Kaiser and Phinney, 1983). Behaviors or overt actions, such as appearance, are relatively concrete. Thus the ability to perceive appearance is followed by an ability to perceive behaviors which, in turn, lead to more abstract processes of attributing personality traits (Barenboim, 1981). Children progress, then, from dichotomous filing systems to the use of more elaborate webs of meaning, connecting appearance styles not only with overt behaviors but also with abstract personality traits (Kaiser, 1989). (See Social Focus 9-1 and Figure 9-4 for more information on cognitive development and appearance perceptions in relation to gender typing.)

With increasing years, children have more consumption experience and are more cognizant of cultural stereotypes (Belk, Mayer, and Driscoll, 1984), but are more flexible in their judgments based on appearance than are younger children (Kaiser, 1989). Progressive socialization and cognitive development allow perceivers to become more adaptable or resilient in their interpretations of appearance. They may recognize that specific trait information about a person (for example, intelligent) is contingent on contextual information. Therefore, perceivers qualify trait descriptions with increased socialization (Leahy, 1976).

In addition to social-cultural perceptions linked to age, structural perceptions of clothes per se are associated with developmental factors. By the approximate age of 5 years, children are able to distinguish specific garment details or features (for example, a sleeve, a ruffle, or a pocket), as well as to see them in relation to the garment whole (Kaigler-Evans and Hulls-Huggins, 1981).

There is some evidence that perceivers become (what is known in Gestalt theory as) less field-dependent with increased age and knowledge of clothing features (Baer, 1979). Persons who are more *field-dependent* are less adept at locating a figure embedded in a larger context. Such perceivers are influenced heavily by background features, or by the Gestalt effect; thus the prevailing field or context sways their perceptions. In contrast, *field-independent* perceivers tend to experience surroundings analytically and are able to detect details or objects as discrete or apart from their backgrounds. Natural cognitive development is likely to promote an ability to become less field-dependent, or more field-in-dependent, with increasing age. [The previously discussed study by Kaigler-

# Cognitive Development and Gender Perception

Children seem to use cultural criteria to develop what we might think of as "mental filing systems" to distinguish between boys and girls in looks, dress, and behavior. Clothes and related cultural objects are among the earliest entries into these filing systems. From a developmental perspective, we can consider that clothes and related cultural objects are visible, tangible, and concrete. So, before children develop the perceptual skills to assign and distinguish among abstract personality traits as they perceive other persons, they are able to discern concrete or obvious differences among individuals. Then, children are able to begin to understand other persons in terms of their actions and behaviors, followed by their more abstract personality traits (Livesley and Bromley, 1973; Barenboim, 1981).

A cognitive-developmental approach to gender perception would suggest that observations inconsistent with basic thought processes are likely to be ignored in the formative stages of comparing males with females. However, in the later stages the subtle complexities and ambiguities of gender may be tolerated and used to refine developing "networks" composed of cultural objects such as clothes, overt behaviors, and abstract traits. Thus, the mental filing systems are likely to break down somewhat as children realize that there are exceptions to the rule— for example, girls can wear jeans, can play actively, and can possess aggressive personality traits. Cognitive-developmental theory would predict that children are more tolerant of ambiguity in gender meanings once they are comfortable with their understanding of gender ideology and realize that gender is a relatively stable aspect of identity (Kohlberg, 1966). In other words, one can break some of the rules and still be a boy or a girl. For example, a girl in middle childhood (between the ages of 7 or 8 years and 10 or 11 years) may no longer feel as great a need to wear a dress for purposes of reaffirming her sexual identity, and the choice of a dress may become increasingly based on contextual considerations.

Research with young girls has shown that with increased age, their degree of cognitive flexibility in gender perceptions increases (Kaiser, 1989). Girls in middle childhood have less need than preschool girls to reaffirm their own female identities through the selection of frilly dresses. Therefore, they are more appreciative of the functional benefits of pants. Along with this cognitive flexibility there appears to be an increased ability by middle childhood to interpret culturally derived gender symbolism in light of social context. Hence, pants are seen as more appropriate for a broader range of play activities, especially active ones. At the same time, gender stereotypes become internalized. Thus, a young girl who is hitting another child is more likely to be expected to wear jeans by girls in middle childhood years, whereas girls under 5 years are just as likely to imagine her wearing a frilly dress. What becomes especially important in the understanding of developing gender perceptions, however, is to consider the ability of the older girls to qualify and put into context their perceptions—to display that they realize stereotypes do not always apply in everyday life. For example, several girls indicated in their comments that a young girl wearing a frilly dress could either be genuinely sweet or snobbish and self-absorbed (Kaiser, 1989). (See Figure 9-4.) Thus, there are ambiguities in the interpretations of gender symbols, and one must rely on context and use one's interpretive processes to make sense of and assign meaning to gender in everyday life.

Style #1

STRONG (93.0)

BRAVE (72.1)

MEAN (55.8)

LIKES TO WIN (47.6)

(52.1)

(61.1)

(44.6)

(51.6)

(40.0)

(40.0)

Style #2

(42.1)

(41.1)

(41.4)

(38.9)

(41.1)

Style #3

(35.1)

(47.4)

PATIENT (74.4)

HONEST (58.1)

SOLVES PROBLEMS (52.2)

LIKES TO HELP OTHERS (51.2)

SHY (51.2)

Style #4

(55.8)

(37.9)

CARES ABOUT HER LOOKS (93.0)

POPULAR (73.8)

SWEET (53.5)

BOSSY (51.2)

*MOST PREFERRED STYLE*

Evans and Hulls-Huggins (1981) also showed that older children were more adept at distinguishing garment details (less field-dependent) than were younger children.] Similarly, junior and senior college students studying clothing were more accurate than lower-division students in their recall of clothing designs associated with the upper and central body areas. Field-independent perceivers, who are likely to be older or more experienced, are able to imprint the image of clothing design and recall it more accurately (Baer, 1979).

How do older adults compare with younger adults in their perceptions of appearance? Unfortunately, few studies have explored older adults as perceivers. Some research, however, indicates that older adults are especially attentive to neatness in appearance and tend to respond favorably (for example, by complying with a request) to people who are tidily and neatly dressed (Lambert, 1972; Judd, Bull, and Gahagan, 1975). Older adults also appear to be conscious of neatness of older actors' and actresses' appearances in the media (Kaiser and Chandler, 1988). In a series of interviews, older adults were asked to comment on appearance features of older adults in magazine advertisements. They generally commented negatively on such appearance cues as a long, unkempt beard or pants that were rumpled and baggy in the crotch. A woman perceiving a photograph of the actor Robert Young, in an ad for decaffeinated coffee, commented: "This is how all men should look: happy, neat, tidy, and making the best of the situation." A photograph of an older female model in a blue dress and matching jacket was also preferred by the older adults: "Now that is me. I have a two-piece dress like that, and I feel good in it. I think she is neat; her hair is neat and very striking." In contrast, an older male model wearing an ill-fitting pants-and-sweater ensemble evoked the following comment: "He looks like an unmade bed."

It is important when interpreting research findings related to age of perceivers to place these findings in their historic context. Socialization emphasizing neatness in appearance may vary in different generational contexts. Thus, older adults in the 1970s and 1980s held certain opinions about appropriate appearances, whereas older adults in the year 2000 or beyond may hold different views. Fashion is part of socialization and is inextricably linked to time and, hence, age. Later, in Social Focus 13-2, older adults' perceptions of fashion will be explored in conjunction with media usage.

---

*FIGURE 9-4*

*This illustration depicts the cluster of behaviors and traits girls associated with four different clothing styles in a study by Kaiser (1989). The clothing-behavior associations were based on a study of 95 girls aged 2 to 10 years. Four years later, 43 of the same girls (now aged 6 to 13 years) made the clothing-trait associations noted here. Clothing-behavior associations are more concrete and tangible than clothing-trait associations. Hence, older girls are able to make abstract associations as required to match style number 3, for example, with the following attributes: patient, honest, solves problems, and the like. The numbers in the illustration refer to the percentage of girls making the association. Courtesy of Clothing and Textiles Research Journal.*

## Social Class

How does social class influence perceivers' judgments of appearance? As the following studies show, there is some evidence of a relation between social class and appearance perception. Indicators of social class typically include income, educational background, and occupation. (Social class will be considered in greater detail in Chapter Thirteen.)

We might expect that persons would vary in their appearance perceptions on the basis of diverse experiences because of the social worlds in which they interact. Personal goals and values are also likely to be influenced by factors such as education and occupation.

Early research in this area indicated that working-class family values differ from those of families with a white-collar worker. Upper-class women in the Midwest during the 1940s were found to be more interested in fashion and more likely to have the leisure time to shop. These women were also likely to admit that they judged others by their clothing. In contrast, women married to working-class husbands were less concerned with fashion (Useem, Tangent, and Useem, 1942). Similarly, in the early 1960s, Rosencranz (1962) found that women with higher income levels and husbands in white-collar positions were more aware of clothing or cognizant of incongruities between appearance and social context.

Evidence indicates that social class influences appearance perceptions at a relatively young age (Mayer and Belk, 1985). In a study of elementary-school-aged children's perceptions of different products, children from higher social classes viewed owners of high-status attire (designer jeans and popular shoes) and a 10-speed bicycle as more wealthy, popular, likely to have new things, and admirable than did lower-social-class children. Children of lower social classes attributed more wealth, popularity, tendency to have new things, and admirability to owners of a dirt bike and video arcade game. Apparently products carry different meanings of social status for children of different social class backgrounds (Mayer and Belk, 1985). Children make more favorable inferences about owners of products associated with, or more likely to be owned by, persons in their own social class (Belk, Mayer, and Driscoll, 1984).

## Occupation

Occupation is one indicator of social class. In terms of appearance perceptions, occupation becomes a critical parameter due to its impact on daily awareness of certain appearance cues. In a study comparing college students from professional level versus working-class families, no differences emerged (Kelley et al., 1982). However, occupational focus was a contributing variable to attitudes about career appearance. Students oriented toward engineering occupations differed from those inclined toward business careers. Respondents who anticipated having more contact with clients (business students) placed more importance on the role of appearance in the occupational world than did engineering students, who were likely to expect less contact with the public. And, regardless of occupational orientation of campus recruiters, who were also studied, they tended to differ from students. Recruiters of both sexes held more favorable views about career appearances than did students of both sexes, and females (whether students or recruiters) held more favorable views than males (Kelley et al., 1982).

Additional research has indicated that a perceiver's frame of reference when evaluating a person's appearance is influenced by occupation. Littrell and Berger (1986) compared law enforcement officers with counselors and found varying levels of perceptual attentiveness to specific appearance details. The two occupational groups differed in the cognitive categories they used to judge the appearance of an adolescent male client in the context of an office visit. The counselors noted fewer detailed appearance cues than did law enforcement officers. Counselors were more likely to notice general aspects of appearance (average looks and overall details), whereas law enforcement officers mentioned more specific items, including details about the boy's jeans, socks, and colors for clothing. Law enforcement officers are more likely to be trained or socialized to pay attention to detailed cues, because their job entails a need to deal frequently with person descriptions. In contrast, counselors are more concerned about a client's general demeanor and outlook. Additionally, counselors were more concerned with whether the client was there on his own volition or because of a referral, whereas the law enforcement officers focused more on the reputation of the client and the nature of the crime or nonstatus offense. The counselors rated the client higher than the police officers did on grooming and fashion. The counselors were also more likely to focus their comments on discipline and personal and vocational concerns:

- He would have come to see me on his own.
- He is being disrespectful to his teacher.
- He is wondering if the engineering school will be interested in the courses he takes or his performance in those courses.

The law enforcement officers were more concerned about the boy's crime record:

- Person has had a few problems with the law before.
- He was involved in some sort of vandalism.

Perceivers of both occupations, however, commented more about the client's attitude about an office visit when he was poorly groomed (Littrell and Berger, 1986).

Research has also shown that whether mothers work outside the home influences their perceptions of portrayals of mothers in advertising (Kaiser, Carstens, and Freeman, working paper) (see Figure 9-5). Mothers at home were more likely than those who worked outside the home to view the mother in Figure 9-5 as putting her job ahead of her family and being more job- than home-oriented when she was wearing a business suit. The mothers who did not work outside the home tended to believe that mothers wearing business

## For the mother who's on the go - a versatile stroller that fits into your lifestyle.

Featuring:
One-hand release handle
Adjustable safety belt
Cushioned seat and backrest

Stroll-Ez®

**FIGURE 9-5**
*Whether or not a mother worked outside the home influenced how she evaluated the mother depicted in this stroller ad (Kaiser et al., working paper). Mothers who worked outside the home were less likely than those who stayed at home to think that this mother would put her job ahead of her family and to evaluate her as unlikely to cry and to be unaware of others' feelings. Photo by Susan B. Kaiser.*

suits were less emotional and more career-oriented women. In contrast, the mothers who worked outside the home had some inside knowledge about juggling home and family concerns, ambition, and emotion. They knew, for example, that one can still care as much about a family or cry just as easily when wearing a suit as when wearing more frilly or feminine attire. These mothers knew that while a suit is associated with a career role, their lives encompass much more than that role alone. Accordingly, they did not distinguish to as great an extent among mothers wearing suits versus more feminine attire, as did mothers who did not work outside the home (Kaiser et al., working paper).

In conclusion, occupational focus is likely to influence individual values, goals, world view, daily experiences, and frame of reference. Accordingly, it has an impact on appearance perception.

Ethnicity is a variable that may or may not influence appearance perception, depending on the context in which appearance is evaluated. For example, no difference as a function of ethnicity was found in a study comparing black Caribbean versus white American subjects' ratings of attractiveness (Maret and Harling, 1985). These subjects were evaluating yearbook photos derived from New Jersey. The researchers explained this lack of a difference on the basis of common media influences.

*Ethnicity*

On the other hand, some differences were found in a study comparing black (African-American) and white (Anglo-American) students' ratings of black and white counselors (Green, Cunningham, and Yanico, 1986). The students evaluated slides in which the appearances had been modified and listened to an audiotape. The female counselors (black and white) wore a skirted suit in the attractive condition and a drab pantsuit in the unattractive condition. The white students tended to rate the physically attractive counselors as making a more favorable impression. Also, there was a distinction in the subjects' perceptions of the counselor's helpfulness. Black students but not white students viewed attractive counselors as being more helpful than unattractive counselors. Likewise, black participants saw unattractive counselors as significantly less likely to be helpful, as compared with white participants. How did the researchers account for this difference? They noted:

> A drably dressed, less attractively groomed professional may violate the expectations of black subjects that pride in one's accomplishments would be accompanied by public display of marks of professional status, such as impeccable grooming and fashionable clothing. White subjects may have found professional status less unusual and, thus, may have been less likely to feel that it necessarily should be accompanied by special attention to personal appearance (Green, Cunningham, and Yanico, 1986, p. 351).

Ethnicity will be discussed in further detail in Chapter Thirteen, in relation to ethnic identity and cultural influence. At this point, however, it is important to note that ethnicity is not always a factor in perception. For example, research has shown that black athletes are not necessarily more prone than white athletes to prefer "attention-getting" styles (Reeder and Drake, 1980). And adolescent black females do not prefer flashier combinations in clothes than do white females (Williams, Arbaugh, and Rucker, 1980). Thus it is important to distinguish between cultural influences that may be linked to ethnicity and socialization, and cultural stereotypes linked to ethnicity—which may have little or no basis in fact.

Aside from perceiver variables linked to gender, age, social class, occupation, or ethnicity, many other variations may result in appearance perception as a function of perceiver characteristics. The following sections will consider self-attributes in relation to appearance perception.

## Projection of Self-Esteem

Lois Dickey (1967) studied the possibility of perceiver self-esteem as a factor in the observations of others. She had subjects describe drawn figures of females' clothed appearances and found that individuals with high self-esteem tended to describe the females in the drawings as confident, whereas persons with low self-esteem were more likely to describe the figures as shy. Basically, her research indicated that the degree of self-esteem attributed to the stimulus persons was a joint function of the perceiver's own (*a*) self-esteem and sense of security, (*b*) degree of identification with the stimulus person, and (*c*) interest and involvement in clothing (Dickey, 1967).

Kathleen Rowold (1984) expanded on this line of research by addressing an additional perceiver characteristic—sensitivity to appearance. We would expect selves-as-perceivers to have a number of unique characteristics influencing their assessments of others, and among a number of subjects we would expect certain characteristics to explain the variability across subjects' responses more adequately than others. In Rowold's study, perceivers' self-esteem accounted for 30 percent of this variability. She pursued other characteristics that might explain more of the variation across subjects' responses and found that an additional 10 to 20 percent could be attributed to the *joint* effects of self-esteem and sensitivity to appearance. When the perceivers looked at clothed appearances (see Figure 9-6), some of the perceivers were more likely than others to distinguish among different styles.

Rowold (1984) also found that subjects with less awareness of clothing features were *more* likely to project self-esteem to the perceived stimulus persons. Perceivers who were less sensitive to appearance were not as likely to use clothes as a guide to perceptions and therefore relied more on their feelings about themselves (self-esteem) than they did the visual cues displayed by others. Similarly, people who were less interested in clothing were more likely to project personal self-esteem to the stimulus person (as shown in Figure 9-6). This work suggests, then, that perceivers vary in the extent to which they actually use others' clothed appearances in evaluating those others' degree of self-confidence. Perceivers who are more sensitive to, and interested in, clothing variations are less likely to project their own self-esteem to others than are perceivers who are less attune to clothing variations. Thus, the impact of a perceiver's self-esteem on perceptions of others is *mediated* by his or her sensitivity to, and interest in, clothing (Rowold, 1984).

A                    B

AT A LUNCHEON

*FIGURE 9-6*
*Following Dickey's (1967) research, Rowold (1984) used these stimuli to see how sensitive perceivers were to appearance styles and to see to what extent they would project their own self-esteem to these stimuli. Perceivers who were less sensitive to differences in appearance styles were less likely to use clothes as a guide to perceptions and more likely, instead, to rely on their feelings about themselves (self-esteem). In contrast, perceivers who were more sensitive to appearance used clothing variations in their judgments more and relied less on self-traits. Courtesy of Kathleen Rowold and* Home Economics Research Journal.

## *Personal Values and Interest in Clothing*

### *Values*

Values are self-organizing principles that guide our thoughts and actions. Culture provides many values for us, which we are socialized to accept; yet values per se are ascribed to individuals. Values are linked to self-concept and self-evaluation. Like the concept of self, values are abstract. In fact, they are probably the most abstract form of social cognition. From these abstract social cognitions we are able to manufacture attitudes and behaviors (Homer and Kahle, 1988). We tend to feel committed to our values, which enable us to understand and compare ourselves with others. Thus, values serve as means for self-evaluation. At the same time, they influence how we perceive others—by organizing our perceptions to pinpoint appearances that we find interesting or attractive, clothes that we view as meaningful or worthwhile, and ideas that we associate with certain appearances. Values induce a selective orientation toward experience itself; they help us to define what is important to us, and they shape our preferences and choices. Yet we often take values for granted; they are most likely to come into focus when our preferences, choices, thoughts, or actions are threatened or challenged in some way (Gordon, 1975).

Let's consider several characteristics of values (Gordon, 1975). First, *values are relatively stable, in the sense that they serve as codes or standards to which we are committed*. This is not to say that values are static. As we have seen, self-concept is not static but rather is a process influenced by social experience and a sense of fluidity as we move from one social context to another. Similarly, values are not static, although they are more stable than other more fleeting beliefs or attitudes that are less central to a sense of self.

A second characteristic of values relates to their dynamic qualities. *Values are energizing forces that serve as the basis for personal goals*. Accordingly, personal clothing choices as well as appearance perceptions are likely to be shaped by values. Third, *values are expressive, and individuals are motivated to communicate them to others*. Appearance serves as a creative outlet for personal expression, so that we can communicate some personal values that may not be easily articulated in conversation. Fourth, *values are receptive, or they shape the way we would like others to respond to us*. Again, the link to personal appearance management is evident, which is shaped not only by the desire for self-expression but also by the social need to communicate in a meaningful manner with others (Gordon, 1975).

Clearly, values underlie appearance communication. They are linked to both appearance management and perception and serve to shape a personal sense of focus in everyday life. They influence not only what we see but also *how* we see. The statements that arise from values, or *value statements*, have two important characteristics that are directly linked to appearance communication. First, value statements are *meaningful*: They provide the means for the expression of likes and dislikes or for discovery (of one's own preferences) and evaluation. Second, value statements are *contextual*. Context and perspective (point of view) are combined in statements that express personal values (Wheelwright, 1960). The meaningful and contextual dimensions of values directly influence aesthetic judgments, the topic pursued in Social Focus 9-2.

Values are central to self-concept, as compared with other personal attributes such as beliefs or attitudes (Rokeach, 1968). The distinctions among attitudes, beliefs, and values might be summarized as follows: Individuals hold countless beliefs, fewer attitudes, and only a handful of basic values.

## *Attitudes*

Whereas values are the central components of belief systems, attitudes are individual clusters of beliefs oriented toward specific stimuli (Rokeach, 1968; Littlejohn, 1978). Attitudes are predispositions to react favorably or unfavorably toward a stimulus; they are more specific referents than are values, which are likely to be the "why" behind a given attitude (Gordon, 1975).

Attitudes are made up of three kinds of elements: cognitive, affective, and behavioral. The cognitive and affective elements are basically perceptual, whereas the behavioral element has the most implications for social action and interaction. The **cognitive** dimension of an attitude includes beliefs or other pieces of in-

Many judgments of appearance are *evaluative*, meaning that value judgments are used in assessing appearance. Evaluative factors of aesthetic objects have been studied by researchers interested in perceptions by having subjects rate them according to adjective scales such as beautiful –ugly, like–dislike, or attractive–unattractive (Berlyne, 1974). We tend to "cluster" our impressions about clothes and other visual art forms. In other words, if we evaluate an article of clothing or a person's appearance favorably on one dimension, then we are likely to find positive attributes in other areas as well. (This tendency is known as a "halo effect.")

Gibbins (1969) studied the responses of adolescent students to clothing and found that fashionability was a dominant factor in their judgments of clothes. This tendency could have a great deal of impact on judgments of others, because fashionability connotes a social stamp of approval and may be less likely to differ among perceivers than "liking" (which is more prone to individual tastes). The evaluative component of clothing has been identified as a dominant factor in people's judgments. This component tends to include adjective pairs such as like–dislike, pleasing–unpleasing, and fashion-oriented terms such as fresh–stale and fashionable–unfashionable (DeLong and Larntz, 1980). Fashionability appears to color our perceptions of what is beautiful or of what we like.

Whisney, Winakor, and Wolins (1979) also reported that preference for clothing styles is closely linked with a perceiver's idea of beauty and of what is current. All of these findings generally support the basic ideas that (1) clothing perceptions are clustered, that is, there is consistency among commonly perceived attributes, and (2) the evaluative component, which includes a sense of fashionability, is fundamental and central to clothing perceptions.

At the same time, it appears that perceivers have the ability to categorize clothing styles on the basis of structural features, or form—that is, silhouette and shape and the part-to-whole relationship. Perceivers then appear to be able to set aside personal preferences and to sort and classify apparel on the basis of objective visual criteria (DeLong and Minshall, 1988).

Thus, values are likely to enter into our perceptions of apparel, thereby shaping what we think is interesting or worthwhile to behold, to wear, or even to study. Nevertheless, apparel has tangible visual characteristics to which we can respond with some degree of objectivity. Understanding the delicate balance between subjective and objective dimensions of consumers' apparel perception remains a challenging, yet richly rewarding task for clothing researchers.

formation about a stimulus. For example, consider the stimuli in Figures 9-7 and 9-8. What do you *know* about these appearances? In Figure 9-7, for example, you may know something about how this hairstyle was derived, that is, the material (gel or glue) that was used to develop the style. Or, you may know something about the social groups that are most likely to wear such a hairstyle. In Figure 9-8, you may know something about the coat pictured—that it is a traditional British style, worn commonly by young girls from upper-class families.

The **affective** dimension of attitudes refers to a perceiver's *feelings* or emotions and likes and dislikes, thereby shaping preferences and tastes. How do you feel about the stimuli in Figures 9-7 and 9-8? Are you shocked, amused, intrigued, disgusted, bewildered, or bored? Do you enjoy looking at them? Do you like or dislike them? All of these feelings relate to *affect*, or emotion. Of course, how you feel about a stimulus at a given point in time is likely to be linked to your current emotional state as well as to your past experiences. For example, research suggests that people who are in love and who have been reminded of their romantic partners are in an emotional state that induces them to rate an appearance of an unknown person more favorably than they might otherwise (Benassi, 1985).

Finally, we can look at the **behavioral** dimension of attitudes through our examples. This dimension addresses a perceiver's intent and readiness to respond to a stimulus. How would you address or approach the male depicted in Figure 9-7? What would you probably say to him? And, might you adopt the hairstyle

**FIGURE 9-7**
*Let's consider the various dimensions of an attitude toward this hairstyle. First, what do you* know *about how this style is created and what it signifies? What you have read, seen, or experienced is likely to influence the* **cognitive** *dimension of your attitude. Second, how you* feel *about the style (whether you like or dislike it) constitutes the* **affective** *dimension. Finally, the* **behavioral** *dimension is linked to how you are likely to* act—*that is, how you will respond toward a person with this hairstyle, or whether or not you will consider trying the style yourself. Photo by Mark Kaiser.*

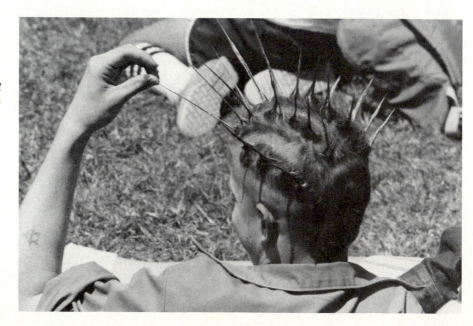

**FIGURE 9-8**
*Attitudes toward this coat are likely to be shaped by cognitive factors such as the tag, which indicates that the coat is made in England and is 100% wool. If you have traveled to England, or have seen movies or books depicting social life there, you may also be aware that the coat is a traditional style commonly associated with young girls from upper-class families. The affective component of your attitude is based on whether or not you are impressed by this, as well as to what extent you find the style attractive. Finally, the behavioral dimension could relate to whether or not you consider buying it for a young girl in your family. Photo by Susan B. Kaiser.*

shown? Would you be likely to buy the coat shown in Figure 9-8 for someone in your family? Any behaviors or actions that are aroused by these clothes and appearances apply to the behavioral dimension of attitudes, that is, to *what one does* as a result of a stimulus.

As we have seen through these examples, attitudes shape appearance perceptions by addressing what we know, how we feel, and how we are predisposed to respond to an article of clothing or an appearance. In turn, attitudes are shaped by more basic and fundamental values, integral to the self-concept. Thus, values and the more specific attitudes to which they refer are linked to appearance communication.

How do attitudes affect the way perceivers evaluate appearances? Several studies have explored gender-related attitudes in relation to appearance perception. It seems that persons who think in a more gender-stereotypical manner are more likely than those who do not think this way to process, store, and recall stimuli in terms of gender-typed criteria. These individuals seem to evaluate themselves as well as others on the basis of gender-typed characteristics (for example, assertiveness versus submissiveness). At the same time, gender-typed attitudes interact in a complex way with other kinds of stereotypical attitudes (for example, attitudes toward attractive versus unattractive people, homosexual versus heterosexual people, or pornography, as we will see in the following studies). In a simulated personnel decision, evaluators who used gender-typed criteria were more likely to give attractive applicants significantly higher hiring recommendations, as compared with "androgynous" raters (who did not use gender-typed criteria for evaluation)(Cash and Kilcullen, 1985). In other words, gender-typed raters were more likely to be biased in favor of attractive candidates and prejudiced against unattractive ones. Both gender-typed and androgynous raters displayed some sexism and beautyism in their choices of applicants, but gender-typed raters applied the "what is beautiful is good" stereotype in more cases, for example, in their evaluations of male applicants. Androgynous raters, in contrast, actually downgraded the attractive men. This study illustrates the complex interactions in perceivers' applications of stereotypes (Cash and Kilcullen, 1985).

Another study exploring the impact of gender-typed attitudes on judgments based on attractiveness focused on differential evaluations of a stimulus person who had violated social norms (Moore, Graziano, and Millar, 1987). Male and female raters with gender-typed attitudes followed the stereotype and assigned a less severe rating to the behavior of a highly attractive stimulus child than they did to a moderately attractive one. Also, it was found that androgynous persons were responsive to attractiveness: they attributed positive social characteristics to both adults and children according to the physical attractiveness stereotype. So, rather than being insensitive to physical appearance, androgynous persons appear to suspend their use of the stereotype when evaluating transgressions. For androgynous persons, social-political conscience may override stereotypic beliefs about appearance and/or arouse a more conscious level of evaluation (Moore, Graziano, and Millar, 1987).

Another study explored differences in raters' associations of appearance with homosexuality, as a function of the raters' own sex and attitudes (Dew, 1985). Female raters with conservative attitudes were more likely to associate homosexuality with women whom they rated lowest in terms of physical appearance, whereas liberal females were less likely to do so. Male raters' attitudes bore little relationship to their evaluations of homosexuality and physical attractiveness. The researchers explained this distinction between male and female raters in terms of the impact of the women's movement, which brings gay and straight women together for a common cause. Because women who are involved in, or who sympathize with, this movement are likely to share common goals, they are less likely than those women who are conservative in their attitudes about gender issues to stereotype homosexuality in terms of appearance (Dew, 1985).

Other research has shown that male subjects differing in attitudes toward pornography (pro and anti) rate female attractiveness differently (Bernstein et al., 1986). The males were shown female models from a variety of sources, ranging from fashion magazines to *Penthouse*, in nude, seminude, and clothed categories. Facial features played less of a role with the pro-pornography males than with the other males when they judged nudes. However, facial features were equally important to all the males when they judged clothed models. Anti-pornography subjects rated all models more negatively than did the other subjects, whereas pro-pornography subjects used different cues in judging nude versus clothed models (Bernstein et al., 1986).

In summary, research reveals that attitudes influence how appearances are perceived, at least as documented in the area of gender-related attitudes. The cognitive, affective, and behavioral dimensions are evident in research studies that call for judgments based on knowledge and emotions about gender issues. Aside from attitudes of a social or political nature, a perceiver's interests are likely to affect his or her evaluations of appearance.

*Interest in Clothing*

How do our interests compare with our values and attitudes? We may describe an interest as the extent to which an individual likes to engage in certain classes of vocational or avocational activities (Gordon, 1975). Vocational activities linked to clothing might include fashion design or illustration, apparel marketing or retailing, or fashion journalism. Avocational activities might include shopping for clothes, experimenting with appearance, and reading fashion magazines. Accordingly, interest in clothes is closely aligned with the behavioral dimension of attitudes in terms of how people spend time, money, and attention relative to clothing. It is also important to note that interest in clothing is critically connected to a wide range of other avocational activities such as sports, music, or even antique cars (see Figure 9-9).

Let's look more closely at interest in clothing per se, or the extent to which an individual is favorably predisposed toward clothes. We have already seen that interest in clothing mediates the degree to which a perceiver's self-esteem influences perceptions of others. But what are some of the tangible clues to a person's

**FIGURE 9-9**
*A perceiver might surmise from this man's T-shirt that
he is interested in antique cars. A perceiver who is
attuned to some of the more subtle aspects of his
appearance may also identify him as an off-duty Air
Force serviceperson. Photo by Joan L. Chandler.*

interest in clothing? If a male becomes known for the tendency to wear only
designer clothes and for his verbal references to the latest issue of a fashion
magazine, observers are likely to infer that he is very interested in clothes. People
who spend a great deal of time, money, and energy on activities related to
appearance management are likely to exhibit a high degree of interest in clothing.
Also, we would expect a relation between a person's level of interest in clothing

and his or her perceptions of others' clothed appearances. There is evidence that females who are interested in clothing and who consider it important are likely to evaluate others favorably when they are attractively dressed, even when the evaluation in question (for example, quality of essay writing) is unrelated to appearance (Lapitsky and Smith, 1981). However, females with an interest in clothing did *not* necessarily make negative judgments of persons dressed in unattractive attire. Similarly, as previously noted, Rowold (1984) found that female perceivers were less likely to project their own self-esteem if they were interested in clothing. So, it seems that interest in clothing mediates projection. Thus, perceivers interested in clothing may be influenced positively but not necessarily negatively by another person's appearance (Lapitsky and Smith, 1981) and may be unlikely to project personal characteristics onto others (perhaps, relying instead on appearance cues). More research is needed in this area to expand our understanding in general and to see if these tendencies apply to male perceivers as well.

It should be clear by now that interest in, and involvement with, clothing is more complex than tangible indicators would suggest, because it is a *multi-dimensional* construct. Let's consider the different dimensions of interest in clothing identified by researchers.

In the early 1960s, Anna Creekmore (1963) developed a measure of interest in clothing. This frequently used measure was analyzed by Gurel and Gurel (1979) to identify and characterize distinct dimensions. The first and most dominant dimension is *concern with personal appearance*. Individuals who express a high degree of concern with how they look are likely to spend a great deal of time, money, and energy pursuing appearance management. Also, they are likely to engage in such activities as shopping or experimentation for purposes of improving their appearances. Whereas concern with personal appearance was identified by Gurel and Gurel (1979) as the most central component of interest in clothing, other distinct and salient dimensions may be identified as well.

A second dimension of interest in clothing is *experimentation with appearance*. Although experimentation may be closely aligned with concern with personal appearance, there is a distinction between the two in the sense that experimentation may be a creative outlet in its own right. An individual who enjoys collecting clothes from museum art shops or antique clothing stores might be likely to score high on this dimension, as might one who enjoys trying out new looks or even shopping for the purpose of entertainment, without necessarily planning to make any purchases. On the other hand, a person who is very concerned with personal appearance may not be willing to risk a change in appearance for the sake of experimentation or creative expression. Once a successful "look" has been identified, he or she may not want to dabble with less proven possibilities. True experimenters, on the other hand, may be continually searching for a new look because they enjoy change, novelty, and aesthetic stimulation. Everyday cultural experiences, including media usage, may provide fruitful hunting grounds for experimenters in search of new looks. For example, music videos may provide ideas about how to wear one's hair or makeup or how to accessorize clothes.

A third dimension associated with clothing interest is *heightened awareness of clothing*. This dimension appears to refer to a focus on the structural details of clothes—the fabrics of which they are made, garment features such as darts or tucks, accessories such as buttons or lace, and the like. An objective, detailed orientation to clothes would be common among people who study or work in the field of clothing and textiles, for example. However, some individuals may have particular preferences in terms of the structural qualities of clothing and not have the background or vocabulary to talk about them. For example, in a study comparing males' and females' descriptions of their favorite clothes, some males focused on garment characteristics that contributed to fit or comfort, but did not necessarily know or found it hard to remember what the specific garments or features they preferred were called.

> *I have a lot of . . . what do you call those shirts? . . . They're not Western but . . . a lot of people wear them with their sleeves rolled up. . . . Gosh, what are those things called? They're always 100 percent cotton.* (Later in the interview, it was clarified that he was talking about flannel shirts.) (Kaiser, 1987).

It would seem that judgments of apparel quality would be related to a heightened awareness of clothing. It might be assumed that an individual who is aware of fashion would be knowledgeable about designer brands and therefore be influenced by them, but this was not the case in a study conducted by Leslie Davis (1985a). Simply being aware of fashion did not necessarily influence judgments concerning the quality of designer-label clothing. Davis measured fashion awareness in terms of exposure to fashion innovation through mass media and retailer communications and through responses to such statements as: "I often window shop to keep current on the latest fashion trends." [Note that this statement is similar in concept to the second dimension of clothing interest—experimentation with appearance. Davis's (1985a) study, although using different measures, further documents the diversity in forms of interest in clothing.]

A fourth dimension of clothing interest is *enhancement of personal security*. At times, clothes may be used to boost morale or to make one feel more self-confident. The concepts of self-monitoring and Goffman's (1959) notion of clothes as appearance-managing props, discussed in Chapter Six, applies to this dimension. Individuals who are concerned with the ability of clothes to enhance their sense of security in social situations would be likely to realize their appearance-managing potential as well as their effect on self-esteem. This dimension of interest in clothing is personal but also serves to connect individuals to others in social contexts. As we saw in Chapter Five, persons who have low self-esteem are likely to be interested in clothes for purposes of enhancing security; in this sense, clothes serve an adaptive function. In contrast, persons with high self-esteem are likely to use clothes in the expressive sense.

A fifth and final dimension of interest in clothing is *enhancement of individuality*. Distinctiveness and uniqueness are likely to be important to a person scoring

high on this dimension. Such a person would enjoy expressing his or her individualism and would probably feel less need to conform with others' appearances
for the purpose of belonging.

Gurel and Gurel (1979) noted that some statements in Creekmore's measure
of clothing interest did not fall into one of the five dimensions resulting from
a statistical procedure known as factor analysis, which produces groupings of
statements to which individuals tend to respond similarly within a given dimension.
Statements not included in the five dimensions pertained to conformity, modesty,
and comfort. These too are types of interests, but they factored out separately.
We will see in the following section on values and interest in clothing that these
statements, as well as other interest-related statements, have been linked to
personal values.

It is important to distinguish the research on interest in clothing from that
focusing more exclusively on interest in fashion. Individuals who keep up with
fashion trends may do so for different reasons, some of which may relate to the
various dimensions of interest in clothing noted earlier. Yet one might be interested
in clothing and appearance without necessarily being concerned with wearing
only the latest fashions.

Sproles and King (1973) sought to measure fashion interest by analyzing
how well individuals keep informed about current fashion trends and how well
they keep their wardrobes up to date. In a series of studies (Sproles and King,
1973), they found that there was a relatively consistent pattern of fashion interest
across populations. Approximately 10 percent of the populations had the highest
level of fashion interest and kept up with most fashion changes. One-third or
more of the subjects expressed a substantial interest in keeping well-informed
abut new fashion trends, although these subjects did not necessarily adopt styles
in each new trend. The remaining consumers tended to follow fashions that
were relatively well-established and to be only mildly interested in fashion. Less
than 15 percent of the individuals in the studies indicated a total lack of interest
in clothing.

In a study of older adults' use of mass media for fashion information, Kaiser
and Chandler (1985) found that older women were more likely than older men
to seek fashion information from sources such as television, newspapers, and
magazines. The older men with high-clothing expenditures were more likely
than the men with low-clothing expenditures to seek fashion information. A
few men, particularly those who spent very little money on clothing, expressed
a lack of interest in clothing in general:

*I never bothered about clothes. I depended on my wife. Now that she has
left this world, it's questionable.*

*Clothes are not important enough to me to spend much time looking at
them or even noticing them.*

A variety of personal characteristics have been studied in relation to interest
in clothing. Some correlates identified in research that did not use Creekmore's

measure of interest in clothing include stereotypic thinking, compliance, insecurity, and social conscientiousness (Aiken, 1963). Perry, Schutz, and Rucker (1983) studied the relation between interest in clothing, using Creekmore's measure, and self-actualization—or the use of personal resources and abilities in a way that maximizes one's potential. Using female college students as subjects, they found a moderate, inverse relation between self-actualization and interest in clothing. As self-actualization increased, interest in clothing decreased, suggesting that individuals who are already maximizing their potential may not "need" clothes to enhance the self. As we have seen, interest in clothing is a multidimensional construct, so individuals with a variety of characteristics may have an interest in clothing for a variety of reasons. In the next section, we will examine research linking basic values to specific types of interest in clothing. This research again used Creekmore's measure, but not in terms of the five dimensions of interest in clothing previously discussed.

## Values and Interest in Clothing

Psychologists Allport, Vernon, and Lindzey (1960) developed a measure of six basic values, based on Spranger's (1928) typology of people's basic orientations. The purpose of the Allport–Vernon–Lindzey test is to rank types of values in order of their importance to an individual. While all individuals hold these categories of values to some extent, they tend to differ in how they prioritize these categories. In studies using college females as subjects, Creekmore (1963) and Sharma (1980) both found correlations between interest in clothing and the six basic values.

*Theoretical* values are those associated with the discovery of truth or the search for knowledge as potential organizing principles for goals or behavior. A person scoring high in theoretical values may enjoy ordering and systematizing knowledge from a variety of sources (for example, from different college courses) to derive specific conclusions or insights. Creekmore (1963) did not find theoretical values to be related to interest in clothing; however, Sharma (1980) found that individuals who were highly concerned with clothing comfort scored high in theoretical values. [Gurel and Gurel (1979) did not identify clothing comfort as a distinct dimension of interest in clothing, but Creekmore's (1963) original measure did include statements tapping the importance of comfort.]

*Economic* values are related to a tendency to view objects in terms of their usefulness or practicality. A person scoring high on economic values might be interested in satisfying basic needs and in avoiding wastefulness in terms of time, money, and energy. For example, a person with strong economic values would probably not appreciate trendy fashions that become obsolete quickly, because such styles represent waste. Creekmore (1963) found that economic values were related to the management of clothing, that is, the purchase and maintenance of clothes in an efficient manner. Sharma (1980) found that individuals guided by economic considerations when buying clothes tended to have the following personality traits: cool, aloof, rigid, submissive, conventional, and self-sufficient. Basically, they were found to be more introverted than persons guided by such considerations as decoration or enhancement of appearance when buying clothes.

Baumgartner (1963) found positive correlations between the amount spent on clothes and the indicated importance of clothes. Female college students spent more on clothing than did males, and students participating in the campus "Greek" system of fraternities and sororities spent more on clothes than did those who did not belong to these groups.

*Aesthetic* values guide a world view of life as a series of events, each with the potential of being enjoyed. Utilitarian benefits of objects or activities are not as important as the pleasures they provide. One need not be an artist to score high on aesthetic values, but they do guide an individual to be interested in perceiving harmony and form, as well as to be aware of one's environment. Aesthetic values were positively correlated with enhancing personal appearance in both Creekmore's (1963) and Sharma's (1980) studies. Sharma (1980) also reported that individuals with aesthetic values were more independent-minded, enthusiastic, individualistic, as well as less critical and rational.

*Social* values are linked to selflessness and regard for others and have been linked to conformity in dress (Creekmore, 1963; Sharma, 1980). This finding suggests that persons who are concerned about others may want to appear similar to those others. In a study by Lapitsky (1961), it was hypothesized that the type of social value stressed in the Allport-Vernon-Lindzey (1960) test (that is, a social value emphasizing a regard for others) is not the only type of social value influencing interest in clothing. A second type of social value might emphasize the need for acceptance and approval by others. This type of social value would be consistent with the dimension of clothing interest stressing the enhancement of security. Lapitsky's (1961) study suggested that this second type of social value is even more likely than the first to be related to conformity in dress.

*Political* values refer to the desire to obtain power or to succeed, exercising influence over others, and gaining recognition. Political values do not necessarily imply a personal interest in social-political issues of the day, although politicians would be likely to score high in political values because they seek recognition and influence. In Creekmore's (1963) study, political values were related to personal concern for the fashionability of one's clothes and to status symbolism. Individuals who dress either in fashionable clothes or in high-status clothes are likely to call attention to themselves and to set themselves apart from others. A dress-for-success ethic appears to be an expression of political values. Sharma (1980) found that persons with high political values were less concerned with comfort, conformity, and economy in terms of clothing, but more concerned with enhancing personal appearance.

*Religious* values are associated with the search for unity among life experiences—or pursuing meaningful connections for an overriding philosophy on life. Mysticism and the supernatural might be of interest to a person with highly religious values. Creekmore (1963) found religious values to be related to concern for modesty in dress, suggesting that inward searching may be disassociated from an outward display of worldliness (see Figure 9-10).

In addition to the six basic values, Creekmore (1963) noted that individuals may hold *exploratory* values, representing a desire to investigate new possibilities for the sake of variety or novelty. Such values may be connected to the dimension

**FIGURE 9-10**
*Religious values are associated with the search for meaningful connections in life experiences in order to achieve an overriding philosophy of life. Hare Krishna followers believe that as they give up their old clothes and adopt the attire of their faith, as shown here, the soul similarly accepts new material bodies, giving up the old and useless ones. Thus, the religious attire becomes a metaphor for Hare Krishna values. Inward searching is emphasized over outward display of material goods. Photo by Larry White.*

of interest in clothing concerned with experimentation. More research is needed to understand the characteristics of persons who pursue appearance management as a possible means for seeking novelty and diversity.

The different values described earlier may be prioritized by individuals, but they may also be integrated into larger systems when they are critically connected in one's outlook. A **value system** involves a clustering or grouping of values that are integrated within one's perspective. For example, some individuals may stress economic values as well as political values and may seek means for "getting ahead" without spending a lot of money, in the most efficient way possible. Similarly, religious and economic values could be connected and evident in a personal preference for a "waste not, want not" philosophy, modest in terms of both a lack of worldliness and expense.

Individuals' values, attitudes, and interest in clothing are likely to be connected to their extent of awareness of appearance in everyday life. Social psychologists frequently use the term **salience** to refer to the perceived value or importance of an object to a person. The concept of salience helps to provide a link between personal, value-laden interest in clothing and awareness of clothing in everyday life. If a person is favorably predisposed toward clothes, then he or she is likely to use them as cues in trying to understand others. Particular types of clothing and appearance cues viewed as having personal meaning and importance are those that are salient.

Awareness is an extremely important concept—necessary, but not sufficient—in relation to appearance communication. Before we can even consider the concept of meaning, we must note whether or not individuals are aware of clothing and appearance cues. Sociologists Glaser and Strauss (1964) coined the phrase *awareness context* to describe everything a person knows about the identities of other persons in a social context, as well as about his or her own identity in the eyes of others. Like clothing and appearance, awareness is essentially linked to social context, as individuals use appearance variously to frame and interpret their experiences.

Individuals vary in the extent to which they are aware of clothing; we have already seen that they differ when they respond to different clothed appearances in research studies. Sensitivity to appearance tends to mediate the influence of self-esteem of a perceiver on judgments of others. All perceivers, consciously or not, are likely to make use of clothing and appearance as they strive to construct (often implicitly) interpretations of social contexts. Helen Douty (1963) noted that perceivers are often not aware, on a conscious level, of the extent to which they use the clothed appearances of others in evaluating those others. Yet the effect can be just as powerful (perhaps more so) as compared with instances when perceivers are highly conscious of their use of appearance cues. Still, there is another level of awareness that becomes an especially salient dimension of communication when appearance management is enacted with certain messages in mind. People who are very aware of differences in clothing and appearance cues may notice subtleties in appearance communication that are lost on other perceivers, as noted in the following male student's comment:

> *I would never dress to stand out like a sore thumb. I would dress so that if there were any differences at all, they would be very subtle and only someone who can maybe appreciate the thing that I can would notice those subtleties (Kaiser, 1987).*

Culture tends to serve as an "umbrella" awareness context, because culture provides, or even consists of, "taken-for-granted but powerfully influential understandings and codes that are learned and shared" (Peacock, 1986, p. 7). We are often not cognizant of awareness context on a conscious level, but in a different cultural context, when one does not know the codes to guide interpretation of a social situation, the lack of an awareness context becomes very clear. Similarly, even in one's own culture it is possible to lack an awareness context. For example, refer back to Figure 9-9. Were you able to interpret from this male's appearance that he is in the United States Air Force? The photographer who took this picture had been in the Air Force herself, and she was able to interpret subtle cues in their context: the haircut, leisure-time clothes, and the proximity of the shopping mall (where he was photographed) to an Air Force base.

Awareness, then, is a prerequisite to meaningful appearance communication. Awareness context is like an abstract stage outlining the conditions, in the minds of participants, to guide interpretation of appearances. If one or more perceivers is not aware of the potential significance of particular appearance cues, then avenues other than appearance communication (such as talking) become more critical to persons' abilities to fit their lines of action together in a meaningful manner. Generally, however, appearance sets the stage for social encounters, albeit on a relatively unconscious level.

## Suggested Readings

Holbrook, M. B. 1986. Aims, concepts, and methods for the representation of individual differences in esthetic responses to design features. *Journal of Consumer Research* 13:337–347.
Holbrook reports on a study of gender differences in perceptions of men's suit styles. Also introduced as variables in the study are distinctions in perceptions based on visualizing and verbalizing tendencies.

Kaiser, S. B., and Phinney, J. S. 1983. Sex typing of play activities by girls' clothing style: Pants versus skirts. *Child Study Journal* 13(2):115–131.
Gender and age differences in young children's perceptions of girls' clothing styles are examined in this study.

Littrell, M. A., and Berger, E. A. 1986. Perceiver's occupation and client's grooming: Influence on person perception. *Clothing and Textiles Research Journal* 4(2):48–55.
Differences in perceptions of a male adolescent's appearance as a function of perceiver occupation are documented. The study also illustrates the usefulness and richness of open-ended response techniques in the study of appearance perception.

Lubner-Rupert, J. A., and Winakor, G. 1985. Male and female style preference and perceived fashion risk. *Home Economics Research Journal* 13:265–266.
This is one of the few studies to examine both men's and women's clothing in one study and to incorporate an analysis of perceiver differences as a function of gender.

Mayer, R. N., and Belk, R. W. 1985. Fashion and impression formation among children. In M. R. Solomon, ed. *The psychology of fashion*, pp. 293–308. Lexington: Heath/Lexington Books.
Variations in children's perceptions of jeans, shoes, and video games are examined in relation to gender and social class.

Sweat, S. J., and Zentner, M. A. 1985. Attributions toward female appearance styles. In M. R. Solomon, ed. *The psychology of fashion*, pp. 321–335. Lexington: Heath/ Lexington Books.
  Differences in males' and females' perceptions of female appearance styles are explored. Also introduced as a variable in the study are psychological preferences as a factor in appearance perception.

# Chapter Ten
## •••
# *Appearance Communication:*
# *A Two-Way Process*

*In this chapter, our focus is on appearance communication as a two-way process. We are interested in the perspectives of both the people who are observed and the observers themselves—in other words, in appearance management and perception as interconnected processes. How are meanings constructed as individuals engage in social interaction? These meanings may be negotiated on the basis of visual appearance as well as verbal and other nonverbal messages. Wearers may either intentionally or unintentionally convey certain messages through their appearance, and perceivers may process appearance messages either in a fairly routine, automatic manner or in a more intrigued and mindful way. Through our interactions with others we create and assign meaning as we jointly arrive at a shared interpretation of one anothers' identities, and of how the situation in which we are interacting should be defined.*

Everyday life is full of social transactions involving communication. Individuals are never totally predictable, because of the spontaneous, responsive part of the self (the I). Accordingly, the manner in which they mesh or connect their lines of action to make sense of the world around them or to establish *meaning* is not entirely predetermined. Therefore, most social interactions involve some degree of negotiation, that is, give and take, interpreting and reinterpreting as necessary, and jointly arriving at social meaning. This type of negotiation not only allows interaction to proceed as individuals adjust their ideas about its "players" and purpose, but it also allows for shared construction of new meanings that individuals are likely to carry with them to subsequent interactions.

In this chapter, we are concerned with communication as a two-way process resulting in mutual constructions of the identities of participants as well as the social context itself. Social cognition, discussed in the previous chapter, is one component of this two-way process, but it deals only with the *appearance perception* side of the equation. Here, we are interested not only in the perceiver's point of view and thought processes, but also in the perspective of the person who *appears*—in the intent of appearance management, not the messages received by perceivers. Of course, appearance communication is somewhat complicated because people simultaneously appear and perceive and tend to perceive themselves as well as others. Also, appearance communication is only a part of the information we convey and receive from one another in social life. Our discussion of appearance communication as negotiation, then, also considers how appearance works with other forms of communication to comprise a network of messages. It is this meshing of messages, along with interpersonal negotiations, that allows us to relate to one another, to share the responsibilities of social life, and to shape social meaning.

## Appearance and Discourse

Symbolic interactionist Gregory Stone (1965) noted that communication involves both *appearance*, which is visual, nonverbal, and nondiscursive, and *discourse*, which includes both verbal and nonverbal discursive messages. Appearance is not only a visual context; it is also a *process* or stage of interaction, according to Stone. The visual context of appearance is highlighted during the appearance stage and serves as a prelude to subsequent interaction. Clothing, in particular, can signify in ways that other codes and channels of communication cannot— in ways that are difficult to describe in words because of the aesthetic nature of its code. This type of communication may at times capture the imaginations of sender and/or receiver. Wilden (1987) notes that information only becomes imaginary in the course of social life or within the larger context of culture. At the same time, information becomes "richer, more complex, more flexible, more ambiguous, and less dependent on close connection: continents or centuries may separate one sender–receiver from another" (Wilden, 1987, p. 172).

Discourse involves verbal and nonverbal messages allowing for shifts and responses in message-making based on give and take among interactants. However, clothing and other appearance cues are omnipresent throughout a social transaction and, thus, are likely to interact with other, more discursive messages. Given that appearance is similar to a "broadcast signal" (Enninger, 1985), it continues to permit, sustain, and delimit the possibilities of discourse (Stone, 1965) and to enter into the negotiation processes of communication once verbal and other nonverbal forms of discourse commence. This quality of appearance communication is illustrated in Figure 10-1.

Because appearance is visual, relies heavily on an aesthetic code, can allude to the imaginary realm, and can convey what words cannot, how do appearance and more discursive forms of communication (conversation, gestures, facial expressions) work together in the course of social interaction? Enninger (1985) notes that clothing codes serve to *mediate* interpersonal meaning during discourse. That is, clothing as well as other forms of appearance intrudes on or interferes with conversation and may also help to settle or arbitrate meaning. Because

**FIGURE 10-1**
*In everyday life, appearance and discourse work together as meaning is negotiated in order for participants to make sense of their interactions. Here an American female customer is completing a purchase from a designer and retailer at Hyper-Hyper boutique in London. Her appearance is similar to that of British youth in the late 1980s, so he is easily able to relate to her. She views his casual yet interesting style of appearance as befitting his creative role. As the two engage in conversation, they begin to compare London with various cities in the United States and learn about one another's cultures and preferences. Thus discourse (back-and-forth conversation) mediates the impressions created initially by their appearances. Yet their appearances continue to communicate right along with discourse, as the two negotiate meaning and understand one another. Photo by Susan B. Kaiser.*

appearance is visual, it "never shuts up" while people are interacting. Therefore, negotiation is accomplished for the most part through discourse, but appearance mediates the meaning of discourse; appearance and discourse work in tandem (see Figure 10-2).

What happens if different types of communication contradict one another—if a sender's gesture or appearance is different from the message he or she conveys verbally? Mehrabian (1981) referred to the combination of verbal and nonverbal messages, which may or may not be compatible with one another, as *mixed communication*. Mehrabian's work suggests that when verbal and nonverbal (discursive) messages conflict, nonverbal cues such as head and body movements (body codes) dominate the impression formed.

Giles and Chavasse (1975) found some support for the idea that clothing can also overpower verbal information. They conducted a field study in which

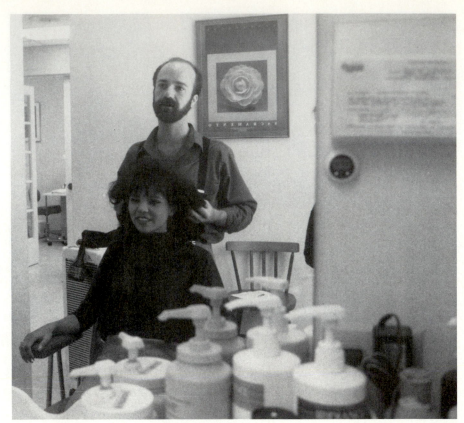

**FIGURE 10-2**
*Appearance and discourse communicate in tandem as this hairstylist and his client negotiate on how he will cut her hair. Visual communication is involved as they study her hair and consider different possibilities (trying to imagine them), and verbal communication takes place in the form of discussion ("Two inches off the side?"). Photo by Susan B. Kaiser.*

a male experimenter in his late twenties acted as a person conducting a survey on economic attitudes in Britain. One hundred middle-aged female consumers in a lower-middle-class neighborhood were asked to complete a brief questionnaire on this topic, and they were asked to return the completed questionnaire to the experimenter in half an hour. There were four experimental conditions: (1) experimenter in formal attire (a shirt, tie, and polished shoes) identifying himself as a research director in a university, (2) experimenter in formal attire identifying himself as an undergraduate student researcher, (3) experimenter in informal attire (a casual sweater and canvas shoes) presenting himself as a research director in a university, and (4) experimenter in informal attire introducing himself as an undergraduate student researcher. To evaluate the effects of these four conditions (high versus low status and formal versus informal attire) on the subjects' responses to the questionnaire, the total number of words written on the returned survey was tallied. Significantly more words were written when the experimenter had been dressed in the more formal clothes. There were no significant status effects as a result of his verbal introduction alone; thus, the style of dress appeared to have more impact on the subjects than did his verbal message. Giles and Chavasse (1975, p. 962) noted that how a person presents himself or herself in terms of appearance is "relatively more powerful than what he (she) claims to be."

We will now focus on appearance and discourse, from the perspectives of the sender and the receiver, and consider when negotiation is most likely to be necessary.

## Sender's Perspective: Intentional versus Unintentional Communication

Let's look first at appearance communication from the viewpoint of the sender or the person who appears. He or she may or may not be aware of the messages that are being given off by that appearance, or how that appearance will be interpreted by others. You will recall from Chapter Seven that appearance messages tend to be ambiguous, that is, several possible meanings may be attributed to a Gestalt (total) appearance or to a specific appearance sign (for example, jeans or hairstyle). Therefore, a sender cannot possibly be aware of all the potential meanings or associations that will come to a perceiver's mind.

It is helpful to note the distinction between messages that (*a*) a sender does not intentionally convey or of which he or she has knowledge, but which are assigned by a perceiver, versus those that (*b*) a sender intends to convey, as part of an impression he or she is trying to create and present to others. In the first instance, the message assigned by the perceiver may be considered **unintentional signification** (Enninger, 1985). The appearance *signifies* to the perceiver but the communication is only unidirectional and involves social cognition on the part of the perceiver without the intent of the sender. In the second instance, if the message intended by the sender is picked up by a perceiver, then we would say **intentional communication** has occurred.

Appearance signification almost always occurs when people interact (although frequently on a preconscious level). Two-way communication, on the other hand, occurs somewhat less frequently, because senders do not always intentionally convey information that is likely to be assigned by perceivers. Enninger (1985) notes that appearance (two-way) communication may be regarded as a by-product of appearance signification (involving social cognition on the part of the perceiver). He compares clothing to words in this respect, indicating that "with words one cannot signify without communicating, while with clothing one can" (Enninger, 1985, p. 85). This difference is based on the fact that clothing and, more generally, appearance are visual and dynamic in terms of meaning change, constructed and reconstructed on a daily basis, and less subject to conventionally established definitions than are words.

Table 10-1 summarizes the sender's point of view in social interaction. This table notes the distinction between appearance alone and appearance combined with discourse, while also considering the consequences of the degree of a sender's knowledge of the message he or she conveys. As the table indicates, a

**TABLE 10-1**
*Sender's Point of View in Appearance Communication*

|  | *Appearance Alone* | *Appearance and Discourse* |
|---|---|---|
| Unintentional Signification | Unknowingly conveys messages to others; no feedback from these messages | Unknowingly conveys messages to others; obtains some feedback from these messages (either verbal or nonverbal) |
| Intentional Communication | Strives to convey a particular message; not aware whether it is conveyed | Strives to convey a particular message; obtains some feedback from success and can use discourse to negotiate desired identity |

key point from the sender's perspective is whether social feedback is received on her or his appearance. Such feedback is supplied only when appearance and discourse are combined, and may come in the form of verbal comments or nonverbal cues (a raised eyebrow, frown, smile, or stare). Feedback may either support or refute an intentional appearance message and has the potential for supplying new information to a receiver in the case of unintentional signification when combined with discursive communication. (Refer back to Figure 10-1 to see an example of unintentional signification versus intentional communication from a sender's perspective.) In this example, the sender (an American tourist) is intentionally dressing similarly to British females her age. Thus, her appearance (as managed and perceived) is an intentional component of communication. The British designer/retailer provides some positive feedback by expressing an interest in her travel plans. Thus, from the sender's perspective, the appearance and discourse, in union, compose an intentional form of communication.

## Receiver's Perspective: Routine versus Intrigued Perceptions

Senders, then, may not always be aware of the messages they convey to perceivers, in part because wearers are not likely to be constantly consumed with their appearances and rely on other more discursive forms of communication to get their messages across during the course of interaction (whereas appearance management generally occurs prior to interaction). In contrast, perceivers are accustomed to viewing others and drawing implicit inferences about them on the basis of appearance. Because appearance is a constant, like a visual broadcast signal, it is consistently there for perceivers to view and use in conjunction with more discursive messages to understand an observed person.

   Therefore, social cognition and processes of appearance signification are relatively constant on the part of perceivers. However, perceivers may or may not be consciously aware of these processes. In familiar contexts, when common appearances are observed, perceivers probably make only implicit or preconscious note of them. In such cases, perceptions may be viewed as relatively *routine and automatic*. They are consistent with a perceiver's desire to simplify his or her perceptions in order to make sense of social life, and the appearances themselves probably mesh with culturally conventional and socially appropriate ones. We have already seen in Chapter Nine that perceivers bring unique qualities to social contexts, and that they are likely to differ in their levels of awareness. All perceivers are likely to experience routine and automatic social cognition; however, some are probably more likely than others to consider given appearances "routine and automatic." More aware perceivers may see subtle variations in appearances that are unknown to those who are less aware.

Let's turn now to another type of perception—one that involves more need for interpretation on a receiver's part. At times, social cognition may be described as involving **intrigued interpretation**. Some appearances, due to their complexity, aesthetic appeal, novelty, incongruity with the social context or the person, or unfamiliar nature, become very salient to perceivers. Such appearances may attract the perceiver's attention, appeal to his or her sensibilities, excite or fascinate, interest or even tantalize, perplex or even confuse. Whether the perceiver finds the appearance visually appealing, he or she is aroused to interpet and to understand (see Figure 10-3).

Table 10-2 summarizes the receiver's point of view in appearance communication. The left side of this table refers to instances of social cognition without discourse (one-way communication). This side refers to the thought processes of the receiver alone. These thought processes may coincide with existing cognitive structures, allowing for easy identification, or they may be stimulated when a given appearance defies simple classification. The visual stimulation that comes from perceiving an appearance that arouses one's interest (for example, on a city street or in a music video) may result in new ideas about ways to dress or new possibilities for understanding other people. Such stimulation can promote fashion change, as people influence one another on a visual level (without necessarily having regard for intended meanings, if any). It can also lead to new hypotheses for interpreting others' appearances, that may or may not be "tested" in subsequent interactions. When appearance alone communicates, a receiver does not have the opportunity to assess potential meanings, but rather is influenced by the aesthetic code—the way the appearance signs work together to create a visual impression. When do receivers view appearances without engaging in discourse? They do so when they view people passing on the street, which may be a potent source of fashion information—all on a nondiscursive and aesthetic level of communication. Most studies of appearance perception use photographs or other visual stimuli to assess receivers' responses.

On the right side of the table, appearance perception is combined with discourse, so the potential exists for appearance to mediate discourse, or vice versa, as the two work in tandem. When responses tend to be routine and

**FIGURE 10-3**
*From a receiver's perspective, perception of the appearance of this Tharu woman in Nepal might be intriguing, requiring some contemplation about the various possible reasons she is wearing this garment on her head. Is she simply trying to keep the sun off of her head? Or, is this a traditional look in her culture? Especially when a perceiver attempts to understand an appearance in a cultural context different from his or her own, concentration and effort are likely to be involved. Photo by Margery Freeman.*

automatic, then a receiver is likely to make an identification of another person, and this response may be mediated through discourse. If, however, responses are more intrigued and interpretive, then the receiver has already realized that his or her cognitive categories or structures are inadequate to deal with the appearance, and therefore is aroused to understand the other person (see Figure 10-3). Negotiation is more likely to occur in this context.

**TABLE 10-2**
*Receiver's Perspective in Appearance Communication*

|  | *Appearance Alone* | *Appearance and Discourse* |
|---|---|---|
| Routine and Automatic | Identification | Identification and mediation |
| Intrigued Interpretation | Stimulation | Negotiation |

## *Sender and Receiver*

Most research focuses on the perspective of the receiver only, some addresses that of the sender, and few actually deal with both. One study pursued the perspective of both sender and receiver, to see how accurate clothing is as a medium of communication (Tseëlon, 1989). British women, not previously acquainted, attended a gathering, dressed in a way that "represented them best." They were asked to judge both themselves and all of the others, using both open-ended responses and a series of adjective scales. It was found that, across the subjects, the average degree of agreement between senders' intentions and receivers' interpretations was about 36 percent. This percentage rose to 56 percent when approximate matchings were calculated (for example, answers such as "she dressed to look *very* affluent" were counted as matching answers such as "she dressed to look *subtly* affluent"). No one guessed all of another woman's messages correctly. (See Figures 10-4 through 10-7 for specific details about the women included in the study.)

This study required women to evaluate one another on the basis of appearance, without the benefit of the kind of discourse necessary to negotiate meaning. In everyday life, appearance communication varies in the extent to which it (*a*) involves the conscious attention or knowledge of the participants, (*b*) interacts with discursive communication, and (*c*) involves social construction and negotiation of meaning as the sender and receiver strive to mesh their interpretations of self and other. A symbolic-interactionist perspective leads us to note that defining and interpreting appearances around us allows us to fit our lines of action with those of others around us (Morrione and Farberman, 1981). We make mental notes to ourselves and try to solve the puzzle posed by appearances that defy automatic processing. Even our own appearances may convey messages that are unknown to us but that may be discovered through social interaction.

Through joint actions with others, the meanings we assign to appearance are socially constructed or mutually defined. It may be necessary for senders and receivers to "work out" their interpretations of one another's appearances so interaction may proceed smoothly. For symbolic interaction or meaningful communication to occur, the meaning they assign to their appearances needs to emerge in somewhat close approximation to one another (Kaiser, 1983–1984). It would be hard to determine if these meanings ever coincide *exactly*, because of the complexity and ambiguity of appearance messages, including their tendency to convey multiple messages simultaneously and because it would be difficult for wearers and perceivers to convey in words (linguistically) a precise meaning. Nonetheless, a jointly constructed, mutual understanding can emerge from intrigued interpretations if participants work at negotiating some understanding that allows interaction to proceed.

Table 10-3 summarizes the preceding discussion, integrating the sender's and receiver's points of view and pointing to contexts in which social construction is most likely to be required or desirable for interaction to proceed. Each of the boxes represents a distinct *appearance communication context*, specifying the potential

**FIGURE 10-4**

*In a study by Tseëlon (1989) in England, about 34 percent of the messages this woman intended to convey through her appearance were exactly consistent with those received by perceivers. About 58 percent of the messages were approximately consistent. She described herself as "a career person" who wore "practical clothes." Others described her as "trying to look young—not succeeding, pleasant," "conservative, proper," "smart, conventional, anxious to please, possibly slightly lacking in confidence." Photo by Efrat Tseëlon.*

**FIGURE 10-5**

*Thirty percent of the messages this woman intended to convey through her appearance were accurately received by perceivers; 60 percent approximated some degree of consistency (Tseëlon, 1989). She described her own clothing as "reasonably smart with attention to detail"; others described her as "a bored housewife," "very smart, quite formal, glamorous and posh," and "neat, likes to please, likes to dress up." Photo by Efrat Tseëlon.*

for meaningful and symbolic interaction to occur. These appearance communication contexts tend to vary in terms of their potential for being *constructivistic*, or promoting negotiation that results in the emergence of new meanings constructed in interaction. One issue that comes to light when viewing this table is: Whose preconceived ideas about the meaning of a sender's appearance are challenged? In order for the sender's ideas to be challenged, some discursive feedback is ordinarily required. (An exception to this rule would be the case of a sender being aroused by another person's appearance and relating or comparing that appearance to his or her own.) In order for the receiver's ideas to be challenged, he or she needs to be intrigued to interpret *or* a routine and "easy" interpretation needs to be proven inadequate during discourse.

**FIGURE 10-6**
*Compared with the women pictured in Figures 10-4, 10-5, and 10-7, this woman's messages through her appearance were less likely to be accurately received (Tseëlon, 1989). Only 14 percent of the messages she intended to convey were accurately received by perceivers; 43 percent approximated some degree of consistency. She described herself as "individual in style, well controlled yet easy-going, chic but not totally aloof, independent, at ease with self and therefore others." Perceivers describe her as "having good taste, affluent, a bit overdone," "stylish and flamboyant, wanting to be noticed," "fashionable, smart, tasteful," and "doesn't want to look dated." Photo by Efrat Tseëlon.*

**FIGURE 10-7**
*Almost half (46 percent) of the messages this woman intended to convey through her appearance were accurately received by perceivers, but 87 percent of these messages were interpreted with an approximate degree of accuracy (Tseëlon, 1989). She described herself in the following way: "This is how I usually dress. I think it conveys to others that I'm fairly casual in my dress. It's probably obvious I'm a student though I'm not consciously portraying this. Comfort!" Others described her as "young, serious, free, limited budget," "college/prep appearance, casual, adventurous, sporty," "'studenty,' not the normal 'high-street' fashion but arty, not too way-out as a student," "casual, comfortable, 'studenty,'" and "active, no-nonsense dressing." Photo by Efrat Tseëlon.*

## Appearance and Negotiation

So, what needs to be negotiated in social life? Most of us enter social contexts with some preconceived notions about what will transpire and how the actors will play their roles. Yet even in contexts that are well-defined in advance by the participants, there are a number of uncertainties or contradictions that may emerge and require negotiation—the give and take of social interaction. The

**TABLE 10-3**
*Sender's and Receiver's Points of View*

| | *Appearance Alone* | *Appearance and Discourse* |
|---|---|---|
| Sender, Intentional<br><br>Receiver, Routine and Automatic | Neither are challenged; receiver uses existing thought processes automatically, and the sender receives no feedback. Meaning is shared but does not consciously pass through any minds; *least constructivistic* (for example, business suit in office context). | Neither are challenged unless discourse happens to produce new insights that change their minds. Most likely, this will not occur because meaning is already shared (for example, business suit in office context). |
| Sender, Unintentional<br><br>Receiver, Routine and Automatic | Neither are challenged; receiver uses existing thought processes automatically, and the sender never knows that a new meaning was assigned to her or his appearance (for example, a business suit in an ad is interpreted in a way never intended by an advertiser). | Sender may come to realize that his or her appearance conveys an unanticipated meaning; therefore, sender is challenged to reevaluate and be motivated to "correct" an impression through discourse, if the unanticipated meaning is not a desirable one. |
| Sender, Intentional<br><br>Receiver, Intrigued Interpretation | Receiver is challenged because of the novel nature of the sender's appearance to him or her; sender is aware that such an effect may occur but receives no feedback. | Receiver is challenged and sender focuses on negotiating the desired impression, assessing the feedback in the process. |
| Sender, Unintentional<br><br>Receiver, Intrigued Interpretation | Receiver is challenged and stimulated by the sender's appearance, but the sender is unaware of this because of a lack of feedback. | Receiver is challenged and, as interaction progresses, the sender is likely to learn about potential unanticipated meanings and negotiate, reassess perceptions of self, and therefore be challenged along with the receiver; *most constructivistic*. |

point is, even if social cognition produces an understanding of the other people in a situation and of the purpose of the situation itself, there is a need for *mutual* construction of meaning in social life, as participants fit their understandings together, fine tune them, and often come away from a context with new insights. And, culture may provide the physical artifacts (clothes and accessories) that we use in appearance communication, as well as the mental images that shape our expectations and recognitions of one another, but we can do a lot with these artifacts and images if desired (Enninger, 1985).

According to symbolic interactionist Gregory Stone (1965), meaning as negotiated through social interaction is always a variable. At one extreme, there may be a total absence of shared understanding. The sender may intend to convey a certain impression, while the receiver assigns an entirely different interpretation that was not anticipated by and undesirable to the wearer. Stone (1965) called this total absence of coexisting responses **non-sense**. For example, the 1988 Olympic gold medalist Florence Griffith-Joyner dressed in striking, unusually styled running attire at track meets leading up to the Olympics. As expressed in the media, she wished to express femininity, as well as a sense of flamboyance and flair, at a level that matched her tremendous athletic ability. If a perceiver happened to view her strictly as a sex object, not even considering her athletic ability or fashion sense, then Stone's (1965) concept of non-sense could be used to characterize this lack of mutual understanding.

At the other extreme, there are cases when the intended and received messages are entirely the same, where there is a total coincidence of responses. To Stone, this type of meaning was **boredom**. In Table 10-3, boredom would be most likely to occur in the box where a sender intentionally conveys a message and a receiver routinely and automatically processes that intended message. Neither the sender nor the receiver are challenged in any way, so there is no need for social construction. Everyday interactions in an office context, where a sender wears a typical business suit and a receiver perceives it as such, would be an example of such an interchange. This is not to say that meaningful communication is precluded: rather, mindful or negotiated interpretations of *appearance* are unnecessary. Interpretations of appearance are instead likely to be relatively unconscious, although discursive forms of communication may require more interpretation. Stone (1965) noted that neither non-sense nor boredom (both extremes on a continuum of meaning) can be approached often in social trans-actions, because either extreme can diminish the possibility that interaction will proceed. In the case of non-sense, appearance becomes something of a barrier to meaningful communication; if there is a *total* deficiency of shared understanding of a sender's appearance, then a receiver does not identify with the sender and assumes they have little in common. On the other hand, boredom seems to preclude the need for continuing communication.

Most social transactions fall somewhere between boredom and non-sense and involve the need for connecting, checking, and refining understandings. For example, an intended sender's message may be received incorrectly yet still be intriguing and promote a receiver's desire to "check out" his or her meaning.

And rarely are responses *totally* the same. Why is this? Stone (1965) noted that the I, the impulsive and responsive part of the self, always injects a certain tentativeness to social interactions, so that rarely are actions fully anticipated or meanings totally predicted. Generally there is some need for interpretation and social construction, and appearance and discourse work together to accomplish this. In some cases, they may even create some degree of confusion, if they contradict one another somewhat, which necessitates further interpretation.

The richest meanings, or those that are most profound, deep, and stimulating, seem to be those that emerge when there is at least some ambiguity about a sender's intent and the "correctness" of a receiver's interpretation. In such cases, responses only more or less coincide, and participants work at negotiating shared understanding. One can imagine the kinds of negotiated meanings that would emerge from interactions with the women pictured in Figures 10-4 through 10-7. Note that, to begin with, senders' intentions and receivers' interpretations only more or less coincide. With further interaction, most likely some common understandings would emerge that would make an impression on both the senders (who would understand themselves better) and the receivers (who would understand the senders better, as well as their own thought processes).

Of course, contexts will vary in terms of the degree of need for negotiation; some interactions and appearances are more routine than others. However, all social interactions are likely to require two problem-solving tasks on the part of participants.

1. There is a need for interactants to *identify and/or negotiate the identities of all participants* (including themselves and one another). They need to understand the *who* of the social context, as well as the qualities that one another bring to the context, and which of those qualities pertain.
2. Interactants need to *identify and/or negotiate a definition of the situation.* This definition becomes the *what* (the purpose) and the *how* (the interaction rules) of the social context (Enninger, 1984).

## Identity Assignment

As we meet one another in daily social encounters, the line between who we *are* and what we *have* is not always clear (Wheelwright, 1960). This is especially true when it comes to personal possessions such as clothes and accessories. Are these consumer objects indicative of who we are? This is one question that senders and receivers implicitly try to answer on a daily basis. Senders have certain attributes or qualities that they wish to convey to others, and receivers have some preconceived thought processes that they use to interpret appearance. Identity may be described as "any aspect of self about which individuals can through symbolic means communicate with others" (F. Davis, 1985, pp. 23–24).

Some constraints are imposed on identity assignments because of cultural and historical meanings and traditions, as well as the prior meanings (derived from previous social contexts) people bring with them to social situations. Some aspects of identity are more open to negotiation than others, and social structure is a factor in prescribing "assumed" identities (Stryker and Gottlieb, 1981). Gender, age, occupation, ethnic background, socioeconomic status, and membership in a social group are examples of such basic, culturally defined identities. These most easily recognized identities can be readily *named* with verbal labels, such as police officer, accountant, baseball player, male, Latino, and middle-aged. An example of identities that intersect is shown in Figure 10-8.

Many identities are not so easily pinned down, however, because we cannot name them and they may be associated with the nonlinguistic, aesthetic qualities of appearance. Even "readily named" identities can be manipulated through appearance management to alter existing preconceptions about what it means to be male, a baseball player, or an accountant. This tenuous characteristic of many identities, as presented and assigned, points to the need for negotiation in social interaction and, more specifically, in social contexts. The negotiation of identities emerges from a central problem for participants—the need to create complementary identities for one another. The following questions become relevant in terms of this problem (Stryker and Gottlieb, 1981):

1. How are the actors presenting themselves?
2. How are the actors "casting" or attempting to present the other actors?
3. How are imposed identities resisted, and how are self-presentations rejected by others?
4. Which aspects of identities and context are open to negotiation?
5. How do actors arrive at some consensus so they may continue to interact?

We are not merely passive recipients of the identities others assign to us; we actively engage in constructing and articulating our identities, and appearance management allows an avenue for this construction and articulation. Appearance rules may apply to some identities that are culturally defined. Often these rules can be described in terms of the *degree* of fit with the identity (Enninger, 1984). For example, a businesswoman is likely to be aware of certain rules that help her to claim a professional identity—a skirt "no shorter than . . .," a hairstyle "no longer than . . .," heels "no higher than . . .," and so on. Part of the need for negotiation even in the case of culturally defined identities stems from this matter of degree in terms of appearance rules, further confounded by fashion change which plays with these rules. Thus dressing to achieve a certain identity often allows for individual experimentation that may stretch the boundaries of appearance rules and involve the need for negotiation.

Identity becomes the *meaning* that individuals interacting attribute to a given individual assuming a role in a particular situation (Burke and Reitzes, 1981). Identity establishes what and where a person is, in social terms (Stone,

**FIGURE 10-8**
*In everyday life, identities tend to converge or intersect. Here, both ethnic and occupational identities may be attributed to these construction workers in mainland China. Photo by Stephen Cunha.*

1965). Because identity is intricately linked to social context, it is *situated* or shaped through situational involvement. Stone noted that identity is *announced* through personal appearance and then *placed* by observers' assessments of that appearance. The identities of all individuals in a social context are situated, allowing them to be drawn together while also setting them apart from one another. Identity is linked to all of the "joinings and departures of social life" (Stone, 1965, p. 223).

Three characteristics of identities may be identified: (1) identities as social products, (2) identities as self-meanings, and (3) identities as symbolic and reflexive (Burke and Reitzes, 1981).

## Identities

### Social Products

Identities are formulated and maintained as the result of social processes. Therefore, we recognize that identities are socially constructed; they are produced through joint interpretations and definitions through three social processes. First, individuals are placed into cultural categories on the basis of appearance. Let's suppose a female wears snugly fitted, brightly colored running tights with a matching cropped top to an exercise class. She thinks of the outfit as fashionable and feels good about herself when she exercises in it. It makes the exercise more fun. A male in the class sees the outfit, however, and thinks of her appearance as sexually attractive. Second, individuals make identifications *of* and possibly *with* one another. Suppose the male greets the female after the class and introduces himself. As he sees her more closely, he identifies her as being not only a sexually attractive female but also as having a pleasant smile. He is actually in the class because he values the form of exercise it provides, but it does not occur to him at this point to identify *with* her for that reason.

Third, self-concepts are validated through the social feedback the individuals provide one another. As the female in our example begins to realize that the male is attracted to her, she evaluates the "program" she presents through her appearance as compared to the "review" she seems to be receiving.

*Symbolic and Reflexive*

Identities are interpreted through processes of social construction, as individuals supply one another with feedback. If the male and female from the preceding example continue to interact, she will have the opportunity to begin to present him with a better understanding of her interpretation of her appearance, and he may come to realize that he identifies with her based on their common goal in the class. She has learned something from his feedback and perhaps has begun to contemplate the consequences of this feedback for how she views herself. He has learned that sexiness is not the only or primary quality associated with her identity and that they have something in common.

*Self-Meanings*

Identities are negotiated in particular situations and organized to produce a concept of self. Based on identities that are socially constructed, individuals may redefine the way they view themselves in certain contexts. These redefinitions are likely to produce new conceptions of person- and situation-appropriate dress. For instance, a female college student who has taken a part-time job as a reading assistant (grader) for a professor may be supplied new self-meanings as the students in the class respond to her in a manner that differs from student-to-student interactions. This student may find that her new role applies only to the particular class in which she is a grader and is thus a situated identity. She may also dress up a little more for that class than for other contexts where she is a "typical" student, because she has different perceptions of self as well as context.

Dramaturgists contend that there is little distinction between our identities and our actions, because our identities situate us in relation to other actors. This is not to say that identities are totally or always prescribed by social scripts, however. Often, they are negotiated through the give and take of social discourse. At the same time, they provide the frame of reference for interpreting a social context and for planning actions accordingly. We take part in the process of identity negotiation as we evaluate others and interpret the feedback (or "reviews") they provide us. The essential connection between identity and appearance, then, is the ability of people interacting to construct common interpretations.

*Role-Taking*

As we have seen, individuals' appearances and identities can never be totally predicted or anticipated. At the same time, people's ability to identify *with* one another, to come to see each other's points of view, helps to diminish the likelihood of "non-sense" (or lack of any jointly constructed meaning) in interaction involving discourse. A social-psychological process that emerges from participants' ability to identify with one another's appearances is *role-taking*. Role-taking is a symbolic-interactionist concept that describes, in the fullest sense of the concept, instances when individuals *mutually* or jointly orient themselves toward one another's identities and actions. Role-taking is a cognitive process that allows a receiver to develop a mental construction of not only a sender's "role" but also his or her identity, linked to the specific context in which interaction occurs (Sherohman, 1977). Role-taking allows receivers to assess where the senders are "coming from" and allows receivers to coordinate their activities and intentions with those of the sender. It allows the receiver to anticipate what the sender will be like in that context.

Role-taking is a slight variation on the theme of being able to identify *with* another person. Appearance becomes more critical in the latter kind of identification process, and often promotes a tendency to engage in role-taking. Together with discourse, appearance may facilitate or preclude role-taking. Since we generally see people's appearances before we begin discursive communication, the ability to identify *with* that appearance can be accomplished before discourse. Once discourse begins, then, part of the verbal role-taking may become redundant (Enninger, 1985).

There are two special cases of role-taking that we can consider at this point. First, individuals may be inclined to identify *with* someone and engage in role-taking when they perceive themselves to be similar to those others. Appearance is one obvious way of assessing similarity. We may presume to have something in common with those who dress like ourselves. Processes of **similarity-attraction**, then, can facilitate role-taking. Second, some individuals are more inclined than others to try to empathize with others, regardless of whether or not they perceive themselves to have something in common—on the surface. **Perspective-taking** involves the tendency to inject more emotion into interaction by feeling with and/or for a sender and giving him or her the benefit of the doubt.

*Similarity-Attraction*

The similarity-attraction hypothesis (Byrne, 1971) suggests that we are attracted to others whom we perceive to be similar to ourselves. In Stone's (1965) terms, we are more likely to identify *with* those who appear similar to ourselves; it is natural that we would assume we have something in common with them. To *like* someone and to be *alike* have the same origins in Old English. A sense of joint belonging or mutual identity may result from feelings of commonality. We also are more likely to be socially at ease in the presence of those similar to ourselves. Similarity-attraction may be partially explained by the idea of *reinforcement* (Hensley, 1981). It is generally gratifying to see others reinforcing our own tastes, as it reaffirms that our appearances are socially acceptable.

Another explanation of similarity-attraction in terms of degree of physical attractiveness is provided by the *matching hypothesis* (Goffman, 1952). This hypothesis suggests that individuals assess their own attributes (for example, appearance, monetary status, possessions) and then select partners who seem "equally matched." Although physically attractive dates may be *preferred* more, men and women of lesser attractiveness appear to *choose* less attractive dates than do highly attractive individuals (Berscheid et al., 1971). The matching hypothesis also seems to apply in some cases to same-sex friendships. Studies have noted that same-sexed close friends tend to be similar in degree of physical attractiveness (Cash and Derlega, 1978).

Apparently individuals are more likely in some cases to help others who are dressed similarly to themselves (Feldman, 1972; Suedfeld, Bochner, and Wnek, 1972; Schiavo, Sherlock, and Wicklund, 1974). Research has also shown that individuals who hold similar characteristics or traits are more likely to purchase similar products such as jeans (Belk, 1978). Hilda Buckley (1983) studied the relation between similarity in dress and two measures of attraction: the extent to which subjects would probably like a stimulus person and the extent to which subjects would enjoy doing schoolwork with the person. She found that as similarity in dress increased, so did the tendency to be attracted to the stimulus person. She noted, however, that the similarity-liking effect is likely to operate only to a certain point (Buckley, 1983). It has been hypothesized that moderate similarity with others generates the highest sense of acceptability (Snyder and Fromkin, 1980). There is a delicate balance between wanting to be like others and striving for uniqueness. Individuals are not likely to want to believe that they are exactly like others. They are likely to believe they are unique in some respects.

What degree of similarity is optimal with respect to processes of fashion influence? To answer this question, a study was conducted in which female college students responded to a series of 16 clothing opinions and to photographs of a female college student who was either very, fairly, slightly, or not similar to them (Leavitt and Kaigler-Evans, 1975). Distinctly lower ratings of agreement were given to new fashion suggestions when they were attributed to a sender judged to be extremely similar to the subjects (receivers). A sender judged to be less similar produced stronger agreement with the "advice." It seems that new ideas about fashion are received better from persons who are less similar to one's self. Although people who dress similarly in terms of fashionability may like each other, they are not necessarily influential with regard to fashion change (Leavitt and Kaigler-Evans, 1975). Some degree of stimulation or arousal is likely to be necessary to induce the kind of arousal required to change one's ideas about what is fashionable. Probably there is an optimal degree of similarity in this regard. The most effective or credible sources of fashion information need to be somewhat similar to message recipients, as well as somewhat different. Usually receivers of fashion messages respond well to persons who are part of their group but who lead or excel in some way (for example, in terms of fashion sense). If the sender of a fashion message is *too* similar to the receiver, the receiver is likely to wonder: Why take fashion advice from a person who is as dowdy as I am?

*Perspective-taking*

It is not necessary to look like someone to be able to understand his or her identity in a given context. Some receivers are more adept at assessing the points of view of others and gauging what others are attending to at a certain point in time and space (Sherohman, 1977). Perspective-taking involves the tendency to try to understand others by imagining their perspectives and often includes some sense of compassion for others. Individuals who engage in perspective-taking tend to be more accurate than those who do not when it comes to judging other people (Bernstein and Davis, 1982).

## Identity in Interaction

Identity is complex and does not emerge in a social vacuum. It is linked to other qualities of the self conveyed through appearance, especially to value, mood, and attitude (Stone, 1965). In addition to *announcing* identities, senders *qualify* these identities by placing some degree of value on them, by expressing personal values, and by posing or creating a mood that can set the tone of interaction (for example, serious or fun). The expression of attitude becomes a means for *activating* identity, suggesting how interaction might proceed. Figure 10-9 shows how value, mood, and attitude intersect in identity negotiations.

## Value

Communication is goal-seeking activity. That communication involves goals also means that it necessarily involves values (Wilden, 1987). "One's clothes impart value to the wearer, both in the wearer's own eyes and in the eyes of others" (Stone, 1965, p. 222). Receivers *appraise* a sender's appearance, and appraisal involves the use of values.

You will recall from the discussion on values in Chapter Nine that they serve as organizing principles influencing individuals' awareness, interests, and aesthetic perceptions in relation to appearance. In that chapter, our focus was on values as *determinants* of appearance management and perception. Here, that focus is still relevant to an understanding of individual characteristics brought to social contexts and therefore influencing appearance communication. Yet our attention in this instance is shifted to the *content* of individual appearances in context, that is, to the expression of value through appearance. The value orientations of humans, then, not only set the stage for appearance communication but also comprise means of personal expression.

In Chapter Nine, the following types of values were discussed: theoretical, economic, aesthetic, social, political, and religious. Combinations of these values may be expressed through certain appearances (see Figure 10-10).

Although there has been little research on the expression of values through appearance, there is evidence that they are related to interest in clothes (Creekmore, 1963; Sharma, 1980). Thus, we would expect some types of values or goals to be displayed through appearance. Stone (1965) noted that *consensual goals*—or those related to wealth, power, and prestige—are likely to be communicated through dress. Such goals would not be that different in concept from political

**FIGURE 10-9**

*How do perceptions of this man's values, mood, and attitude interact with one another as a receiver considers his appearance at a "Whole Earth" festival? Let's assume that a perceiver (a potential customer) interprets that this man is driven by a profit motivation but also enjoys expressing his creativity, that his mood is not too serious, and that his attitude toward life is low-key and relaxed. How will the potential customer interact with him based on these perceptions? He or she may be likely to make some jokes, but realize that the social transaction is still framed in a business context. During the course of the interaction, the initial perceptions may be modified through the mutual processes of negotiation. Photo by Wendy Dildey.*

values and the corresponding use of status symbols (Creekmore, 1963). However, we should exercise caution in predicting others' values on the basis of appearance, because in some instances circumstantial factors may induce individuals to express some values at the expense of others. For example, one might enjoy dressing uniquely or creatively (because of aesthetic values), yet view "dress-for-success" clothes (linked to political values) as a better alternative, particularly in a job interview.

Nonetheless, some research suggests that clothes reflect basic value orientations. Unger and Raymond (1974) conducted a study to see how accurately a person's race and attire could predict values. Research observers classified black (African-American) and white (Anglo-American) male college students who wore either deviant ("hippie") or conventional attire on a college campus in the early 1970s into one of four groups: black conventional, black deviant, white conventional, and white deviant. The 30 males in each of the groups were administered a measure of values focusing on personal qualities deemed most important. Re-

**FIGURE 10-10**
*Both religious and social values are communicated through this Jewish boy's wearing of the* yarmulke *at a New York parade celebrating an Israeli holiday. His personal beliefs as well as his social identification with the Jewish community are conveyed. Photo by Susan B. Kaiser.*

gardless of race, the males who wore deviant attire valued independence, imagination, and lovingness more than the conventionally attired males. The conventionally dressed students ranked higher on ambition and obedience. The white males valued lovingness, broadmindedness, honesty, and forgivingness more than the black males, who were more likely to value independence, intelligence, courage, and logic. Thus, both race and attire were indicative of basic values with respect to personal qualities.

*Mood*

Mood is comparable to feelings of pride about one's appearance (Stone, 1965), with reference to a set of values that serve to guide self-evaluations. A receiver may respond to a sender's appearance by *appreciating* the ambience, feeling, or spirit it brings to a social context (see Figure 10-11).

How accurately can clothes communicate a sender's mood or the mood he or she strives to convey? Little research has been conducted in this area, probably due to the fluctuating and transitory nature of mood. Mood is an intangible quality that is difficult to study or measure. A person's mood at the time of measurement may not be the same as it was when he or she got dressed that day. Thus clothes selected at an earlier point in time may not always reflect current mood, which may fluctuate. As we saw in Chapter Five, fluctuation in mood, as in the case of depression, may be linked to clothing selections on a daily basis.

Some authors have suggested that color may be more closely aligned with mood than is texture or clothing style (Ryan, 1966). Perceivers may use visible cues such as bright colors or grooming to interpret and define mood in a given situation. Still, a brightly colored shirt chosen during a cheerful mood in the morning may no longer reflect the way a man feels after a hard day at work. It is likely, however, that his demeanor may show that he is not very concerned about his appearance as he rides home on the bus. To the extent that the clothing symbols used are discursive, he may modify his appearance in relation to his mood. For instance, he could remove his jacket, loosen his tie, and roll up the sleeves of his bright shirt, thereby expressing that he is tired, is less interested than he was at work about being "on stage," and is now ready to relax. Nonverbal cues such as facial expression or the way one sits also communicate mood.

Another way we can consider mood, however, is to look to the nonlinguistic and aesthetic nature of appearance codes and consider the feelings they may arouse that cannot be easily put into words. Appearance may express, in an imprecise and intangible manner, the degree of anxiety, excitement, and respect participants have for one another in a social context.

This section highlights attitudes in terms of *behavior*, as contrasted with the discussion in Chapter Nine focusing on the cognitive and affective components

### *Attitude*

**FIGURE 10-11**
*Clothes can be used to create a sense of mood. This street musician in San Francisco probably wants to create a context of fun, joviality, and creativity. Photo by Mark Kaiser.*

of attitudes shaping how perceivers respond to clothes. Let's review the three components of attitudes by considering Figure 10-12.

Stone (1965) used a symbolic-interactionist perspective to describe attitudes used by perceivers in estimating the past, present, and future activities of a wearer. He noted that attitudes are *proposed* by those who manage appearance (develop "programs") and *anticipated* by the reviewers of that appearance. In this way, appearance *substitutes* for past and present action and, at the same time, poses clues enabling reviewers to anticipate what is about to occur. Loyalty to places, sports teams, or favorite rock stars holding cherished significance can be displayed through symbolic colors or slogans. In this way, past actions are expressed, and the context in which meaningful clothes are worn to display such loyalty most likely affects the nature of the appearance communication. Attitudes proposing information about present and future actions are essentially linked to identity and context.

**FIGURE 10-12**
*We can review the various dimensions of attitudes (cognitive, affective, and behavioral) by considering this young girl's T-shirt. We also want to consider the communicative aspects of the T-shirt. The cognitive dimension of a perceiver's attitude may relate to what he or she knows about the arms race and the social-political possibilities for a freeze on arms. The perceiver's affect is linked to how he or she feels about this issue and how emotion-laden these feelings are. Behavior toward this young girl or (more likely) her parents may be influenced by the perceiver's cognition and affect. For example, the topic of world peace may be introduced in a conversation. From this girl's perspective, we can also consider her own attitudes toward the T-shirt and what it represents, as well as how she internalizes the responses of perceivers. Photo by Susan B. Kaiser.*

*FIGURE 10-13*
*How are this boy's attitudes toward sports conveyed by his clothes and posters? It is relatively easy to detect a strong interest on his part. Photo by Susan B. Kaiser.*

In addition to conveying details about or substituting details for our actions, attitudes can be visually displayed so as to reveal a wearer's opinions and to set the stage, in a general sense, for the type of discourse that is likely to follow. Wearers can convey their attitudes toward specific clothing styles by actually wearing them, of course, but they can also propose attitudes toward other cultural artifacts, figures, and issues of the day (see Figure 10-13).

Some research suggests that attitudes vary in terms of accuracy in communication, or agreement between wearer intent and observer perception. Historic and cultural contexts are likely to impact the extent of explicitness of attitudinal appearance messages. In the early 1970s—a time when social-political attitudes were relatively straightforward or explicit—Kness and Densmore (1976) found that hippie dressers (long hair, unpressed jeans and shirt, and sandals or bare feet) were less concerned with status symbolism in dress than were conservative dressers (short, trimmed hair and straight-cut pants, sweaters or pressed tailored shirt, shoes, and socks). Hippie dressers characterized clothes as bothersome and tended to stress the importance of comfort. They expressed the following beliefs: (1) The business world should not force its appearance-related values on workers; and (2) freedom in personal choice of dress is important. In contrast, conservative dressers indicated concern about the importance of personal appearance in peer groups and expressed their enjoyment from wearing traditional or conservative clothes. Basically, this research indicated that in the 1970s, at

*Social-Political Attitudes*

least, it was possible to predict a student's social-political attitudes on the basis of dress.

These findings were also supported in a study by Buckley and Roach (1974). The researchers studied the clothing and social-political attitudes of male and female university students and found that the students' attitudes toward social and political issues (for example, the military draft, black power, woman's lib, the FBI, abortion, the Pentagon, and Wall Street) were perceived by the subjects to be communicated through clothes. The students espousing countercultural beliefs (the hippies) especially identified with clothes that symbolized their attitudes. Both the countercultural and conservative students displayed consistency between attitudes and overt behavior (as measured by responses to photographs of clothing and to clothing actually worn).

Attitude similarity was found to be a factor in a study of females' perceptions of variations in male hairstyles (Peterson and Curran, 1976). Females who preferred the short-haired males were conservative, whereas those preferring the appearance of the long-haired males were more liberal. Hair length in males was seen as a cue to social-political attitudes, and the females identified most with those whom they perceived to be similar to themselves.

In studies conducted in field settings, perceived similarity in social-political attitudes was found to be important in obtaining political support for certain causes in the early 1970s. Part of this research interest stemmed from the "Clean for Gene" phenomenon that emerged during Eugene McCarthy's 1968 presidential campaign. This phenomenon seemed to be based on the assumption that a "deviant" or hippie appearance on the part of campaigners might alienate people who might otherwise support a political cause. Apparently, research indicated "deviant" dress was considered by perceivers to be indicative of more liberal political attitudes, while "conventional" dress was associated with conservative attitudes (Darley and Cooper, 1972). Hippie-appearing experimenters received significantly more signatures to a petition calling for an end to the Vietnam War from hippie passers-by (Suedfeld, Bochner, and Matas, 1971; Keasey and Tomlinson-Keasey, 1973).

It seems that similarity in dress is likely to be most important in social-political contexts such as requesting signatures on a petition when the perceived similarity in beliefs is not as important, that is, when the subject has little belief in the petition or when the petition is not as controversial (Bryant, 1975). It is interesting to note that one study found the attitude-similarity effect did not hold true in the case of males perceiving females (Walsh, 1977). It seems that male students in the 1970s, whether hippie or not, were more likely to respond favorably (by signing a petition for a bicycle path) to a female who was dressed in conventional attire, as opposed to hippie attire (Walsh, 1977). It is possible that straight females may have appeared more "feminine" than hippie females, and that sexual attraction was stronger than similarity-attraction (in terms of attitudes) in this study. This possibility leads us to question how sexual attitudes are communicated through appearance.

Clothing appears to be a less accurate indicator of sexual attitudes than of social-political attitudes. Mathes and Kempher (1976) asked university students to indicate the frequency with which they wore various apparel items. The students also provided information on their sexual attitudes and behavior (for example, as related to premarital sex), as well as on their beliefs about how often sexually liberal versus conservative students wear various clothing styles. The cognitive elements of their attitudes (their beliefs) were evident as they identified a variety of styles associated with liberal sexual attitudes and behaviors. The appearance cues for males included going barefoot, wearing open shirts or sandals, going shirtless, or wearing net shirts. The cues for females included cut-offs, hip-hugger pants, hoop earrings, midriffs, work shirts, going braless, blue jeans, hot pants, halter tops, sandals, and going barefoot.

*Sexual Attitudes*

The correlations among the items of dress worn by the subjects (demonstrating the behavioral component of attitudes), their attitudes toward premarital sexual relations, and their reported number of sexual partners indicated that, for men, clothing is not a valid cue to sexual attitudes and/or reported behavior. For the females, there were some moderate correlations between cut-offs and midriffs and attitudes toward sexual relations. There were also moderate correlations between women's tendencies to wear midriffs, work shirts, and no bra and the reported number of different sexual partners. These findings suggest that there may be a slight relation between female attire and sexual attitudes and behavior. However, there were many items of dress that subjects *believed* to be indicative of sexual attitudes and behavior that were not so in actuality. Therefore, a distinction should be made between attributed sexual attitudes on the basis of clothing and actual attitudes held, because fewer clothes were accurate indicators of sexual attitudes than were identified as such.

In another study, both males and females were evaluated in terms of qualities associated with revealing versus nonrevealing clothes (Abbey et al., 1987). The stimulus persons (either a male or a female) were pictured in the social context of an empty classroom, seated at a desk near either a male or female as though they were comparing notes after class. The females in the revealing clothing conditions wore an outfit that was not likely to be appropriate classroom attire—a low-cut blouse, a slit skirt, and high-heeled shoes. In the nonrevealing conditions, the females wore a blouse buttoned to the neck, a skirt without a slit, and boots. Males with revealing attire wore a shirt with the top three buttons undone and tight-fitting slacks. In the nonrevealing clothing conditions, they wore a shirt buttoned to the neck and loose-fitting slacks. Females in revealing clothes were perceived as sexier, more seductive, more flirtatious, more promiscuous, less considerate, and less sincere than those wearing nonrevealing clothes. Those wearing revealing clothes were rated higher on sexual-related trait attitudes regardless of the gender of the partner in the pictured context. Both male and female targets were perceived as more kind and warm when they wore nonrevealing clothes. The male sender's attire, however, was not associated with sexual ratings as the female's was. He was evaluated as more cheerful, friendly, humorous, warm, and marginally more kind when his attire was non-revealing, but there seemed to be little consensus among the receivers as to what makes men look sexy or revealing.

The studies on communication of sexual attitudes through clothing point to a problematic area in gender relations (see Social Focus 10-1). That clothes more accurately convey social-political attitudes than they do sexual attitudes could be related to the fundamental cultural category of gender. Gender stereotypes, being linked to cultural ideology, are likely to endure longer than stereotypes linked to social-political issues of the day. Clothing indicative of conservative or liberal political views probably have become more ambiguous since the 1970s. Symbols of sexual attraction, on the other hand, reflect relatively enduring stereotypes that cut across changing fashions.

## Definition of the Situation

In addition to serving as a facilitator in the negotiation of identity, appearance plays a vital part in helping individuals define and interpret social situations. Identities are intricately linked to the contexts in which they are negotiated, but it is important to consider not only *who* is interacting but also *what* they are attempting to accomplish and *how* they go about it. W. I. Thomas (1924), who is known for the concept of **definition of the situation**, noted that if humans define situations as real, then they are real in their consequences. In other words, reality is socially constructed, and our perceptions are largely responsible, as they are meshed with those of others, in shaping the course of our actions and interactions. People often enter situations with some preconceived ideas about what will transpire and about the identities of the people involved (for example, who they are and how they will act). When these expectations are relatively strong and the individuals proceed with a set of assumptions in mind, their definitions of situations may become **self-fulfilling prophecies** (Merton, 1949). In fact, appearance management is enacted with situations in mind, in advance of those situations. Clothes are even used as markers at times to gauge the tone of an upcoming event, as when invitations specify "casual attire," "toga party," or "costume only." If party-goers expect to have a "wild and crazy" time, and the clothes are part of that prescription, then they proceed with that assumption in mind and most likely have a wild and crazy time, unless something or someone challenges that definition.

Human behavior is never totally predictable. Mead's (1934) concept of the dialogue within the self, between the I and the me, is relevant to this point. You will recall from Chapter Five that the I provides for spontaneity and impulsivity, whereas the me is responsible for incorporating the collective attitudes of others. Inevitably in some contexts, someone in a social gathering will have different preconceived ideas about a situation, and the need for negotiation becomes apparent. Discrepancies in preconceived definitions of a situation are probably most common in contexts that are not routine or that are new to the participants

# Appearance Communication and Miscommunication: The Case of Attitudes and Sexuality

How accurately does appearance communicate a person's sexual attitudes? Accuracy can become a serious issue in the context of female senders and male receivers. There is a high degree of potential for miscommunication—with dire consequences in some instances.

Females do not necessarily tend to wear clothing items for the single purpose of appearing sexually attractive for men (McCullough, Miller, and Ford, 1977). However, males tend to focus more on sensuality in their perceptions of women's appearances than do women (Kaigler-Evans and Damhorst, 1978). Men tend to view some items of clothing (DeLong, Salusso-Deonier, and Larntz, 1983) and shoes (Kaiser, Schutz, and Chandler, 1987) as sexier than do women.

Based on a study of the evaluations of 20 males and 20 females on the attractiveness of female models, Williamson and Hewitt (1986) concluded that a woman does appear more attractive to a man in subtle forms of sexually alluring attire such as a mini skirt. However, blatant forms of sexually alluring attire such as unbuttoned shirts or no bra in a wet T-shirt do *not* increase a woman's attractiveness in the eyes of men and *reduce* it in the eyes of women.

Zellman and Goodchilds (1983) asked 14- to 18-year-old adolescents "whether a girl's low-cut top, shorts, tight jeans, or see-through clothes meant she wanted to have sex, and whether similar meaning was implied if a guy wore an open shirt, tight pants, jewelry, or tight swim trunks" (p. 58). The male adolescents perceived each of these types of clothing as more indicative of sexual interest or availability than did female adolescents. (Yet both males and females perceived males' clothing to be less indicative of sexual intent than they did females' clothing.) It seems that females are likely to wear clothes with the *intent* of appearing fashionable, stylish, or similar to their peers. However, males may focus, instead, on the sexiness in the appearance, and this appears to occur without an overload of cues. Thus men appear to overestimate the sexual intent or attitude pronouncements of women they perceive (Abbey et al., 1987). More research is needed in everyday contexts to determine the factors that may either intensify or reduce the tendency for this degree of overestimation to occur.

Some studies have focused specifically on the context of rape, in which attitude miscommunications based on appearance have violent consequences. These studies have suggested perceivers expect a female who goes outdoors wearing provocative clothing and assuming a nonaggressive posture to be susceptible to rape (Terry and Doerge, 1979). In another study, males tended to be more likely than females to attribute greater responsibility to a female rape victim (Kanekar and Kolsawalla, 1980). Additionally, the perceived provocativeness of the victim's clothes directly affected her perceived responsibility. These findings were reinforced and amplified in a later study incorporating three conditions of dress: highly provocative (see-through mesh dress), provocative (mini-length dress), and non-provocative (jeans worn with a bulky sweater) (Lewis and Johnson, 1989). The most highly provocative attire was associated with a greater degree of "responsibility" than were the other two styles. Moreover, males were more likely to assign this responsibility than were women (Lewis and Johnson, 1989). Clearly, appearance perceptions can be linked to serious social issues, and there is a need for further research to identify these linkages, so as to foster an awareness of the ramifications of gender-based power relations. If, for example, a man in an expensive suit is mugged on his way home from work, are perceivers likely to attribute responsibility to him because he appears prosperous (and is therefore "asking for it")? How do judgments of a woman's sexuality differ from those of a man's success? The point is that neither males nor females are likely to dress in order to become victims of a crime.

(for example, a party or social gathering, a night club, or a foreign country). Let's suppose a male college student goes to a party that he knows several other Young Republicans and business majors will be attending. (He fits both of these descriptions.) He finds when he reaches the apartment where the party is to be held that many of the attendees are dressed in punk attire (spiked, colored hair, black leather, spiked wrist bands, and the like). Verbal discourse and negotiation are required for him to reconstruct a definition of the situation. If this male and the other party-goers can get past the differences in their appearance and engage in conversation, they may find they actually have more in common than they have presumed. In the process, their ideas about the meanings of one another's appearance are likely to change. In this context, the participants need to work at defining the situation so interaction can proceed.

Assumed definitions of situations come to the surface when clothes disrupt or appear incongruent with any of the participants' expectations. An angry female bank customer who is trying to get a checking account straightened out may find it difficult to remain serious about the situation if she is met at the window by a teller dressed in a Halloween costume. The normally serious, staid environment of a bank may be transformed into a jovial, relaxed, and informal setting through the introduction of costumes. In such a case, the clothes enable a redefinition of the situation.

How can we study people's attempts to define situations? Among the techniques that have been used, *projective* measures seem to be promising in illustrating the richness and complexity of people's interpretations. Such measures allow receivers to relax their defenses and project their own psychological feelings onto imaginary characters and situations. When subjects are asked directly, they may not really be aware of their grooming motives and emotions, and they may attempt to rationalize or "explain away" any apparent contradictions or embarrassing tendencies. A projective approach, on the other hand, has the potential to break through subjects' anxieties about dealing with sensitive or personal subjects and allow them to freely and creatively express their feelings (Rook, 1985b). This technique has been found to be especially conducive to exploring individuals' interpretations of grooming rituals (Rook, 1985b) and the degree of formality in office contexts (Damhorst, 1984–1985).

As we attempt to understand how people use appearance to define the situations in which they find themselves, it is helpful to delineate some of the variables appearance defines in social contexts. The next section deals with these variables, which help to elucidate the *what* of social interaction.

## Social Variables Defined by Dress

Some social variables are often defined by apparel cues, particularly when the setting lacks specificity or when the apparel cues are out of context in a given setting. The following social variables are defined by dress, as individuals socially construct their interpretations of a situation: (1) degree of formality, (2) identities of and relationships among participants, (3) degree of familiarity with the situation, (4) degree of salience (personal commitment and meaning) the situation has for the participants, and (5) possibilities for overt action.

Clothes serve as a strong cue to the degree of formality in a situation and help to shape how individuals interact. A British study examined the effects of formal versus casual attire by using a researcher who requested subjects to write responses on a questionnaire. It was noted that the subjects used a more formal writing style in their responses when the researcher (with a standard British accent) was dressed formally (skirt, blouse, and buttoned coat) than when she was dressed casually (jeans, rugby shirt, and open coat) (Giles and Farrar, 1979). Thus the experimenter's attire served to define the (research) situation as a formal one in the minds of the subjects.

*Degree of Formality*

Degree of dress formality tends to be part of a culture's repertoire, especially for such contexts as church attendance and special dances or functions, as opposed to picnics or joining neighborhood games of touch football. Yet there may be subtle nuances producing different preconceived definitions of the degree of formality even in some of these "standard" formal versus informal contexts, because each group may develop its own cultural expectations.

Damhorst (1984–1985) found that formality was a strong cue in subjects' interpretations of a hypothetical situation presented to them in line drawings, from which they were asked to construct stories or scenarios. The subjects used the sex of the senders as well as the degree of formality in their attire to construct an interpretation of the situation. (See Figure 10-14 for a related situation.)

Given that identity is entangled with social context, we would expect the same appearance style to hold different meanings and to invoke disparate identity placements when the context varies, and research documents this assertion. A

*Identities of and Relationships among Participants*

**FIGURE 10-14**
*How might a student perceiver walking by these campus recruiters' desk at a career fair define the situation in terms of formality? The recruiters' appearances are likely to set the stage for interaction, but the degree of formality will be negotiated as a student interacts with them. Note the difference between the level of formality in the female's and the male's appearances. Photo by Wendy Dildey.*

tie, for example, has been found to increase an observer's impression of a student's intelligence when it is worn to a job interview, but to decrease such an impression if worn to a lecture (where it is less appropriate) (Rees, Williams, and Giles, 1974). In this case, identity placements are tempered by the student role and concomitant conditions under which it is appropriate to alter that role. Given that identity is situated, it is defined and placed according to such conditions.

As identities are negotiated through the course of interaction, clothes enable participants to align their actions on the basis of their relationship to one another. Possibilities for such relationships include similarity and equality versus asymmetry and hierarchy. Mary Lynn Damhorst (1984–1985) found that the *differences* in the degree of formality of stimulus persons interacting in an office context tended to increase the subjects' certainty about the meaning of a man's suit (dominance). (See Social Focus 10-2 for a discussion on the issue of formality similarities or differences as well as other issues in the counseling context; also see Figure 10-15.)

A perceived romantic relationship between persons may also emerge from appearance cues—especially from a female's appearance. When a female stimulus person wore revealing attire (as opposed to nonrevealing attire), she was more likely to be judged to be romantically involved with a male seated with her in a classroom (comparing notes after class) (Abbey et al., 1987). The couple was also perceived to be more sexually attracted to one another. Males' clothing variations produced no differences in this regard (Abbey et al., 1987). Both

*FIGURE 10-15*
*The identities of and relationship between this student (left) interested in an internship and the internship counselor (right, also a student) are shaped in part by their clothes. Although this is not a job interview, the student on the left dressed up, because she defined the situation in terms of the need to make a good impression. To the counselor on the right, this is a part-time job in an informal setting, and she has dressed accordingly. The differences in their definitions of the situation are "worked out" as they interact. Photo by Molly Greek.*

# Appearance Communication in Counselor–Client Interactions

Early perceptions and expectations on the part of a client entering a counseling context are likely to contribute to a counselor's effectiveness as well as to the ultimate outcome of the interaction. First impressions of a counselor, like any first impressions, are part of the appearance phase of interaction described by Gregory Stone (1965). During this phase, identities are established and mobilized to set the stage for the discourse (discussions) to follow.

Several studies have examined counselor attractiveness as a variable in client perceptions, and the results suggest that—once again—appearance is an important factor in social interaction. A male counselor is evaluated as more competent, trustworthy, and helpful with a variety of problems if his appearance is attractive rather than unattractive (Cash et al., 1975). The same results have been found with female counselors; positive perceptions and expectations are associated with attractiveness (Lewis and Walsh, 1978). Attractiveness does not appear to be a substitute for skill on the part of a counselor, but it does play a role in the initial stage of counseling (Paradise, Zweig, and Conway, 1986).

Some research has focused on clothing as a variable that can mediate perceptions of counselor attractiveness. Degree of formality in counselor attire has been a focal point of much of this research. The principle behind the selection of formality as a variable is linked to the idea that it is important for a counselor to strike a delicate balance between appearing competent and expert (so his or her advice will be followed), and avoiding a look that creates too much social distance (and, hence, contributes to a client's feelings of discomfort or anxiety). An important factor in social distance, of course, is the client's attire. Research suggests that clients feel less anxious when their counselors dress a little more—but not *too* much more—formally than they themselves typically dress (Hubble and Gelso, 1978). For example, a sweat shirt and jeans appear to be too casual for a male counselor's attire, even when the clients are students who typically wear very casual attire. A casual sport shirt and slacks, however, appear to reduce anxiety in student clients who typically dress in a very casual manner. In contrast, students who typically dress formally to some degree appear to feel comfortable with a counselor wearing formal attire (a jacket and tie). Thus, it seems that the most effective attire for reducing anxiety is "a little better" than what the clients themselves usually wear, without appearing *too* different (Hubble and Gelso, 1978).

Other research suggests that the impact of formality versus informality in a counselor's clothing is diminished when the client is highly ego-involved in the counselor–client discussion, for example, when parents are being counselled regarding how to improve their children's reading skills (Wasserman and Kassinove, 1976).

Of course, dress is only one factor in the counseling context. Dress was manipulated along with the office setting and role behavior in a study by Kerr and Dell (1976). A female counselor wore either an attractive dress or tailored pantsuit with hose and dress shoes, or clean blue jeans and a casual shirt, walking shoes, and bright socks. Her behavior was either expert and logical in approach or warm and responsive, and the office setting included the display of either credentials and textbooks or "sensitivity" posters and a humorous mural. The extent to which the counselor was perceived as warm or responsive was influenced almost exclusively by her behavioral style. However, attire did interact with role behavior in the clients' determinations of expertness. When the expert-role behavior was adopted, there was a distinction between professional attire and casual attire. The professional attire condition resulted in a more expert evaluation than the casual attire condition.

In another study, one black (African-American) and one white counselor dressed in either a skirted suit (attractive condition) or a drab pantsuit (unattractive condition) (Green, Cunningham, and Yanicko, 1986). Makeup and hairstyle were also manipulated to alter the degree of attractiveness according to the condition. Both black and white clients (students) rated the attractive counselor more favorably than the unattractive counselor, regardless of the student's or the counselor's race. However, the black students were more likely than the white students to expect the attractive counselor to be more helpful.

Thus, it seems that clothes can enhance a counselor's ability to adopt a certain professional style, to reduce client anxiety, and to strengthen client confidence. However, there are a number of contextual factors that influence the extent to which these effects may be realized. Moreover, there are numerous dimensions along which counselors can modify their appearances. Research by Littrell, Littrell, and Kuznick (1981) has indicated that the formal–informal

## *Social Focus 10-2 (continued)*

dress dimension is not the singlemost important dimension for assessing meaning in counselors' attire. There are other important layers of meaning, including fashionability. Thus, negotiations of the meanings of appearance between clients and counselors, like all negotiations of meaning, are likely to be dynamic processes of social construction, mediated by verbal discussion and other contextual factors.

males and females associated the seductively dressed female's attire with a romantic or sexual relationship. However, the males thought that the pictured female was more seductive, sexy, and promiscuous than the female raters did, regardless of whether that female was pictured with a male or female. It seems that males' cognitive contexts or thought processes when perceiving females overpowered the social context in assigning qualities to the pictured female.

A study in a laboratory experimental context also found that the gender of individuals interacting factors into how receivers define a situation (Barnes and Rosenthal, 1985). This study sought to assess the effects of an experimenter's physical attractiveness and attire in same- and mixed-sex dyads. Raters observed experimenters but were unable to see with whom the experimenters were interacting. The behavior of the experimenter was evaluated in terms of smiles, glances, dominance, warmth, anxiety, and talkativeness. Experimenters' talking behavior changed as a function of their attractiveness, attire, and to whom they were talking (a male or a female). It seems that both males and females treat females differently than they treat males, though as perceivers we can better see changes in another's behavior when that behavior is directed toward someone of our own sex (Barnes and Rosenthal, 1985).

Therefore, physical attractiveness, attire, and gender may interact with each other in a manner that may unintentionally affect the laboratory experimental context. Their interaction with one another could also play an important function in everyday communication in dyadic interactions, since both females and males appear to behave differently in opposite- versus same-sex dyads. Also, a sender's physical attractiveness may become a less potent predictor of a receiver's evaluations when there is a great deal more information available about the sender—namely, the sender's attire and the identity (gender) of the person with whom the sender is interacting. More research is needed to pursue these possibilities in everyday contexts. (See Figure 10-16.)

*Degree of Familiarity*    Some situations, as participants enter them, seem familiar or commonplace, whereas others suggest that one is about to have a unique, unfamiliar, or bizarre experience. The clothed appearances of others in a situation provide the clues enabling one to define a situation as familiar versus unfamiliar. Familiarity with clothing cues, such as a business suit, appears to increase a perceiver's degree of certainty as to the definition of a situation (Damhorst, 1984–1985).

**FIGURE 10-16**
*Appearances are likely to be a factor in how this man and woman interact as they enjoy a picnic along the Seine River in Paris. Appearances, along with the setting, help to develop a tone or mood for the occasion—perhaps one of romance. Photo by Susan B. Kaiser.*

Culture generally provides some mental blueprints for interpreting the clothes in a situation (McCracken, 1986), and when those clothes are unfamiliar to a person entering a context, he or she is likely to infer that the situation will also produce a new or first-time experience. Traveling in a foreign country often invokes such a response (see Figure 10-17), but moving into social circles or contexts that are unfamiliar within one's own country can also produce a sense

**FIGURE 10-17**
*How familiar is this context to a tourist in this mountain village of Colombia? The clothes may serve to define a situation of unfamiliarity, suggesting to the tourist that some other aspects of his or her experiences at the market (for example, knowing how to buy or barter) may also be unfamiliar. Photo by Carla M. Freeman.*

of culture shock. In some cases, a situation may be unique to many participants, perhaps because they all had different preconceptions and thus have dressed very differently. Vernon (1978) refers to situations such as these having "phantom norm definitions"—where no real group consensus exists, but each participant assumes there exists one that is unfamiliar only to himself or herself. Eventually, the participants are likely to construct a shared definition of the situation out of the dramaturgical ambiguity that ensues, that is, if they are to continue to interact. Thus, if *everyone* dresses differently and there is a lack of consensus or shared definition to begin with, active construction is necessary and it is possible that "anything goes" for the time being in terms of appearance. (Later, some kind of group look will probably emerge.) Research on active constructions emerging from individuals aligning their interpretations and definitions of a situation, and the relation of these processes to appearance norms, is needed if we are to understand fully the dynamics of appearance in social contexts.

*Salience*

Individuals are likely to communicate their degree of regard for a situation through appearance management. If a person gives a party that was intended to be formal and has indicated this formality to guests, then he or she is likely to feel slighted if they come in shorts and T-shirts. In this case, they may not be displaying the same degree of salience to the situation that the party host or hostess is, or at least he or she may perceive that to be the case. Negotiation through discourse will be necessary if the guests are likely to indicate that the party is important to them (if it is).

Situations that are likely to be considered especially salient by senders, as they prepare for interaction, are parties hosted by one's boss, a male meeting his girlfriend's parents for the first time, or a young child's first day of kindergarten. Job interviews are typically defined as important by the interviewer and interviewee (in particular). Advice in personnel literature often underscores the importance of the *appearance* phase in job interviews. Common wisdom suggests that interviewers make their selection decisions during the first four minutes of interaction, resulting primarily from nonverbal cues (Hatfield and Gatewood, 1978). Traditionally, the appearance of an applicant and an application form or resumé have been salient factors in the final personnel decision (Springbett, 1958).

*Possibilities for Overt Action*

Mode of dress prescribes possibilities for overt actions in a practical way. The utilitarian nature of apparel cues dictates to some extent the degree to which individuals can engage in physical activity. High heels can be a damper if a female on a date is spontaneously invited to hike through the woods. In contrast, wearing sweats while lying on the couch watching television may come in handy if one gets the sudden urge to exercise (or if an aerobics program begins).

Research with young children indicates young girls' choice of attire expresses possibilities for overt actions and defines a play situation accordingly. Girls who wear pants are *perceived* as more likely to engage in such active play as climbing trees, whereas girls who wear skirts are associated with such traditionally feminine contexts as playing with dolls (Kaiser and Phinney, 1983; Kaiser, Rudy, and

**FIGURE 10-18**
*Possibilities for overt action are defined in part by this girl's clothes. At her parents' insistence, she has put on her helmet to ride her bike, but unfortunately she is wearing no shoes and her skirt could get caught in the bicycle spokes or chain. Photo by Susan B. Kaiser.*

Byfield, 1985; Kaiser, 1989). However, in reality, a preschool girl's attire appears to have little influence on whether or not she plays with dolls or engages in more physically active behaviors such as riding a tricycle (Kaiser, Rudy, and Byfield, 1985). (See Figure 10-18.)

## Understanding Appearance Communication

We have seen that identities and contexts are socially constructed and negotiated in everyday life. Meaning is "neither inferred nor externally predetermined; it is negotiated" (Stryker and Gottlieb, 1981, p. 447). The critical point from a contextual perspective is not whether meaning is valid or correct when measured against some objective standard. Instead, the critical point is whether or not senders' and receivers' inferences and interpretations come to be shared or interconnected as a result of the dynamic interplay between appearance and discourse.

How can we extend our understanding of appearance communication—a fascinating yet elusive and taken-for-granted area of study? First, it is important for the study of appearance perception (the most commonly researched side of the appearance communication equation) to extend beyond trait perception (Hamilton, 1981; Damhorst, in press). There is a need for a broader research agenda in terms of inferences based on appearance, to understand how situations are defined, redefined, and transformed into new situations. This process of **contextualizing**, which includes a sensitivity to situational dynamics (Morrione and Farberman, 1981), can promote the development of new methodologies and insights to understand the richness in meanings linked to appearance in and across situations.

Second, there is a need to answer a critical question: What is open to negotiation in terms of appearance in everyday life? Everyday life is not totally undetermined or likely to be entirely open to negotiation (Stryker and Gottlieb, 1981). Rather, there are likely to be some social-structural constraints that suggest, establish, or demand how interaction is to proceed and appearances are to be managed and interpreted. At the same time, we know that social interactions cannot be totally predetermined and that appearance affords an outlet for creative expression, experimentation, and self-understanding. Therefore, there is a need to determine how appearance rules are constructed, or how the distinctions between *can*, *should*, and *must* are negotiated (Enninger, 1983).

In Part Four, the social processes leading to the development of social structure and constraints will be examined. By using a contextual perspective, we can explore the cultural and historical ideologies that influence how we manage and interpret appearance, as well as the social-psychological processes contributing to the emergence of new meanings of appearance. Without communication there is no memory, and without memory there is no life. A contextual perspective provides people with a way to take this memory into account, while also allowing them to be open to novelty, diversity, cooperation, and the future (Wilden, 1987). All of these elements are vital to any study of the changing meanings of appearance and processes of social and fashion change.

## Suggested Readings

Abbey, A., Cozzarelli, C., McLaughlin, K., and Harnish, R. 1987. The effects of clothing and dyad sex composition on perceptions of sexual intent: Do women and men evaluate these cues differently? *Journal of Applied Social Psychology 17*:108–126.
This study provides an understanding of the implications of appearance communication in everyday life, especially as related to gender relations.

Barnes, M. L., and Rosenthal, R. 1985. Interpersonal effects of experimenter attractiveness, attire, and gender. *Journal of Personality and Social Psychology 48*:435–446.
This article reports on an experimental study that examined how perceivers define a situation

in relation to physical attractiveness and attire in same- and mixed-sex dyads. The complex interactions of a number of variables are illustrated.

Stone, G. P. 1965. Appearance and the self. In M. E. Roach and J. B. Eicher, eds. *Dress, adornment, and the social order*, pp. 216–245. New York: John Wiley & Sons.
In this classic article on appearance as a social process, Stone provides a framework for appearance communication based on wearer's "programs" and perceiver's "reviews." He also addresses socialization of the self in relation to clothing and notes how the self is developed and sustained through appearance in everyday life.

# Part Four
...
# Appearance and Culture

WE have now seen how appearance is linked to self-concept and self-presentation (Part Two), as well as to communication and behavior toward others (Part Three). In this part, we will address how we *collectively* use clothes and appearance styles as forms of expression. Social meanings associated with clothes do not emerge in a vacuum or as the result of the interpretations of just one or two people. There may be some idiosyncratic interpretations of appearances, known only to one or two, but in fact many meanings are shared with larger numbers of persons. The ideas of shared meaning and collective representation become relevant when we consider that clothes and appearance allow us to fit our lines of action with those of others and to express our desire to be part of something bigger—in short, to belong.

Inasmuch as clothing and appearance refer to networks of meanings and values, they are connected to a whole gamut of collective norms. Clothing and appearance messages, then, become a part of the social-historical nature of a group of people. These messages represent that group's **culture** and obtain their value in that context (Barthes, 1972). Culture facilitates shared meanings and provides the means for their creation.

Hence, culture is a concept that enables us to understand shared meaning and collective representation through appearance. There are two ways we can consider this concept. First, we can look at culture as a larger umbrella or context that provides blueprints for appearance management and perception. Culture provides a frame of reference—a perspective—that allows us to make sense of the world around us (McCracken, 1988). Although it is true that we experience everyday life within the shared symbolic order that the larger context of culture represents (Geertz, 1973), we must also recognize social-psychological processes that work to sustain and re-create culture. Appearance communication is the product not only of the fashion industry and its cultural allies (advertisers and retailers), but it is also the result of a group of people's negotiated understandings in relation to clothing and appearance. Each individual replenishes and supplies meaning to clothing and appearance (Delaporte, 1980). In the process, the meanings supplied by the culturally constituted world are not only received but also dislocated, revised, and reestablished in relation to group life.

The culture-as-umbrella approach is useful for understanding the influence of cultural context upon social interactions. Yet alone the concept of culture as umbrella or blueprint provider is not adequate to understand collective behavior linked to appearance. Blueprints for human behavior do not just materialize in the ether. Where did they come from in the first place? Also, blueprints are not fixed in stone but rather are subject to modification, especially in the realm of fashion change. Therefore, it is important that we integrate our discussion of the *influence of culture on the social meanings of appearance*, with a consideration of the *social processes leading to shared cultural meaning*.

A *social-psychological* approach to culture from a contextual perspective leads us to focus upon the dynamics of collective behavior, as people fit their lines of action together and, in the process, *create* culture, especially in the context of small groups. This "culture-in-the-making" approach draws heavily from a symbolic-interactionist perspective and focuses on how people communicate to develop shared understandings. This approach begins to address the topic of culture by describing the process by which culture is created and spread, and by attempting to answer the question: How and where is culture generated, and how do individuals learn about it (Fine, 1987, p. 124)? By focusing on individuals as they interact in smaller groups and develop aspects of group life to refer to in their interactions, we can address how ideas emerge, how appearance styles are created and assigned meaning, and how a set of shared understandings emerge. Through the creation of culture, such understandings are developed as group members share common appearance styles and other possessions, activities and motivations, and ways of thinking (Fine, 1987, p. 124). From this perspective, we may view culture as a "structure of feeling," and the emotions and values linked to shared understandings are grounded in the social contexts in which they are developed and experienced. From a social-psychological perspective, it is important to address how individuals relate to the "structure of feeling" and shared understandings that compose culture and take part not only in their creation but also in their enactment in everyday life.

Culture may be studied at different levels of analysis—in group life, in formal organizations, or in societies. In Chapter Eleven, we will begin our exploration of culture by first examining it at its most "micro" level (the group), then delving into culture in organizational life. Then we will address culture in the context of different types of societies, and consider how societal variations influence shared meanings and structures of feeling (in Chapter Twelve). *Whereas culture is a relatively abstract concept that describes the mental and physical artifacts that people value, society may be described as a large collectivity of people.* We can actually count and describe the people in a society. As compared to an organization, a *collectivity* such as a society tends to be larger, less structured, and lacking defined procedures for recruiting and identifying members (Turner and Killian, 1972). Appearance styles that emerge are therefore likely to be more spontaneous and informal in societies. At the same time, there is more ambiguity about what is expected of an individual who is likely to belong to numerous groups and organizations.

In addition to group and organizational memberships, individuals are socially placed into categories provided by culture. Cultural categories linked to gender, physical appearance, age, social class, and ethnicity are discussed in Chapter Thirteen. These categories are culturally coded in terms of appearance expectations. Individuals experience a convergence of cultural categories in the form of their identities, because they naturally fall into multiple categories at once. Cultural categories influence and are sustained and modified in the course of appearance management and perception. A contextual perspective enables us to connect cultural categories with identity constructions on a daily basis, with cognitive categories people use to understand others, and with social constructions of meaning.

# Chapter Eleven
### ...
# *Appearance in Group and Organizational Culture*

*Members of groups and organizations share a common culture. By being part of the group we learn the meanings of group symbols and can even take part in the development and transformation of these symbols (and their meanings). Each group has its own beliefs, behaviors, and customs that provide important socializing functions. Group habits involving clothing and appearance can give individuals guidelines or a source of reference for understanding the self. Collectively, group members can express cohesiveness and mutual interests through clothing and appearance. Similarly, in the more formalized and larger-scale organizational culture, an individual's clothing is indicative of collective processes. However, in organizations there tend to be more established rules and traditions linked to standards of formality and hierarchical structure. Uniforms may be regarded as a "special case" of organizational culture. In this chapter, the implications of group and organizational cultures for individual expression, as well as individual influences on these cultures, are explored.*

Shared usage and understanding of clothes can cultivate a sense of interconnectedness among members of a group. In the process, the kind of "structure of feeling" that fosters the emergence of culture becomes evident. In this chapter, we will consider the emergence and maintenance of culture in group and organizational life. Our focus on the expressive dimensions of culture includes both the material side of culture, including its products, its signifiers, or its artifacts; and the nonmaterial side of culture, including its abstract concepts, its ideology, its values (what is *signified*). Part of the experience of culture involves its tendency to send messages to itself, and these messages acquire meaning or significance for individuals in everyday contexts. Moreover, people themselves are responsible for the creation and transformation of culture through the dynamics of interactions and interpretations and reinterpretations of cultural messages.

The contribution of social-psychological processes to the emergence and realization of culture becomes evident as we examine its characteristics.

## Characteristics of Culture

At whatever level of social organization we examine culture, we can detect four basic qualities that characterize this structure of feeling or "set of shared artifacts and understandings." Culture is (1) transmitted, (2) learned, (3) shared, and (4) transformed.

Every group, organization, or society has its own set of shared artifacts and understandings that are conveyed to and through its members. In other words, group values are passed along through members, and only by belonging to a group and internalizing its understandings can we partake in the transmission of its culture by communicating our interpretations of these understandings to others. That is, we *learn* about culture through socialization into a group, organization, or society; we *share* culture and take part in its development and transformation as we interpret its messages and join our actions with those of others around us; and we simultaneously *transform* and *transmit* culture through processes of negotiation (change) and accommodation (continuity). Thus culture represents both the complexity and the consistency that make up the meshing of individual actions that occurs in group life. To scrutinize these characteristics of culture in greater depth, let's turn our attention to culture in the most "micro" of contexts—the small group.

## Group as Idioculture

Out of group life emerges meaningful artifacts and traditions. Each group has its own "lore" or idioculture, that is, a "system of knowledge, beliefs, behaviors, and customs shared by members of an interacting group" (Fine, 1987, p. 125). Idioculture is to group as culture is to a larger society. An idioculture can emerge within mainstream culture, or within a more specific subculture (for example, punk). The key idea is that idioculture is associated with group life, and it is subject to all the idiosyncratic nuances that emerge therein. Idioculture provides members with a point of reference to serve as the basis for further interaction and understandings. Group members share experiences and can refer to these experiences with some assurance that other group members frame their social realities similarly. This approach to the study of culture stresses how it is localized in the context of group life. An idioculture consists of a group's patterns of behavior or communication that have significance for its members. For example, an idioculture may consist of nicknames, jokes, beliefs, clothing styles, and gestures (Fine, 1987, p. 126). Symbolic-interactionist Gary Alan Fine studied idiocultures of groups of preadolescent males, in the form of Little League teams. He notes that an idioculture does not necessarily exist at the inception of a group; rather, the culture begins to be formed from the "opening moments of group interaction," as group members begin to obtain information about one another. Part of this information includes individual appearances. Through processes of visual and verbal negotiation, a "group look" may emerge along with other forms of shared understandings. A group may have a desired *public* image along with a more privatized (idiocultural) understanding of appearance style. Moreover, collective processes pinpoint the negotiations by which an acceptable *group* look (as opposed to an acceptable *individual* look) can emerge (see Figure 11-1). And, social control over an individual's appearance and actions is likely to be evident in a group context. In the next section, we will consider some characteristics of groups and examine how they exert influence with respect to appearance.

## Personal Appearance and Group Dynamics

Groups provide important socializing functions for individuals. They are a primary source of information about the social order and serve a mediating function between the individual and the larger society. In other words, groups intervene between individual preferences and societal expectations. As we will see in the following sections, much of the research conducted with groups has involved adolescents, and most likely there is a reason underlying this research focus. During adolescence, persons place a great deal of emphasis on appearance and use it as a gauge or criterion for self-evaluation. Ideas about appropriate appearances

**FIGURE 11-1**
*A group "look" tends to emerge as people get to know each other and are influenced by one another's appearance. The look this group of friends has negotiated includes the wearing of Rastafarian knitted caps (tams) and going shirtless. Photo by Mark Kaiser.*

are linked to group values as individuals compare and assess themselves in relation to others. Although such comparisons and assessments occur throughout the life cycle, they are likely to be especially acute in the transitional period of adolescence, when the need to belong is combined with a strong emphasis on appearance concerns. Some theorists believe that a sense of individuality can emerge only once persons have come to understand group values and then learn how they can relate to these values while still establishing a sense of uniqueness.

Group norms or habits related to clothing and appearance are likely to exercise some constraints on an individual. At the same time, an individual is generally free to add some additional "touches" to group-condoned appearances. These touches may even be incorporated into a group look if the innovating individual is respected by his or her peers. However, it is important to keep in mind that group values and norms, while serving as a source of reference and a means of social control, almost never coincide completely with those of an individual.

## Group Cohesiveness and Acceptance

In small groups, there is a tendency for members to engage in frequent interaction and to define one another as members. Small groups tend to share norms concerning matters of mutual interest, and a system of interlocking roles is likely to arise either informally or formally. A group "superego" tends to evolve, as the members identify *with* one another and are mutually rewarded by their membership. This results in a collective perception of group unity that causes the members to act in a unified manner toward the outside world (Cartwright and Zander, 1968).

The most important attribute of a group, then, is its cohesiveness or the degree of mutual interest among members. Through appearance, group members can express their mutual interests, shared agenda, and collective tastes. Group satisfaction generally emerges from rewards received by group members. These rewards promote a sense of cohesiveness, as members convey to one another that they share a common perspective. Clothing and appearance provide a visible basis for assigning and receiving rewards in the form of compliments and group recognition; they also promote a sense of cohesiveness as a group "look" emerges.

A cohesive group may be more likely to develop consensus about whether a new individual, seeking membership into the group, will be likely to "fit" in, and this quality of a cohesive group may make it easier for a new person to join a group, assuming that person understands and is able to express the group values and norms. Joanne Eicher studied female high school friendship groups over a 4-year period and examined (1) reciprocal friendship structures, wherein choices of friendship were returned, (2) mutual pairs, involving a reciprocated choice of two persons, and (3) "isolates," or persons who had no reciprocated friendship choices (Littrell and Eicher, 1973). The majority of the isolates who chose to belong to cohesive reciprocal friendship groups eventually became members of those groups. None of the isolates who aspired to belong to less cohesive reciprocal friendship groups became members of their chosen groups. When isolates held opinions on clothing, appearance, and social acceptance similar to those of the groups to which they chose to belong, they were more likely to become members of those groups than if they held unlike opinions. The movement from social isolation, then, to social acceptance was facilitated by two factors: (1) the higher degree of cohesiveness in the group to which one aspired and (2) the display of dress, appearance, and social-acceptance opinions shared by that group. The following comments by freshman girls illustrate their thoughts on how a new girl in school can be socially accepted:

> *When a new person arrives at the school they are either accepted or rejected because of their manner of dress, general looks, and the way they conduct themselves. Therefore, it would be wise for a new girl to pay close attention to all three of these criteria.*

> *She should direct her interests toward the popular groups by dressing as well as they do (Littrell and Eicher, 1973, p. 197).*

Girls with unconventional appearances are less likely to be accepted as members of a high school group than they are as personal friends by some of the group members. High school females in the early 1970s, for example, were able to imagine being personal friends with someone who wears mismatched and unconventional socks or who has messy hair (Allen and Eicher, 1973). However, these females were more likely to be doubtful that a female with such an appearance would fit into the groups to which they belonged. Thus a conforming appearance is perceived to be more relevant to group membership than to a personal friendship (Allen and Eicher, 1973).

How does a group "look" emerge to the extent that it influences the acceptance of new members? Let's look at several mechanisms. First, certain individuals are likely to bring to the group context their own interpretations of individual and group values. Through visual and verbal communication and processes of negotiation, certain looks will be adopted over others. Yet a little bit of one person's look is likely to be combined with part of another person's, and through this combining and recombining of appearance elements, a negotiated look is likely to evolve that signifies group values. A certain appearance code is likely to emerge that governs what items of clothing are worn together, how hair is groomed, and how clothes are altered (for example, ripped jeans and rolled-up sleeves or pants) to convey that one is a member of a group (see Figure 11-2). The code that emerges may be subtle and complex, to the extent that "outsiders" attempting to emulate the group look without a good understanding of it may be derogated.

Another factor that is likely to influence the emergence of a group look is the degree of power or authority some group members exert over others. Some persons will be more persuasive or compelling than others in their representations of group values.

Power may stem from either direct or indirect sources (Littlejohn, 1978). Direct power stems from the ability to control rewards or punishments for others in a group, whereas indirect power may stem from a previous reputation. Clothing

*Power and Influence*

**FIGURE 11-2**
*Imagine that this group consists of friends traveling together in Bavaria. They bought these knicker-styled pants, shoes, and socks at the same time, and a group look—framed in a vacation-with-friends context—has emerged. Photo by Susan B. Kaiser.*

and appearance may represent either form of power. For example, the direct power of a group leader may be symbolized through the wearing of certain badges of that power. Or, styles adopted by that leader may influence other group members *because* he or she is a leader. On the other hand, clothing and appearance may also indirectly accelerate a group member's degree of power. This type of power, obtained through a visual appreciation of a person, is in the hedonic mode (as contrasted to the direct, agonic mode discussed in Chapter Three). Hedonic power stems from indirect means, such as interpersonal attraction (Lips, 1981; Freedman, 1986). Some group members gain recognition by virtue of their appearances, rather than by direct action or forcefulness. These members may serve to create and interpret the appearance code that governs a group look, and to become a resource in the arena of personal appearance while not necessarily exerting the same degree of influence in other arenas. A person's appearance is likely to influence the extent to which his or her degree of power is *socially constructed*. If a person appears to have leadership qualities, then group members may be more likely to respond toward him or her on that basis and allow for the development or expression of such qualities.

The attractiveness of high school students' clothes is likely to be related to their tendency to assume leadership roles. Although female leaders are likely to be especially aware of clothing norms, some research has suggested that attractive clothing may actually be more important to male than to female adolescent leaders (Morganosky and Creekmore, 1981). Perhaps females, whether leaders or not, are *expected* to be attuned to appearance styles, whereas males are more likely to be able to distinguish themselves through such an awareness. More research is needed in this area to ascertain the relative importance of appearance among males in groups.

The type of power that emerges in a group is likely to be linked to the form of influence that group exerts over its members. Three types of group influence may be distinguished: informative, normative, and reference.

A group exerts informative influence when individuals actually seek information from a particular group and that group successfully supplies details or facts about the idioculture of the group, including details about its forms of expression and its social knowledge. At the earliest moments of group interaction, an idioculture does not exist. However, once the members begin to share information about themselves and to typify themselves as individuals, the stage is set for the development of a known culture. This known culture consists of the pool of background information that becomes part of a group's idioculture (Fine, 1987, p. 131). Since group members have been members of other groups in the past, they bring prior knowledge and past experiences to the group context, and through social interaction a *known* culture is socially constructed for the new group. The known culture is that which exercises informational group influence. As Fine (1987) notes, creativity is rarely a problem in the development of a known culture. This is true because creativity reflects novel combinations of previously familiar elements and bits of information. Thus, known culture includes the types of opinions and tastes that come to be shared, the type of information that is routinely exchanged, and the common experiences and understandings that are realized and reflected through appearance. An individual attempting to enter a group must master certain elements of this known culture before being accepted. Based on his research with preadolescent males and group life, Fine (1987) developed the following proposition, along with two corollaries, pertaining to "known culture" and informational group influence:

*Informative Group Influence*

**Proposition:** *Knowledge and acceptance of a group's idioculture is a necessary and sufficient condition for distinguishing members of a group from non-members (p. 128).*

*Corollary 1:  The greater the perceived difference between the public image implicated by an item in a group's idioculture and the group's desired public image, the more the group will attempt to shield that information from its public (p. 129).*

*Corollary 2:  A group becomes significantly less open when a nonmember is present. Groups attempt to hide their idioculture until it is believed that the newcomer can be trusted not to reveal the secrets of the group (p. 130).*

Thus group life involves shared knowledge and understandings and may also entail a desire to shield "inside" information from outsiders. This tendency particularly applies when the group engages in behaviors or endorses values that are not condoned or understood by the general public. For example, gangs may code their membership in terms of colors (red for "Bloods" and blue for "Crips") and engage in violent activities and/or drug-peddling. Thus, wearing the wrong color in the wrong neighborhood may lead to violent repercussions, and even outsiders in areas of high gang involvement would be aware of the critical aspects of color symbolism (for purposes of safety). Other more subtle forms of coding would be unfamiliar to most individuals outside of the gang. These subtle forms would be part of the known culture that is heavily guarded by gang members.

*Normative Group Influence*

Normative group influence pertains to the ongoing process of appearing before others in the group and receiving reinforcement or criticism through social feedback. In this way, group members come to understand what the group will and will not condone or tolerate in the form of appearance and behavior. A kind of Gestalt-like, group "mind" emerges that serves as a source of continual feedback for group members. This form of feedback is based on the concept of generalized other or collective understanding of group norms and values (previously discussed in Chapter Five).

The idea of normative group influence parallels Fine's discussion of *appropriate* culture. Cultural elements such as styles of appearance that are consistent with patterns of interaction in a group make up its appropriate culture (Fine, 1987, p. 134). High-status members may find that their personal status is conducive to the emergence of the group norms they wish to establish. For example, Fine noted that Little League boys tended to want to look like those ballplayers with whom they identified. Also, there was a tendency for the boys to strive to maintain a professional team image for games. In contrast, boys who came to games with mismatched socks or dirty uniforms were teased (Fine, 1987, p. 92). However, what also emerged from the group experience was a network of social influence. A hairstyle could gain or lose legitimacy as a function of the group members' standings.

Several members of the Beanville Rangers got wiffles (short haircuts) after Wiley, the second-most-popular boy on the team, got one and was proud of it. This fad continued (with one or two boys newly shaved each day) until Rich, the most popular boy on the team, publicly claimed that he thought the haircut looked stupid, although he deliberately excluded Wiley from this evaluation.

After Rich's announcement, only one low-status boy had his hair cut in that fashion, and the team was highly critical of his tonsorial style, saying it looked horrible and, further, it wasn't a *real* wiffle. Similar sociometric processes affected clothing conformity, such as wearing wrist-bands or sneakers at games and wearing shorts or removing one's shirt at practice (Fine, 1987, p. 136).

Individuals may or may not actually belong to the groups that supply reference group influence, which contributes a means for self-evaluation as individuals compare their values and appearance to those of a reference group. Although individuals frequently compare themselves with others in a group to which they belong, they may also compare themselves with people or groups who serve as a point of reference but with whom they do not interact on a regular basis. For example, junior-high females are more likely to use not only their peers but also older, high-school females as a source of reference; in contrast, their mothers are likely to exert less referential influence (Kernan, 1973). *Reference Group Influence*

Similarly, in a study of British boys who join soccer fan groups, 9- and 10-year-old boys were found to use older males as reference groups, borrowing some symbols of allegiance such as scarves and accessories (Marsh, 1985). Members of this older reference group, called the "Rowdies," wore scarves tied around their wrists, thin T-shirts even in the middle of the winter, heavy boots, and skinhead hairstyles. This group was known for its group chants and energetic, active response to the game. By the time the male soccer fans had become members of the next group, the "Graduates" (in their early 20s), they tended to dress similarly to others their own age and had relinquished many of the "Rowdy" symbols. This socialization to groups was explained in the following way by the researcher:

> Personal identity is worked for—is undertaken as a project—and thus patterns of complex social interaction can be understood in terms of such projects. These projects involve, first, the establishment of social identities. Such is the flexible nature of our societies that where limited opportunities for social identity exist within the "official" culture, alternative sources may be found in "unofficial" cultures. Having established social identities which provide for reputation, dignity, and recognition, personal identity can be achieved through giving individual expression to required role performance. We can also bend the rules a little, but first those rules have to be learned through conformity. To be individuals we have first to be "one of the boys" (Marsh, 1985, p. 29).

Thus reference group influence may be regarded as a means for developing a sense of social identity or a feeling of interconnectedness with others with whom one may or may not interact. Through this type of influence, individuals can assess their own values with those of others and then evaluate which of these values should be incorporated into individual identity.

Who is likely to provide reference group influence in relation to styles of clothing that are fashionable? By its very nature, an avant-garde or fashion-forward (futuristic) clothing style is ambiguous in the extent to which it will gain acceptance. Research on conformity indicates that individuals are more likely to conform to a group position if the type of judgment in question is ambiguous in nature (Davis, 1984b). In such a case, individuals may be uncertain about how "correct" their judgments are and are therefore more likely to refer to others for guidance. A current, popular clothing style may be easily labelled as fashionable, then, whereas a style that is presented as potentially fashionable in the future is more difficult to assess. (This latter type of assessment is required of retail buyers as they make their judgments on buying trips. What will the public accept? The buyer is asked to make such a prediction.) Greater conformity results for the more ambiguous judgments of future fashionability than for judgments of present fashionability. Moreover, individuals who are highly self-conscious conform more to judgments of future fashionability than to judgments of present fashionability. In contrast, persons who are low in self-consciousness conform equally to both (Davis, 1984b). Thus, self-consciousness works jointly with ambiguity in the type of judgments requested to affect the degree of social influence exerted.

The media may provide a parasocial form of reference group influence when direct social sources becomes less readily available. For example, older persons who have retired may in some cases have fewer opportunities to interact with people on a daily basis. Thus they may implicitly turn to sources such as television or other media for information about what is socially appropriate or fashionable attire. Older men, for example, appear to find sources of reference in the form of older actors or public figures in news and talk shows. In contrast, older females are more likely to be influenced by women near their age on soap operas or by younger female characters in "real-life" roles such as news commentators (Kaiser and Chandler, 1985). Reference group influence, then, is not always readily available from individuals who are similar to ourselves. It may be necessary at times to adapt appearance messages from individuals who seem unlike ourselves but with whom we can relate on some level.

## Group Life in Context

It is important to remember that group norms, values, and "looks" are created and negotiated through processes of social interaction. Symbolic interactionists focus on the social construction of group values and the negotiations based on continual interpretations. As a group look emerges, it allows for categorization of persons as members of a group, on a cognitive level. From a cultural perspective, we can address culture by considering how appearance codes emerge and are sustained or modified. By combining the symbolic-interactionist, cognitive, and cultural perspectives into a contextual framework, we can keep in mind that a group is, in and of itself, a context of everyday life that integrates: (1) symbolic and constructivistic processes based on social interaction, (2) cognitive assessment of individuals as members versus nonmembers, and (3) the emergence of idioculture with its own distinctive appearance codes.

Groups are dynamic entities. They can flourish or perish in response to the degree of success in individuals' attempts to fit their lines of action together or to develop a sense of group cohesiveness. As groups become larger, members will find it more difficult to interact with one another. Accordingly, the impact of appearance symbolism will be altered in some way. Whereas appearance symbolism may be readily understood as part of a small group's known culture, it may result in more diffuse interpretations (and less direct negotiation) as a group increases in size and/or its members begin to join other groups. Thus, if appearance symbolism is to remain a sense of consistency on a larger scale, it may need to become increasingly formalized. In the next section this idea will be considered in the context of organizational life.

## Appearance in Organizations

### Characteristics of Organizations

Social life today tends to be self-consciously organized; some degree of organization is apparent in political, occupational, and even religious realms (Hamilton and Biggart, 1985). In organizational life, individual behavior tends to be governed by established rules of procedure that are often backed by the force of tradition (Turner and Killian, 1972). Organizations can be characterized by four qualities (Berelson and Steiner, 1964). First, a context of *formality* tends to prevail, which promotes the collective goals, policies, or procedures and rules that give form to the organization. Second, organizations have *hierarchical structures* that tend to be maintained so that the individuals in power can sustain their influence. Third, organizations consist of *relatively large numbers of people*, to the extent that it becomes almost impossible to have close interactions with all of them. Although these individuals perform different functions in the organization, some cooperative relations do exist that tend to be somewhat formalized. Fourth, organizations tend to *last longer than a lifetime.*

### Clothing Symbolism and Organizational Culture

The German sociologist Max Weber (1947) provided some of the earliest theoretical work on human institutions. He developed a theory of **bureaucracy** to explain the abstract type of large-scale, formal organization characterized by order, impersonality, rationality, and a hierarchical structure. He noted that organizations vary in the extent to which bureaucracy is found. In the historical development of complex organizations, a kind of bureaucratic authority emerged, differing in character from the feudal authority (based on the medieval political system) found in past centuries (Joseph, 1986, p. 32).

Why do organizations tend to prevail in modern society? They may do so because they are efficient, consistent with social values, or tradition-bound. Organizations may also last because of their popularity.

Every organization is likely to develop a culture with a distinctive set of values, and these values are either likely to be expressed through uniforms or be expected to "rub off" on organizational members so that they will conform to a formal or informal dress code. First, we will consider how some organizations use uniformity to achieve their goals. Then we will explore dress codes in organizational life.

### Uniforms

Sociologist Nathan Joseph (1986) studied organizational culture in relation to clothing norms and noted that a uniform is possible only after an organization has distinguished or differentiated itself from other groups. Thus, *organizational differentiation* is a prerequisite for uniforms: "An organization can communicate sartorially only if it is a separate entity" (Joseph, 1986, p. 35). Joseph stated that organizational differentiation occurred quite late in the history of many uniformed organizations. For example, the United States naval force began on an ad hoc basis early in the history of the country. At the point of each ship's voyage, individuals were recruited, and the same pool of individuals could be found on naval ships as on merchant ships. It was not until late in the nineteenth century that the need arose for a larger pool of trained individuals for the navy. Standardized, occupational clothing that was functional for work and based on only informal patterns was worn by both naval personnel and merchants. This clothing was replaced by a distinctive naval uniform around the middle of the nineteenth century (Joseph, 1986, p. 36).

Some organizations tend to need uniforms for purposes of identification, visibility, and expression of organizational roles. Yet uniforms function as much more than signaling devices. They can develop a complex degree of symbolism that is inextricably linked to the contexts in which they are embedded. Ironically, however, the popularity of organizations often tends to derive initially from borrowed symbolism. That is, organizations are likely to adopt symbols from groups of individuals in other contexts, so as to impart "a distinctive militaristic, scientific, or religious tinge" to organizational culture (Joseph, 1986, p. 32). In this way, symbols such as uniforms become **metaphors** for such ideologies as militarism, science, or religion. A metaphor is a representation of meaning that borrows from another context, so that the qualities associated with one context will be assigned in another context as well. For example, the Salvation Army adopted uniforms because the public at large was favorable toward the army and its symbolism. Therefore, uniforms were not adopted because the Salvation Army was especially militaristic but rather because it wanted to be associated with the feelings of good will ascribed to the military at the time it was founded (see Figure 11-3).

Once an organization has distinguished itself from other groups and has developed a uniform, a system or code for interpreting the requirements of the organization by "reading" its uniforms is likely to emerge. Since an organization becomes a context in and of itself, the meanings assigned to its uniforms are derived from that context. For example, the Guardian Angels organization in New York City developed its own uniform to convey power and courage— necessary qualities for members who are "guardians" of the public's safety. Red berets and medals signify organizational membership.

An individual who wears a uniform tends to be assigned a particular *role set*. Uniforms not only allow outsiders to identify individuals as members of the organization, but also enables insiders to interpret their rank, duties, and privileges. As in any other social context, perceivers interpret clothing based on their taken-for-granted knowledge of social reality. An important part of that social reality includes the social statuses and relationships among individuals, often defined by clothing. A basic relation of power, or "who controls whom," is conveyed through organizational use of uniforms.

**FIGURE 11-3**
*Salvation Army uniforms serve to convey an organizational ideology in this London station. Photo by Susan B. Kaiser.*

Power includes compelling wearers to dress in clothing not of their own selection and, significantly, to emit inaccurate messages. Employees have at times been obliged to adopt an occupational uniform which presented a desired image of the organization. In some instances, the message is that of sexual attractiveness or even availability, primarily of women, which was very often not the meaning desired by the wearer (Joseph, 1986, p. 40).

Power relationships are complicated in that they imply a reciprocity: In order for some to have power, others must have a lack of power. Thus, there is responsibility on the part of both individuals who have power and those who do not (Joseph, 1986, p. 42). People in organizations establish formal and informal norms to control behavior. However, people in organizations do not necessarily follow rules in a mindless manner. And, even though obedience supplies a foundation for power, obedience and power are not opposites. Instead, in dramaturgical terms, they "stage role performances in order to produce calculated results" (Hamilton and Biggart, 1985). Thus an analysis of uniform requirements in organizations should include an understanding of why people obey. Organization theorists contend that people obey to be effective, powerful, reliable, and accountable. In organizational life, power and obedience are not opposite phenomena; instead, they are intertwined as part of the social reality that is negotiated. Thus private, individual goals and interests become inseparable from individual enactments of organizational roles (Hamilton and Biggart, 1985). For example, the concepts of role distance and role embracement, discussed in Chapter Six, are evident in individuals' ways of wearing their uniforms (see Figure 11-4).

Some uniforms within an organization are imbued with a special status of organizational status display. Culture tends to entrust clothing with messages that cannot be conveyed in other (verbal) ways (McCracken, 1988). Uniforms of some individuals derive their importance as "repositories for values," such as honor or pride. Likewise, individuals enacting certain statuses or roles within

**FIGURE 11-4**
*This boy conveys a certain degree of role distance through the act of modifying his Cub Scout uniform. The goals and values of the Cub Scout organization, the identity of his specific troop, as well as his personal achievements are all conveyed through uniform codes. Yet he elects to present his own message, to convey that the uniform does not refer to his only identity, and to personalize his appearance. Photo by Linda Boynton.*

the organization function as "curators or promulgators of symbols" (Joseph, 1986, p. 42). Who are the individuals who wear these value-laded uniforms that are so expressive (and nonlinguistic)? Again it is necessary to return to power relationships within the organization for understanding. The role of some individuals within the organization is to indicate the power, wealth, or values of the organization—in short, to display its image and what it represents—through their attire. This type of role parallels the concept of **vicarious consumption** (Veblen, 1899). Some individuals use, display, or waste goods and services as surrogates of others, based on a relationship of power. Thus individuals who wear particularly expressive, colorful, or symbolic uniforms within an organization indirectly convey the power of others within the organization (Joseph, 1986, p. 42). Color guards in military organizations and uniformed hostesses or receptionists in hotels or restaurants perform these types of expressive roles that incorporate a vicarious form of appearance communication.

Dress codes may either be formalized in written form or informally accepted as part of organizational roles and relationships. Whether written or not, dress codes are likely to emerge as part of everyday negotiation and communication in organizational contexts where uniforms are not worn. Dress codes generally consist of setting limits on the styles of "street" or everyday clothes that may be worn within the context of the organizational culture. The type of code varies according to the degree of contact with the public, the region, and the cultural and historical context of the organization (Joseph, 1986, p. 144). Moreover, codes are intricately linked to gender in organizational life. Whereas males have traditionally had the power as well as an understood white-collar appearance style—the ubiquitous business suit—for corporate contexts, females have historically had an ambiguous appearance code to follow. (Clothing issues for women in corporate organizational life are discussed in Social Focus 11-1.)

When dress codes *are* written, changing fashions become problematic and may require continual assessment and updating of the code. Many organizations find that social control generally operates to produce conformity without a formal, written dress code, as individuals take their cues from one another and negotiate an organizational reality.

Organizational image and values are often likely to assume more significance in the type of clothes worn than are utilitarian concerns. One study compared organizations' dress codes with their inclinations toward energy conservation and comfort issues (Sommer, Kaiser, and Sommer, 1987). In order to determine whether temperature- or image-effective clothes were valued more in organizations, office managers and personnel in 28 firms in Northern California were interviewed. Most of the firms had a generally accepted set of dress standards (written or unwritten) that were primarily aimed at promoting the image of the organization. Necessary office wear for men included ties as a general rule, and managers and supervisors were expected to wear suits or sport jackets and slacks. For women, nylon hosiery was required, and female managers or supervisors had to wear suits, dresses, or pantsuits. Secretarial and clerical personnel were expected to dress similarly to managers, although more latitude was permitted. For instance, male secretarial and clerical personnel might get by without a coat, and women could wear slacks and a blouse. The study showed that the idea of a connection between dress standards and energy usage was new or unfamiliar to most of the individuals interviewed. Appearance management, on an organizational scale, was a prevailing motive behind the clothing norms.

Collective management of impressions often is the goal of bureaucratic organizations. Individuals in large organizations cannot interact personally with one another. Therefore, many contacts within the organization are likely to be on a first-impression basis. The general impression that is frequently desired by management is one of seriousness, decisiveness, and dependability. (See Social Focus 11-1 for a discussion of how these characteristics are perceived in female managers' appearances.) Appearance becomes an issue because it may not always

*Organization Dress Codes*

# First Impressions of Women in the Organizational Context

Historically, women have not had a straightforward business "uniform" code to follow. As increasing numbers of women have entered the work force, especially in the twentieth century, a dilemma of sorts has become evident. Especially in first-impression contexts that become so critical in large organizations, both women and men want to make good impressions on others, especially those who have control over their futures. Appearance can have an important impact in hiring decisions as well as in other short-term interactions, especially when other information about an individual is minimal or incomplete. Although men have a fairly established code of business attire and are likely to be viewed as both attractive and competent if they follow this code, women seem to be forced in some organizational contexts to make a choice between aesthetics and creativity versus competence.

Thus, during the 1970s and early 1980s, "dress for success" advice for women was rampant in the popular literature, and conservative skirted business suits were prevalent. At the same time, clothing scholars pursued research to identify the personality characteristics associated with different styles of women's attire, so as to determine the implications for the professional context.

Several studies indicated that a woman makes a stronger businesslike impression in a skirted suit (Rucker, Taber and Harrison, 1981; Forsythe, Drake and Cox, 1984; Workman, 1984–1985). Managerial characteristics such as forcefulness, self-reliance, dynamism, aggressiveness, and decisiveness were found to be associated more with certain suit and blouse combinations than with a feminine dress (Forsythe, Drake and Cox, 1984). The addition of a jacket appears to add a businesslike touch to a woman's appearance (Rucker, Taber, and Harrison, 1981; Scherbaum and Shepherd, 1987).

Male, but not female, businesspersons associated women in jackets that were dark (as opposed to light) in color with more potency (qualified, expert, powerful, professional, bold, and the like), in a study by Damhorst and Pinaire Reed (1986). Typically, the researchers noted, women have had more freedom to experiment with color, whereas men have been socialized to recognize and adopt the dark business suit as a sign of corporate power and achievement.

> Clothing meanings . . . change with time. As a greater number of women enter management level jobs, busi-nessmen may become accustomed to a variety of colors in women's dress, and meaning of color value may diminish or change for men. Conversely, women may adopt traditional, darker colors in business dress, and the meanings they assign to color could shift toward agreement with men (Damhorst and Pinaire Reed, 1986, p. 96).

Another study documented that the color code is still more rigid for males than it is for females in business attire (Scherbaum and Shepherd, 1987). However, within the latitude in women's business attire there appears to be an emergent aesthetic code, as shown in a study of campus recruiters' perceptions of attire appropriate for retail interviews. In this study, the 26 suit styles rated as most appropriate tended to have classic tailoring, natural to boxy silhouettes, neutral or duller colors, low contrast, skirt length right below the knee, neck emphasis, and limited accessories. On the other hand, the less appropriate suits had at least one extreme element, either a highly clothes- or body-dominant silhouette, an unconventional combination of textures or colors, or attention-grabbing, trendy, or outdated elements (Damhorst, Eckman, and Stout, 1986).

Aside from impressions of competence or being businesslike, it is important to consider other meanings conveyed by clothes in organizational contexts. For example, a woman may be viewed as very serious and capable, yet unfriendly or unimaginative. Some research has suggested that there is a downside to women's adoption of a business "uniform." A blazer may be a good intellectual cue, increasing the respect a perceiver has for a woman; however, the addition of a blazer also tends to decrease likability (Lennon and Miller, 1984). A classic suit tends to convey a conventional and dominant impression, but also may be perceived as contributing to a slightly standoffish or somewhat unapproachable air (Sweat and Zentner, 1985). Moreover, research shows that although a suit with a plain white blouse elicits impressions of competence, a woman wearing a dress may be perceived as creative:

> To be dressed in a suit is to have creativity downplayed any observable differences in the total clothing outfit limited to slight variations in color and texture or small details in cut. To wear a dress is to introduce a far greater range in variations from a norm, perhaps cueing inferences to creativity and independence (Johnson and Roach-Higgins, 1987).

## Social Focus 11-1 (continued)

Thus many factors must be taken into account before concluding what type of attire a woman should wear in the organizational context. The extent to which creativity is an important attribute in one's position is important, along with considerations about how critical informal contacts can be in business. Often, consequential decisions are made in informal contexts (for example, in the bar or on the racquetball court), and a woman who tries too hard to make a serious impression may diminish her opportunities to interact on this level. Basically, it seems that women are faced with some tough, double-edged choices in the business world; to some extent it becomes a question of choosing between being taken seriously versus being perceived as creative and sociable. Hopefully, a delicate balance or compromise can be negotiated in everyday organizational contexts, in which women can weigh and assess all of the social variables involved.

The complexity in women's choices is further increased by some differences in the perceptions of males and females concerning women's business attire. Studies focusing more on overall style than on color have suggested that women's business attire influences female perceivers more than it does male perceivers (Rucker, Taber, and Harrison, 1981). DeLong, Salusso-Deonier, and Larntz (1983) found that males evaluated women's business attire less positively and social attire more positively than did females. Females were also more likely to differentiate between business and social attire. Sweat and Zentner (1985) found that females were more stereotypical in their responses than were males. That is, female perceivers viewed the classic business suit as more conventional and dominant than did male perceivers, suggesting that females may think this style has more of an impact on males than it actually does. It should also be noted that the perceivers in the studies by Rucker, Taber, and Harrison (1981), DeLong, Salusso-Deonier, and Larntz (1983), and Sweat and Zentner (1985) were college students, and females who are preparing to pursue careers may be more concerned about these cues than women who are well-established in their careers.

A business suit worn in the early stages of a woman's career may represent a kind of compensation symbolism. That is to say, until a woman has become comfortable and established in her career role, a business suit may be adopted in part to complete a professional self-image. Once a woman has become more settled in her career and has less need to complete such a self-image, she is likely to feel freer to experiment with appearance (Solomon and Douglas, 1985). Rather than taking her cue primarily from her work associates (who may be predominantly male) as she did earlier in her career, she is likely to feel freer to pursue fashion ideas in magazines and other media (Rabolt and Drake, 1985).

There is another, deeper interpretation of the practice of women borrowing symbolism from males. By engaging in a form of imitative behavior, women may actually reinforce that the masculine model of business attire is the "right" one. Thus by adopting *the* "authority" look, women may actually be reinforcing their subordinate status in organizational culture (McCracken, 1985).

In a broader cultural context, it had become apparent by the 1980s that the skirted business suit had become an emblem or stereotype. In business and general interest magazines between the 1960s and 1980s, there was a significant increase in portrayals of women in skirted business suits. Still, the suit did not replace all of the other acceptable options for women to wear. And in contrast to changes in the images of women, there were no significant differences in how men have been portrayed in these ads (Saunders and Stead, 1986):

> The skirted suit is perceived as the female equivalent of the suit worn almost universally by businessmen and executives. Possibly, by imitating men, women are conveying the impression that to succeed they must transform themselves into copies of men—not only in terms of behavior, attitudes, values and skills, but also in dress. The impression conveyed may be that women can only succeed if they imitate men. . . . In the short term, as with men, the use of the business uniform can facilitate acceptance of women by creating the necessary impression of competence. In the long term, women who have become successful may need to seek a form of dress that does not merely ape that of men (pp. 203–204).

Thus there will be a continuing need for a negotiation of aesthetic codes that signify appropriate business attire for women. As designers, retailers, and consumers create and interpret these codes, the *relational* aspects of male and female interactions will need to be considered along with the organizational realities that they construct in everyday life.

be possible in large organizations, in particular, to discern which persons are really competent in their jobs. When such ambiguity exists in the evaluation of others' competence on the basis of their abilities, clothing and personal grooming assume added significance.

There are several important reasons for appearance management both individually and collectively in organizational contexts (Klein and Ritti, 1980). First, there is a lot of mobility in bureaucratic organizations. Especially in the earlier phases of one's career, there is a tendency to be in a position no more than 1 or 2 years at a time. It is often common for an individual to dress for the next higher position, so that perceivers will associate him or her with that position. However, it may be inadvisable to "outshine" one's supervisor to the extent that a lack of deference to his or her authority is expressed. Second, many critical business interactions take place outside of one's own immediate territory or department. Thus, individuals tend to be evaluated primarily on the basis of personal presentation (appearance) rather than on personal surroundings (an impressive desk or office). Third, it is often difficult to assess an individual's motivation or ability in an objective manner in a large organization. Therefore, concrete or visible cues such as appearance take on further consequence. Perceived credibility, in particular, becomes a critical part of an individual's enactment of his or her role within the organization.

With the kind of increased depersonalization that is characteristic of bureaucratic organizations, there is a greater tendency for people to be viewed largely in relation to their roles. Individuals are categorized and evaluated on the basis of the positions they assume, and the resulting stereotypes are likely to include expectations for clothes. For instance, sales representatives within a large "high-tech" organization may be stereotyped as being crisp and hard-hitting. Their attire is likely to be sharp and high-powered, because they are expected to make favorable first impressions for the organization in order to sell the product. In contrast, engineers within the same organization may be typed as thoughtful and methodical. They may be expected to be too "preoccupied" with their thoughts to pay much attention to appearance. Advertising people, on the other hand, may be expected to dress in a somewhat more colorful or individualistic style so as to demonstrate, or give the appearance of, creativity. Whether organizational stereotypes are true is not as important as their consequences. If people *expect* such appearances, then they may be troubled by "inconsistent" impressions. The organizational philosophy underlying appearance norms may also be traced to power relationships. Whereas one large high-tech organization may stipulate specific forms of clothing according to hierarchies within the organization, another organization producing high-tech goods may emphasize that managers working in the production area may (in fact, should) dress somewhat similarly to the workers, in order to promote a sense of esprit de corps. Expectancies about an individual's appearance, as we will see in the next section, are not only linked to role and organizational philosophy but are further shaped by the type of organization to which he or she belongs.

## *Organizational Cultures: Ideal Types*

The culture of an organization consists of its ideology or belief structure, system of knowledge, values, rules, and day-to-day rituals. The concept of culture derives from the agricultural idea of cultivation—as a process of tilling and cultivating the land (Morgan, 1986, p. 112). In the context of organizational life, culture becomes a metaphor for the process of cultivating and enacting goals, everyday practices, and symbolism based on an underlying philosophy and sense of purpose.

Organizations are similar to miniature societies with their own cultures and subcultures (distinct cultures within the larger cultures). Some organizations may promote an ethos of working together as a team, with little emphasis on hierarchical variations, whereas other organizations may be segmented along lines of power or goals, with distinct subcultures. Individuals seeking meaning in their lives may develop subcultures to find a place within the larger organizational culture (Morgan, 1986, p. 127). Such subcultures may function similarly to friendship groups or other social groupings.

Organizational cultures and subcultures emerge as individuals in organizations mesh their ideas, symbols, and values to derive shared meaning and shared understandings—to create a sense of organizational reality. Culture provides the glue that connects individuals and therefore holds the organization together (Morgan, 1986, p. 128).

Different organizations may use appearance in diverse ways in accordance with their cultures and senses of reality. Appearance can carry a great deal of weight in organizational life, as roles are enacted and hierarchies are developed and maintained. Most people in organizations quickly learn the accepted appearance and clothing styles that facilitate advancement to the top ranks. Yet clothing in organizational culture cannot be explained entirely in terms of image building and impression management. Instead, it is important to consider the relation between clothing and the sense of social reality within an organization's culture. Attempts to distort this reality by symbolic manipulation that is insincere or cynical are likely to be uncovered if they contrast too greatly with the shared meanings that compose this reality (Joseph, 1986, p. 12).

To understand the different types of organizational cultures, we can use the concept of **ideal type**. This term refers to a category or type that may not exist exactly as described but that provides a hypothetical means for conceptual classification. Ideal types of organizational cultures can provide the means for comparing functions of appearance and clothing in diverse symbolic contexts. Five ideal types of organizational cultures can be identified: service, economic, protective, associative, and religious (Strother, 1963).

*Economic Organizations*

Economics organizations are engaged in the production or distribution of goods or services in return for money. Appearance management and corporate image are likely to be important in economic organizational culture, at least to the extent that profit margins are influenced by first impressions. Retail stores are a good example of economic organizations. Employees are generally expected to dress neatly, fashionably, and in accordance with store image. In an apparel store or department, sales managers and associates are encouraged or required to wear the kinds of clothes that the store features. Across economic organizations, however, different cultures are likely to emerge as linked to philosophy and history. Different retail organizations, for example, may develop cultures based on merchandising philosophy and desired public image.

As consumer psychologist Michael Solomon (1987) noted, uniforms in economic organizations can affect employees as well as customers. When employees interact with both insiders (coworkers) and outsiders (customers and vendors), they are caught between two groups with often conflicting goals. There may be a danger, from the organization's perspective, that employees will begin to identify more with the customer's needs than with the organization's. A uniform serves to remind employees of their primary allegiance (to the organization) while also presenting a consistent image to customers. Thus, organizations may adopt uniforms to minimize role confusion and to convey their philosophy to the public.

Organizations such as banks, accounting firms, telephone companies, and even hospitals provide services to clients, often with an underlying profit motivation in mind. (See Social Focus 11-2 for a discussion of hospital culture and clothing symbolism.)

## Service Organizations

Service organizations provide benefits or services to clients and tend to lack an overriding profit motivation. A governmental agency, for example, provides services to citizens and is subsidized primarily by taxes. Therefore, goods or services are not produced with the intent of making a profit. The image that members of public sector organizations convey is likely to be different from that projected by members of an economic organization. Neatness and competence are probable goals in public employees' appearances, but constraint from blatant signs of prosperity through the wearing of visibly expensive clothes is likely to be exercised (see Figure 11-5).

City organizations may be examined as examples of organizations composed of personnel who provide a range of services for the citizens of a city. City organizations may be viewed as "municipal corporations," with city residents as the owners and clients whose cooperation and favor are sought. In a study of 21 officials from cities in California, clothing was examined as a means of communication both within the organizational culture and in its image among taxpayers (the organization's major constituency) (Kaiser, 1982). Several important functions of clothing were identified by elected officials and city administrative and staff personnel: (*a*) avoiding a "slick" image, (*b*) dressing in relation to one's role within the organization, and (*c*) conveying open communication with the public.

## Avoidance of a Slick Image

Overdressing is to be avoided in city organizations. As one official remarked, "You have to project an austere image to the public. It's expected in public

■■■ *Social Focus 11-2*
# The Hospital as an Organizational Context

A hospital is generally an economic organization with a strong service orientation. Thus the organization wants its employees to convey an impression of efficiency, competence, cleanliness, and caring.

Status hierarchies become evident through clothing codes, although in recent years there has been increasing ambiguity surrounding these codes. Let's focus here on the appearances associated with physicians and nurses.

One of the most authoritative figures in a hospital has typically been the physician. The traditional symbol of the physician—the white coat—originated in scientific laboratories, operating rooms, and modern hospitals. Part of the meaning assigned to this garment is tied to the role of healing. The cultural significance of "whiteness" is related not only to the authority of the physician, but also to a nexus of meanings: life, purity in the sense of absence of malice and unaroused sexuality, superhuman power ("cleanliness is next to godliness"), and candor or justice (Blumhagen, 1979).

As there was a historical shift in the health profession from the home visit to the hospital or clinic, there was a corresponding use of the white lab coat, which served to legitimize forms of behavior (for example, physical checkups) that might otherwise be considered socially taboo. White was used in hospitals to symbolize this shift toward professionalism, from an organizational perspective. The white coat has maintained its association with laboratory science, distinguishing the wearer from healing cultists and quacks.

In addition to the white lab coat, other symbols such as stethoscopes, head mirrors, and black bags have traditionally surrounded the physician, rendering credence to his or her role. In medical journals and newspaper comics, these symbols abound, reinforcing stereotypes about physicians' appearances. The most frequently used symbol, however, is the white coat (Blumhagen, 1979).

For some patients, the white lab coat's symbolism may be overpowering. Pediatricians and psychiatrists often wear pastel or lightly colored coats or normal street clothes in order to lessen the social distance between themselves and their patients. The issue of whether the lab coat should be worn with patients is one that has been debated in medical schools and professional journals. One reason for its continued use by some physicians has been its function in distinguishing physicians from other personnel in the hospital (Morens, 1976). Identification in conjunction with the hierarchical structure in the hospital organization, then, appears to be an important factor in its continued use.

To determine actual attitudes about physicians' attire, a study of 404 adult patients, residents, and staff physicians was conducted (Gjerdinger, Simpson, and Titus, 1987). Clothing items that received positive responses from this group as a whole were traditional items such as a dress, dress shoes, and nylons for female physicians; and a shirt and tie for male physicians. For both males and females, identifying items such as the white lab coat and a name tag were favored. Negative responses were associated with casual items such as blue jeans, scrub suits, athletic shoes, clogs, and sport socks. Especially feminine items such as prominent ruffles, patterned hose, or dangling earrings were viewed as inappropriate for female physicians. Long hair and earrings on male physicians also received negative evaluations.

Thus a traditional look was favored overall. However, when patients were asked to evaluate physicians' attire, they were not as discriminating in their attitudes as the physicians were themselves. The patients tended to rate the traditional items somewhat less positively and the casual items somewhat less negatively, as compared with the physicians. However, patients rated three items more positively than did the physicians: name tags, visible stethoscopes, and groomed mustache. Clearly, identification was an important factor to the patients. The researchers concluded from this study that male physicians should wear short hair, a shirt and tie, a white coat with a name tag, dress pants, and shoes. A female physician should wear a white coat over a dress or skirt and blouse, a name tag, lipstick, nylons, and dress shoes (Gjerdingen, Simpson, and Titus, 1987).

A debate surrounding traditional role symbols has been ongoing in the nursing profession as well. In this case, the symbols in question are the white cap and uniform. Pediatric nurses started wearing colored uniforms or street clothes at work because of the belief that the typical white uniform may be frightening to some children. The reactions of nurses to this change have been mixed (Howe, 1969). Some nurses feel they appear more approachable, involved, and effective in colored uniforms or street clothes as opposed to uniforms, whereas others feel less professional

## Social Focus 11-2 (continued)

and less likely to inspire their patient's confidence. It appears from research that nurses are more likely to have strong feelings about the desirability or undesirability of white uniforms than are patients (Goldberg, Offer, and Schatzman, 1961). In a study on the effect of nurses' street clothes on psychiatric patients, nurses made such statements as "I felt so funny" or "I felt just like a visitor" (in street clothes). They had to remind themselves that they were on the job as they adjusted to the transition from uniforms to street clothes. Therapists made such comments as "The nurses have very poor taste in clothes" and "I had never noticed Miss B's legs before." Most patients agreed that they liked the nurses in street clothes once they had become accustomed to it. Only a few patients indicated that they felt more comfortable with the nurses in uniform (Goldberg, Offer, and Schatzman, 1961).

Other research has indicated that nurses' attitudes toward role symbols (for example, uniform and cap) are related to their attitudes about the nursing role in general (Lafferty and Dickey, 1980). Socialization to the nursing role is a factor in their attitudes toward traditional role symbols. Nurses with a baccalaureate degree appear to reject these symbols more frequently than do those without a degree. Nurses who express unfavorable attitudes toward role symbols appear to feel that nurses should be more autonomous (less dependent) and less accepting of traditional role limitations (Lafferty and Dickey, 1980).

By the mid 1970s, the traditional nurse's uniform had become increasingly ineffective as professional clothing, for several reasons. First, there was a general decline in the prestige of uniforms in general, including such categories as military and religious uniforms as well as those in the medical profession. Second, there was a growing emphasis on "power" dressing among professionals in the larger culture. Third, many nonprofessional workers' dress resembled that of nurses, who lost a sense of identification. Fourth, there were greater numbers of men pursuing the nursing profession, and the traditional uniform seemed less appropriate. Finally, increasing numbers of nurses were found in more diverse clinical roles and management positions, and the uniform no longer served as a reliable indicator of role performance (Kalisch and Kalisch, 1985).

The lack of uniforms in hospitals caused concern for some nursing professionals, because of confusion over roles and identification:

> Endorsement of the traditional full uniform as a cluster of symbols to represent nursing to the public is no longer viable. . . . At the same time, the confusion that reigns within the vacuum surrounding nurse clothing of the mid 1980s is a marketing nightmare. It is virtually impossible to differentiate RNs in the crowd of hospital workers (Kalisch and Kalisch, 1985, p. 893).
> Nurses emphasize that they are the most visible image of the hospital. Hospital marketers are now realizing how true that is. . . . Most nurses don't want to return to rigid, paternalistic dress codes . . . [But] nursing means business, and nursing brings business. Your investment in the right clothes is a part of the image business (Fashion '86, 1986).

Due to the increasing ambiguity in nurses' appearances perhaps, a survey of 339 nurses suggested a trend in hospitals toward the idea of dress codes in some form (Fashion Feedback, 1985). The majority indicated that some type of uniform was required at their place of work. Over one-half indicated they could not wear colored uniforms where they work (42 percent could). An overwhelming majority preferred white anyway (Fashion Feedback, 1985).

Thus, there appears to be a swing in attitudes toward a more traditional approach to appearances in the medical profession, although clearly some of the old stereotypes are no longer a viable option, largely due to changes in gender relations in the hospital context. For both physicians and nurses, appearance continues to be an important sign of "legitimacy" and identity. At the same time, traditional symbols are continuing to be scrutinized and evaluated, as the need for a negotiation of appropriate symbols prevails.

**FIGURE 11-5**
*This division chief in a state agency dresses in a manner that is consistent with the goals of his (service) organization. At the same time, he is able to express some degree of individuality and distinctiveness through the wearing of red suspenders. Photo by Mark Kaiser.*

work." A sensible, tailored look was most preferred by the officials. One parks and recreation director reported that a citizen observed the director's expensive three-piece suit and implied through his comments that the director was digging into the "public trough" to make such purchases. Taxpaying citizens may resent highly polished and lavish appearances on the part of public employees, feeling that they are subsidizing them. This philosophy of understated competence may be contrasted with economic organizations' tendencies to stress their success to outsiders.

Clothing can help create an "open atmosphere," which is consistent with the effect that must be conveyed in service organizational culture. One city manager noted that he must be able to communicate with a broad range of groups within the community, and the topic or group with whom he meets tends to dictate the style of dress worn. For instance, a blue three-piece suit might be more suitable for meeting with a group of local bankers or high-tech industry representatives, whereas a slightly less formal suit of lighter colors might be preferable for meetings with human service groups or lower income community groups.

*Open Communication with the Public*

In city organizations, as in organizations of all types, stereotypes tend to emerge to characterize particular groups or subcultures within the larger organization. Elected officials (mayors and city council members) have more latitude in appearance choices than city staff. Several individuals remarked that elected officials could use clothing as a "mark" to be remembered, as they "partly set out to create an image of themselves as individuals. . . . to establish that separate identity."

*Dressing for One's Role*

City staff, who are supported primarily by taxes, have less latitude than elected officials. The city manager, or head of the organization, tends to set the tone for other employees. Generally, city managers dress for the community and the internal organization and strive to dress in a manner that promotes a sense of conservatism, which is symbolic of fiscal responsibility. One individual commented: "I think they reflect their own individualism. I think a lot of them have enough ego strength that they can wear anything they want to, and there are some that feel their public role or the public appearance is important, so they'll gear toward that."

Various department head positions are associated with different stereotypes emerging from function and role. City attorneys and finance directors are generally regarded as the most formal and are expected to wear suits. In fact, one individual commented that a "sincere" blue-striped suit was seen as a sign of a finance director in the city, and anyone else who wore such a suit was teased for masquerading as a finance director. Some of the stereotypes people have about the clothing of lawyers and accountants in the private sector apply as well in city organizations, although it is likely to be recognized that cities often allow more latitude in dress standards than do private corporations.

Parks and recreation directors are viewed as casual, comfortable, and colorful dressers. One director commented, however, that contrary to popular belief, most of them are seldom seen in "sweatshirts with whistles." Police chiefs are regarded as appearing the most regimented and polished, as formal dressers who seldom wear uniforms. Fire chiefs are more likely to wear their uniforms on a regular (weekly) basis than are police chiefs (Kaiser, 1982). This distinction between fire and police chiefs may be attributed in part to differences in public perceptions of police versus fire departments. (Fire departments enjoy a very favorable public image, whereas the public image of police departments can be more ambiguous.) These kinds of departments actually compose subcultures within the city organization; the nature of their clothing symbolism will be discussed in more detail in the following section on protective organizations.

## Protective Organizations

Protective organizations provide services as needed but do not depend upon continuous client need. Police and military organizations fall into this type of organizational culture. Their primary function is to defend the public, and they always strive to remain prepared for this function as the need arises.

A well-regimented appearance is expected in protective organizations, because such an image is viewed as a sign of efficiency and competence. Uniforms are considered to be integral to the organizational culture that orders priorities, demands compliance for the sake of the public's safety, and creates and maintains a hierarchy (see Figure 11-6). We can examine the means by which uniforms exert control over organizational members by looking at the following characteristics of uniforms: (1) emblematic of organization, (2) revealing and concealing status position, (3) certifying legitimacy, and (4) suppressing individuality (Joseph, 1986, pp. 66–68).

**FIGURE 11-6**
*In a protective organization such as a campus fire department, the relationship between members is clearly conveyed through uniforms. The man in the white shirt is the supervisor of the firefighter on the right. Photo by Wendy Dildey.*

   *1. Uniform as emblem of organization.* A uniform depicts the properties of the organization in tangible form. It becomes a badge or representation of the organization itself. Thus one can disgrace a uniform by behaving in a manner that is unbecoming to organizational goals. In the military, one may salute "the uniform and not the man," due to the uniform's embodiment of organizational culture (Joseph, 1986, p. 66).
   In police departments, organizational culture needs to combine an image of competence and authority with one of positive public relations. Authority cues can include hats (Volpp and Lennon, 1988) as well as certain clothing styles. Research has indicated the traditional navy blue uniform is positively received by most people (Mauro, 1984). Officers in traditional uniforms were perceived as having better judgment and as being more competent, helpful,

honest, fast, and active than police officers in "modern" uniforms, combining gray slacks and dark blue blazers. Similarly, officer-directed assaults have actually declined in Menlo Park, California, since the police department returned to the traditional navy uniform in 1977. Between 1969 and 1977, the police officers had worn the experimental style including blazers (Mauro, 1984). Research by Gundersen (1987) however led him to conclude that "a change to blazer and slacks would lose nothing while increasing the public's perceptions of a department so attired" (p. 194). He based this conclusion on a comparison of students' perceptions of line drawings of three uniform styles. The blazer uniform was seen as more professional than the more standard uniforms. In comparing Mauro's (1984) and Gundersen's (1987) findings, it is important to consider what context of impressions a police organization wants to convey. What is more important—a sense of professionalism or a sense of authority, and can some acceptable compromise be attained? The social context in which the uniform is perceived influences the need for a specific impression (Addison, 1981; Muchmore, 1975). Therefore, it may be difficult to recommend one style of uniform over another for *all* contexts. Cultural context must be considered as well. Research in New Zealand indicated that police officers in uniforms were evaluated as more competent, reliable, intelligent, and helpful than those who wore civilian clothing. At the same time, they were viewed as more tense when in uniform than when in civilian clothing (Singer and Singer, 1985).

Historic context may also influence public perceptions of police uniforms. For example, some of the data from studies in the 1970s suggested that public perceptions of police uniforms were not necessarily favorable in all contexts (Muchmore, 1975; Tenzel and Gizanckas, 1973). Later studies have produced more favorable assessments of uniforms, in New Zealand (Singer and Singer, 1985) as well as in the United States (Mauro, 1984). Such a shift in attitudes may parallel the increased conservatism and concern about crime in the 1980s. Similarly, a study in the 1980s indicated that males are perceived as more attractive in military uniforms than in other forms of attire (suit, slacks and sweater, and jeans and shirt) (Hewitt and German, 1987). Basically, more formal styles of clothing, with military uniforms constituting the most formal, were preferred over less formal styles. Military uniforms may connote power or control (Hewitt and German, 1987), but it is possible that the socially conservative climate of the times promotes more favorable evaluations of this style.

*2. Uniforms reveal and conceal status position.* A uniform conceals all identities an individual may have except one—membership in an organization. Thus organizational membership is the single status that is revealed by a uniform; all other statuses may become irrelevant in a uniformed context. Army regulations have discouraged uniformed officers from displaying any signs of a domesticated identity as indicated by carrying packages such as grocery bags. In a uniform, organizational membership assumes a kind of master status (Joseph, 1986, p. 67).

*3. Uniforms certify legitimacy.* When an individual wears a uniform, the organization certifies that he or she is representative of the organization and that the organization assumes responsibility for his or her actions (Joseph, 1986, p. 85).

   ***4. Uniforms suppress individuality.*** A uniform may lead to a sense of depersonalization as it ensures conformity to organizational ideology (Joseph, 1986, p. 68). The individual becomes a member of the organization, and his or her own interests and values become subordinate to organizational goals.

   In cases where individuals in protective organizations have sought to express their individuality and have been denied the right to do so, the courts have generally ruled against the individuals, in favor of the organization. For example, the courts have ruled that facial hair on firemen, for example, could interfere with equipment use, and long hair may pose a fire hazard. Police officers have generally been required to follow police department grooming codes, based upon judges' statements that police officers should be neat and disciplined so as to gain public respect, that uniformed officers are more recognizable to the public, and that uniforms create an esprit de corps for policemen. On the other hand, the courts ruled in favor of a male who had been denied admission to a police department on the basis of his habit of practicing nudism on weekends, because the department's actions infringed on the applicant's constitutional rights (Maher and Slocum, 1986).

   Military hair codes may promote dissatisfaction among individuals, especially in eras when longer hair is fashionable. Pragmatic issues such as safety and hygiene may be cited as organizational reasons for very short military hairstyles, but these appearance codes may also refer to political ideology, connotations of masculinity, and the promotion of discipline (Joseph, 1986, p. 90).

## Associative Organizations

Associative organizations meet social needs and provide means of mutual member identification and interaction. Many associative organizations are social in nature (for example, fraternities or sororities). Symbols such as Greek letters on sweatshirts promote a sense of affiliation among organization members. The culture of a social organization, in fact, may be based on the benefits of belonging to a larger entity.

   Socialization and education are social needs that associative cultures also provide. Issues of dress in schools shed light on organizational culture in associative institutions. Private or parochial schools often have dress codes that result in a uniform appearance. Proponents of such standards of dress contend that they facilitate educational goals. The following reasons for school uniforms have been offered: (*a*) increased discipline and respect for the teacher, (*b*) promotion of group spirit (esprit de corps), (*c*) a belief that academic standards are maintained by uniformity, (*d*) the easing of family budgeting problems, and (*e*) blurring social-class distinctions among students. However, students have not always accepted these reasons as outweighing the authoritarianism and deindividualization that uniforms represent to some. When the question of abolishing a school uniform was raised in a New Zealand secondary school, two-thirds of the parents were in favor of retaining the uniform and only a slight majority of the students wanted to abolish it (Barrington and Marshall, 1975). Therefore, there is likely to be some ambivalence about the wearing of school uniforms, as the pros and cons are weighed.

In the 1980s, a resurgence of interest in school uniforms and dress codes resulted from public school concerns about the wearing of designer brands (and the corresponding increased competitiveness), punk styles, T-shirts with certain kinds of messages printed on them, and gang symbolism. Concerns were expressed about the characterization of lifestyles condoning drugs, alcohol, violence, vulgarity, and disrespect for authority (Elliot, 1984). Another perspective on this issue addresses the legal and historical and contextual issues at play:

> The conditions are ripe for revival of the hair patrol and the dress code vigilantes. The arguments for curtailing today's faddish punk look are memorialized in the legal briefs of two decades ago, when educators justified rules against long hair for boys on the grounds that the hair reflected a poor attitude, made it hard to tell the boys from the girls, and destroyed moral fiber. . . . For every school executive these days who finds a student's rainbow-spiked hair a threat to discipline and the "basic educational mission," there are half a dozen lawyers eager to make a *cause celebré* out of that student's suspension. How much of your school budget would you like to spend litigating the constitutional right of a female student to wear a Mohawk hairstyle or a male student to wear an earring? (Splitt, 1986)

Whereas dress codes are generally developed to *proscribe* or prohibit certain clothes or grooming practices considered objectionable, uniforms *prescribe* a certain standard and style of attire. In a public grade school in Baltimore, Maryland, school uniforms were generally well-received by teachers and students alike. These uniforms were not mandatory, but 95 percent of the parents purchased them (Valentine, 1987). The coordinator of the uniform program was quoted as saying, "Children can get destroyed with concern about clothes instead of education." Additionally, she added, uniforms can instill a sense of pride in the self and the school, while also eliminating competition and expense. The other side of the argument points to the issue of free public education as being equated with students' freedom of choice. According to this line of reasoning, part of the goal of education is to teach independent and critical thinking, and freedom of choice and individualism in appearance parallel these thinking skills.

An issue related to clothing and dress codes in schools is the influence of attractiveness on a student's experiences. There is some evidence that less attractive high school students perform better on IQ and achievement tests. These students may attempt to compensate for physical appearance by excelling in other areas, such as academics (Moran and McCullers, 1984). Given the emphasis on attractiveness and popular attire among adolescents, appearance may be a factor that either detracts from the learning process or promotes critical thinking skills as a lesson in social life. More research is needed to examine the implications of these possibilities in greater depth.

The appearances of teachers have been an issue in some schools as well. Some individuals argue that teachers should symbolize the social distance between themselves and their students through dress. Others agree but stress the importance of role modeling. Individuals arguing against dress codes for teachers contend that the codes violate individual rights.

The issue of the regulation of teachers' appearances has been considered by the courts in a number of cases. Cases occurring between 1967 and 1976 primarily involved high school teachers who refused to comply with dress codes issued by school authorities. The majority of complaints involved males, and the most common issue pertained to facial hair. The judges generally ruled in favor of the teachers' preferences for facial hair, because the school restrictions were characterized as arbitrary, unenforceable, and/or racially discriminatory. In some cases, teachers were unaware of expectations and subsequent sanctions. Appearance was also viewed by some judges as unlikely to interfere with job performance (Maher and Slocum, 1986). Moreover, the First Amendment insures free speech as a basic individual liberty. It was argued by some attorneys that grooming is a kind of symbolic speech (Fischer, 1978). Yet legal distinctions have been made between the regulation of grooming (for example, beards and mustaches) and clothing styles. Although the courts have traditionally ruled in favor of school boards trying to implement dress codes for teachers in matters of attire, the same rulings have not necessarily applied to grooming, with the following rationale: Clothes can be changed after work hours, whereas a haircut or shaved-off beard cannot be quickly replaced and thus should not be controlled by the school board. Control of grooming practices, therefore, may constitute interference into teachers' private lives. Cases concerning clothing were related to such issues as the need to wear a jacket and tie, and the license to wear a mini skirt or a black armband. Judges tended to rule against the teachers in these instances (Maher and Slocum, 1986).

Probably the most important point related to the question of uniforms and dress codes in schools pertains to the degree of participation of members themselves. The available evidence suggests that a suitable compromise can be achieved when school authorities, parents, teachers, and students work together and communicate with one another. A uniform or standard of dress that is forced on students, teachers, or staff without their involvement in the process may be more detrimental to the organizational culture than the diversity that emerges from freedom of choice. For example, a school district in northern California negotiated with staff in order to establish uniforms for cafeteria, custodial, grounds, campus supervision, maintenance, and bus driving personnel (Di-Geronimo and Gustafson, 1985). By including the staff in the negotiation process, the advantages of providing uniforms at district expense could be discussed along with the benefits of a professional appearance.

Another issue related to appearance styles in educational contexts (associative organizations) is to what extent these styles influence the learning process. How are teachers perceived, for example, as a function of dress? Are they perceived as "easier" or more competent in one form of dress or another? Research in Tennessee indicated that a female high school teacher wearing a soft, feminine style of dress was perceived as more approachable and more likely to offer assistance in an emergency or to allow students to make up work (Reeder and

King, 1984). In contrast, an image of a teacher wearing a skirted, tailored suit was perceived as most capable with maintaining classroom order, most desirable as a homeroom teacher, and one with whom students could discuss personal problems. This teacher in a tailored suit seemed to be judged as having leadership qualities and as being trustworthy and capable. Teachers wearing a simple skirt, blouse, and vest, or a masculine-appearing pantsuit received the lowest ratings by the high school students; they were judged as least intelligent and most old-fashioned (Reeder and King, 1984). Other research has suggested that teachers who wear fashionable clothing tend to exercise a controlled manner of teaching style, emphasizing lecture and demonstration techniques. In contrast, teachers who wear less fashionable clothes tend to emphasize group discussion (Rosenblatt, 1980). Another study revealed that the same college instructor was evaluated more positively by American students in a class (clothing construction) where she wore Western attire (a dress or skirted suit), as compared with one in which she wore East Indian attire (for example, a sari). The students approached her more frequently when she was in Western attire than when she wore East Indian clothes (Chowdhary, 1988b).

This study relates to a larger appearance-related issue in large institutions such as college campuses—stereotyping. (See Figure 11-7.) Because all students on a campus cannot possibly interact with one another and there is a natural

**FIGURE 11-7**
*A major university is an associative organization that allows a fairly high degree of latitude and freedom in dress norms. Still, it becomes quite common to categorize or stereotype people on the basis of their appearances. Whom would you expect to be a professor in this picture? Photo by Carla M. Freeman.*

cognitive tendency to place people in social categories, students are likely to be classified by such factors as college major. Accordingly, appearance imagery evolves to represent these classifications. For example, informal styles such as jeans and overalls were judged in a study on a California campus as more likely to be worn by animal science majors, followed by art, engineering, psychology, and textiles. The reverse order applied to the wearing of a pantsuit or skirted suit. That is, textiles majors were most expected to wear these items, and animal science least. Thus, a formal–informal continuum applied to the majors. Across majors, however, jeans were judged as the most generally accepted symbols of student attire. For professors, suits were seen as the most likely attire, but this differed by department, with animal science and art professors being expected to dress more casually than engineering, psychology, or textiles professors (Rucker et al., 1982).

Religious organizations deal with collective beliefs about supernatural forces. Such organizations have traditionally used forms of vestments to promote organizational and spiritual goals. In the Catholic church, mass vestments have historically served to symbolize the conscious change from "earthly to ordained man" (Mayer-Thurman, 1975, p. 14). Symbolism related to holiness, cleanliness, and purity has also prevailed in Catholic uniforms for priests and nuns. In the context of a college classroom, a professor/priest's Roman collar and black suit worn by Catholic priests are symbolic of moral commitment and social isolation (Coursey, 1973). These clothes have become symbolic of authority and leadership as well, because they represent the ability to communicate with the deity. In compliance with this symbolism, priests are afforded respect in public contexts (Bouska and Beatty, 1978). Similarly, nuns in uniform are treated with respect in counseling contexts. Research has shown that students spend more time responding to questions posed by a nun wearing her habit than to the same nun in lay dress. Also, students respond more conservatively in the presence of a nun's habit (Long, 1978).

*Religious Organizations*

    The history of ecclesiastical dress points to the importance of liturgical vestments in concurrence with religious ideology and in the celebration of ritual ceremony. As the Catholic church gained authority, it called for greater distinctions of rank through sumptuosity and color of clothing (Mayo, 1984). Liturgical vestments also provide a visual and symbolic focus for worship and convey the mission of the church (Littrell and Evers, 1985). When the priest's role was less clear during the 1960s—a time when issues such as lay participation in the church and the role of the priest were discussed—the chasubles worn by priests exhibited greater diversity in certain design characteristics. That is, changes in chasuble design seemed to parallel an organizational shift from priests as superiors to laypersons to one of interaction among equals. In the 1970s, a shift from a king to a shepherd role was symbolized by lower percentages of embellishment, fewer motifs per garment, and a simpler border and organization of design (Littrell and Evers, 1985). Thus changes in organizational culture and ideology were accompanied by design alterations.

Not surprisingly, changes in the priest's role during the 1960s and 1970s coincided with shifts in the nun's role and a broadening of appearance options. A nun's habit represents her religious dedication and influences how laypersons respond toward her (Long, 1978). In the 1970s, some nuns shed their habits and turned to modest street dress, whereas others maintained the habit because of its association with spiritual discipline (see Figure 11-8).

In a study of lay Catholics' perceptions of nuns with or without habits, the subjects with the more progressive religious beliefs and liberal political views were more receptive to nuns wearing street clothes, whereas more traditional and conservative subjects preferred the traditional habit. Seventy-three percent of the lay Catholics indicated a need for the change in clothes, whereas only 51 percent stated that they would prefer dealing with a nun who wore lay dress. Thus, there was some expressed reluctance to the clothing changes on the part of nearly one-half of the subjects; females over 30 years of age with a high school education were among those who were least receptive to the change (Baer and Mosele, 1970).

Some authors have suggested that the move in the 1970s toward more contemporary clothing was symbolic of a corresponding increased awareness on the part of nuns of the limitations of a role as a meek teacher or nurse; as their conceptions of themselves changed, so did the attire of some (Melamed, Silverman, and Lewis, 1975). The traditional habit was a uniform that served as a constant reminder that a nun's religious role shaped others' responses toward

**FIGURE 11-8**
*These nuns on vacation in Bavaria wear somewhat modified habits, in part, to reflect their involvement in a religious organization. Photo by Mark Kaiser.*

**FIGURE 11-9**
*The identities of these Buddhist monks are clearly conveyed through their bright gold attire and hairstyles. These symbols of religiosity serve to set them apart from others, and also serve the needs of their religious organization. Photo by Stephen Cunha.*

her. Along with increasing freedom and individuality in dress, nuns have been allowed to express their personalities and to form individualized self-concepts (San Giovanni, 1978).

In general, religious organizations tend to be characterized by their use of clothing to symbolize religious beliefs. The emphasis is generally on styles that set the religious leaders apart from lay members in accordance with organizational role, as well as on symbols that communicate religious beliefs (see Figure 11-9).

Beyond the social constraints and realities of organizational culture, some institutions demand total compliance.

## Total Institutions

**Total institutions** are places where large numbers of like-situated individuals reside and work in a context cut off from the wider society for an appreciable period of time (Goffman, 1961a). Collectively, these individuals lead enclosed, formally administered lives. Total institutions, then, are organizations in which the everyday social realities are highly structured. Among the organizations that may fall into this category are prisons, military training camps, and religious convents. A common theme in total institutions is the maintenance of the status quo through the use of uniforms and through barriers to social interaction with the outside world. Typically, activities are scheduled for the individual and carried out in conjunction with *groups* of people. All aspects of life are conducted in the same place and under the same single authority. Goffman (1961a) described total institutions in terms of their depersonalizing qualities, that is, as a "forcing house for changing persons, as a natural experiment on what can be done to the self" (p. 12).

Prison codes provide a prime example of the use of clothing to promote the goals of a total institution. Prisons are designed to exert control over individuals. On admission, inmates become a part of the system, as the self is stripped of usual belongings, or *identity kits*. Despite the uniformity required in prisons, however, inmates find means for developing variations in their appearances. Research indicated that a prison code dictating a uniform of brown pants, shirt, and shoes for men was altered in private quarters; the institution allowed this unless the privilege was taken to an extreme. The more personal clothing a man owned, the more likely he was to have status and independence (Ramsey, 1976).

When confronted with uniform regulations that inhibit self-expression, individuals tend to respond by "making do," or making adaptations whenever possible (Goffman, 1961a). For example, in Ramsey's (1976) research, inmates from a particular city could be recognized by several cues based on making do. Jail hats were worn with the bill turned to the side and tipped slightly. Afro hairstyles were parted down the middle or to one side. Prison trousers were deliberately cut about six inches too short. Black Muslims were identified by neatly pressed clothes, the wearing of "stocky" caps with a small turned-up cuff, and short hair with a sharp line where the hair met the scalp. Sunglasses were popular and appeared to be a symbol of hostility and boredom. The wearing of two earrings distinguished the homosexual prisoners, whereas one earring was a personal expression of masculinity. It was common for young, attractive heterosexual inmates to make an effort to appear unshaven and dirty.

Goffman (1961a) also found that "make-do's" were common in mental hospitals. He studied mental patients at a time when uniforms were commonly worn in institutions and noted that hospital-issue khaki pants were often carefully tailored into neat summer shorts. One patient discovered the little-known fact that a team of seamstresses were hired by the hospital to repair the "one-size-fits-all" uniforms and found a way to have his shirts and pants tailored to a good fit (by "trading" these services for a small sum of money or a few cigarettes). Make-do's that allowed the patients to transport their various belongings were important symbols of status. One patient who was an engineer fashioned a purse out of a discarded oilcloth, developing intricate compartments for his comb, toothbrush, writing paper, pencil, soap, facecloth, and toilet paper. The purse was attached to the underside of his belt. He also sewed an extra pocket on the inside of his jacket to carry a book (Goffman, 1961a, pp. 251–252).

Thus, clothing in total institutions is likely to be socially controlled through the use of uniforms. Yet the human capacity for creativity and resourcefulness often results in means for modifying appearance to express personal and group values. This capacity becomes a critical component in our study of culture, whether in the group or organizational context, or in the context of society.

## Suggested Readings

Fine, G. A. 1987. *With the boys: Little League baseball and preadolescent culture*. Chicago: The University of Chicago Press.
  This book is based on an ethnographic study of Little League baseball culture. The concept of idioculture is presented and illustrated in the context of group behavior. Several examples of negotiated ideas and practices related to clothing are provided.

Jasper, C. R., and Roach-Higgins, M. E. 1988. Role conflict and conformity in dress. *Social Behavior and Personality 16*: 227–240.
  This article draws from a study of 5,475 American Catholic priests. It documents that priests who conformed to church regulations with respect to dress in the late 1960s differed from nonconformists in their beliefs about the priest's role and other opinions about the religious organization.

Joseph, N. 1986. *Uniforms and nonuniforms: Communication through clothing*. New York: Greenwood Press.
  This book delves into the issue of clothing as a form of communication, providing a number of rich examples of the relation of clothing to organizational culture. The historical basis for uniforms in a variety of organizational contexts are discussed as well.

Maher, P. M., and Slocum, A. C. 1987. Freedom in dress: Legal sanctions. *Clothing and Textiles Research Journal 5*(4): 14–22.
  The concept of freedom in dress is explored in relation to court cases and the types of legal sanctions imposed.

Solomon, M. 1987. Standard issue. *Psychology Today 21*(12): 30–31.
  Solomon discusses why many organizations have a desire for their employees to wear uniforms.

# Chapter Twelve
### ...
# *Society, Appearance, and Fashion*

*Societies are composed of larger numbers of people than are groups and organizations. Societies may vary from relatively simple to very complex and heterogeneous systems. A society is shaped by historical and developmental factors (for example, industrialization and urbanization). These factors influence the types of clothing styles that are worn. Similarly, the culture of a society expresses its ideas and values about appearance and fashion. When societies become large and complex, subcultures tend to emerge within the larger "mainstream" culture. Cultural trends and impulses that may be described as "postmodern" are discussed in this chapter, as they parallel life in postindustrial societies.*

Social groups and organizations contribute to the interlocking networks that compose society. Society is a macrolevel, social infrastructure and is a concept that is often (although not necessarily) equated with a nation. As we have seen in Chapter Eleven, organizations are often too large for all of their members to interact with one another on a day-to-day basis. Because society is much larger in scope and diffuse in nature, it is often impossible for individuals to interact with one another at all. In this chapter, we will pursue a cultural and historical comparison of fashion and appearance in societies.

Just as a group or an organization generally has a distinctive culture, often a society can be characterized as having its own culture as well (see Figure 12-1). However, as we will see, once a society becomes large and complex, there is a strong likelihood that it will not only have a "mainstream" culture but also will be composed of some distinctive "sub-societies" (groups of people who embody a certain population) with their own cultures (subcultures). Thus there may be a generalized "structure of feeling" in addition to particular cultures (subcultures) within that general structure.

The concept of society is important to social-psychological studies, because human societies are made up of selves. Human actions are jointly constructed

**FIGURE 12-1**
*A certain "structure of feeling" is conveyed through the aesthetic codes of a culture. Visitors to India are struck by the vibrant colors in the clothes. Photo by Stephen Cunha.*

as individuals in groups and organizations link their actions with those of others. Symbolic interactionist Herbert Blumer (1969a) describes societies as composed of acting units, or "collectivities whose members are acting together on a common quest, or organizations acting on behalf of a constituency" (p. 85).

Clothing and appearance serve to identify and differentiate the acting units within a society, whether these units are individuals who dress uniquely, groups or organizations with collective symbols, or subcultures with distinctive appearance styles. However, the structure of feeling that parallels the size and complexity of collectivities of people also impacts appearance and participation in the fashion process. Many factors influence the rise of fashion. We will begin our discussion of society, appearance, and fashion by considering the historical and cultural contexts in which fashion first emerged.

## Social Structure and the Emergence of Fashion

The French sociologist Jean Baudrillard (1983) provides a framework for analyzing fashion historically, focusing on shifts in what he calls "orders of appearance" and "laws of value." He identifies three eras that have emerged since the Renaissance: (1) the "classical" period, from the Renaissance to the Industrial Revolution, (2) the "industrial" era, and (3) the latter half of the twentieth century (postindustrial).

Historians generally agree that the beginnings of fashion change in Western civilization may be linked with the rise of cities and the middle class. During the Renaissance, elements of the feudal order began to break down. Signs of prestige and wealth "naturally" placed a person into a social category, but as open competition in the order of appearance emerged, "counterfeit" images challenged the source of power (Baudrillard, 1983).

Several factors contributed to the rise of fashion: city life, a class structure allowing for social mobility, the rise of capitalism, and industrialization all seem to have had a tremendous impact on fashion as we know it today. A city, by definition, is larger than a town or village, dense and heterogeneous in population, and inclusive of a wide range of nonagricultural specialists (Sjoberg, 1960). Cities first appeared, scholars generally agree, in the Mesopotamian river basin and in Meso-America (independently). In the preindustrial city, class structure was clearly symbolized by manners, dress, and speech. The feudal elite (who had generally been born into the agrarian aristocracy) tended to relay their superiority through clothes that signified their wealth based on a lack of need to work. Although every complex social order uses dress to mark status, especially rigid and pervasive norms were evident in the realm of many preindustrial cities (Sjoberg, 1960, pp. 127–128). At the same time, competition emerged in the form of imitation of the elite. Historically, the feudal elite took measures to ensure the maintenance of their power, just in case commoners might be able to obtain "counterfeits" of their prized symbols. Still, the cities of the Renaissance were places where individuals could compete through appearance management. **Sumptuary laws**, designed to preserve the existing social order's power structure through the use of clothing restrictions, were enacted to maintain class distinctions (Phillips and Staley, 1979) and to delineate certain groups. In medieval Europe, Jews and prostitutes were forced to wear distinctive signs to set them apart from the rest of society (Sjoberg, 1960). In Renaissance Italian cities (in the fifteenth century), Jewish women were required to wear earrings, which were viewed as a sign of social stigma—a form of discrimination toward a minority group (Hughes, 1986). In Elizabethan England, sumptuary laws prohibited commoners from wearing gold or silver cloth, velvet, furs, and other luxury materials. Many European feudal cities mandated that prostitutes were to remain unveiled, so they could be distinguished from "respectable women," who covered their heads in public. In feudal cities of the East and West (for example, in Japan and France), the hierarchical nature of traditional society was clearly and rigidly prescribed (Steele, 1988). In Korean feudal cities, commoners were forbidden to wear long, flowing sleeves—a sign of dissociation from manual work. This type of symbolism was still important in Seoul, Korea, around 1900: elite gentlemen wore a distinctive head covering, the headband of which was so tightly bound around the temples that it clearly indicated his inability to engage in physical labor (in which commoners would be involved) (Sjoberg, 1960).

Thus differentiation among social groups became a fundamental aspect of city life. The concept of fashion change may be identified as early as the fourteenth century. In such politically independent and economically advanced cities as Milan, Florence, and Venice, Italy, fashion change was equated with the expansion

**FIGURE 12-2**
*This garment is actually the predecessor of modern men's clothing. The short doublet and tights replaced the coat of chain mail during the Renaissance (fourteenth century) in Italian cities. The style spread to France and then to other countries such as Germany, where this style was worn around 1480. Illustration by Molly Greek.*

of trade and the breakdown of feudal society (Wilson, 1985; Steele, 1988). In 1340 in Italy, the birth of modern men's clothing may be traced to the popularity of the short doublet and tights, which replaced the coat of chain mail and was adopted first by middle-class adolescent fashion leaders (Steele, 1988, pp. 18–19). Italian cities during this era were beginning to reveal signs of **capitalism** (an economic system based on the free play of market forces), and fashion innovation and competition were on the rise.

> Even the society of the Renaissance was "modern" in its tendency towards secular worldliness, its preoccupation with the daily, material world, and its dynamism. Characteristic of that world was its love of the changing mode, and a wealthy middle class that already competed in finery with the nobility. From its beginnings fashion was part of this modernity (Wilson, 1985, p. 60).

The concept of fashion spread from Italy to the court of Burgundy in France, which is generally recognized as the "cradle of fashion" (Steele, 1988, p. 19). In the fifteenth century, the dukes of Burgundy had much more wealth and power than the kings of France. Thus regional fashion centers in France and Italy had been established. (See Figure 12-2 for an example of European men's fashion during the fifteenth century.) By the reign of Louis XIV (from 1660 to 1715), the textile industry had become the foundation of the fashion industry in France, in competition with the Italian industry. In Paris, truly modern fashion emerged in the early 1700s as garments were produced by tailors and dressmakers for the courtiers at the palace of Versailles, for the wealthy bourgeois (the upper class, in control over the means of production), and for the increasing numbers of foreign visitors. Even some of the princesses and ladies of the court wanted to turn their backs on the traditional, aristocratic styles and dress instead in Parisian styles (Steele, 1988, p. 25). At the same time, aristocratic styles were imitated by fashionable city dwellers. Thus, between the fourteenth and eighteenth centuries, struggles for status and freedom of expression through appearance were apparent in city life (Wilson, 1985). Of course, there was still a different norm of dress (functional, utilitarian) in agrarian or rural life.

## Era of Industrialization

In the late 1700s, the Industrial Revolution in England brought mechanization and a new structure of feeling to city life. Capitalism was brought to a new level, and cities were now contexts in which social mobility was more feasible and assessment of social standing was increasingly complicated. In the early stages of urban-industrial centers, wealthy and poor individuals often lived side by side (Wilson, 1985, p. 26). Fashion was even more important than it was in preindustrial cities, as street life offered a wider array of circulating images. Involvement in fashion seemed to become a strategy for re-creating the fragmented self (Wilson, 1985). Yet along with the rise of capitalism, males opted to be out of the fashion competition as they became increasingly involved in the world of commerce. The clothes of the rural aristocracy in England (riding clothes) were adopted by male members of the rising middle class (Wilson, 1985; Steele, 1988), and a fundamental distinction between men's and women's appearances emerged to parallel the distinction between public and private (domestic) spheres. London, where the capitalist economy was more advanced, became the center of men's wear, whereas Paris remained the center of women's fashions.

Along with urbanization and industrialization is an ethos of modernity, covering the gamut of lifestyles and affecting technology, social organization, art, production, and fashion. The invention of the sewing machine around the middle of the 1800s revolutionized the possibilities for producing clothes at volume levels. However, this was one area of "progress" and modernity that was not readily embraced by all consumers.

Until the middle of the nineteenth century, fashionable clothes had largely been affordable by the wealthy only. Until the end of the 1800s, most clothes were made at home; it was not until well into the 1900s that the term *store-bought* evoked other than purely negative connotations. As manufacturing gradually improved and the idea of mass-produced clothes became more acceptable, ready-to-wear clothing overcame some of the stigma of cheapness that originally had been assigned to it. An increased awareness of fashion trends on the part of the New York apparel industry, along with improved methods for meeting them, was a big step in this direction. There was a progression from the mere copying of Parisian designs to the original development of American fashions.

According to Baudrillard (1983), the commercial law of value emerged in the context of the industrial era. A new generation of signs and objects was created, without the tradition of caste (see Figure 12-3). Signs were not necessarily modeled after the aristocracy. Rather, the new signs were produced on a large

**FIGURE 12-3**
*Skirts and blouses for working women were mass-produced around the turn of the century. These women are telephone operators. Courtesy of the Pacific Telephone Collection, City of Sacramento, Museum and History Division.*

scale; the issue of their origin or uniqueness was no longer as important (Baudrillard, 1983). Along with industrialization, an ideology embracing rationality and science and technology emerged. This utilitarian ideology, valuing that which is perceived as useful over that which is viewed as unnecessarily frivolous, has shaped much of our contemporary ambivalence about fashion, according to Elizabeth Wilson (1985). On the one hand, we embrace the manner in which fashion seems to reflect modernity and progressiveness, but on the other hand, we sense that it is impractical and wasteful. Industrial capitalism promotes a desire for the new and a realm of competition, "repeatedly throwing up ambiguous rebels whose rebellion never is a revolution, but instead a reaffirmation of the self" (Wilson, 1985, p. 183).

Thus the rise of fashion has been closely associated with a nexus of competition and differentiation in city life, capitalism, and industrialization. Associated with some of these elements may be diverse structures of feeling, which are considered in the next section.

## Gemeinschaft *versus* Gesellschaft

The cultures of collectivities of people have been classified and characterized by anthropologists and sociologists on the basis of technology and social interactions. Although such characterizations may not exactly reflect the nature of a given collectivity, as we saw in Chapter Eleven, *ideal types* are abstract constructs that enable us to characterize and compare. The German sociologist Ferdinand Tönnies (1853–1936) identified a basic conceptual distinction between **Gemeinschaft** (community) and **Gesellschaft** (society) (Tönnies, 1940). A feeling of *Gemeinschaft* is evident when people are able to associate with one another in informal ways, perhaps even on a face-to-face basis. Small, traditional communities united by a common ancestry are conducive to relationships that are intense and personal. In contrast, *Gesellschaft* is characteristic of more businesslike, impersonal relationships and bonds based on rational self-interests directed toward a particular goal (Tönnies, 1940). Anthropologist Robert Redfield (1930), who was influenced by Tönnies's work, characterized societies as based on the premise that increased heterogeneity and disorganization are related to increased size of communities or cities. Redfield conducted field studies in Mexico in the 1930s and 1940s and noted that the primary cultural variations among the Mexican people were not due to regional differences, but to urban versus rural lifestyles. Small, isolated communities are characterized by cultural homogeneity, the relative importance of families, and the development of rituals that express collective beliefs and attitudes. Religion is stronger in small, isolated communities. In larger communities, there is increased heterogeneity and anonymity with decreased emphasis on traditional rituals. The following discussion of *Gemeinschaft*- and *Gesellschaft*-like collectivities integrates some of Redfield's ideas, in addition to those of clothing scholars Mary Ellen Roach and Joann Eicher (1973). (See the description of their work in the Suggested Reading section at the end of the chapter.)

Tönnies (1940) believed that human will—the basis for volition, hopes and goals, discipline, and self-control—may be characterized either as natural or rational. Natural will guides social thinking and interactions in *Gemeinschaft*-like contexts, whereas rational will is associated with *Gesellschaft*. *Natural will* is unconditional, whereas *rational will* revolves around processes of exchange. *Gemeinschaft*-based, natural will applies when individuals are motivated by what they can do for one another. Close relationships with others in one's society are perceived to be a supernatural gift. Individuals *want* to identify with one another and express their sense of belonging, therefore they dress similarly with others, at least those who share the same age and gender categories. Though Tönnies and some other scholars have expressed regret about the loss of *Gemeinschaft*-like social interactions in complex, modern societies, there are often costs to individuals in *Gemeinschaft* contexts that should not be overlooked. *Gemeinschaft* ties may restrict individuality, spontaneity, and creativity, because there is a high degree of social control (Hess, Markson, and Stein, 1985). People know each other well enough to keep an eye on one another.

The way of life in a *Gemeinschaft* context is relatively orderly and often revolves around family and kinship. Sentimentality, fellowship, and meaningful interactions are the hallmarks of *Gemeinschaft*. An expressive mode of thinking is used; Tönnies (1940) compared *Gemeinschaft* to the innocence and idealism of youth.

Appearance symbolism is likely to be relatively enduring, because there is a focus on tradition and conformity for the sake of community. *Gemeinschaft*-like style of dress tends to be guided by tradition and may consist of folk costume. Folk costume is a form of dress that (a) outwardly identifies the folk (*Gemeinschaft*-like) community and (b) expresses the individual's relationships to and within that community (Yoder, 1972). Folk costume serves to convey the following information about the wearer and his or her culture:

1. Festive and professional functions (for ritual patterns, see Figure 12-4)
2. Social class and status
3. Region, nationality, and religion (See Figure 12-5)
4. Age of the wearer
5. Distinguishing markers between married and unmarried people
6. Gender and sexuality as linked to social function and morality
7. Distinction between rural and urban
8. "Aesthetic, erotic, and magical functions" (Bogatyrev, 1976)

The social meaning of appearance signs is likely to become quite elaborate as structural qualities of fabrics and garments serve to code cultural messages. Tradition and cultural aesthetics are valued and preserved through folk costumes, and much information is conveyed visually in the process of social life. Meaning is shared and commonly understood. There is less change in clothing styles, because a great deal of time may be invested in the construction of a single garment. Somewhat unique stylistic variations within a framework of conformity

## *Gemeinschaft*

**FIGURE 12-4**
*Folk costumes help to create a festive context for community traditions, as shown in this Joan of Arc parade in Orléans, France. Photo by Clyde W. Benke.*

**FIGURE 12-5**
*This Guatemalan woman's attire and the fabric she is weaving convey regionality. Each village has its own distinctive textile patterns. Photo by Katharine Hoag.*

**FIGURE 12-6**
*The Amish have managed to maintain a sense of* **Gemeinschaft** *(community) within the larger context of mainstream North American culture. Their clothes serve to convey the social separation from worldly persons; note the difference between the appearances of the Amish family on the left and the tourists on the right at the National Zoo in Washington, D.C. Although the Amish communicate* Gemeinschaft*-like ties to one another in a very distinctive way, such ties may be developed in more subtle ways among group members, even in very complex societies. Photo by Lillian W. Low.*

may be possible due to handcrafted fabrics and individual touches in garment construction.

Although we can see evidence of *Gemeinschaft* in historical (pre-urban-industrial) contexts (see Figure 12-6), a *Gemeinschaft*-like structure of feeling is also apparent in some contemporary, small-scale societies or communities. (See Social Focus 12-1 for a discussion of the *Gemeinschaft*-like qualities of Amish society within the larger, heterogeneous American society.)

In contrast to *Gemeinschaft*, *Gesellschaft* (society) is characterized by a structure of feeling influenced by commercialization and industrialization. Table 12-1 summarizes the differences between *Gemeinschaft* and *Gesellschaft*. As indicated, rational will characterizes a *Gesellschaft* society. A collective consciousness of authority arises from status relationships. Individuals calculate means and the appropriateness of means to an end. People orient their actions toward one another in relation to systems of exchange and rationality.

Urbanization and industrialization are equated with the emergence of *Gesellschaft*; people move increasingly from rural areas or villages to urban areas, as factories—a product of an industrial revolution—provide new opportunities for jobs. There is a simultaneous division of labor, and people become acquainted with the notion of bureaucracy, discussed in Chapter Eleven.

*Gesellschaft*

# *Gemeinschaft*-like Qualities of Amish Society

Amish society illustrates many of the characteristics of *Gemeinschaft*. Individuals in this society live in communities in Pennsylvania (especially Lancaster County) and in parts of the Midwest. They are descendants of the Anabaptist Protestants in sixteenth-century Europe, who came to North America to escape religious persecution. Today, the Amish have a distinctive culture, or subculture, within the larger context of North American society.

Consistent with *Gemeinschaft* values, the Amish are uncomfortable with the idea of change and value tradition. Many of the customs and small-scale technologies that were common in rural society during the nineteenth century in North America are retained in Amish life. There is a strong sense of "we-ness," and people know that they can count on one another for help and support in times of need. They do things for one another because they truly desire to do so. It is not necessary for basic goals in life to be stated as matters of doctrine, because these goals do not tend to be questioned. Rather, they are understood and implied by the acts that go along with living in a homogeneous, closely knit society.

Some of the unique characteristics of Amish life are (*a*) distinctiveness, (*b*) smallness of scale, (*c*) homogeneous cultural patterns, and (*d*) strain toward self-sufficiency (Hostetler, 1980, pp. 8–17). These characteristics tend to be illustrated in Amish clothing styles. The Amish are highly visible; their clothes and grooming serve to separate them from the outside world. Men wear long beards without mustaches, and wear distinctive "broadfall" trousers. Solid fabrics are worn, and wristwatches are forbidden. Frock coats are worn for church. Men's suit coats and vests have closures of hooks and eyes rather than buttons (which are considered to be too decorative). They do not wear ties. Common accessories are a hat and suspenders, justified on the basis of utility rather than adornment.

Women do not cut their hair and wear it in a bun covered by a prayer cap. They do not wear makeup, jewelry, or shorts and slacks. Instead, they wear modest dresses with aprons, with black bonnets and shawls or overdresses for outerwear. Black stockings and black, laced shoes are worn when going away from the home. Purple is a favorite dress color among Amish women in Lancaster County, although other shades of blue are also common (Scott, 1986).

Smallness of scale is typified by life being organized on a human scale, rather than on an organization scale.

Face-to-face interactions make up the basis for social life, and clothing symbolizes a sense of unity and local culture (as contrasted to mass media culture in the larger society). There is a preference for traditional and shared knowledge, for example, as related to agriculture, construction and crafts, needlework, and quilting. Critical thought has little place in Amish life.

Finally, there is a strain toward self-sufficiency—a preference for what is natural and for living off the soil. For this reason, the Amish prefer to go barefoot around the home during warm weather months. Based on a fairly strict division of labor based on gender, women display self-sufficiency in such activities as cooking, sewing clothes for family members, and pursuing crafts activities such as needlework or quilting (Hostetler, 1980). Although needlework is an outlet for aesthetic and creative expression, it is justified on the basis of the resulting objects' utility in the home.

Thus the use value of objects is valued and emphasized. In contrast, ornaments and finery are considered to be contrary to biblical principle. Popular clothing styles are viewed as worldly and contrary to God's will. Fashion change, in general, is regarded as promoting a system of exchange and profit, rather than extolling the virtues of how objects are used.

> They feel the world is controlled largely by Satan and the forces of evil. And so, they reason, conformity to the fads and fashions of popular society indicates identity with the world's system. . . . Economically, they judge the fashion industry to be a deceitful, greedy force. Keeping up with the latest styles is seen as wasteful, planned obsolescence (Scott, 1986, p. 6).

A major part of the usefulness of dress is identifying the community of believers. The sense of fellowship engendered by this symbolism was characterized by one Old Order Amish man in the following way:

> Seeing a fellow plain person when far from home is like hearing your own language spoken while traveling in a foreign land. There is an immediate bond of fellowship even though the person might be a total stranger (Scott, 1986, p. 6).

Since the 1950s, however, the Amish have had increasing contact with the outside world, especially through

# Social Focus 12-1 *(continued)*

contacts with tourists who are fascinated with the sub-culture. Thus, the exchange value of traditional Amish objects such as quilts has become a factor in their creation. Modifications in quilt designs have resulted from these exchanges, to satisfy tourist demands. (This topic will be discussed in Chapter Sixteen; Figure 16-14 provides an example of an Amish quilt produced for tourists.) Consequently, quilts in the more traditional patterns, predating 1940, are highly valued by collectors for their design and workmanship. More recent quilts may be distinguished on the basis of whether they were designed for sale versus for home use. Traditional designs are used exclusively in Amish homes (Boynton, 1986a).

Similarly, a study of Amish consumer behavior patterns indicates that the Amish interact with the outside world, but are still able to maintain traditional lifestyles—with a preference for occupations that require working with their hands (Wilkens and Hsu, 1987). Forty-eight percent of the Amish men in this study were farmers, whereas 26 percent pursued farming as a secondary occupation. Other Amish men were carpenters, shed or cabinet makers, furniture refinishers, blacksmiths, and the like. The Amish tend to avoid frequent shopping trips, as time is considered to be precious. A single shopping trip every week or two or three is considered to be sufficient. Amish wives tend to dominate decision making in terms of grocery and clothing purchases, whereas the decisions are shared with the spouse in relation to furniture, shelter, or reading materials (Wilkens and Hsu, 1987).

Thus the Amish are not immune to the social and cultural forces of the larger American society. Still, they are able to maintain a sense of *Gemeinschaft* through a community structure rich in symbolism and meaning.

---

*TABLE 12-1*
Gemeinschaft *versus* Gesellschaft

| Gemeinschaft | Gesellschaft |
|---|---|
| **Organizational Structure** | |
| Small scale (sense of community) | Large scale (society) |
| Values manual labor | Values mechanized labor |
| Free will guides interactions | Rational will guides interactions |
| Personal and emotional associations (face to face) | Abstract and categorical associations (organizations) |
| **Culture and Clothing and Appearance** | |
| Tradition-oriented | Change-oriented |
| Folk costume | Fashion change |
| Use value is stressed | Exchange value is stressed |
| Handcrafted items as valued possessions and expressions of culture | Consumer culture stressing "use up" rather than "use" |
| Symbolism relatively explicit and elaborate | Symbolism relatively ambiguous and complex and diffuse |
| Richly developed and shared symbols | Symbolic meaning always in dispute because of societal tensions |
| Strongly patterned meanings (homogeneity) | Diverse and ambiguous meanings (heterogeneity) |
| Conformity for the sake of continuity and community | Conformity for the sake of commodity aesthetics and search for collective identity |

Ethnographic studies support the idea that villagers who migrate to the city and begin to wear urban clothes return to village (folk) costume when they return to the village so as to avoid standing out from the more *Gemeinschaft*-like community (Bogatyrev, 1976). Also, the function of attire may vary between village and urban contexts, even though the styles may merge and thus appear similar or identical.

> For example, in Russian villages during the prewar period galoshes were very much in style, but villagers, primarily young people, did not wear them in bad and muddy weather but on sunny holidays only. In the city the dominant function of galoshes was to protect the feet from moisture and mud; in the village, however, the dominant function was aesthetic. For example, there is a song that goes as follows: "All lads look fine in galoshes but my sweetheart, even without galoshes, is neat and handsome all the time" (Bogatyrev, 1976).

Bogatyrev (1976) notes that an ethnographer who examines the function of village versus urban costume must pay attention to distinctions of this sort. Such distinctions may reflect, in part, the shift in structure of feeling between *Gemeinschaft* and *Gesellschaft*.

In some societies, modernization has been more or less induced by intercultural contact or governmental intervention. Traditional aspects of culture tend to be deemphasized in these cases, as they may not be congruent with the current emphasis on productivity and newness. This modernization is often, but not always, symbolized through the abandonment of traditional folk costumes for mass-produced clothing. In Muslim cultures, it has frequently been the males who have adopted the appearance styles of Western businessmen, whereas females have at least initially maintained their traditional modes of dress. Just as American females became responsible in the urban-industrial historical context for maintaining morality in the home, Muslim women have had the charge of concealing themselves in public for the sake of sexual morality (Mernissi, 1987). (See Figure 12-7.)

A shift between *Gemeinschaft* and *Gesellschaft* aesthetic codes may be analyzed by looking at traditional, handcrafted textiles and apparel that were once hand-crafted for their use value for one's own family or friends, but are now produced as commodities, for their exchange value (see Social Focus 12-1 for a discussion of this in relation to Amish quilts). Industrialization, which is often equated with *Gesellschaft*, leads to mass production of apparel and, at least initially, to simpler structures. Handcrafted touches are more difficult to provide because of rising labor costs. The artistic value of clothing diminishes in terms of how it was defined in the context of *Gemeinschaft*. Manufacturers realize that by eliminating design features such as hand embroidery and replacing them with mechanized techniques, it is possible to reduce labor costs and speed up the production process. The result is a lack of uniqueness such as that found in slightly imperfect, one-of-a-kind works done by hand, in which no two motifs are exact duplicates.

As more traditional styles are replaced by styles dictated by fashion, which changes at a relatively rapid pace, there is a concomitant shift in, or loss of, the

**FIGURE 12-7**
*The meaning of the veil* (chadora) *worn by Muslim women in Iranian society is multidimensional. After the revolution, social-political overtones and maintenance of sexual morality became prominent themes in the* chadora's *symbolism, as women wearing Western dress were regarded as "loose" and less sympathetic to the revolutionary cause. Photo by Tommy Wiberg/ Photoreporters.*

elaborate symbolism of clothing (Roach and Eicher, 1973, p. 183). Much of this change is based on industry's profit motivation and the realization that planned obsolescence of styles can lead to the sale of new and different styles. At the same time, the social structure is conducive to fashion change, which can symbolize and anchor the rapid social change that individuals seem to be feeling in their lives (Blumer, 1969b).

With rapid changes in style, there is not enough time for new, elaborate systems of meaning to develop across an entire, large-scale society. Rather, meaning tends to be constructed in smaller social groups, organizations, or subcultures. At the same time, some cultural stereotypes seem to linger (for example, gender stereotypes tend to die hard).

In the emerging *Gesellschaft* societies in Great Britain and the United States in the nineteenth century, the increasing emphasis on exchange value and the doctrine of utilitarianism pervaded social thought and influenced emerging clothing styles of males, in particular (Wilson, 1985). This doctrine of utilitarianism is consistent with the concept of rational will. The separation between public and private (domestic) spheres emerged along with urbanization and industrialization, as males left the home or farm to work in factories or in other entrepreneurial enterprises, whereas females mainly stayed at home and performed domestic and childrearing functions. A work ethic and striving for success and modernity characterized capitalistic growth. For males, these values were applied to business ventures or other industrial concerns. Females, on the other hand, were increasingly evaluated, by self and others, in terms of interpersonal attraction (finding a husband), followed by their homes and children (Banner, 1983). Male attire, accordingly, was utilitarian and rational in appearance. Black suits were worn in the nineteenth century and set the stage for the modern business suit. A "dress for success" philosophy that stresses seriousness and competence may be consistent with the *Gesellschaft* structure of feeling, as evident primarily in men's attire from the nineteenth century to the present.

Systems of exchange are likely to be more complex in a *Gesellschaft* context, and there is a greater awareness of the benefits or possible gains derived from certain actions. Money becomes increasingly important, as does an ethic of progress and modernity. People tend to move to urban settings and may not get to know one another well enough to have a sense of community. Thus, more emphasis is placed on material wealth and less is placed upon face-to-face interactions with others in society. Tönnies (1940) believed that *Gesellschaft* characteristics were typical of a cynical philosophy, and thus related to maturity and education. Yet his ideas have been qualified by other writers who point out that it is an oversimplification to characterize *Gesellschaft*-like city life as alienating and totally impersonal. Autonomous interactions in cities do not necessarily reflect a lack of meaning or order (Lofland, 1973; Karp, Stone, and Yoels, 1977). Strangers confront one another with a strong sense of the present, rather than the past (and corresponding traditions). There is a degree of risk in the role of city stranger, but there also are special opportunities for broader interactions. If persons feel they can handle city street life with competence and savvy, a heightened sense of personal control may be experienced. Thus impersonal contexts may become more comprehensible and meaningful (Reitzes, 1986). In the realm of appearance and fashion, the role of city stranger may provide some exciting opportunities for experimentation, because of diminished social control and increased visual stimulation that parallels the vast array of people-images. Individuals not only may make identifications *of* one another (placing one another in social categories), but also may identify *with* the urban context, in the form of "the infusion of self into place" (Reitzes, 1986, p. 170). Although identification *of* is largely a cognitive exercise, identification *with* includes evaluative and emotional attachments. Images of downtown as a crowded, busy place are not necessarily evaluated negatively (Reitzes, 1986). Face-to-face encounters with strangers seldom result in close, personal relationships, but in the visual realm of appearance communication, these encounters may be meaningful to the extent that they stimulate the imagination and promote attachment to a sense of (urban) place.

## Summary

The concepts of *Gemeinschaft* and *Gesellschaft* are useful for characterizing the shifts in structures of feeling that parallel the rise of urbanization, capitalism, and industrialization. These processes tend to promote fashion change. Yet we have seen from our historical overview that fashion change is a complex phe-nomenon, influenced by a variety of factors that converge in specific cultural contexts. Thus it is important *not* to use these constructs to attempt to classify all societies in one way or another. Many societies today still contain elements of both. For example, in some rural areas of countries such as France one may find a *Gemeinschaft*-like spirit abiding in communities with a strong sense of locality and tradition. Cities and communities across the United States hold farmers' markets and other related events or traditions. These can foster a sense of *Gemeinschaft* by promoting face-to-face interactions between the producer and consumer of goods, as well as a sense of community (see Figure 12-8). Other societies display a complex mixture of industrial and preindustrial methods (see Figure 12-9). The constructs of *Gemeinschaft* and *Gesellschaft* do enable us to characterize different orientations in human will and in the value of products, but they should not be used to obscure the complexities that are inherent in all aspects of human life (Lofland, 1988).

## Postindustrial Society and Postmodern Culture

To return to Baudrillard's (1983) historical framework, the third era (following the classical and industrial eras) is postindustrial. The societies that were among

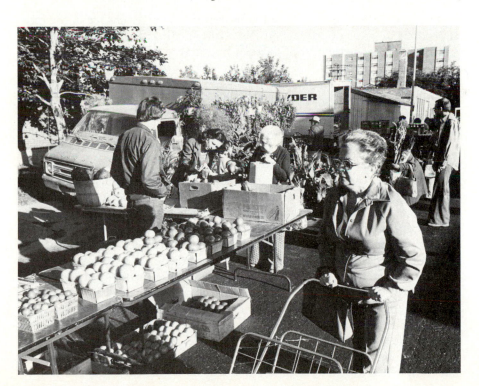

**FIGURE 12-8**
*A sense of Gemeinschaft can be constructed in the form of community gatherings such as this farmer's market in Evanston, Illinois. Photo by Robert Sommer.*

**FIGURE 12-9**
*Note the complex mixture of "preindustrial" and "postindustrial" signs in this picture. In this setting in Nepal, traditional and Western clothing coexist. Photo by Stephen Cunha.*

the first to develop textile and fashion industries no longer engage in the most labor-intensive areas of production (for example, the sewing of apparel pieces together). These postindustrial societies find it very difficult to compete with societies whose labor costs are much lower. Thus, many postindustrial societies "farm out" the more labor-intensive aspects of production that they can no longer afford to countries where the labor costs are not as high. Imported apparel products become a real threat to the domestic industry, as developing countries with lower labor costs become very competitive.

In postindustrial societies, there are increasing attempts to automate because of the expense of labor costs. At the same time, there is a backlash against the consistent theme of commercialization, and consumers may have a renewed respect for handcrafted items, which manufacturers try to simulate mechanically.

The concept of "mass" society emerged to characterize postindustrial societies and describe how media and other widespread mass influences diffuse individuals' abilities to construct a sense of self. However, appearance management also provides the means for "fashioning" or reconstructing a sense of self. Some theorists contend that mass society is something of a myth—that individuals still need to construct their own realities and may actually need to work harder at it in a postindustrial society (Bell, 1956). Futurists have identified ways in which postindustrial societies become increasingly "demassified." Similarly, some predict that apparel production in postindustrial societies will someday be accomplished by consumers themselves—through the use of personal computers and computer-activated laser cutters that cut out a garment to consumer specifications. Thus, customized apparel could become available on a high-technological basis (Toffler, 1980).

Social and intellectual thought about postindustrial society has also revolved around the emergence of **postmodern culture**. Postindustrial is to society as postmodern is to culture. What is happening in postmodern culture? Postmodernism has been described as a "transforming shift in (culture's) 'structure of feeling'" (Fuller, 1983), a "general sensibility" (Gitlin, 1989), and a "new cultural logic in its own right" (Jameson, in Stephanson, 1987). In art as well as in fashion, music, literature, and other aspects of popular culture, there is a common structure of feeling. In a store window of Barney's in New York, "fashion meets art." One window depicts a mannequin wearing an outfit designed by Claude Montana, in front of a takeoff on an Ed Ruscha painting that is block lettered: "she was born in Montana." Clothes designed by Jean Paul Gaultier, which are postmodern in and of themselves, are shown behind a wall of Brillo boxes, which resembles a design by Andy Warhol (Hochswender, 1988). What does this all mean? Some writers contend that we are "hip deep in postmodernism" (Gitlin, 1988). Postmodernism in the arts seems to correspond with postmodernism in everyday life. In postmodern fashion, many different styles can coexist peacefully; eclecticism is the order of the day. In postmodern life in general, a similar ethos can be uncovered:

> Eclecticism is the degree zero of contemporary general culture: one listens to reggae, watches a western, eats McDonald's food for lunch and local cuisine for dinner, wears Paris perfume in Tokyo and "retro" clothes in Hong Kong; knowledge is a matter for TV games. It is easy to find a public for eclectic worlds (Lyotard, 1988, p. 76).

Sociologist Todd Gitlin (1989) notes postmodernism "is more than a buzzword or even an esthetic; it is a way of seeing, a view of the human spirit and an attitude toward political as well as cultural possibilities. . . . In style, more than style is at stake"(p. 52). To understand what postmodernism is as an aesthetic movement, however, it is helpful to look at two earlier movements to which it responds: realism and modernism (Gitlin, 1988). Realism was an important movement of nineteenth-century art; the goal was to mirror reality and to display unity and continuity. High culture was viewed as more "valuable" than popular culture as part of this aesthetic, and when individuals were portrayed in art, their place in society and history was clearly indicated.

In contrast, modernism emerged in the early part of the twentieth century and spoke with many voices, perspectives, and materials. Fragments were juxtaposed to create works—to remake life. In the process, continuity was disrupted, and the individual subject in art became dislocated. High culture quoted popular culture. Perhaps in fashion, the "flapper" style of the 1920s epitomizes the modernist movement (See Figure 12-10).

Then along came postmodernism, which seems to be "indifferent to consistency and continuity altogether" (Gitlin, 1988, p. 35).

## *EVENING DRESSES c. 1927-29*

Long earrings

Low 'V' shaped neckline edged with sequins

Low square neckline

Wide shoulder straps cut in one with bodice

Low waistline emphasized by heavy sequined design

Inset squares of shiny satin squaring to a point low on hip

Scalloped hemline dipping to back

Hemline curving at C/F and in handkerchief points from sides to back

Dress of fine tulle covered with gold sequins, over-pattern of silver sequins, c. 1927

Silver kid shoes with round jet buckles

Black lace dress with flesh-coloured silk underdress, uneven hemline, c. 1928-29

**FIGURE 12-10**
*Modernist fashion of the 1920s parallelled modernist art.*

It self-consciously splices genres, attitudes, styles. It relishes the blurring or juxtaposition of forms (fiction–nonfiction), stances (straight–ironic), moods (violent–comic), cultural levels (high–low). It disdains originality and fancies copies, repetition, the recombination of hand-me-down scraps. It neither embraces nor criticizes, but beholds the world blankly, with a knowingness that dissolves feeling and commitment into irony. It pulls the rug out from under itself, displaying an acute self-consciousness about the world's constructed nature. It takes pleasure in the play of surfaces and derides the search for depth as mere nostalgia (Gitlin, 1989, p. 52.)

Let's look at some examples of postmodernism in a variety of cultural media. These might include Andy Warhol's multiple-image paintings and photorealism, Disneyland, Las Vegas, suburban strips, shopping malls, the movie *Star Wars*, David Byrne, "Max Headroom," MTV, "Miami Vice," and news/talk shows providing us with a "backstage" look at the image-making of political candidates and celebrities (Gitlin, 1988). Also included under the postmodernist umbrella would be music videos, video games depicting sports and other kinds of strategic games, a Barbie video game that revolves around a fashion show, Barbie or Jem dolls with their friends on a "rocker stage" (representing female rockers in cartoons and/or music videos; see Figure 12-11), the Barbie doll game or news shows (simulating television; see Figure 12-12), and Epcot center (the Disney center in Florida that has a strong global or international theme; one can visit a number of "countries" in a matter of hours). In other words, what we have in postmodern culture are numerous "representations of representations"; in the process of all of these representations, many theorists contend, our picture of reality is altered.

To place postmodernism in a cultural and historical context, we can consider some of the theories that have emerged to explain it. Theorist Fredric Jameson

*FIGURE 12-11*
*Barbie dolls can be used to simulate (represent) almost anything in the postmodern cultural context, depending on how they are staged. The point is that the staging becomes an end in and of itself. It took about two hours to put this stage together, dress the dolls, and situate them with their instruments. What happens now? Photo by Susan B. Kaiser.*

**FIGURE 12-12**
*Barbie dolls are joined by Ken to participate in a staged game show. In the postmodern cultural context, representations become simulations of something (a game show) that is itself a simulation. Photo by Joan L. Chandler.*

(1983) characterizes postmodernism as an ideology that expresses the global-economic nature of capitalism; he describes postmodernism as a "global shopping center," similar to an eclectic blend of cross-cultural commodities (Jameson, in Stephanson, 1987). (The social-psychological implications of the global economy will be considered in greater detail in Chapter Sixteen.) Postmodernism has also been linked to (1) advances in the physical sciences (quantum theory and microphysics) that have undermined a sense of certainty and continuity and (2) the impact of television on social thinking. Yet these explanations do not necessarily reveal why some of the postmodernist aesthetic trends have only recently surfaced, because some of the developments to which they refer have been in the process of developing for a number of years (Gitlin, 1989). Gitlin (1989) notes that postmodernism probably represents a convergence of several forces and contends that it is no accident, perhaps, that postmodernism seems to have been born in the United States. American culture has had an eclectic logic for a number of years. Juxtaposition has been characteristic of its "polyethnic culture (less a melting pot than a grab bag)." Gitlin (1989) notes that over 150 years ago, Alexis de Tocqueville characterized the United States as a "marketplace jamboree"—as a variety show with a laissez-faire philosophy (where anything goes). To the extent that postmodernism can be described as having American cultural roots, the historical context of post-1960s in the United States has also contributed to this cultural phenomenon. Post-1960s culture can be described as post-Vietnam, post-New Left, posthippie, post-Watergate: "History was ruptured, passions have been expended, belief has become difficult; heroes have died and been replaced by celebrities" (Gitlin, 1989, p. 58). Some cultural sentiments (for example, the Vietnam War and the assassinations of leaders), Gitlin contends, had been repressed because they have been too painful. Thus, a kind of numb I've-seen-it-all postmodernist attitude resulted.

Gitlin (1989) identifies these postmodernist currents as being especially concentrated among individuals born in the 1950s and 1960s (the post-World-War II "baby boomers"): "To grow up post-1960s is an experience of aftermath, privatization, weightlessness; everything has apparently already been done" (Gitlin, 1989, p. 58). Hence, culture engages in a "process of recycling; everything is juxtaposable to everything else because nothing matters" (Gitlin, 1989, p. 58). So, postmodernism's seemingly cavalier attitude about history is paradoxical because postmodernism "turns out to be all too embedded in (guess what) history" (Gitlin, 1988, p. 36). Nevertheless, an attitude lacking in a historical consciousness of the past characterizes postmodernism, despite the recycling of historical signs (which are stripped from their historic contexts). In an interview, Jameson noted, "Objects fall into the world and become decoration again; visual depth and systems of interpretation fade away; and something peculiar happens to historical time" (Jameson, in Stephanson, 1987, p. 30).

Postmodern recycling of signs may be based in part on mixed emotions about modern life, incorporating some feelings of nostalgia for the past, but not really wanting to give up the conveniences of modern life. For example, tie-dyed T-shirts, reminiscent of the late 1960s, reemerged in the late 1980s along with other signs of nostalgia and unresolved emotions from that previous era (peace symbols, rock musical groups, the Beatles, and movies about the Vietnam War). In the late 1960s tie-dyed T-shirts were valued because people could produce these styles themselves, in response to or rejection of mass-produced commodities and the "establishment." In contrast, young people wearing tie-dyed T-shirts in the 1980s were unlikely to relate to that base of reference underlying the historic context of the 1960s; the *look* was what was sought. The styles were stripped from their previous context, became signifiers without a historic referent, and were worn in new appearance contexts that characterize postmodern aesthetics (combining the old and the new).

Some critics contend that what is occurring in aesthetic life today may be regarded as a means of recuperating from the effects of industrial capitalism (Fuller, 1983; Wilson, 1985). In the process of industrialization and a philosophy of utilitarianism, the aesthetic dimensions of everyday life were devalued. Some postmodernist theorists regard postmodernism as indicative of a "closer, purer version of capitalism" than was evident during industrialization (Jameson, in Stephanson, 1987, p. 38). At any rate, aesthetic eclecticism may be democratic in some respects, but that does not mean we can glamorize all fashion as populist (Jameson, in Stephanson, 1987, p. 37). Rather,

> Fashion is a branch of aesthetics, of the art of modern society. It is also a mass pastime, a form of group entertainment, of popular culture. Related as it is to both fine art and popular art, it is a kind of performance art (Wilson, 1985, p. 60).

"Late capitalist" (postindustrial) society may also be characterized in terms of the link between signification and the marketplace. Baudrillard (1981) theorizes that in a capitalist economic context, within the sign, the signifier becomes increasingly more important or inflated as compared with the signified (the idea it is supposed to represent). Similarly, exchange value supersedes use value. Thus signifiers ( for example, images, clothes, and hairstyles) and exchange value develop a dynamic interplay as governed by codes (Baudrillard, 1981, p. 146). (See Social Focus 12-2 for a discussion of the children's apparel market in relation to the postmodern cultural context.)

A study of advertisements in popular United States magazines between 1900 and 1980 revealed little evidence of a progressively more luxurious and comfortable lifestyle. Instead, advertising is now especially likely to portray consumption as *an end in itself* rather than as a means to consumer well-being. Also, advertising appeals to luxury and pleasure increased in frequency, whereas practical and functional appeals declined (Belk and Pollay, 1985). These findings are consistent with Baudrillard's (1981, 1983) ideas about fashion, simulation, and exchange value.

Thus, postmodern culture may be characterized as a structure of feeling involving aesthetic trends (art, architecture, music, and fashion) and social thought. It involves the convergence of old (traditional) and new (modern) elements and codes, inevitably producing a recycling of signs from previous historic contexts. Postmodern culture, however, frames the signs in a context that has little to do with the past, that juxtaposes elements in an eclectic manner, and that places increasing emphasis on the *signifier* portion of the sign (as discussed in Chapter Seven).

In fact, Baudrillard (1983) characterizes the postmodern context as one of *simulation*. Signs are not as much produced as they are *reproduced*. Baudrillard (1975) contends that along with an emphasis on exchange value in its most extreme forms, we use commodities to organize our daily existences. Culture does not dictate the meanings of new clothing styles, and consumption becomes a kind of process of labor. Consumers need to work at supplying and constructing meaning to make sense of social life. The potential for mixing, matching, and juxtaposing appearance signs to create totally new looks is tremendous in post-modern cultural contexts. Resulting looks are ambiguous in meaning, and consumers need to work actively to construct meaning through their social interactions (Kaiser, Nagasawa, and Hutton, 1989). An increasing amount of communication relative to appearance and fashion is visual, as individuals inspire one another by their looks on the street, particularly in large cities. Looks are represented for the sake of representation and do not necessarily refer to specific cultural ideologies in a way that can be verbalized. Punk aesthetics and music video imagery are good examples of postmodern culture that involves complex combinations of elements for the sake of visual impact. The heterogeneity of appearances in city life and mass media may be at once visually stimulating and conducive to a sense of ambivalence about modernity and a corresponding uneasiness and tension about social identities. Baudrillard (1976) describes modernity as something

# The Children's Apparel Market

In the 1980s, children's clothing lines became increasingly fashion- and image-conscious. A well-dressed child seemed to become the ultimate status symbol. This tendency is consistent with the postmodern cultural context, in which increasing emphasis is placed on display and simulation. In a sense, a child's appearance can become a simulation of fashionability. That the clothes will be quickly outgrown necessitates continual replacement and benefits a marketplace emphasizing exchange value over use value.

Part of the trend toward increasing fashion-consciousness in children's wear may be attributed to post-World War II baby boomers becoming parents and creating a new baby "boomlet" (Henry, 1986). From 1980 through 1985, the rising birthrate marked the first major population increase since 1970. The children's wear industry became particularly enamored with older, more educated, and affluent parents (Feibus, 1986). The children's wear market stabilized by the late 1980s, but one additional contributing factor to the profitability of this market has been the relatively high percentage of first births out of total births (about 40 percent in 1985). The arrival of a first child tends to stimulate more purchasing activities than subsequent births. Furthermore, women are having children later, during high earning years, and having smaller families so that more money is available per family member (Infants Still Growing, 1985).

The children's wear market has become increasingly competitive and diverse. Retailers have been particularly aware of the importance of the infant business as a foundation of the children's wear department, because this area makes initial impressions on new parents and has a very viable gift component to it. Many children's wear manufacturers count on the grandparent business at key times, such as the holiday season, and "inject an extra dose of frilliness" in girls' clothing at that time of year (McLean, 1986). Rucker, Boynton, and Park (1986) conducted a study of purchases of children's items around the Christmas season. They found that the younger the shopper, the more likely the purchase was to be a nongift. Gift items tended to be fancier or more embellished than nongift items, although price of the item was not a significant predictor of gift versus nongift items. Male adults tended to show more of a tendency to purchase high-price gift items than did female adults, and the probability of purchasing a high-priced gift increased with age. Twenty-two percent of the shoppers were over 50 years of age, and 89 percent of the sample were female (Rucker, Kim, and Ho, 1987). The males were more likely to purchase toys, furnishings, or equipment, whereas females purchased more of the clothing. Men were especially unlikely to purchase nongift, day-to-day clothing items for children (Rucker, Boynton, and Park, 1986).

The children's apparel marketplace represents an amalgamation of cultural symbols adults may select for purposes of displaying children's sex, socioeconomic status, and parental taste. It is important when looking at this market to take into account the degree of its diversity, as well as the distinctions between gift versus nongift purchases, male adult versus female adult purchasers, and parents versus grandparents or other consumers. More stores are striving to appeal to the children themselves, especially as the baby boomlet has begun to experience a decline and the children are increasingly self-reliant in their purchase and use of products in the marketplace. Numerous apparel companies have developed children's lines as counterparts to their junior and women's lines—hence The Gap spawns GapKids, Esprit begats Esprit Kids, Benetton creates Benetton 012, and so on (Gill, 1989).

of a myth in the postindustrial context. He believes that we are simulating continuous change through commodities but are not "progressing" in a linear, straightforward manner to the extent that we were during periods of industrialization (Baudrillard, 1983).

In summary, postmodern culture may be linked to a variety of cultural messages and individual emotions about modern life. Before we can fully understand why people may feel ambivalent, it is necessary to look at some of the other aspects of culture that promote these kinds of emotions. The next chapter will address the cultural categories of gender, physical appearance, age, social class, and ethnicity and examine their impact on social hierarchies and interactions. Then, in Part Five, we will examine how tensions related to these categories provide a continual source of design inspiration, as fashion plays with cultural codes.

## *Suggested Readings*

Balkwell, C. 1986. On peacocks and peahens: A cross-cultural investigation of the effects of economic development on sex differences in dress. *Clothing and Textiles Research Journal 4*(2): 30–36.
> Balkwell presents a study of 161 preindustrial cultures and addresses whether men dressed as elaborately as women. She found that economic activities associated with agrarian societies were linked with more ornate females, whereas men tended to be more than or equally ornate as females in folk societies with less advanced economic activities.

Baudrillard, J. 1983. *Simulations*. Trans. by P. Foss, P. Patton, and P. Beitchman. New York: Semiotext(e).
> Baudrillard provides a framework for understanding historical eras in relation to fashion and meaning.

Gitlin, T. 1989. Postmodernism defined, at last! *Utne Reader*, July/Aug., 52–61.
> Gitlin provides a very useful description and analysis of postmodernism, including a number of examples of the postmodern impulse in contemporary life.

Roach, M. E., and Eicher, J. B. 1973. *The visible self: Perspectives on dress*. Englewood Cliffs: Prentice-Hall.
> This book focuses on sociocultural dimensions of dress and includes a discussion of societal differences and their implications for clothing. Four types of societies are characterized: folk, agrarian, urban-industrial, and mass.

Scott, S. 1986. *Why do they dress that way?* Intercourse, PA: Good Books.
> Scott examines dress symbolism among Amish and Mennonite religious groups. This book provides a number of rich examples of social thinking that parallels the concept of *Gemeinschaft*.

Steele, V. 1988. *Paris fashion: A cultural history*. New York: Oxford University Press.
> Steele traces the cultural and historical development of fashion in Paris. Also included is a discussion of the initial emergence of fashion in fourteenth-century Italy and fashion as interconnected with city life and social class.

# Chapter Thirteen
### ...
# Cultural Categories, Appearance, and Social Stratification

> Considered as a whole, the system of American clothing amounts to a
> very complex scheme of cultural categories and the relations between
> them, a veritable map—it does not exaggerate to say—of the cultural
> universe.
>
> —SAHLINS, 1976, p. 179

> Clothing reveals both the themes and the formal relationships which
> serve a culture as orienting ideas and the real or imagined basis
> according to which cultural categories are organized. . . . The principles
> of a world are found woven into the fabric of its clothing.
>
> —McCRACKEN, 1988, p. 60

*Culture is an abstract concept that becomes more concrete when we look at
its implications for groups of individuals. Culture may be organized
conceptually in terms of cultural categories and cultural principles. In this
chapter, we will consider the cultural principle of social stratification (system
of social and economic inequity) in relation to cultural categories composed
of classifications of people. Specifically, we will focus on gender, physical
attractiveness, age, social class, and ethnicity as cultural-categorical
constructs. Particularly in societies in which first-impression encounters are
critical due to higher numbers of short-term interactions that affect one's
personal and professional life, these cultural categories as reflected through
appearances influence how people respond to one another. Cultural
categories also may account for differences in media and advertising
imagery, as well as consumer behavior toward dress.*

Culture tends to provide individuals with frameworks for understanding themselves
and their relationships with others. One common tendency is for culture to
divide the world as we know it into categories or manageable segments. Although
time, space, and nature may be divided into smaller components by virtue of
culture, our attention in this chapter will focus on *cultural categories* relative to
the human community, that is, how people are distinguished, classified, and
socialized on the basis of differences that are culturally relevant. A culture's
material objects make these categories more concrete and lend expression to
them (McCracken, 1988, p. 73). The *meanings* of these categories may not be
easily verbalized, but through appearance codes people can construct some
interpretations of them. Clothes help to establish the "basic coordinates into

which a world has been divided by culture" (McCracken, 1988). Let's look at some examples of how clothes and appearance styles are used in this way. The culture of a high school may be based in part on some distinctions in social groups that may have labels (jocks, punks, and stoners). In this chapter, we will consider the fundamental categories of gender, physical attractiveness, age, social class, and ethnicity. Most cultures make distinctions among individuals on the basis of these categories, and because these distinctions often lead to unequal access to prestige, privileges, or power, we will consider these cultural categories as they relate to the concept of **social stratification**, or socioeconomic inequality. In this way, cultural categories are intertwined with social structure and organization. Essentially, cultural categories pertain to the structure of feeling, as well as the values, beliefs, and artifacts associated with the various structural components of a society. Social stratification linked to cultural categories has a daily impact on the lives of people. This impact is entwined in a complex nexus of physical appearance, clothing, and fashion change. Thus appearance management and appearance perception are essentially linked to cultural categories.

Appearance management is a process of identity expression, and identity, in turn, is influenced by a convergence of cultural categories. We fall not only into one category but into many, as discussed in Chapter Five in relation to the concept of social location. In some social contexts, we may wish to emphasize one identity more than another, and appearance management may allow for this type of expression. Moreover, we may resist *appearing* to fall into some cultural categories that carry less social honor in our society. For example, the media emphasize in American culture that women should fight the visible signs of aging by dyeing their hair to conceal the gray and by using special creams to prevent or remove wrinkles. The cultural category of old age, these advertisements promise, may be denied through the use of appearance-managing products. Part of the complexity in assessing cultural categories from the perspective of appearance management stems from the somewhat blurry boundaries between some categories (for example, young versus old age). We can use appearance management as a device to emphasize or deemphasize cultural categories.

Appearance perception is similarly affected by the complex convergence of visually perceived cultural categories. From a contextual perspective, we would want to consider how cultural categories influence our own thought processes, or our own *cognitive categories*. What do we expect from others on the basis of the categories that culture provides? What images do we associate with these cultural categories and their manner of convergence? For example, what mental picture is conjured by the description "attractive, older, upper-class white male" as compared with that of "attractive, young, upper-middle-class, black male"? When do we focus on one category more than another, that is, how important is age as compared to social class, or gender as compared to ethnicity? These are all questions that a contextual perspective would lead us to address by considering how cultural ideology affects our judgments of one another, and by addressing the influence of social context on these judgments. Additionally, this approach allows us to consider how cultural categories influence social cognition, as well as how thought processes may be altered by symbolic interaction. Boundaries between cultural categories may be either intentionally blurred or delineated on the basis of appearance management, and then appearance perception is influenced by the degree of clarity versus ambiguity in cultural and cognitive categories. For example, the message in the advertisement featured in Figure 13-1 is ambiguous and invites the consumer to draw his or her own conclusions about its meanings. How would you interpret the advertisement's message about gender relations, for example? How might the cultural category of gender be defined, or what are its implications for the use of hair products? What is the relationship between the male and the female depicted? There are probably numerous interpretations and scenarios that could be developed on the basis of this advertisement, many of which pertain to the boundaries and relations between the cultural category of gender.

There is a lot of room for negotiation and social construction, especially in complex societies. On the one hand, our judgments in these societies are simplified by short-cut thought processes, because we have a greater need to derive some semblance of order out of a confusing array of images. On the other hand, that confusing array of images, as well as the symbolic ambiguity that may be presented in a single appearance context, promotes the need for us to *rethink* the relevance of our cognitive categories in the midst of social change (see Figure 13-2).

## Cultural Principles and Social Stratification

Cultural categories are governed by *cultural principles*. These principles refer to the *ideology* (ideas or values) behind the categories (McCracken, 1988). Why, for example, do males and females dress differently? Why are some appearance styles associated more with one social class or ethnic group than another? Cultural principles are the organizing ideas and rationales behind cultural categories. Hence, cultural principles are linked to the *nature*—the how and why—of the differences between cultural categories. We can also tie cultural principles to aesthetics. For example, a principle of looking natural was representative of the hippie cultural category (McCracken, 1988).

Grant McCracken (1988) contends that clothing is a particularly valuable source of evidence as we attempt to study cultural principles. Although cultural categories can be linked to *linguistic* or verbal categories (for example, male versus female, young versus old, and physically attractive versus physically un-attractive), cultural principles are harder to verbalize (McCracken, 1988, p. 60). That is, people are not likely to want to talk about cultural principles such as social inequities, and/or these inequities are likely to be so ingrained in their modes of thinking because of socialization that they are hardly conscious of them.

Before proceeding with a discussion of social stratification as it pertains to cultural categories, it is important to distinguish among the elements of strat-

*Concepts*

**FIGURE 13-1**
*Advertisers often create a context of ambiguity in an ad, in part so that different consumers can read what they want to read into it. (In other words, there is a message for everyone.) How would you interpret the cultural meaning of gender on the basis of the images of the man and woman in this ad? Image by R. Madden, photo by W. Seng.*

ification: status, prestige, privilege, and power. **Status** involves a person's position in a social hierarchy. **Prestige** involves the evaluation applied by perceivers to a person's position in a status hierarchy. Such an evaluation may involve social recognition, respect, admiration, or deference if the observed person is considered to have a relatively high position on a status hierarchy. Prestige may be distinguished from status in that status is the position on a continuum of social honor, whereas prestige involves the evaluations made of a person based on others' perceptions of this position. Prestige may be viewed as an *estimation* of a person's worth. It may be an illusion, because it is largely a perception. However, whether a symbol rendering prestige is illusionary or real is not important; what is important

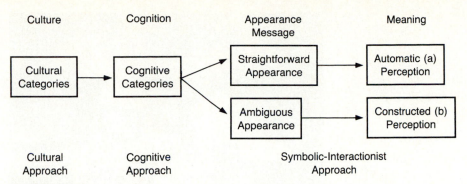

**FIGURE 13-2**
*Cultural categories, continuity and change: a contextual model. (a) Existing ideology thrives— leads to continuity in categories.(b) Need for social construction and potential change in category boundaries—may lead to restructured cognitive categories and eventually cultural categories (if sufficient numbers of people engage in these social-cognitive processes).*

is how a wearer and a perceiver assign meaning to a particular symbol. That is, status symbolism is socially interpreted and negotiated between wearers and perceivers. (See Figure 13-3.) Status characteristics such as dress tend to lead to differential expectations of wearers' behavior and identities, resulting in diverse levels of prestige (Greenstein and Knottnerus, 1980). In the absence of explicit cues relevant to a person's attributes, cues such as dress may be used to infer such attributes.

In order for status to be present, at least two persons must be involved: one to *claim* the status and one to *honor* it. A symbolic-interactionist perspective, with its emphasis on meaning, is helpful in considering the claiming and honoring of status. Although status is frequently thought of in economic terms, there are other forms of status that are influenced by a person's abilities. For example, a letter sweater may symbolize athletic ability in a high school and thus may be honored despite the relative lack of economic symbolism. This chapter will emphasize status and prestige as they relate to cultural categories, that is, perceivers' evaluations or meanings associated with cultural categories.

**Privilege** refers to the social distribution of goods, services, or other beneficial commodities, so that the individuals in a given social hierarchy receive those advantages and deprivations associated with their stratum. These components may be economic or social in nature. Those with the money—one reward of the social system—can afford symbols that are consistent with their social station (for example, a diamond necklace for a wealthy woman). Moreover, certain systems of stratification have symbols of privilege associated with the higher ranks (for example, the male business suit).

**Power** refers to the ability of individuals to exert their will on members of a lower stratum. Marks of honor tend to be indicative of power. The social dynamics of fashion may be related not only to class conflict but also to other

**FIGURE 13-3**
*The degree of status and prestige in an occupational context is negotiated, in part, by means of appearance management and perception. Gender is a factor in this negotiation, along with socioeconomic aspects. The female construction worker has painted flowers on her helmet to personalize it. Photo by Wendy Dildey.*

cultural categories in which power is ritualized. In the context of appearance symbolism, cultural categories become part of a ritual of power (Simon-Miller, 1985, p. 79).

When power is *legitimate*, or consistent with the rules of the organization or society, it constitutes a form of authority that is condoned by the social system. The use of clothing such as uniforms can legitimize and convey power (Bickman, 1974; Dean, Willis, and Hewitt, 1975). The distribution of power, like that of the other elements of stratification, has important consequences for social interactions. The exercise of power may be linked to signs of legitimacy, attractiveness, wealth, and many other appearance cues that are interpreted and negotiated in everyday life.

## Multiple-Hierarchical Model

We will now focus on cultural categories that can be characterized as being associated with *diffuse status characteristics*, that is, generalized ideas about people in a given category based on their position in a social hierarchy and indicated by social cues such as appearance. Diffuse status characteristics activate patterns of widely shared cultural beliefs (Webster and Driskell, 1983).

Status hierarchies may be based on a variety of characteristics associated with cultural categories, including signs of being male versus female or young versus old, skin color, or symbols of social class. A *multiple-hierarchical model* of stratification recognizes that hierarchies are interrelated in their consequences (Jeffries and Ransford, 1980). A multiple-hierarchical approach allows us to consider the degree of prestige associated with appearance images based on a convergence of cultural categories (see Figure 13-4).

Cultural categories based on systems of social stratification are likely to be ideological in nature. In other words, some individuals in some cultural categories have a vested interest in maintaining the status quo—keeping life as it is in terms of social hierarchies. Yet, the picture of cultural categories is not complete if we focus only on ideology (values and beliefs) as the basis for the development and maintenance of hierarchical boundaries. It is also important to consider the cultural images or messages that we may see on a daily basis in the media or everyday life. Processes of socialization and almost unconscious practices that contribute to social hierarchies should also be considered, including how individuals respond to one another in first-impressions situations. In this way, we can examine how cultural categories become transformed into cognitive categories, and, in turn, become linked to interpersonal encounters.

**FIGURE 13-4**
*Cultural categories of social class, age, ethnicity, and gender converge to render a certain degree of prestige to an individual or group of individuals. These are well-to-do school children in Chengdu, China. Photo by Stephen Cunha.*

As we look at each of the systems of cultural categories that may be characterized as diffuse status characteristics, it becomes evident that there is much overlap among the categories. For example, the process of aging is more problematic for a female than for a male in terms of status, because attractiveness is considered more important for females, and is perceived as diminishing with age more for females than for males. At times, one cultural category may assume more significance than another in accordance with social context. Also, it is important to remember that lifestyle variables (for example, values, attitudes, and how people spend their time and money) may be more important than the cultural category per se. Yet ideologically, we may still *think* about the categories as the basis for variations among people.

## Gender

> Every known society recognizes and elaborates some differences between the sexes, and although there are groups in which men wear skirts and women wear pants or trousers, it is everywhere the case that there are characteristic tasks, manners, and responsibilities primarily associated with women or with men.
>
> —ROSALDO, 1974, p. 18

Insofar as gender is socially constructed and culturally defined, it is a diffuse (and pervasive) status characteristic. Gender was discussed in greater detail in Chapter Three to illustrate the contextual perspective. Here, we will focus on cultural messages conveyed about gender and how individuals respond to one another on the basis of gender stereotypes. You will recall that although the term *sex* refers to biological differences among humans (male versus female), *gender* describes the social and cultural differences. What we perceive as masculine versus feminine, or how we think males should appear and act as compared to females, is ideological in nature and linked to the concept of gender.

Why do we construe gender as a basis for social stratification? Clearly, the privileges doled out by society fall into the hands of males more often than females. Males hold more power in government and private corporations. Females earn only $.60 to every $1.00 earned by males. Females have historically had a status of "second sex" or "other" as compared with males (DeBeauvoir, 1953). Whereas there may be, or have been, some egalitarian societies cross-culturally, anthropologists agree that there have never been societies in which women have publicly had power and authority outshining men (Rosaldo and Lamphere, 1974). That is, some degree of male dominance generally exists cross-culturally. This type of dominance is called *patriarchy*. More often than not, women have been viewed as "essentially uninteresting and irrelevant" and "in some way subordinate to men" (Rosaldo, 1974, p. 18). Everywhere, from the societies that may be considered egalitarian to those in which gender stratification is most marked, men have been the "locus of cultural value" (Rosaldo, 1974, p. 20).

With respect to appearance and clothing, then, a key issue in stratification pertains to the *meanings* associated with masculinity and femininity in a culture, as well as to the culturally coded differences that lead to inequities. What then are the inequities? Both males and females have had access to power with appearance management as a ticket to some advantages, but the nature of the gender paths varies. As discussed in Chapter Three, male power has traditionally been more direct and forceful—in the *agonic mode*, whereas the power that females have obtained may be characterized more often than not as more indirect or covert—in the *hedonic mode*. It is questionable whether hedonic power, which is based largely on personal appearance, is, in fact, an advantage to females as a whole.

> Beauty enhances the power of women even while diminishing it. As a primary source of social influence, appearance is paradoxically a major cause of female weakness. . . . Signals of power are confounded with signals of gender, creating a dominance hierarchy that rests on sex differences. As women learn to channel energy into being seen rather than into being strong, attracting becomes a substitute for acting (Freedman, 1986, p. 72).

Feminists have noted that much of the problem stems from the tendency for females to be *objectified* (turned into objects) by this relative focus on the importance of appearance. The media, for example, historically have presented a narrow interpretation of women's roles. Those roles that have been presented overemphasize *looking* at women rather than paying attention to their abilities. In a content analysis of magazines, women were shown to be underrepresented in ads depicting people in the workplace. Instead, women were found in more decorative roles (Courtney and Lockeretz, 1971). One recurring theme in the media has been that of woman as the alluring instrument of destruction for men (Dispenza, 1975). This theme may take the form of women selling cars or other products on the basis of their sexual appeal to men, who are vulnerable to feminine charms. Since most advertisers are men, they may be convinced that what sells a product to men is consistent with what sells a product to women (Dispenza, 1975).

Not surprisingly, when we compare young, single male and female consumers, a pattern emerges of their orientations toward clothing in the marketplace, which is consistent with cultural principles and gender socialization. Single American women are more "into" clothing shopping than are their male counterparts. Women often seem to enjoy shopping to the point of recreation, and therefore place greater weight on almost all clothing information sources (Bruner, 1988). Hence, a major question that emerges when we consider advertising aimed at women pertains to the images that hold the most meaning for them, as compared with those for men. Feminists have helped to raise the consciousness of both men and women in this respect.

Still, the theme of women as decorative objects pervades mass media. In fact, this theme may be identified as a cultural principle that has resulted in a *media format* (Altheide and Snow, 1979). We can see evidence of these formats in such diverse media as Saturday morning television cartoons and music videos. (See Figure 13-5 and Social Focus 13-1.)

How do cultural messages about the meaning of gendered appearances assume relevance in our everyday lives? Do people really respond differently toward us when we dress in styles that are more faithful to cultural expectations than when we dress in styles that stretch the boundaries of gender expectations? Some field studies were conducted in the 1970s to explore these issues at a time when the feminist movement was having a strong impact on the emergence of new images for women. One image commonly associated with feminists at this time was a mode of dress similar to that worn by working-class males—jeans and work shirts. Wearing feminist attire, as opposed to more traditionally feminine attire, was evaluated in the context of asking strangers for help.

In one study, two women, one tall and large and the other short and petite, dressed either in masculine attire (a man's shirt, jeans, tennis shoes, and straight hair) or in feminine attire (a ruffled blouse, high heels, and curled hair) (Harris and Bays, 1973). Either a neutral request ("Do you have change for a dime?") or a feminine request ("My shopping cart is stuck. Can you help me?") was made. The females were helped more often when they wore the feminine dress, but not necessarily because of their body types. The effect of the dress was greater on male than on female respondents. Additionally, there was a context effect based on the type of request. The feminine dress was more influential in producing compliance to the request for help with the shopping cart, but not for the neutral request of change for a dime (Harris and Bays, 1973). The shopping cart request was probably considered to be more consistent with the stereotype of the "damsel in distress."

A similar study was conducted in which a female experimenter asked for directions in downtown Indianapolis, approaching 90 middle-aged men (Miller and Rowold, 1980). Thirty of the men were approached while the experimenter was wearing a man-tailored blouse with no bra (feminist condition); 30 were approached when she was in the feminine or sensuous condition (wearing a tube top); and the remaining 30 were approached when she was in a traditional feminine blouse with a bra. When the experimenter was wearing a tube top, 70 percent of the men provided detailed directions. When she was wearing the man-tailored shirt, she received detailed directions from 50 percent of the men. The feminine blouse with a bra yielded detailed directions 40 percent of the time. Both an attire-role consistency effect and an attraction or sensual effect may have influenced the men's responses. Thus going braless probably confounded the issue of dressing in more masculine attire, because it most likely added to the sensuality of the impression.

A later study suggested that the political views of an attractive woman have a greater impact on helping behavior than that of an unattractive woman (Wilson and Dovidio, 1985). A highly attractive feminist woman was helped *less* frequently than was an equally attractive traditional-looking woman, but the feminist orientation of an *unattractive* woman did not influence rates of helping. Perceivers

**FIGURE 13-5**
*A variety of images of women as portrayed in music videos. The media serve to define and redefine cultural categories of gender. Photo by Wendy Dildey.*

# Images of Women in Music Videos

The electronic machine eats up images of
women: even (*most of all?*) emancipation from
the patriarchal world of gender ideology is
experienced simultaneously as domination *and*
freedom. For feminists in the mediascape it's
no longer "either/or," but "both/and."
— KROKER AND COOK, 1986

Music videos present a wide array of female images (see Figure 13-5). Are these images positive or negative? In line with the thinking of Kroker and Cook (1986), the answer is probably "both/and." Research on this question has taken two forms: analysis of the content of the videos per se as well as interviews with viewers. First, let's look at some of the findings from studies employing the technique of content analysis.

It is common for music videos to use women exclusively as decorative objects. In these productions, women are portrayed for purposes of background decoration, often clad in bathing suits, underclothing, or highly seductive clothing. Part of the paradox in these images is that the clothing worn is frequently quite innovative, but nevertheless reinforces traditional gender roles (Vincent, Davis, and Boruszkowski, 1985). Innovation can be represented in the form of androgyny, in which appearances combine traditional elements of male and female appearances resulting in ambiguous gender identity. Almost one-quarter (22.6 percent) of the observations in one study identified androgynous appearances. Also common were the use of provocative clothing (31 percent) and costuming (to portray characterizations beyond those associated with contemporary garb; 19 percent) (Baxter et al., 1985).

How do adolescents actually interpret these styles? To explore this issue, Kaiser and Damhorst (working paper) had male and female adolescents sort 75 photographs of MTV women (both performers and nonperformers) into piles on the basis of appearance cues. Then, the respondents described and interpreted the resulting clusters of images. These clusters revolved around the following appearance elements: (1) hair with a kind of "structured wildness" (spiked or very full), (2) soft, full hair with full lips or open mouths, (3) young, wholesome ("girl next door") looks, (4) blondes with rounded facial and bodily features with clothing and hair resembling Marilyn Monroe or other 1950s stars (Madonna and Belinda Carlisle), (5) business suits or tailored clothes signaling "working women," (6) costumes often including hats, (7) glitzy showgirl or Egyptian costumes, (8) middle-aged and/or

overweight women, (9) emphasis on such accessories as silver baubles or hoop earrings, often coupled with heavy makeup, and (10) breast-revealing swimsuits. Both male and female respondents' comments about these appearance styles often emphasized the power of attractiveness as well as somewhat traditional notions of femininity. Yet they did not tend to differentiate the women and their attractiveness on the basis of ethnicity. In general, the adolescents constructed nontraditional interpretations of appearance along with traditional ones.

"Dress like" and "wanna be" behavior among female adolescents are some of the most visible signs of the impact of video imagery. Cultural definitions of what it means to be female may be both reinforced *and* disrupted, in the media as well as in everyday life. In the 1980s, rock singers Cyndi Lauper and Madonna were identified as "key figures of style imitation because of the ways their dress and use of the body violate the discourse of femininity" (Lewis, 1987, p. 369). Feminists have credited Lauper with moving feminism beyond conformity to individuality, rebellion, and freedom, on the basis of her personal philosophy, illustrated by her unconventional hair and dress styles. In contrast, Madonna's image is often ridiculed by feminists, despite her popularity with young women. Yet this "either feminist or not" contrast probably oversimplifies the issue, as described in the following description of Madonna:

Admonished for making a sexual spectacle of herself, her "slut" presentation is, in actuality, marred by the indifference she projects toward men and the self-assurance she displays as an image of her own creation. Her style combines the very trappings of the discourse of femininity—wedding dress, undergarments—with its counterimage—material desires, blasphemous use of religious symbols, sexual lures (Lewis, 1987).

Female teenage fans may actually interpret Madonna's image in a feminist way, as the following comment suggests: "She gives us ideas. It's really women's lib, not being

## Social Focus 13-1 (continued)

afraid of what guys think (Skow, Booth, and Worrel, 1985). Thus, Madonna's images may be interpreted as being both a celebration and a violation of traditional femininity—at once in a given appearance.

Hence, the content and interpretations of female imagery in music videos point to some larger questions about what it means to be and appear female in the traditional sense versus what it means to be and to appear feminist, and whether or not the two are necessarily mu-

tually exclusive. Female adolescents and preadolescents may cling to some familiar forms of femininity as they explore perceptions of sexuality. But these young women may use their charms creatively and independently, combining the use of these charms with a bit of rebellion against adult norms and a desire to move away from images of childhood. The result may be dress that conveys a combination of shock value, sexuality, and experimentation.

---

seemed to have noticed a feminist T-shirt (with the slogan, "The best man for the job is a woman.") more when it was worn by an attractive woman (whose appearance was enhanced by grooming and makeup) than when an unattractive woman wore it. Consequently they responded more negatively toward her (were less likely to help) than they did to an unattractive woman. An attractive woman who expresses a feminist orientation may contradict social expectations (Wilson and Dovidio, 1985).

The stimulus characteristics (appearance cues) and contexts having an impact on the everyday experiences of both females *and* males deserve further study and clarification (Piliavin and Unger, 1984; Fedler, 1984). More attention needs to be paid in research to contexts in which appearance is clearly a factor in gender stratification. (It is still debatable as to what being helped with a stuck shopping cart, for instance, says about gender stratification.) One study along these lines explored the issue of service priority in department stores (Stead and Zinkhan, 1986). The results indicated that male customers received more prompt service than did female customers, regardless of the clerk's or the department's gender. Moreover, men in business attire were more likely to receive service priority over men in casual dress. In contrast, business attire did not improve service for female customers. It is possible that female gender is such a strong social cue that even professional dress does not increase a woman's prestige. Or, it may be that male customers are few enough in comparison to females that they are given preferential treatment because of their special minority status. Female customers, regardless of their attire, may just be part of the familiar herd.

Thus, either consciously or unconsciously, perceivers respond differently toward males and females, and the available evidence indicates that these responses are consistent with cultural messages about the value of males and females and about how they should appear.

## Physical Attractiveness

Beauty is a greater recommendation than any letter of introduction.
                                                              —ARISTOTLE

The picture is not pretty. Physical attractiveness touches practically every corner of human existence and it does so with great impact.
                                                              —PATZER, 1985

At first glance, it may seem strange to think of physical attractiveness in the context of cultural categories. To be sure, cultural attractiveness categories are not as clear-cut as gender categories. Rather, attractiveness is like a continuum (from unattractive to attractive). However, physical attractiveness is clearly a diffuse status characteristic insofar as the world appears to be a better place for attractive people, because they are perceived as possessing almost all types of social advantages that can be measured (Webster and Driskell, 1983). Most research on physical attractiveness has involved comparisons of people in high and low or high, medium, and low levels or categories. Thus research has enabled us to develop profiles of people to the extent that we can, in reality, construe people as falling into categories of attractiveness.

Several issues related to the study of attractiveness should be addressed before we delve further into the available evidence. First, the notion of physical attractiveness has not always been conceptualized in a consistent manner. Most researchers have focused primarily on "facial attractiveness"; others have included some other physical and dress-related features as well. The ingredients of beauty have not been clearly stated or identified (Berscheid and Walster, 1974). Moreover, such a definition is likely to be difficult because good looks are probably assessed by perceivers in a Gestalt or global manner rather than by focusing on singular elements (Huston and Levinger, 1978). Second, the extent to which appearance management influences ratings of physical attractiveness has not been adequately addressed. Even in studies where only facial photographs are used as stimuli, it is likely that makeup, jewelry, or hairstyle influence observers' ratings. There is evidence that when clothing is manipulated as a variable in ratings of physical attractiveness, evaluations are influenced by clothing cues (Buckley, 1983; Brown, Cash, and Noles, 1986; Hill, Nocks, and Gardner, 1987).

Third, physical attractiveness research has often been conducted in laboratory situations. Although such conditions are desirable from the standpoint of experimental control, there are some related disadvantages (Bickman and Hencky, 1972). Laboratory situations are schematized so as to restrict social responses to fragments of behavior, extracted from their larger context in everyday life. Such an extraction may change the character of the social responses studied. For example, in many studies perceivers evaluate photographs of individuals previously determined as being either high or low in physical attractiveness, using sets of adjective scales to assess their personality characteristics. Whether or not we can extrapolate from first-impression ratings of photographs to instances in everyday life when we interact with people varying in attractiveness is debatable. Perceptions are based not only on snapshot views of others, but also on other verbal and nonverbal characteristics. Finally, college students probably have been overused in experimental studies. Their responses may not always be representative of the larger population, which includes individuals of more diverse ages and socioeconomic and ethnic backgrounds.

Nevertheless, there is an impressive amount of evidence that consistently points to the cultural advantages of attractiveness. In recent years, the literature in this area has burgeoned, and researchers have begun to develop more sophisticated ways of explaining and studying the phenomenon of physical attractiveness. (Space does not allow an exhaustive review of the literature in this area. For good summaries, see *The Physical Attractiveness Phenomena* by Patzer, 1985, and *Mirror, Mirror: The Importance of Looks in Everyday Life* by Hatfield and Sprecher, 1986.) What we will address here, however, is the link between physical attractiveness and culture, and the impact of physical attractiveness on interpersonal encounters.

To some extent, culture probably sends us some conflicting messages about the value of physical attractiveness. On the one hand, we are bombarded with media images and advertisements stressing the value of beauty. On the other hand, we are taught as we grow up that "Beauty is only skin deep and mostly in the eye of the beholder" (Sergios and Cody, 1985). It seems in most cultures, however, that beholders not only agree that what is beautiful is good, but also as to what is beautiful per se (Patzer, 1985). Published works from around the world clearly indicate that physical attractiveness is beneficial across cultural contexts. Most of the research in this area has been conducted in the United States (in the twentieth century, especially since the 1960s). However, there is enough cross-cultural evidence to reveal that the status of physically attractive people is not unique to the United States in the present context (Patzer, 1985).

We might expect, however, that in postmodern cultures there would be a greater emphasis on attractiveness, given the increased emphasis on appearances (and signifiers in general, as discussed in Chapter Twelve). Also, the structure of feeling associated with *Gemeinschaft*-like culture might differ from that of *Gesellschaft*-like culture. If people interact with one another intimately, rather than on the basis of fleeting encounters, we would expect the impact of physical attractiveness to diminish. Familiarity tends to mediate the effects of physical appearance (Styczynsky and Langlois, 1977). As we get to know people on a personal level, we are likely to judge them on qualities other than appearance. Generally, it seems that people evaluate others whom they know as being more attractive. In other words, perceivers are more generous when they rate the physical attractiveness of people with whom they are familiar. This "knowing" factor especially appears to apply when the person being rated is somewhat average in degree of attractiveness (Cavior, Miller, and Cohen, 1975).

The most pervasive finding in the literature is that physically attractive individuals are perceived as masters of their fates. Attractive people are judged to be more responsible for positive outcomes of chance events, whereas unattractive people have been seen as more responsible for negative outcomes (Turkat and Dawson, 1976). Thus there are differences in how people *think* about attractive and unattractive people. When perceivers evaluate attractive others, a "halo effect" appears to operate. These perceivers reason that if an unknown person is attractive, he or she must have other desirable qualities as well. Thus attractive people are evaluated as being warmer and more sensitive than unattractive people (Dion, Berscheid, and Walster, 1972; Lombardo and Tocci, 1979), for example. Several themes may be identified across the numerous studies on attractiveness (Webster and Driskell, 1983):

*1.* Attractiveness produces a wide range of effects, with beautiful people having a number of advantages over ugly people in a variety of contexts: (*a*) in advertisements (Kahle and Homer, 1985); (*b*) in the courtroom, as evident from both laboratory simulations (Efran, 1974; Sigall and Ostrove, 1975) and actual courtrooms (Stewart, 1985); (*c*) in the classroom (Kehle, Bramble, and Mason, 1974; Salvia, Algozzine, and Sheare, 1977); (*d*) in obtaining help (Wilson, 1978; Harrell, 1978); and (*e*) in getting elected to public office—a direct advantage for males (Sigelman et al., 1986) and an indirect advantage for females, being mediated by perceived femininity, dynamism, niceness, and age (Sigelman, Sigelman, and Fowler, 1987).

However, there are some contextual qualifications to these advantages. In the context of juridical judgments, attractiveness seems to affect sentencing but not conviction or acquittal (Stewart, 1985). Additionally, accused swindlers are assigned harsher punishments when they are attractive (as opposed to unattractive), because the ability to swindle is likely to be enhanced by the power of beauty. A beautiful female swindler may be regarded as taking advantage of her "God-given gift" (Sigall and Ostrove, 1975).

*2.* Attractiveness effects identified by research often pertain to skills at performing something. That is, attractive people are viewed as doing something better than unattractive people, in a variety of contexts: producing a happy marriage, finding partners in adultery, writing essays, or getting people to agree with them. There are a few contextual exceptions to this rule, however. Attractive people are *not* expected to excel at parenting (Dion, Berscheid, and Walster, 1972), perhaps because they are thought to focus on themselves and their beauty, whereas parenting is associated with *giving*. Additionally, in the context of evaluations of attractive females pursuing some male-dominated professions, research has suggested some "beauty as beastly" effects. Females who are very attractive may be associated with the female stereotype (the beautiful damsel in distress or all beauty and no brains) in contexts where males have generally dominated (such as in management). (See Social Foci 8-1 and 11-1 for more details about the importance of appearance for female managers.) A related consideration, however, is that both male and female attractive executives have been thought to have achieved their positions because of their social skills rather than their competence (Wilson et al., 1985).

*3.* Attractiveness affects not only perceived abilities but also interaction. It seems that attractive people are actually more successful than unattractive people at counseling (as was discussed in a Social Focus 10-2), selling products, wielding influence, and at being liked after a get-acquainted conversation (Wilson and Henzlik, 1986). Attractive people are accorded more *deference* (respect or appreciation) than are unattractive people, as evidenced by such perceiver behaviors as the allowance of more personal space. In this connection, an interesting distinction has been found between simulated laboratory research and actual behavior on sidewalks (Powell and Dabbs, 1976; Dabbs and Stokes, 1975). It seems that on sidewalks, attractive people were assigned deference because they are viewed as somewhat "unapproachable" because of a "beauty as power" effect. More physical distance is allowed between a passer-by and an attractive confederate (research participant). In contrast, in a laboratory setting, perceivers were more likely to want to stand closer to a poster of an attractive female's face than that of an unattractive female's face (Powell and Dabbs, 1976). The researchers explained this difference between laboratory and field research findings as follows:

> Beauty in the abstract, as in a picture, is attractive and inspires all manner of positive attribution. But beauty in the flesh provokes a different reaction. In our society beauty implies a certain power and status. We suggest that Ss (subjects) on the sidewalk in our study had mixed motives. Beauty was attractive and they would have liked to approach it, but even with the tacit invitation to come forward and be interviewed they were hesitant (Powell and Dabbs, 1976, pp. 63–64).

*4.* The effects of attractiveness and success appear to be reciprocal. That is, attractive people are *perceived* as better at most things and as more successful than are unattractive people. And, people who are better and more successful *become*, by virtue of those traits, more attractive to others (Webster and Driskell, 1983). Thus what is beautiful is good *and* what is good is beautiful.

The link between cultural messages about physical attractiveness and actual interpersonal relations is an important one to consider from a contextual perspective. The media are likely to have a strong impact on the importance of attractiveness in everyday life. How often do we see unattractive people falling in love in movies? How often do we see unattractive people at all in the media? Potent cultural messages are conveyed to us through the media, as we may come to equate romance with beauty, for example. Studies have revealed that romantic opportunities are enhanced by physical attractiveness (Walster, Aronson, and Abrahams, 1966; Brislin and Lewis, 1968) and that males are especially concerned about the attractiveness of female companions (Byrne, Ervin, and Lamberth, 1970). Attractive males, themselves, are expected to possess heterosocial skills (Neumann, Critelli, and Tang, 1986).

Moreover, males who are higher self-monitors (a concept discussed in Chapter Six) are more likely than low self-monitors to be influenced by the physical attractiveness of their potential partners. High self-monitors are likely to be tuned in to attractiveness cues and to structure their romantic relationships accordingly (Glick, 1985). This tendency to prefer an attractive romantic partner also applies to male homosexual dating behavior and partner selection (Sergios and Cody, 1985), especially in first-impression contexts such as bars and discos (Sergios and Cody, 1985). Some social psychologists have noted that we tend to be attracted to individuals who provide us with pleasure or "rewards" (Aronson, 1988). A **reward-attraction effect** is likely to apply in some contexts to perceptions of physical attractiveness. Thus we may seek the companionship of attractive others because of their aesthetic reward value. Another mediating factor is described by Goffman's "matching hypothesis" (Goffman, 1952), which suggests that individuals assess their own attributes (for example, appearance, monetary status, and possessions) and then select partners who seem "equally matched." This hypothesis has received support in terms of heterosexual romantic involvement. That is, people seem to choose to date others who are comparable in degree of attractiveness (Berscheid et al., 1971). When differences *do* exist, females who are less attractive than their male partners seem to have to compensate in some other way (such as in personality) to achieve some equity; however, this equity explanation does not necessarily apply to less attractive males (Feingold, 1981). There is evidence in a variety of contexts that physical attractiveness as a status characteristic is likely to be more potent for females than for males. As such, it is a complex status characteristic with mixed meanings. Dating back at least as far as the nineteenth century in the United States, the theme of beauty for women has been equated not only with morality but also with power. Women were expected to use their beauty to advance their own interests, primarily in the context of heterosexual relationships. Some cultural ambivalence about beauty in terms of morality was also evident:

> Beauty represented neither morality nor goodness, but rather a means of self-aggrandizement through "admiration, homage," and, ultimately, association with a powerful man. Woman was not only an Eve figure, but also an individual obsessed with self, with physical relationships with men (Banner, 1983, p. 13).

Feminists and moral reformers in this historic context stressed honesty and devotion as forms of beauty, whereas commercial fashion leaders emphasized dress, hairstyle, and physical conformity to prevailing ideals. Beauty became a part of the reality of women's separate culture (Banner, 1983, p. 13).

A stereotype of "what is beautiful is good is sex-typed" still operates in many social contexts. Although good looks are an asset for both males and females, for women they are likely to be more than just a pleasant bonus. Appearance management, rather, is likely to be a major concern throughout women's lives. Is this necessarily an advantage or disadvantage? Let's look at one view on this subject:

> Women in our culture probably learn early to take stock of the strengths and weaknesses of their appearance and to take whatever steps are possible to bring their appearance up to established standards. The frequency with which women are urged to wear "flattering" makeup, hairstyles, clothes, and colors implies, logically, that they can and have assessed where their natural endowments, or previous habits along these lines, fall short. . . . Men are much more restricted

than women in what they can do to improve their attractiveness via hair and clothing, and indeed may feel that excessive attention to such matters is un-masculine. These factors could provide men with less reinforcement for accurate self-evaluation (Rand and Hall, 1983, p. 362).

Physical attractiveness differs from some other diffuse status characteristics (such as gender) to the extent that it can be an *achieved* characteristic. Although heredity does determine facial attractiveness and other physical predispositions, attractiveness is still a malleable concept. Clothing, cosmetics, plastic or recon-structive surgery, diet, and exercise can all influence the degree of perceived attractiveness. Some sociologists predict that as (and if) status characteristics such as gender and ethnicity fall into disuse because of social change, attractiveness may assume even more significance (Webster and Driskell, 1983).

# *Age*

A distinguished middle-aged woman points to brown spots on her hands and exclaims, "They call these age spots. I call them *ugly*! But, what's a woman to do?"

—DOWNS AND HARRISON, 1985

Beauty sells. Most likely, as women, in particular, begin to perceive visible signs of aging, they will also be confronted with advertising pitches promising to obliterate these signs. Some product is inevitably available to cover or remove the age spots, to cover the gray in one's hair, or to remove or reduce wrinkles in the skin. A content-analytic study revealed that whereas older women were found in some television commercials for cosmetics, they were never found in commercials for clothing (Downs and Harrison, 1985).

What is the cultural message about age and the degree of honor bestowed in relation to appearance and fashion? North Americans in general, and women in particular, are expected to fight aging every step of the way, and the cosmetics industry thrives on this expectation. For women, whose primary source of power has traditionally been in the hedonic mode (appearance-related), the process of aging is especially problematic. Fashion, however, is associated with the cultural category of youth, especially since the 1960s. Thus, age is intricately linked to the cultural categories of gender and attractiveness. The cultural category of age, like that of attractiveness, is *relative* in basis. Both of these categories can be actively manipulated through appearance management. Although we may associate some age categories with tangible numbers of years, individuals may appear much different than their true age. Another complicating factor is: How do we know when we are old? When Ronald Reagan was President of the United States, he was actually older than some other politicians for whom age became more of an issue (such as California Senator Alan Cranston). It is the *appearance* of age, rather than chronological age, that seems to matter most in the worlds of politics, media, and fashion. For example, fashion model agencies frequently hire very young women (teenagers) and make them up to appear a few years older, whereas the few older female models who are likely to be successful are likely to appear much younger than they are.

When we look at the cultural category of age and consider its impact on status in society, it is important to consider generational factors, or historic context, to determine the meaning of age. The median age of the American population increased from 20 in 1960 to 30 years in 1980, because of the post-World-War-II "baby-boom" generation. This generation had a profound impact on fashion change in the 1960s and 1970s, and, as it ages, Western cultural perceptions of age are likely to change as well. The median age of a society's population is likely to have an impact on its role models and fashion influentials. By the year 2000, the median age in the United States will be 37 years (Behling, 1985).

French sociologist Pierre Bourdieu (1984) noted the importance of age categories for fashion change in French culture:

> The newcomers to the field, young couturiers or designers endeavoring to win acceptance of their subversive ideas, are the "objective allies" of the new fractions and the younger generation of the dominant fractions of the bourgeoisie, for whom the symbolic revolutions of which vestimentary and cosmetic outrages are the paradigm, are the perfect vehicle for expressing the ambiguity of their situation as the "poor relations" of the temporal powers (p. 233).

Thus, a youthful orientation toward that which was "real" and "genuine" in the late 1960s resulted in the selling of such styles as combat trousers, Canadian trappers' jackets, Japanese martial-art kimonos, and safari jackets at inflated prices in "in" boutiques (Bourdieu, 1984). Since the 1960s in Great Britain, working-class youth have set a number of fashion trends through their participation in subcultures. (This is discussed further in Chapters Fourteen and Fifteen). Research suggests that fashion involvement has been more age- than class-oriented in England since the 1960s (Horowitz, 1982). Moreover, younger British women are affected more by the excitement motive connected with fashion change, as compared with older British women, who are more likely to be concerned with the economy motive. Young consumers are especially apt to lean toward style rather than quality considerations, to be influenced more by mass media, and to be less sensitive than older people to status symbols associated with social class (Horowitz, 1982).

To understand the cultural category of age and its meaning for women, especially, in American culture, it is helpful to turn to history. As historian Lois Banner (1983) describes the situation in the nineteenth century, older women were assigned to a special sphere that was distinct from that of younger women. Once a woman reached her thirties, and especially if she was married, she was considered old. Her sphere of influence was restricted to family cohesion and governance. She was not expected (or even really allowed) to be concerned about her appearance any longer; that was part of a younger, unmarried woman's sphere. Thus an "older" woman was likely to tuck her hair up into a cap to renounce her sexuality, wear dull colors, and have her teeth pulled rather than capped (because of the expense) if they began to decay. Older women were excluded from social pleasures and certainly from social influence. Men, in contrast, were often still considered youthful in their thirties and even in their early forties. There were no mandatory retirement policies, and males could be distinguished politicians and statesmen into their later years. (The image of Uncle Sam reflects this cultural category for men.) There was a prevailing joke in the nineteenth century that "any man would gladly exchange his wife of 40 for two 20s" (Banner, 1983, p. 220). As the nineteenth century progressed, young women became more and more interested in personal beauty, and attitudes about the appearance of old age probably became increasingly negative. In contrast, in France at this time, older women could be considered attractive and relatively influential.

By the twentieth century, the cultural categories of age for women had been radically altered, thanks in large part to the separate and disparate agendas of feminists and the cosmetics industry. Now women were faced with a rather cruel paradox: They were now free to dress and act as they pleased, but they were also vulnerable to the exploitation of the commercial culture of beauty. Dropping age barriers for women in the realm of personal appearance was liberating, on the one hand, but indicative of new restrictions and new penalties, on the other. The cultural prohibitions against striving to look young were dropped, and, given that white hair, wrinkles, and sagging muscles had been viewed with disdain for some time, women were primed for the change. They could now diet and exercise, dye their hair, wear corsets, and put on creams and makeup to conceal wrinkles.

> Why was it that innumerable products were marketed for women to stave off old age, but nothing was advertised for men? The truth of the matter was . . . that they did not have to look young to be appreciated. . . . American society had come to approve older women's participation in public affairs outside the home, but such participation had not brought a new respect for the physical appearance of old age. . . . The commercial beauty culture played a powerful role in standardizing the connection between beauty and youth. To have conceded that older women were intrinsically beautiful would have been to destroy a potentially immense market before the exploitation of it had ever begun (Banner, 1983, p. 225).

Thus, females in the twentieth century have been socialized to value appearance throughout their lives. Although the fashion industry caters primarily to the young, research on older female consumers indicates that their interest in fashion does not necessarily decline with age. Research has indicated that the older female fashion consumer is likely to buy a garment to match accessories already in her wardrobe, in a store she has previously patronized (Martin, 1976). She is likely to have identified at least one color she will not buy and have definite fabric and garment care predispositions. Two-thirds of the women in Martin's (1976) study exhibited a positive degree of fashion consciousness and indicated a desire to keep up to date with fashion. Studies in the 1980s have also indicated that most older women wish to remain current with respect to fashion trends. A national survey indicated that older female consumers enjoy shopping, especially where they are known by store personnel. They are not especially price-conscious, nor do they tend to shop around (Lumpkin and Greenberg, 1982). Accordingly, they are likely to seek fashion information from different sources. [See Social Focus 13-2 for a discussion of older adults' (including older men's) use of media for fashion information.]

Despite older women's interests, in particular, in clothing, the literature reports some problems on their part in finding preferred clothes that fit. A Swedish study of 750 women (aged 65 to 80) indicated that about 50 percent of them did not fit into the common size range (Rosenblad-Wallin and Karlsson, 1986). Clothes are manufactured, both in size and in design, for younger women. Thus 46 percent of the women reported difficulties in finding clothes that fit, and 51 percent reported that it was hard to find clothes that were modern in style. The women spent as much money as younger women did on their clothes. Three-fourths of the women were of the opinion that there is an obvious need for a new kind of clothing with a better correspondence to their fit and preference requirements. Some complained of being forced by the marketplace into an "old lady style of dressing" (Rosenblad-Wallin and Karlsson, 1986).

In an American study of women between the ages of 30 and 75+ years, it was found that the older women were less aware than the younger women of the alterations needed for proper fit. They were not likely to perceive a need for garment alterations if they thought the garment was attractive and felt comfortable (Hogge and Baer, 1986).

Little research has been conducted to determine older men's needs and preferences with respect to clothing. One study comparing males between the ages of 20 and 60 years indicated that the younger men were not influenced to any greater degree by brand label of dress slacks than were the older men, in terms of their perceptions of quality (Behling and Wilch, 1988).

More research is needed to assess some of the social trends that could very well reshape cultural categories associated with age, not only for women, but also for men. It seems that men as well as women are becoming more concerned about maintaining a youthful appearance, although inequities still clearly exist as a function of gender. In this connection, there may be a socioeconomic bias in images of older men, in particular, in the media (Kaiser and Chandler, 1985). Social class, the topic of the following section, is a factor in this bias.

## Social Class

The interest the different classes have in self-presentation, the attention they devote to it, their awareness of the profits it gives and the investment of time, effort, sacrifice and care which they actually put into it are proportionate to the chances of material or symbolic profit they can reasonably expect from it.
—BOURDIEU, 1984, p. 202

# Older Adults' Use of Media for Fashion Information

Fashion is equated in many Western societies with youthfulness. For women, in particular, beauty is perceived as diminishing with increased age in these societies. Nevertheless, interest in fashion is not necessarily adversely affected by socialization to old age (Martin, 1976; Lumpkin and Greenberg, 1982).

Newspapers have been a traditional source of fashion information, and many older female fashion consumers appear to rely on them for this purpose (Martin, 1976; Lumpkin and Greenberg, 1982; Kaiser and Chandler, 1985). Yet it appears that older adults notice and appreciate some of the clothing styles they see on television as well, and thus are likely to derive some ideas from this medium. News and talk shows and daytime and evening soap operas are among the types of television programs that have well-dressed individuals, in the eyes of older adults (Kaiser and Chandler, 1985). Content analysis of soap operas indicates that older characters tend to be attractive and well-dressed (Cassata, Anderson, and Skill, 1980). Similarly, older adults seem to appreciate the neatness depicted by older males wearing well-tailored suits in news and talk shows (Kaiser and Chandler, 1985), as well as in magazines (Kaiser and Chandler, 1988).

Some older adults, however, seem to feel a sense of alienation toward fashion change. With increased age, older adults were more likely to disagree with the following statements in a study by Kaiser and Chandler (1984):

*I enjoy reading about mass media accounts of what people in the public eye are wearing.*
*It is fun to keep up with fashion.*

In part, some of these negative feelings toward fashion and the media may stem from the "young is beautiful" ideology. Women's fashion magazines typically do not feature models over 40 years of age, unless one turns to magazines catering to older women. Research has suggested that intent to purchase a style is actually slightly higher among older respondents when they view that style on a younger, as opposed to an older, model (Steinhaus and Lapitsky, 1986). Part of this might be explained by conditioning in the media, and a desire on the part of older women to perceive themselves as wearing youthful styles. At the same time, the cultural equation of youth with fashionability is perpetuated by the pervasiveness of youthful-appearing models—many of whom are in their teens made up to look like adults. Other research has indicated that a style is perceived as more fashionable when it is viewed on a young, as compared to a middle-aged, model (Lennon, Clayton, and Larkin, 1989).

Older women appear to be selective about the fashion information they filter through the media, however. Selection of women's clothing styles was found to be related to media exposure in a study by Usha Chowdhary (1988a). Yet media exposure was associated with the selection of classic styles rather than the latest styles. Chowdhary explained this finding by noting that classic styles are more reminiscent of the 1930s and 1940s, when the older adults in her study would have been youths. Thus socialization during youth may be likely to have a continuing influence on style perceptions in later life. This idea raises some questions about the preferences of older adults in the future. Will older adults who were youths in the 1960s and 1970s have a preference for informal styles such as jeans and T-shirts, or some facsimile thereof? Will those who were young in the 1980s be interested in "put together" styles emphasizing separates and accessories? And, how will the media portray older adults in the future? It is important when talking about age to consider the historical and fashion context in which individuals experience life changes.

Social class is a difficult concept. It is not easy to measure, and some philosophical and ethical worldviews may prevent us from confronting the concept directly. In American society, especially, there is a discomfort associated with the idea of social class due to an underlying sense of frontier spirit designed to escape the fixed social stations in Europe (Domhoff, 1983). Although in England, for example, a rigid class structure provided some fixed standards of taste for the social classes, in the more fluid American society, there were several ingredients contributing to confusion in the realm of class display: (1) the universal striving for success, (2) the lack of a titled aristocracy, and (3) the modest past of most Americans (Banner, 1983, p. 54). In twentieth-century England as well, the challenge to upper-class-dictated fashion has been acute. A youth culture emerged out of the working classes, and since the 1960s a variety of subcultures has represented a form of rebellion and a search for excitement in the realm of style. The influence of this youth culture has been realized far beyond the boundaries of the working class, especially among youth (Horowitz, 1982, pp. 635–636).

The 1980s brought a fresh perspective to the concept of social class and its implications for taste (Bourdieu, 1984) and consumption (Coleman, 1983), after a period during the late 1960s and 1970s when the concept fell out of favor in academic circles. During the late 1960s and 1970s, the effects of the civil rights and women's movements were felt, and social class did not seem to be as vital a cultural category as did ethnicity and gender. Moreover, lifestyle choices did not seem to coincide very neatly with conventional wisdom about social class. There was confusion in the realm of status symbolism as to what conveyed signs of high versus low class. This confusion has been attributed to a kind of **conspicuous counterconsumption** (Simon-Miller, 1985)—the counterculture's answer to the meaning of style, which was a form of **parody display**, according to John Brooks (1981) in the book *Showing Off in America*: "The most effective status seeking style is mockery of status seeking" (p. 270).

To understand the basis for much of our thinking about social class in relation to appearance and fashion, let us turn to the ideas of Thorstein Veblen, who wrote around the turn of the century (1899). In his influential book, *The Theory of the Leisure Class*, he sought to critique the social inequities he saw in American culture. In particular, he expressed disdain for the cultural bias in favor of "leisure" display. His idea of leisure differs from our twentieth-century images of sports, hot tubs, and rock concerts. Instead, he spoke of leisure in the context of conspicuously displaying that one need not work: Our dress, therefore, in order to serve its purpose

> effectually, should not only be expensive, but it should also make plain to all observers that the wearer is not engaged in any kind of productive labor. . . . No apparel can be considered elegant, or even decent, if it shows the effect of manual labor on the part of the wearer, in the way of soil or wear (Veblen, 1899, p. 120).

The visible signs of "leisure" in Veblen's day were the patent-leather shoe, the top hat, and the walking stick for men. (See Figure 13-6.) None of these

*FIGURE 13-6*
*Conspicuous leisure is conveyed in white-collar attire. In Veblen's (1899) terms, the concept of conspicuous leisure encompasses signs of nonphysical labor. The business suit worn by professional men has been a traditional symbol of conspicuous leisure in the context of nonphysical work. This is a staged 1922 "replay" of financiers in 1849. Courtesy of the City of Sacramento, Museum and History Division.*

items were intrinsically useful or functional. Patent-leather shoes that were shiny and clean showed that the wearer had not engaged in manual labor. For women, the display of "leisure" was especially acute, because Veblen noted that "it has in the course of economic development become the office of the woman to consume vicariously for the head of the household; and her apparel is contrived with this object in view" (Veblen, 1899, p. 126). Women displayed their status through feminine bonnets, shoes with a French heel, long hair, and the corset (Veblen, 1899, p. 121).

Veblen identified several critical functions of dress, from a social-class perspective:

1. **Conspicuous leisure**— the display of a wearer's lack of need to engage in "productive" (manual) labor.
2. **Conspicuous consumption**—tangible evidence of the cost of one's apparel, indicating an ability to afford to spend freely on clothes.
3. **Conspicuous waste**—the display of frivolous spending, on styles that will quickly fall out of favor in terms of fashion, based on the apparel industry's tendency to make styles obsolete before they are worn out.

Veblen's ideas have influenced a number of writers, including sociologist Georg Simmel (1904), who used the idea of conspicuous consumption to develop a theory of class structure and fashion (to be discussed in Chapter Fifteen). Quentin Bell, author of *On Human Finery* (1978), added the concept of **conspicuous outrage** to Veblen's scheme. This concept describes those individuals who can afford to display their indifference to some social standards, or indicate that they are "above" such things. There is a deliberate wearing of clothes, in this connection, that does not conform to mainstream cultural norms regarding "good taste." Alison Lurie (1976) describes conspicuous outrage with the following examples.

> It is Conspicuous Outrage which causes persons to appear at parties given by those to whom they feel (or wish to feel) superior in casual or strikingly untidy dress, thus silently announcing to all who see them that they are slumming. The same ploy is frequently, and perhaps more understandably, adopted by artists who have been invited to dinner by their patrons—whose wardrobes are sure to offer much more in the way of conspicuous consumption (p. 521).

Several writers have critiqued Veblen's ideas, noting the numerous contradictions in the display of social class, especially in American society. Historian Lois Banner (1983) indicates that class structure, even in the nineteenth century, was more complex than Veblen's descriptions would suggest. Elizabeth Wilson (1985) points out that Veblen's works are motivated by a utilitarian bias—that which is not "useful" is deemed by Veblen as inconsequential and unappealing. Wilson notes that fashion should be regarded in terms of aesthetics, not merely utilitarian value, and to undermine aesthetic codes at the expense of function is to underestimate the power of fashion. Nevertheless, Veblen pointed out some major inequities and double standards based on social class—cultural shortcomings based on stratification. Although he may have oversimplified the picture in many respects, he nevertheless sensitized us to the issue of dress as a visible means of stratification.

If we look at the historic context in which modern conceptions of fashion materialized, the importance of class structure becomes clearer. In American society, since at least 1800, the fashion picture was influenced not only by the upper classes, as Veblen's ideas would suggest, but also by the middle and working classes. Old wealth "has the security to abjure engaging in the kind of conspicuous consumption that characterizes the nouveau riche" (Banner, 1983,

p. 7). Individuals in the elite classes could elect to innovate in a variety of areas—not just fashion display.

In New York City in the nineteenth century, housing patterns were not yet sorted out by social class. This contributed to a perplexing message about fashionability. Middle-class boarding houses and working-class tenements were adjacent to upper-class mansions. The class challenge to high fashion was both visible and direct. The newly "well-to-do" who had come from modest backgrounds had been socialized to wear clothes of dark fabrics, designed to conceal dirt or the quality of the material. These middle-class women were now attracted to bright colors and visual display, and they enjoyed a new freedom in fashion while also challenging the fashion leadership of the upper classes.

Some working-class women also challenged the elite control of fashion. Women who worked in the dressmaking business, for example, could follow fashion through the remaking of existing garments (adding a bow here or there or replacing sleeves to reflect new styling). Dressmakers' assistants especially challenged the control of fashion in the 1850s; they had special access to fashion information that was still coming primarily from Paris. They enjoyed wearing bright colors and decorations, defying "all laws of harmony and taste" (Banner, 1983, p. 75). Unlike the "genteel" image of the upper-class woman in this historic context, the working-class women were plump, hearty, and vivacious. They wore their skirts shockingly short (above the ankle) and were often confused with prostitutes, who had to find other codes to display their status.

How did the upper classes respond to these fashion challenges by the middle and working classes? To some extent, the wealthy sought to introduce styles that the middle classes could not afford. For example, cashmere shawls were very expensive because they were woven by hand from the rare fleece of Kashmir goats, having originally been brought to Europe during the Napoleonic wars. Upper-class women also brought very finely woven, expensive handkerchiefs trimmed with lace; as a sign of conspicuous leisure they would hold these in the tips of their fingers as they shopped in the fashionable stores of New York City. Yet the textile industry challenged the "eliteness" of even these signs of wealth. Increasingly, fine machine-made lace was produced to emulate the more expensive laces made by hand, and in Paisley, England, fine imitations of the cashmere shawl were developed. In response,

> ultimately, certain sectors of the upper classes dropped completely out of the competition, made simplicity their hallmark, left fashion competition to others, and added another confusing element to the fashion scene (Banner, 1983, p. 77).

The struggle has continued in the twentieth century, with new challenges and complexities. Still, some theorists maintain that different social classes hold values and tastes that are distinctive to their processes of socialization. One of these theorists is the French sociologist Pierre Bourdieu (1984), who helped bring a renewed appreciation and critical approach to the topic of social class based on an extensive study of taste in French culture. Marketing researcher Richard Coleman (1983) holds, with Bourdieu, that the picture is complex, but worthy of study if we are to understand the relation between social class and style. Coleman identifies four main status distinctions in late-twentieth-century America: upper Americans, middle class, working class, and lower Americans. He associates these distinctions with specific values and lifestyles, although he notes there are exceptions and contradictions in some areas. For purposes of comparison, let's explore these distinctions drawing from Bourdieu's (1984) data on French culture, as well as from existing evidence in American culture.

## Upper Americans

The lifestyles of upper Americans (approximately the upper sixth of the nation) appear to have changed more dramatically than those of the people in the classes below. The concept of upper American includes individuals in the upper-upper class from the past, who may still be pursuing a traditionally aristocratic lifestyle, lower-uppers who display their wealth in a flamboyant manner, and upper-middles who can afford some of the luxuries of life. Traditionally, the upper-upper class has emphasized a culture molded after the British aristocracy. School blazers and ties (preppy styles), somewhat esoteric sports such as squash and lacrosse, and the building of character were emphasized in the educational system that was distinct to this group; it still is, in the realm of prep schools and debutante balls (Domhoff, 1983). The Junior League was founded around 1900 to contribute to social reforms; participation in civic and volunteer activities, especially for women, represented not only conspicuous leisure but also an ethic of social responsibility (Domhoff, 1983). Some of these traditions have lingered, according to Coleman (1983). Yet some important shifts have occurred, as described in the following:

> Upper America is now a vibrant mix of many life styles, which might be labeled post-preppy, sybaritic, counter-cultural, intellectual, political, and so on. Such subdivisions are usually of more importance for targeting messages and goods than are the horizontal, status-flavored, class-named strata (Coleman, 1983, p. 271).

Thus, upper America may include conservatives and liberals, socially conscious consumers and those who are more concerned with maintaining the status quo, and intellectuals as well as rich and famous individuals who abhor what is traditional. Self-expression is likely to be more prized among these individuals than in previous generations, because the class is more diverse and complex. Income for most upper Americans is not sufficient to afford all of the luxuries of life at once, so priorities are inevitable. Only a "lucky few" need not worry about picking and choosing the goods and services that are most important to them. (See Figure 13-7.)

## Middle Class

The middle class has traditionally been associated with wanting to "do the right thing" and buying "what's popular":

*FIGURE 13-7*
*An upper-class mother and son in Colombia. Photo by Carla M. Freeman.*

They have been very concerned with fashion all along, following—with affordable modification—the recommendations of "experts" in the print media. When families of this class have increased their earnings to manage it, better living has meant—and still seems to mean—a "nicer home" in a "nicer neighborhood," . . . spending more money on "worthwhile experiences" for the children, and aiming them toward a college education; shopping at more expensive stores for clothing with "one of the better brand names"; and constant concern over the appearance of public areas in one's home—i.e., wherever guests may visit and pass judgment (Coleman, 1983, p. 272).

In French culture, Bourdieu (1984) also characterizes the middle class as appearance-conscious and traces this consciousness to the "middle status." He notes that the middle classes are "committed to the symbolic" and that their concern for appearance, sometimes disguised as arrogance, is also a source of their pretension, a permanent disposition towards the bluff or usurpation of social identity which consists in anticipating "being" by "seeming," appropriating the appearances so as to have the reality, the nominal so as to have the real, in trying to modify the positions in the objective classifications by modifying the representation of the ranks in the classification or of the principles of classification (Bourdieu, 1984, p. 253).

To the extent that this profile is accurate in American as well as in French culture, individuals in the middle class are likely to be viewed as somewhat artificial by members of the social classes above and below them (Bourdieu, 1984). Yet the middle class probably has the most to gain in terms of social mobility, in a practical sense, and may also express some concern about holding onto what it already has. Thus Bourdieu attributes the emphasis on "seeming" or appearances, among middle-class individuals, to the somewhat ambiguous place of their class in the social structure.

In this connection, American sociologist C. Wright Mills (1951) pointed out that "middle" positions (beneath more independent employees and above blue-collar workers) are often associated with prestige that is relatively unstable and ambiguous in nature. He noted examples of the tendency for middle-class workers (for example, sales associates in department stores) to experience a form of "status panic," resulting in the borrowing of prestige from one's place of work (such as a store with a positive fashion image). In the lower ranks of the middle class, in particular, salary itself may be insufficient compensation. In fact, the salaries of working-class individuals may often be higher than those of middle-class workers in the lower ranks.

In the United States, interviews in the 1970s suggested an increased spirit of individualism in middle-class lifestyles, due possibly to the "do your own thing" ethic of the earlier decade and to the increasing self-expressiveness in upper America. Coleman (1983) notes that the "stuffiness" of the 1950s has diminished in terms of middle-class self-presentation. There is a greater tendency to enjoy life, to eat out more, to relax public dress codes, and to emphasize family vacations. He characterizes a trend toward a shift from "possessions–pride" toward "activities–pleasure."

## *Working Class*

Working-class Americans are often described as "family folk," intimately linked to their relatives and more narrow (*Gemeinschaft*-like) geographic perspectives in terms of home and work. Working-class loyalties are displayed in relation to local sports heroes, vacation patterns, patriotism, and pride in industrial accomplishments (Coleman, 1983). In the 1980s, the domestic industry declined when confronted with foreign competition. However, renewed cultural appreciation for working-class values was emphasized, and the plight of the loyal and patriotic worker was highlighted by rock singer Bruce Springsteen, by movies about life in factories (including songs such as "Working Class Man"), and by "Americana" fashions such as blue jeans, denim jackets, and red bandanas. Perhaps a kind of genuineness, a *Gemeinschaft*-like sense of community has been associated with this class, the plight of which is relatively uncertain in postindustrial society.

Like the other social classes, however, a mixture of values and lifestyles may be seen in the working classes.

In French culture, Bourdieu (1984) distinguished between the working class focus on "being" and the middle class attention to "seeming." He stressed that working-class people place a higher priority on function, as compared with a greater emphasis assigned to aesthetics on the part of the upper classes.

Similar results have been reported in American studies. One such example was found in a sociological study of a small Midwestern town with an upper- and working-class dichotomy in the 1940s (Useem, Tangent, and Useem, 1942). The upper-class women were found to be more interested in fashion and more likely to have the leisure time to shop. They admitted to judging others by their clothing. In contrast, the working-class women regarded the upper-class women as being overly concerned with superficial matters such as fashion and appearances and reported that they were more involved in "genuine" tasks such as church work, childrearing, or visiting neighbors. They were less concerned with fashion. In a study of American mothers in the 1980s, Michelle Morganosky (1987) found that women in the higher income groups tended to place less importance on functionality in clothes and more importance on aesthetics, as compared with the women in the lower income groups.

Bourdieu (1984) also noted a tendency for the working class to be attentive to the strength, as opposed to the shape, of men's bodies—in a manner that is consistent with this emphasis on functionality and the priority assigned to *being* rather than seeming. As in Banner's (1984) description of working-class women in nineteenth-century America, working-class French women emphasized body slenderness less than women in higher classes. Additionally, Bourdieu found a regard for the domestic world as a place of freedom, where the distinction between visible (top) clothes and underclothing was not as important as it was in the upper classes.

> Ignoring the bourgeois concern to introduce formality and formal dress into the domestic world, the place for freedom—an apron and slippers (for women), bare chest or a vest (for men)—they scarcely mark the distinction between top clothes, visible, intended to be seen, and underclothes, invisible or hidden—unlike the middle classes, who have a degree of anxiety about external appearances, both sartorial and cosmetic, at least outside and at work (to which middle-class women more often have access) (Bourdieu, 1984, p. 201).

Bourdieu also noted the distinction between occupational attire of office workers and manual workers—a form of opposition between (white-collar) business attire and the blue overall (the distinctive mark in French culture of the farmer and industrial worker) (see Figure 13-8). Within the American working class, higher levels of education have been found to relate to males wearing formal clothing to work and to their wives preferring quality rather than quantity of clothes. The status of the husbands' degree of job advancement was related to educational level, wearing formal clothes to work, and the wives' preferences for quality over quantity. Moreover, the higher the employee's job satisfaction,

**FIGURE 13-8**
*A working-class man in Paris. Overalls have been a distinctive mark of French working-class culture (Bourdieu, 1984). Photo by Susan B. Kaiser.*

the more likely he was to dress formally (Kundel, 1976). Bourdieu (1984) noted that using a smock and apron (a working-class woman's uniform) is found much less often in the upper classes, whereas dressing gowns or pajamas were rarer in the working classes than in the upper classes. Manual workers bought more handkerchiefs, vests (undershirts), and underwear than the middle and upper classes.

### Lower Americans

Individuals classified by Coleman (1983) as lower Americans consist of individuals who are barely surviving in the economic system. They tend to hover around the poverty line and may or may not be employed. If they are employed, their wages are likely to be based on the minimum wage. Together, the employed and unemployed individuals in this category account for approximately one-fifth of the adult population, but less than 10 percent of the disposable income. They have been referred to as the "new poor," and public attention has turned to the plight of downwardly mobile individuals (frequently single mothers) and, especially, the homeless. Little research on clothing problems or possible feelings of deprivation has been conducted. This area is in great need of further study.

### Measurement of Social Class

A major issue in the study of social class is how to measure it adequately. Income does not correlate well with social class, because working-class individuals may have higher incomes than those in the middle class. [There is an adage cited by Coleman (1983) that blue-collar workers have "more money than class" and white-collar workers have "more class than money."] The number of workers in the family, as well as the age of the workers, confounds the use of income as an indicator of social class. The issue of whether income or social class is a better predictor of consumption should probably be rephrased as "how class affects use of income" (Coleman, 1983, p. 265).

The primary indicator of social class has typically been occupation—traditionally, of the male head of the household (Engel and Blackwell, 1982). However, with over one-half of the women in the United States in the workforce, this indicator alone obviously is not sufficient. Therefore, newer methods of gauging social class factor in the occupations of both heads of household. Thus, the measurement of social class by means of occupation is increasingly complex. In instances where husbands' and wives' occupations are unequal in status, it becomes more necessary to consider family relations and dynamics. Level of education is another social-class indicator that interacts in complex ways with occupation and family relations.

The advantages of using occupation as an indicator of social class relate to researchers' abilities to evaluate the prestige of an occupation. In terms of occupational clothing, the distinction between white-collar and blue-collar attire provides for a relatively straightforward classification for men. This distinction is not as clear-cut for women. That is, stereotypes of women's appearances in occupations are more subtle and less predefined than are those about men's work apparel. Nevertheless, status differences exist that can be observed in occupational contexts (Kanter, 1977).

Clothing researchers have documented the value of focusing on employment as a distinguishing characteristic in the attitudes of American women. When a female's lifestyle includes employment, the evaluative criteria used in relation to clothing is different in configuration from that applied to social contexts. For example, comfort, appropriateness, quality, and attractiveness are likely to be especially important considerations for career apparel. Working women appear to be relatively self-confident consumers who desire to be physically attractive and fashionable (Cassill and Drake, 1987). Employed women also differ from women who are not employed outside the home in terms of their search patterns for the selection of apparel (Shim and Drake, 1988). Most of the research with clothing concerns of working women has focused on white-collar workers, and, to a certain extent, there may be a social-class distinction in relation to women's employment patterns. There is a need for a better understanding of the meanings work clothes hold for women, across occupation status lines. Whereas for men the white-collar versus blue-collar distinction is quite obvious, for women status distinctions in appearance are likely to be more subtle and context-dependent. The issue of how gender and social class interconnect is one worthy of further study in clothing and appearance research.

Studies of first impression based on visible signs of social class reinforce the idea that the essence of social class is "the way a person is treated by others and, reciprocally, the way that person treats others" (Engel and Blackwell, 1982). The ubiquitous business suit, the sign of the white-collar world, has been associated, in particular, with the display of deference (respect) for the wearer in field studies

(Lefkowitz, Blake, and Mouton, 1959; Bickman, 1972; Fortenberry et al., 1978).

In first-impression situations, as described earlier, the obvious (blue- versus white-collar) as well as the subtle (quality and taste) signs of social class have been evident. Yet in attempting to relate the variable of social class to other characteristics, the research picture is even more complex. A variety of additional factors such as education, area of residence, and income of all family members needs to be assessed, along with more qualitative indicators of taste and values such as those studied by Bourdieu (1984) through intensive interviews.

The need to be aware of instances when social class does *not* adequately explain consumer behavior is also apparent. Marketing research combining a focus on values and lifestyles with more tangible indicators (income and age) has indicated, for example, that some cultural categories of consumers seem to cut across lines of income, age, occupation, or region. A group identified as "ultraconsumers" by nationwide marketing research in the United States, for example, is based on similarity in attitudes toward success and an insatiable desire for the new (Lebow, 1986). It makes up 25 percent of the American population and is characterized as between the ages of 21 and 50. This category seems to fall primarily into Coleman's (1983) scheme of upper Americans, but also includes persons from the middle classes and excludes some upper Americans who are less fashion-oriented. Forty-four percent of ultraconsumers own or use top designer clothing. This classification of consumers tends to be career-oriented and places a high priority on earning to afford what they enjoy. It does *not*, however, fit the picture of the young, restless, and wealthy consumer stereotype of the "yuppie" (young, upwardly mobile professional, usually in an urban context). Attitudinally and demographically, the "ultraconsumer" classification reveals the inadequacy of the yuppie stereotype (Lebow, 1986).

## *Ethnicity*

> This shattering of traditional styles of beauty continues. Its extension is based partly on the commercial realization that ethnic cultures with substantial buying power exist. But the increasing sophistication of businessmen and advertisers in targeting specific consumer populations alone cannot explain the continuing democratization of beauty. . . . The very self-absorption of the last two decades itself may underlie the continuing democratization of beauty standards by implicitly validating each individual's claim to beauty.
>
> —BANNER, 1983, p. 290

Ethnicity is a cultural category that may be visible on the basis of such physical attributes as skin color, eye shape, hair texture, or facial features. Additional cues pertain to grooming and clothing styles (see Figure 13-9). Whereas ethnicity (like gender) is a cultural concept referring to that which is socially constructed, *race* (like sex) is a biological concept. However, the concept of race cannot be defined scientifically because of the variations within *phenotypes* (categories based

***FIGURE 13-9***
*A black (African-American) woman in the latter part of the nineteenth century. Courtesy of the California State Library Collection, City of Sacramento, Museum and History Division.*

on physical attributes) (Hess, Markson, and Stein, 1985). Thus our discussion will revolve around variations based on socialization within ethnic cultural categories, and the corresponding potential for inequities relative to prevailing standards of attractiveness and fashionability.

In the 1960s, for the first time in American history, non-European models were presented for purposes of cultural emulation. Donyale Luna was the first black (African-American) model to be featured in general-circulation fashion magazines such as *Vogue*. The civil rights movement was a major factor in this shift in cultural imagery. The slogan "black is beautiful" came to penetrate even the white (Anglo-American) consciousness, as many black persons proudly wore their hair naturally in a style called "Afro." By the end of the 1960s, this style had become a fashionable look for white Americans as well—often achieved with permanents. By the 1970s, black and Asian-American women had advanced to the finals of the Miss America pageant. The Miss Universe contest presented an even broader array of ethnic appearances (Banner, 1983, pp. 289–290). The standardization of physical appearance ideals had broken down somewhat; more racial and ethnic looks could be viewed as attractive from a cultural perspective. Yet inequities still persist to some extent on the beauty front. Similarly, social stratification based on such factors as skin color has diminished but certainly has not disappeared. We will now focus on ethnicity as a cultural category in terms of appearance imagery and clothing preferences, especially in relation to *actual*, rather than stereotypical, understandings.

## African-American Consumers

The first black (African-American) millionaire was a woman, Madame C. J. Walker. She made her fortune by discovering a way of straightening her hair and establishing a chain of beauty salons to market her invention (Banner, 1983, p. 14). Black-owned cosmetic companies now hold about 50 percent of the black market share. Black consumers buy approximately five times as many cosmetics as the general market; they also are high consumers of hair-care products. Since the middle of the 1970s, however, the overall market share for black-owned companies has diminished as the "giants" of the industry, such as Revlon, have emerged with even greater force (Spratlen and Choudhury, 1987).

Although black consumers are often stereotyped as spending more on clothes than other consumers, research on this topic produces mixed results (Dardis, Derrick, and Lehfeld, 1981; Shaw, Lazer, and Smith, 1987). In general, stereotypes based on ethnic cultural categories frequently fail to receive straightforward support in the research literature. Although there may sometimes be a "kernel of truth" in stereotypes about ethnic cultural categories, actual tendencies and preferences are often more complex than the stereotypes would suggest. Black females, for example, do not especially prefer "flashier" combinations. They *do* prefer "truer" hues or more intensity in some colors, probably because these colors complement their skin tones (Williams, Arbaugh, and Rucker, 1980). Blue and red have been identified as preferred colors, but black was also identified as a popular color among black consumers in the late 1980s, when it was a fashionable color in general (Liebman, 1987). Thus, it is important that researchers aiming to identify preferences clearly note the influences of fashion and distinguish these from factors related to ethnicity.

Research has indicated that white university students *perceived* black male athletes as wearing more attention-getting clothes than their white counterparts, yet the *actual* clothing preferences of black athletes were not as extreme as the perceptions would suggest (Reeder and Drake, 1980). In contrast, there was no discrepancy between white students' perceptions of white male athletes' attire and the actual preferences of white male athletes. It is also important to note that black male athletes who preferred more attention-getting clothes exhibited higher feelings of self-concept (Reeder and Drake, 1980). Some research has suggested that black consumers have allowed clothing to influence their social participation more than have white consumers (Kelley et al., 1974).

In the context of a Southern high school, research indicated that black students accepted other black students socially, and white students accepted white students socially (Drake and Ford, 1979). Whereas black males participated more in organized activities, such as sports, than did white males, white females participated in more organizational activities than did black females. Black freshmen were more negative (in terms of social acceptance) toward white female freshmen than they were toward black female freshmen. In contrast, black sophomores held more favorable attitudes toward black and white sophomores. A year of constant contact in a school setting may have accounted for this more favorable attitude. Black students who felt deprived in terms of their own clothing were less self-accepting. White students, on the other hand, tended to regard "dressing for others" as more important than the black students (Drake and Ford, 1979).

In a later study among white and black college females, there were significant differences on three variables: adequacy of money, use of sexually attractive clothing, and self-esteem (Ford and Drake, 1982). The two groups were similar on three other variables: body satisfaction, attitude toward unusual clothing, and flair in clothing. Regardless of ethnicity, self-esteem was related to body satisfaction. The black females scored higher than white females on the use of sexually attractive clothing, especially when at leisure but also when attending class or going out on a casual date. The researchers explained some of these differences on the basis of heterosexual competition. The sex ratio and dating practices were more problematic for black females, as compared to white females. That is, white females had more dating opportunities. Ford and Drake (1982) found that the two groups were most alike in their low use of sexually attractive clothing for a job interview, a context for which a more widely understood mode of dress is culturally accepted. In an earlier study, both black and white females had reported relatively infrequent use of clothing items that they *perceived* to be sexually attractive to males (McCullough, Miller, and Ford, 1977). Social context, however, was not included as a variable in this study; the inclusion of social context in the later study helped to clarify the issue.

## Latino Consumers

Latino consumers (descending from Latin-American countries) make up the fastest growing minority group in America. They have been characterized as being more brand loyal than non-Latino consumers and as being influenced by family relationships (Saegert and Hoover, 1985). Another factor that impinges on Latino consumer behavior is the degree of *acculturation*, a process by which the members of a minority internalize the norms and values of the majority, without necessarily being admitted into intimate groupings (Hess, Markson, and Stein, 1985). Therefore, to understand this cultural group's consumer behavior more fully, it is critical that broader contextual factors be incorporated into the discussion.

Karen Kaigler-Walker and Mary Ericksen (working paper) explored the relation between level of acculturation and clothing perceptions of Latino-Texan women. No differences were found between Mexican (from Mexico) and white-

Texan women in their evaluations of Anglo-American clothes for social and business contexts. However, there were differences with respect to perceptions of Anglo-American casual clothes. There was a tendency for the Latino-Texan women, like the Mexican women, to perceive the Anglo-American casual "shopping" style as inappropriate. This difference may be attributed in part to a greater tendency toward formality in female appearance styles in Latino culture. A low degree of acculturation was related to preferences for root-cultural styles and a lack of certainty about dominant (Anglo-American) culture appropriateness, especially for casual contexts. Thus, the Latino-Texan American women, although adopting prevailing Anglo-American symbols in many respects, still tended to be influenced in some ways by their cultural roots. In a later study in southern California there was a tendency for these findings to be confirmed in terms of a relation between acculturation and clothing perceptions (Kaigler-Walker, Ericksen, and Mount, 1989).

Some differences among adolescent black, white, and Latino-Texan females were found in a study of clothing satisfaction in West Texas. Among Latino-Texan females, socioeconomic status and the number of shoes in their wardrobes contributed most to satisfaction with clothing. Among the white females, feelings of social security and the number of dressy and casual dresses in their wardrobes contributed most to their clothing satisfaction. The black females tended to hold values and opinions that differed somewhat from those of the other two groups. Among these females, feelings of being liked and accepted or belonging were the most important predictors of satisfaction with their clothes (Kness, 1983).

## Asian-American Consumers

The Asian-American consumer market (over 5 million in 1986) has traditionally been considered too small to warrant a separate marketing effort. Moreover, this market encompasses diverse cultural orientations (for example, Japanese, Chinese, and Korean). However, the importance of this market, especially in certain parts of the United States such as the West Coast, is becoming apparent to marketers (Lee and Cooke, 1987).

Some research has indicated differences in color preferences between white and Asian-American females (Rucker, Kim, and Ho, 1987). The Asian females tended to prefer pale pink, as well as pale orange and purple, for lingerie for a wedding trip. Overall, the differences in color preference pertained to tints, but not hues or shades. There were more similarities than differences with respect to the wedding context, but more differences overall in color preference (Rucker, Kim, and Ho, 1987). The differences that did exist may be explained, in part, on the basis of cultural differences in orientation toward femininity.

Another study determined some differences among the different cultural groups composing the more inclusive market of Asian-American consumers (Forney and Rabolt, 1986). Since the latter part of the nineteenth century in America, many Asian-Americans (as well as individuals in other ethnic groups) have lain aside their ethnic identity to embrace American mainstream culture (see Figure 13-10). Yet since the 1960s there has been increased interest in ethnic traditions such as holidays. In a study in the 1980s in San Francisco,

*FIGURE 13-10*
*Asian-American men in the early part of the twentieth century. Courtesy of the Folsom Historical Society Collection, City of Sacramento, Museum and History Division.*

there was general agreement among minority groups that cultural heritage is important. Ethnic-specific clothing was indicated as being worn on special holidays although not typically in everyday contexts. Those individuals with a higher level of ethnic identity also reported wearing and identifying with items of ethnic dress. Among the Japanese-American students, there was a relation between ethnic identity and use of ethnic market sources, including fashion magazines, fashion shows, and sales associates. The same finding did not hold for the Chinese-American students. This finding in terms of the Japanese-American students may be linked to the current fashion scene in Japan, with which Japanese-American students may identify. Prominent Japanese designers such as Issey Miyake are likely to contribute to a source of ethnic pride. Researchers Judith Forney and Nancy Rabolt (1986) note that ethnic identity is not a static concept but is likely to be influenced by current trends, even in different countries.

## Continuity and Change in Categorical Boundaries

Now that we have looked at the various cultural categories that may contribute to status hierarchies, it should be clear that (1) these categories converge in dynamic ways; (2) individuals may exercise a great deal of control through appearance management, on a daily basis, to shape the extent to which they either fall neatly into these categories or to which they stretch the boundaries;

and (3) social perceptions are shaped and reshaped on the basis of forces linked to appearance, clothing, and fashion. In Part Five, we will see that these types of negotiations in everyday life contribute to cultural continuity (maintenance of ideology) as well as to change (transformations in ideology). Chapter Fourteen will discuss the tensions and dynamics across cultural categories in relation to the forces of continuity and change.

## Suggested Readings

Banner, L. W. 1983. *American beauty*. Chicago: The University of Chicago Press.
Banner provides a social-historical treatment of the fashion and beauty cultures in the United States, focusing especially on New York City. This work serves to illustrate the elaborate connections among attractiveness, age, gender, and social class.

Bourdieu, P. 1984. *Distinction: A social critique of the judgement of taste*. Cambridge: Harvard University Press.
Bourdieu provides data on the relation between social class and judgments of taste in French culture. Numerous examples of preferences, expenditures, and attitudes with respect to clothing are provided.

Fox-Genovese, E. 1987. The empress's new clothes: The politics of fashion. *Socialist Review 17*(1): 7–32.
The politics of gender, social class, and ethnic symbolism through dress are characterized using a critical approach.

Hatfield, E., and Sprecher, S. 1986. *Mirror, mirror: The importance of looks in everyday life*. Albany: State University of New York Press.
A very useful analysis of "good looks" is provided. A variety of terms related to attractiveness are conceptualized, and measures for examining perceptions of appearance (one's own, as well as others') are described.

Patzer, G. L. 1985. *The physical attractiveness phenomenon*. New York: Plenum Press.
Patzer reviews a number of studies related to the physical attractiveness phenomenon and discusses the need for programmatic research addressing it.

# *Part Five*
# ...
# *Culture Change and Continuity*

Modernity is a code, and fashion is its emblem.
— BAUDRILLARD, 1976

*H*OW do we know when our lives have really changed—when the new styles we wear really represent new ideas or values? According to some writers, like the French sociologist Jean Baudrillard (1976; 1981), modernity itself is a kind of myth. Fashion provides us with an illusion of change, he says, while nothing fundamental has been changed in the social order. At the same time, we have seen that the cultural categories we use to derive thought processes (cognitive categories) to understand other people may be altered somewhat as the boundaries between these categories are blurred and confused by perplexing appearance messages. Yet some ideologies seem to be quite resistant to change, and new styles may actually serve to represent older ideologies in an updated way. Thus the issue of continuity and change is a central component of any understanding about culture, and in this part we will delve into these issues by considering the micro and macro forces that lead to change while also constraining that change.

As we saw in Chapter Thirteen, there are some inherent tensions between cultural categories such as male versus female, old versus young, and others. These tensions are linked to ambivalences and are culturally coded in the midst of the fashion process. Conflicting desires for identification (with others) and differentiation (from others) also compel the fashion process. These topics will be considered in Chapter Fourteen.

Thus we are likely to attempt to distinguish ourselves from one another, but we also have a need to express our commonalities. Such is the dilemma inherent in cultural life, and it is given form in fashion change. In Chapter Fifteen, we will consider some of the major theories that have attempted to explain the perplexing phenomenon of fashion, considering both cultural change and social-psychological processes.

The concept of postmodernism was introduced earlier (in Chapter Twelve) in relation to the eclectic blend of appearance elements in many cultures today. Postmodernism is apparent in the global context, and appearance communication is a worldwide process influenced by an eclectic blending of appearance signs that are often stripped from their specific cultural contexts. Thus as we consider the global context of clothing and appearance, a major dilemma emerges that parallels the issues of identification and differentiation. How can we convey our tendency toward a "global village" through our appearance and still maintain some sense of locality in our cultural identities? Chapter Sixteen will delve further into this dilemma.

# Chapter Fourteen
...
# Cultural Dynamics and Identity Construction

*Cultural categories may promote underlying tensions or ambivalences in a society. These ambivalences provide creative fuel for fashion change and personal experimentation with appearance, as designers and consumers may juxtapose symbols of masculinity and femininity, youth and old age, and high and low status. Such juxtapositions are likely to create appearances that are novel and ambiguous—in other words, that do not necessarily fit neatly into the categories culture provides for us. As perceivers' cognitive categories are challenged by ambiguous appearances, changes in ways of thinking about appearance contribute to the modification of cultural categories. These changes in ways of thinking are compatible with the postmodern cultural context, in which there is not necessarily a single acceptable "look," but rather multiple, simultaneously acceptable looks. Identification and differentiation become critical, interdependent processes, allowing us to dress like some people and unlike others, while still having the potential to express a sense of self.*

As we saw in Chapter Thirteen, cultural categories form the basis for social differences within a society, and appearance styles lend expression to these differences. However, cultural categories are neither fixed nor constant; rather, they are malleable and alterable in response to individual and social-psychological processes. The boundaries between cultural categories change, and appearance provides a fruitful arena for expressing and redefining what it means to be male versus female, or young versus old. Cultural categories and their social meanings are alterable because culture itself is dynamic. In this chapter, we will address the underlying principles that contribute to individuals' identity constructions within the dynamic context of culture. Basic ambivalences related to cultural categories (for example, the interplay of masculinity and femininity in gender symbolism) are presented along with a consideration of the fundamental micro

453

and macro processes of identification and differentiation. We want to appear like others to some degree, but we also want to be unique as individuals.

Let's begin our discussion of cultural dynamics and identity construction by focusing on the instability and ambivalence related to cultural categories.

## Cultural Ambivalence and the Meaning of Style

### Instabilities in Cultural Categories

What cultural categories *mean* in everyday life changes in conjunction with individual acts of appearance management and social interactions. Thus, culture does not "feed" meanings to individuals "on a platter." Although some meanings are part of culture's "structure of feeling," they assume significance through everyday rituals and interactions. Still other meanings emerge from individual acts of creative expression and social interpretations of these acts. Regardless of the source, however, the meanings of appearance styles are susceptible to variation and transformation.

Three characteristics of cultural categories in contemporary North America, as well as in many other postindustrial societies throughout the world, help to clarify the instabilities that lead to changing representations through appearance (McCracken, 1986):

*1.* Cultural categories tend to be indeterminate. They are often indefinite, imprecise, and ambiguous. There is a lack of clarity in terms of where one category begins and another ends. Through appearance management, individuals can blur the distinctions between cultural categories. For example, we can look at instances where rock stars have crossed traditional gender boundaries, often to create some intrigue and ambiguity (see Figure 14-1). As the symbolic-interactionist perspective tells us, symbolic ambiguity often leads to the most intriguing or mindful interpretations, because appearances that are hard to categorize simply are not only troublesome in a cognitive sense but also fascinating and arousing in a symbolic sense. A cognitive perspective indicates that the difficulties associated with dissonance in our thought processes are weighed against a desire for novelty and stimulation. A contextual framework encourages us to consider the contexts in which we formulate judgments of appearance. In the case of rock stars' appearances, some arousal and shock value may be expected on the part of the viewing and listening audience. And, although individuals in the audience may not necessarily rush out and try these styles themselves, their *thought processes* are likely to be altered as they reformulate their cognitive categories in accordance with changing cultural categories. For example, the idea of males wearing earrings, or even eyeliner, has become more acceptable in the last 10 years. It is almost as though we have mental filing systems with appearance cues filed in certain categories (male versus female). At times we will realize that we either need to move one card into the other file or make a duplicate so that the appearance cue can go either way.

**FIGURE 14-1**
*Gender bending (blurring of cultural categories of male and female) has been something of a tradition in the world of rock. In the 1970s, singer Patti Smith noted, "Gender is irrelevant when we're talking about art at the highest level." (She began her career as a poet.) A female rock singer was still a novelty at that time and, perhaps to compensate, Smith turned herself into a "nearly flawless mixture of the sensibilities and visual styles of Mick Jagger, Keith Richards, and Bob Dylan" (Simels, 1985, p. 68). Photo by Larry White.*

**2.** In addition to being indeterminate, cultural categories often seem to have a kind of "elective" quality. Let's look at age categories, which probably illustrate this point most clearly. These categories are indeterminate not only because it is unclear as to what chronological age brackets compose each category, but also because even if age brackets were clearly delineated, individuals may naturally or, with some effort, look similar to those in another category. Young girls can look older than their age through the use of makeup, hairstyling, and dress. Older women, on the other hand, may use these devices as strategies for appearing younger than their age. The cultural ideology behind these attempts to alter the appearance of age was discussed in Chapter Thirteen. Here our concern is with the implications of individual acts of appearance management for cultural categories. Our conceptions of what age *means* are altered as individuals can appear in ways that defy rigid boundaries.

To the extent that individuals have some freedom to buy and wear the clothes they want and to alter their appearances through grooming, they can elect to "belong" to cultural categories. This elective quality varies somewhat by cultural categories, but the point is that individuals can *appear* to belong to cultural categories. By managing their appearances to do so, they can emphasize those categories they wish to emphasize—frequently those that are more salient to their identities. And, they can strive to "fit" into a category neatly by conforming to traditional conceptions about how people in that category look, or they can strive to blur the boundaries between categories by juxtaposing elements from more than one category.

*3.* Cultural categories are subject to continual and rapid change. Stereotypes may emerge to classify individuals but then fade from the collective consciousness as they no longer seem to apply or clarify. For example, the cultural category of "yuppie" was created in part by the media to characterize individuals of the same age category (post-World-War-II "baby boomers") who were also upwardly mobile and shared certain lifestyles, values, and preferences. Although the yuppie stereotype may never have fully "fit" reality, it did serve as a kind of reference group for purposes of comparison. As individuals in this age category consumed certain products (compact disc players, BMWs, health food), they could ask themselves whether or not they were, or wanted to be, "typical" yuppies. Once some aspects of the yuppie stereotype were exposed as being mythical, it faded from the public consciousness and the media lost its fascination with this short-lived cultural category that actually represented a blending of two more stable categories (age and social class, framed in a specific cultural and historic context).

As we examine the instability of cultural categories in modern societies, the following question arises: What cultural and social-psychological forces influence these instabilities? Part of the answer, at least, may lie in uncertainties about social identity on the part of groups of individuals, as well as in the politics of style itself. The politics of style are linked not only to struggles between social classes but also, more widely, to the tenuous nature of cultural categories and what they represent. Simon-Miller (1985) notes that cultural anthropology can contribute to an understanding of the politics of style by reminding us that power often becomes ritualized, as people classify one another routinely and (almost) unconsciously.

Anthropologists view consumption as being inextricably linked to power, but note that power may be held, represented, and enacted in a variety of ways (Douglas and Isherwood, 1979). To the extent that cultural categories are based on ideological principles, these categories thrive best when individuals do not question them—or when they are *beneath* individuals' levels of consciousness (Hebdige, 1979, p. 11). To unravel the ideological dimensions of cultural signs, the codes through which meaning is organized must be revealed and deciphered. How are these codes developed in the first place?

We must first consider how power is distributed in our society. That is, we must ask which groups and classes have how much say in defining, ordering and classifying the social world. For instance, if we pause to reflect for a moment, it should be obvious that access to the means by which ideas are disseminated in our society (i.e., principally the mass media) is *not* the same for all classes. Some groups have more say, more opportunity to break the rules, to organize meaning, while others are less favourably placed, have less power to produce and impose their definitions of the world on the world (Hebdige, 1979, p. 14).

This is not to say that ideological principles underlying the meaning of style are inflexible, but rather that people in some cultural categories have more of a vested interest in maintaining the status quo in appearance styles. For example, successful men in professional positions may benefit, in terms of power relations, from the continuing popularity of business suits. That is, their status is secured and reinforced by a commonly understood, potent symbol.

Through appearance management and display, however, people can vie for preferred identities and participate in a kind of cultural "dialogue" on the preferred meanings associated with cultural categories (for example, masculinity versus femininity, high versus low status, youthful versus mature). Style is one arena in which opposing definitions and interpretations can clash with dramatic force (Hebdige, 1979, p. 3). Do individuals participate in this dialogue consciously? In many cases, they probably do not become involved in the discourse of style to struggle with meanings on a conscious level. For example, a woman who wears a conservative gray business suit with a white blouse and a little black tie may not deliberately be trying to look like a man, but she may well be caught up in the ritual or everyday practice of competing—of striving to being taken seriously—in a traditionally masculine context. As more women assume positions of power in the corporate world, the instabilities between gender categories are likely to be manifest in different ways, to reflect new kinds of struggles and negotiations. Thus, it is often important to distinguish between what is meant by the *collective search for identity* on the part of groups of individuals who share common goals and characteristics, and *individual expressions of identity*, which may or may not be consciously derived or managed. Do individuals in cultural categories with less power necessarily strive to "move out" of their social positions? The answer to this question is neither simple nor straightforward, because people tend to have mixed emotions about identities linked to cultural categories, as we will see in the following section.

## Culturally Coded Identity Ambivalences

Sociologist Fred Davis (1988) suggests that shifting cultural moods and style-selection processes are incited by what he calls "identity ambivalences." To understand this concept, first it is necessary to understand what we mean by ambivalence. Ambivalence refers to the conflicting or contradictory emotional and psychological attitudes that we experience in everyday life. We may feel one way on Monday and another on Tuesday about issues related to gender, for example. Imagine a woman who works as an accountant for a conservative firm.

To be taken seriously, she feels she needs to wear a conservative gray or navy suit. Therefore, her attitude toward this suit revolves around her career and her future. At the same time, she often becomes bored with the suit and longs to rekindle her interest in fashion in her precareer days. Such feelings may not be on a conscious level on her part. Yet if we look at general shifts in the style choices of large numbers of women in similar situations—on a *collective* level— then we can see that she is not alone in her feelings of ambivalence.

Many women who wore business suits in the corporate world in the late 1970s and early to middle 1980s embraced the "dress-for-success" ethic (viewing clothing as instrumental to career advancement). However, women who espoused the goals of the women's movement were more likely than women who did not support this movement to endorse the dress-for-success ethic and to reveal an interest in fashion (wanting to dress in the latest styles and having an interest in experimenting with different clothing styles) (Koch and Dickey, 1988). Thus, it is not surprising that by the late 1980s, large numbers of women were eschewing traditional gray or navy suits and incorporating more color and style into their career wardrobes. Endorsing the idea of dressing in styles that emulate men's business wear in order to be taken seriously in a traditionally male world conflicted with years of female socialization promoting an interest in fashion and "color." Accordingly, different sentiments and cultural values to which women had been exposed were likely to contribute to "inner voices" that would "clash, or at the very least, talk past each other. 'Whom do I wish to please and in so doing whom am I likely to offend? What are the consequences of appearing as this kind of person as against that kind? Does the image I believe I convey of myself reflect my true innermost self or some specious version thereof?'" (Davis, 1988, p. 25).

Davis (1988) believes that ambivalences "have come over the course of centuries to be deeply etched into the culturally encoded identity formulas through which Western men and women conceive of themselves" (p. 24). The mixed emotions or ambivalences individuals perceive in their identities provide a continual resource on which fashion designers can draw for inspiration.

> Among the more prominent ambivalences underlying such fashion-susceptible instabilities are the subjective tensions of youth versus age, masculinity versus femininity, androgyny versus singularity, inclusiveness versus exclusiveness, work versus play, domesticity versus worldliness. . . . Fashion's code modifications seem constantly to move within and among the symbols by which clothing encodes these tensions, now highlighting this, muting that, juxtaposing what was previously disparate (Davis, 1985, pp. 24–25).

You will note that many of the ambivalences indicated by Davis are linked to cultural categories such as gender, age, and social status. These categories foster identity ambivalences that are evident in many cultures today in which rapid social and fashion change are evident. In more stable societies of both the past and present, cultural categories are likely to be more delineated and durable; accordingly, these societies are not as likely to experience continual or rapid fashion change. (See Social Focus 14-1 for a discussion of identity ambivalences related to gender.)

Through style variations, then, culture may send messages to itself about (*a*) the discourse or struggle across cultural categories and (*b*) collective ambivalences about these categories and what they represent. As style becomes an arena for expression, revolt, and identification, it displays that culture is not necessarily based on a "one-track" structure of feeling.

The idea of mass culture has been proposed at various times to characterize aspects of modern life that may be depersonalizing: one-way communication from mass media to the individual, loneliness, anonymity, conformity, loss of community (*Gemeinschaft*-like) ties, and secondary relations among people. The media, for example, may promote a kind of thinking that is category-responding (Vernon, 1978), thereby perpetuating stereotypes encouraging categorization of people and symbols. We know from a cognitive perspective that humans create categories and then respond to these socially created, symboled phenomena in order to simplify their worlds. However, this tendency to create categories and thus to oversimplify interpersonal perceptions is counterbalanced by the fact that people in complex societies realize that it is hard to know all aspects of culture. Ambiguities in appearances are likely to emerge in part from identity ambivalences. For example, the juxtaposition of different signs (earrings with football uniforms, business suits with high heels), when first encountered by perceivers, may defy simple categorization. Hence, humans must *concentrate* to fit their lines of action together, in some contexts more than others. A symbolic-interactionist perspective leads us to consider the idea that symbolic ambiguity may lead to the richest constructions of meaning, because of the need for more mindful, aware, or aroused interpretations.

Thus, depersonalizing characteristics may appear to be present in postindustrial (*Gesellschaft*-like) societies, but there are also likely to be ambivalences and instabilities, as we have seen, that challenge a unidimensional mass culture. If there are some depersonalizing aspects of large-scale *Gesellschaft*-like societies, they are probably due not to the complexity and modernity inherent in these types of societies, but rather to certain (albeit unstable) conditions in the economic, political, or social order.

*Alienation* involves one's frustrated responses to economic and sociological processes that are beyond the control of the individual and that affect his or her perceptions of identity. A sense of meaninglessness is one component of alienation (Seeman, 1959). Sociologist Orrin Klapp (1982) argues that there is a meaning lag in postindustrial societies that accounts for some of the meaninglessness confronting some people. His basic thesis is that in an information society largely influenced by the mass media, a sense of meaning does not necessarily follow the processing of information. Because of an abundance of "noise" inherent in this form of heterogeneous society, it is difficult to receive or find meaning in all of the information and images with which individuals are bombarded on a daily basis. Alienation is the loss of identification with

## The Myth of Mass Culture

## Gender Ambivalence in Fashion and Rock Music

In the history of Western fashion no greater symbolic tension can be found than that generated by the desire, sometimes overt though more often repressed, of each sex to emulate the clothing and associated gender paraphernalia of the other.

—DAVIS, 1988, p. 27

Although more often than not the tendency has been for masculine versus feminine ambivalence to reveal itself in the form of females borrowing signs of male status and masculinity (as in the dark business suit) (Davis, 1988), males have also participated in the symbolic struggle of gender ambivalence. Perhaps some of the most dramatic images of "gender bending" on both the masculine and feminine sides of the equation have been evident in the appearances of rock musicians.

As one of the "subthemes" or stories in rock, androgyny aims to blur distinctions, traditional or otherwise, between the sexes. Yet in appearance management, signs of gender cannot be blended or dissolved. Rather, androgyny is constructed by means of juxtaposition and opposition. A male face adorned with makeup, coupled with an elaborate hairstyle and earrings, for example, calls into question traditional notions about masculinity versus femininity. The history of rock and roll is replete with examples of gender benders. During the 1950s, performer Little Richard was rarely seen or photographed without lipstick, the wildest hairstyles, and the heaviest makeup. Long hair on males was popularized by the Beatles and other rock groups of the 1960s. And, the 1970s brought the visually dramatic gender ambivalence of David Bowie:

After a period of stringent self-analysis, immersions in Tibetan Buddhism, classes with an undistinguished mime artist, and mingling with the Warhol crowd in New York, Bowie decided to turn himself into the reincarnation of Katharine Hepburn. This got him noticed during various promotional visits to the States; how could it not? By the time he had found high-powered management and readied himself for an American concert debut, he had at last developed a genuinely striking character to portray: the first homosexual rock star from outer space, a/k/a Ziggy Stardust (Simels, 1985).

Linked to the context of the English New Romantic Movement, David Bowie continued to construct new appearances into the 1980s, and facilitated the making of a *concept* of "constantly recreating your look" or "neurotic chameleoning" (Simels, 1985). The Eurythmics, Boy George, Michael Jackson, Prince, and many other rock musicians (see Figure 14-1) have participated in this process of continually reconstructing the self-image, and gender has been a predominant theme that has been explored, tested, and ruptured.

What a star she was. What a *hairdo* she had!

There are full grown legends about Annie Lennox's hostile coiffure, the one she wore on the way to fame. . . . Annie's haircut made a big contribution to the vogue for gender confusion. Most participants were men who looked like women. Lennox was the reverse. . . . As an image and as a celebrated voice, this ambivalence—this sparkling noncommitment— is the key to the Lennox performance and hence the Eurythmics' celebrity impact. Juxtaposing a neutral, businessman's threads with a jarring, alluring head and facial impact (scarlet lips and a luxurious smile), Lennox became a glistening alien, an outsider in disguise (Hill, 1986).

Androgynous dressing reveals a lack of commitment to traditional gender ideology and, in a larger context, a noncommitment to a single look. At the same time, a strong commitment is made to the idea of continually constructing a sense of self—a theme that ambivalence fuels. It is perhaps this theme that has been fostered most in everyday life, whether or not consumers engage in the act of gender bending. More dramatically, gender ambivalence in the rock world may be characterized as a blending of poetry and packaging, melding and marketing, and shock and sales. Thus the gender ambivalence is embedded in a nexus of cultural ambivalence about producing the self and profiting in the process.

cultural symbols due to a lack of significance or meaning of these symbols for an individual or a group (Becker, 1967). Clothing styles are likely to exist that cannot be interpreted by much of a complex society's population, but rather that are understood only in smaller scale group "idiocultures" (as discussed in Chapter Eleven).

Consumers may not readily be able to interpret new clothing styles until they interact with people who have adopted them and come to negotiate a sense of understanding. Some styles never seem to infiltrate the population because they are too far "out of step" with people's lives. For example, the "midi" style of the early 1970s was soundly rejected by the consuming female population, and the revival of the mini skirt in the 1980s did not work in the lives of career women, who would agree to somewhat shortened skirts but not to the extreme extent that the fashion industry was promoting.

In any event, the concept of mass culture is not supported by the diversity in clothing styles, which will appeal to different segments of the population and be interpreted in various ways even by those people who do adopt them—all because meaning still tends to be negotiated in everyday social interactions. In other words, there tends to be a lack of widespread cultural consensus on the meanings of clothing styles. Thus, while people within certain cultural categories (for example, the young) may still conform for the same reasons they did in the 1950s, for example, *the styles they conform to* are much more diffuse and eclectic than they were back then. Today, each young person has to work out his or her own image in the context of social relations, so although "apparel still proclaims" the man and the woman, "the proclamation is noisier and less uniform" than it was around the middle of the twentieth century.

To some extent, mass media may serve to counterbalance the "noisiness" in clothing styles. One function of mass media is that of *cultural transmission*, through the impersonal communication of lifestyles and symbols that cannot always be communicated through interpersonal relations because of (a) rapid social change and (b) increased anonymity (Wright, 1960). However, the media today are also diffuse or "demassified"; people are likely to tune in to media that are most relevant to their lives and interests. For example, music videos are likely to be more watched by some age groups than others. Specialized magazines in the marketplace cater to specific lifestyles, values, sports and leisure interests, and fashion preferences.

Despite (and perhaps because of) this diversity, the media can reduce feelings of alienation and continue the socialization of individuals who are not in direct contact with others on a daily basis. However, the media may also standardize images of certain cultural categories by promoting stereotypical images. For example, the media tend to overemphasize a link between youth and beauty, especially for women. Accordingly, some older adults may feel a sense of alienation toward fashion (Kaiser and Chandler, 1984).

Thus, there are conflicting indicators and ideas as to what constitutes mass culture, whether or not it exists, or, if it does, if it is inherently negative in its consequences from the standpoint of the individual. Daniel Bell (1956) attributes the concept of mass culture to the romantic protest against the effects of industrialization and argues that culture is as important in people's lives in *Gesellschaft*-like societies as it is in *Gemeinschaft*-like ones. The concept of mass culture implies that superior groups make the important decisions that make an impact on the lives of other, less powerful groups, and as we have seen, cultural categories may operate on this basis. For example, mass media may perpetuate existing stereotypes about women, older adults, and ethnic minorities who are often not only underrepresented but also misrepresented. Yet consumer capitalism does not merely create homogeneous mass taste but rather it generates a variety of tastes, audiences, and consumers (Swingewood, 1977).

Moreover, distinctions between **high culture** and **popular culture** tend to become somewhat blurred in postindustrial societies. What do we mean by high culture versus popular culture? The concept of high culture refers to the fine arts such as "classical" art, music, and literature, whereas popular culture embraces romance novels, television shows, music videos, rock music, and fashionable clothing styles affordable to most people in a society. Some critics of the mass culture concept argue that whereas nineteenth-century societies in the process of becoming industrialized were still "dominated by poverty, ignorance and exclusiveness with high culture triumphant," the twentieth century's emergence of postindustrial societies has resulted in more democratic cultures (Swingewood, 1977, p. 95). At the same time, the media can and do perpetuate existing stereotypes about women and men, young and old people, and so on. But if we look at the eclectic array of appearances that people may strive to create, and consider the increasing number of style alternatives both in the media and in everyday life, then we can see that fashion in general is more pluralist than it was prior to industrialization. The (late) capitalist marketplace associated with postmodern culture benefits from the breadth in personal choices.

The range of products and activities subject to fashion change, for example, is continually widening. Almost *everything* seems to be susceptible to fashion change: automobiles, foods, hobbies, places to travel, music, slang, points of view, and types of exercise, as well as clothing styles. Sociologists Orrin Klapp (1966) and Fred Davis (1988) agree that fashions in postindustrial societies are symptomatic of a collective restlessness about identity. Klapp notes that there will be a variety of reactions to the more predominant styles of the day. These reactions may be outlined as follows.

*Ego Screaming*    Ego screaming is an individual reaction to prevalent clothing styles, characterized by an attempt to create shock value and to demand attention. This attention is not necessarily desired for purposes of approval or disapproval, but rather for the sake of *being noticed* per se.

We live in an era of free identity experimentation, and the conditions are ripe for a variety of forms of expression. Individual interpretations of fashion allow for a form of ego differentiation, which can become a more powerful motive for dressing than class differentiation. Thus, ego screamers may actually embrace some form of fashion and exaggerate it. Ego screamers are not necessarily

**FIGURE 14-2**
*Some punk appearance styles of the 1980s were designed for purposes of shock value or* **ego screaming**. *Appearance was an avenue for testing the reactions of perceivers. Photo by Larry White.*

left totally to their own devices; in fact, they may actually create a distinct idioculture, in which they derive a group look or a kind of "collective ego" that is different from that expressed by outsiders.

What are some examples of ego screaming in the recent past? Some punk and postpunk appearances have been generated with the intent of creating shock value (see Figure 14-2). Similarly, some of the bright colors associated with the early new-wave styles may have been worn to achieve this kind of effect. Also, mohawk hairstyles with brightly colored tips of the 1980s may have been designed initially with a reaction of astonishment or awe in mind.

Dandyism is a particularly unique form of symbolic protest against the social order and the corresponding styles that this order seems to dictate. A dandy develops an inordinate focus on style, often unique or exaggerated in the context     *Dandyism* of mainstream culture. A dandy's style implies that "nothing else matters." Unlike the classic dandy, who was a fashion leader, the dandy may seek a form of fantasy and escapism through style. Individuals with this perspective tend to reject drudgery and sameness in the social order. They may object to the routine aspects of everyday life, viewing them as mechanical and tedious. Dandies prefer to live for display, and they enjoy standing out from the crowd and not fitting into the prevailing mold. Although ego screamers also enjoy standing out in a crowd, they are more likely than dandies to do so because they desire to shock. Dandies, in contrast, respond to the idea that appearance can be spectacular, striking, and romantic (perhaps as a form of escape).

Some examples of individuals who adopt the dandy philosophy might include such performers as Liberace, Elton John, Prince (see Figure 14-3), and Cyndi

FIGURE 14-3
*Dandyism*—*an ethos of appearance as display*—*is conveyed through styles of dress such as this one worn by Prince. Illustration by Michelle Dildey.*

Lauper. The "New Romantic" British subculture of the 1980s also probably endorsed this ethic; individuals in this scene frequented nightclubs where "dressing to the hilt" was the order of the day, and, for the evening at least, a world of fantasy could be created.

Instead of trying to outshine popular fashion addicts as do ego screamers and dandies, some individuals react to popular fashion by overtly displaying their indifference to, and evasion from, social norms. Although Klapp (1969) used the term *negligence* to describe this evasion from social norms, perhaps *studied indifference* is a more appropriate term. *Negligence* implies a relatively passive approach to appearance management, but even indifference to the prevalent mode of dress is likely to be expressed in a relatively active attempt to appear as though one does not care. Of course, this kind of response in and of itself may become fashionable among individuals in some circles. Hippie styles of the late 1960s and early 1970s featured ragged blue jeans, T-shirts, long hair, and beards—indicative of a studied indifference. Hence, negligence need not refer to a lack of effort on the part of individuals. Instead, these individuals may display that they are immune to the dictates of popular styles, and they have chosen to drop out of the realm of style competition. Within the new realms that individuals of like mind create through this response, new styles emerge (for example, tie-dyed T-shirts, work shirts decorated with hand embroidery; both of these styles required a fairly high degree of involvement on the part of the person who tie-dyed or handcrafted them).

*Studied Indifference*

The Rastafarian subculture draws from the experiences of black people in Jamaica and Great Britain and represents a religion distinct from white Christianity. Rastafarians respond to suffering in the ghetto culture of the West Indies and Great Britain by refusing to deny their stolen identity and by turning poverty into a form of expression. Reggae music and appearance styles (dreadlocks, woolen hats called tams, and the wearing of red, green, and gold—the colors of the Ethiopian flag representing deliverance through exodus to Africa) became the means of subcultural expression of not only alienation but also ethnic identity (Hebdige, 1979).

See Figure 14-4 for an illustration of a white American who espouses Rastafarian philosophy and desires to create an individualistic lifestyle centered around self-sufficiency and nonparticipation in the capitalist marketplace. He refers to his appearance as representing a "complete absence of style": In his eyes, he is displaying indifference to the prevailing popular styles. At the same time, he is part of a whole network of style symbolism based on a distinct ethic.

Some individuals mock or degrade styles of the day by symbolically expressing their feelings of ambivalence about these styles. Mockery may be based on feelings of disdain tinged with some degree of infatuation; otherwise, why bother to respond to the style at all? In the late 1960s, antiwar protesters donned old army fatigues and modified them by adding other symbols of the antiwar movement, including arm bands and political buttons. These garments were obviously worn out of context. The appearance context was different from a

*Mockery*

**FIGURE 14-4**
*Studied indifference becomes an appearance message in and of itself. Photo by Miho Hongo.*

military look, because long hair and jeans were worn with the fatigue jackets. The social context of protest was also quite different from the military context. And, the cultural and historical context was distinct as well, because many of the fatigues came from army surplus from previous wars (for example, World War II and the Korean War).

The preppy styles of the early 1980s were also mocked by individuals with a disregard for the Ivy League lifestyle—in short, for the snobbishness that they felt the preppy styles represented. Thus, "anti-preppies" collected alligators from polo-styled shirts—the emblem of "preppydom"—or defaced these styles in some way. For example, male college students mocked the preppy style by cutting off the bottoms of their name-brand, polo-styled shirts to create midriff styles. The reaction of some real preppies to this mockery of their symbolism was quite intense in some cases.

Mockery of the established fashion industry's dictates was expressed forcefully by punks of the late 1970s who used style as a form of revolt. The whole idea of fashion was turned upside down as objects "borrowed from the most sordid of contexts found a place in the punks' ensembles" (Hebdige, 1979, p. 107):

> Lavatory chains were draped in graceful arcs across chests encased in plastic bin-liners. Safety pins were taken out of their domestic "utility" context and worn as gruesome ornaments through the cheek, ear or lip. "Cheap" trashy fabrics (PVC, plastic, lurex, etc.) in vulgar designs (e.g., mock leopard skin) and "nasty" colors, long discarded by the quality end of the fashion industry as obsolete kitsch, were salvaged by the punks and turned into garments (fly boy drain-pipes, "common" mini-skirts) which offered self-conscious commentaries on the notions of modernity and taste. Conventional ideas of prettiness were jettisoned along with the traditional feminine lore of cosmetics. Contrary to the advice of every woman's magazine, makeup for both boys and girls was worn to be seen. Faces became abstract portraits: sharply observed and meticulously executed studies in alienation. Hair was obviously dyed (hay yellow, jet black, or bright orange with tufts of green or bleached in question marks), and T-shirts and trousers told the story of their own construction with multiple zips and outside seams clearly displayed. Similarly, fragments of school uniform (white nylon shirts, school ties) were symbolically defiled (the shirts covered in graffiti, or fake blood; the ties left undone) and juxtaposed against leather drains or shocking pink mohair tops. The perverse and the abnormal were valued intrinsically (Hebdige, 1979, p. 107).

*Puritanism*

Puritanism involves a moralistic rejection of the notion of fashion and its corresponding materialism, worldliness, and economic waste. Like the English Puritans and American pilgrims from whom they get their name, today's puritans seek to demonstrate that they do not need fashion to lead meaningful lives. Persons who endorse the puritan philosophy delineate themselves from people who need fashion for this purpose. Some religious groups fall into this category. For example, Black Muslims criticize blacks (African-Americans) who, they feel, overemphasize fashionability in dress. Black Muslim men tend to wear conservative suits, whereas women cover their bodies completely and wear no makeup other than face powder. The goal is to create a sense of self-respect among blacks rather than copy what they consider to be white styles.

Amish and Mennonite religious groups also ratify a puritan philosophy in their everyday lives (see Figure 14-5 for an example of Mennonite women's dress; Amish people's dress was depicted in Figure 12-6). Any styles that reflect worldliness are rejected in favor of clothing and appearance styles that deemphasize pride and emphasize a sense of humility (Scott, 1987). Paradoxically, working so hard to maintain an appearance that deemphasizes personal pride may become a source of group-centered pride in and of itself (Boynton, 1989).

Orthodox          Married          Unmarried

*FIGURE 14-5*
*Attire worn by Holdeman Mennonite women displays a philosophy of* **Puritanism** *in the form of a rejection of material and worldly values. The more orthodox a woman is, the plainer her dress is (Boynton, 1989). (See Social Focus 16-2 for more information about Holdeman Mennonite women.) Illustration by Mary Lou Carter.*

*Implementing Strategic Reactions*

The reactions to mass culture outlined above are not necessarily mutually exclusive. For example, punk rockers could be characterized both as ego screamers and as mockers of the establishment. The personal reasons for reacting to popular styles by endorsing individualistic styles may vary among persons within a specific group that endorses similar styles. Also, individual responses may be complex and incorporate a variety of motives. Moreover, the same motive for reacting to popular fashions may be expressed through a variety of clothing and appearance styles, as we have seen. Thus, these reactions represent *strategies* for establishing a sense of identity. Ironically, stylistic reactions to mass culture—to the extent that there is one—often influence mainstream fashions and thus lose their original and ideological significance. Participation in this process of style "wars," therefore, may continue as individuals who wish to distinguish themselves from the masses find new avenues for expression.

One concept that clarifies how individuals striving to express themselves can accomplish this goal is **bricolage** (Lévi-Strauss, 1966). *Bricolage* is a French word referring to the idea of "do-it-yourself"—of finding solutions to problems by examining, using, and combining cultural signs in ways in which they were not initially intended. In the process, new contexts for usage are created. A **bricoleur**, then, is analogous to a "handyperson," who finds tools and various odds and ends in a bag or work environment that provide design solutions. In a sense, bricolage is individual expression at its height. Early punk aesthetics as described earlier in the quote by Hebdige (1979) made use of safety pins and lavatory chains—common, everyday objects that were never intended initially for purposes of appearance management. These objects become incorporated into the arena of style revolt.

The bricoleur is adept at creating and problem-solving, but in somewhat unconventional ways. He or she makes do with whatever objects are available, develops new connections among objects, and uses them to "think" about the world (Lévi-Strauss, 1966). Hebdige (1979) connects this concept to the British mod subculture (see Figure 14-6 for a late 1980s' American interpretation of the mod look).

> The mods could be said to be functioning as bricoleurs when they appropriated . . . commodities by placing them in a symbolic ensemble which served to erase or subvert their original straight meanings. Thus . . . the motor scooter, originally an ultra-respectable means of transport, was turned into a menacing symbol of group solidarity. In the same improvisatory manner, metal combs, honed to a razor-like sharpness, turned narcissism into an offensive weapon. . . . More subtly, the conventional insignia of the business world—the suit, collar and tie, short hair, etc.—were stripped of their original connotations—efficiency, ambition, compliance with authority—and transformed into "empty" fetishes,

*FIGURE 14-6*
*Personal appearance and mode of transportation influenced by the mod subculture. Photo by Steven Wilson.*

objects to be desired, fondled and valued in their own right (Hebdige, 1979, pp. 105–106).

Thus, any objects become fair game for appearance management in the act of bricolage, and accessorizing becomes an art in itself. Hence, the strategic response of bricolage may reflect an individualistic means of personalizing what the fashion industry has to offer. By creating and constructing unique appearances, individuals can move away from conventional rules of appearance management and create new looks or forms of expression. The nature of bricolage as a response to popular or conventional style, then, is to use the tools at hand (both those intended for appearance management and those that are not) to create a unique appearance context. In the process, individual signs are stripped from their old contexts and then combined with other signs to create a personally meaningful whole. (See Figure 14-7.)

**FIGURE 14-7**
*Bricolage is the process of using everyday objects (not intended to be worn) as accessories. This student has added safety pins as well as the plastic tractor feed from a computer printer to his wardrobe—all in the spirit of using the tools on hand to construct a distinctive look. Photo by Wendy Dildey.*

Individuals who engage in bricolage, as well as any individuals who wish to distinguish themselves from the masses, often do so in numbers—*collectively*. In the process, they create new meanings through group negotiations based on both visual and verbal communication. And, they find new forms of identification while also differentiating themselves from the larger society. The interdependent social processes of identification and differentiation are fundamental components of everyday life interpretations of the meaning of style and are examined in the following section.

## Identification and Differentiation

Stylistic responses on the part of individuals and groups of individuals to prevailing popular fashions, as we have seen, can represent a variety of motives and ideologies. Culture can engage in a kind of discourse or dialogue to sort out these styles (creating new cultural categories) as well as to derive means of integration.

The sociologist Georg Simmel (1904) noted that identification and differentiation are major forces driving the course of fashion change. Similarity in dress can both "unite" members of the same group and "segregate" them from members of other groups (Simmel, 1904; Snyder and Fromkin, 1980). On a collective level, these forces seem to reflect a cultural dialogue based on identity ambivalences (Davis, 1988) and the interplay among cultural categories. We might say that identification and differentiation are cultural principles or ideologies that are embedded deeply in a culture's collective consciousness. Together, these principles represent a struggle that can be understood by considering the concept of **hegemony**. Hegemony relates to dominance and, specifically, refers to a context in which individuals in certain cultural categories hold power over individuals in other subordinate cultural categories. This power is not enacted through direct coercion but through indirect means, for example, by promoting certain meanings that are taken for granted and are natural, and therefore do not seem to have ideological significance (S. Hall, 1977; Hebdige, 1979). We do not tend to question the meaning of a traditional business suit, for example, but rather unconsciously accept it as a sign of power (of one class over another or one gender over another).

Hegemony is not static and fixed; on the contrary, it has to be "won, reproduced, sustained" (S. Hall, 1977). Hegemony is a "moving equilibrium" that is tentative and likely to give rise to feelings of ambivalence, on a cultural level. Thus business suits may be viewed as a sign of authority and power, but may also be devalued by some who view them as indicative of sameness and bureaucracy. Hegemony is challenged by processes such as bricolage, especially when enacted through subcultures. This challenge is not direct but rather is expressed "obliquely," through style.

Just as there are macro cultural processes that promote a dynamic interplay between identification and differentiation, there are micro social-psychological processes that lead individuals to struggle between conflicting desires to express their uniqueness and to appear like others. Thus the distinction between individuality and conformity is often tenuous. Most individuals express both simultaneously by conforming to, or endorsing, some ideologies within a particular group while also expressing some degree of individuality within that group. At the same time, the group tends to evolve a look that somehow reflects or reacts in relation to larger mainstream cultural values and also displays a sense of uniqueness.

If we take a very micro perspective and look at the self (as discussed in Chapter Five), then we can examine the interplay between the "I" and the "me." You will recall that the I contributes to an individual sense of spontaneity and expression, whereas the me incorporates a generalized understanding of group or societal attitudes. The I and the me develop a dialogue in the self, just as a cultural dialogue or discourse emerges and contributes to the ambivalence about identification and differentiation. The dialogues within the self and within a culture are mediated in group life, as people interact with one another and negotiate meaning.

## Conformity

Conformity may be defined as a change in an individual's behavior or attitude in order to achieve consistency based on real or imagined group pressure (Kiesler and Kiesler, 1970). A symbolic-interactionist approach to conformity and social control would lead us to consider the importance of self-control in this process. That is, the self considers the consequences of deviating from the norm because of the me, or the internalized attitudes of others. Conformity becomes a way of reducing anxiety and gaining social acceptance by expressing the ability to identify with other people. Some other positive aspects of conformity include loyalty—to an organization, university, or country—and a sense of solidarity with others. People who dress similarly to others communicate that they are a group and have certain attributes or attitudes in common.

Certain individuals, more than others, find a sense of security in conformity. Research shows that individuals who conform in terms of clothing are likely to have conforming personalities as well (Gurel, Wilbur, and Gurel, 1972). They are also more likely to be restrained and submissive, that is, they "give in" to the social order (Aiken, 1963). A desire to be accepted by others is generally a motivating factor to conform with others in appearance. People who value conformity in dress want to maintain harmonious relations and to express their affiliation with others (Taylor and Compton, 1968). Some research has shown that males who are very clothes-conscious tend to value the social advantages of clothing more than the aesthetic aspects. In contrast, females who are very clothes-conscious tend to be inhibited, loyal, and conforming (Rosenfeld and Plax, 1977).

Assuming a person strives to conform in terms of dress, there may still be confusion about when he or she is really conforming and, if so, with whom. Whose ideas have the most influence—those of one's social group, those of larger society, or those of the fashion industry?

Research suggests that **informative social influence** is more likely to be provided by "experts," whereas **normative social influence** is more likely to be exerted by one's peers (Davis and Miller, 1983). In one study, fashion experts were more influential in changing the opinions (that is, inducing conformity) of research participants than were other potential reference groups (peers, house-wives, or career women) (Davis and Miller, 1983).

**Other-directedness** is a concept proposed by sociologist David Riesman (1953) to describe a quality in an individual that involves sensitivity to the expectations and preferences of others. A person with this orientation is likely to conform with others' expectations and preferences. In contrast, **inner-directedness** is more closely related to nonconformity, or a tendency to possess an internalized set of goals, with less concern for the expectations of others. Individuals who are inner-directed may seek, within themselves, forms of self-expression. A disadvantage of conforming may be a sense of feeling stifled or experiencing boredom or monotony. Any tendencies of this sort, however, are frequently offset by the inclination on the part of many individuals to express individuality as well as conformity.

Individualism is considered to be a basic philosophy in Western civilization, although it has been manifest and conceptualized in a variety of ways in different cultural and historical contexts (Lukes, 1973). Among French socialists, individualism has typically been contrasted with an ideal social order based on cooperation, association, and harmony (Lukes, 1973, p. 10). Among German Romantics, individualism was conceived as an ethic of uniqueness, originality, and self-realization (Lukes, 1973, p. 17). In the United States, individualism was evident in a pioneer spirit that came to extol the virtues of capitalism and democracy. Individual freedom has been valued if not sanctified. In contrast, some other cultures (for example, in the Far East) have a different kind of orientation to individualism (see Social Focus 14-2).

*Individuality*

What are the risks associated with expressions of individuality? In a high school context, research indicates that conformity with the norm of one or more groups is more conducive to peer acceptance than is individuality (Creekmore, 1980). Furthermore, several field studies have indicated that strangers respond more favorably to people who are conventionally, as opposed to "differently," dressed (Crassweller, Gordon, and Tedford, 1972; Schiavo, Sherlock, and Wicklund, 1974).

In addition to cultural ideology stressing individuality for purposes of personal freedom and creativity, there are physical and psychological forces that promote the basic human need to strive for some degree of uniqueness. We are born with distinct physical attributes, for one thing. In fact, the variation of the human body becomes evident when individuals try to find shoes, bras, hats, belts, and pants that fit their bodies exactly. Thus each human being is composed of "a highly idiosyncratic physical makeup" (Snyder and Fromkin, 1980).

In terms of psychological uniqueness, there are many contexts (for some individuals, more than others) in which there may be a desire to appear and feel different. We have already seen (in Chapter Nine) that people are attracted to similar others. Yet social psychologists Snyder and Fromkin (1980) note that this type of interpersonal attraction is counterbalanced by a desire for uniqueness.

# Individuality and Conformity in Japan

As we consider the countervailing forces of individualism and conformity in another cultural context, it is important to attempt to frame our understanding of these forces carefully. That is to say, the *meanings* of individuality and conformity within a cultural context must be considered along with the tangible or concrete expressions of them that we can observe. What *looks* like conformity from an outsider's perspective may not be viewed in the same way within a culture.

Much has been written about the homogeneity of the Japanese. To the foreign executive who has just visited Japan, Japanese businessmen may all look alike: dark suits, black shoes, black hair, short stature, undistinguished ties of the same cut and company pins on the lapel. On a school visit, students are seen wearing the same uniform. Shopping at a large department store, the female assistants are dressed alike, bend up and down in unison and chime together, "irasshaimase!" (Mouer and Sugimoto, 1986, p. 192).

Leonard Koren (1984), author of *New Fashion Japan*, notes that in Japanese society there are certain looks that go with different social worlds and lifestyles. On a visible level, a high degree of conformity may be ascertained within these groups:

Being Japanese is all about belonging, and acting the part. If you're a banker you'll work near Tokyo Station and wear a blue suit. If you're a gangster you'll work the game parlors in Shinjuku and, under your loud polyester shirt, maybe sport a tattoo. If you're young and with it, you'll parade around Aoyama, Shibuya, and Harajuku in your trendy designer fashions, and pretty much look like everyone else (Koren, 1984, p. 17).

Characteristic of postmodern Japanese culture is diversity and plurality *across* groups. Conformity is expressed *within* the group context, where looks are negotiated in everyday life, just as they are in Western cultures. In Japanese culture, there is an especially high level of consensus and intragroup harmony, however, that stems from a sense of voluntary commitment or loyalty on the part of group members (Mouer and Sugimoto, 1986).

Thus, to dress in a certain style or to conform to a given fashionable look is to express commitment to a group concept. But there is also an aesthetic dimension to this process that must be understood within its cultural context.

Imitation in Japan does not have the stigma that it does in the West. It is a social act, not a confession of feeble imagination. In a traditional art like brush painting, the learner copies the master's composition stroke by stroke. Fashion in Japan works much the same way. It is not a matter of finding the look that suits "me" best. Rather it is making the choices that will take the "fashion" to its most perfect state, be it preppie, avant garde, or white-collar. One can charitably say that the Japanese have elevated looking properly smart to a high enough art so as to supplant any desire for eccentric self-expression (Koren, 1984, p. 18).

This is not to say that individualism is unimportant in Japanese culture. To the contrary, individualism is highly valued and is evident in a variety of ways. One has only to visit a Japanese store to witness the tremendous product differentiation, reflecting outlets for a range of choices in accessories, that taps into diverse intellectual and aesthetic contexts. Similarly, within the context of wearing the traditional kimono, there is variation not only in the style itself but also in the way one chooses to wear it (Mouer and Sugimoto, 1986).

Expressing too much conformity for the purpose of pleasing everyone else is equated with timidity and lack of self-confidence. In Japanese childrearing, much emphasis is placed on producing creative and self-reliant individuals. Similarly, children are encouraged to record their unique existences in diaries and journals. There is a cultural concern with biography (Mouer and Sugimoto, 1986, pp. 197–198).

Individualism is expressed through a unique integration of appearance style and behavioral style. Just as there is not a single way one can look and dress because of the eclecticism in Japanese society, there is not only one way to behave in public contexts, as the following description of individuals on a train reveals:

A ride on any train toward the end of the day on a warm summer evening will reveal two facets of that identity: one is the full expression of one's self and the other is obliviousness to others. Someone opens the window; someone else gets on at the next station

## *Social Focus 14-2 (continued)*

and closes it. A slightly overweight young woman wears a red T-shirt embossed with green lettering reading "slippery when wet." The music from her radio is contained by headphones, but her body wiggles limply and she smiles blandly.

Next to her is a middle-aged businessman; dressed in a high-quality suit, he wipes sweat from his forehead, studies the daily financial newspaper and then takes out a textbook on Japanese chess. Across the aisle another middle-aged salary man chews gum noisily; picking his nose and flicking his diggings onto the floor, he reads a pornographic magazine. The cover-girl is tied in a contorted posture, but the contents seem to arouse the man's sexual fantasies. Another man stands, despite the fact that there are empty seats; actually he half sways from the hand-belts overhead. In a low but contented voice he sings the refrain to a karaoke (melody) he had only half-finished at the last bar. At the far end, four students are dressed for mountain climbing. They talk and laugh loudly, joking about events in class earlier in the week.

Part way down the aisle on the other side rides a young boy and his girl friend. Wearing his all-black leather pants and an embroidered shirt with a safari cut, his key holder hanging conspicuously at his side, he is too young to be called a chinpira (a young punk) and is probably a banchō (head of a gang) at a junior high school. He may feel out of place, but he doesn't flinch and pretends not to notice that his leather pants

don't breathe and are the major reason his shirt is soaking with perspiration. If he were older and more confident, he might ignore the no-smoking sign. His arm is propped up on the aluminum reinforcement pipe and he curls his hair with the end of his index finger. His girl friend, in black slacks but a colorful shirt, rocks her ankles back and forth, her high cork sandals serving as a fulcrum. She sits quietly; her fingers dance up and down his smooth arm. They never talked once during the twenty minutes they rode the train (Mouer and Sugimoto, 1986, pp. 193–194).

In this public context, people represent distinctive signs of individualism and coexist peacefully, consistent with the "golden rule"—*jūnin toiro* (different strokes for different folks). In recent years, an additional rule has been added: *karasu no katte desho* (literally, "as the crow pleases"). In other words, one can have his or her own reasons for doing things and need not explain these reasons. Thus it is unnecessary for everyone to behave according to a logic that everyone else can understand (Mouer and Sugimoto, 1986, p. 195).

Therefore, the paradox of individualism and conformity is alive and well in Japan, just as it is in Western culture. Yet the aesthetic and social-psychological dimensions of individualism and conformity must be viewed within their distinctive cultural context.

---

Accordingly, they have developed the **uniqueness theory** to address this tendency. To perceive the self as *too* similar to others, they note, is to feel a threat to a person's sense of uniqueness (p. 13). Thus, "birds of a feather do *not always* flock together." In some social contexts, "birds want to be different from a flock," and "some birds may want to be more different than others" (Snyder and Fromkin, 1980, p. 26). That is, individuals vary in the extent to which they need to feel unique or different. Moreover, the "pursuit of difference" is not a pursuit of *total* difference but rather one of *some* sense of difference from others (p. 37). Thus, the uniqueness theory predicts that when the degree of perceived similarity with others becomes very high, then some negative emotional responses will follow and people will attempt to reestablish their differences (p. 53).

Through the use of products such as clothing, we can strive to emphasize uniqueness. Frequently, advertisements encourage us to become unique individuals by buying and using their products (Snyder and Fromkin, 1980, p. 118). Some manufacturers and retailers specialize in separates that can be coordinated in a variety of ways so an individual can create a distinctive look. Perfume advertisements promote the myth that a scent becomes "uniquely yours" as it reacts with your body chemistry. Paradoxically, by complying with the advertising appeals to be unique, we may actually realize that our tastes are becoming similar to those of others.

Keeping up with the latest trends in fashion may be conceptualized in terms of *acceptable deviance* from the norm—in other words, individuals who wear the most current styles must balance between deviating from the norm enough not to be entirely predictable and conforming enough to the norm to be acceptable in one's social circles (Harman, 1985). There is a certain degree of irony in this delicate balancing act (as shown in Figure 14-8). This balancing act is a form of "rule-bending," and often it is necessary to *know* the rules before one can *bend* them without negative results. There are legitimate ways to bend the rules. For example, research indicates that people who emphasize aesthetics—form and harmony—in their value structures tend to be less likely to emphasize conformity in dress. Rather, they are likely to lean toward individualism and self-sufficiency (Taylor and Compton, 1968).

On a collective level, fashion is "custom in the guise of departure from custom" and a form of "adventurous safety" (Sapir, 1931). On an individual level, fashion becomes a way of making self-statements in the face of pressures to conform at the societal level. Individuals such as dandies and ego screamers who carry these statements to an extreme are likely to be viewed with a combination of awe and ridicule. On the other hand, individuals who are "old-fashioned" also become outsiders in fashionable circles. Thus, being fashionable may be conceptualized as "acceptably deviating . . . between the two forms of unacceptable deviance—being outrageous and being old-fashioned—to become the rule, the socially-prescribed behavior" (Harman, 1985, p. 9).

In their research, Snyder and Fromkin (1980) demonstrated that we value our clothing in part because everyone else is not wearing the same thing. Individuals who have a higher need for a self-definition of uniqueness, moreover, are especially likely to see scarce objects as more desirable. Individuals who had a high need for uniqueness displayed greater preferences for leather boots when these boots were thought to be available only to a few other persons than when they were perceived as being available to large numbers of other persons. This preference was not expressed by research participants with a low need for uniqueness (as evident from scores on a test Snyder and Fromkin developed).

How do individuals achieve a sense of uniqueness in a society where clothes are mass-produced? Georg Simmel (1904) noted that individuality in consumption is possible to the extent that a person selectively chooses among the objects he or she desires, thus limiting the number of objects to which value or meaning is attached. Injecting a "personal touch" becomes a mechanism for coping in the marketplace (Mills, 1951). Social and fashion trends seem to indicate an increasing range of options for individuals in the marketplace. Through the vast variety of separates and the infinite numbers of combinations that may be created to form unique appearance contexts, individuals can express a sense of uniqueness

**FIGURE 14-8**
*Dressing fashionably can be a form of **acceptable deviance**. Note how the headcovering worn by this mannequin resembles a punk mohawk hairstyle. Photo by Susan B. Kaiser.*

while also conforming to a general fashion ideology of "do-it-yourself" stylistic self-expression.

Futurist Alvin Toffler (1980) contends that production is becoming increasingly demassified, and apparel manufacturers are finding means for promoting individual distinctiveness. The common, mass-produced T-shirt, for example, may serve as a medium for customized designs or slogans applied through the use of economical, fast-heat presses. Only one T-shirt is imprinted at a time, thus allowing for an individualized design. The result is a broad range of shirts facetiously identifying such characteristics as the wearer's musical taste, drinking habits, or sense of humor. T-shirts obtained from unusual places (for example, in foreign travels) also serve to set a person apart, especially when the words printed are in a foreign language.

Technological advances in the apparel industry, such as the computer-based laser cutter, allow manufacturers to cut fewer numbers of pattern pieces for apparel at one time while maintaining high production speed. Toffler predicts that it will become possible for consumers to design their own clothes and have them produced by manufacturers, all without leaving their homes. He anticipates that consumers will be able to feed their measurements and style preferences into a computer that will instruct a laser cutter to produce a single garment, cut exactly to individualized dimensions from a personally selected or designed fabric.

Thus the fashion industry may more or less respond to the dynamic interplay between conformity (identification) and individuality (differentiation). Still, given that there are cultural and social constraints that operate on the individual, it is important to consider individuals' states of mind when electing to dress like or unlike others.

## Freedom in Dress

Individuals are likely to have the freedom to decide if they want to conform or to deviate with respect to appearance management. Freedom in dress is not the opposite of conformity, then, but is rather a separate dimension of appearance management (Lowe and Buckley, 1982). Freedom in dress may be characterized in three ways: (1) as an individually or subjectively defined state of mind; (2) in terms of the various phases involved in the process of "dressing freely": (*a*) purposeful planning, (*b*) the execution of the plan (wearing the clothes that were planned for certain contexts), and (*c*) enjoyment of the results; and (3) on the basis of restrictions and satisfactions related to clothing (Lowe and Anspach, 1973).

Restrictions in dress may be economic, social, or perceptual. Female college students have been found to feel restricted economically in terms of clothing choices. Social restrictions related to the college experience may include the student role, a lack of self-confidence in apparel selection, and a degree of dissatisfaction with previous clothing choices. Students who had had negative clothing-related experiences were more likely to feel restricted, whereas students with the fewest restrictions related to clothing felt freer about their clothing choices. Additionally, the lack of aesthetic perceptual abilities was found to confine individuals' sense of freedom in dress. Such perceptual abilities may be linked to the ability to coordinate interesting appearance contexts, for example. Individuals who have these perceptual abilities may be able to overcome economic restrictions by using originality (for example, sewing their own clothes or shopping at thrift or discount stores) and creativity in appearance management (Lowe and Anspach, 1978).

Satisfaction with one's clothing choices appears to be a more positive factor in freedom in dress than restrictions are negative factors. Satisfaction in relation to clothing choices appears to be influenced more by social-psychological than by economic considerations (Lowe and Dunsing, 1981). To be able to have some choice and to be able to capitalize on that choice contribute to the state of mind known as freedom in dress (Lowe and Buckley, 1982).

Just as individuals vary to the extent that they experience a sense of freedom in dress, they also differ in their degree of involvement with fashion change. In the following chapter, we will explore the micro- and macro-level forces that promote change in and involvement with fashion. As we have seen, both types of forces contribute to dynamic struggles and instabilities, leading us to walk a tightrope in terms of individual choices and cultural constraints. With this in mind, we can now examine in greater depth the idea of fashion as a *process* that must be examined within its cultural and historical, social, and cognitive contexts.

## *Suggested Readings*

Davis, F. 1988. Clothing, fashion and the dialectic of identity. In D. R. Maines and C. J. Couch, eds. *Communication and social structure*. Springfield: Charles C Thomas.
  Davis describes his theory of identity ambivalence, focusing primarily on gender. He illustrates the theory with examples drawn from the fashion media and fashion history.

Hebdige, D. 1979. *Subculture: The meaning of style*. London: Methuen.
  Hebdige uses a cultural perspective (drawing from semiotics and cultural studies) to examine the emergence and meaning of style in subcultures. Clothing in British subcultures (for example, mod, punk, and Rastafarian) is described in rich detail.

McCracken, G. 1986. Culture and consumption: A theoretical account of the structure and movement of the cultural meaning of consumer goods. *Journal of Consumer Research* 13:71–84.
  This article by McCracken includes a description of the concepts of cultural categories and cultural principles, and relates them to consumption behavior.

Sawyer, C. H. 1987. Men in skirts and women in trousers, from Achilles to Victoria Grant: One explanation of a comedic paradox. *Journal of Popular Culture* 21(2): 1–16.
  This article deals with the topic of gender ambivalence by exploring the issue of why cross-dressing by men in popular culture is considered humorous, whereas the same phenomenon

by women is not. Sawyer draws a fascinating parallel between humor and power in gender relations, using dress as a focal point.

Wilson, E. 1985. *Adorned in dreams: Fashion and modernity*. London: Virago Press.
Wilson discusses a number of themes that pertain to the concept of ambivalence in relation to fashion in modern (or postmodern) life. One chapter focuses on ambivalences that are basic to fashion and feminism.

# Chapter Fifteen
## ...
# Fashion Change: Social-Psychological Processes in Cultural and Historical Context

Fashion is custom in the guise of departure from custom. . . . The personal note which is at the hidden core of fashion becomes superpersonalized.

—SAPIR, 1931

Fashion is one of the most accessible and one of the most flexible means by which we express . . . ambiguities. Fashion is modernist irony.

—WILSON, 1985, p. 15

*In this chapter, the focus is on fashion change as it pertains to a nexus of cultural and social-psychological processes. Why and how does fashion change? Various theoretical perspectives are reviewed and critiqued in this chapter, including theories pertaining to class struggle, collective identity, consumer behavior in the fashion marketplace, and subcultures. These theories have been developed in different historical, cultural, and intellectual contexts. The challenge of explaining fashion change across historical and cultural contexts remains. It is suggested that cultural ambivalence, as linked to underlying tensions across cultural categories, has some potential for explaining the continual creative fuel that has become embedded in Western civilization and beyond.*

Fashion is a dynamic collective process, yet it influences individuals' lives in a distinctly personal way. It is through the process of fashion that new styles are created, introduced to a consuming public, and popularly accepted by that public (Sproles, 1979). Individual creativity and ambivalences pertaining to issues of individuality and conformity bring fashion to a very personal level. People differ in their level of involvement with fashionable objects or in the extent to which they keep abreast of fashion trends. Yet few people are immune to the implications of the fashion process when it comes to changes in shared meanings of appearance styles or to the availability of clothes that may or may not suit individual needs.

What do we mean by fashion? Some define it simply as a prevalent style of a particular group at a particular time. In other words, it may be linked to a specific cultural and historical context, in which there is general acceptance of a given style or look. Does this type of definition capture the essence of fashion? According to Fred Davis (1985), it is critical that we also include the idea of *change*, or shifts in meaning, between "the relationship of signifier and signified, albeit always bearing in mind that in dress the relationship between 'signifiers' and the referents, attributes, or values thereby 'signified' is generally much less uniform or exact than is true of written or spoken language."

> In any case, **fashion** . . . must be made to refer to some alteration in the code of visual conventions by which we read meanings of whatever sort and variety into the clothes we and our contemporaries wear. The change may involve the introduction of wholly new visual, tactile, or olfactory signifiers, the retrieval of certain old ones which have receded from but still linger in memory or a change in the accenting of familiar signifiers; but change there must be to warrant the appellation **fashion** (Davis, 1985, pp. 21–22).

Whether or not a code modification is accepted determines if it will succeed or "merely pass from the scene as a futile symbolic gesture" (Davis, 1985, p. 22). Why then are aesthetic codes altered, and how do people come to accept these alterations? The answers to these questions are neither simple nor straightforward. The answers are inevitably embedded in a nexus of cultural ambivalence, cultural category tensions, aesthetic codes, modernity, processes of visual and verbal communication, and social-psychological forces, all within a cultural and historical context.

Theoretical explanations linking fashion change strictly with (*a*) capitalist cultural conspiracy, designed to make our wardrobes continually obsolete, or (*b*) individual boredom fail to account for the complex social-psychological, aesthetic, and cultural forces by which an idea enters a designer's mind and may or may not eventually become fashionable.

The idea of a capitalist conspiracy suggests that rapid change in clothing styles is a plot by the fashion industry to build obsolescence into its products so as to increase sales. However, history reveals that the "gatekeepers" of fashion cannot ram new styles down the throats of consumers. Moreover, there is evidence that the fashion process is *not* necessarily accelerating in conjunction with modern advancements in production, distribution, and communication. Rather, the fashion industry appears "to adjust to psychosocial constraints in the environment," and aesthetic codes are a part of this environment (Lowe and Lowe, 1985).

Still there is probably some element of truth to the conspiracy explanation. Granted, "the image-making business" depends on individuals striving to look (and be) thinner, younger, more athletic, or beautiful than they are. We might say that the basic motives of designers, manufacturers, and retailers are not all that different from those of fashion consumers. All desire greater success (Giddon, 1985). Fashion may not reap equal privileges to all cultural categories and to competing social values; however, it cannot be identified with any single group or institution. For that reason alone, the conspiracy explanation of fashion does not work (Fox-Genovese, 1987, p. 27).

Similarly, the "boredom" explanation for fashion change is too simplistic in nature. Individualism-centered models of fashion change tend to emphasize the pursuit of novelty or excitement-seeking as a motivating factor in style adoption. A cognitive approach would lead us to believe that we seek stimulation, but a boredom explanation does not explain the *social* aspects of fashion. The boredom explanation, like the uniqueness theory (Snyder and Fromkin, 1980), *does* help to explain individual variations from general fashion trends, however (Sproles, 1985).

Similarly, we know that social pressures to conform can influence style choices (Davis and Miller, 1983), but it is important not to place exclusive emphasis on conformity to explain fashion change. A blend, balance, or juxtaposition of identification and differentiation (as discussed in Chapter Fourteen) is one of several keys to understanding fashion change. At this point, we will turn our attention to some of the major theories that have dealt with fashion change, recognizing that rarely does any single explanation provide a complete picture.

## Class Struggle Theories

Fashion and class stratification have been linked by some writers. Thorstein Veblen (1899) viewed fashion change as the result of a class struggle for social superiority. Class leadership, he felt, was displayed through the conspicuous consumption and waste associated with fashion. Veblen noted that the upper classes seemed to flaunt the fact that they did not need to engage in manual labor (as discussed in Chapter Thirteen). The "leisure class" could maintain its position in the social hierarchy by adopting new styles sooner than the lower classes.

Sociologist Georg Simmel (1904) was influenced by Veblen's ideas on fashion and stratification. Simmel identified the two fundamental processes of imitation (emulation in Veblen's terms) and differentiation. In order for fashion to change, Simmel reasoned, there must be someone (the upper-class elite) to imitate, and the class structure must be open to allow this process. Simmel's (1904) **trickle-down theory** was based on the idea that the elite could maintain its position in the social hierarchy by adopting new styles for purposes of obtaining distinction. Once the lower classes began to imitate these styles, the elite had to abandon them and turn to new ones in order to assert and maintain their superiority. Grant McCracken (1985) points out that one advantage of the trickle-down theory is its predictive power; it gives advance warning and predicts a consequence—differentiation on the part of the upper classes. Yet does this prediction come true? Many exceptions to this trickle-down process have been noted in recent fashion history, as we will see in later sections of this chapter.

Even when the predictions do come true, perhaps the term *trickle down* itself is a misnomer. In actuality, the dynamics described by Simmel (1904) could more accurately be described as an upward "chase and flight" pattern (McCracken, 1985). The subordinate social group may seek out elite status markers and attempt to claim them, and then a superordinate social group flees on to new ones. Thus in terms of a precipitating dynamic, it is an *upward* movement that compels fashion change (McCracken, 1985), with each level or social grouping seeking a kind of "higher ground." The styles themselves may trickle down (see Figure 15-1), but the drive for social mobility was the major impetus behind the fashion process, according to Veblen and Simmel.

The problem was, and still is, that it is somewhat difficult to tell by sight who the upper classes are in the mobile society of the United States. Moreover, as we saw in Chapter Twelve, by the 1850s, the upper classes, at least in the United States, did not always set the prevailing style (Banner, 1983, p. 66). Some sectors of the upper classes simply withdrew from the fashion competition and focused their energies in other areas (for example, charity and civic cultural activities). Moreover, it seems that emulation of the upper classes, as the "fundamental engine of fashion," has broken down in the twentieth century (Lowe and Lowe, 1985). However, certain aspects of Veblen's and Simmel's ideas may still be regarded as very insightful, but need to be applied with a different "twist." We need to identify the basic concepts that identify the forces at play in fashion change and to determine if they are still relevant. If so, they need to be recast, reframed, or reevaluated to fit the current temporal context. For example, class differentiation may actually take the form of status denial on the part of the "fashionable elite."

> Veblen's model may in fact still be relevant: buying Goodwill jeans instead of Calvin Kleins, a Lacoste shirt without the logo, refusing to own a television set, and preferring a Jeep Wagoneer to a Cadillac, is in fact a parody display or reverse ostentation. Veblen still applies: as conspicuous consumption becomes associated with the mainstream, the upscale segment shifts into what might be called conspicuous counterconsumption (Simon-Miller, 1985, p. 74).

Social-psychological and cultural forces related to power and display are still relevant to fashion change. What is outdated in Veblen's theory is the idea that the ruling class is the leisure class that exclusively dictates fashion. Today, the social elite, which is not necessarily synonymous with the wealthiest elite, can perpetuate itself to some extent by using fashion. Yet, individuals from any social class who desire to participate in the fashion process may do so, through a variety of means and forms of expression (see Figure 15-2). Simon-Miller (1985) notes that consumption may serve as an alternative to social protest. Consumption can mask class conflict and perpetuate the status quo. "Instead of changing their actual environment, people, through fashion, change only its packaging" (Simon-Miller, 1985, p. 74). French theorist Baudrillard (1981) would agree with Simon-Miller. He contends that, consistent with postmodern culture, we are caught up in a kind of *simulation* of change in terms of social structure.

**FIGURE 15-1**
*The trickle-down process of fashion diffusion is illustrated in these national chain store "knock-offs" of the concepts of "units" or multiple separates that can be combined in an infinite variety of ways. Photo by Joan L. Chandler.*

**FIGURE 15-2**
*In the early 1980s, the preppie look that had originated in the upper classes became a popular style on college campuses, as shown here. In response to this widespread "co-opting" of the preppie look, some upper-class youth distinguished themselves by intentionally "dressing down." Photo by Carla M. Freeman.*

The formal logic of fashion imposes an increased mobility on all the distinctive social signs. Does this formal mobility of signs correspond to a real mobility in social structures (professional, political, social)? Certainly not. Fashion—and more broadly, consumption, which is inseparable from fashion—masks a profound social inertia. It itself is a *factor* of social inertia, insofar as the demand for real social mobility frolics and loses itself in fashion, in the sudden and often cyclical changes of objects, clothes, and ideas (Baudrillard, 1981, pp. 50–51).

Thus, a variety of perspectives may be taken to explore fashion and class stratification. A key issue today is whether fashion change really represents major shifts in social structure or whether it conceals (by glossing over) existing inequities.

Nevertheless, what is clear is that fashion change is influenced by struggles and instabilities. One of the key contributions of Simmel's (1904) work on fashion involved his insights on the duality and interplay between imitation and demarcation. In this connection, we can update or revise the trickle-down theory in two major ways. First, we can recognize that social class is not the only cultural category in which struggles and instabilities exist. Tensions among cultural categories also exist in the areas of gender, ethnicity, age, and physical attractiveness. Second, we can acknowledge that aesthetically coded influences do not necessarily fit a "top down" model. Since the 1960s, there have been numerous examples of styles that originated from sources other than the upper elite (for example, from the streets and from subcultures). Thus the term *trickle down* does not fit the realities of fashion change. The metaphor of a tug-of-war, with opposite cultural categories at either end, may more adequately characterize the competition for aesthetic codes. We will come back to these issues in a later section on cultural categories and ambivalence.

## Collective Selection Theory

In the 1960s, symbolic interactionist Herbert Blumer (1969b) critiqued Simmel's (1904) class struggle approach to fashion change, on the grounds that it is better-suited to explanation of fashion change in the seventeenth and eighteenth centuries in Europe than to that of fashion change today. Blumer (1969b) noted that to be *fashionable* per se is not necessarily within the control of the elite. To be fashionable in and of itself is to command a source of prestige.

> The efforts of an elite class to set itself apart in appearance takes place inside of the movement of fashion instead of being its cause. The prestige of elite groups, in place of setting the direction of the fashion movement, is effective only to the extent to which they are recognized as representing and portraying the movement. The people in other classes who consciously follow the fashion do so because it is the fashion and not because of the separate prestige of the elite group. . . . *The fashion mechanism appears not in response to a need of class differentiation but in response to a wish to be in fashion, to be abreast of what has good standing, to express new tastes which are emerging in a changing world* (Blumer, 1969b, pp. 281–282). (Emphasis in the original)

Research supports the idea that fashionable attire is perceived as socially desirable. Individuals wearing currently fashionable clothes seem to evoke favorable responses in perceivers, including evaluations of sociability (Johnson, Nagasawa, and Peters, 1977). Interpersonal distance in social interaction can be modified by clothing manipulations. If a person does not wear a current style, he or she may be rejected or labeled as "different" before having a chance to prove his or her worth as an individual (Workman, 1987).

Blumer's theory of collective selection revolves around the effort of individuals *in numbers* to choose from among competing styles or models those that are most in tune with emergent tastes—those that "click" or "connect" (Blumer, 1969b, p. 282). Far from viewing fashion change as based on capitalist conspiracy, Blumer (1969b) indicated that fashion functions in postindustrial societies to enable people to cope with the rapid pace of social change. As consumers collectively select styles from a large array of possible choices, they cast ballots in the marketplace. Those styles that are selected appear to be in step with the *Zeitgeist*, or spirit of the times. Thus Blumer indicated that fashion performs an important socialization function at the societal level as well as a social-psychological purpose at the individual level. *Fashion may help people adjust to the rapid pace of life in postindustrial society by rendering visibility or providing form to that pace*. This tendency, Blumer noted, may be linked to temporal (historical) context:

1. Fashion can symbolically provide individuals with a mechanism for detaching from the past (see Figure 15-3).
2. Fashion can allow people to deal (cope) with the stresses of the present in an orderly way, by helping to define what is appropriate in a world of uncertainties. In this way, people can express a positive interest in being part of the times—in *belonging* with the present.
3. Fashion can prepare people for the immediate future by providing a sense of anticipation or a clue to emerging issues and tastes (see Figure 15-4). This aspect of fashion may seldom be on the conscious level, but the shopping process itself is future-oriented.

Fashion may be "therapeutic" in another sense. Sociologist Peter Berger (1977) pointed out that some degree of "triviality" is a fundamental requirement in people's lives. All aspects of everyday life cannot assume full and serious attention. Some sense of fantasy or aesthetic stimulation from rigorous daily routines is necessary. Although it is debatable as to whether fashion is trivial, there are likely to be some aspects of it, at least, that facilitate this type of release from everyday tensions. To undermine the aesthetic codes and pleasures associated with fashion change is to ignore a critical component of this complex social phenomenon.

Elizabeth Wilson (1985) notes that "modern individualism" can be characterized as a state of "exaggerated yet fragile sense of self—a raw, painful, condition" (p. 12), just as Orrin Klapp (1969) argued that individuals collectively search for a sense of identity. Hence, fashion can give us something to hold on to; it can provide an anchor enabling us to connect with time. At the same time it anchors us and allows us to feel a part of something bigger in a given (albeit fleeting) historic context, it also allows us some room to roam and express individuality. (Imagine a boat that is anchored but is still able to move around a little bit within a given space.) Thus, the interplay between individuality and conformity, or identification and differentiation, is an important aspect of participation in the fashion process. Collective selection does not necessarily contradict individual selection in the realm of fashion.

*FIGURE 15-3*
*Although fashion*
*symbolically provides*
*individuals with a*
*mechanism for detaching*
*from the past, in the*
*postmodern cultural context*
*there is an ambivalence*
*about time, and signs of the*
*past can be stripped from*
*their historic contexts and*
*worn in the present*
*(Kaiser, Nagasawa, and*
*Hutton, 1989). This*
*woman dresses in a 1950s-*
*style outfit for 1950s day at*
*her office. Photo by Mark*
*Kaiser.*

Some researchers of fashion change have pointed out that Blumer's (1969b) theory of collective selection should be qualified, because fashion is not simply driven by the desire to adapt to a changing world.

> Not only is (the fashion process) a way in which taste is "collectivized" thereby avoiding anarchy in a changing world, but also, the fashion process imposes limits on the magnitude of the rate of change and sometimes, the direction that change may take. . . . Fashion change is neither purely autonomous nor

**FIGURE 15-4**
*Buying new clothes can provide a person with a sense of anticipation about the near future. With respect to the far future, some designers draw upon a sense of vision to develop an interpretation. Often this vision draws from the past, as well. The designer of this outfit, Kate Lindsay, described her work in the following way: "My work expresses a personal fantasy of the clothing of the future . . . Geometry, juxtaposed with the human form, intrigues me, as does the blending of historical costume references with materials and shapes of the New Age.' My goal is to allow the wearer and the viewer to slightly remove themselves from the present moment and experience a new futuristic mood." Courtesy of Kate Lindsay, photography by John Skalicky.*

**FIGURE 15-5**
*Collective selection of popular styles is mediated by factors such as preferences for certain baseball teams. Fashion can be influenced, then, by the current popularity of sports teams (especially when they are winning), as well as political events, movies, and many other cultural stimuli. Photo by Susan B. Kaiser.*

simply driven by exogenous forces. Fundamentally, it is a blend of the two, woven from disparate threads into a pattern as yet not clearly discerned. We see the fashion process as in part following an inner logic of stylistic development whose foundation must lie in social-psychological constructs. However, this process is mediated by the social institutions in which it is embedded (Lowe and Lowe, 1985, pp. 202–205).

Thus, collective selection is likely to be tempered or moderated by aesthetic trends, social structure, and the inner workings and social world of the fashion industry, as well as social-psychological processes (such as identification and differentiation). Political and economic tensions can also induce and shape the course of fashion change (Lowe and Lowe, 1985). (See Figure 15-5 for an example of another kind of mediation of the collective selection process.)

## *Mass Market Theory and Fashion Diffusion*

Marketing theorists such as Charles King (1963) have typically agreed with Blumer's assertion that top down fashion models such as Simmel's (1904) do not necessarily apply to consumer acceptance in the marketplace, especially since the 1960s. Like Blumer, marketing theorists tend to agree that no longer does class differentiation characterize the fundamental basis for fashion change (King and Ring, 1980). King (1963) proposed the **mass market** (also called **simultaneous adoption**) theory to explain the *horizontal* diffusion of fashion. He noted that styles diffuse *across* given classes or groups in a society. King contends that new styles and consumer information about these styles are made available to social classes at the same time. Basic conditions associated with a postindustrial society (for example, mass production and mass media), as well as within the fashion industry itself, account for the simultaneous availability of new styles. For example, a sportswear firm may have two or more price lines. In the top line, the materials used may be more expensive or more details requiring additional labor costs may be included. In the moderately priced line, the same basic style may exist but in different materials and with fewer details. These two price lines are likely to hit the marketplace at the same time.

Fashion leadership, then, is tied to interpersonal influence within a social world of some sort. A social world is defined by symbolic interactionists as a diffuse and loosely bounded level of social organization, characterized by a system of practices that have evolved into a perceived sphere of interest and involvement for participants (Unruh, 1979). A social world may consist of a group, a subculture, an organization, or an informal network. A person's social world may be related more closely to lifestyle patterns and value systems than to socioeconomic status.

The simultaneous adoption process relies on two subprocesses. First, fashion innovators, or influentials, adopt new styles and introduce them to the public. Innovative persons interpret styles and give them visibility within their own social worlds. Second, within these worlds, processes of interpersonal influence converge as early adopters interact and "spread" the fashion message visually as well as verbally in some cases (as they explain their interpretations to others).

These subprocesses rely heavily on the social-psychological forces described by Simmel (1904)—imitation and differentiation. Fashion followers provide the function of imitation (of fashion leaders), whereas fashion innovators are likely to continue to seek out new and different styles to distinguish themselves and maintain their status as innovators. These social-psychological processes have been characterized in terms of *adoption* and *diffusion* models (Rogers, 1983), with fashion leaders as change agents providing a vital role. Thus, marketing and consumer behavior research on the fashion process has typically focused on characterizing those individuals who are more inclined to adopt new styles. A major goal has been to understand how and why consumers vary with respect to the stage of a style's life cycle in which they are likely to adopt the style. Consumer "types" have often been characterized as fashion innovators, fashion opinion leaders and early conformists, mass market consumers, late fashion followers, and fashion isolates or laggards (Sproles, 1979, p. 351). (See Figure 15-6 for a graph illustrating this process.)

The early adopters, or change agents, in the diffusion process include the innovators and the fashion opinion leaders. Early conformists also could conceivably fall into this broad area of adoption. The mass market consumers adopt the

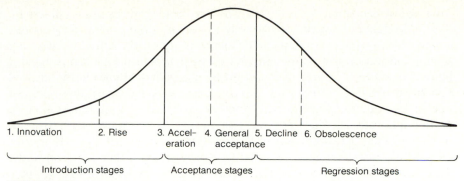

**FIGURE 15-6**
*Fashion innovators adopt a new style in the innovation stage of its cycle. Opinion leaders and early conformists then adopt the style and contribute to its rise. Mass market consumers adopt the style during the acceptance stages, then the late fashion followers adopt it during its decline. Finally, fashion isolates and laggards adopt the style once it has entered the stage of obsolescence. Adapted from Sproles (1979).*

style at the peak of its cycle. Fashion retailers attempt to stock a style in large quantities immediately prior to this stage of fashion acceptance. The late fashion followers adopt the style as it gradually begins to decline. The fashion isolates and laggards adopt it in its final stages, when retailers are drastically marking down the style in an attempt to clear it out of the store and make room for newer styles. Fashion isolates are consumers who are late adopters because they are not exposed to many of the influences that lead to an awareness of or interest in the style. Fashion laggards, on the other hand, adopt the style without overwhelming interest, either because it is very cheap at this stage, or because there is a great deal of social pressure to do so.

The goal of fashion marketers is to provide the right merchandise at the right time, in the right place, and in the right assortments and quantities to satisfy consumer demand. In order for this feat to be accomplished, marketers need to have a good understanding of the target consumers' preferences and characteristic behavioral patterns. Particular emphasis, therefore, must be geared toward creating awareness and interest on the part of fashion "change agents." These change agents, in turn, influence other consumers within their own social worlds. In the following sections we will look at some of the research identifying characteristics of fashion consumers.

## Fashion Innovators

Fashion innovators are the earliest communicators of a new style or look to other fashion consumers. Fashion innovators may or may not be influential in causing others to respond favorably toward the style, but they at least create an initial degree of awareness. They provide both *visual display* and *initial exposure* of the style. How can researchers identify fashion innovators in order to study them? Several measures of fashion innovation have been used. One of these involves independent judges or peers, who rate the individuals in a social system. This procedure only works satisfactorily in a small social system (for example, a high school) so that everyone can be identified. Another method for assessing fashion innovation is a self-designating measure in which a person is asked if he or she perceives himself or herself to be innovative. Studies have indicated that the correlation between the perceived measures and actual ownership of new styles is quite low, however. Another problem with self-report data on fashion innovation is that consumers' intentions to buy a new style may not mesh with their actual purchases (Reynolds and Darden, 1973). Perhaps, for example, the styles do not look good to consumers once they see them in the store and, perhaps, try them on. Or, perhaps consumers would like to buy a new style but cannot afford to do so. Fashion adoption, moreover, may be difficult to assess empirically because of the distinction between the *purchase* of a new style and the *wearing* of a new style (Winakor and Goings, 1973). Fashion preference does not always seem to correlate with buying behavior.

One reason for the lack of consistency between what people say about themselves and what they do may be related to the importance of fashion awareness as a stage that precedes the process of fashion adoption. If a male thinks he is innovative in adopting a new sweater style, for example, it may be that it is because he has just become *aware* of the style. Earlier adopters may now think of that style as well-established.

Two other means for evaluating degree of fashion innovation include longitudinal and cross-sectional research. Longitudinal research involves the study of consumers' behavior over time, in an attempt to analyze the timing of adoption (Reynolds and Darden, 1973). Such research may consist of consumers' recollections of the adoption date or, for a more reliable measure, actual records that have established the adoption date. Probably the most widely used measure of fashion innovation is the cross-sectional method, which categorizes a sample of consumers along a continuum based on the number of new items they have purchased. Fashion innovativeness has also been measured in terms of the degree of consumers' willingness to accept new fashion innovations. This can be tested by assessing recognition or acceptance of visual stimuli from the most recent fashion magazines, as compared with those from an earlier time (for example, 5 years earlier) (Gorden, Infante, and Braun, 1985).

What characteristics do fashion innovators possess? Research has explored demographic factors (social class, age, and income) as well as lifestyle and personality variables. Some researchers have found that a higher family income is related to a higher degree of innovation in female college students (Painter and Pinegar, 1971; Mason and Bellenger, 1973–1974). Yet most studies have not found an association between socioeconomic status and level of innovation (King, 1963; Grindereng, 1967; Schrank and Gilmore, 1973). In a study of Korean female college students, fashion innovators were distributed evenly across socioeconomic levels (Kim and Schrank, 1982). Thus, little support for trickle-down or class differentiation theory has been provided. The inconsistencies across some studies might suggest that socioeconomic factors affect innovation in a context-bound way, that is, they may influence the adoption of some, but not all, new styles. These inconsistencies may also stem from the fact that researchers have often defined and measured fashion innovation in varying ways.

In terms of social-psychological characteristics of fashion innovators, they appear to be more inner-directed than noninnovators (Painter and Pinegar, 1971). That is, innovators are not likely to need or seek conformity with others to as great an extent as other fashion consumers. As Rogers (1983) has pointed out, innovators underconform with social norms. It takes some inner direction and individuality to dare to be the first to adopt a new style. There is a degree of *social-psychological risk* associated with wearing new styles. Social-psychological risk incorporates the aesthetic appeal of a style as well as other social and psychological concerns. This type of risk appears to be more important to consumers than the more pragmatic economic or performance risks of a style (Minshall, Winakor, and Swinney, 1982). What are the social-psychological risks and how do they affect fashion innovators? For one thing, a style an innovator wears may never actually catch on. Moreover, the "stamp of approval" from the fashion establishment may mean little to perceivers who are relatively unaware of new styles. Therefore, an innovator who interacts with unaware perceivers may need to inform them that a style really *is* current—in the height of fashion ("It appeared in *Vogue* this month.") It is likely, however, that a fashion innovator will *seek* to be different by continually keeping up with new styles and will set himself or herself apart from later fashion adopters.

It appears that fashion innovators feel more socially secure and, not surprisingly, are more interested in fashion than later fashion adopters (Grindereng, 1967; Schrank and Gilmore, 1973). In a Korean study, it was found that fashion innovators held significantly more positive attitudes toward change than did late adopters (Kim and Schrank, 1982). This tendency is consistent with the possibility that innovators may be more tolerant of ambiguity than noninnovators (Lennon and Davis, 1987). Sharron Lennon and Leslie Davis (1987) found a positive, though small, relation between innovativeness and cognitive complexity. Cognitive complexity describes the manner in which people respond to conflict, uncertainty, rule structure, and authority. On a conceptual level, it may be equated with a tolerance for ambiguity. Individuals functioning at a high level of cognitive complexity (including fashion innovators, as suggested by this study) do not tend to compromise their values to please others or to conform. Likewise, they tolerate uncertainty, ambiguity, and difference of opinion. A low level of cognitive complexity, on the other hand, is equated with concern for behaving in a socially acceptable manner and expressions of anxiety about incorrect action.

In terms of innovator lifestyle, other research has shown that participation in social organizations such as sororities is positively related to the degree of fashion innovation displayed by female college students (Painter and Pinegar, 1971; Mason and Bellenger, 1973–1974). Of particular interest to fashion marketers are the findings that female college students who are innovators read more magazines (especially fashion magazines) than do noninnovators (Painter and Pinegar, 1971) and attend more fashion shows each year (Mason and Bellenger, 1973–1974).

Other research has addressed the issue of *communicator style* of fashion innovators. Communicator style refers to the verbal and nonverbal style of interaction that signals how literal meaning should be taken, interpreted, and filtered or understood. Female students were studied in relation to their recognition or acceptance of visual fashion stimuli (Gorden, Infante, and Braun, 1985). Students who were high in fashion innovativeness, as measured by this form of acceptance, were more likely than those low in fashion innovativeness to have communicator style characteristics of animation, friendliness, impression-leaving, and drama. Animation and drama characteristics of communicator style pertain to the degree of exaggeration or "color" of communication content. Impression-leaving incorporates both discursive and nondiscursive elements, and involves a high degree of energy and active communication on the part of the innovator. If an innovator exerts energy in this way, then there is an expectation that he or she will leave an impression on others. Friendliness relates to outgoingness and related qualities. Thus, it seems that expressive behavior, social sensitivity, and a high awareness and energy level are "part of a consistent personal communicator statement" of fashion innovators. The researchers concluded that "the mental image that is held suggests a strong, dramatic impression-making identity" (Gorden, Infante, and Braun, 1985, p. 173).

## Fashion Opinion Leaders

Opinion leaders in fashion serve to *legitimize* (give a stamp of approval to) a style for fashion followers. In other words, opinion leaders tend to influence others in their social worlds. Fashion followers have respect for opinion leaders' levels of taste and senses of social appropriateness.

Research has suggested that persons are attracted to similarly dressed others according to the fashionability of their clothing style (Reed, 1979). It probably also follows that opinion leaders do not really deviate from the social norms of their groups. They are probably more likely to be current within a range of accepted norms. Opinion leaders may adopt slightly modified or toned-down versions of a style or look after innovators have received the attention of others. For this reason, opinion leaders are sometimes referred to as *editors of fashion*. They play a major role in providing the needed impetus for others' adoption processes.

Most researchers have studied opinion leadership by using a self-designating opinion leadership scale (Rogers and Cartano, 1962), with the assumption that an individual's perception of his or her own opinion leadership is what determines behavior. An example of a question used in a measure of fashion opinion leadership is: "Compared with your circle of friends, are you less likely, about as likely, or more likely to be asked for advice about fashion in clothing?" (Brett and Kernaleguen, 1975).

Studies of different demographic characteristics of opinion leaders in fashion have produced findings such as the following: (1) Socioeconomic background is not necessarily related to opinion leadership; it seems that opinion leaders influence others in their social worlds who are likely to be at the same socioeconomic level (King, 1963; Schrank and Gilmore, 1973; Kim and Schrank, 1982). (2) Female fashion opinion leaders tend to be young and well-educated (Summers, 1970).

Lifestyle characteristics of opinion leaders have been studied as well. As we might expect, fashion opinion leaders appear to be relatively sociable. Among both male and female opinion leaders, participation in sports, attendance in sorority and club meetings, major, fashion awareness, and self-esteem may all contribute to fashion opinion leadership. Female opinion leaders are likely to be physically mobile, cosmopolitan, gregarious, and active in social organizations. They may even be more interested in clothing than fashion innovators in some cases; perhaps they feel conscientious about their role in influencing others (Schrank and Gilmore, 1973). They are not necessarily socially insecure but they value conformity in dress (Schrank and Gilmore, 1973). However, the fashion-opinion leadership role may be related to performance anxiety (Brett and Kernaleguen, 1975). To some extent, fashion opinion leaders may dress to bolster their self-concept and to compensate for feelings of anxiety. Knowing that one is influencing others may be used to bolster one's sense of self-competence. In contrast to the finding that fashion innovators may function at a higher level of cognitive complexity, Lennon and Davis (1987) found that fashion opinion leaders may actually function at somewhat lower levels of cognitive complexity than those who were not high in fashion opinion leadership.

Fashion opinion leaders display a high degree of self-monitoring behavior. It seems that the fashion opinion leadership role may be associated with attention-seeking and individuality expressed for purposes of controlling social situations (Davis and Lennon, 1985). Moreover, self-monitoring fashion consumers appear to be more willing to pay higher amounts for name-brand products (Guess and Jordache) when an advertisement stresses image than do those with low self-monitors (Lennon, Davis, and Fairhurst, 1988).

Fashion opinion leadership is also related to public self-consciousness or an awareness of self as a social object and a concern with self-presentation (Miller, Davis, and Rowold, 1982). Opinion leaders may feel the need to direct others and may show competitive exhibitionist tendencies (Summers, 1970). They are highly involved in keeping up with fashion trends and perceive themselves as doing so.

In a study comparing American and Korean fashion consumer behaviors, the strength of correlation between an attitude toward change and both (*a*) fashion innovation and (*b*) fashion opinion leadership was greater for the Korean respondents (Schrank, Sugawara, and Kim, 1982). The researchers surmised that adoption of fashion may present a greater degree of change for Korean college students than it presents for American college students. Americans may take change for granted more than do Koreans. Once fashion change is established as an institution within a cultural context, the norms supporting fashion change may become more independent of general cultural norms (Schrank, Sugawara, and Kim, 1982).

*Innovative*
*Communicator*

In some cases, one individual may be both a fashion innovator and a fashion opinion leader. Thus, while fashion innovation and fashion opinion leadership are distinct conceptually, and different social-psychological profiles may be established on the basis of research, some studies have found moderate-to-strong correlations between these two constructs (Schrank and Gilmore, 1973; Kim and Schrank, 1982; Lennon and Davis, 1987). The manner in which these two constructs are measured undoubtedly influences the extent to which they have been found to be correlated, if at all.

Yet, there does seem to be some credence to the idea that *some* individuals, at least, are both innovators and opinion leaders. Such individuals are dual-change agents who are likely to be quite influential in the diffusion process. These persons may be called **innovative communicators**. In a study of male college students who were innovative communicators, it was found that they tended to be in a higher socioeconomic class, were more likely than noninnovators to be business majors, and were especially unlikely to be engineering majors (Baumgarten, 1975). They were both physically and socially active. They had a strong preference for rock music but were not necessarily moviegoers. The innovative communicators were very likely to read magazines and newspapers, including fashion magazines such as *Gentleman's Quarterly* and *Esquire*. Over 80 percent of these fashion leaders read *Playboy* regularly.

These innovative communicators were extremely appearance-conscious and possessed the personality traits of exhibitionism, narcissism (self-love), and impulsivity (which is likely to be a factor when shopping). They spent a relatively high amount of money on clothes, knew a lot about styles and brands, and owned brand-name items. They appeared to possess some of the characteristics of both the fashion innovator and the fashion opinion leader (Baumgarten, 1975).

*Fashion Followers*

Although relatively little research has focused on the characteristics of fashion followers per se, there is considerable evidence that consumers as a whole who are particularly susceptible to personal influence have some commonalities (Robertson, 1971). They are more likely than opinion leaders to be other-directed or to look to others for behavioral guidelines rather than rely on their own value systems. People in transitional life stages may also be more susceptible to interpersonal influence. This might apply to college freshmen, newlyweds, individuals in new careers, or recently widowed or divorced individuals. There is also some evidence that easily influenced consumers tend to be relatively anxious with respect to social affiliations.

Fashion followers have been found to be influenced to a greater extent by consumer-dominated sources (opinion leaders) than they are by marketer-dominated sources (media) (Polegato and Wall, 1980). In the early stages of their careers, females are more likely to rely on co-workers for information about appropriate attire, whereas later in their careers, they are more likely to turn to media such as magazines (Rabolt and Drake, 1985). It has not been possible to distinguish female college students who are fashion leaders from those who are followers on the basis of demographic characteristics, rendering further credence to the idea that leaders and followers are in the same social circles or socioeconomic groups (Polegato and Wall, 1980).

What are some of the other characteristics that influence involvement with fashion? Fashion awareness is one aspect of such involvement that has been explored. It may be described as knowledge of whether styles depicted in fashion sketches are in or out of style. (This type of awareness has also been used by some researchers, as noted earlier, as a factor in determining fashion innovation.) Obviously, fashion awareness is an important concept because it is likely to precede interest, evaluation, trial, and adoption or rejection of a style (Rogers, 1983).

*Other Characteristics*

In a survey of 1,950 business women, individuals who exhibited high fashion awareness derived more pleasure from (and devoted more time to) shopping for clothing and purchased more clothing on impulse as compared with those persons having low fashion awareness. Individuals who were low in fashion awareness showed greater concern with the economic aspects of clothing acquisition than did persons revealing high fashion awareness (Horridge and Richards, 1984).

Fashion awareness has also been found to be associated with the following characteristics of female consumers: readership of fashion magazines, age, marital status, education, income, and courses taken related to fashion. Specifically, women who read *Vogue* and *Harper's Bazaar* were significantly more aware of current fashions than individuals who read other fashion magazines. Women who were 25 years of age or under and those in the 26 to 35 age group possessed more fashion awareness than the older groups, ranging to 65 years of age. Those who had never been married were more fashion-aware than those who were married, divorced, or widowed. Additionally, there was some evidence that fashion awareness tended to increase along with education and income (Horridge, Khan, and Huffman, 1981).

Some research has characterized shopping behavior in terms of fashion-related issues (Lumpkin and McConkey, 1984). Individuals who shop at department stores appear to be more fashion-conscious and to enjoy the shopping experience more than do discount store shoppers. (It should be noted, however, that some "discount" stores carry designer apparel, so one must be cautious about making generalizations on the nature of discount store shopping.) Specialty store shoppers appear to place more importance on apparel brand and quality and tend to judge store personality as an important criterion. Both specialty and department store shoppers may be fashion-conscious and/or innovative (Lumpkin and McConkey, 1984).

Large-scale marketing surveys with both male and female consumers have enabled researchers to differentiate between *style-oriented consumers*, whose interest lies in cut or style of a garment, how interesting it is, and its appearance or quality, and *pragmatic consumers*, who are concerned mostly with the ease of care or low cost of maintaining their clothes (the "use" value). Approximately

43 percent of American adults may be described as pragmatic, as compared with the 19 percent who could be characterized as style-oriented consumers (Gadel, 1985). Style-oriented consumers buy clothes more often and account for a higher share of clothing purchases. Appearances mean a lot to these consumers, who are very interested in styling, but do not necessarily follow the latest fashion trends. Over 60 percent of style-oriented consumers are female, but men are represented as well. Style-oriented consumers do not differ significantly from the population as a whole in other demographic characteristics. A little more than one-half identify themselves as upper middle or upper class (Gadel, 1985).

Similarly, research using Illinois mothers has indicated fashion-oriented consumers (who prefer "product or style newness") tend to value quantity over quality, buy from want rather than need, and are not likely to return garments to a store and complain when dissatisfied (Morganosky, 1987). In contrast to these fashion-oriented individuals, functionally oriented individuals were significantly more likely to value (low) cost over convenience and need over want. Individuals in high income groups tended to place less importance on functionality and more importance on aesthetics. However, there were no differences based on household income in relation to valuing fashion (Morganosky, 1987)

Several studies have delved into personality traits of fashion consumers. In one study, male and female college students were asked to respond to the statement, "I should love to be a clothes designer," which was meant to examine interest in the field of fashion (Rosenfeld and Plax, 1977). Males with this interest were characterized as cooperative, sympathetic, warm, helpful, impulsive, irritable, and demanding. They were also conformists who sought encouragement from others. Females with this type of fashion interest, however, were described as irrational, uncritical, stereotypic in their thinking, quick, expressive, and ebullient. Thus, different personality profiles emerged on the basis of gender. Further research is needed to clarify differences in males' and females' orientations toward fashion (Rosenfeld and Plax, 1977).

Another study investigated predisposition to fashion in relation to personality characteristics (Pinaire Reed, 1979). Individuals with a high predisposition were somewhat less dogmatic than those with a low predisposition. High dogmatics would be expected to be less open to change than low dogmatics, so early adopters might be expected to be less dogmatic. Individuals with a high predisposition toward fashion also tended to be higher in Machiavellian tactics than individuals with a low predisposition. A Machiavellian personality relates to the tendency to manipulate others, and clothes may be used by some as a means of controlling the impressions they convey to others as a form of manipulation.

## Summary

Research on processes of style adoption and on characteristics of fashion consumers has clarified our understanding of the fashion process. Still needed, however, is a clearer understanding of the *meaning* of fashion to different groups of consumers. Such an understanding must incorporate consideration of fashion consumers' characteristics as well as the stage (temporal context) in which styles are perceived.

In a step toward this direction, George Sproles (1985) summarized some of the different theoretical perspectives on fashion and identified six sequential phases.

*1. Invention and introduction* involve the generation of an idea in a designer's, or in a "fashion bricoleur's," head. Consequently, a noticeable style or look is created. The inspiration for this "invention" can come from any source, including a subculture, an art movement, ethnic styles, trends of nostalgia, or any creative individual's insights. "At any given time alternative styles and ideals of beauty compete for attention" (Sproles, 1985, p. 65). Not only must a style or look be "created," but it must also be made available to the consuming public, usually by retailers of fashion. (For an exploration of the idea of retailing as a social world, see Social Focus 15-1.)

*2. Fashion leadership* is evident when a small proportion of the most fashion-conscious consumers adopt a style and introduce it to the public. These leaders experiment with the style, possibly incorporating it into a new look or concept, and provide the visual communication of the style as they introduce it to individuals within their own social worlds. You will recall that fashion innovators, who are most closely associated with this stage, are likely to strive to differentiate themselves from other fashion consumers. Thus, they provide the *differentiation* or *demarcation* function described by Simmel (1904).

*3. Increasing social visibility* of the style occurs as it is endorsed by some other fashion-conscious consumers, especially fashion opinion leaders.

*4. Conformity within and across social groups* emerges as a style achieves social legitimacy, and the compelling forces of conformity (identification or imitation) and mass marketing help to spread it.

*5. Social saturation* is evident when the style has become very commonplace—overused as a cliché. This point of saturation sets the stage for its eventual decline.

*6. Decline and obsolescence* of the style occur as new fashion alternatives are introduced as replacements, and use of the old fashion recedes. By this time, innovators have already begun to experiment with newer styles and looks and are likely to be providing visual exposure to them.

As we evelute these stages, the following question may emerge: What triggers or compels the passage from one fashion cycle to another? (Simon-Miller, 1985). Moreover, we know that cycles of fashion do not neatly follow one another sequentially. Rather, the cycles often overlap and are further confounded because buying and wearing styles are substantively different processes.

Existing diffusion research, as we have seen, has tended to focus almost exclusively on the early stages of a style's adoption. More research is needed to address the later stages of the fashion process, for example, to explore the meaning of style to fashion followers. What is also needed to advance our understanding of mass market theory and fashion diffusion is research that explores the interconnectedness among diffusion constructs, for example, change

# Retailing as a Social World

Retailers play a pivotal role in determining which apparel styles and accessories are made available to consumers. During the invention and introductory stages of the fashion cycle, retailers serve as **gatekeepers** who filter out some styles offered by manufacturers and attempt to supply a meaningful context (through store displays and advertisements) for the styles that they *do* select.

> Fashion is nothing more and nothing less than the systematic encryption, transmission, and interpretation of social meaning. A fashion item itself is only a vehicle that transports cultural information to its destination—the consumer. It is, however, a vehicle that makes many stops along the way. Proposals for the appropriate "payload" to be transported are put forth by design specialists, the most successful of whom function as "cultural telepaths" by virtue of their ability to detect the wants and whims of the public. These proposals compete in the creative marketplace; some are selected to be given physical form by manufacturers and imbued with symbolic form by advertisers. Retailers in turn act as filters by screening out potentially unpopular models and adding additional layers of meaning to the product. Finally, consumers vote with their dollars for those vehicles which will provide the best social mileage (Solomon, 1985, p. xi).

From a symbolic-interactionist perspective, fashion retailing may be regarded as a social world in which the participants are involved with timely, symbolic products. The concept of social world refers to an amorphous and diffuse unit of social organization characterized by a common sphere of interest and involvement for participants (Unruh, 1979). In this case, the common sphere of interest and involvement is fostered by attending "market week" at apparel marts—where manufacturers present their styles to retailers, by reading common fashion publications, and by interacting with the ultimate consumer.

Blumer (1969b) noted that fashion is a process of collective selection in which retail buyers are immersed in a common world of intense stimulation. As they pay careful attention to consumer demand and aim to provide a linkage between the manufacturer and the consumer in the fashion distribution process, retailers are likely to develop common sensitivities and appreciations for similar styles. Their choices may not always match those that the consumer would make if given the opportunity to make decisions at the manufacturing level, in part because retailers are influenced by internal organizational factors such as store image, profitability, and consumer satisfaction in the aggregate (Taylor, 1985). Weighing all of these factors, along with aesthetic choices, a delicate balance of merchandise assortment is assembled for presentation to the consumer.

Within fashion retailing per se, some diverse "cultures" of sorts may be identified. Retail activities may be viewed along a cultural continuum, ranging from high culture to popular culture (Hirschman and Wallendorf, 1982). High-cultural products include those with more intangible qualities such as prestige and fashionability, as compared with popular-cultural products. Thus more effort is required from retailers to create or foster intended meanings of high-cultural products, for consumers who demand and expect more than utilitarian value.

Retailers are confronted with the implicit tasks of predicting the tasks in which consumers will wear apparel and accessories, the meanings consumers will assign to them, and the extent to which their own preferences and interpretations differ from consumers. Research has indicated that employees in high-cultural shoe stores are more discriminating in their assessments of such qualities as prestige and fashionability (Kaiser et al., 1985). Retailers as a whole, however, were aware that some of the dimensions of their interpretations of shoes tended to differ from those of consumers. Although retailers may serve as gatekeepers in initially selecting those products that are to become available to consumers, they can do little to control consumers' assignment of meaning to those products that continue to emerge after these products leave the store.

agents' characteristics and competing initiatives such as the marketing actions of innovating firms and the actions of competitors (Gatignon and Robertson, 1985). Also needed is an understanding of processes by which styles emerge not strictly from designer's heads but also from consumers and groups of individuals themselves—as in the case of bricolage (discussed in Chapter Fourteen). Particularly as we explore the idea of "looks" (Gestalt appearances) rather than just styles (individual garments), instances of *consumer* creativity become very salient. Mass market theory has inspired a great deal of research on characteristics of consumers based on their role in the fashion process, but its focus has perhaps led researchers to dwell unduly on the adoption of clothes as a commodity rather than as a form of self-expression. To discover more about the *meaning* of fashion to consumers, their acts of appearance management must be considered. In the next section, we will consider the theoretical perspectives on styles that emerge from "the streets."

## *Subcultural Leadership Theories*

By now it should be apparent that styles do not simply trickle down from the upper to the lower social classes. Neither do they emerge strictly nor originally from the fashion industry itself. As we saw in Sproles's (1985) description of the invention and introduction stage of the fashion process, ideas can spring from a variety of sources of inspiration. Often, fashion designers may be in the position of *interpreting* the looks they see on the streets and then of basing their designs on these interpretations (visual concepts). The industry can never totally predict what consumers will do with specific garments and/or accessories once they take them home and begin to experiment with them. Using individual creativity and experimenting with the "tools and props" on hand, consumers participate in the development of style.

Thus theorists attempting to explain fashion change have explored processes by which ideas and looks emerge from consumers themselves, and not necessarily from those in the upper classes (Field, 1970; Blumberg, 1974). The phenomenon of "status float" (trickle-up), for example, has been used to describe an upward flow of fashion to the middle and upper social classes from blue-collar workers, ethnic groups, and the young (Field, 1970).

Many of these ideas and looks emerge from subcultures within a larger society. As we examine the influence of subcultures on fashion change,

it becomes necessary to distinguish between true leadership and mere visibility caused by sensational dress. Typically a subculture leads simply by its ability to invent new styles creatively. Eventually the unique style becomes admired by the larger population for its creativity, artistic excellence, or relevance to current life-styles. Then the style diffuses into mass population, sometimes as a result of mass marketing (Sproles, 1985, p. 61).

There is a great deal of evidence that the hippie subculture or counterculture of the late 1960s and early 1970s influenced mass fashion. America's "radical youth," associated with the New Left movement, tended to adopt an appearance style that was a kind of metaphor of rural dress. Blue denim jeans, jackets, and overalls could be linked to styles of the rural nineteenth-century farmers and cowboys of America. By the 1970s, blue jeans had become status symbols, with visible designer labels to "document" their worth (Lind and Roach-Higgins, 1985). Thus Veblen's (1899) idea of conspicuous consumption applied to blue jeans once they entered the realm of fashionability and status. In contrast, when they had been associated with the counterculture, they had been a form of conspicuous counterconsumption.

In the 1960s, a time when youth made up a large segment of the population, it became clear that the cultural category of age had replaced the cultural category of social class with respect to processes of imitation and differentiation promoting fashion change. In England, the youth culture's influence on fashion could be connected more with working-class culture than with middle-class culture (Horowitz, 1982). However, fashion seemed to be speaking more to age than to class, as a whole. Fashion also seemed to place more emphasis on providing personal satisfaction and excitement (valued especially by youth) through its frequent innovations (Horowitz, 1982). This perspective on fashion is consistent with Blumer's (1969b) emphasis on the *prestige of fashion*.

A major issue emerges as we consider the influence of subcultures on fashion. It becomes important to identify the extent to which subcultural appearance codes represent "violations of the authorized codes through which the social world is organized" (Hebdige, 1979, p. 91). And, if these newer codes represent "violations," "noise," or "interference" as compared to the status quo, then why and how does mainstream culture become influenced by these "renegade" aesthetic codes? Also, to return to the point raised by Sproles (1985) with respect to the issue of *leadership* versus *visual inspiration*, it is important to recognize that subcultures may adopt aesthetic codes for purposes of *differentiation* from other subcultures and mainstream culture itself. Style in this sense may be a form of revolt, but subcultures are not necessarily wanting to be imitated by mainstream culture. In fact, they may resist this type of "legitimation" of their styles and looks. Once the fashion industry appropriates some of their aesthetic codes, they may either strive to seek new forms of expression to differentiate themselves once again, *or* they may go ahead and pursue a more conventional form of appearance management.

Thus the point of social protest and subcultural differentiation—the power of appearance symbolism—seems to emerge from stylistic shock value. Once a style or look has been co-opted by the fashion industry and has become culturally legitimized, it loses its potency.

The diversion of social protest into the realm of fashion only confirms the political impotence of youthful protest against closing opportunities and social despair. . . . For what fashion can always co-opt is the outrageous. Since its business is novelty, is its always having to be replaced, shock constitutes one of the tools of the trade (Fox-Genovese, 1987, p. 9).

How does fashion co-opt subcultural style? It is important to recognize that a style may become mainstream fashion, based on the visual inspiration subcultures provide fashion designers who are looking for outrageous, whimsical, or shocking looks. These looks then are interpreted and produced as *commodities* (Hebdige, 1979). Processes of visual communication, interpretation, and appropriation thus lead to

> the process of production, publicity and packaging which must inevitably lead to the defusion of the subculture's subversive power. . . . Each new subculture establishes new trends, generates new looks and sounds which feed back into the appropriate industries (Hebdige, 1979, p. 95).

What happens to the meaning of these styles or looks in the process of becoming a commodity? Transformed into commodities, these styles or looks "arrive at the marketplace already laden with significance" (Hebdige, 1979, p. 95) but now they have been removed from their subcultural contexts. Thus they largely become stripped of their meaning and value to the subculture, since the whole idea in the subcultural context was to break aesthetic rules. Now that the styles seem legitimate, their subcultural *use value* diminishes. In contrast, their *exchange value*, on a mass industry scale, is what counts. As Baudrillard (1981) would note, an interplay between the *signifier* (style or look) and its exchange value is now evident. What is less important is what was *signified* by the style or look in the first place—its ideological value and use value in the eyes of the subculture's members. Examples of this process can be seen in Figures 15-7 and 15-8. Social Focus 15-2 delves into punk and post-punk subcultures in relation to the "incorporation" of style.

In addition to considering the stylistic influence of subcultures, it is also important to assess if any of their values have an impact on the larger culture. In some case, there may be an *ideological form* of diffusion (Hebdige, 1979). Initially, "style in particular provokes a double response: it is alternately celebrated (in the fashion page) and ridiculed or reviled (in those articles which define subcultures as social problems")" (Hebdige, 1979, p. 93).

However, eventually some aspects of a subculture's ideology may be appropriated into mainstream culture. There is likely to be a time lag between a subcultural style becoming a commodity and recognition by the larger society that a change has actually taken place (if indeed it has). It takes time for the various segments of the community to comprehend or appreciate that new meanings are emerging or have emerged (Lind and Roach-Higgins, 1985). For example, we can consider the influence of reggae music and some aspects of Rastafarian style on popular music and fashion. Such influences may serve as signs that our world is increasingly becoming a "global village," a tendency that is consistent with postmodernism (to be discussed in Chapter Sixteen). Similarly, the feminist movement of the 1960s was symbolized by the "natural look" (long,

**FIGURE 15-7**
*Subcultural symbols can become part of mainstream fashion, as shown in this model's "dreadlock" hairstyle influenced by the Rastafarian subculture. She achieved this style with much effort, a crimping iron and curling iron, and lots of gel. Photo by Wendy Dildey.*

straight hair, no makeup, and no bra) and some imagery borrowed from working-class male culture (blue work shirts and jeans). The "natural look," in particular, was co-opted by the fashion and beauty industries, which began to produce bras with natural bustlines and cosmetics that enhance one's features while maintaining a "natural" look. Unquestionably, feminist ideologies have had a tremendous impact on society as well and have contributed to a rethinking of gender categories.

That subcultures have some influence not only on the styles we wear but also on some of our ideas is indicative of some larger currents in modern life. As we saw in Chapter Fourteen, cultural ambivalence seems to be woven into the fabric of postindustrial society.

**FIGURE 15-8**
*British designer Zandra Rhodes developed an expensive interpretation of punk style in this 1977 black jersey evening dress decorated with beaded safety pins and chains. Courtesy of the Trustees of the Victoria and Albert Museum.*

# The Punk Aesthetic and Fashion

The seventies. The "Me Decade." The "natural look" was in, and everyone tried to look like Cheryl Tiegs. Such mediocrity in style deserved to end with a vengeance. The fashion scene was ready for a jolt, and when the punks took to the streets in the late seventies, they created a look so radically different and unlike anything seen before that "new" was an understatement.

—HOFLER AND ZARCO, 1985

The diffusion of punk style occurred by means of a co-opting of the new aesthetic code. By means of "production, publicity and packaging . . . punk innovations were fed back directly into high fashion and mainstream fashion" (Hebdige, 1979, p. 95):

> Punk clothing and insignia could be bought mail-order by the summer of 1977, and in September of that year *Cosmopolitan* ran a review of Zandra Rhodes' latest collection of couture follies which consisted entirely of variations on the punk theme. Models smouldered beneath mountains of safety pins and plastic (the pins were jewelled, the "plastic" wet-look satin) and the accompanying article ended with an aphorism—"To shock is chic"—which presaged the subculture's imminent demise (Hebdige, 1979, p. 96).

Once the innovations of a subculture are translated into commodities, their ideological meanings are transformed. When the general public can *buy* signs of punk, the "do-it-yourself and be outrageous" idea loses some of its significance.

> You can now buy the signs of Punk, and in very expensive, if slightly transposed, forms. And there is a kind of escalation in matters of style: the better something is made, the better it looks. There is a

painful irony in social rebels' having to view the signs of their rebellion sported in exquisite materials by those they thought they were rebelling against. It is only human to want to be able to buy the superior version. An Annie Lennox may brilliantly press the style to its limits and beyond, but fashion is already catching up with her, already identifying her as merely an especially dramatic version of itself. She has lost her power to shock, and is losing her power to command attention (Fox-Genovese, 1987).

Punk subcultural meanings became frozen with much of the political value lost, but there were very tangible alterations of larger, cultural aesthetic codes. What remained was a new aesthetic and a new, eclectic way of wearing as well as seeing. The punk aesthetic demanded a look at the everyday world in a new context.

In the early 1980s, the French designer Jean Paul Gaultier interpreted the punk aesthetic in terms of a subversion of the whole idea of fashion. He interspersed mannequins with "real" models of all shapes and sizes, presented underwear (corsets) as outerwear, and combined elements of appearance that conventionally didn't match (Wilson, 1985, pp. 132–133). Similarly, British designer Vivienne Westwood's version of punk in the late 1970s reflected her way of thinking that anything is possible and that seemingly disparate materials and objects can be combined. Thus cashmere can go with plastic, styles from the past can become futuristic, socks can fall down, and bras can be worn over dresses (McDermott, 1987). Punk left its mark in bright colors, painted faces, and androgynous hairstyles (Fox-Genovese, 1987). Yet, more generally, it led the larger postmodern culture to question the aesthetic codes aligned with traditional ideologies. In the process, there have been modifications in how we dress and construct our realities in everyday life.

## Ambivalence Theories

There are . . . collective currents that impinge on our sense of self at different times during our lives and at different historical moments. . . . Because we are subject to many of the same conditions of life, a great many of us experience in our persons similar yearnings, tensions, concerns, and discontents, which regardless of how we apprehend them, seek some form of expression (Davis, 1985, p. 24).

Ambivalence theories on fashion, emerging in the 1980s, address the instabilities relating not only to social class but also to other cultural categories such as age, gender, and ethnicity, as we saw in Chapter Fourteen (see Figure 15-9). Fred Davis (1985, 1988) indicates that identity ambivalence is a fundamental factor contributing to fashion change. Kaiser, Nagasawa, and Hutton (1989) contend that the concept of ambivalence also applies to feelings about time (nostalgia for the past versus desire to be current) (see Figure 15-10) and capitalism (wanting clothing commodities but thinking that we may spend too much on them and that marketers' profit margin is higher than it should be), as well as other issues.

FIGURE 15-9
Cultural ambivalence about age can be examined by considering the historical relations between youth and maturity. Do adults want children, at times, to behave and appear like "miniature adults," and do children themselves want to do so, as shown here? Also, how and why do adults strive to maintain a youthful appearance? Courtesy of the Frederick Beauchamp Collection, City of Sacramento, Museum and History Division.

**FIGURE 15-10**
*Cultural ambivalence about time and history reveals itself in a borrowing of signs of the past (1960s tie-dyed T-shirts, long hair, and friendship bracelet), interpreted in new ways and combined in new contexts that may have little to do with the spirit of the past from which they were derived. Photo by Michelle Small.*

Part and parcel of cultural ambivalence is the dynamic modification of the *aesthetic code*. That is, cultural ambivalence is likely to propel individuals to experiment with appearance, and ambiguous looks are likely to emerge in the process. The meanings of these looks must then be negotiated in everyday life, as the look (appearance style) becomes accepted (fashionable). Underlying feelings of ambivalence, however, are not resolvable; therefore the process of fashion continues (Kaiser, Nagasawa, and Hutton, 1989).

When a cultural category's own aesthetic code influences that of another cultural category, the process is neither a "willy nilly" kind of appropriation, nor a "wholesale adoption" of a style or look. Rather, this influence is likely to be based on careful, although frequently unconscious, selection of and playing with stylistic elements.

Who is least likely to experiment with aesthetic codes? According to one writer on fashion change, it is important to note that "the only remaining rules concern men's dress at the highest levels of business and government" (Fox-Genovese, 1987). Perhaps those who *have* the most and, therefore, have the *most to lose* are least likely to experiment with aesthetic codes. Yet even among upper-class white males there is some room for code modification, albeit subtle.

For example, the "power" tie has alternated from red to yellow to other colors (for example, turquoise).

Baudrillard (1981) identifies *ambivalence as the principle on which the logic of symbolic exchange is based* (p. 123). Ambivalence, he contends, is somewhat obscured by a dominant aesthetic code (for example, a business suit), and fashion change results from a "rupture" of the existing code when certain individuals or groups lend expression to their ambivalence. Aesthetics in the postmodern sense, he suggests, no longer has anything to do with the categories of beauty and ugliness; the confusion between the two, he contends, is strategic (Baudrillard, 1981, p. 187). This confusion in itself may be linked to the concept of ambivalence. For example, the punk aesthetic was based on a principle of disharmony and shock value. A logic of *difference* (for example, moral versus immoral and old versus new) is deeply etched in fashion change:

> Fashion is one of the more inexplicable phenomena, so far as these matters go: its compulsion to innovate signs, its apparently arbitrary and perpetual production of meaning—a kind of meaning drive—and the logical mystery of its cycle are all in fact the essence of what is sociological. The logical processes of fashion might be extrapolated to the dimension of "culture" in general—to all social production of signs, values and relations (Baudrillard, 1981, pp. 78–79).

Since Baudrillard regards ambivalence as a "rupture of value," it would follow that styles representing this rupture would be ambiguous. Moreover, meaning can be difficult to decipher because a signifier may refer to any number of potential signifieds (Baudrillard, 1981, p. 149).

Ambivalence also gives rise simultaneously to distinction and conformity in what is one of the great paradoxes of fashion. By buying and wearing appearance signs, individuals and groups search for a place in the social order (Baudrillard, 1981, p. 38). It no longer is enough to possess certain styles; now there is a need to underscore one's possessions and to show how well he or she possesses them (p. 42). For example, in the 1980s accessories became extremely important aspects of appearance management. People would wear multiple bracelets, earrings, watches, pins, and other articles of jewelry, as though to underscore the idea of accessorizing.

To partake in the fashion process, and especially to become immersed in it, is to engage in a kind of bricolage in order to organize one's own existence and to invest it with meaning. In postmodern fashion, it is not always so much what particular garment is consumed (purchased and worn) as it is a process of consuming a code or a system of garments and related accessories. "It is no longer a question of 'being' oneself but of 'producing' oneself" (Baudrillard, 1975, p. 19). Individuals reflect on themselves, and consumption becomes a "mirror of production" (Baudrillard, 1975, p. 19). That is, to consume is to begin to produce again, as consumption becomes a system of self-production that is integrated into everyday activities (Baudrillard, 1968). Individuals can enjoy the self's value and meaning, and engage in self-expression and self-accumulation "whose form escapes the self" (Baudrillard, 1975).

Fascination with the aesthetic code, according to Baudrillard (1975), is pervasive in postmodern life. In fact, it is so powerful that it has taken on a kind of life of its own. Not everyone will elect to play with the aesthetic code, to bend the rules, to experiment with accessories and styles (Baudrillard, 1981, p. 48). You will recall tht some consumers are quite style-sensitive, whereas there are others for whom style is not as important (Gadel, 1985). Innovative and creative people are most likely to play with the aesthetic code *"in order not to be understood by the majority,"* at least not initially. The goal is distinction (Baudrillard, 1981, p. 48).

Part of the passion in postmodern aesthetics entails looking for new rules and categories (Lyotard, 1988, p. 81). Behind this passion and quest for the code is ambivalence (Baudrillard, 1981; Davis, 1985; Kaiser, Nagasawa, and Hutton, 1989). Not all individuals will experience it equally or on a similarly conscious level, but ambivalence provides a continual source of stimulation for designers and fashion bricoleur-consumers alike. Ambivalence promotes a sense of **play** (Derrida, 1970, p. 263). Individuals can engage in this process of play and thereby participate in a postmodern cultural discourse about the meaning of style. Postmodernism has been described as a "rich and creative movement, of the greatest play and delight," but a form of aesthetic play that is committed "to surface and to the *superficial* in all senses of the word" (Bennington and Massumi, in the introduction to Lyotard, 1988, p. xviii).

Baudrillard may go too far in some of his assertions about fashion and postmodern life. For example, Elizabeth Wilson (1985) has criticized Baudrillard for what she considers to be a utilitarian bias, that is, he, like Veblen (1899), critiques social values on the basis of a lack of use value. Like Veblen, Baudrillard (1981) feels that fashion tends to disguise fundamental inequities in the social order. (Some other theorists, in contrast, tend to regard postmodernism as democratic.)

At any rate, part of the value in Baudrillard's critique of fashion lies in his emphasis on the importance of aesthetic codes and their ability to assume their own logic. He is able to link an understanding of late capitalism with cultural symbols, by combining semiotics with everyday-life behavior in the form of consumption (Poster, 1975).

Although they may differ on some points, Baudrillard (1981) and Wilson both agree that cultural ambivalence exists and is linked to capitalism and aesthetic codes.

> We both love and hate fashion, just as we love and hate capitalism itself. . . .
> We live as far as clothes are concerned a triple ambiguity: the ambiguity of capitalism itself with its great wealth and great squalor, its capacity to create and its dreadful wastefulness; the ambiguity of our identity, of the relation of self to body and self to the world; and the ambiguity of art, its purpose and meaning (Wilson, 1985, pp. 14–15).

The challenge in our attempts to understand fashion as a process is to explore the means by which people use appearance to construct a sense of self and to negotiate the meaning of style in social life. Although it may not be possible to resolve ambivalence, the process of constructing appearances in everyday social and personal processes makes art accessible and meaning dynamic.

## *Suggested Readings*

Blumer, H. 1969b. Fashion: From class differentiation to collective selection. *Sociological Quarterly 10*:275–291.
   In this classic article, Blumer developed a theory of collective selection. He criticized the traditional class-oriented explanation of fashion change and called for an understanding of fashion based on a sensitivity to emerging tastes and collective processes.

McDermott, D. 1987. *Street style*. New York: Rizzoli.
   McDermott delves into British textile and apparel designs of the 1970s and 1980s, and considers their social and aesthetic implications.

Solomon, M. R., ed. 1985. *The psychology of fashion*. Lexington: Heath/Lexington Books.
   This book of readings is based on a "Psychology of Fashion" conference held in New York in the summer of 1984. A number of articles deal with theoretical issues, research findings, and marketing implications relative to the study of fashion.

Sproles, G. B. 1985. Behavioral sciences theories of fashion. In M. R. Solomon, ed. *The psychology of fashion*, pp. 55–70. Lexington: Heath/Lexington Books.
   In this article, Sproles summarizes and classifies the variety of theoretical approaches to the study of fashion.

# Chapter Sixteen
## ...
# Global Influences and Identity Expression

The new electronic interdependence recreates the world in the image of global village.

—MARSHALL McLUHAN, 1967

Does this mean massive homogenization of culture, of the decorative arts, of clothing? It is possible. The possibility should urge us to capture and record the individuality, the richness and the uniqueness of current civilizations of the world before these are obscured by the melting pot of international communications.

—LAUGHLIN, 1985

*Today we find ourselves in a global context of fashion and appearance communication. A kind of global-cultural eclecticism exists in the fashion marketplace and the realm of media imagery. What are the implications of this globalization of appearance and clothing fashion? Multiple looks with a variety of stylistic influences are stripped from their cultural contexts and become part of a larger fashion influence process. These trends could lead to a more democratic sense of global understanding. At the same time, there may be a diminishing of a sense of locality and cultural identity. Different anthropological perspectives on culture may guide our inquiry on cultural and global issues in different directions. The crux of the issue is as follows: How can we decide what is the same (universal) and what is different when we compare cultures, especially in a postmodern, global context? The implications for individual expressions of identity are discussed.*

When we speak of fashion and appearance communication today, we speak of a global context. Fashion commodities and visual images are shared across cultural boundaries, because of the international character of apparel production and retailing, and electronic media (movies, television, and music videos), respectively. Influences on fashion are drawn from a variety of ethnic and cultural sources, combined and recombined, and cast in new social and cultural contexts.

The aesthetic and visual inspiration offered by a "global village" is likely to be both enriching in the context of cross-cultural appreciation and problematic in the context of intracultural preservation of tradition and uniqueness. On a personal level, the implications of this dilemma are embedded in the expression of identity.

Clothing and personal appearance can be valuable tools in the study of different cultures for a number of reasons. One of these reasons is based on the concepts of acculturation and assimilation. In today's world, appearance communication is not limited within social systems. The degree of intercultural contact is ever-increasing, and *styles in dress diffuse across social systems* as well as within them. Does this mean that meanings are shared across cultural contexts? Not necessarily. Even among individuals in complex societies, the meanings of given styles or looks are not necessarily shared. Thus, across cultural contexts, with the likelihood of language and other cultural barriers, the potential for misunderstandings and misinterpretations are increased even further.

An outside observer may find it difficult to comprehend, in a visual sense, aesthetic codes, much less moral or ethical codes. The visual and aesthetic nature of clothes offers exciting prospects for cross-cultural appreciation. At the same time, appearance styles that are not viewed as aesthetically pleasing, within one's own cultural framework, may implicitly become barriers to further communication or understanding. More than ever, it is probably necessary for meaning to be constructed at a local level, within a person's social worlds, within a specific cultural context. Thus, the nature of appearance communication in a cross-cultural context is even more mysterious and intricate than in a given cultural context. Should we attempt such an understanding?

> Clothing and adornment are universal features of human behavior and an examination of what they reveal, and attempt to conceal, contributes to our knowledge about the fabric of cultures and to our understanding of the threads of human nature (Cordwell and Schwarz, 1979, p. 1).

## Postmodernism in the Global Village

In an interview, postmodern theorist Fredric Jameson described late capitalism as a "global multinational culture which is decentered and cannot be visualized, a culture in which one cannot position oneself" (Jameson, in Stephanson, 1987). One can fly into international airports, stay in international hotels, and shop in malls with multinational retail chain stores (for example, Benetton). In the process, one can lose a sense of space and cultural context.

At the same time, the eclectic blend of cultural and ethnic elements in fashion, music, and other stylistic forms is staggering. Cultural pluralism seems to thrive within given cultural contexts and within the global context. A juxtaposition of cultural elements, on an international scale, may be compared either to a "grab bag" or a "melting pot" (Gitlin, 1989). In the world marketplace, according to Baudrillard (1981, p. 113), all values—labor, knowledge, social relations, culture, and nature—are transformed into a form of economic exchange value. Signifiers (that is, clothes and images) can float freely from one cultural context to another; in the process, what is signified is lost and/or altered.

The goal from a postmodernist perspective seems to be to strive for "the best of both worlds"—a celebration of local traditions and a new cross-cultural understanding: "What is wanted here is therefore a new relationship between a global cultural style and the specificity and demands of a concrete local or national situation" (Jameson, in Stephanson, p. 40). Hence, the ultimate challenge in a world of multinational fashion is to discover the processes of acculturation, assimilation, and accommodation that blend postmodernist culture with the specifics of local-cultural contexts and to remember the individual and his or her quest for identity and social meaning in the process. Postmodernism can be stimulating, challenging, and democratic on the one hand, but exploitative on the other. In the visual arts, as it is with fashion, postmodernism involves a compilation and recombination; it is a kind of "immigrant diversity" that represents the "oneness of the world" (Gitlin, 1989). In the global shopping center, ironically, brand names and familiar styles seem to furnish "a kind of cultural home"—an anchor, albeit an international one (Gitlin, 1989). (See Figure 16-1.)

The danger in the postmodern global context, of course, is "a loss of the autonomy of culture, a case of culture falling into the world" (Jameson, in Stephanson, 1987, p. 37). (See Figure 16-2.) This poses a new theoretical problem: How can (and should) we define and characterize cultural systems? Jameson describes postmodernism in the global context as a pervasive capitalist

**FIGURE 16-1**
*Familiar T-shirt and sweatshirt styles, coupled with English words, can provide a kind of cross-cultural anchor for an American tourist in Paris. The global, postmodern context blurs many of the stylistic distinctions across specific cultural contexts, yet* interpretations of a given *style are still likely to vary as a function of cultural viewpoint. Photo by Susan B. Kaiser.*

**FIGURE 16-2**
*Seeing English words on a sweatshirt in a non-English-speaking cultural setting reminds us that there seems to be a loss of the autonomy of specific cultures in the global context. Photo by Margery Freeman.*

system (driven by a profit motivation). This global-capitalist context may be democratic in some respects, but it can also represent a "cannibalizing of styles" (exploitation of cultural symbols, stripped from their local contexts; see Figure 16-3). A sense of history or tradition may be lost in the process (Stephanson, 1987). From Baudrillard's (1981) perspective, the sphere of the code with which fashion and other media play makes up the basis on which global capitalism is founded.

How can we accomplish an understanding of cultural specificity in a global, postmodern context? New challenges are posed for cross-cultural researchers, and any student of clothing, appearance, and fashion cannot ignore global influences, even if his or her attention is focused in a specific cultural context.

## World Views on Culture

Aesthetic expression through appearance display may facilitate cross-cultural understanding, or may pose artificial barriers to such an understanding. The perspective, or "world view," guiding cross-cultural study influences the framework within which clothing and appearance, as other cultural phenomena, are interpreted. In this connection, we can consider three world views on culture: universalism, evolutionism, and relativism. These world views are anthropological models that shape a researcher's interpretations of the apparent diversity of human understandings (Shweder and Bourne, 1984).

## Universalism

The universalist philosophy involves a commitment to the view that diversity in the human experience is more apparent than it is real. "Exotic" idea systems, this perspective suggests, are really more like our own than it would seem at first glance. Thus a sense of homogeneity across cultural contexts is sought. Clothing and appearance are likely to be regarded as "apparently different but really the same" (Shweder and Bourne, 1984).

The advantage of such a perspective is the sense of democracy that it promotes. In other words, different cultures are likely to be perceived as "equal" because they are not all that different. However, cultural diversity is sacrificed for the sake of this sense of equality. The methodological approach leads a researcher to look for underlying, abstract likenesses beneath concrete, visible appearances (see Figure 16-4).

Such a level of abstraction in the quest for universality can provoke a "thrill or recognition that comes from resemblance" (Shweder and Bourne, 1984). Critics of this approach, however, would point out that rather than moving us toward the "essentials of the human situation," it moves us away from them

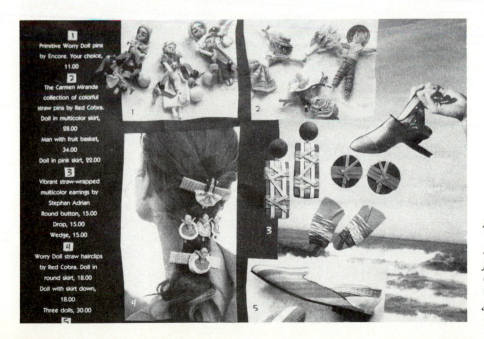

**FIGURE 16-3**
*Worry-doll jewelry shows how signs can be stripped from their (Guatemalan) cultural context and turned into commodities in the global marketplace. Photo by Wendy Dildey.*

**FIGURE 16-4**
*A universalist approach to the study of culture would lead us to look for similarities across cultures. For example, a universalist might focus on the similarity between this Bhutani girl's jewelry and headcovering, and appearance styles adopted in other cultures and subcultures. Yet focusing too much on these similarities may lead us to miss the richness of meanings in their local contexts. Photo by Katharine Hoag.*

(Geertz, 1973, p. 39). Instead anthropologist Clifford Geertz (1973) promotes a sensitivity to cultural context and the social processes within it that can be "thickly described" (p. 14). Using this approach, we can strive toward a rich understanding of the embeddedness of appearances as used by people to construct a sense of social reality. Universalism, on the contrary, can obscure our understanding of complex variations in meanings of appearances, even (and especially) when they look similar on the surface. At the same time, universalism may also lead to powerful (perhaps global) context-rich universal generalizations in some cases, and should not be undermined when it contributes to such an understanding (Shweder and Bourne, 1984).

*Evolutionism*    The evolutionist philosophy espouses a commitment to the view that "alien" idea systems are truly different from our own. In fact, they differ in a special way—in terms of a hierarchical order. Cultural diversity is expected, and cultures are "ranked" in the process, with some cultures (probably the researchers') viewed as more advanced than others. A "different but unequal" perspective is endorsed (Shweder and Bourne, 1984). The concept of hegemony (discussed in Chapter Fourteen), describing power of certain cultures over others, applies here in a global context.

How would a researcher rank cultural differences? First, cultures are likely to be characterized along a developmental continuum, from "primitive" to "advanced." Second, a "normative cultural model" (again, probably the researcher's own) is treated as the endpoint of development. Third, diverse beliefs and understandings are characterized as steps or developmental stages toward a "normative" endpoint (Shweder and Bourne, 1984).

This perspective allows for the existence of cultural diversity, but it does so in a very undemocratic way. The major pitfall of this approach lies in the selection of a normative cultural model. Who is to say which culture is normative, or which kind of understanding is better or worse than another kind? This perspective promotes a tendency to perceive the ideas of others through the "filter" of one's own concerns. Moreover, this perspective is essentially ahistorical in the sense that it is naively assumed that history can be hypothetically reconstructed on the basis of cross-cultural observation. For example, a researcher might falsely make assumptions about the dress of "primeval" Europeans on the basis of historically known "savages." Even more problematic is the assumption that Europeans are morally and aesthetically superior, as a cross-cultural understanding of appearance is discussed in the context of *mutilations* of primitives, as contrasted with the *fads and fashions* of Euro-Westerners (Roach-Higgins, 1986, p. 66). (See Figure 16-5.)

## Relativism

Cultural relativists would point out that evolutionism leads to **ethnocentrism**—"the taking of our own culture's standards as an objective, natural reality to be used in judging other cultures" (Cancian and Cancian, 1974, p. 2). In contrast, cultural relativism is based on the idea that a kind of cultural filter (such as a system of cultural categories) exists that "colors" our perceptions. Part of the meaning of culture is the acceptance of categories or a filter through which we interpret the world around us. Individuals from different cultures, then, may construct an interpretation of the same reality in very different ways. Hence, everything is relative to everything else. There is no "objective" reality. Who is to say what the "real" world looks like? For example, a cultural relativist would note the difficulties in assessing masculine versus feminine appearances in a different cultural context, because the whole filter through which these activities are viewed is likely to be clouded by one's own gender within his or her own culture (see Social Focus 16-1 and Figure 16-6).

The dilemma posed by cultural relativism is: How can one decide what is the same and what is different? Being almost the converse of universalism, this perspective emphasizes differences and the difficulty of "establishing sameness" (Cancian and Cancian, 1974, p. 2).

**FIGURE 16-5**
*An evolutionary approach to the study of culture might
lead a person to look at this Tibetan child's sheepskin
clothing as a form of dress that will "evolve" into
another style. The danger in this kind of thinking is
that it suggests some cultures can be used as gauges
against which others are measured, and what is missed
in the process is a sensitivity to the richness of meanings
in their cultural contexts. Photo by Stephen Cunha.*

The objective of cross-cultural study is to strike a compromise between
cross-cultural differences and similarities. Cultural relativism is pluralist in the
sense that a "different but equal" philosophy is espoused. It is assumed that
idea systems outside one's own culture are different and display a certain coherency
that can be understood but not judged. Therefore, equality *and* diversity are
pursued. Thus the aspirations are essentially democratic in nature, as relativists
strive to preserve the integrity of differences while also establishing the equality
among diverse structures of feeling. In this connection, two rules of thumb are
applied to cross-cultural study: (*a*) the contextualization rule and (*b*) the principle
of arbitrariness (Shweder and Bourne, 1984). **Contextualization** is a conceptual
framework promoting an understanding of appearances and ideologies within
their contexts. This framework is consistent with the concept of **holism**, which

# Cultural Relativism: The Case of Islamic Women's Appearances

> Say to the believing women, that they
> cast down their eyes . . . and reveal not
> their adornment . . . and let them cast
> their veils over their bosoms.
>
> — KORAN, SURA XXIV:31

The veil was given only passing mention in the Ko-ran—Islam's holy book—but veiling is an ancient custom that may be traced back to India and Persia. It was adopted by Arabia's nomadic tribes, who enforced a strict code of female modesty (Alireza, 1987). Today the women of such conservative centers of Islam as the Arabian Peninsula, Saudi Arabia, and Afghanistan still cover themselves completely, whereas many upper-class women in the more Westernized areas—Turkey, Syria, Jordan, Tunisia, Lebanon, and parts of Egypt—have virtually abandoned the veil. Some Muslim women have lifted their veils for purposes of convenience and others reveal more complex emotions about this issue:

> "It's terrifying letting your veil go—coming out into the open for the first time," says a Moroccan medical student living in Boston. "The last thing I want a man to think is that I'm some oversexed female." In contrast, and expressing a more political view, Egyptian film-maker Laila Abou-Saifi says, "When you hide your face you annul your person, you cancel out your personality. I understand the need to identify with history, but men are wearing whatever they like—why does symbolism always fall on the backs of women?" (Manny, 1981, p. 61).

Is the veil worn today by Islamic women for privacy and protection from male harassment, or is it a symbol of oppression? A cultural-relativist perspective leads us to recognize that persons from different cultures are likely to interpret appearance and construct a sense of reality in diverse ways. There is no *objective* reality; rather, appearance must be understood within the appropriate cultural context. It is necessary to understand how the parts of a culture fit together into a whole before attempting to understand the meaning of those parts.

The Islamic fundamentalist movement that was initiated in the 1970s restored, and often demanded, the revival of the wearing of the veil for women. This revival can be linked to gender and class relations.

> Beyond the strong obsession with religion, the violent confrontations going on in the Muslim world are about two eminently materialistic pleasures: exercise of political power, and consumerism. . . . While the men seeking power through religion and its revivification are mostly from newly urbanized middle- and lower-middle-class backgrounds, unveiled women on the contrary are predominantly of the urban upper and middle class (Mernissi, 1987, p. xi).

The "covering" of women has tremendous symbolic significance throughout the Middle East; however, the manner in which head coverings are used and the meanings to which they refer vary from place to place. In Iran, the fundamentalist government that overthrew the Shah insisted that women cover themselves with the traditional *chador*—a black garment that conceals from head to toe. In Egypt, the *carsaf* has been adopted by some feminists as a symbolic shield against being treated as sex objects. In Turkey, there is a basic ideological conflict between the ideas of progressive nationalism versus Islamic identity. Hence female university professors and students are reprimanded for wearing head scarves associated with Islamic fundamentalism (Olson, 1985). In Malaysia as well, where Islam is the official religion but where 47 percent of the population are not Muslims, the government has taken steps to ban female civil servants and university students from covering the face during work. There is concern about the influx of fundamentalist ideas that are more radical than the form of Islamic ideology customarily espoused in that country (Aznam, 1985).

Clearly, as we attempt to understand the meanings of veiling in different Islamic cultures, it is important to contextualize this understanding and to avoid using Western cultural categories of gender to interpret these meanings.

> We often hear and read about women's marginalization, women's deprivation, and women's exclusion from modernity in the Third World. This kind of leftist self-serving, hasty analysis, which could be called the "Cassandra" syndrome, has led to simplistic generalizations about how bad the state is and how neglected women are. And this weepy line leaves us unable to understand why all the political actors in the Muslim world are so obsessed with women and their clothes (Mernissi, 1987, pp. xxviii–xxix).

Sociologist Fatima Mernissi (1987) notes that Islamic religion is *not* actually rooted in a principle of the biological

## *Social Focus 16-1 (continued)*

or ideological inferiority of women; in fact, the whole system is based on the assumption that women are powerful and dangerous sexual beings. Gender inequality, then, is a function not of the religious foundation but instead on the social order designed to restrain women's power. What is feared is *fitna*—disorder or chaos. There is concern that beautiful women cause men to lose their self-control, and thus the veil is used as a means for symbolically and spatially separating the sexes. Women are viewed as better able to control their sexual impulses than are men. Thus, public contexts such as city streets become social constructions of male space, and the veil is used to express the invisibility of women. The veil protects women from men and men from women.

> The Muslim ethic is against women's ornamenting themselves and exposing their charm; veils and walls were particularly effective anti-seduction devices. Westernization allowed ornamented and seductively clad female bodies to appear on the streets. It is interesting that while Western women's liberation movements had to repudiate the body in pornographic mass media, Muslim women are likely to claim the right to their bodies as part of their liberation movement. Previously a Muslim woman's body belonged to the man who possessed her, father or husband. The mushrooming of beauty salons and ready-to-wear boutiques in Moroccan towns can be interpreted as a

forerunner of women's urges to claim their own bodies (Mernissi, 1987, p. 168).

Underneath the veils and cloaks worn by some Islamic women are a variety of forms of aesthetic expression. For example, in Saudi Arabia:

> Today's apparel could be anything imaginable because everything imaginable is available, but veil and cloak lend anonymity and appearances are deceiving. Underneath might be a high-society lady in haute couture, a high schooler togged in blue jeans and a T-shirt, a villager in colorful cotton, or an old-time lady in her old-time dress. Anything goes, but the outer layer—with slight variations, perhaps—remains the same. It is a shock to see sedate cloaked figures peeling to leotards in a fitness center to do routines popular the world over. Some to whom the concept is new have tried to remain modest and decorous in their wraps while pedaling bikes or walking treadmills, until the machinery demonstrates its nasty tendency to gobble loose flaps of material and long veils attached to quite long hair (Alireza, 1987, p. 449).

Aesthetic, political, religious, and social dimensions must all be considered when interpreting the meanings of Islamic veils. What is needed is a sensitivity to the specific cultural contexts in which these meanings arise, as well as to the social circumstances shaping the everyday realities of Islamic women.

---

pertains to understanding and elaborating the implications of "part–whole" relationships. Each part is characterized by the particular relationships into which it is embedded. Parts are interconnected by relationships; they are also altered in the context of relationships. Holism can facilitate an understanding of specific signs within an appearance context (as discussed in Chapter Seven). For example, veils worn by Muslim women are only part of their appearances (see Social Focus 16-1 and Figure 16-6). These appearances, which are contexts in and of themselves, must be understood in the context of social relations. And specific cultural contexts within the Muslim religion may frame the meanings of the veil differently. In other words, it is not possible to understand phenomena in the abstract, as isolated fragments. Contextual clarification is sought prior to making a judgment. Signs are not stripped from their contexts but rather are interpreted as components of larger wholes.

**FIGURE 16-6**
*A cultural-relativistic approach to the study of culture cautions us against trying to interpret or understand the meanings of symbols from other cultures using our own culture's viewpoint or "filter." The veil worn by this Muslim Moroccan woman refers to a complex state of gender relations that are framed very differently in Moroccan culture than they are in North American culture (Mernissi, 1987). Photo by Carl Frank/Photo Researchers, Inc.*

**Arbitrariness** is a concept describing how equally rational people can look out on the same world and arrive at different understandings. That is to say, meaning is arbitrarily assigned based in part on one's cultural perspective. The world view of cultural relativism cautions us about the cultural and cognitive categories we are likely to take for granted but nevertheless use to group objects or people together (see Figure 16-7 for an example of this problem from a cross-cultural perspective).

Cultural relativism views the individual as context-dependent, embedded in a network of cultural categories and meanings. However, in a global, postmodern context, it may be difficult to know how to place the self within a larger framework. The distinction between the cultural and the larger global context may become blurred. For example, refer back to Figure 16-3 and consider the example of Central American "worry dolls." If the accessories shown in the ad are worn by a young Guatemalan woman who is very fashion-conscious, it becomes necessary to sort out whether she wears worry-doll jewelry because of its tie to local culture or because such jewelry is fashionable in the global-capitalist marketplace.

**FIGURE 16-7**
*The colorful knitted hat worn by this Peruvian Indian man might be regarded as feminine when regarded within a North American framework, but such an interpretation is based on arbitrary cultural categories that do not necessarily apply in another cultural context. Photo by Stephen Cunha.*

Additionally, the philosophy of individualism or autonomy in the United States, for example, can make it difficult to place the self in context, and there may be some social-psychological costs associated with this philosophy:

> There are costs to having no larger framework within which to locate the self. Many in our culture lack a meaningful orientation to the past. . . . Many lack a meaningful orientation to the future. We are going nowhere—at best we view ourselves as "machines" that will one day run down. . . . Cut adrift from any larger whole, the self has become the measure of all things, clutching to a faith that some "invisible hand" will sleight of hand right things in the end (Shweder and Bourne, 1984, p. 194).

One might argue, however, that in the postmodern context fashion provides a contextualizing function in a global sense. This assertion would be consistent with Blumer's (1969b) theory of collective selection (discussed in Chapter Fifteen) as well as with the tendency of ambivalence theories to note how fashion gives form to unresolved tensions. For example, to return to the worry-doll illustration (Figure 16-3), imagine that you are a tourist in Guatemala. You meet a young Guatemalan woman wearing a worry-doll barrette that is similar to one you are wearing. Thus you realize that you have something in common; you identify with her and, in the process, realize how you can place yourself within the global context. (Of course, you also probably realize that a sense of local culture is less easy to establish.)

To compare specific cultures with respect to contextualizing potential, we can consider the distinction between high-context and low-context cultures (E. T. Hall, 1977). In **high-context** cultures, social cues are clearly and richly embedded in a culturally prescribed context. A wealth of cues are provided with respect to what "social scripts" individuals must, should, or can follow. In **low-context** cultures, fewer cues and clearcut "social scripts" are prescribed.

One of the functions of culture is to serve as a "highly selective screen" between people and the outside world. Culture designates what we should pay attention to and what we should ignore. As a cognitive perspective suggests, we cannot pay attention to everything because reality is too complex to be fully comprehended. Therefore, we selectively perceive people's appearances, for example, to make sense of everyday life and to construct a sense of social reality.

Thus, according to Edward Hall (1977) cultural context provides the framework for social perceptions, along with the social situation and a person's own perspective. Cultures vary in the extent to which they provide context for the interpretation of appearance messages. In a high-context culture, there is less context needed in everyday perceptions because the culture already provides a rich coding system that is readily understood. In a low-context culture, on the other hand, individuals need to work harder at creating and maintaining contexts for interpretation of messages. Although it is inappropriate to categorize cultures, in a straightforward manner, as high versus low context, it is useful to use these concepts to compare cultures, which fall somewhere on a continuum between high and low context. North American culture, for example, is low context, in part, because of the complex melting pot of other cultures. In the postmodern era, cultures probably move closer toward the low-context end of the continuum, because the pace of change is so rapid and the eclectic blend of signs is so complex to interpret. Thus individuals need to construct their own contexts for interpretation.

From the standpoint of social cognition, it also becomes important to assess the factors facilitating versus negating cross-cultural understanding. Ethnocentrism may directly influence social cognition. Especially in the visual realm of communication, an outside observer may apply the wrong cultural categories or principles to an interpretation.

Attribution in a high-context culture may tend to overemphasize individual deviations from cultural norms. In contrast, in a low-context culture, subtle contextual cues may be missed because perceivers expect individuals to be "free agents" (Ehrenhaus, 1982). (Social Focus 16-2 and Figure 16-8 provide descriptions and examples of appearance communication in a high-context culture.)

## Diversity in Cultural Patterns

Through *material culture*, the categories and principles of a culture can be identified in the form of concrete and tangible objects. Clothing, in this respect, "makes culture material in diverse and illuminating ways" (McCracken, 1988, p. 61). In so doing, "that which is implicitly or covertly required by one's cultural system" is "that which is preferred or wanted" (Hamilton and Hamilton, 1989).

We can examine variations in clothing across cultures on the basis of the following patterns: technical, aesthetic, moral, and ritualistic (Roach and Eicher, 1965). **Technical patterns** are directly related to a society's material culture,

# High-Context Culture: The Case of Holdeman Mennonites

In a high-context culture, elaborate systems of appearance symbolism are developed in which subtle visible differences may be quite meaningful and revealing. "Social scripts" are closely followed and understood, along with appearance norms. As part of her graduate studies in clothing and sociology, Linda Boynton (1989) conducted ethnographic research for a number of years among Holdeman Mennonites living in the central valley of northern California and identified some characteristics of a high-context culture in this group.

Currently, there are approximately 10,000 Holdeman Mennonites, most of whom live in North America (Scott, 1986, p. 35). This religious group was started by a Mennonite in Ohio. Mennonites, like Amish religious groups, have common roots in the European Protestant Reformation; these groups were persecuted and migrated to the United States by way of Pennsylvania in the eighteenth century.

The ethnoreligious (cultural) context of Holdeman Mennonites includes a commitment to continual separation from the outside (non-Mennonite) world. Mennonites, like the Amish (discussed in Social Focus 12-1), are born into a tradition of "plain clothes," based on the belief that they are "in this world but not of it" (Boynton, 1986b). This belief, as transformed into appearance-managing practices, is defined differently by various Amish and Mennonite groups. Although the Amish adopt a distinctive costume to symbolize that they are not worldly, Holdeman Mennonites keep their clothes plain, but closer to the styles of the times. Still, clothing and appearance management serve to visually separate Mennonites from nonplain people who wear fashionable clothing. In addition to symbolizing separation from worldly individuals, plain clothes connote modesty, humility, religious commitment through compliance to rules, and the belief in allowing the "inner virtue of the heart to shine through" (Scott, 1986, p. 16).

Gender separation is one of the most important contextual meanings of Holdeman Mennonite attire, based on the belief that God's order of creation is as follows: God-Christ-man-woman (Scott, 1986, p. 100). There are clear guidelines for appropriate appearance management as determined by sex and life stage. As one woman in Boynton's (1989) research noted, "When I put on Men-nonite clothing, I put on all of the church's rules." Indeed, even details in clothing and appearance that would be almost imperceptible to an outside observer are extremely meaningful indicators of religiosity among Holdeman Mennonites, and this type of symbolism is most evident among women.

Women never wear pants or shorts because of strict gender distinction, and makeup and jewelry are not worn because of their worldly connotations (Scott, 1986). The subservience of women is symbolized by the devotional head covering, which conceals uncut hair that is pinned up on the back of the head. After a woman is baptised during adolescence, she wears the head covering for as long as she stays a member of the church. The head covering consists of a three-cornered black scarf folded into a round shape around a bun hairstyle.

In public, Holdeman Mennonite women wear simple, home-sewn, shirtwaist dresses with fitted bodices buttoned down to the natural waistline (refer to Figure 14-5). The skirt is hemmed below the knee. Either short or long sleeves may be worn on an everyday basis, although long sleeves are worn for church. Dresses are made in subdued colors, either in solid or small, floral-patterned fabrics. Orthodox or extremely devout women will tend to wear even more subdued colors than other women and may be more likely to wear solid colors rather than prints. Fit is another subtle indicator of a woman's status. Unmarried women tend to wear their dresses more closely fitted to the body than do married women. The styles worn by married and unmarried women, however, are basically identical.

A woman who had been a minister's daughter and had left the church 18 years prior when she was a young adult explained the intricate religious symbolism adopted by women as follows:

> If your clothes are straight down the line as to the rules of the group then everyone can see that you are submitting your will to the church. The Mennonite dress is like a uniform—it indicates that you're keeping everything under control. This is why everyone watches what everyone else is wearing and how they are wearing it, because clothing shows acceptance of all the rules of the church (Boynton, 1989, p. 18).

**FIGURE 16-8**
*In a high-context culture such as the Karen hill tribe in northwest Thailand, clothing has traditionally conveyed a wealth of information about a woman's marital status. This woman's blouse and skirt are designed to indicate that she is an adult female, which in Karen culture is equated with "adult married female" (Hamilton and Hamilton, 1989). Photo by J. W. Hamilton.*

including the types of natural and synthetic materials available for the production of textiles and apparel, as well as the means for producing textiles and apparel (see Figure 16-9). **Aesthetic patterns** refer to the artistic codes or symbolic means of expression that help to compose the nonlinguistic structure of feeling in a society. **Moral patterns** of culture reflect the socially learned ethics and values that impinge on such issues as sexuality in appearance, traditions, and

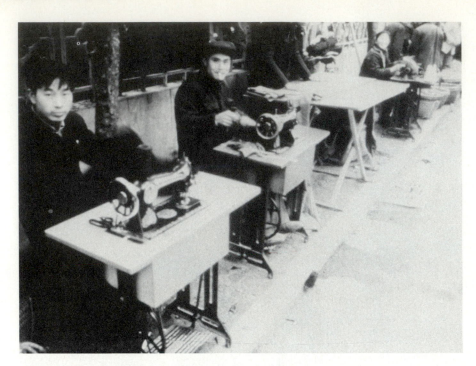

**FIGURE 16-9**
*Technical patterns of apparel production in mainland China. Photo by Stephen Cunha.*

habits (see Figure 16-10). **Ritualistic patterns** include culturally patterned activities that are taken seriously by participants, including ceremonies marking changes in individual status (for example, graduation ceremony or wedding) or community festivals or parades. A **rite of passage** is a ceremony marking a change in an individual's life status (see Figure 16-11), whereas a **rite of intensification** is a community-based ritual (see Figure 16-12).

Variations among cultures may also be examined in the context of technology, social structure, and ideology (infrastructure, structure, and superstructure). The "culture of clothing" may be evaluated in relation to these three "layers" (Hamilton, 1987). (See Figure 16-13.) *Technology* refers to material culture, or the physical things used to enable people to adapt to their physical and social environments. This includes fiber, yarn, or fabric, and the techniques by which they are constructed. Technology parallels Roach and Eicher's (1965) concept of technical patterns. *Social structure* refers to socially established arrangements, norms, or behaviors on how humans organize themselves into roles and groups. Gender and other appearance-related distinctions pertain to the social structure of a culture. *Ideology* refers to the beliefs and values a culture holds. "It is a set of cognitive rules, explicit or implicit, which define good and bad, right and wrong, appropriate or inappropriate" (Hamilton, 1987, p. 3). Roach and Eicher's (1965) concept of moral patterns would fall into the realm of ideology, because these patterns deal with issues of socially accepted clothing—what is appropriate, modest, indecent, shocking, or illegal.

**FIGURE 16-10**
*Moral patterns, including ideas about modesty, vary across cultural contexts. In some parts of Europe it is fairly common to see both boys and girls going shirtless in the summertime. Photo by Mark Kaiser.*

Let's turn our attention to aesthetic codes and patterns and examine how they undergo modification in the global postmodern context, in the midst of intercultural contact. To understand this process, we can focus on the impact of tourism on handcrafted textiles, as well as the interpretations of these artifacts by their creators and consumers.

Aesthetic patterns or codes may be modified for purposes of exchange value (salability). The aesthetic tastes of Cuna Indians living on the islands off the

**FIGURE 16-11**
*Rite of passage to married life is depicted in this traditional Korean wedding photograph including the extended families of the bride and groom. Courtesy of Soyeon Shim.*

**FIGURE 16-12**
*Rite of intensification in the form of a community parade complete with folk costumes and a tribute to Joan of Arc, a cultural and historical figure honored annually in a parade in Orléans, France. Photos by Clyde W. Benke.*

| IDEOLOGY |
| SOCIAL STRUCTURE |
| TECHNOLOGY |

| ECONOMIC ORGANIZATION |
| POLITICAL ORGANIZATION |
| FAMILY/KINSHIP ORGANIZATION |
| SOCIALIZATION |
| IDEOLOGICAL ORGANIZATION |
| ARTS AND AESTHETICS |
| COMMUNICATIONS |

**FIGURE 16-13**
*In Jean Hamilton's (1987) model of the "culture of clothing," she identifies ideology, social structure, and technology as three components of culture that cut across various forms of social organization, as shown here.*

Atlantic coast of Panama were studied to examine variations between Cuna women's preferences and their perceptions of Westerners' preferences (Hirschfeld, 1977). In this way, the effect of preferences and perceptions on value systems in the production of traditional *molas* was explored. The mola is a rectangular panel of reverse appliqué worn on the front and back of Cuna blouses. Twenty Cuna women of varying ages were surveyed on their perceptions of 34 photographs of molas. They were asked to select the three styles that they (*a*) preferred for personal use and (*b*) believed to be most salable to Westerners. The most important considerations in selecting a mola for personal use appeared to be greater complexity and reduced symmetry in design. These design features appeared to be more important than color considerations, although there were some color preferences as well—black as a primary color, with bright reds and yellows as secondary colors. In contrast, the molas considered to be most salable were characterized by color brightness—deep red as a primary color, with bright yellows for secondary colors. The Cuna women considered Westerners to choose molas by subject matter and by color, as opposed to design complexity. In mola production, then, a kind of dialectic, or system of conflict, appears to operate.

The mola is produced not only for personal use and ethnic expression by Cuna women, but also for sale to Westerners. A kind of compromise appears to exist that incorporates both of these value systems. This study indicated that foreign trade or intercultural contact due to tourism has an impact on clothing designs deemed as traditional. Other research has documented the same phenomenon, as Figure 16-14 reveals.

Some research suggests, however, that aesthetic codes need not necessarily be altered in order to enhance exchange value. In a study of midwestern consumers' preferences for Hmong textiles (reverse appliqué), it was found that the Hmong need not feel they must adopt only the colors popular in the United States (Slaybaugh, Littrell, and Farrell-Beck, in press). Many consumers appreciate the colors and designs unique to the Hmong textile tradition. Potential use value, on the other hand, may be a limiting factor for some consumers. For example, some of the traditional Hmong colors do not match the colors in American consumers' homes, and the nature of the product (handcrafted pillow versus dress, for example) needs to be considered along with aesthetic codes.

What do handcrafted textiles *mean* to the tourists themselves? These meanings were assessed in a study in which 98 frequent travelers were asked: "From all

*FIGURE 16-14*
*Amish quilts produced for tourists tend to differ from those crafted for use in the Amish home. In this quilt produced for sale, the corner blocks and inner border are traditional, but the lone star figure in the middle is not. The* concept *of having a focal point in the middle of a quilt is a traditional Amish quilting practice, however, so in fact this quilt represents a blending of both traditional and nontraditional elements (Boynton, 1986a). Photo by Linda Boynton.*

of your travels, what handcrafted textiles or clothing item(s) have you purchased that is most special or meaningful to you?" and "Why is the textile craft special to you; what meaning does the textile hold?" The responses were classified into five categories: (1) use value, (2) reminder of shopping experience, (3) associations with place and culture, (4) recollections of place and culture, and (5) intrinsic qualities (for example, beauty, workmanship, age, or investment value) (Littrell and Beavers, 1987).

## Acculturation and Assimilation

The concept of **acculturation** refers to the process by which members of a distinct culture internalize the values and behavioral patterns of a majority society but are not admitted to intimate groupings. In contrast, the concept of **assimilation** goes one step further. It encompasses the process by which individuals in a culture or subculture are accepted into major social institutions and more personal groupings (Hess, Markson, and Stein, 1985).

More often than not, cultural change as a function of intercultural contact begins with a change in technology. Technological change, in turn, brings about some alterations in the social-structural relations required to make the best use of that technology. Then, new ideologies emerge to give sanction to the new technology and social structure. Thus, technology may be regarded as the foundation or bottom layer of a culture's social structure and ideology, as shown in Figure 16-13. It constitutes the principal interface between culture and nature (Hamilton, 1987). Similarly, social structure is likely to lay the foundation for ideology.

Moral patterns in dress from another culture may be among the last to be adopted by persons outside that culture, because they often are linked to valued aspects of the culture's ideology, for example, as connected to religion. Standards of modesty, tied to the Islamic religion, are a major factor preventing many Islamic women from going out in public in Western-style dress, especially since religious fundamentalism has surfaced in the Islamic world. However, the practice of women wearing veils and concealing their bodies cannot be explained by religion alone. Social structure (including gender relations) is also an important factor, as noted in Social Focus 16-1.

In instances when one society conquers another, the moral patterns of the dominant culture may be thrust on the conquered individuals. Being forced to wear clothes that conflict with one's moral patterns is symbolic of the demoralizing aspects of such a situation. Christians who settled in South and East Africa found it difficult to deal with the sight of the natives' half-naked bodies. They placed a taboo on such exposure for their house servants and gardeners (von Ehrenfels, 1979).

Aesthetic and ritualistic patterns may also be replaced by, or blended with, new ones with some reluctance. Traditional or folk costumes are likely to be retained, however, at least for special occasions.

Several variables are likely to be considered as individuals from one culture debate the adoption of clothing styles from another culture (Rogers and Shoemaker, 1971). Let's examine the following variables: observability, relative advantage, comparability, complexity, and ability to put to trial.

*Cross-Cultural Adoption Criteria*

*1. Observability.* Because clothes are so visible and observable, they are likely to have an early influence on individuals in the process of acculturation. When Japanese immigrants settled in British Columbia at the turn of the century, they adopted Western dress fairly readily. Outward display of adaptation to the local lifestyle was seen as a means of reducing ethnic discrimination (Batts, 1975).

*2. Relative advantage.* Some cultures have abandoned traditional or folk dress for Western dress, with the notion that the latter is more indicative of "progressiveness." Ironically, "ethnic" or folk dress has been popular in postindustrial societies, influencing fashion at various times. Such attire may be seen as "genuine." In a global, postmodern context such an interchange of aesthetic codes and an eclectic blending of elements would be expected and, as discussed earlier, the advantages and disadvantages of this type of cultural blending and replacement are debatable.

*3. Comparability.* How congruent is the new style with existing belief and value systems and individual and cultural needs?

*4. Complexity.* Is the style or look difficult to understand or use? Can indigenous styles be modified to become more appealing to those outside the culture? Design concepts used in Korean silk textiles have changed with increased intercultural contact. Symbolic, individual motifs have been replaced by more pattern-oriented or geometric designs. Traditional motifs have become much less prevalent in the process (Kwon, 1979). Thus the complexity of some cultural aesthetic codes may be reduced in the face of intercultural contact, as discussed in the context of tourism and textile and apparel traditional crafts.

*5. Ability to put to trial.* Can the style be tried on a small-scale basis? Many Westerners have adopted "ethnic" costumes, frequently representing a combination of cross-cultural elements, on an experimental basis. Folkloric or ethnic apparel may seem more authentic and classic than styles that rapidly change in postindustrial societies.

To explain how an artifact or idea external to a culture is assimilated into that culture, Eicher and Erekosima (1980) developed the concept of **cultural authentication**. Cultural authentication is the process by which this assimilation occurs by accommodative change of the external object or idea into a *valued* indigenous object or idea. In other words, through cultural authentication, a culture can turn an unfamiliar object or idea into a familiar, valued one. In research among the Kalabari people in Nigeria, Erekosima and Eicher (1981) were able to demonstrate four levels of cultural authentication in relation to the Kalabaris' use of imported cloth: (1) *selection*—borrowing or using the cloth as it existed; (2) *characterization*—"naming" the cloth; (3) *incorporation*—the exclusive owning of a specific cloth by a particular group (for example, a family);

and (4) *transformation*—creating a modified cloth that has an additional design cut on it (using a process of lifting threads with a needle and snipping them off with a razor). At the transformed level of cultural authentication, creative adaptation is displayed, and the resulting "localized" product is highly valued and prized.

The concept of cultural authentication has also been illustrated in the context of the material culture of native American tribes of the Great Lakes region from the mid-eighteenth to the mid-nineteenth centuries (Pannabecker, 1988). Silk ribbon from Europe was incorporated into ribbon-garnished dress that we now think of as Indian.

## Cultural and Individual Identity

Cultural identity is one of many forms of identity that individuals may express through clothing. Cultural or subcultural identity may be developed, displayed, or ignored by individuals. Acculturation and assimilation continue to take place *within* many societies, as individuals of diverse cultural heritages introduce aesthetic codes and ideologies. We might argue that acculturation and assimilation continue on a worldwide basis as well, as processes of imitation and differentiation become international means of sorting out meaning in the postmodern global context. In the midst of the resulting bombardment of multicultural images and aesthetic codes, how can individuals and cultures maintain a sense of locality or specificity, and do they choose to do so?

**Symbolic ethnicity** is characterized by (1) a nostalgic allegiance to a specific culture (as one's root culture) and (2) a love for, and pride in, a tradition that can be experienced without being incorporated into everyday behavior (Gans, 1979). Third or fourth generations of different ethnic groups in the United States, for example, may embrace root-cultural symbols as visible signs of their heritage. Such signs may serve to provide a sense of *symbolic self-completion* (Wicklund and Gollwitzer, 1983) to complete an aspect of one's identity in which there may be some need for expression (see Figure 16-15).

## Contextual Perspective on Cultural Identity

More than ever, perhaps, it is necessary for individuals to *work* at constructing their identities. Assessment of ethnic identity needs to take into account the global context and worldwide fashion influence of root cultures today (Forney and Rabolt, 1985–1986). Given the eclectic range of possibilities for personal expression, individuals may intermingle and juxtapose diverse appearance signs. The potential for symbolic ambiguity is tremendous. Here is where a contextual perspective can help us to keep the "big picture" in mind. Appearance contexts are constructed and visually negotiated on an individual and interpersonal level,

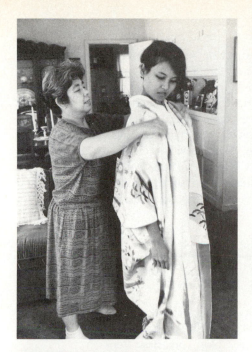

**FIGURE 16-15**
*Symbolic ethnicity is represented by this student's interest in trying on a traditional Japanese kimono. While she is from Tokyo, she has actually only worn a kimono at one other time in her life (as a young girl at a special ceremony). Thus she needs a great deal of assistance from her friend who learned the art of kimono dressing in Japan before coming to the United States about 20 years ago. Photos by Carla M. Freeman and Susan B. Kaiser.*

and they derive their meaning as a function of *social constructions* in specific contexts, all within a cultural as well as a larger global context.

Individuals strive to map their positions in space and time, cognitively and symbolically. Ambivalence surrounding the continuity and change in cultural categories gives rise to a host of symbolic tensions through fashion and aesthetic expression, the meanings of which are initially uncertain but continually challenging in the realm of meaning construction. Social-psychological processes of identification and differentiation intersect within the self, within the group and organizational context, within a subcultural and/or larger societal context, and cross-culturally, as the interplay between locality and globalism continues.

## Suggested Readings

Erekosima, T. V., and Eicher, J. B. 1981. Kalabari cut thread and pulled-thread cloth. *African Arts 14*(2):48–51, 87.
This article describes a particular imported cloth with openwork designs worn by the Kalabari people, in relation to the concept of cultural authentication.

Geertz, C. 1973. *The interpretation of cultures*. New York: Basic Books.
Geertz elaborates on how culture should be conceptualized and studied by means of thick description to achieve an interpretive understanding.

Hamilton, J. A. 1987. Dress as a cultural sub-system: A unifying metatheory for clothing and textiles. *Clothing and Textiles Research Journal 6*(1):1–7.
In this article, Hamilton presents a culturally based model for the study of dress as a dynamic, interacting system that is unbounded by time and space.

Hamilton, J. A., and Hamilton, J. W. 1989. Dress as a reflection and sustainer of social reality: A cross-cultural perspective. *Clothing and Textiles Research Journal 7*(2):16–22.
This paper describes an interpretation of female dress of the Karen, a hill tribe in northwest Thailand, based on ethnographic research.

Roach, M. E., and Eicher, J. B., eds. 1965. *Dress, adornment, and the social order*. New York: John Wiley & Sons.
This book of readings incorporates a number of classic articles on dress. Roach and Eicher describe the patterns by which the similarities and differences across cultures can be examined: technical, aesthetic, moral, and ritualistic.

# References

Abbey, A., Gozzarelli, C., McLaughlin, K., and Harnish, R. 1987. The effects of clothing and dyad sex composition on perceptions of sexual intent: Do women and men evaluate these cues differently? *Journal of Applied Social Psychology* 17:108–126.

Aboulafia, M. 1986. *The mediating self: Mead, Sartre, and self-determination*. New Haven: Yale University Press.

Abramov, I. 1985. An analysis of personal color analysis. In M. R. Solomon, ed. *The psychology of fashion*, pp. 211–223. Lexington: Heath/Lexington Books.

Adams, F. M., and Osgood, C. E. 1973. A cross-cultural study of the affective meanings of color. *Journal of Cross-Cultural Psychology* 4(2):135–156.

Adams, G. R. 1977a. Physical attractiveness research: Toward a developmental social psychology of beauty. *Human Development* 20:217–239.

Adams, G. R. 1977b. Physical attractiveness, personality, and social reactions to peer pressure. *Journal of Psychology* 96:287–296.

Adams, G. R. 1978. Racial membership and physical attractiveness effects on preschool teachers' expectations. *Child Study Journal* 8:29–41.

Adams, G. R., and Cohen, A. S. 1974. Children's physical and interpersonal characteristics that affect student-teacher interactions. *Journal of Experimental Education* 43:1–5.

Adams, G. R., and Crane, P. 1980. An assumption of parents' and teachers' expectations of preschool children's social preference for attractive or unattractive children or adults. *Child Development* 51:224–231.

Adams, G. R., and LaVoie, J. C. 1975. Parental expectations of educational and personal-social performance and childrearing patterns as a function of attractiveness, sex, and conduct of the child. *Child Study Journal* 55:125–142.

Adams, M. J. 1988. Large (size) and growing. *Stores*, July, 11–26.

Addison, C. J. 1981. *The effect of evaluation and apprehension on attitude change in the presence of a police uniform*. Ph.D. dissertation, University of Denver.

Agnew, R. 1984. The effect of appearance on personality and behavior: Are the beautiful really good? *Youth and Society* 15(3):285–303.

Aiken, L. R. 1963. The relationship of dress to selected measures of personality in undergraduate women. *Journal of Social Psychology* 59:119–128.

Alicke, M. D., Smith, R. H., and Klotz, M. L. 1986. Judgments of physical attractiveness: The role of faces and bodies. *Personality and Social Psychology Bulletin* 12:381–389.

Alireza, M. 1987. Women of Saudi Arabia. *National Geographic*, Oct., pp. 423–453.

Allen, C. D., and Eicher, J. B. 1973. Adolescent girls' acceptance and rejection based on appearance. *Adolescence* 8(29):125–138.

Allen, D. E., Guy, R. F., and Edgley, C. K. 1980. *Social psychology as social process*. Belmont: Wadsworth.

Allor, M. 1987. Projective readings: Cultural studies from here. *Canadian Journal of Political and Social Theory 111*(1–2):124–128.

Allport, G. W. 1968. *The person in psychology: Selected essays*. Boston: Beacon Press.

Allport, G., Vernon, P., and Lindzey, G. 1960. *Study of values*. Boston: Houghton-Mifflin.

Altheide, D. L., and Snow, R. P. 1979. *Media logic*. Beverly Hills: Sage.

Anorexia: The starving disease epidemic. 1982. *U.S. News and World Report*, Aug. 30, 47–48.

Aronson, E. 1988. *The social animal* 5th ed. San Francisco: W. H. Freeman.

Asch, S. E. 1946. Forming impressions of personality. *Journal of Abnormal Social Psychology 41*:258–290.

Aznam, S. 1985. Lifting the veils. *Far Eastern Economic Review 127*(12):22–23.

Baer, D. J., and Mosele, V. F. 1970. Political and religious beliefs of Catholics and attitudes toward lay dress of Sisters. *Journal of Psychology 74*:77–83.

Baer, M. 1979. Visual recall of dress design determined by perceptual style. *Home Economics Research Journal 7*:292–303.

Balkwell, C. 1986. On peacocks and peahens: A cross-cultural investigation of the effects of economic development on sex differences in dress. *Clothing and Textiles Research Journal 4*(2):30–36.

Bandura, A. 1986. *Social foundations of thought and action: A social cognitive theory*. Englewood Cliffs: Prentice-Hall.

Banner, L. W. 1983. *American beauty*. Chicago: The University of Chicago Press.

Bardack, N. R., and McAndrew, F. T. 1985. The influence of physical attractiveness and manner of dress on success in a simulated personnel decision. *Journal of Social Psychology 125*:777–778.

Barenboim, C. 1981. The development of person perception in childhood and adolescence: From behavioral comparisons to psychological constructs to psychological comparisons. *Child Development 52*:129–144.

Barnes, M. L., and Rosenthal, R. 1985. Interpersonal effects of experimenter attractiveness, attire, and gender. *Journal of Personality and Social Psychology 48*:435–446.

Barr, E. D. 1934. *A psychological analysis of fashion motivation*. New York: Archives of Psychology.

Barrington, J. M., and Marshall, G. N. 1975. School administration and educational rituals: A case study of participative decision making. *Journal of Educational Administration 8*(1):93–98.

Barthes, R. 1972. *Mythologies*. London: Jonathan Cape Ltd.

Barthes, R. 1983. *The fashion system*. Trans. by M. Ward and R. Howard. New York: Hill and Wang.

Bartley, L., and Warden, J. 1962. Clothing preferences of women sixty-five and older. *Journal of Home Economics 54*:716–717.

Bassett, R. E. 1979. Effects of source attire on judgments of credibility. *Central States Speech Journal 30*(3):282–285.

Batts, 1975. Clothing style of Japanese immigrants in British Columbia, Canada. *Costume 9*:51–52.

Baudrillard, J. 1968. *Le systeme des objets*. Paris: Gallimard.

Baudrillard, J. 1975. *The mirror of production*. Trans. by M. Poster. St. Louis: Telos Press.

Baudrillard, J. 1976. *L'echange symbolique et la mort*. Paris: Gallimard.

Baudrillard, J. 1981. *For a critique of the political economy of the sign*. Trans. with intro. by C. Levin. St. Louis: Telos Press.

Baudrillard, J. 1983. *Simulations*. Trans. by P. Foss, P. Patton, and P. Beitchman. New York: Semiotext(e), Inc.

Baumeister, R. F. 1986. *Public self and private self*. New York: Springer-Verlag.

Baumgarten, S. A. 1975. The innovative communicator in the diffusion process. *Journal of Marketing Research* 12(1):12–18.

Baumgartner, C. W. 1963. Factors associated with clothing consumption among college freshmen. *Journal of Home Economics* 55:218.

Baxter, R. L., De Riemer, C., Landini, A., Leslie, L., and Singletary, M. W. 1985. A content analysis of music videos. *Journal of Broadcasting and Electronic Media* 29:333–340.

Beale, S., Lisper, H.-O., and Palm, B. 1980. A psychological study of patients seeking augmentation mammaplasty. *British Journal of Psychiatry* 136:133–138.

Beck, S. B., Ward-Hull, C. I., and McLear, P. M. 1976. Variables related to women's somatic preferences of the male and female body. *Journal of Personality and Social Psychology* 34:1200–1210.

Becker, E. 1967. *Beyond alienation: A philosophy of education for the crisis of democracy*. New York: G. Braziller.

Becker, E. 1975. The self as a focus of linguistic causality. In D. Brissett and C. Edgley, eds. *Life as theater: A dramaturgical sourcebook*. Chicago: Aldine.

Beehr, T. A., and Gilmore, D. C. 1982. Applicant attractiveness as a perceived job-relevant variable in selection of management trainees. *Academy of Management Journal* 25:607–617.

Behling, D. 1985. Fashion change and demographics: A model. *Clothing and Textiles Research Journal* 4(1):18–24.

Behling, D., and Wilch, J. 1988. Perceptions of branded clothing by male consumers. *Clothing and Textiles Research Journal* 6(2):43–47.

Belk, R. W. 1978. Assessing the effects of visible consumption on impression formation. In H. K. Hunt, ed. *Advances in consumer research* vol. 5. Ann Arbor: Association for Consumer Research.

Belk, R. W. 1987. Identity and the relevance of market, personal, and community objects. In J. Umiker-Sebeok, ed. *Marketing and semiotics: New directions in the study of signs for sale*, pp. 151–164. Berlin: Mouton de Gruyter.

Belk, R., Mayer, R., and Driscoll, A. 1984. Children's recognition of consumption symbolism in children's products. *Journal of Consumer Research* 10:386–397.

Belk, R. W., and Pollay, R. W. 1985. Images of ourselves: The good life in twentieth century advertising. *Journal of Consumer Research* 11:887–897.

Bell, D. 1956. *Work and its discontents*. Ann Arbor: University Microfilms.

Bell, Q. 1978. *On human finery* 2d ed. New York: Schocken Books.

Bem, D. 1967. Self-perception: An alternative interpretation of cognitive dissonance phenomena. *Psychological Review* 74(3):183–200.

Bem, D. 1972. Self-perception theory. In L. Berkowitz, ed. *Advances in experimental social psychology* vol. 6. New York: Academic Press.

Benassi, M. A. 1985. Effects of romantic love on perception of strangers' physical attractiveness. *Psychological Reports* 56:355–358.

Berelson, B., and Steiner, G. A. 1964. *Human behavior: An inventory of scientific findings*. New York: Harcourt, Brace & World.

Berger, J. 1972. *Ways of seeing*. London: British Broadcasting Corporation.

Berger, P. L. 1963. *Invitation to sociology: A humanistic perspective*. Garden City: Doubleday.

Berger, P. L. 1977. *Facing up to modernity*. New York: Basic Books.

Berger, P. L., and Luckmann, T. 1966. *The social construction of reality*. Garden City: Doubleday.

Berkowitz, L., and Frodi, A. 1979. Reactions to a child's mistakes as affected by her/his looks and speech. *Social Psychology Quarterly* 42(4):420–425.

Berlyne, D. E., ed. 1974. *Studies in the new experimental aesthetics*. New York: John Wiley & Sons.

Bernstein, I. H., Huang, M.-H., Teng, G., and Lin, T.-D. 1986. Effects of attitudes toward pornography upon male judgements of female attractiveness. *Perception and Psychophysics 39*(4):287–293.

Bernstein, W. M., and Davis, M. H. 1982. Perspective-taking, self-consciousness, and accuracy in person perception. *Basic and Applied Social Psychology 3*(1):1–19.

Berscheid, E., Dion, K., Walster, E., and Walster, G. W. 1971. Physical attractiveness and dating choice: A test of the matching hypothesis. *Journal of Experimental Social Psychology 7*:173–180.

Berscheid, E., and Walster, E. 1974. Physical attractiveness. In L. Berkowitz, ed. *Advances in Experimental Social Psychology* vol. 7, pp. 157–213. New York: Academic Press.

Bickman, L. 1972. The effect of social status on the honesty of others. In L. Bickman and T. Hencky, eds. *Beyond the laboratory: Field research in social psychology* pp. 102–104. New York: McGraw-Hill.

Bickman, L. 1974. The social power of a uniform. *Journal of Applied Social Psychology 4*:47–61.

Bickman, L., and Hencky, T., eds. 1972. *Beyond the laboratory: Field research in social psychology*. New York: McGraw-Hill.

Blumberg, P. 1974. The decline and fall of the status symbol: Some thoughts on status in a post-industrial society. *Social Problems 21*(4):480–497.

Blumer, H. 1969a. *Symbolic interactionism: Perspective and method*. Englewood Cliffs: Prentice-Hall.

Blumer, H. 1969b. Fashion: From class differentiation to collective selection. *Sociology Quarterly 10*:275–291.

Blumhagen, D. W. 1979. The doctor's white coat: The image of the physician in modern America. *Annals of Internal Medicine 91*:111–116.

Bogatyrev, P. 1976. Costume as sign. In L. Matejka and I. R. Titunik, eds. *Semiotics of art: Prague School contributors*, pp. 13–19. Cambridge: MIT Press.

Bordieri, J. E., Solodky, M. L., and Mikos, K. A. 1985. Physical attractiveness and nurses' perceptions of pediatric patients. *Nursing Research 34*:24–26.

Bourdieu, P. 1984. *Distinction: A social critique of the judgement of taste*. Cambridge: Harvard University Press.

Bouska, M. L., and Beatty, P. A. 1978. Clothing as a symbol of status: Its effect on control of interaction territory. *Bulletin of Psychonomic Sociology 11*(4):235–238.

Boynton, L. L. 1986a. The effect of tourism on Amish quilting design. *Annals of Tourism Research 13*:451–465.

Boynton, L. L. 1986b. *The plain people: An ethnography of the Holdeman Mennonites*. Salem: Sheffield.

Boynton, L. L. 1989. Religious orthodoxy, social control and clothing: Dress and adornment as symbolic indicators of social control among Mennonite women. Paper presented at the meeting of the American Sociological Association, San Francisco, August.

Brandt, A. 1980. Self-confrontations. *Psychology Today 14*(6):78–101.

Brett, J. E., and Kernaleguen, A. 1975. Perceptual and personality variables related to opinion leadership in fashion. *Perceptual and Motor Skills 40*:775–779.

Brislin, R. W., and Lewis, S. A. 1968. Dating and physical attractiveness: Replication. *Psychological Reports 22*:976.

Brissett, D., and Edgley, C. 1975. *Life as theater: A dramaturgical sourcebook*. Chicago: Aldine.

Brocken, C. 1969. Body image and habit change in religious women. Ph.D. dissertation, Loyola University.

Brooks, J. 1981. *Showing off in America: From conspicuous consumption to parody display*. Boston: Little, Brown.

Brown, T. A., Cash, T. F., and Noles, S. W. 1986. Perceptions of physical attractiveness among college students: Selected determinants and methodological matters. *Journal of Social Psychology 126*(3):305–316.

Brownmiller, S. 1984. *Femininity*. New York: Linden Press.

Bruner, G. C. 1988. Singles and sex-roles: Are there differences in the clothing prepurchase process? *Clothing and Textiles Research Journal* 7(1):3–9.

Bryant, N. J. 1975. Petitioning: Dress congruence versus belief congruence. *Journal of Applied Social Psychology* 5:144–149.

Buckley, H. M. 1983. Attraction toward a stranger as a linear function of similarity in dress. *Home Economics Research Journal* 12:25–33.

Buckley, H. M. 1985. Toward an operational definition of dress. *Clothing and Textiles Research Journal* 3(2):1–10.

Buckley, H. M., and Roach, M. E. 1974. Clothing as a nonverbal communicator of social and political attitudes. *Home Economics Research Journal* 3:94–101.

Burgard, D. 1986. Movers and shakers. *Radiance*, Winter, p. 8.

Burke, K. 1975. The five key terms of dramatism. In D. Brissett and C. Edgley, eds. *Life as theater: A dramaturgical sourcebook*, pp. 370–375. Chicago: Aldine.

Burke, P. J., and Reitzes, D. C. 1981. The link between identity and role performance. *Social Psychology Quarterly* 44:83–92.

Byrne, D. E. 1971. *The attraction paradigm*. New York: Academic Press.

Byrne, D., Ervin, C. R., and Lamberth, J. 1970. Continuity between the experimental study of attraction and "real life" computer dating. *Journal of Personality and Social Psychology* 16:157–165.

Campbell, K. E., Kleim, D. M., and Olson, K. R. 1986. Gender, physical attractiveness, and assertiveness. *Journal of Social Psychology* 126:697–698.

Cancian, F. M., and Cancian, F. 1974. Cultural relativism. Module for General Learning Press.

Carter, E. 1984. Alice in the consumer wonderland. In A. McRobbie and M. Nova, eds. *Gender and generation*, pp. 185–214. London: Macmillan Education Ltd.

Cartwright, D., and Zander, A., eds. 1968. *Group dynamics: Research and theory*. New York: Harper & Row.

Cash, T. F., and Derlega, V. L. 1978. The matching hypothesis: Physical attractiveness among same-sexed friends. *Personality and Social Psychology Bulletin* 4:240–243.

Cash, T. F., Begley, P. J., McCrown, D. A., and Weise, B. C. 1975. When counselors are heard but not seen: Initial impact of physical attractiveness. *Journal of Counseling Psychology* 22(4):273–279.

Cash, T. F., and Kilcullen, R. N. 1985. The aye of the beholder: Susceptibility to sexism and beautyism in the evaluation of managerial applicants. *Journal of Applied Social Psychology* 15:591–605.

Cash, T. F., Winstead, B. A., and Janda, L. H. 1986. The great American shape-up: We're healthier than ever, fitter than ever . . . but less satisfied with how we look. *Psychology Today* 20(4):30–37.

Cassata, M. B., Anderson, P. A., and Skill, T. D. 1980. The older adult in daytime serial drama. *Journal of Communication* 30(1):48–49.

Cassill, N., and Drake, M. F. 1987. Employment orientation's influence on lifestyle and evaluative criteria for apparel. *Home Economics Research Journal* 16(1):23–35.

Cavior, N., Miller, K., and Cohen, S. H. 1975. Physical attractiveness, attitude similarity, and length of acquaintance as contributors to interpersonal attraction among adolescents. *Social Behavior and Personality* 3(2):133–141.

Chapkis, W. 1986. *Beauty secrets: Women and the politics of appearance*. Boston: South End Press.

Chernin, K. 1981. *The obsession: Reflections on the tyranny of slenderness*. New York: Harper & Row.

Chowdhary, U. 1988a. Self-esteem, age identification, and media exposure of the elderly and their relationship to fashionability. *Clothing and Textiles Research Journal* 7(1):23–30.

Chowdhary, U. 1988b. Instructor's attire as a biasing factor in student's ratings of an instructor. *Clothing and Textiles Research Journal* 6(2):17–22.

Chowdhary, U., and Beale, N. V. 1988. Plus-size women's clothing interest, satisfactions and dissatisfactions with ready-to-wear apparel. *Perceptual and Motor Skills* 66:783–788.

Clifford, M. M., and Walster, E. 1973. Research note: The effect of physical attractiveness on teacher expectations. *Sociology of Education* 46:248–258.

Coleman, R. P. 1983. The continuing significance of social class to marketing. *Journal of Consumer Research* 10:265–280.

Collins, R. 1986. Reflections on the death of Goffman. *Sociological Theory* 4:196–213.

Comer, R. J., and Piliavin, J. A. 1972. The effects of physical deviance upon face-to-face interaction: The other side. *Journal of Personality and Social Psychology* 23:33–39.

Compton, N. H. 1962. Personal attributes of color and design preferences in clothing fabrics. *Journal of Psychology* 54:191–195.

Compton, N. H. 1964. Body-image boundaries in relation to clothing fabric and design preferences of a group of hospitalized psychotic women. *Journal of Home Economics* 56(1):40–44.

Conner, B. H., Peters, K., and Nagasawa, R. H. 1975. Person and costume: Effects on the formation of first impressions. *Home Economics Research Journal* 4(1):32–41.

Constantinople, A. 1979. Sex-role acquisition: In search of the elephant. *Sex Roles* 5:121–133.

Cooley, C. H. 1902. *Human nature and the social order*. New York: Charles Scribner's Sons.

Cooper, J., Darley, J. M., and Henderson, J. E. 1974. On the effectiveness of deviant and conventional-appearing communicators: A field experiment. *Journal of Personality and Social Psychology* 29:752–757.

Cordwell, J. M., and Schwarz, R. A., eds. 1979. *The fabrics of culture: The anthropology of clothing and adornment*. The Hague: Mouton.

Corliss, R. 1982. The new ideal of beauty. *Time*, August 30, pp. 72–73.

Coughlin, E. K. 1989. In face of growing success and conservatives' attacks, cultural-studies scholars ponder future directions. *The Chronicle of Higher Education*. January 18, pp. 4, 5, 12.

Coursey, R. D. 1973. Clothes doth make the man, in the eye of the beholder. *Perceptual and Motor Skills* 36:1259–1264.

Courtney, A. E., and Lockeretz, S. W. 1971. A woman's place: An analysis of the roles portrayed by women in magazine advertisements. *Journal of Marketing Research* 8:92–95.

Crassweller, P., Gordon, M. A., and Tedford, W. H., Jr. 1972. An experimental investigation of hitchhiking. *Journal of Psychology* 82:43–47.

Creekmore, A. M. 1963. Clothing behaviors and their relation to general values and to the striving for basic needs. Ph.D. dissertation, Pennsylvania State University.

Creekmore, A. M. 1974. Clothing related to body satisfaction and perceived peer self. *Research Report 239*, Michigan: Technical Bulletin, Michigan State University Agricultural Experiment Station.

Creekmore, A. M. 1980. Clothing and personal attractiveness of adolescents related to conformity, to clothing mode, peer acceptance, and leadership potential. *Home Economics Research Journal* 8(3):203–215.

Crisp, A. H., and Kalucy, R. S. 1974. Aspects of the perceptual disorder in anorexia nervosa. *British Journal of Medical Psychology* 47:349–361.

Cuber, J. F. 1963. *Sociology: A synopsis of principles*. New York: Appleton-Century-Crofts.

Dabbs, J. M., Jr., and Stokes, N. A. 1975. Beauty is power: The use of space on the sidewalk. *Sociometry* 38, 551–557.

Damhorst, M. L. 1985. Meanings of clothing cues in social context. *Clothing and Textiles Research Journal* 3(2):39–48.

Damhorst, M. L. 1989. A contextual model of clothing sign systems. Paper presented at the Colloquium on the Body and Clothing as Communication, Institute of Marketing Meaning, July, Indianapolis.

Damhorst, M. L., Eckman, M., and Stout, S. 1986. Cluster analysis of women's business suits. In *ACPTC Proceedings*, *National Meeting*, p. 65. Monument, CO: Association of College Professors of Textiles and Clothing.

Damhorst, M. L., Littrell, J. M., and Littrell, M. A. 1987. Adolescent body satisfaction. *Journal of Psychology 121*:553–562.

Damhorst, M. L., and Pinaire Reed, J. A. 1986. Clothing color value and facial expression: Effects on evaluations of female job applicants. *Social Behavior and Personality 14*(1): 89–98.

Damhorst, M. L. In press. In search of a common thread: Classification of information communicated through dress. *Clothing and Textiles Research Journal.*

Dannenmaier, W. D., and Thumin, F. J. 1964. Authority status as a factor in perceptual distortion of size. *Journal of Social Psychology 63*:361–365.

Dardis, R., Derrick, F., and Lehfeld, A. 1981. Clothing demand in the United States: A cross-sectional analysis. *Home Economics Research Journal 10*(2):212–222.

Darley, J. M., and Cooper, J. 1972. The "clean for Gene" phenomenon: The effect of students' appearance on political campaigning. *Journal of Applied Psychology 2*:24–33.

Davis, F. 1982. On the "symbolic" in symbolic interaction. *Symbolic Interaction 5*:111–126.

Davis, F. 1985. Clothing and fashion as communication. In M. R. Solomon, ed. *The psychology of fashion*, pp. 15–27. Lexington: Heath/Lexington Books.

Davis, F. 1988. Clothing, fashion and the dialectic of identity. In D. R. Maines and C. J. Couch, eds. *Communication and Social Structure*. Springfield: Charles C Thomas.

Davis, L. L. 1984a. Clothing and human behavior: A review. *Home Economics Research Journal 12*:325–339.

Davis, L. L. 1984b. Judgment ambiguity, self-consciousness, and conformity in judgments of fashionability. *Psychological Reports 54*:671–675.

Davis, L. L. 1985a. Effects of physical quality and brand labeling on perceptions of clothing quality. *Perceptual and Motor Skills 61*:671–677.

Davis, L. L. 1985b. Perceived somatotype, body-cathexis, and attitudes toward clothing among college females. *Perceptual and Motor Skills 61*:1199–1205.

Davis, L. L. 1985c. Sex, gender identity, and behavior concerning sex-related clothing. *Clothing and Textiles Research Journal 3*(2):20–24.

Davis, L. L., and Lennon, S. J. 1985. Self-monitoring, fashion opinion leadership, and attitudes toward clothing. In M. R. Solomon, ed. *The Psychology of Fashion*, pp. 177–182. Lexington: Heath/Lexington Books.

Davis, L. L., and Lennon, S. J. 1988. Social cognition and the study of clothing and human behavior. *Social Behavior and Personality 16*(2):175–186.

Davis, L. L., and Miller, F. G. 1983. Conformity and judgments of fashionability. *Home Economics Research Journal 11*(4):337–342.

Dean, L. M., Willis, F. N., and Hewitt, J. 1975. Initial interaction distance among individuals equal and unequal in rank. *Journal of Personality and Social Psychology 32*:294–299.

Dearborn, G. 1918. The psychology of clothing. *Psychological Review Monographs 26*: 1–72.

DeBeauvoir, S. 1953. *The second sex*. New York: Alfred A. Knopf.

Delaporte, Y. 1980. Le signe vestimentaire. *L'Homme 20*(3):109–142.

DeLong, M. R. 1987. *The way we look: A framework for visual analysis of dress*. Ames: Iowa State University Press.

DeLong, M. R., and Larntz, K. 1980. Measuring visual response to clothing. *Home Economics Research Journal 8*(4):281–293.

DeLong, M. R., and Minshall, B. C. 1988. Categorization of forms of dress. *Clothing and Textiles Research Journal 6*(4):13–19.

DeLong, M. R., Salusso-Deonier, C., and Larntz, K. 1983. Use of perceptions of female dress as an indicator of role definition. *Home Economics Research Journal 11*(4): 327–336.

Denzin, N. K. 1970. Symbolic interactionism and ethnomethodology. In J. D. Douglas, ed. *Understanding everyday life*, pp. 261–284. Chicago: Aldine.

Denzin, N. K. 1977. *Childhood socialization*. San Francisco: Jossey-Bass.

Derrida, J. 1970. Structure, sign, and play in the discourse of the human sciences. In R. Macksey and E. Donato, eds. *The language of criticism and the sciences of man: The structuralist controversy*, pp. 247–272. Baltimore: Johns Hopkins Press.

Deseran, F. A., and Chung, C. 1979. Appearance, role-taking, and reactions to deviance: Some experimental findings. *Social Psychology Quarterly 42*:426–430.

Dew, M. A. 1985. The effect of attitudes on inferences of homosexuality and perceived physical attractiveness in women. *Sex Roles 12*:143–155.

Dickey, L. E. 1967. Projection of the self through judgments of clothed figures and its relation to self-esteem, security-insecurity, and to selected clothing behaviors. Ph.D. dissertation, Pennsylvania State University.

DiGeronimo, J., and Gustafson, G. A. 1985. How about uniforms? *Thrust 14*:48.

Dillon, L. S. 1980. Business dress for women corporate professionals. *Home Economics Research Journal 9*(2):124–129.

Dion, K. K. 1973. Young children's stereotyping of facial attractiveness. *Developmental Psychology 9*(2):183–188.

Dion, K. K., and Berscheid, E. 1974. Physical attractiveness and peer perception among children. *Sociometry 37*:1–12.

Dion, K. K., Berscheid, E., and Walster, E. 1972. What is beautiful is good. *Journal of Personality and Social Psychology 24*:285–290.

Dion, K. K., and Stein, S. 1978. Physical attractiveness and interpersonal influence. *Journal of Experimental Social Psychology 14*:97–108.

Dipboye, R. L., Arvey, R. D., Terpstra, D. E. 1977. Sex and physical attractiveness of raters and applicants as determinants of resumé evaluations. *Journal of Applied Psychology 62*:288–294.

Dispenza, J. E. 1975. *Advertising the American woman*. Dayton: Pflaum Publishing.

Domhoff, G. W. 1983. *Who rules America now? A view for the 80s*. Englewood Cliffs: Prentice-Hall.

Douglas, J. D. 1970. Understanding everyday life. In J. D. Douglas, ed. *Understanding everyday life*, pp. 3–44. Chicago: Aldine.

Douglas, M., and Isherwood, B. 1979. *The world of goods*. New York: Basic Books.

Douty, H. I. 1963. Influence of clothing on perception of persons. *Journal of Home Economics 55*:197–202.

Douty, H. I., and Brannon, E. L. 1984. Figure attractiveness: Male and female preferences for female figures. *Home Economics Research Journal 13*:122–137.

Downs, C. A., and Harrison, S. K. 1985. Embarrassing age spots or just plain ugly? Physical attractiveness stereotyping as an instrument of sexism on American television commercials. *Sex Roles 13*:9–19.

Drake, M. F., and Ford, I. M. (1979). Adolescent clothing and adjustment. *Home Economics Research Journal 7*:283–291.

Dubbert, J. 1979. *A man's place: Masculinity in transition*. Englewood Cliffs: Prentice-Hall.

Dubler, M. L., and Gurel, L. M. 1984. Depression: Relationships to clothing and appearance self-concept. *Home Economics Research Journal 13*:21–26.

Dunlap, K. 1928. The development and function of clothing. *Journal of General Psychology 64*–78.

Dworkin, S. H., and Kerr, B. A. 1987. Comparison of interventions for women experiencing body image problems. *Journal of Counseling Psychology 34*:136–140.

Ebeling, M., and Rosencranz, M. L. 1961. Social and personal aspects of clothing for older women. *Journal of Home Economics* 53:464–465.

Eco, U. 1979. *A theory of semiotics*. Bloomington: Indiana University Press.

Efran, M. G. 1974. The effect of physical appearance on the judgment of guilt, interpersonal attraction and severity of recommended punishment in a simulated jury task. *Journal of Research in Personality* 8:45–54.

Ehrenhaus, P. 1982. Attribution theory: Implications for intercultural communication. In M. Burgoon, ed. *Communication yearbook* vol. 6. Beverly Hills: Sage.

Ehrenreich, B. 1983. *The hearts of men: American dreams and the flight from commitment*. New York: Anchor Press.

Eicher, J. B. 1981. Influence of changing resources on clothing, textiles, and quality of life: Dressing for creativity, fun, and fantasy. In *ACPTC Combined Proceedings*, pp. 36–41. Reston, VA: Association of College Professors of Textiles and Clothing.

Eicher, J. B., and Erekosima, T. V. 1980. Distinguishing non-Western from Western dress: The concept of cultural authentication. In *ACPTC Proceedings, National Meeting*, pp. 83–84. Reston, VA: Association of College Professors of Textiles and Clothing.

Eisele, J., Hertsgaard, D., and Light, H. K. 1986. Factors related to eating disorders in young adolescent girls. *Adolescence* 11:283–290.

Eiser, J. R. 1980. *Cognitive social psychology*. London: McGraw-Hill.

Elliot, D. A. 1984. Return of the dress code. *American Secondary Education* 13:26.

Elliot, G. C. 1986. Self-esteem and self-consistency: A theoretical and empirical link between two primary motivations. *Social Psychology Quarterly* 49:218–297.

Elman, D. 1977. Physical characteristics and the perception of masculine traits. *Journal of Social Psychology* 103:157–158.

Engel, J. F., and Blackwell, R. D. 1982. *Consumer behavior* 4th ed. Chicago: The Dryden Press.

Enninger, W. 1983. Kodewandel in der Kleidung: Sechsundzwanzig Hypothesenpaare. *Zeitschrift fur Semiotik* 5:23–48.

Enninger, W. 1984. Inferencing social structure and social processes from nonverbal behavior. *American Journal of Semiotics* 3(2):77–96.

Enninger, W. 1985. The design features of clothing codes: The functions of clothing displays in interaction. *Kodikas/Code* 8(1/2):81–110.

Erekosima, T. V., and Eicher, J. B. 1981. Kalabari cut thread and pulled-thread cloth. *African Arts* 14(2):48–51, 87.

Fallon, A. E., and Rozin, P. 1985. Short reports: Sex differences in perceptions of desirable body shape. *Journal of Abnormal Psychology* 94:102–105.

Farren, M. 1985. *The black leather jacket*. New York: Abbeville Press.

Fashion '86: 1986. Nursing means business. *American Journal of Nursing* 86 (Aug.), pp. 954, 956–959.

Fashion feedback. 1985. *American Journal of Nursing* 85 (Aug.), p. 894.

Fat, flashy—and fashionable. 1984. *Ms.*, Mar., pp. 101–103.

Feather, B. L., Kaiser, S. B., and Rucker, M. 1988. Mastectomy and related treatments: Impact of appearance satisfaction on self-esteem. *Home Economics Research Journal* 17:129–139.

Feather, B. L., Kaiser, S. B., and Rucker, M. 1989. Breast reconstruction and prosthesis use as forms of symbolic completion of the physical self. *Home Economics Research Journal* 17:216–227.

Feather, B. L., and Lanigan, C. 1987. Looking good after your mastectomy. *American Journal of Nursing* 87:1048–1049.

Feather, B. L., Martin, B. B., and Miller, W. R. 1979. Attitudes toward clothing and self-concept of physically handicapped and able-bodied university men and women. *Home Economics Research Journal* 7:234–240.

Feather, B. L., Rucker, M., and Kaiser, S. B. 1989. Social concerns of post-mastectomy women: Stigmata and clothing. *Home Economics Research Journal* 17:289–299.

Fedler, F. 1984. Studies show people still willing to help a stranger, but especially a woman. *Psychological Reports 54*:365–366.

Feibus, R. 1986. Changing tastes mark kid's wear market. *California Apparel News*, August 15–21, p. 28.

Feingold, A. 1981. Testing equity as an explanation for romantic couples "mismatched" on physical attractiveness. *Psychological Reports 49*:247–250.

Feldman, R. E. 1972. Response to compatriot and foreigner who seek assistance. In L. Bickman and T. Hencky, eds. *Beyond the laboratory: Field research in social psychology*, pp. 44–55. New York: McGraw Hill.

Felson, R. B. 1985. Reflected appraisal and the development of the self. *Social Psychology Quarterly 48*:71–78.

Festinger, L. 1954. A theory of social comparison processes. *Human Relations 7*:117–140.

Festinger, L. 1957. *A theory of cognitive dissonance*. New York: Harper & Row.

Field, G. A. 1970. The status float phenomenon: The upward diffusion of innovation. *Business Horizons 13*(August):45–52.

Fine, G. A. 1987. *With the boys: Little League baseball and preadolescent culture*. Chicago: The University of Chicago Press.

Fischer, L. 1978. The civil rights of teachers in post-industrial society. *High School Journal 61*(8):380–392.

Fisher, B. A. 1978. *Perspectives on human communication*. New York: Macmillan.

Fisher, S. 1968. Body image. In D. Sills, ed. *International encyclopedia of the social sciences* vol. 2. New York: Macmillan.

Fisher, S. 1986a. *Development and structure of the body image* vol. 1. Hillsdale: Lawrence Erlbaum.

Fisher, S. 1986b. *Development and structure of the body image* vol. 2. Hillsdale: Lawrence Erlbaum.

Fisher, S., and Cleveland, S. 1968. Body boundary and perceptual vividness. *Journal of Abnormal Psychology 73*:392–396.

Flügel, J. C. 1950. *The psychology of clothes*. London: Hogarth Press (first published in 1930).

Foltyn, J. L. 1989. The importance of being beautiful: The social construction of the beautiful self. Ph.D. dissertation, University of California at San Diego.

Foote, N. 1975. Concept and method in the study of human development. In D. Brissett and C. Edgley, eds. *Life as theater: A dramaturgical sourcebook*, pp. 23–31. Chicago: Aldine.

Foote, S. 1989. Challenging gender symbols. In C. B. Kidwell and V. Steele, eds. *Men and women: Dressing the part*, pp. 144–157. Washington: Smithsonian Institute Press.

Ford, I. M., and Drake, M. F. 1982. Attitudes toward clothing, body, and self: A comparison of two groups. *Home Economics Research Journal 11*:187–196.

Forney, J. C., and Rabolt, N. J. 1986. Ethnic identity: Its relationship to ethnic and contemporary dress. *Clothing and Textiles Research Journal 4*(2):1–8.

Forsythe, S. M., Drake, M. F., and Cox, C. A. 1984. Dress as an influence on the perceptions of management characteristics in women. *Home Economics Research Journal 13*(2):112–121.

Fortenberry, J. H., MacLean, J., Morris, P., and O'Connell, M. 1978. Replications and refinements: Mode of dress as a perceptual cue to deference. *Journal of Social Psychology 104*:139–140.

Fox-Genovese, E. 1987. The empress's new clothes: The politics of fashion. *Socialist Review 17*(1):7–32.

Franklin, C. W. 1984. *The changing definition of masculinity*. New York: Plenum Press.

Franks, D. D., and Seeburger, F. F. 1980. The person behind the word: Mead's theory of universals and a shift of focus in symbolic interactionism. *Symbolic Interaction 3*:41–58.

Freedman, R. 1986. *Beauty bound*. Lexington: Heath/Lexington Books.

Freeman, C. M., Kaiser, S. B., and Chandler, J. L. 1987. Perceptions of functional clothing by able-bodied people: The other side. *Journal of Consumer Studies and Home Economics 11*:345–358.

Freeman, C. M., Kaiser, S. B., and Wingate, S. B. 1985. Perceptions of functional clothing by persons with physical disabilities: A social-cognitive framework. *Clothing and Textiles Research Journal 4*(1), 46–52.

Freeman, H. R. 1985. Somatic attractiveness: As in other things, moderation is best. *Psychology of Women Quarterly 9*(11):311–322.

Friedan, B. 1983. *The feminine mystique*. New York: W. W. Norton & Co. (first published in 1963).

Fujiwara, Y. 1986. Clothing interest in relation to self-concept and self-esteem of university women. *Journal of Home Economics of Japan 37*:493.

Fuller, P. 1983. *Aesthetics after modernism*. London: Writers & Readers.

Gadel, M. S. 1985. Commentary: Style-oriented apparel customers. In M. R. Solomon, ed. *The psychology of fashion*, pp. 155–157. Lexington: Heath/Lexington Books.

Gans, H. J. 1979. Symbolic ethnicity: The future of ethnic groups and cultures in America. *Ethnic and Racial Studies 2*(1):1–20.

Garfinkel, H. (1967). *Studies in ethnomethodology*. Englewood Cliffs: Prentice-Hall.

Garner, D. M., Garfinkel, P. E., Stancer, H. C., and Moldofsky, H. 1976. Body image disturbances and anorexia nervosa and obesity. *Psychosomatic Medicine 38*:327–336.

Gatignon, H., and Robertson, T. S. 1985. A propositional inventory for new diffusion research. *Journal of Consumer Research 11*:849–867.

Geertz, C. 1973. *The interpretation of cultures*. New York: Basic Books.

Georgoudi, M., and Rosnow, R. L. 1985. Notes toward a contextualist understanding of social psychology. *Personality and Social Psychology Bulletin 11*:5–22.

Gergen, K. J. 1985. Social psychology and the Phoenix of unreality. In S. Koch and D. E. Leary, eds. *A century of psychology as science*, pp. 528–557. New York: McGraw-Hill.

Gibbins, K. 1969. Communication aspects of women's clothes and their relation to fashionability. *British Journal of Social and Clinical Psychology 8*:301–312.

Gibbins, K., and Schneider, A. 1980. Meaning of garments: Relation between impression of an outfit and the message carried by its component garments. *Perceptual and Motor Skills 51*:287–291.

Giddon, D. B. 1985. Ethical considerations for the fashion industry. In M. R. Solomon, ed. *The psychology of fashion*, pp. 225–232. Lexington: Heath/Lexington Books.

Giles, H., and Chavasse, W. 1975. Communication length as function of dress style and social status. *Perceptual and Motor Skills 40*:961–962.

Giles, H., and Farrar, K. 1979. Some behavioral consequences of speech and dress style. *Journal of Social and Clinical Psychology 18*:209–210.

Gill, P. 1989. Treating kids as customers. *Stores*, Mar., pp. 13–26.

Gilligan, C. 1982. *In a different voice: Psychological theory and women's development*. Cambridge: Harvard University Press.

Gilmore, D. C., Beehr, T. A., and Love, K. G. 1986. Effects of applicant sex, applicant physical attractiveness, type of rater and type of job on interview decisions. *Journal of Occupational Psychology 59*:103–109.

Gitlin, T. 1988. Hip deep in post-modernism. *The New York Times Book Review*, Nov. 6, pp. 1, 35–36.

Gitlin, T. 1989. Postmodernism defined, at last! *Utne Reader*, July/Aug., pp. 52–61.

Gjerdingen, D. K., Simpson, D. E., and Titus, S. L. 1987. Patients' and physicians' attitudes regarding the physician's professional appearance. *Archives of Internal Medicine 147*:1209–1212.

Glaser, B. G., and Strauss, A. L. 1964. Awareness contexts and social interaction. *American Sociological Review 29*:669–679.

Gleghorn, A. A., Penner, L. A., Powers, P. S., and Schulman, R. 1987. The psychometric properties of several measures of body image. *Journal of Psychopathology and Behavioral Assessment 9*:203–218.

Glick, P. 1985. Orientations toward relationships: Choosing a situation in which to begin a relationship. *Journal of Experimental Social Psychology 21*:544–562.

Goffman, E. 1952. On cooling the mark out: Some aspects of adaptations to failure. *Psychiatry 15*:451–463.

Goffman, E. 1959. *The presentation of self in everyday life*. Garden City: Doubleday.

Goffman, E. 1961a. *Asylums: Essays on the social situation of mental patients and other inmates*. Garden City: Doubleday.

Goffman, E. 1961b. *Encounters: Two studies in the sociology of interaction*. Indianapolis: Bobbs-Merrill.

Goffman, E. 1963. *Stigma*. Englewood Cliffs: Prentice-Hall.

Goldberg, A., Offer, D., and Schatzman, L. 1961. The role of the uniform in a psychiatric hospital. *Comprehensive Psychiatry 2*:35–43.

Gollwitzer, P. M., and Wicklund, R. A. 1985. Self-symbolizing and the neglect of others' perspectives. *Journal of Personality and Social Psychology 48*:702–715.

Gorden, W. I., Infante, D. A., and Braun, A. A. 1985. Communicator style and fashion innovativeness. In M. R. Solomon, ed. *The psychology of fashion*, pp. 161–175. Lexington: Heath/Lexington Books.

Gordon, L. V. 1975. The psychological study of values. In L. Gordon, ed. *The measurement of interpersonal values*. Chicago: Science Research Association.

Grant, C. L., and Fodor, I. G. 1986. Adolescent attitudes toward image and anorexic behavior. *Adolescence 11*(82):269–281.

Gray, S. H. 1977. Social aspects of body image: Perception of normalcy of weight and affect of college undergraduates. *Perceptual and Motor Skills 45*:1035–1040.

Green, C. F., Cunningham, J., and Yanico, B. J. 1986. Effects of counselor and subject race and counselor physical attractiveness on impressions and expectations of a female counselor. *Journal of Counseling Psychology 33*:349–352.

Greenberg, J., Pyszczynski, T., and Solomon, S. 1986. The causes and consequences of a need for self-esteem: A terror management theory. In R. Baumeister, ed. *Public self and private self*, pp. 189–212. New York: Springer-Verlag.

Greenstein, T. N., and Knottnerus, J. D. 1980. The effects of differential evaluations on status generalizations. *Social Psychology Quarterly 43*(2):147–154.

Grindereng, M. P. 1967. Fashion diffusion. *Journal of Home Economics 59*:171–174.

Gundersen, D. F. 1987. Credibility and the police uniform. *Journal of Police Science and Administration 15*:192–195.

Gurel, L. M., and Gurel, L. 1979. Clothing interest: Conceptualization and measurement. *Home Economics Research Journal 7*:274–282.

Gurel, L. M., Wilbur, J. C., and Gurel, L. 1972. Personality correlates of adolescent clothing styles. *Journal of Home Economics 64*:42–47.

Hall, E. T. 1977. *Beyond culture*. Garden City: Doubleday.

Hall, S. 1977. Culture, the media, and the "ideological effect." In J. Curran et al., eds. *Mass communication and society*. New York: Arnold.

Hall, S. 1982. The rediscovery of "ideology": Return of the repressed in media studies. In M. Gurevitch et al., eds. *Culture, society, and the media*. London: Methuen.

Hallenbeck, P. N. 1966. Special clothing for the handicapped: Review of research and resources. *Rehabilitation Literature 27*:34–40.

Hamid, P. N. 1968. Style of dress as a perceptual cue in impression formation. *Perceptual and Motor Skills 26*:904–906.

Hamilton, D. L. 1981. Stereotyping and intergroup behavior: Some thoughts on the cognitive approach. In D. L. Hamilton, ed. *Cognitive processes in stereotyping and intergroup behavior*, pp. 83–114. Hillsdale: Lawrence Erlbaum.

Hamilton, G., and Biggart, N. 1985. Why people obey: Theoretical observations on power and obediance in complex organization. *Sociological Perspectives 28*(1):3–28.

Hamilton, J. A. 1987. Dress as a cultural sub-system: A unifying methatheory for clothing and textiles. *Clothing and Textiles Research Journal* 6(1):1–7.

Hamilton, J. A. 1988. The interplay of theory and research in discerning the social meaning in dress: Implications for understanding in merchandising. In R. Kean, ed. *Theory building in merchandising*, pp. 32–39. Lincoln: College of Home Economics, University of Nebraska.

Hamilton, J. A., and Hamilton, J. W. 1989. Dress as a reflection and sustainer of social reality: A cross-cultural perspective. *Clothing and Textiles Research Journal* 7(2):16–22.

Hanks, M., and Poplin, D. E. 1981. The sociology of physical disability: A review of literature and some conceptual perspectives. *Deviant Behavior* 2:309–328.

Harman, L. D. 1985. Acceptable deviance as social control: The cases of fashion and slang. *Deviant Behavior* 6:1–15.

Harp, S. S., Stretch, S. M., and Harp, D. A. 1985. The influence of apparel on responses to television news and anchorwomen. In M. R. Solomon, ed. *The psychology of fashion*, pp. 279–291. Lexington: Heath/Lexington Books.

Harrell, W. A. 1978. Physical attractiveness, self-disclosure, and helping behavior. *Journal of Social Psychology* 104:15–17.

Harris, M. B., and Bays, G. 1973. Altruism and sex roles. *Psychological Reports* 32:1002.

Harrison, R. P. 1981. *The cartoon: Communication to the quick*. Beverly Hills: Sage.

Harrison, R. 1985. Clothing as communication: The nonverbal dimension. In *ACPTC Combined Proceedings*, p. 208. Monument, CO: Association of College Professors of Textiles and Clothing.

Hartmann, G. W. 1949. Clothing: Personal problem and social issue. *Journal of Home Economics* 41(6):295–298.

Hassan, M. D. 1976. Tattoos and body image: Tattooed and non-tattooed incarcerated narcotics addicts differentiated by Barrier scores and internal-external locus of control. Ph.D. dissertation, California School of Professional Psychology.

Hatfield, E., and Sprecher, S. 1986. *Mirror, mirror: The importance of looks in everyday life*. Albany: State University of New York Press.

Hatfield, J. D., and Gatewood, R. D. 1978. Nonverbal cues in the selection interview. *Personnel Administration* 23(1):35–37.

Hayes, D., and Ross, C. E. 1987. Body and mind: The effect of exercise, overweight, and physical health and well-being. *Journal of Health and Social Behavior* 27:387–400.

Hebdige, D. 1979. *Subculture: The meaning of style*. London: Methuen.

Heider, F. 1958. *The psychology of interpersonal relations*. New York: John Wiley & Sons.

Heilman, M. E., and Saruwatari, L. R. 1979. When beauty is beastly: The effects of appearance and sex on evaluations of job applicants for managerial and nonmanagerial jobs. *Organizational Behavior and Human Performance* 23:360–372.

Henley, N. M. 1977. *Body politics: Power, sex, and nonverbal communication*. Englewood Cliffs: Prentice-Hall.

Henry, G. M. 1986. High fashion for little ones. *Time* 127:60.

Hensley, W. E. 1981. The effects of attire, location, and sex on aiding behavior: A similarity explanation. *Journal of Nonverbal Behavior* 6(1):3–11.

Hess, B. B., Markson, E. W., and Stein, P. J. 1985. *Sociology* 2d ed. New York: Macmillan.

Hewitt, J., and German, K. 1987. Attire and attractiveness. *Perceptual and Motor Skills* 64:558.

Hildebrandt, K. A., and Fitzgerald, H. E. 1978. Adults' responses to infants varying in perceived cuteness. *Behavioral Processes* 3:159–172.

Hill, D. 1986. *Designer boys and material girls: Manufacturing the '80s pop dream*. Poole, UK: Blandford Press.

Hill, E. M., Nocks, E. S., and Gardner, L. 1987. Physical attractiveness: Manipulation by physique and status displays. *Ethology and Sociobiology* 8:143–154.

Hillestad, R. 1980. The underlying structure of appearance. *Dress* 5:117–125.

Hirschfeld, L. A. 1977. Cuna aesthetics: A quantitative analysis. *Ethnology* 16(2):147–166.

Hirschman, E. C., and Wallendorf, M. R. 1982. Characteristics of the cultural continuum: Implications for retailing. *Journal of Retailing* 58(1):5–21.

Hochswender, W. 1988. Patterns. *New York Times*, Nov. 1, p. B-6.

Hoelter, J. W. 1985. A structural theory of personal consistency. *Social Psychology Quarterly* 48(2):118–129.

Hofler, R., and Zarco, C. 1985. *Wild style*. New York: Simon & Schuster.

Hogge, V. E., and Baer, M. M. 1986. Elderly women's clothing: Acquisition, fit and alterations of ready to wear garments. *Journal of Consumer Studies and Home Economics* 10:333–341.

Holbrook, M. B. 1986. Aims, concepts, and methods for the representation of individual differences in esthetic responses to design features. *Journal of Consumer Research* 13:337–347.

Hollander, A. 1976. Fashion in nudity. *Georgia Review* 30(3):642–702.

Holman, R. H. 1980. A transcription and analysis system for the study of women's clothing behavior. *Semiotica* 32(1/2):11–34.

Homer, P. M., and Kahle, L. R. 1988. A structural equation test of the value-attitude-behavior hierarchy. *Journal of Personality and Social Psychology* 54(4):638–646.

Hongo, M., and Kaiser, S. 1989. Male endorsers in advertisements: Cultural stereotypes and appearance messages. Paper presented at the Colloquium on the Body and Clothing as Communication, International Institute on Marketing Meaning, July, Indianapolis.

Horn, M. J. 1965. *The second skin*. Boston: Houghton-Mifflin.

Horn, M. J., and Gurel, L. M. 1981. *The second skin* 3d ed. Boston: Houghton-Mifflin.

Horowitz, T. 1982. Excitement vs. economy: Fashion and youth culture in Britain. *Adolescence* 17(67):227–236.

Horridge, P. E., Khan, S., and Huffman, K. E. 1981. An assessment of fashion awareness of females based on selected demographic factors. *Journal of Consumer Studies and Home Economics* 5:301–310.

Horridge, P., and Richards, L. 1984. Relationship of fashion awareness and clothing economic practices. *Home Economics Research Journal* 13(2):138–152.

Hostetler, J. A. 1980. *Amish society* 3d ed. Baltimore: The Johns Hopkins University Press.

Howe, J. 1969. What's all this about colored uniforms? *American Journal of Nursing* 69:1665–1667.

Hubble, M. A., and Gelso, C. J. 1978. Brief reports: Effect of counselor attire in an initial interview. *Journal of Counseling Psychology* 25(6):581–584.

Hughes, D. O. 1986. Distinguishing signs: Earrings, Jews and Franciscan rhetoric in the Italian Renaissance city. *Past and Present* 112:3–59.

Hurlock, E. B. 1929. *Motivation in fashion*. New York: Archives of Psychology.

Huston, T. L., and Levinger, G. 1978. Interpersonal attraction and relationships. *Annual Review of Psychology* 29:115–156.

Hutton, S. S. 1984. State of the art: Clothing as a form of human behavior. *Home Economics Research Journal* 12(3): 340–353.

Infants still growing. 1985. *Women's Wear Daily* (Special Issue: "For the Young"). July, p. 24.

Jackson, D., and Huston, T. L. 1975. Physical attractiveness and assertiveness. *Journal of Social Psychology* 96:79–84.

Jacoby, S. 1986. Do you have color anxiety? *Ms.* May, pp. 64–66, 114–116.

James, W. 1890. *The principles of psychology*. New York: Holt, Rinehart and Winston.

Jameson, F. 1983. Postmodernism and consumer society: In H. Foster, eds. *The anti-aesthetic: Essays on postmodern culture*, pp. 111–125. Port Townshend: Bay Press.

Jasper, C. R., and Roach-Higgins, M. E. 1987. History of costume: Theory and instruction. *Clothing and Textiles Research Journal* 5(4):1–6.

Jasper, C. R., and Roach-Higgins, M. E. 1988. Role conflict and conformity in dress. *Social Behaviour and Personality* 16:227–240.

Jeffries, V., and Ransford, H. E. 1980. *Social stratification: A multiple hierarchy approach*. Wellesley: Allyn and Bacon.

Joffe, C. 1971. Sex role socialization and the nursery school: As the twig is bent. *Journal of Marriage and the Family* 33:467–475.

Johnson, B. H., Nagasawa, R. H., and Peters, K. 1977. Clothing style differences: Their effect on the impression of sociability. *Home Economics Research Journal* 6(1):58–63.

Johnson, K. K. P., and Roach-Higgins, M. E. 1987. Dress and physical attractiveness of women in job interviews. *Clothing and Textiles Research Journal* 5(3):1–8.

Johnson, R. 1986–1987. What is cultural studies anyway? *Social Text* 16:38–80.

Jones, E. E., and Davis, K. E. (1965). From acts to dispositions: The attribution process in person perception. In L. Berkowitz, ed. *Advances in Experimental Social Psychology* vol. 2, pp. 219–266. New York: Academic Press.

Joseph, N. 1986. *Uniforms and nonuniforms: Communication through clothing*. New York: Greenwood Press.

Judd, N., Bull, R. H. C., and Gahagan, D. 1975. The effects of clothing style upon the reactions of a stranger. *Social Behavior and Personality* 3(2):225–227.

Kahle, L. R., and Homer, P. M. 1985. Physical attractiveness of the celebrity endorser: A social adaptation perspective. *Journal of Consumer Research* 11:954–961.

Kaigler-Evans, K. 1979. Perceived similarity of sources' and receivers' innovativeness: Facilitators of transmission of information about fashion. *Perceptual and Motor Skills* 49:243–246.

Kaigler-Evans, K., and Damhorst, M. L. 1978. Impression formation: Use of descriptors of personal traits. *Perceptual and Motor Skills* 46:903–906.

Kaigler-Evans, K., and Hulls-Huggins, M. J. 1981. Awareness of clothing of preschool children. In *ACPTC Combined Proceedings*, p. 93. Reston, VA: Association of College Professors of Textiles and Clothing.

Kaigler-Walker, K., and Ericksen, M. K. Working paper. Appearance as a symbolic indicator of acculturation of Hispanic-American women. Southwest Texas State University.

Kaigler-Walker, K., Ericksen, M. K., and Mount, J. 1989. Acculturation and social class as related to Hispanic-American women's perception of clothing/appearance products. Paper presented at the Bi-annual World Marketing Congress (Academy of Marketing Science), July, Singapore.

Kaiser, S. B. 1982. Clothes can say a lot; contribution of clothing to communication in city government. *Western City* 58:18–22.

Kaiser, S. B. 1983–1984. Toward a contextual social psychology of clothing: A synthesis of symbolic interactionist and cognitive theoretical perspectives. *Clothing and Textiles Research Journal* 2:1–9.

Kaiser, S. B. 1987. Appearance management and identity: Contextual dimensions of creativity. Paper presented at the meeting of the Western Social Science Association (Symbolic Interaction Section), Apr., El Paso.

Kaiser, S. B. 1989. Clothing and the social organization of gender perception: A developmental approach. *Clothing and Textiles Research Journal* 7(2):46–56.

Kaiser, S. B., 1990. Mother-daughter relations, appearance socialization, and gender issues. Progress report submitted to the center for Consumer Research, University of California, at Davis.

Kaiser, S. B., Carstens, S., and Freeman, C. Working paper. Perception of mothers' appearance styles. University of California, Davis.

Kaiser, S. B., and Chandler, J. L. 1984. Fashion alienation: Older adults and the mass media. *International Journal of Aging and Human Development* 19:199–217.

Kaiser, S. B., and Chandler, J. L. 1985. Older consumers' use of media for fashion information. *Journal of Broadcasting and Electronic Media* 29:201–207.

Kaiser, S. B., and Chandler, J. L. 1988. Audience responses to appearance codes: Old-age imagery in the media. *Gerontologist* 28:692–699.

Kaiser, S. B., Chandler, J. L., Freeman, C. M., and Carstens, S. C. 1986. Appearance forms and sex-role ideology: A characterization of females on Saturday morning television. Paper presented at the meeting of the Pacific Sociological Association, Apr., Denver.

Kaiser, S. B., and Damhorst, M. L. Working paper. Adolescents' categorizations and interpretations of music video females' appearances. University of California at Davis and Iowa State University.

Kaiser, S. B., and Damhorst, M. L. eds. Forthcoming 1990. *Critical linkages in textiles and clothing: Theory, method, and practice*. Monument, CO: Association of College Professors of Textiles and Clothing.

Kaiser, S. B., and Freeman, C. M. 1989. Meaningful clothing and the framing of emotion: Toward a gender-relational understanding. Paper presented at the meeting of the Society for the Study of Symbolic Interaction, Aug., San Francisco.

Kaiser, S. B., Freeman, C. M., and Wingate, S. B. 1985. Stigmata and negotiated outcomes: Management of appearance by persons with physical disabilities. *Deviant Behavior* 6:205–224.

Kaiser, S. B., and Khan, S. 1980. Clothing for the aged: A potential market. *Texas Home Economist* 47:14.

Kaiser, S. B., Nagasawa, R. H., and Hutton, S. S. 1989. Toward a theory of fashion and the social construction of meaning: Symbolic-interactionist insights and initiatives. Paper presented at the Gregory Stone Symposium, Feb., Arizona State University.

Kaiser, S. B., and Phinney, J. S. 1983. Sex typing of play activities by girls' clothing style: Pants versus skirts. *Child Study Journal* 13(2):115–131.

Kaiser, S. B., Rudy, M., and Byfield, P. 1985. The role of clothing in sex role socialization: Person perceptions versus overt behaviors. *Child Study Journal* 15:83–97.

Kaiser, S. B., Schutz, H. G., and Chandler, J. L. 1987. Cultural codes and sex-role ideology: A study of shoes. *American Journal of Semiotics* 5(1):13–34.

Kaiser, S. B., Schutz, H. G., Chandler, J. L., and Lieder, L. M. 1985. Shoes as sociocultural symbols: Retailers' versus consumers' perceptions. In M. R. Solomon, ed. *The psychology of fashion*, pp. 127–141. Lexington: Heath/Lexington Books.

Kaiser, S. B., Wingate, S. B., Freeman, C. M., and Chandler, J. L. 1987. Acceptance of physical disability and attitudes toward personal appearance. *Rehabilitation Psychology* 32:51–58.

Kalisch, B. J., and Kalisch, P. A. 1985. Dressing for success. *American Journal of Nursing* 85:887–893.

Kanekar, S., and Kolsawalla, M. B. 1980. Responsibility of a rape victim in relation to her respectability, attractiveness, and provocativeness. *Journal of Social Psychology* 112:153–154.

Kantor, R. M. 1977. *Men and women of the corporation*. New York: Basic Books.

Karp, D. A., Stone, G. P., and Yoels, W. 1977. *Being urban: A social psychological view of city life*. Lexington: Heath/Lexington Books.

Kassarjian, H. H. 1963. Voting intentions and political perception. *Journal of Psychology* 56:85–88.

Keasey, C. B., and Tomlinson-Keasey, C. 1973. Petition signing in a naturalistic setting. *Journal of Social Psychology* 89:313–314.

Kefgen, M., and Touchie-Specht, P. 1986. *Individuality in clothing selection and personal appearance* 4th ed. New York: Macmillan.

Kehle, T. J., Bramble, W. J., and Mason, E. J. 1974. Teachers' expectations: Ratings of student performance as biased by student characteristics. *Journal of Experimental Education* 43(1):54–60.

Kehret-Ward, T. 1987. Combining products in use: How the syntax of product use affects marketing decisions. In J. Umiker-Sebeok, ed. *Marketing and semiotics: New directions in the study of signs for sale*, pp. 219–238. Berlin: Mouton de Gruyter.

Kelley, E. A., Daigle, C. W., La Fleur, R. S., and Wilson, L. J. 1974. *Adolescent dress and social participation. Home Economics Research Journal* 2(3):167–175.

Kelley, E., Blouin, D., Glee, R., Sweat, S., and Arledge, L. 1982. Career appearance: Perceptions of university students and recruiters who visit their campuses. *Home Economics Research Journal* 10:253–263.

Kelley, E., and Sweat, S. 1983–1984. Correspondent inference: Theoretical framework for viewing clothed appearances. *Clothing and Textiles Research Journal* 2:49–55.

Kelley, H. 1973. Processes of causal attribution. *American Psychologist* 28:107–128.

Kernaleguen, A. 1978. *Clothing designs for the handicapped*. Alberta: University of Alberta Press.

Kernaleguen, A. P., and Compton, N. H. 1968. Body-field perceptual differentiation related to peer perception of attitudes toward clothing. *Perceptual and Motor Skills* 27:195–198.

Kernan, J. B. 1973. Her mother's daughter? The case of clothing and cosmetic fashions. *Adolescence* 8:343–350.

Kerr, B. A., and Dell, D. M. 1976. Perceived interviewer expertness and attractiveness: Effects of interviewer behavior and attire and interview setting. *Journal of Counseling Psychology* 23:553–556.

Kidwell, C. B., and Steele, V., eds. 1989. *Men and women: Dressing the part*. Washington: Smithsonian Institution Press.

Kiesler, C. A., and Kiesler, S. B. 1970. *Conformity*. Reading: Addison-Wesley.

Kim, M., and Schrank, H. L. 1982. Fashion leadership among Korean college women, Part 1. *Home Economics Research Journal* 10:227–234.

King, C. W. 1963. Fashion adoption: A rebuttal to the "trickle-down" theory. In S. A. Greyser, ed. *Toward scientific marketing*, pp. 108–125. Chicago: American Marketing Association.

King, C. W., and Ring, L. 1980. Fashion theory: The dynamics of style and taste, adoption and diffusion. In J. Olson, ed. *Advances in consumer research*, pp. 13–16. Ann Arbor: Association for Consumer Research.

Klapp, O. 1969. *Collective search for identity*. New York: Holt, Rinehart & Winston.

Klapp, O. E. 1982. Meaning lag in the information society. *Journal of Communication* 32(2):56–66.

Kleck, R. 1968. Physical stigma and non-verbal cues emitted in face-to-face interaction. *Human Relations* 1:9–28.

Kleck, R., Ono, H., and Hastorf, A. H. 1966. The effects of physical deviance upon face-to-face interaction. *Human Relations* 19:425–436.

Klein, S. M., and Ritti, R. R. 1980. Impression management in organizational life. In S. M. Klein and R. R. Ritti, eds. *Understanding organizational behavior*, pp. 150–171. Boston, MA: Kent Publishing Co.

Kleinke, C. L., and Staneski, R. A. 1980. First impressions of female bust size. *Journal of Social Psychology* 110:123–124.

Kness, D. 1983. Clothing deprivation feelings of three adolescent ethnic groups. *Adolescence* 18:659–674.

Kness, D., and Densmore, B. 1976. Dress and social-political beliefs of young male students. *Adolescence* 11:431–442.

Koch, K. E., and Dickey, L. E. 1988. The feminist in the workplace: Applications to a contextual study of dress. *Clothing and Textiles Research Journal* 7(1):46–54.

Kohlberg, L. 1966. A cognitive-developmental analysis of children's sex-role concepts and attitudes. In E. E. Maccoby, ed. *The development of sex differences*, pp. 82–173. Stanford: Stanford University Press.

Koren, L. 1984. *New fashion Japan*. Tokyo: Kodansha International.

Koulack, D., and Tuthill, J. A. 1972. Height perception: A function of social distance.

*Canadian Journal of Behavioral Science* 4:50–53.

Kroker, A., and Cook, D. 1986. *The postmodern scene: Excremental culture and hyperaesthetics*. New York: St. Martin's Press.

Krebs, D., and Adinolfi, A. A. 1975. Physical attractiveness, social relations and personality style. *Journal of Personality and Social Psychology* 31:245–253.

Kundel, C. 1976. Clothing practices and preferences of blue-collar workers and their families. *Home Economics Research Journal* 4(4):225–234.

Kunzle, D. 1977. Dress reform as antifeminism: A response to Helene E. Roberts's "The exquisite slave: The role of clothes in the making of the Victorian woman." *Signs* 2:570–579.

Kwon, H. 1979. Changing function of symbolism in design of Korean silk textiles. *Home Economics Research Journal* 8:16–26.

Lafferty, H. K., and Dickey, L. E. 1980. Clothing symbolism and the changing role of nurses. *Home Economics Research Journal* 8:294–301.

Lambert, S. 1972. Reactions to a stranger as a function of style of dress. *Perceptual and Motor Skills* 35:711–712.

Lapitsky, M. 1961. Clothing values and their relation to general values and to social security and insecurity. Ph.D. dissertation, Pennsylvania State University.

Lapitsky, M., and Smith, C. M. 1981. Impact of clothing on impressions of personal characteristics and writing ability. *Home Economics Research Journal* 9:327–335.

Laughlin, J. 1985. Developing a global perspective: Premises, probabilities, possibilities, and planning for action. In *ACPTC Combined Proceedings*, pp. 9–17. Monument, CO: Association of College Professors of Textiles and Clothing.

Laver, J. 1937. *Taste and fashion from the French revolution until today*. London: George G. Harrap and Company Ltd.

Lavers, A. 1982. *Roland Barthes: Structuralism and after*. London: Methuen.

Lavrakas, P. J. 1975. Female preferences for male physiques. *Journal of Research in Personality* 9:324–334.

Lawson, L. R., Pedersen, E. L., and Markee, N. L. 1987. Body cathexis and self-image courses. In *ACPTC Combined Proceedings*, p. 123. Monument, CO: Association of College Professors of Textiles and Clothing.

Leahy, R. L. 1976. Developmental trends in qualified inferences and descriptions of self and others. *Developmental Psychology* 12:546–547.

Leahy, R. L., and Shirk, S. R. 1985. Social cognition and the development of the self. In R. L. Leahy, ed. *The development of the self*, pp. 123–150. Orlando: Academic Press.

Leavitt, C., and Kaigler-Evans, K. 1975. Mere similarity versus information processing: An exploration of source and message interaction. *Communication Research* 2:300–306.

Lebow, J. 1986. Big beauties search reflects larger outlook. *Women's Wear Daily*, Aug. 26, p. 21.

Lechelt, E. C. 1975. Occupational affiliation and ratings of physical height and personal esteem. *Psychological Reports* 36:943–946.

Lee, M., and Cooke, E. F. 1987. Asian Americans: Demographics of an ignored target market. In R. L. King, ed. *Minority marketing: Issues and prospects* vol. 3, pp. 87–91. Charleston: Academy of Marketing Science.

Lefkowitz, M., Blake, R. R., and Mouton, J. S. 1959. Status factors in pedestrian violation of traffic signals. *Journal of Abnormal and Social Psychology* 51:704–706.

Lennon, S. 1988. Physical attractiveness, age, and body type. *Home Economics Research Journal* 16:195–203.

Lennon, S. J., Clayton, R., and Larkin, J. 1989. Age, body type, and clothing fashion. Paper presented at the Colloquium on the Body and Clothing as Communication, International Institute on Marketing Meaning, July, Indianapolis.

Lennon, S. J., and Davis, L. L. 1987. Individual differences in fashion orientation and cognitive complexity. *Perceptual and Motor Skills* 64:327–330.

Lennon, S. J., and Davis, L. L. 1989. Clothing and human behavior from a social cognitive framework. Part I: Theoretical perspectives. *Clothing and Textiles Research Journal* 7(4):41–48.

Lennon, S., Davis, L. L., and Fairhurst, A. 1988. Evaluations of apparel advertising as a function of self-monitoring. *Perceptual and Motor Skills* 66:987–996.

Lennon, S. J., and Miller, F. G. 1984. Salience of physical appearance in impression formation. *Home Economics Research Journal* 13:95–104.

Lennon, S. J., and Miller, F. G. 1984–1985. Attire, physical appearance, and first impressions: More is less. *Clothing and Textiles Research Journal* 3(1):1–8.

Lerner, R. M., Iwasaki, S., Chihara, T., and Sorell, G. T. 1981. Self-concept, self-esteem, and body attitudes among Japanese male and female adolescents. In S. Chess and A. Thomas, eds. *Annual progress in child psychiatry and child development*, pp. 495–507. New York: Brunner/Mazel Inc.

Lerner, R. M., and Karabenick, S. A. 1974. Physical attractiveness and self-concept in late adolescents. *Journal of Youth and Adolescence* 3:307–316.

Lerner, R. M., Karabenick, S. A., and Meisels, M. 1975. Effects of age and sex on the development of personal space schemata towards body build. *Journal of Genetic Psychology* 127:91–101.

Lerner, R. M., Karabenick, S. A., and Stuart, J. L. 1973. Relations among physical attractiveness, body attitudes, and self-concept in male and female college students. *Journal of Psychology* 85:119–129.

Lerner, R. M., and Lerner, J. V. 1977. Effects of age, sex, and physical attractiveness on child-peer relations, academic performance, and elementary school adjustment. *Developmental Psychology* 13:585–590.

Lerner, R. M., Orlos, J. B., and Knapp, J. R. 1976. Physical attractiveness, physical effectiveness, and self-concept in late adolescents. *Adolescence* 11:313–326.

Lettich, J. 1986. Spectators turning to authentic athletic wear. *Apparel World*, Mar., pp. 35–38.

Lévi-Strauss, C. 1966. *The savage mind*. Chicago: The University of Chicago Press.

Lewin, K. 1935. Dynamic theory of personality. New York: McGraw-Hill.

Lewis, K. N., and Walsh, W. B. 1978. Physical attractiveness: Its impact on the perception of a female counselor. *Journal of Counseling Theory* 25:210–216.

Lewis, L. 1987. Form and female authorship in music videos. *Communication* 9:355–377.

Lewis, L., and Johnson, K. K. P. 1989. Effect of dress, cosmetics, sex of subject, and causal inference on attribution of victim responsibility. *Clothing and Textiles Research Journal* 8(1):22–27.

Liebman, M. M. 1987. A conceptual framework for examining color preference, importance and categorization in a multiattribute context among blacks. In R. L. King, ed. *Minority marketing: Issues and prospects* vol. 3, pp. 57–63. Charleston: Academy of Marketing Science.

Lind, C., and Roach-Higgins, M. E. 1985. Fashion, collective adoption, and the social-political symbolism of dress. In M. R. Solomon, ed. *The psychology of fashion*, pp. 183–192. Lexington: Heath/Lexington Books.

Lips, H. 1981. *Women, men, and the psychology of power*. Englewood Cliffs: Prentice-Hall.

Littlejohn, S. W. 1978. *Theories of human communication*. Columbus: Charles E. Merrill.

Littrell, M. A., and Beavers, M. 1987. Textile handcrafts: Meanings for tourist consumers. In *ACPTC Combined Proceedings*, p. 41. Monument, CO: Association of College Professors of Textiles and Clothing.

Littrell, M. A., and Berger, E. A. 1986. Perceiver's occupation and client's grooming: Influence on person perception. *Clothing and Textiles Research Journal* 4(2):48–55.

Littrell, M. A., Damhorst, M. L., and Littrell, J. M. In press. Clothing interests, body satisfaction, and eating behavior of adolescent females: Related or independent dimensions? *Adolescence*.

Littrell, M. A., and Eicher, J. B. 1973. Clothing opinions and the social acceptance process among adolescents. *Adolescence 8*(30):197–212.

Littrell, M. A., and Evers, S. J. 1985. Liturgical vestments and the priest role. *Home Economics Research Journal 14*:152–162.

Littrell, M. A., Littrell, J. M., and Kuznick, A. 1981. Formal/informal dimension in perceptions of counselors' dress. *Perceptual and Motor Skills 53*:751–757.

Livesley, W. J., and Bromley, D. B. 1973. *Person perception in childhood and adolescence*. New York: John Wiley & Sons.

Lofland, L. H. 1988. *A world of strangers: Order and action in urban public space*. New York: Basic Books.

Lofland, L. H. 1988. Communication and construction: The built environment as message and medium. In D. R. Maines and C. J. Couch, eds. *Communication and social structure*, pp. 307–322. Springfield: Charles C Thomas.

Lombardo, J. P., and Tocci, M. E. 1979. Attributions of positive and negative characteristics of instructors as a function of attractiveness and sex of instructor and sex of subject. *Perceptual and Motor Skills 48*:491–494.

Long, T. J. 1978. Influence of uniform and religious status on interviewees. *Journal of Counseling Psychology 25*:405–409.

Lowe, E. 1984. Aesthetic rules in women's apparel: Empirical fact or fantasy. *Journal of Consumer Studies and Home Economics 8*:169–181.

Lowe, E. D., and Anspach, K. A. 1973. Toward a definition of freedom in dress. *Home Economics Research Journal 1*:246–250.

Lowe, E. D., and Anspach, K. A. 1978. Freedom in dress: A search for related factors. *Home Economics Research Journal 7*:121–127.

Lowe, E. D., and Buckley, H. M. 1982. Freedom and conformity in dress: A two-dimensional approach. *Home Economics Research Journal 11*:197–204.

Lowe, E. D., and Dunsing, M. M. 1981. Clothing satisfaction determinants. *Home Economics Research Journal 9*(4):363–373.

Lowe, E. D., and Lowe, J. W. G. 1985. Quantitative analysis of women's dress. In M. R. Solomon, ed. *The psychology of fashion*, pp. 193–206. Lexington: Heath/Lexington Books.

Lubner-Rupert, J. A., and Winakor, G. 1985. Male and female style preference and perceived fashion risk. *Home Economics Research Journal 13*:265–266.

Lukes, S. 1973. *Individualism*. Worcester, Great Britain: Billing and Sons.

Lumpkin, J. R., and Greenberg, B. A. 1982. Apparel shopping patterns of the elderly consumer. *Journal of Retailing 58*:68–89.

Lumpkin, J. R., and McConkey, C. W. 1984. Identifying determinants of store choice of fashion shoppers. *Akron Business and Economic Review 15*(4):30–35.

Lundholm, J. K., and Littrell, J. M. 1986. Desire for thinness among high school cheerleaders: Relationship to disordered eating and weight control behaviors. *Adolescence 21*:573–579.

Lurie, A. 1976. Arts in society: The dress code. *New Society*, Dec. 9, pp. 520–521.

Lyotard, J.-F. 1988. *The postmodern condition: A report on knowledge*. Trans. by G. Bennington and B. Massumi. Minneapolis: University of Minneapolis Press.

MacCannell, D., and MacCannell, J. F. 1982. *The time of the sign: A semiotic interpretation of modern culture*. Bloomington: Indiana University Press.

McArthur, L. Z., and Post, D. L. 1977. Figural emphasis and person perception. *Journal of Experimental Social Psychology 13*:520–535.

McCall, G. J., and Simmons, J. L. 1966. *Identities and interactions*. New York: Free Press.

McCracken, G. 1985. The trickle-down theory revisited. In M. R. Solomon, ed. *The psychology of fashion*, pp. 39–54. Lexington: Heath/Lexington Books.

McCracken, G. 1986. Culture and consumption: A theoretical account of the structure and movement of the cultural meaning of consumer goods. *Journal of Consumer Research 13*:71–84.

McCracken, G. 1988. *Culture and consumption*. Bloomington: Indiana University Press.

McCullough, E. A., Miller, M. F., and Ford, I. M. 1977. Sexually attractive clothing: Attitudes and usage. *Home Economics Research Journal 6*:164–170.

McDermott, C. 1987. *Street style*. New York: Rizzoli.

McGuire, W. J. 1985. Toward social psychology's second century. In S. Koch, and D. E. Leary, eds. *A century of psychology as science*, pp. 558–590. New York: McGraw-Hill.

McKeachie, W. J. 1952. Lipstick as a determiner of first impressions of personality. *Journal of Social Psychology 36*:241–244.

McLean, C. 1986. The kidswear business grows up. *California Apparel News*. May 9–15, p. 6.

McLean, F. P. 1978. The process of aging related to body cathexis and to clothing satisfaction. Ph.D. doctoral dissertation, Utah State University.

McLuhan, M. 1967. *The medium is the message*. New York: Random House.

McPeek, R. W., and Edwards, J. D. 1975. Expectancy disconfirmation and attitude change. *Journal of Social Psychology 96*:193–208.

McReady, A. 1987. The forgotten woman: Large-size profits. *Women's Wear Daily* (Supplement: Best of Group III/Dallas), Jan., p. 42.

McRobbie, A., and Nava, M., eds. 1984. *Gender and generation*. London: Macmillan Education Ltd.

Maher, P. M., and Slocum, A. C. 1986. Freedom in dress: The legal view. *Home Economics Research Journal 14*:371–379.

Maher, P. M., and Slocum, A. C. 1987. Freedom in dress: Legal sanctions. *Clothing and Textiles Research Journal 5*(4):14–22.

Mahoney, E. R., and Finch, M. D. 1976. The dimensionality of body cathexis. *Journal of Psychology 92*:277–279.

Manning, P. K. 1987. *Semiotics and field work*. Newbury Park: Sage.

Manny, L. 1981. Behind the veil. *Odyssey*. Public Broadcasting Associates.

Manz, W., and Lueck, H. E. 1968. Influence of wearing glasses on personality ratings: Crosscultural validation of an old experiment. *Perceptual and Motor Skills 27*:704.

Maret, S. M., and Harling, C. A. 1985. Cross-cultural perceptions of physical attractiveness: Ratings of photographs of whites by Cruzans and Americans. *Perceptual and Motor Skills 60*:163–166.

Markus, H., Hamill, R., and Sentis, K. P. 1987. Thinking fat: Self-schemas for body weight and the processing of weight relevant information. *Journal of Applied Social Psychology 17*:50–71.

Marsh, P. 1985. Identity: An ethogenic perspective. In R. C. Trexler, ed. *Persons in groups*, pp. 17–30. Binghamton: Medieval and Renaissance Texts and Studies.

Martin, C. D. 1976. A transgenerational comparison: The elderly fashion consumer. *Advances in Consumer Research 3*:453–456.

Martin, C. L., and Halverson, C. F. 1983. The effects of sex-typing schemas on young children's memory. *Child Development 54*(3):563–574.

Mason, J. B., and Bellenger, D. 1973–1974. Analyzing high fashion acceptance. *Journal of Retailing 49*(4):79–88.

Mathes, E. W., Brennan, S. M., Haugen, P. M., and Rice, H. B. 1985. Ratings of physical attractiveness as a function of age. *Journal of Social Psychology 125*:157–168.

Mathes, E. W., and Kempher, S. B. 1976. Clothing as a nonverbal communicator of sexual attitudes and behavior. *Perceptual and Motor Skills 43*:495–498.

Mauro, R. 1984. The constable's new clothes: Effects of uniforms on perceptions and problems of police officers. *Journal of Applied Social Psychology 14*(1):42–56.

May, J. K., and Koester, A. W. 1985. Clothing purchase practices of adolescents. *Home Economics Research Journal* 13:226–236.

Mayer, R. N., and Belk, R. W. 1985. Fashion and impression formation among children. In M. R. Solomon, ed. *The psychology of fashion*, pp. 293–308. Lexington: Heath/ Lexington Books.

Mayer-Thurman, C. 1975. The significance of mass vestments. *Arts and Artists* 10:14–21.

Mayo, J. 1984. *A history of ecclesiastical dress*. New York: Holmes & Meier.

Mead, G. H. 1934. *Mind, self, and society*. Chicago: The University of Chicago Press.

Mehrabian, A. 1981. *Silent messages* 2d ed. Belmont: Wadsworth.

Melamed, A. R., Silverman, M. S., and Lewis, G. J. 1975. Personal orientation inventory: Three year follow-up of women religious. *Review of Religious Research* 16:105–110.

Mernissi, F. 1987. *Beyond the veil: Male-female dynamics in modern Muslim society* 2d ed. Bloomington: Indiana University Press.

Merton, R. 1949. *Social theory and social structure: Toward the codification of theory and research*. Glencoe: Free Press.

Michelman, S. O., and Michelman, J. D. 1986. Public, private, and secret self: A multidisciplinary approach to the study of dress and body markings. In *ACPTC National Proceedings*, p. 128. Monument, CO: Association of College Professors of Textiles and Clothing.

Mick, D. G. 1986. Consumer research and semiotics: Exploring the morphology of signs, symbols, and significance. *Journal of Consumer Research* 13:196–213.

Mick, D. G., and Politi, L. G. 1989. Consumers' interpretations of advertising imagery: A visit to the hell of connotation. In E. C. Hirschman, ed. *Interpretive Consumer Research*, pp. 85–96. Provo: Association for Consumer Research.

Miller, F. G. 1982. Clothing and physical impairment: Joint effects on person perception. *Home Economics Research Journal* 10:265–270.

Miller, F. G., Davis, L. L., and Rowold, K. L. 1982. Public self-consciousness, social anxiety, and attitudes toward the use of clothing. *Home Economics Research Journal* 10:363–368.

Miller, F. G., and Rowold, K. L. 1980. Attire, sex roles, and responses to requests for directions. *Psychological Reports* 47:661–662.

Millman, M. 1980. *Such a pretty face: Being fat in America*. New York: W. W. Norton & Co.

Mills, C. W. 1951. *White collar: The American middle classes*. New York: Oxford University Press.

Minshall, B., Winakor, G., and Swinney, J. L. 1982. Fashion preferences of males and females, risks perceived, and temporal quality of styles. *Home Economics Research Journal* 10:370–378.

Miyamoto, S. F., and Dornbusch, S. M. 1956. A test of interactionist hypotheses of self-conception. *American Journal of Sociology* 61:399–403.

Moore, J. S., Graziano, W. G., and Millar, M. G. 1987. Physical attractiveness, sex role orientation, and the evaluation of adults and children. *Personality and Social Psychology Bulletin* 13:95–102.

Moran, J. D., and McCullers, J. C. 1984. A comparison of achievement scores in physically attractive and unattractive students. *Home Economics Research Journal* 13:36–40.

Morens, D. M. 1976. White coats 34 years ago. *The New England Journal of Medicine* 294(10):564–565.

Morgan, E. 1972. *The descent of woman*. New York: Stein & Day.

Morgan, G. 1986. *Images of organization*. Beverly Hills: Sage.

Morganosky, M. 1984. Aesthetic and utilitarian qualities of clothing: Use of a multidimensional clothing value model. *Home Economics Research Journal* 13:12–20.

Morganosky, M. 1987a. Aesthetic, function, and fashion consumer values: Relationships to other values and demographics. *Clothing and Textiles Research Journal* 6(1):15–28.

Morganosky, M. 1987b. Aesthetic and utilitarian qualities of clothing: Use of a multi-dimensional clothing value model. *Home Economics Research Journal* 13:12–20.

Morganosky, M., and Creekmore, A. M. 1981. Clothing influence in adolescent leadership roles. *Home Economics Research Journal* 9:356–362.

Morrione, T. J., and Farberman, H. A. 1981. Conversation with Herbert Blumer: I. *Symbolic Interaction* 4:113–137.

Morris, B. J. 1985. The phenomenon of anorexia nervosa: A feminist perspective. *Feminist Issues* 5:89–99.

Morse, S., and Gergen, K. J. 1970. Social comparison, self-consistency, and the concept of self. *Journal of Personality and Social Psychology* 16:148–156.

Mosher, D. L., Oliver, W. A., and Dolgan, J. 1967. Body image in tattooed prisoners. *Journal of Clinical Psychology* 23:31–32.

Mouer, R., and Sugimoto, Y. 1986. *Images in Japanese society*. London: KPI.

Muchmore, J. M. 1975. The uniform: its effect. *The Police Chief* 42:70–71.

Musa, K. E., and Roach, M. E. 1973. Adolescent appearance and self-concept. *Adolescence* 8:385–394.

Muuss, R. E. 1986. Adolescent eating disorders. *Adolescence* 21:257–267.

Nagasawa, R. H., Kaiser, S. B., and Hutton, S. S. 1989. Theoretical development in clothing and textiles: Are we stuck in the concrete? *Clothing and Textiles Research Journal* 7(2):23–31.

Neumann, K. F., Critelli, J. W., and Tang, C. 1986. Male physical attractiveness as a potential contaminating variable in ratings of heterosocial skill. *Journal of Social Psychology* 126:813–814.

Noles, S. W., Cash, T. F., and Winstead, B. A. 1985. Body image, physical attractiveness, and depression. *Journal of Consulting and Clinical Psychology* 53:88–94.

Novotny, H., and Walsleben, E. 1986. Department stores buy into large size market. *California Apparel News*, Oct. 31–Nov. 6, pp. 24–25.

Nystrom, P. H. 1928. *Economics of fashion*. New York: The Ronald Press Company.

Olson, E. A. 1985. Muslim identity and secularism in contemporary Turkey: "The headscarf dispute." *Anthropological Quarterly* 58:161–171.

Paek, S. L. 1986. Effects of garment style on the perception of personal traits. *Clothing and Textiles Research Journal* 5(1):10–16.

Painter, J. J., and Pinegar, M. L. 1971. Post-high teens and fashion information. *Journal of Marketing Research* 8:368–369.

Pancer, S. M., and Meindl, J. R. 1978. Length of hair and beardedness as determinants of personality impressions. *Perceptual and Motor Skills* 46:1328–1330.

Pannabecker, R. K. 1988. The cultural authentication of ribbon: Use and test of a concept. *Clothing and Textiles Research Journal* 7(1):55–56.

Paoletti, J. B. 1985. Ridicule and role models as factors in American men's fashion change, 1880–1910. *Costume* 19:121–134.

Paoletti, J. B. 1987. Clothing and gender in America: Children's fashions, 1890–1920. *Signs* 13(1):136–143.

Paoletti, J. B., and Kregloh, C. L. 1989. The children's department. In C. B. Kidwell and V. Steele, eds. *Men and women: Dressing the part*, pp. 22–41. Washington: Smithsonian University Press.

Paradise, L. V., Zweig, J., Conway, B. S. 1986. Effects of expert and referent influence, physical attractiveness, and gender on perceptions of counselor attributes. *Journal of Counseling Psychology* 33(1):16–22.

Patzer, G. L. 1985. *The physical attractiveness phenomena*. New York: Plenum Press.

Peacock, J. L. 1986. *The anthropological lens: Harsh light, soft focus*. Cambridge: Cambridge University Press.

Perry, M. O., Schutz, H. G., and Rucker, M. H. 1983. Clothing interest, self-actualization, and demographic variables. *Home Economics Research Journal* 11:280–288.

Peterson, D., and Curran, J. P. 1976. Trait attraction as a function of hair length and correlates of subjects' preferences for hair style. *Journal of Psychology* 93(2):331–339.

Pettigrew, T. F. 1981. Extending the stereotype concept. In D. L. Hamilton, ed. *Cognitive processes in stereotyping and intergroup behavior*, pp. 303–331. Hillsdale: Lawrence Erlbaum.

Phillips, J. W., and Staley, H. K. 1979. Sumptuary legislation in four centuries. In L. M. Gurel and M. S. Beeson, eds. *Dimensions of dress and adornment* 3d ed. Dubuque: Kendall/Hunt.

Piliavin, J. A., and Unger, R. K. 1985. The helpful but helpless female: Myth or reality? In V. E. O'Leary, R. K. Unger, and B. S. Wallston, eds., *Women, gender, and social psychology*, pp. 149–189. Hillsdale: Lawrence Erlbaum.

Pines, H. A. 1983. The fashion self-concept: Structure and function. Paper presented at the Eastern Psychological Association meeting, Philadelphia.

Pines, H. A., and Kuczkowski, R. 1987. A self-schema for clothing. Paper presented at the American Psychological Association meeting, New York City.

Pines, H. A., and Roll, S. A. 1984. The fashion self-concept: "Clothes that are me." Paper presented at the Eastern Psychological Association meeting, Baltimore.

Polegato, R., and Wall, M. 1980. Information seeking by fashion opinion leaders and followers. *Home Economics Research Journal* 8:327–338.

Polhemus, T. 1978. Introduction. In T. Polhemus, ed. *The body reader: Social aspects of the human body*, pp. 21–29. New York: Pantheon Books.

Pond, M. 1985. *Shoes never lie*. New York: Berkley Books.

Poster, M. 1975. Introduction. In J. Baudrillard. *The mirror of production*. St. Louis: Telos Press.

Powell, P. H., and Dabbs, J. M. 1976. Physical attractiveness and personal space. *Journal of Social Psychology* 100:59–64.

Power, T. G., Hildebrandt, K. A., and Fitzgerald, H. E. 1982. Adults' responses to infants ranging in facial expression and perceived attractiveness. *Infant Behavior and Development* 5:33–44.

Probyn, E. 1987. The anorexic body. *Canadian Journal of Political and Social Theory* 11:111–119.

Quereshi, M. Y., and Kay, J. P. 1986. Physical attractiveness, age, and sex as determinants of reactions to resumés. *Social Behavior and Personality* 14:103–112.

Quin, C. O., Robinson, I. E., and Balkwell, J. W. 1980. A synthesis of two social psychologies. *Symbolic Interaction* 3:59–88.

Rabolt, N. J., and Drake, M. F. 1985. Information sources used by women for career dressing decisions. In M. R. Solomon, ed. *The psychology of fashion*, pp. 371–385. Lexington: Heath/Lexington Books.

Ramsey, S. J. 1976. Nonverbal communication: Prison codes. *Journal of Communication* 26:39–45.

Rand, C., and Hall, J. A. 1983. Sex differences in the accuracy of self-perceived attractiveness. *Social Psychology Quarterly* 46:359–363.

Rasband, J. 1983. *Color crazed*. Provo, UT: Judith Rasband.

Redfield, R. 1930. *Tepoztlan: A Mexican village*. Chicago: The University of Chicago Press.

Reed, J. A. Pinaire. 1979. Interpersonal attraction: Fashionability and perceived similarity. *Perceptual and Motor Skills* 48(2):571–576.

Reeder, E., and Drake, M. F. 1980. Clothing preferences of male athletes: Actual and perceived. *Home Economics Research Journal* 8:339–343.

Reeder, E. N., and King, A. C. 1984. Are teachers dressing for success? *Illinois Teacher*, May/June, 212–213.

Rees, D. W., Williams, L., and Giles, H. 1974. Dress style and symbolic meaning. *International Journal of Symbology* 5:1–8.

Reitzes, D. C. 1986. Urban identification and downtown activities: A social psychological approach. *Social Psychology Quarterly* 49:167–179.

Reynolds, F. D., and Darden, W. R. 1973. Fashion theory and pragmatics: The case of the midi. *Journal of Retailing* 49:51–62.

Richards, M. L. 1981. The clothing preferences and problems of elderly female consumers. *Gerontologist* 21:263–267.

Richmond, M. L. 1986. Learning to love large sizes. *California Apparel News*, Oct. 31–Nov. 6, p. 31.

Riesman, D. 1953. *The lonely crowd: A study of the changing American character*. Garden City: Doubleday.

Riverol, A. R. 1983. Myth America and other misses: A second look at the American beauty contests. *Et Cetera* 40:207–217.

Roach, M. E., and Eicher, J. B., eds. 1965. *Dress, adornment, and the social order*. New York: John Wiley & Sons.

Roach, M. E., and Eicher, J. B. 1973. *The visible self: Perspectives on dress*. Englewood Cliffs: Prentice-Hall.

Roach, M. E., and Musa, K. E. 1980. *New perspectives on the history of Western dress*. New York: Nutriguides.

Roach-Higgins, M. E. 1986. Theories of dress: Evolutionary myths and miasma. In *ACPTC National Proceedings*, p. 66. Monument, CO: Association of College Professors of Textiles and Clothing.

Roberts, H. E. 1977. The exquisite slave: The role of clothes in the making of the Victorian woman. *Signs* 2:554–569.

Robertson, T. S. 1971. *Innovative behavior and communication*. New York: Holt, Rinehart & Winston.

Rogers, E. 1962. *Diffusion of innovations*. New York: Free Press.

Rogers, E. M. 1983. *Diffusion of innovations* 3d ed. New York: The Free Press.

Rogers, E. M., and Cartano, D. 1962. Methods of measuring opinion leadership. *Public Opinion Quarterly* 26:435–441.

Rogers, E. M., and Shoemaker, F. F. 1971. *Communication of innovations: A cross-cultural approach* 2d ed. New York: Free Press.

Rokeach, M. 1968. *Beliefs, attitudes, and values: A theory of organization and change*. San Francisco: Jossey-Bass.

Rook, D. W. 1985a. Body cathexis and market segmentation. In M. R. Solomon, ed. *The psychology of fashion*, pp. 233–241. Lexington: Heath/Lexington Books.

Rook, D. W. 1985b. The ritual dimension of consumer behavior. *Journal of Consumer Research* 12:251–264.

Rosaldo, M. Z. 1974. Woman, culture and society: A theoretical overview. In M. Z. Rosaldo and L. Lamphere, eds. *Woman, culture, and society*, pp. 17–42. Stanford: Stanford University Press.

Rosaldo, M. Z., and Lamphere, L. 1974. Introduction. In M. Z. Rosaldo and L. Lamphere, eds. *Woman, culture, and society*, pp. 1–15. Stanford: Stanford University Press.

Roscoe, B., Callahan, J. E., and Peterson, K. L. 1985. Physical attractiveness as a potential contributor to child abuse. *Education* 105:349–353.

Rosen, S. 1985. Is romance dysfunctional? *International Journal of Women's Studies* 8:250–265.

Rosenberg, M. 1985. Self-concept and psychological well-being. In R. L. Leahy, ed. *The development of the self*. Orlando: Academic Press.

Rosenblad-Wallin, E., and Karlsson, M. 1986. Clothing for the elderly at home and in nursing homes. *Journal of Consumer Studies and Home Economics* 10:343–356.

Rosenblatt, S. 1980. The relationship of clothing to perceived teaching styles. *College*

*Student Journal 14*:230–236.

Rosencranz, M. L. 1950. Sociological aspects of clothing studied. *Journal of Home Economics 42*(3):206.

Rosencranz, M. L. 1962. Clothing symbolism. *Journal of Home Economics 54*:18–22.

Rosencranz, M. L. 1965. Social and psychological approaches to clothing research. *Journal of Home Economics 57*(1):26–29.

Rosenfeld, L. B., and Plax, T. G. 1977. Clothing as communication. *Journal of Communication 27*:24–31.

Rosenwasser, S. M., Adams, V., and Tansh, K. 1983. Visual attention as a function of sex and apparel of stimulus object: Who looks at whom? *Social Behavior and Personality 11*:11–15.

Rossi, S. R., and Rossi, J. S. 1985. Gender differences in the perception of women in magazine advertising. *Sex Roles 12*:1033–1039.

Rowold, K. L. 1984. Sensitivity to the appearance of others and projection as factors in impression management. *Home Economics Research Journal 13*:105–110.

Rubin, J., Provenzano, F., and Luria, Z. 1974. The eye of the beholder: Parents' views on sex of newborns. *American Journal of Orthopsychiatry 44*:512–519.

Rucker, M. H., Boynton, L., and Park, M.-Y. 1986. Gift versus regular purchases: The children's market. In J. G. Saegert, ed. *Proceedings of the Division of Consumer Psychology*, pp. 129–134.

Rucker, M., Hughes, R., Utts, J., and Bruno, N. 1982. Clothing stereotypes of the college campus: The jeaning of America. In *ACPTC Combined Proceedings*, pp. 291–292. Reston, VA: Association of College Professors of Textiles and Clothing.

Rucker, M. H., Kim, Y.-J., and Ho, H. 1987. Evaluation of color preferences: A comparison of Asian and White consumers. In R. L. King, ed. *Minority marketing: Issues and prospects* vol. 3, p. 64. Charleston: Academy of Marketing Science.

Rucker, M., Taber, D., and Harrison, A. 1981. The effect of clothing variation on first impressions of female job applicants: What to wear when. *Social Behavior and Personality 9*:53–64.

Rumsey, N., Bull, R., and Gahagan, D. 1986. A developmental study of children's stereotyping of facially deformed adults. *British Journal of Psychology 77*:269–274.

Ryan, M. S. 1965. Perception of self in relation to clothing. In M. E. Roach and J. B. Eicher, eds. *Dress, Adornment, and the Social Order*, pp. 247–249. New York: John Wiley & Sons.

Ryan, M. S. 1966. *Clothing: A study in human behavior*. New York: Holt, Rinehart & Winston.

Saegert, J., and Hoover, R. J. 1985. A catalog of hypotheses about Hispanic consumers. In W. D. Hoyer, ed. *Proceedings of the Division of Consumer Psychology*. Los Angeles, CA: American Psychological Association.

Sahlins, M. 1976. *Culture and practical reason*. Chicago: University of Chicago Press.

Salvia, J., Algozzine, R., and Sheare, J. B. 1977. Attractiveness and school achievement. *Journal of School Psychology 15*:60–67.

Samuels, C. A., and Ewy, R. 1985. Aesthetic perception of faces during infancy. *British Journal of Developmental Psychology 3*:221–228.

San Giovanni, L. 1978. *Ex-nuns: A study of emergent role passage*. New Jersey: Ablex.

Sapir, E. 1931. Fashion. In *Encyclopedia of the Social Sciences* vol. 6. New York: Macmillan.

Saunders, C. S., and Stead, B. A. 1986. Women's adoption of a business uniform: A content analysis of magazine advertisements. *Sex Roles 15*:197–205.

Saussure, F. 1959. *Course in general linguistics*. Trans. by W. Baskin. New York: Philosophical Library.

Sawyer, C. H. 1987. Men in skirts and women in trousers, from Achilles to Victoria Grant: One explanation of a comedic paradox. *Journal of Popular Culture 21*(2):1–16.

Scherbaum, C. J., and Shepherd, D. H. 1987. Dressing for success: Effects of color and layering on perceptions of women in business. *Sex Roles 16*:391–399.

Schiavo, R. S., Sherlock, B., and Wicklund, G. 1974. Effect of attire on obtaining directions. *Psychological Reports 34*:245–246.

Schlenker, B. R. 1986. *Impression management* 2d ed. Monterey: Brooks/Cole.

Schloderer, B. 1986. Designers discover large-size market. *California Apparel News*, Oct. 31–Nov. 6, p. 31.

Schneider, D. J. 1973. Implicit personality theory: A review. *Psychological Bulletin 79*:294–309.

Schrank, H. L., and Gilmore, D. L. 1973. Correlates of fashion leadership: Implications for fashion process theory. *Sociological Quarterly 14*:534–543.

Schrank, H. L., Sugawara, A. I., and Kim, M. 1982. Comparison of Korean and American fashion leaders: Part 2. *Home Economics Research Journal 10*:235–240.

Schreier, B. 1989. Introduction. In C. B. Kidwell and V. Steele, eds. *Men and women: Dressing the part*, pp. 1–15. Washington, D.C.: Smithsonian Institution Press.

Schwartz, H. 1986. *Never satisfied: A cultural history of diets, fantasies, and fat*. New York: Free Press.

Scott, S. 1986. *Why do they dress that way?* Intercourse, PA: Good Books.

Sebeok, T. 1985. Pandora's box: How and why to communicate 10,000 years into the future. In M. Blonsky, ed. *In signs*, pp. 448–466. Baltimore: Johns Hopkins University Press.

Secord, P. F., and Jourard, S. M. 1953. The appraisal of body cathexis: Body-cathexis and the self. *Journal of Consulting Psychology 17*:343–347.

Seeman, M. 1959. On the meaning of alienation. *American Sociological Review 24*:783–791.

Seid, R. Pollack. 1989. *Never too thin: Why women are at war with their bodies*. Englewood Cliffs, NJ: Prentice-Hall.

Sergios, P., and Cody, J. 1985. Importance of physical attractiveness and social assertiveness skills in male homosexual dating behavior and partner selection. *Journal of Homosexuality 12*:71–84.

Serpe, R. T. 1987. Stability and change in self: A structural symbolic interactionist explanation. *Social Psychology Quarterly 50*:44–55.

Shakin, M., Shakin, D., and Sternglanz, S. H. 1985. Infant clothing: Sex labeling for strangers. *Sex Roles 12*:955–964.

Shannon, E., and Reich, N. 1979. Clothing and related needs of physically handicapped persons. *Rehabilitation Literature 40*(1):2–6.

Sharma, R. S. 1980. Clothing behaviour, personality, and values. *Psychological Studies 25*(2):137–142.

Shaw, E. H., Lazer, W., and Smith, A. E. 1987. Macro consumption patterns of black American households. In R. L. King, ed. *Minority marketing: Issues and prospects* vol. 3, pp. 3–7. Charleston: Academy of Marketing Science.

Sherohman, J. 1977. Conceptual and methodological issues in the study of role-taking accuracy. *Symbolic Interaction 1*:121–131.

Sherry, J. F., Jr. 1987. Advertising as a cultural system. In J. Umiker-Sebeok, ed. *Marketing and semiotics: New directions in the study of signs for sale*, pp. 441–461. Berlin: Mouton de Gruyter.

Shim, S., and Drake, M. F. 1988. Apparel selection by employed women: A typology of information search patterns. *Clothing and Textiles Research Journal 6*(2):1–9.

Shweder, R. A., and Bourne, E. J. 1984. Does the concept of person vary cross-culturally? In R. A. Shweder and R. A. LeVine, eds. *Culture theory*, pp. 158–199. Cambridge: Cambridge University Press.

Sigall, H., and Ostrove, N. 1975. Beautiful but dangerous: Effects of offender attractiveness and nature of the crime on juridic judgment. *Journal of Personality and Social Psychology 31*:410–414.

Sigelman, C. K., Thomas, D. B., Sigelman, L., and Ribich, F. D. 1986. Gender, physical attractiveness, and electability: An experimental investigation of voter biases. *Journal of Applied Social Psychology 16*:229–248.

Sigelman, L., Sigelman, C. K., and Fowler, C. 1987. A bird of a different feather? An experimental investigation of physical attractiveness and the electability of female candidates. *Social Psychology Quarterly 50*:32–43.

Silverstein, B., Perdue, L., Peterson, B., and Kelly, E. 1986. The role of the mass media in promoting a thin standard of bodily attractiveness for women. *Sex Roles 14*: 519–532.

Simels, S. 1985. *Gender chameleons: Androgyny in rock'n'roll*. New York: Timbre Books/ Arbor House.

Simmel, G. 1904. Fashion. *International Quarterly 10*:130–155. [Reprinted in *American Journal of Sociology 62* (May 1957):541–558.]

Simon-Miller, F. 1985. Commentary: Signs and cycles in the fashion system. In M. R. Solomon, ed. *The psychology of fashion*, pp. 71–81. Lexington: Heath/Lexington Books.

Singer, M. S., and Singer, A. E. 1985. The effect of police uniform on interpersonal perception. *Journal of Psychology 119*:157–161.

Sjoberg, G. 1960. *The preindustrial city: past and present*. New York: Free Press.

Skow, J., Booth, C., and Worrel, D. 1985. Madonna rocks the land. *Time*, May 27, pp. 74–77.

Slade, P. D. 1977. Awareness of body dimensions during pregnancy: An analogue study. *Psychological Medicine 7*:245–252.

Slade, P. D., and Russell, G. F. M. 1973a. Awareness of body dimensions in anorexia nervosa: Cross-sectional and longitudinal studies. *Psychological Medicine 3*:188–199.

Slade, P. D., and Russell, G. F. M. 1973b. Experimental investigations of body perception in anorexia nervosa and obesity. *Psychotherapy and Psychosomatics 22*:359–363.

Slaybaugh, J., Littrell, M. A., and Farrell-Beck, J. In press. Consumers of Hmong textiles. *Clothing and Textiles Research Journal*.

Smathers, D. G., and Horridge, P. E. 1978–1979. The effects of physical changes on clothing preferences of elderly women. *International Journal of Aging and Human Development 9*:273–278.

Smith, G. J. 1985. Facial and full-length ratings of attractiveness related to the social interactions of young children. *Sex Roles 12*:287–293.

Smith, J., and Krantz, M. 1986. Physical attractiveness and popularity in children: A methodological refinement and replication. *Journal of Genetic Psychology 147*:419–420.

Snyder, M. 1987. *Public appearances, private realities: The psychology of self-monitoring*. New York: W. H. Freeman.

Snyder, C. R., and Fromkin, H. L. 1980. *Uniqueness: The human pursuit of difference*. New York: Plenum Press.

Solano, C. H. 1979. Actor-observer differences in attribution: A replication. *Psychological Reports 44*:583–586.

Solomon, M. R., ed. 1988. *The psychology of fashion*. Lexington, MA: Heath/Lexington Books.

Solomon, M. 1987. Standard issue. *Psychology Today 21*(12):30–31.

Solomon, M. R., and Assael, H. 1987. The forest or the trees?: A Gestalt approach to symbolic consumption. In J. Umiker-Sebeok, ed. *Marketing and semiotics: New directions in the study of signs for sale*, pp. 189–217. Berlin: Mouton de Gruyter.

Solomon, M. R., and Douglas, S. P. 1985. The female clotheshorse: From aesthetics to tactics. In M. R. Solomon ed., *The Psychology of Fashion*, pp. 387–401. Lexington: Heath/Lexington Books.

Solomon, M. R., and Douglas, S. 1987. Diversity in product symbolism: The case of female executive clothing. *Psychology and Marketing 4*:189–212.

Solomon, M. R., and Schopler, J. 1982. Self-consciousness and clothing. *Personality and Social Psychology Bulletin 8*:508–514.

Sommer, B. A., Kaiser, S. B., and Sommer, R. 1987. Clothing factors in energy conservation. *Journal of Consumer Studies and Home Economics 11*:195–205.

Sommer, B. A., Gemulla, P., and Sommer, R. Working paper. Time on our hands— Wristwatch messages. University of California at Davis.

Sontag, M. S., and Schlater, J. D. 1982. Proximity of clothing to self: Evolution of a concept. *Clothing and Textiles Research Journal 1*(1):1–8.

Splitt, D. A. School law. 1986. *The National Educator*, December, p. 5.

Spranger, E. 1928. *Types of men*. Germany: Max Niemeyer Verlag, Halle.

Spratlen, T. H., and Choudhury, P. K. 1987. Black-white differences in the consumption of cosmetics: Aggregate and sociocultural dimensions. In R. L. King, ed. *Minority marketing: Issues and prospects* vol. 3, pp. 41–45. Charleston: Academy of Marketing Science.

Springbett, B. M. 1958. Factors affecting the final decision in the employment interview. *Canadian Journal of Psychology 12*:13–22.

Sproles, G. B. 1979. *Fashion: Consumer behavior toward dress*. Minneapolis: Burgess.

Sproles, G. B. 1985. Behavioral science theories. In M. R. Solomon, ed. *The psychology of fashion*, pp. 55–70. Lexington: Heath/Lexington Books.

Sproles, G. B., and King, C. W. 1973. *The consumer fashion change agent: A theoretical conceptualization and empirical investigation*. Institute for Research in the Behavioral, Economic, and Management Sciences. Purdue University, Paper No. 433, Dec.

Stabb, J. C. 1985. Clothing as communication: Wearable art. In *ACPTC Combined Proceedings*, pp. 208–209. Monument, CO: Association of College Professors of Textiles and Clothing.

Staffieri, J. R. 1967. A study of social stereotype of body image in children. *Journal of Personality and Social Psychology 7*(1):101–104.

Staffieri, J. R. 1972. Body build and behavioral expectancies in young females. *Developmental Psychology 6*(1):125–127.

Starr, F. 1891. Dress and adornment. *Popular Science Monthly 39*:787–801.

Stead, B. A., and Zinkhan, G. M. 1986. Service priority in department stores: The effects of customer gender and dress. *Sex Roles 15*:601–611.

Steele, V. 1985. *Fashion and eroticism*. New York: Oxford University Press.

Steele, V. 1988. *Paris fashion: A cultural history*. New York: Oxford University Press.

Steele, V. 1989a. Appearance and identity. In C. B. Kidwell and V. Steele, eds. *Men and women: Dressing the part*, pp. 6–21. Washington: Smithsonian Institution Press.

Steele, V. 1989b. Clothing and sexuality. In C. B. Kidwell and V. Steele, eds. *Men and women: Dressing the part*, pp. 42–63. Washington: Smithsonian Institution Press.

Steele, V. 1989c. Dressing for work. In C. B. Kidwell and V. Steele, eds. *Men and women: Dressing the part*, pp. 64–91. Washington: Smithsonian Institution Press.

Steinhaus, N. H., and Lapitsky, M. 1986. Fashion model's age as an influence on consumers' attitudes and purchase intent. *Home Economics Research Journal 14*:294–305.

Stephanson, A. 1987. Regarding postmodernism—A conversation with Fredrick Jameson. *Social Text 17*:29–54.

Stephan, C. W., and Langlois, J. H. 1984. Baby beautiful: Adult attributions of infant competence as a function of infant attractiveness. *Child Development 55*:576–585.

Stewart, J. E. 1985. Appearance and punishment: The attraction-leniency effect in the courtroom. *Journal of Social Psychology 125*:373–378.

Stone, G. P. 1965. Appearance and the self. In M. E. Roach and J. B. Eicher, eds. *Dress, adornment, and the social order*, pp. 216–245. New York: John Wiley & Sons.

Stone, G. P. 1977. Personal acts. *Symbolic Interaction 1*(1):2–19.

Straus, R. A. 1981. The theoretical frame of symbolic interactionism: A contextualist, social science. *Symbolic Interaction 4*:261–272.

Strother, G. B. 1963. Problems in the development of a social science of organization. In H. J. Leavitt, ed. *The social science of organizations: Four perspectives*. Englewood Cliffs: Prentice-Hall.

Stryker, S. 1980. *Symbolic interactionism: A social structural version*. Menlo Park: Benjamin/Cummings.

Stryker, S. 1987. The vitalization of symbolic interactionism. *Symbolic Interactionism* 50:83–94.

Stryker, S., and Gottlieb, A. 1981. Attribution theory and symbolic interactionism: A comparison. In J. H. Harvey, W. Ickes, and R. F. Kidd, eds. *New directions in attribution research* vol. 3, pp. 426–458. Hillsdale: Lawrence Erlbaum.

Styczynsky, L. E., and Langlois, J. H. 1977. The effects of familiarity on behavioral stereotypes associated with physical attractiveness in young children. *Child Development* 48:1137–1141.

Suedfeld, P., Bochner, S., and Matas, C. 1971. Petitioner's attire and petition signing by peace demonstrators: A field experiment. *Journal of Applied Social Psychology* 1(3):278–283.

Suedfeld, P., Bochner, S., and Wnek, D. 1972. Helper-sufferer similarity and a specific request for help: Bystander intervention during a peace demonstration. *Journal of Applied Social Psychology* 2(1):17–23.

Summers, J. O. 1970. The identity of women's clothing fashion opinion leaders. *Journal of Marketing Research* 7:178–185.

Sweat, S., and Zentner, M. A. 1985. Attributions toward female appearance styles. In M. R. Soloman, ed. *The Psychology of Fashion*, pp. 321–335. Lexington, MA: Heath/Lexington Books.

Swingewood, A. 1977. *The myth of mass culture*. Atlantic Highlands: Humanities Press.

Taylor, L. C. and Compton, N. H. 1968. Personality correlates of dress conformity. *Journal of Home Economics* 60:653–656.

Taylor, M. J., and Cooper, P. J. 1986. Body size overestimation and depressed mood. *British Journal of Clinical Psychology* 25(2):153–154.

Taylor, R. A. Lesher. 1985. Do retail buyers short-circuit profit-making items in the apparel industry? In M. R. Sullivan, ed. *The psychology of fashion*, pp. 143–153. Lexington, MA: Heath/Lexington Books.

Taylor, S. 1981. A categorization approach to stereotyping. In D. L. Hamilton, ed. *Cognitive processes in stereotyping and intergroup behavior*, pp. 83–114. Hillsdale: Lawrence Erlbaum Associates.

Tenzel, J. H., and Gizanckas, V. 1973. The uniform experiment. *Journal of Police Science and Administration* 1:421–424.

Terry, R. L., and Doerge, S. 1979. Dress, posture and setting as additive factors in subjective probabilities of rape. *Perceptual and Motor Skills* 48:903–906.

Tharin, L. 1981. Dress codes, observed attire, and behavior in a recreational setting. Unpublished senior thesis, University of California at Davis.

Theodorson, G. A., and Theodorson, A. G. 1969. *A modern dictionary of sociology*. New York: Crowell Collier Press.

Thomas, W. I. 1924. *The unadjusted girl*. London: Routledge.

Thompson, J. K. 1986. Larger than life. *Psychology Today* 70:38–39, 42, 44.

Thompson, S. K. 1975. Gender labels and early sex role development. *Child Development* 46:339–347.

Thompson, S. K., and Bentler, P. M. 1971. The priority of cues in sex discrimination by children and adults. *Developmental Psychology* 5:181–185.

Tish-Knobf, M. K. 1985. Primary breast cancer: Physical consequences and rehabilitation. *Seminars in Oncology Nursing* 1:214–224.

Toffler, A. 1980. *The third wave*. New York: William Morrow and Co.

Tönnies, F. 1940. *Fundamental concepts of sociology*. Trans. by C. P. Loomis. New York: American Book Co. (Original work published as *Gemeinschaft and Gesellschaft*.)

Troiden, R. R. 1984. Self, self-concept, identity, and homosexual identity: Constructs in need of definition and differentiation. *Journal of Homosexuality* 10:97–109.

Tseëlon, E. Communicating via clothes. Ph.D. dissertation, Oxford University, 1989.

Tucker, L. A. 1982. Effect of a weight-training program on the self-concepts of college males. *Perceptual and Motor Skills 54*:1055–1061.

Turkat, D., and Dawson, J. 1976. Attributions of responsibility for a chance event as a function of sex and physical attractiveness of target individuals. *Psychological Reports 39*:275–279.

Turner, B. S. 1984. *The body and society*. New York: Basil Blackwell Publisher.

Turner, R., and Killian, L. M. 1972. *Collective behavior* 2d ed. Englewood Cliffs: Prentice-Hall.

Tyrchniewicz, M. E., and Gonzales, C. A. 1978. The relationship between specific clothing variables and self-concept of adult women. *Canadian Home Economics Journal 28*(3):189–196.

Unger, R., and Raymond, B. 1974. External criteria as predictors of values: The importance of race and attire. *Journal of Social Psychology 93*:295–296.

Unruh, D. R. 1979. Characteristics and types of participation in social worlds. *Symbolic Interaction 2*(2):115–129.

Useem, J., Tangent, P., and Useem, R. H. 1942. Stratification in a prairie town. *American Sociological Review 7*:331–342.

Valentine, P. W. 1987. Uniforms in public school aim at social leveling. *San Francisco Chronicle*, Sept. 3, p. 29.

Vaughan, J. L., and Riemer, J. W. 1985. Fabricating the self: The socialization of fashion models. *Sociological Spectrum 5*:213–229.

Veblen, T. 1899. *The theory of the leisure class*. New York: Macmillan.

Vernon, G. M. 1978. *Symbolic aspects of interaction*. Washington: University Press of America.

Vincent, R. C., Davis, D. K., and Boruszkowski, L. A. 1985. Sexism on MTV: A content analysis of music videos. Paper presented at the meeting of the International Communication Association, Chicago, Illinois.

Volpp, J. M., and Lennon, S. J. 1988. Perceived police authority as a function of uniform hat and sex. *Perceptual and Motor Skills 67*:815–824.

von Ehrenfels, U. R. 1979. Clothing and power abuse. In J. M. Cordwell and R. A. Schwarz, eds. *The fabrics of culture*, pp. 399–403. The Hague: Mouton Publishers.

von Uexkull, T. 1984. Semiotics and the problem of the observer. *Semiotica 48*:187–195.

Walsh, E. J. 1977. Petition signing in town and on campus. *Journal of Social Psychology 102*:323–324.

Walster, E., Aronson, V., and Abrahams, D. 1966. Importance of physical attractiveness on dating behavior. *Journal of Personality and Social Psychology 4*(5):508–516.

Warden, J., and Colquett, J. 1982. Clothing selection by adolescent boys. *Journal of Home Economics 74*:37–40.

Wass, B., and Eicher, J. 1964. Clothing as related to role behavior of teen-age girls. *Quarterly Bulletin 47*(2):206–213.

Wass, B., and Eicher, J. 1980. Analysis of historic and contemporary dress: An African example. *Home Economics Research Journal 8*(5):318–326.

Wasserman, T., and Kassinove, H. 1976. Effects of type of recommendation, attire and perceived expertise on parental compliance. *Journal of Social Psychology 99*(1):43–50.

Weber, M. 1947. *The theory of social and economic organization*. New York: Oxford University Press.

Webster, M., Jr., and Driskell, J. E. C., Jr. 1983. Beauty as status. *American Journal of Sociology 89*:140–165.

Wegner, D. M., and Vallacher, R. R. 1977. *Implicit psychology: An introduction to social cognition*. New York: Oxford University Press.

Weinraub, M., Clemens, L. P., Sockloff, A., Ethridge, T., Gracely, E., and Myers, B.

1984. The development of sex role stereotypes in the third year: Relationships to gender labeling, gender identity, sex-typed toy preference, and family characteristics. *Child Development 55*:1493–1503.

Wellman, D. 1988. The politics of Herbert Blumer's sociological method. *Symbolic Interaction 11*:59–68.

Westermarck, E. A. 1921. *History of human marriage*. London: Macmillan.

Wheeler, P. T., Adams, G. R., and Nielsen, E. C. 1987. Effect of a child's physical attractiveness on verbal scoring of the Wechsler Intelligence scale for children (revised) and personality attributions. *Journal of General Psychology 114*:109–116.

Wheelwright, P. E. 1960. *The way of philosophy* 2d ed. New York: Odyssey Press.

Whisney, A. J., Winakor, G., and Wolins, L. 1979. Fashion preference: Drawings versus photographs. *Home Economics Research Journal 8*(2):138–150.

Whyte, W. H., Jr. 1957. *The organization man*. Garden City: Doubleday Ancor Books.

Wicklund, R. A., and Gollwitzer, P. M. 1982. *Symbolic self-completion*. Hillsdale: Lawrence Erlbaum.

Wilden, A. 1987. *The rules are no game*. New York: Routledge and Regan Paul.

Wildman, R. W., Wildman, R. W., Brown, A., and Trice, C. 1976. Note on males' and females' preferences for opposite-sex body parts, bust sizes and bust-revealing clothing. *Psychological Reports 38*:485–486.

Wilkens, H. T., and Hsu, M. M. 1987. Consumer behavior patterns of the Old Order Amish in south-central Pennsylvania. In R. L. King, ed. *Minority marketing: Issues and prospects* vol. 3, pp. 83–86. Academy of Marketing Science.

Williams, J., Arbaugh, J., and Rucker, M. 1980. Clothing color preferences of adolescent females. *Home Economics Research Journal 9*:57–63.

Williams, R. 1986. The uses of cultural theory. *New Left Review 158*, July/Aug., pp. 19–31.

Williamson, S., and Hewitt, J. 1986. Attire, sexual allure and attractiveness. *Perceptual and Motor Skills 63*:981–982.

Wilson, D. W. 1978. Helping behavior and physical attractiveness. *Journal of Social Psychology 104*(2):313–314.

Wilson, E. 1985. *Adorned in dreams: Fashion and modernity*. London: Virago Press.

Wilson, M., and Dovidio, J. F. 1985. Effects of perceived attractiveness and feminist orientation on helping behavior. *Journal of Social Psychology 125*:415–420.

Wilson, M., Crocker, J., Brown, C. E., Johnson, D., Liotta, R., and Konat, J. 1985. The attractive executive: Effects of sex of business associates on attributions of competence and social skills. *Basic and Applied Social Psychology 6*:13–23.

Wilson, P. R. 1968. Perceptual distortion of height as a function of ascribed academic status. *Journal of Social Psychology 74*:97–102.

Wilson, T. P. 1970. Normative and interpretive paradigms in sociology. In J. D. Douglas, ed. *Understanding everyday life*, pp. 57–79. Chicago: Aldine.

Wilson, W., and Henzlik, W. 1986. Reciprocity of liking following face-to-face encounters with attractive and unattractive others. *Psychological Reports 59*:599–609.

Winakor, G., and Goings, B. D. 1973. Fashion preference: Measurement of change. *Home Economics Research Journal 1*:195–209.

Wingate, B. A., and Christie, M. J. 1978. Ego strength and body image in anorexia nervosa. *Journal of Psychosomatic Research 22*(3):201–204.

Wingate, S. B., Kaiser, S. B., and Freeman, C. M. 1986. Salience of disability cues in functional clothing: A multidimensional approach. *Clothing and Textiles Research Journal 4*(2):37–47.

Woods, W. A., Padgett, T. C., and Montoya, M. I. 1987. An aesthetic factor in apparel choice. In J. G. Saegert, ed. *Proceedings of the Division of Consumer Psychology*. Washington: American Psychological Association.

Woods, W. P., and Heretick, D. M. L. 1983–1984. Self-schemata in anorexia and obesity. *Imagination, Cognition, and Personality 3*(1):31–48.

Workman, J. E. 1984–1985. Effects of appropriate and inappropriate attire on attributions of personal dispositions. *Clothing and Textiles Research Journal* 3(1):20–23.

Workman, J. E. 1987. Fashionable versus out-of-date clothing and interpersonal distance. *Clothing and Textiles Research Journal* 5(3):31–35.

Wright, C. R. 1960. Functional analysis and mass communication. *Public Opinion Quarterly* 24:605–620.

Yarmey, A. D., and Johnson, J. 1982. Evidence for the self as an imaginal prototype. *Journal of Research in Personality* 16:238–246.

Yoder, D. 1972. Folk costume. In R. D. Dorson, ed. *Folklore and folklife: An introduction*. Chicago: University of Chicago Press.

Zahr, L. 1985. Physical attractiveness and Lebanese children's school performance. *Psychological Reports* 56(1):191–192.

Zakia, R. D. 1986. Adverteasement. *Semiotica* 59(1/2):1–11.

Zakin, D. F., Blyth, D. A., and Simmons, R. G. 1984. Physical attractiveness as a mediator of the impact of early pubertal changes for girls. *Journal of Youth and Adolescence* 13:439–450.

Zellman, G., and Goodchilds, J. 1983. Becoming sexual in adolescence. In E. R. Allgeier and N. B. McCormick, eds. *Changing boundaries: Gender roles and sexual behavior*, pp. 49–63. Palo Alto: Mayfield.

Zerubavel, E. 1982. Personal information and social life. *Symbolic Interaction* 5(1):97–109.

# Author Index

# Subject Index